A NORTON CRITICAL EDITION

James Joyce

A PORTRAIT OF THE ARTIST
AS A YOUNG MAN

AUTHORITATIVE TEXT
BACKGROUNDS AND CONTEXTS
CRITICISM

Edited by

JOHN PAUL RIQUELME
BOSTON UNIVERSITY

Text Edited by

HANS WALTER GABLER
WITH WALTER HETTCHE

W. W. NORTON & COMPANY • *New York* • *London*

For Marie-Anne

". . . a Flower of the mountain yes. . . ."

W. W. Norton & Company has been independent since its founding in 1923, when William Warder Norton and Mary D. Herter Norton first published lectures delivered at the People's Institute, the adult education division of New York City's Cooper Union. The Nortons soon expanded their program beyond the Institute, publishing books by celebrated academics from America and abroad. By mid-century, the two major pillars of Norton's publishing program—trade books and college texts—were firmly established. In the 1950s, the Norton family transferred control of the company to its employees, and today—with a staff of four hundred and a comparable number of trade, college, and professional titles published each year—W. W. Norton & Company stands as the largest and oldest publishing house owned wholly by its employees.

Composition by Binghamton Valley.
Manufacturing by the Maple-Vail Book Group, Binghamton.
Book design by Antonina Krass.
Production manager: Ben Reynolds.

Library of Congress Cataloging-in-Publication Data

Joyce, James, 1882–1941.
    A portrait of the artist as a young man: authoritative text, backgrounds and contexts, criticism / James Joyce; edited by John Paul Riquelme; text edited by Hans Walter Gabler with Walter Hettche.
        p.   cm. — (A Norton critical edition)
    includes bibliographical references.
    ISBN-13: 978-0-393-92679-8 (pbk.)
    ISBN-10: 0-393-92679-6 (pbk.)

1. Young men—Fiction. 2. Artists—Fiction. 3. Dublin (Ireland)—Fiction. 4. Joyce, James, 1882–1914. Portrait of the artist as a young man. I. Riquelme, John Paul. II. Gabler, Hans Walter, 1938– III. Hettche, Walter, 1957– IV. Title.
PR6019.O9P63   2007

823'.912—dc22   2006047242

W. W. Norton & Company, Inc., 500 Fifth Avenue,
New York, N.Y. 10110
www.wwnorton.com

W. W. Norton & Company Ltd., Castle House,
75/76 Wells Street, London W1T 3QT

5 6 7 8 9 0

Contents

Criticism   305

Preface

by John Paul Riquelme

During my first semester in college, decades ago, I was asked by an energetic Irish-American teacher, Gerald O'Grady, to read *A Portrait of the Artist as a Young Man* and some essays by the American theorist and critic Kenneth Burke. Like Stephen Dedalus in Joyce's narrative, I was facing a difficult initiation into adult life, yet I did not understand Joyce's challenging book when I tried to read it then, for the first time. Because I found it compelling, I reread the book several times during the following semester, trying to make better sense of it, without much success. It distracted me from other assignments; it left a permanent impression.

This edition of *A Portrait* is meant for all those students and other readers who recognize the book's achievement in its effect on them and who wish to understand the work more fully. The edition provides information and perspectives that may deepen readers' own conclusions about the book's implications, which are various and debatable. The annotations provided for the text are factual rather than interpretive.

The Text

The text of the narrative presented here is the authoritative version, established by Hans Walter Gabler with Walter Hettche, originally published with full editorial apparatus by Garland Publishing (1993). Included with that text is a selection of key notes from the Garland edition concerning textual variants. These notes, placed at page bottom, are meant to allow the interested reader easy access to options that were available during the editorial process. As Gabler explains in his "Introduction: Composition, Text, and Editing," Joyce's handwritten fair copy of the entire narrative, currently in the collection of the National Library of Ireland, provided the "copytext," that is, the base text that was modified editorially. The text is, as Gabler puts it, "eclectic," a necessarily composite version, because textual changes were grafted onto the fair copy, changes warranted by later documents in the book's history. I am grateful to Gabler for allowing us to make more widely available the results of his careful editing work, including the selections from his textual notes for the Garland edition. "Why and How to Read the Textual Notes," which follows the "Editorial Introduction," explains the enabling character of the notes for the reading process. In his introduction, Gabler discusses briefly the relevant composition and publication history of Joyce's book, including the particular prepublication documents that have survived. Readers interested in obtaining more details about that history will find ample, illuminating discussion in the longer introduction to the Garland edition and in Gabler's essay "The Genesis of *A Portrait of the Artist as a Young Man*."[1]

Backgrounds and Contexts

In the late 1940s and the 1950s, the period just after their author's death, Joyce's works received substantial positive critical attention. They were considered valuable largely on the basis of readings that involved attention to literary form and to so-called symbols, with little or no attention to historical and political contexts. At that time, modern literature had yet to be interpreted in light of empire-building and colonization. The literary canon was also narrower than it is now. For example, the writings of Oscar Wilde (1854–1900), one of Joyce's most important precursors, were still not widely discussed (a lingering effect of the scandal surrounding his conviction for acts of "gross indecency"). Half a century later, critical approaches to literature attend more fully to issues of historical and social context, and the canon has changed. But reliable historical materials concerning many of our greatest modern writers have not been readily available to readers who are not specialists. The "Backgrounds and Contexts" section of this edition addresses that situation for Joyce's narrative by providing information about Irish history, especially political history, with an emphasis on significant events of the nineteenth century. This is the political history that Joyce would have grown up with and that his artist protagonist, Stephen Dedalus, knows from the inside. The documents concerning Irish history carry forward through 1916, the year of the Easter Rising, which marked a crucial turning point in Ireland's becoming a nation. The Easter Rising and *A Portrait of the Artist as a Young Man* are both products of Irish historical directions that emerged, on the streets of Dublin and in print, in 1916. Both signal something new and significant. The chronology that opens "Backgrounds and Contexts" provides a slightly longer historical perspective, reaching back to the Insurrection of 1798 and forward to the 1937 Constitution of Ireland.

---

1. *Critical Essays on James Joyce's "A Portrait of the Artist as a Young Man,"* ed. Philip Brady and James F. Carens. New York: G. K. Hall, 1998, 83–112.

The fourteen illustrations within the section reflect graphically the history of violence—literal, political, and psychological—that informs Stephen Dedalus's world. These visual texts include prejudicial English political cartoons that represent the Irish, and in particular their political leader, Charles Stewart Parnell (1846–1891), as monstrous. The violence of internal Irish political disagreement is reflected in the language and the cover of an anti-Parnell pamphlet, *The Discrowned King of Ireland*. The extreme pressures on the young are evident in the physical torments depicted in the woodcuts from *Hell Opened to Christians*, a pamphlet that could have been distributed at retreats such as the one Stephen participates in (Part III). The retreat's description of serpents devouring the souls of sinners finds an aesthetic counterpart in the *Laocoön* sculpture group, reproduced here, which plays a key role in Stephen's thinking about art.

Irish cultural revival provides an additional frame of reference for reading *A Portrait*. The writings of Douglas Hyde (1860–1949) and John Millington Synge (1871–1909) help illustrate the options Joyce faced and presented to Stephen, because both Hyde and Synge emphasize native Irish culture and because both took comparatively moderate stances on cultural politics. Though Joyce relocated to the Continent, he paid continuing attention to Irish culture. Displaying a similar cosmopolitanism, Stephen Dedalus is not interested in becoming fluent in Gaelic. He is headed toward Europe, not the west of Ireland. His thinking about Ireland deserves comparison with Synge's descriptions of traditional Irish living on the isolated Aran Islands off the west coast. Indeed, Joyce would have known Synge's book *The Aran Islands* (1907), aspects of which he evokes in his presentation of Stephen.

Sharing Joyce's education by Jesuits, Stephen comes to know well and to practice for a time the rigorous spiritual exercises recommended and formulated by St. Ignatius Loyola, the founder of the Jesuit religious order. Excerpts from *The Spiritual Exercises*, including the meditation on hell, are provided as material that Stephen would know by heart or nearly so. (*Hell Opened to Christians* would have been a supplement to *The Spiritual Exercises*.)

Finally, the relevant contexts include aesthetic matters. As Joyce reached maturity, he encountered the immensely influential Aesthetic movement, whose most important English advocate was Walter Pater (1839–1894). Every aspiring artist in the English-speaking world during the 1890s read Pater's writings attentively. His response to Leonardo's *Mona Lisa* (*La Gioconda*) and his suppressed and then revised and reissued closing to *Studies in the History of the Renaissance* (1873–93) were among the most widely read belle-lettristic passages of the late nineteenth century. Joyce imitates aspects of Pater's elaborate style late in Part IV, where it informs

Stephen's thoughts. Oscar Wilde was influenced by Pater, but became an aesthete of a different kind. He was also the most successful Irish writer of the generation preceding Joyce's and Stephen's. When Joyce gave a title to his narrative about the artist, he may have had in mind Wilde's *The Picture of Dorian Gray* (1891), excerpts from which are provided.

Criticism

Joyce's works have attracted substantial attention from other writers, artists, theorists, and literary critics. Any selection from the wide, voluminous commentary on *A Portrait of the Artist as a Young Man* will necessarily be highly selective, even with regard to the kinds of commentary that have appeared. In this edition, the "Criticism" section presents work by three generations of commentators on both sides of the Atlantic. The critical commentaries are nearly all essays that have not been readily available through reprintings. I have given equal emphasis to work by groundbreaking interpreters during 1950–75 (Kenneth Burke, Umberto Eco, Hugh Kenner, and Hélène Cixous, who are respectively American, Italian, Canadian, and French); by a next wave of critics whose readings of Joyce respond to poststructuralist thinking, to style, and to feminism (myself, Karen Lawrence, Maud Ellmann, and Bonnie Kime Scott); and by younger critics who develop the discussion by focusing on gender identity, nation, religion, and history, including postcolonial history (Joseph Valente, Marian Eide, Pericles Lewis, and Jonathan Mulrooney). The "Selected Bibliography" presents suggestions for further research.

Acknowledgments

An edition of this kind results from collaborative efforts. I was fortunate to receive generous assistance from colleagues who exceed in number the limits of my memory, the space I have to thank them, and my ability to express my gratitude adequately. Primary among them is Hans Walter Gabler, whose careful, thoughtful, always well-informed attention to detail led to publication of the authoritative text of Joyce's narrative, which is here reprinted. He invariably responded patiently and supportively to the needs of this new edition, which he regularly anticipated. Equally important among the patient collaborators who made the work possible is Carol Bemis at W. W. Norton & Company. She, her colleague, Brian Baker, and many others at Norton provided timely, energetic assistance and imaginative ideas. In particular, during copyediting Kurt Wildermuth enabled numerous improvements through his canny, meticulous attention to the volume's details. His commitment, goodwill, and tact made the final stage of the work especially rewarding.

When I began work on this volume, I circulated a questionnaire concerning its possible contents to two dozen colleagues who teach and write about Joyce. I am grateful for the illuminating responses to that questionnaire, and to my other requests for information and advice, from Derek Attridge, Murray Beja, Christine van Boheemen, Rosa Maria Bollettieri Bosinelli, Richard Brown, Gregory Castle, Kevin Dettmar, Enda Duffy, Michael Patrick Gillespie, Michael Groden, Suzette Henke, Marjorie Howes, Nico Israel, Scott Klein, Patrick McGee, Jonathan Mulrooney, Vincent Pecora, Jean-Michel Rabaté, Bonnie Kime Scott, and Joseph Valente. Gregory Castle and Jonathan Mulrooney provided advice throughout the editing process, Castle primarily concerning critical commentaries and Mulrooney primarily concerning Joyce's relation to Catholicism. Howard Gray, S.J., shared his knowledge of St. Ignatius. William Brockman clarified some textual matters. Ellen Esrock, who translated Umberto Eco's commentary, clarified an aspect of the translation. The explanatory notes for the text are based on my independent research, but annotating a text as frequently commented on as Joyce's involves awareness of what other scholars have done. I consulted annotations by Chester Anderson, James Atherton, Seamus Deane, Don Gifford, and Jeri Johnson, whose efforts I acknowledge with thanks.

I was able to complete much of the work on the edition during a research leave in 2005 generously granted by the College of Arts and Sciences and the Humanities Foundation of Boston University. Special thanks go to Jeffrey Henderson, dean of CAS, and Katherine O'Connor, director of the Foundation, for their confidence and support. I also wish to thank my colleague Fred S. Kleiner, professor of art history and archaeology at Boston University, for explaining the strange history of the *Laocoön* sculpture group. Lindsey Gilbert, Mary Lawless, and Holly Schaaf, doctoral students in English in my department, provided dedicated assistance through their careful proofreading.

I am grateful to the journals, publishers, institutions, and individuals who gave permission for materials to appear, especially Anthony Burke, Hélène Cixous, Carol Kealiher, and Robert Young. Rhoda Bilansky, the head of Interlibrary Loan at Mugar Memorial Library, Boston University, frequently obtained for extended use books and essays that were not locally available, including items that I never expected to see without travel to distant libraries. I received assistance as well from the staff of the British Library and the National Library of Ireland (Leabharlann Náisiúnta na hÉireann). At the National Library, Bernie McCann of Reprographics Services arranged for the copying of items in deteriorated, barely reproducible condition. Joanna Finegan, Curator of Prints and Drawings, and her colleague, Colette O'Flaherty, authorized reproduction of the library's copy of the 1916 Proclamation and expedited delivery of the image.

Reproducing many of the illustrations for this volume would have been impossible without the resources and cooperation of the NLI.

My deep thanks for support on a daily basis go to my partner, Marie-Anne Verougstraete, who rendered all the illustrations for the edition, many of them from difficult originals. More importantly, she believed that the work on the edition was worth the time I spent to do it.

Sources for the Annotations

Anderson, Chester G. "Explanatory Notes." *A Portrait of the Artist as a Young Man: Text, Criticism, and Notes*. Ed. Chester G. Anderson. New York: Viking, 1968.

Catholic Encyclopedia. www.newadvent.org. [Cited as *Cath. Enc.*]

Connolly, S. J. *The Oxford Companion to Irish History*. Oxford, Eng.: Oxford UP, 1998.

Encyclopaedia Britannica, Eleventh Ed. London and New York: Encyclopaedia Britannica, 1910. [Cited as *Enc. Brit.*]

Gifford, Don. *Joyce Annotated: Notes for* Dubliners *and* A Portrait of the Artist as a Young Man. Second Ed. Berkeley: U of California P, 1982.

Holy Bible, the Douay Version of the Old Testament, the Confraternity Edition of the New Testament. New York: P. J. Kenedy & Sons, 1950. [This English version of the Bible was chosen as more appropriate than the King James Version for Joyce's text because the Douay-Confraternity translation is accepted by the Roman Catholic Church.]

Joyce, P. W. *English as We Speak It in Ireland*. 1910; rpt. Dublin: Wolfhound P, 1979.

Lalor, Brian, ed. *The Encyclopedia of Ireland*. New Haven and London: Yale UP, 2003.

Letters of James Joyce. Vol. I, corrected. Ed. Stuart Gilbert. New York: Viking, 1966. Vols. II–III. Ed. Richard Ellmann. New York: Viking, 1966.

Michael, Ian. *The Teaching of English, from the Sixteenth Century to 1870*. Cambridge, Eng.: Cambridge UP, 1987.

Mullin, Katherine. *James Joyce, Sexuality and Social Purity*. Cambridge, Eng.: Cambridge UP, 2003.

Oxford English Dictionary. Second Ed. Ed. J. A. Simpson and E. S. C. Weiner. Oxford, Eng.: Clarendon, 1989. [Cited as *OED*.]

Shakespeare, William. *The Norton Shakespeare, Based on the Oxford Edition*. Ed. Stephen Greenblatt, et al. New York and London: W. W. Norton & Company, 1997.

Sullivan, Kevin. *Joyce among the Jesuits*. New York: Columbia UP, 1957.

Introduction: Composition, Text, and Editing[†]

by Hans Walter Gabler

The seminal invention for *A Portrait of the Artist as a Young Man* was Joyce's narrative essay "A Portrait of the Artist."[1] The essay survives in Joyce's hand in a copybook belonging to his sister Mabel and bears the date 7/1/1904.[2] Submitted to the literary magazine *Dana* (as likely as not in the very copybook), it was rejected within less than a fortnight. According to Stanislaus Joyce in his *Dublin Diary*, the rejection spurred Joyce on to conceiving of an autobiographical novel, the opening chapters of which he supposedly wrote in the space of a couple of weeks.[3] Stanislaus also tells us that, as the brothers sat together in the kitchen on James Joyce's twenty-second birthday, February 2, 1904, James shared his plans for the novel with him, and he claims that he, Stanislaus, suggested the title *Stephen Hero*.

Joyce scholars have followed Richard Ellmann (*JJ*, 144–49) in taking Stanislaus's account altogether at face value. We have all persistently overlooked May Joyce's letter to James of September 1, 1916, in which she recalls James's reading the early chapters to their mother when they lived in St. Peter's Terrace, with the younger siblings put out of the room. May used to hide under the sofa to listen until, relenting, James allowed her to stay (*Letters* II, 382–83). This intimate memory puts the beginnings of Joyce's art in a different

---

[†] Revised excerpt from "Introduction," *A Portrait of the Artist as a Young Man*, ed. Hans Walter Gabler with Walter Hettche. New York and London: Garland, 1993.

1. "A Portrait of the Artist" is most conveniently available in James Joyce, *Poems and Shorter Writings*, ed. Richard Ellmann, A. Walton Litz, and John Whittier-Ferguson. London: Faber and Faber, 1991, 211–18. The original is photographically reprinted in James Joyce, *A Portrait of the Artist as a Young Man. A Facsimile of Epiphanies, Notes, Manuscripts, and Typescripts*, prefaced and arranged by Hans Walter Gabler. New York and London: Garland Publishing, Inc., 1978 (vol. [7] of *The James Joyce Archive*, 63 vols., general editor Michael Groden), 70–85.

2. That is, January 7, 1904.

3. Stanislaus Joyce, *The Complete Dublin Diary*, ed. George H. Healey. Ithaca: Cornell UP, 1971, 11–13.

perspective. It suggests that he started his autobiographical novel almost a year earlier than has hitherto been assumed, probably some
months at least before August 1903, when his mother died. The impulse thus seems to have sprung immediately from his first experience of exile in Paris in 1902–03. "A Portrait of the Artist," of
January 1904, can appear no longer as seminal for *Stephen Hero*.
Rather, defined as the conceptual outline for *A Portrait of the Artist
as a Young Man* that it has always been felt to be, it stands as Joyce's
first attempt to break away from his initial mode of autobiographical
fiction. Against Stanislaus Joyce's idealizing of his brother's tri-
umphant heroism in defying *Dana*, we sense instead the stymying
effect of that first public rejection. Digging his heels in and continuing to write *Stephen Hero* was a retarding stage, even perhaps a
retrogression, in Joyce's search for a sense of his art and a narrative
idiom all his own. *Stephen Hero* was to falter by mid-1905, by which
time Joyce was freeing himself from its fetters through *Dubliners*.[4]

With eleven chapters of *Stephen Hero* written and its immediate
continuation conceived, Joyce left Dublin with Nora Barnacle, his
future wife, on October 8, 1904, for Trieste and Pola. Short narratives, too, were fermenting in his head. In the course of 1904, he
had published three stories in *The Irish Homestead*: "The Sisters,"
"Eveline," and "After the Race." They were the beginnings of
Dubliners, to be enlarged into a book-length collection in Trieste. In
their exile, too, James and Nora soon found themselves to be expec-
tant parents. During Nora's pregnancy, Joyce carried *Stephen Hero*
forward through its "University episode," now the novel's only surviving fragment. Yet, closely coinciding with the birth of Giorgio
Joyce, he suspended work on it in June 1905.[5] From mid-1905, he
turned wholly to writing *Dubliners*. The protracted endeavor,
throughout 1906, to get the collection published ran persistently
foul even as, in 1906–07, he capped the sequence with "The Dead."

The Emerging Novel

The time devoted to writing *Dubliners* was the gestation period of a
fundamentally new conception for Joyce's autobiographical novel.
Suspending it in 1905 had, as became apparent by 1907, been

---

4. Hans Walter Gabler, *The Rocky Roads to* Ulysses. The National Library of Ireland Joyce
Studies 2004, no. 15. Dublin: National Library of Ireland, 2005.
5. The "University episode" fragment of eleven chapters—XV through XXV—was posthumously edited (erroneously as chapters XV through XXVI) by Theodore Spencer in 1944
and subsequently augmented by the text of a few stray additional manuscript pages
(James Joyce, *Stephen Hero*, ed. from the Manuscript in the Harvard College Library by
Theodore Spencer. A New Edition, Incorporating the Additional Manuscript Pages in the
Yale University Library and the Cornell University Library, ed. John J. Slocum and Herbert Cahoon. New York: New Directions, 1963). The *James Joyce Archive*, vol. [8], collects
and reprints photographically the "University episode" and the stray manuscript pages.

tantamount to aborting the sixty-three-chapter project of *Stephen Hero* in favor of beginning afresh a novel in five parts and naming it *A Portrait of the Artist as a Young Man*. The first part was written between September 8 and November 29, 1907. Reworked from *Stephen Hero*, it omitted entirely the seven initial chapters of that novel—those dealing with Stephen's childhood—and opened immediately with Stephen's going to school (cf. *JJ*, 64). We may assume[6] that this early version of Part I, of autumn 1907, included neither the overture of the novel as eventually published ("Once upon a time . . . *Apologise*." [Part I, lines 1–41]) nor the Christmas-dinner scene ([I, 716–1151]; this at first apparently belonged to Part II of *A Portrait*, as drafted from materials reworked from *Stephen Hero*). By April 7, 1908, the new novel had grown to three parts, but was making no further progress. It was therefore sections of a work he had grown despondent about that in early 1909 Joyce gave a fellow writer to read. The reader was Ettore Schmitz, or Italo Svevo, at the time Joyce's language pupil. The supportive criticism he set out in a letter of February 8, 1909 (*Letters* II, 226–27), suggests that he had been given Parts I through III, plus a draft opening of Part IV, in versions prior to those known from the published book. Specifically—if inference may be trusted—the Christmas-dinner scene was still a section of Part II, and the conclusion of Stephen's confession in Part III was yet unwritten.

Schmitz's response encouraged Joyce to complete Part IV and begin Part V. Yet this precipitated an apparently more serious crisis. Sometime in 1911, Joyce threw the entire manuscript as it then stood—313 manuscript leaves—in the fire.[7] Instantly rescued by a family fire brigade, it apparently suffered no real harm and was kept tied up in an old sheet for months before Joyce "sorted [it] out and pieced [it] together as best [he] could" (*Letters* I, 136). This reconstruction involved developing and rounding off Part V, thoroughly revising Parts I through III, and shaping the novel as a whole into a stringent chiastic, or midcentered, design. It was an effort of creation and re-creation occupying Joyce for over two, if not three, years. On Easter Day 1913, he envisaged finishing the book by the end of the year, but completing it spilled over into 1914. The surviving fair copy bears the date line "Dublin 1904 | Trieste 1914" on its last page. Yet the date "1913" on the fair copy's title page indicates

6. For what follows, see my in-depth analysis in "The Genesis of *A Portrait of the Artist as a Young Man*," *Critical Essays on James Joyce's "A Portrait of the Artist as a Young Man*," ed. Philip Brady and James F. Carens. New York: G. K. Hall, 1998, 83–112.
7. It was not the *Stephen Hero* manuscript, therefore, as a persistent legend would have it, but an early *A Portrait* manuscript that was thus given over to the flames, a fact that a careful reading of Joyce's letter to Harriet Shaw Weaver of January 6, 1920, confirms (*Letters* I, 136).

that Joyce's Easter Day confidence was sufficiently well founded. The design and much of the text were essentially realized in 1913.

Joyce left the manuscript behind in Trieste when he moved to Zurich in 1915. He retrieved it in 1919 and presented it to Harriet Shaw Weaver (1876–1961) for Christmas (*Letters* I, 136), in gratitude for her support as his publisher and generous patron since 1914. Weaver saw to it that her Joyce manuscripts went into public holdings. The entire work-in-progress lot of *Finnegans Wake* papers in her trust should, she felt, go to Ireland. But Nora Joyce strongly objected. Consequently, the British Museum in London received them. In 1952, Weaver gave the fair copy of *A Portrait of the Artist as a Young Man* to the National Library of Ireland.

The Serialization

On December 15, 1913, the American poet and critic Ezra Pound (1885–1972) wrote to Joyce from London asking whether he had anything publishable that Pound could place for him in any of the British or American journals with which Pound had connections.[8] He had heard about the young Irish writer exiled in faraway Trieste through Joyce's fellow Irishman, then in London, the poet and playwright W. B. Yeats (1865–1939). During those vital years of his passion to discover the new writers and promote the new literature, Pound was specifically associated with *The Egoist* (formerly titled *The Freewoman* and *The New Freewoman*) under the editorship of Dora Marsden. With the concurrent prospect of the British publisher Grant Richards's finally publishing *Dubliners*, Joyce wanted Pound and *The Egoist* to consider his new novel. *The Egoist* began to serialize *A Portrait of the Artist as a Young Man* in brief fortnightly installments on, as it happened, February 2, 1914, Joyce's thirty-second birthday. Continuing through the spring and summer of 1914 and for an entire year into World War I (despite recurring difficulties then in delivering typescript copy from Austro-Hungarian enemy territory to London), the serialization finished on September 1, 1915.

Owing to objections the British printers made for fear of prosecution for obscenity, *The Egoist* employed three printing houses in succession, and even so the text underwent cuts from censorship in production. The first paragraph of Part III, a couple of sentences in the bird-girl conclusion to Part IV, a brief dialogue exchange about farting, and the occurrence (twice) of the expletive "ballocks" in Part V were affected. Joyce did not read proof on the *Egoist* text. Nor, beyond Part II, did he receive the published text to read until sometimes many weeks or months after publication. (The wartime

8. *Pound/Joyce: The Letters of Ezra Pound to James Joyce, with Pound's Essays on Joyce.* Ed. Forrest Read. New York: New Directions, 1967, 17–18.

disturbances in communication were the obvious reason.) Nevertheless, he instantly spotted the censorship cuts in the published text. In
Zurich, within neutral Switzerland, he was cut off from all the notes
and manuscripts he had left behind in war-embroiled Trieste. Yet
from a prodigious memory—a faculty that was essential to Joyce's
writing throughout his life—he reprovided faultlessly words and sentences missing in the *Egoist* installments; with great determination,
he insisted on an entirely uncensored text for the book publication.

Toward the First Edition

In the spring of 1915, several months before the end of the *Portrait*
installments in *The Egoist,* Harriet Weaver, assisted by Ezra Pound,
embarked upon a protracted search for a British publisher of the
novel in book form. Grant Richards had the right of first refusal,
contracted with the publishing of *Dubliners,* and declined. Martin
Secker and, after long deliberation, Gerald Duckworth followed
suit. Ezra Pound's attempts to interest John Lane—who in 1936 was
to publish *Ulysses*—were unsuccessful. Duckworth's rejection of
January 1916 was based on a reader's report from Edward Garnett,
which documents how categorically *A Portrait*'s construction and
style were beyond the expectations, and therefore the powers of
perception, of even a most esteemed literary reader of the time.[9]
Eventually, Harriet Weaver became a publisher and founded The
Egoist Ltd. expressly to publish *A Portrait of the Artist as a Young
Man* as a book. Yet, just as the established British publishers had
refused to take on the novel, British printers now proved unwilling
to touch it uncensored. (The then-recent legal proceedings against
D. H. Lawrence's *The Rainbow* no doubt influenced their attitude.) Weaver's remaining hope was to arrange with an American
partner to supply her with import sheets for a British edition. The
promise of a satisfactory arrangement with John Marshall collapsed
when Marshall absconded to Canada. It was with B. W. Huebsch of
New York that a joint venture finally succeeded.

The Book Editions

B. W. Huebsch had become aware of Joyce through Grant Richards,
who throughout 1916 negotiated with Huebsch to publish *Dubliners*
in the United States with sheets imported from England. (The edition was brought out in December 1916, only a few weeks before
that of *A Portrait.*) He was alerted to *A Portrait* through E. Byrne
Hackett, an Irish-American bookseller and small-scale publisher to
whom, on Ezra Pound's recommendation, Harriet Weaver had sent a

9. Garnett's report is quoted in *JJ,* 403–04.

set of uncorrected tearsheets, that is, the relevant columns cut from
The Egoist. Hackett forwarded these to Huebsch, who on June 16,
1916,[1] offered "to print absolutely in accordance with the author's
wishes, without deletion" (*Letters* I, 91). Providing him with copy to
allow him to do so was now, in the middle of World War I, a trans-
atlantic challenge involving efforts at communication between New
York, London, and Zurich. John Marshall held a fully marked-up
printer's copy, with corrections by Joyce in Parts I and II, author's
corrections transferred into Parts III and IV by Harriet Weaver from
lists Joyce had sent her, and Part V in the original typescript. But
Marshall had disappeared, and all attempts to retrieve his set for
Huebsch failed. (From this calamity, our greatest loss is that of the
original Trieste typescript of Part V.) Weaver sent Huebsch a substitute copy with Parts III and IV marked up according to Joyce's lists,
but Parts I, II, and V corrected merely through her recollection of
Joyce's changes or, with respect to Part V, just her unaided impressions. Huebsch wisely refused to start printing from this copy, awaiting rather the receipt of Parts I, II, and V in exemplars Weaver had
concurrently sent to Joyce to freshly mark up. These reached New
York on October 6, and on October 17 Huebsch confirmed that the
book was in the printer's hands. No proofreading other than
Huebsch's house-proofing was feasible. Joyce was pressing for publication in 1916; this was even stipulated in the publishing contract.
On December 29, a few copies were bound, to justify the date, "1916,"
on the first edition title page. In January 1917, the edition entered
the American market, and 768 sets of sheets (for the 750 ordered) arrived in London to be bound and marketed by The Egoist Ltd.

Joyce found the first edition in need of extensive correction. By
April 10, 1917, he had drawn up a handwritten list of "nearly 400"
changes, which he sent to his literary agent, J. B. Pinker, to be typed
with a carbon copy, so that, for safety's sake, two exemplars could be
forwarded by separate mailings to New York. Yet by the time they
arrived, Huebsch had already printed "a second edition from the
first plates" unaltered. Weaver, who was also considering a second
edition, refrained from extending her joint venture with Huebsch
when she discovered that freshly imported sheets would not include
Joyce's changes. She marked up instead an exemplar of the English
first edition (American sheets) as printer's copy for the reset English
second edition, published under the imprint of The Egoist Ltd. in
1918. (Weaver eventually gave this copy to the Bodleian Library

---

1. This was a year to the day after Joyce had written a postcard from Trieste to his brother
Stanislaus, who, less protected by influential friends than James, had been interned as an
enemy alien in a camp in Lower Austria. (James therefore wrote the card in rather shaky
German [*Selected Letters,* 209].) He had written, so he informed his brother, the first
chapter of his new novel, *Ulysses*—which was destined, as we now know, to be set on June
16, 1904.

in Oxford, where it is now shelved.) The "third English edition," published under the Egoist imprint in 1921, was, properly speaking, another issue of the first American edition, using more sheets imported from the United States.

In 1924, the publishing firm Jonathan Cape took over *A Portrait of the Artist as a Young Man* and published the "fourth English edition," which, in strict bibliographical terms, was the book's third edition. With the proofing and revising of *Ulysses* (1922) fresh in his memory, Joyce proofread the Jonathan Cape *Portrait* more thoroughly and consistently than any other of his books after their first publication. On July 11, he reported from Saint-Malo on work done before he left Paris, which involved resisting suggested censorial cuts[2] and insisting on the removal of the "perverted commas . . . by the sergeant-at-arms" (*Letters* III, 99–100). Cape complied on both counts—that is, he agreed to print without cuts and to remove the quotation marks and reset all dialogue with opening flush-left dialogue dashes. Joyce appears to have read three rounds of proof on the Cape edition. This marked the end of his attention to the text of *A Portrait of the Artist as a Young Man*.

This Edition

This Norton Critical Edition is a copy-text edition of *A Portrait of the Artist as a Young Man*.[3] The copy-text it is based on is provided by Joyce's fair-copy holograph, held by the National Library of Ireland and photographically reprinted in *The James Joyce Archive*. The surviving fragments of the typescript, the few *Egoist* galleys preserved, the *Egoist* serialization (1914–15), the first edition (B. W. Huebsch, 1916), the second edition (The Egoist Ltd., 1918), and the third edition (Jonathan Cape, 1924) have been collated against the fair copy; and the marked-up *Egoist* tearsheets, Joyce's lists of corrections, and Harriet Weaver's marked-up printer's copy for the 1918 British edition, as well as published and unpublished correspondence itemizing textual changes, have been checked. This comprehensive survey has been the basis for preparing the edited text.[4] Fundamentally, the edited text maintains the wording, spelling, and

---

2. Sylvia Beach, the American expatriate writer whose Parisian bookshop, Shakespeare and Company, published *Ulysses* in 1922, records her "amazement at the printer's queries in the margins." Sylvia Beach, *Shakespeare and Company*. London: Faber and Faber, 1960, 56.
3. That is, our edition has been constructed according to one of several alternative models of editing, other such models being, for instance, the diplomatic edition, the documentary edition, or the genetic or genetically oriented edition, as exemplified by James Joyce, *Ulysses. A Critical and Synoptic Edition*. 3 vols. Prepared by Hans Walter Gabler with Wolfhard Steppe and Claus Melchior. New York: Garland, 1984, [2]1986.
4. Except for letters, all manuscript materials relevant to the constitution of the text have been photographically reprinted in *The James Joyce Archive*, vols. [7], [9], and [10].

punctuation of its copy-text, although it emends obvious slips of the pen and authorial copying errors. Yet onto the copy-text it also grafts: first, Joyce's revisions on the typescript, in the serialization and in the book editions of 1916, 1918, and 1924; second, his restyling of capitalization and compound formation without hyphens (i.e., compounds in one word or two words) in the book editions; third, the styling of speech with dialogue dashes, as insisted on for the Jonathan Cape edition of 1924. Such editorial overwriting of the copy-text in terms of authorial revision and restyling later in time than the copy-text defines the edited text as a critically eclectic one.

The present edition adopts the edited text together with essentials of the apparatus from the Garland Critical Edition of 1993.[5] For a scholarly edition presents itself to its readers always as a network of discourses. Meshed with the edited text are commonly at least three further discursive strands, namely the so-called apparatus (that is, collation lists and notes answering to the editing); the explanatory material, or commentary; and the editorial introduction, essential particularly for arguing the rationale of the editing and for outlining the design of the edition. Each of these strands is represented in the present edition. Taking over the edited text wholly from the critical edition has also meant preserving the through line numbering for each part that, independent of book paginations, was devised identically for the Garland and Vintage editions of 1993. The present "Editorial Introduction," in its turn, is a revision and modification of the introduction in the Garland edition. The textual footnotes in this edition, furthermore, merge the three parts of the Garland edition's apparatus (i.e., its notes at the foot of the text pages, plus its appended "Emendation of Accidentals" and "Historical Collation" lists). Moreover, this Norton Critical Edition features prominently the fourth strand of a scholarly edition's constituent parts, the commentary. In fact, it does so doubly, both with bottom-of-the-page annotations and by means of the appended sections headed "Backgrounds and Contexts" and "Criticism."

Select Bibliography

Anderson, Chester G. "The Text of James Joyce's *A Portrait of the Artist as a Young Man.*" *Neuphilologische Mitteilungen* 65 (1964): 160–200.

Ellmann, Richard. *James Joyce.* Oxford, Eng.: Oxford UP, 1982 (*JJ*)

Gabler, Hans Walter. "Towards a Critical Text of James Joyce's *A*

---

5. James Joyce, *A Portrait of the Artist as a Young Man,* ed. Hans Walter Gabler with Walter Hettche. New York and London: Garland, 1993. There, the section "This Edition," on pages 10–18 within the introduction, discusses in detail the copy-text-editing rationale and procedures resulting in the edition's edited text.

Portrait of the Artist as a Young Man." *Studies in Bibliography* 27 (1974): 1–53.

Gabler, Hans Walter. "The Genesis of *A Portrait of the Artist as a Young Man.*" *Critical Essays on James Joyce's "A Portrait of the Artist as a Young Man."* Ed. Philip Brady and James F. Carens. New York: G. K. Hall, 1998, 83–112.

Gabler, Hans Walter. *The Rocky Roads to* Ulysses. The National Library of Ireland Joyce Studies 2004, no. 15. Dublin: National Library of Ireland, 2005.

Joyce, James. *A Portrait of the Artist as a Young Man.* Critical Ed. Ed. Hans Walter Gabler with Walter Hettche. New York and London: Garland, 1993.

Joyce, James. *A Portrait of the Artist as a Young Man.* Ed. Hans Walter Gabler with Walter Hettche. New York: Vintage, 1993.

Letters of James Joyce. Vol. I. Ed. Stuart Gilbert. New York: Viking, 1957, 1966. (*Letters* I)

Letters of James Joyce. Vols. II–III. Ed. Richard Ellmann. New York: Viking, 1966. (*Letters* II and III)

Selected Letters of James Joyce. Ed. Richard Ellmann. New York: Viking, 1975. (*Selected Letters*)

The James Joyce Archive. 63 vols. General editor Michael Groden. New York and London: Garland, 1977–79. Vol. [7]: *A Portrait of the Artist as a Young Man. A Facsimile of Epiphanies, Notes, Manuscripts, and Typescripts.* Prefaced and arranged by Hans Walter Gabler; vols. [9] and [10]: *A Portrait of the Artist as a Young Man. A Facsimile of the Final Holograph Manuscript.* Prefaced and arranged by Hans Walter Gabler.

Why and How to Read the Textual Notes

by Hans Walter Gabler and John Paul Riquelme

Readers of this edition should have little difficulty in drawing their gains from the annotations, contextual materials, and critical essays. But readers might benefit from some pointers on why and how to read and study the textual notes.

The copy-text for this edition is not a draft but a fair copy. Although it is not a document in which Joyce first wrote the text, the fair copy of *A Portrait of the Artist as a Young Man* shows distinct traces of continued writing in revisions that focus, or freshly generate, critically interpretable meaning. Such instances are recorded in the textual notes, and a decoding of the notes' formulaic foreshortenings opens the records up to interpretation. For instance, we find recorded, at Part I, lines 101–02 and lines 282–83, that Joyce originally used different numbers when, on the eve of Stephen Dedalus's sickness during his first term in Clongowes Wood College, Stephen changes from "seventyseven" to "seventysix" the number on a slip of paper inside his desk in the study-hall. Joyce erased something in the manuscript in both places. The total erasure at 101–02 is indicated by a ◇ in the footnote; but at 282–83, enough of the erased writing remains discernible to suggest that the word first written was "thirty." In itself, this information seems inert. But since we are reading not for information but to better understand and interpret a fictional text, we relate Joyce's minute revision of the numbers to the narrative. Because the next sentence at lines 283–84 talks about the Christmas vacation being far away, we may assume that the numbers count the days left until Christmas. Yet more significantly, this dating makes Stephen's sickness coincide with the death of the great Irish statesman Charles Stewart Parnell (1846–1891). Synchronizing historical time and fictional time, the parallel anchors Stephen's fantasy identifications with Parnell and Christ in the narrative's very structure.[1]

Throughout, the textual notes provide readers with the opportunity to understand aspects of the process by which the language for the narrative they are reading came into being through writing, revision, and editing. They also provide instances of verbal differences among the versions consulted during the establishing of the text printed in this edition. Some of the notes enable us to recognize Joyce's changes to the handwritten fair copy, as we have seen, or to a later typed or printed version, as part of his composing process. Some of those changes were corrections, such as the addition of a word that had been dropped during the transcribing of the fair copy from an earlier document or during the composing of new material for the fair copy. Other changes involved rewording that resulted in different meanings, through either substitution or addition of language. In effect, we have access to part of the writer's creative process. The notes also record differences between the fair copy and later versions of the text in typescript, in printed editions, or in changes that Joyce directed to be made. The changes may be corrections to errors committed by the typist or by printers, or they may reflect Joyce's decisions to modify the narrative's language. In either case, the differences can bring out contrasting meanings that affect our understanding of the passage's implications. We have access through the notes to processes of textual production between handwritten copy and printed versions, including this one. Those processes, which involve decisions made by the writer and his editors, extend a dimension already contained in the narrative, which in Part V presents Stephen Dedalus's process of composing his poem. Joyce has memorably evoked for us there the act of writing out by hand the text that Stephen is composing, but he has also given us the finished text as it is set up as a printed document.[2] The double vision of Stephen's poem as process and as result is one of the book's most vivid effects. The textual notes allow the reader to experience at points throughout the narrative, not just in the section concerning the poem, some of the oscillations between

1. For a detailed analysis, see Hans Walter Gabler, "The Genesis of *A Portrait of the Artist as a Young Man,*" *Critical Essays on James Joyce's "A Portrait of the Artist as a Young Man,"* ed. Philip Brady and James F. Carens. New York: G. K. Hall, 1998, 106–08; or the essay "The Christmas Dinner Scene, Parnell's Death, and the Genesis of *A Portrait* . . . ," *James Joyce Quarterly* 13 (1976): 27–38.

2. The process of writing the "Villanelle" section itself into Part V has been analyzed from the fair copy in Gabler, "The Genesis of *A Portrait of the Artist as a Young Man,*" 95–96. For an interpretive commentary concerning the relation of printed text to the acts of composing, writing out by hand, and reading, see John Paul Riquelme, "The Villanelle and the Source of Writing," *Teller and Tale in Joyce's Fiction,* Baltimore and London: Johns Hopkins UP, 1983, 73–83.

the writer's handwritten text and the version that ultimately emerges as a published document.

The textual notes in this edition are an ample selection drawn from the footnotes pertaining to the establishing of the text editorially, as well as from the "Historical Collation" list in the 1993 Garland Critical Edition of *A Portrait of the Artist as a Young Man*. Some of the information from the "Historical Collation" not already also contained in the 1993 footnotes, concerning differences between versions of the text, has been shifted to the footnotes of this edition. The notes open with a line number and the reading in question from the line indicated. This so-called lemma is marked off by a square bracket. After the bracket follows a document indicator, marked off by a semicolon, for the source of the reading of this edition. Where the source is the copy-text—that is, Joyce's autograph fair-copy manuscript—the indicator (MS) is commonly absent, since implied, though it is given where especially warranted. For example, the first textual note for Part I begins:

12 *geen*] MS;

This means that in line 12, the word *"geen"* is written thus (with an *r* missing, as in a child's speech) in the fair copy; and a reason for emphasizing the MS spelling is that the conventional word ("green") appears in all published versions, prior to the text in this edition, established from that MS.

When the edition departs from its copy-text, the source of the adopted reading is always given. For example, the seventh textual note for Part I—

106 thrown--haha] aEg; jumped MS, Eg

—means that the language of line 106 from "thrown" through "haha" ("thrown his hat on the haha") has been accepted as a change away from the copy-text, that is, the MS, which contains only "jumped." As the "a" before the source indicator ("Eg") reports, Joyce changed the language on that later printing of the text, namely, in this case, the serial publication in *The Egoist*. In rare instances, the textual editors have decided uniquely for the critical edition not to retain the language of the MS, even though no document verifies Joyce's desire to have the change made. Such emendations of the MS are marked by "e"; if a document partially supports the change, it is mentioned after a colon. Any revision in the manuscript, such as a deletion, insertion, or cancellation, is indicated using the system presented in "Symbols and Sigla" (p. xxx). For example, the note to IV, lines

385–86, places "the--keys" (followed by "MS") between superscript numerals and raised limit marks, as follows:

385–386 the--keys,] ⁷¹ the--keys ¹ᴦ MS

This note indicates that all the language from "the" through "keys" ("the power of the keys") was added to the MS during the first level of revision. The addition is visible on the page of the manuscript here reproduced, written in above the sixth line of handwriting (p. xxix). Such additions happen to be more frequent in Part IV than in the other parts. They are traces of the fact that the fair copy of Part IV is older than the fair copies of the other parts, and that therefore more instances of a later-stage revision are to be found on the MS for Part IV.[3] The note provides a reason and a basis for the reader to compare the passage before the addition was made to the passage.

Beyond documenting sources of readings, the notes frequently also report the language's textual history through typescript (TS) and *Egoist* serialization (Eg), as well as through the American first (16) and the British first and second editions (18 and 24). This record has been deemed especially pertinent where a departure in transmission from Joyce's MS has persisted into Chester G. Anderson's Viking edition (64), even though that first attempt at a critical edition was based on the rediscovery of the MS. For example, the first note for Part I, cited above, continues after "MS;" as follows:

green Eg–64

This note means (as indicated above) that the other published editions, from *The Egoist* through the 1964 edition, print "green," while the MS has "geen." Only exceptionally does the present edition give a textual history of its readings where the 1964 edition already reasserted Joyce's MS or a warranted change to it. The full textual record may be found in the 1993 Garland Critical Edition.[4]

In the printing of this edition, finally, as in the Garland and Vintage editions of 1993, end-of-line hyphenation occurs in two modes. The sign "=" marks a division for mere typographical reasons. Words so printed should always be cited as one undivided word. The regular hyphen indicates an authentic Joycean hyphen.

---

3. See Gabler, "The Genesis of *A Portrait of the Artist as a Young Man*," section I, especially pp. 85–86.
4. On only one occasion has an editorial decision of 1993 been reversed. At V. 2096 this edition does not follow the copy-text's 'wenchers'; considering that form now an authorial slip of the pen, it emends according to all published texts and reads 'wenches'.

man. No King or emperor on this earth has the power of the priest of God. No angel or archangel in heaven, no saint, not even the Blessed Virgin, has the power of a priest of God, the power, the authority, to make the great God of Heaven come down upon the altar and take the form of bread and wine. What an awful power, Stephen! —

A flame began to flutter again on Stephen's cheek as he heard in this proud address an echo of his own proud musings. How often had he seen himself as a priest wielding calmly and humbly the awful power of which angels and saints stood in reverence! His soul had loved to muse in secret on this desire. He had seen himself a young and silent-mannered priest, entering a confessional swiftly, ascending the altar-steps, incensing, genuflecting, accomplishing the vague acts of the priesthood which pleased him by reason of their semblance of reality and of their distance from it. In that dim life which he had lived through in his musings he had assumed the voices

MS page for IV.382–402.

Symbols and Sigla

The symbols employed in the apparatus sections of this edition describe characteristic features of the writing and indicate sequences of correction and revision within the fair copy that provides the edition's copy-text.

⟨ ⟩   authorial deletion in the course of writing

⌐¹TEXT NEW¹⌐   text inserted/changed at first level of revision

⟨⌐¹⌐TEXT OLD⟩   text cancelled at first level of revision

⌐¹⟨TEXT OLD⟩ TEXT NEW¹⌐   text replaced at first level of revision

The symbols ⌐ ⌐ delimit an area of change; a given number indicates the level, an additional letter identifies the agent ("A"=author; "s"=scribe)

∅   space reserved in the autograph

◇   erasure

□   illegible character(s) or word(s)

| line division in document

The document sigla employed in the apparatus sections are: MS, TS, Eg, 16, 18, 24, 64, as summarized above (p. xxviii) and again identified in the opening textual footnote.

Following the lemma bracket in the emendations,

e   indicates a unique emendation in this edition;

e: indicates a unique emendation partially supported by the document identified after the colon;

a   prefixed to a document sigla (e.g., aEg, a16) indicates an authorial correction/revision in or to the document identified by the sigla.

The Text of
A PORTRAIT OF THE ARTIST
AS A YOUNG MAN

Edited, with Textual Notes, by

HANS WALTER GABLER
WITH WALTER HETTCHE

Explanatory Notes by

JOHN PAUL RIQUELME

Et ignotas animum dimittit in artes.[1]

Ovid, Metamorphoses. VIII.188.

---

1. "He turned his mind toward unknown arts" (Latin). The Roman poet Ovid (Publius Ovidius Naso, 43 BCE–17 CE) is presenting the decision of Daedalus, the legendary Athenian artist and inventor, to move beyond the limits of the known in his attempt to escape with his son, Icarus, from their island prison. After Daedalus had constructed a wooden device that made it possible for Queen Pasiphaë of Crete to have intercourse with a bull, her husband, King Minos, had Daedalus build a labyrinth to contain the Minotaur, the half-human, half-bull creature born of the union. Daedalus flew out of the labyrinth and escaped to Sicily with wings made in part of wax, but his son died after disregarding Daedalus's warning not to fly too close to the sun.

I

Once upon a time and a very good time it was there was a moocow coming down along the road and this moocow that was coming down along the road met a nicens little boy named baby tuckoo . . . . .

His father told him that story: his father looked at him through a glass:[1] he had a hairy face.   5

He was baby tuckoo. The moocow came down the road where Betty Byrne lived: she sold lemon platt.[2]

> O, the wild rose blossoms
> On the little green place.   10

He sang that song. That was his song.

> O, the geen wothe botheth.

When you wet the bed first it is warm then it gets cold. His mother put on the oilsheet. That had the queer smell.

His mother had a nicer smell than his father. She played on   15
the piano the sailor's hornpipe for him to dance. He danced:

> Tralala lala
> Tralala tralaladdy
> Tralala lala
> Tralala lala.   20

Uncle Charles and Dante clapped. They were older than his father and mother but uncle Charles was older than Dante.

Dante had two brushes in her press.[3] The brush with the maroon velvet back was for Michael Davitt and the brush with the green velvet back was for Parnell.[4] Dante gave him a cachou[5]   25
every time he brought her a piece of tissue paper.

The Vances lived in number seven. They had a different

Copy-text: Holograph manuscript MS 920 and MS 921 at the National Library of Ireland (MS); Collated texts: proofs and published text of the serialization in *The Egoist*, London 1914–15 (Eg); first edition, New York 1916 (16); second edition, London 1918 (18); third edition, London 1924 (24); 1964 Viking edition in the 1968 Viking Critical Library printing (64).

12 *geen*] MS; green Eg–64 [see pp. xxvii–xxviii]

1. Eyeglass or lens (*OED*); monocle.
2. Platted, or plaited (that is, intertwined), strands (*OED*) of lemon candy.
3. A cupboard for clothes and other personal belongings (*OED*).
4. The Irishmen Michael Davitt (1846–1906) and Charles Stewart Parnell (1846–1891) were the most influential nationalist political leaders in the 1880s, when the narrative opens, during campaigns for land-tenants' rights and Home Rule (limited autonomy) for Ireland.
5. A breath freshener and candy in the form of a pill made of cashew nut, licorice extract, and sugar (*OED*).

father and mother. They were Eileen's father and mother.
When they were grown up he was going to marry Eileen.

He hid under the table. His mother said: 30
—O, Stephen will apologise.

Dante said:
—O, if not, the eagles will come and pull out his eyes.

> *Pull out his eyes,*
> *Apologise,*   35
> *Apologise,*
> *Pull out his eyes.*
>
> *Apologise,*
> *Pull out his eyes,*
> *Pull out his eyes,*   40
> *Apologise.*

◆ ◆ ◆

The wide playgrounds were swarming with boys. All were
shouting and the prefects[6] urged them on with strong cries. The
evening air was pale and chilly and after every charge and thud
of the footballers[7] the greasy leather orb flew like a heavy bird   45
through the grey light. He kept on the fringe of his line, out of
sight of his prefect, out of the reach of the rude feet, feigning to
run now and then. He felt his body small and weak amid the
throng of players and his eyes were weak and watery. Rody
Kickham was not like that: he would be captain of the third   50
line[8] all the fellows said.

Rody Kickham was a decent fellow but Nasty Roche was a
stink. Rody Kickham had greaves in his number and a hamper
in the refectory.[9] Nasty Roche had big hands. He called the
Friday pudding dog-in-the-blanket. And one day he had asked: 55
—What is your name?

Stephen had answered:
—Stephen Dedalus.

Then Nasty Roche had said:
—What kind of a name is that?   60

And when Stephen had not been able to answer Nasty
Roche had asked:

---

30 He (NEW PARAGRAPH)] NO PARAGRAPH 16–64   59 Then] aEg; The MS, Eg

6. Senior students or teachers given the authority to supervise.
7. Probably playing rugby, though "orb" suggests the round ball, rather than the oval rugby
   ball, that would be appropriate for Gaelic football, which was revived in the 1880s.
8. Youngest (for boys under thirteen) of three groups in the school, by contrast with the
   "lower" line (ages thirteen–fifteen) and the "higher" one (ages fifteen–eighteen).
9. Shin guards (*OED*) in a numbered cubby or small locker, and a food container in the dining area.

—What is your father?

Stephen had answered:

—A gentleman.   65

Then Nasty Roche had asked:

—Is he a magistrate?[1]

He crept about from point to point on the fringe of his line,
making little runs now and then. But his hands were bluish
with cold. He kept his hands in the sidepockets of his belted   70
grey suit. That was a belt round his jacket. And belt was also to
give a fellow a belt. One day a fellow had said to Cantwell:

—I'd give you such a belt in a second.

Cantwell had answered:

—Go and fight your match. Give Cecil Thunder a belt. I'd like   75
to see you. He'd give you a toe in the rump for yourself.

That was not a nice expression. His mother had told him
not to speak with the rough boys in the college. Nice mother!
The first day in the hall of the castle[2] when she had said good=
bye she had put up her veil double to her nose to kiss him: and   80
her nose and eyes were red. But he had pretended not to see
that she was going to cry. She was a nice mother but she was
not so nice when she cried. And his father had given him two
fiveshilling pieces for pocket money. And his father had told
him if he wanted anything to write home to him and, whatever   85
he did, never to peach on a fellow.[3] Then at the door of the
castle the rector had shaken hands with his father and mother,
his soutane[4] fluttering in the breeze, and the car had driven off
with his father and mother on it. They had cried to him from
the car, waving their hands: 90

—Goodbye, Stephen, goodbye!

—Goodbye, Stephen, goodbye!

He was caught in the whirl of a scrimmage[5] and, fearful of
the flashing eyes and muddy boots, bent down to look through
the legs. The fellows were struggling and groaning and their   95
legs were rubbing and kicking and stamping. Then Jack
Lawton's yellow boots dodged out the ball and all the other

71 jacket.] pocket. Eg–64

1. A member of the local judiciary; spread throughout Ireland outside Dublin, magistrates
   were frequently Protestants, but by the late decades of the nineteenth century, Catholics
   were sometimes appointed.
2. Central structure of Clongowes Wood College, founded 1814, the first and most prestigious boys' school established in Ireland by the Society of Jesus, a Roman Catholic religious order also know as the Jesuits.
3. Inform on an accomplice or associate (OED).
4. As a Roman Catholic priest, the head of the school, or rector, would have worn the traditional ecclesiastical outer garment, "a long buttoned gown or frock, with sleeves" (OED).
5. "A tussle for the ball among players (in various games)" (OED).

boots and legs ran after. He ran after them a little way and then
stopped. It was useless to run on. Soon they would be going
home for the holidays. After supper in the studyhall he would   100
change the number pasted up inside his desk from seventyseven
to seventysix.[6]

It would be better to be in the studyhall than out there in the
cold. The sky was pale and cold but there were lights in the
castle. He wondered from which window Hamilton Rowan   105
had thrown his hat on the haha[7] and had there been flowerbeds
at that time under the windows. One day when he had been
called to the castle the butler had shown him the marks of the
soldiers' slugs in the wood of the door and had given him a
piece of shortbread that the community[8] ate. It was nice and   110
warm to see the lights in the castle. It was like something in a
book. Perhaps Leicester Abbey was like that. And there were
nice sentences in Doctor Cornwell's Spelling Book.[9] They were
like poetry but they were only sentences to learn the spelling
from.   115

> Wolsey died in Leicester Abbey[1]
> Where the abbots buried him.
> Canker is a disease of plants,
> Cancer one of animals.

It would be nice to lie on the hearthrug before the fire,   120
leaning his head upon his hands, and think on those sentences.
He shivered as if he had cold slimy water next his skin. That
was mean of Wells to shoulder him into the square ditch[2] be=
cause he would not swop his little snuffbox for Wells's sea=
soned hacking chestnut,[3] the conqueror of forty. How cold and   125
slimy the water had been! A fellow had once seen a big rat
jump plop into the scum. He shivered and longed to cry. It

---

101 seventyseven] aEg; ⌐|⟨◇seven⟩ seventy-seven|⌐ MS; seventy-seven Eg   102 seventysix.]
a Eg; ⌐| ⟨◇six.⟩ seventy-six.|⌐ MS; seventy-six. Eg   106 thrown--haha] aEg; jumped MS, Eg
106 had(2)] Eg; were MS   127–128 He--home.] ABSENT Eg–64

6. Days remaining until Christmas. On Joyce's changes to the manuscript here, see pp.
   xxv–xxvi.
7. Archibald Hamilton Rowan (1751–1834), an Irish nationalist imprisoned for sedition in
   1794, stopped at Clongowes Wood Castle (before it was a school) while escaping to France
   and reputedly threw his hat into the dry moat, or haha, around the Castle to mislead his
   pursuers.
8. Priests and other members of the order living and working together at the college.
9. In the middle of the nineteenth century, James Cornwell (1812–1902) published a number of
   books for instruction in grammar and composition, including *The Young Composer* (Michael).
1. Thomas Wolsey (c. 1474–1530), cardinal and lord chancellor of England, died at an
   abbey near Leicester in England on his way to trial for treason, having failed to secure
   from the pope a divorce for King Henry VIII from Catherine of Aragon.
2. The cesspool for the square, or urinal, behind the dormitory (Anderson).
3. Chestnut tied to a string to enable hacking, or striking against another chestnut until one
   breaks.

would be so nice to be at home. Mother was sitting at the fire
with Dante waiting for Brigid to bring in the tea. She had her
feet on the fender and her jewelly slippers were so hot and they
had such a lovely warm smell! Dante knew a lot of things. She
had taught him where the Mozambique Channel was and what
was the longest river in America and what was the name of the
highest mountain in the moon. Father Arnall knew more than
Dante because he was a priest but both his father and uncle
Charles said that Dante was a clever woman and a wellread
woman. And when Dante made that noise after dinner and
then put up her hand to her mouth: that was heartburn.

A voice cried far out on the playground:

—All in!

Then other voices cried from the lower and third lines:

—All in! All in!

The players closed around, flushed and muddy, and he went
among them, glad to go in. Rody Kickham held the ball by its
greasy lace. A fellow asked him to give it one last: but he
walked on without even answering the fellow. Simon Moonan
told him not to because the prefect was looking. The fellow
turned to Simon Moonan and said:

—We all know why you speak. You are McGlade's suck.[4]

Suck was a queer word. The fellow called Simon Moonan
that name because Simon Moonan used to tie the prefect's false
sleeves behind his back and the prefect used to let on to be
angry. But the sound was ugly. Once he had washed his hands
in the lavatory of the Wicklow Hotel and his father pulled the
stopper up by the chain after and the dirty water went down
through the hole in the basin. And when it had all gone down
slowly the hole in the basin had made a sound like that: suck.
Only louder.

To remember that and the white look of the lavatory made
him feel cold and then hot. There were two cocks that you
turned and water came out: cold and hot. He felt cold and then
a little hot: and he could see the names printed on the cocks.
That was a very queer thing.

And the air in the corridor chilled him too. It was queer and
wettish. But soon the gas would be lit and in burning it made a
light noise like a little song. Always the same: and when the
fellows stopped talking in the playroom you could hear it.

It was the hour for sums. Father Arnall wrote a hard sum on
the board and then he said:

169 he] ABSENT Eg–64

4. Sycophant; someone who sucks up to another (schoolboy slang; *OED*).

—Now then, who will win? Go ahead, York! Go ahead, Lan=   170
caster![5]

Stephen tried his best but the sum was too hard and he felt
confused. The little silk badge with the white rose on it that
was pinned on the breast of his jacket began to flutter. He was
no good at sums but he tried his best so that York might not   175
lose. Father Arnall's face looked very black but he was not in a
wax:[6] he was laughing. Then Jack Lawton cracked his fingers
and Father Arnall looked at his copybook and said:

—Right. Bravo Lancaster! The red rose wins. Come on now,
York! Forge ahead!   180

Jack Lawton looked over from his side. The little silk badge
with the red rose on it looked very rich because he had a blue
sailor top on. Stephen felt his own face red too, thinking of all
the bets about who would get first place in elements,[7] Jack
Lawton or he. Some weeks Jack Lawton got the card for first   185
and some weeks he got the card for first. His white silk badge
fluttered and fluttered as he worked at the next sum and heard
Father Arnall's voice. Then all his eagerness passed away and
he felt his face quite cool. He thought his face must be white
because it felt so cool. He could not get out the answer for the 190
sum but it did not matter. White roses and red roses: those
were beautiful colours to think of. And the cards for first place
and second place and third place were beautiful colours too:
pink and cream and lavender. Lavender and cream and pink
roses were beautiful to think of. Perhaps a wild rose might be   195
like those colours: and he remembered the song about the wild
rose blossoms on the little green place. But you could not have
a green rose. But perhaps somewhere in the world you could.

The bell rang and then the classes began to file out of the
rooms and along the corridors towards the refectory. He sat   200
looking at the two prints of butter on his plate but could not
eat the damp bread. The tablecloth was damp and limp. But he
drank off the hot weak tea which the clumsy scullion, girt with
a white apron, poured into his cup. He wondered whether the
scullion's apron was damp too or whether all white things were   205
cold and damp. Nasty Roche and Saurin drank cocoa that their
people sent them in tins. They said they could not drink the tea;

5. The House of York, whose emblem was the white rose, and the House of Lancaster, whose
   emblem was the red rose, opposed each other during the civil war in England later known
   as the War of the Roses. Ireland sided with York. Lancaster won.
6. Not angry (slang; *OED*).
7. As opposed to third *grammar,* the other division of the third line, the youngest students;
   the *elements* class studied spelling, grammar, writing, arithmetic, geography, history, and
   Latin (Gifford).

that it was hogwash. Their fathers were magistrates, the fel=
lows said.

All the boys seemed to him very strange. They had all fa=   210
thers and mothers and different clothes and voices. He longed
to be at home and lay his head on his mother's lap. But he
could not: and so he longed for the play and study and prayers
to be over and to be in bed.

He drank another cup of hot tea and Fleming said: 215
—What's up? Have you a pain or what's up with you?
—I don't know, Stephen said.
—Sick in your breadbasket, Fleming said, because your face
looks white. It will go away.
—O yes, Stephen said.   220

But he was not sick there. He thought that he was sick in his
heart if you could be sick in that place. Fleming was very
decent to ask him. He wanted to cry. He leaned his elbows on
the table and shut and opened the flaps of his ears. Then he
heard the noise of the refectory every time he opened the flaps   225
of his ears. It made a roar like a train at night. And when he
closed the flaps the roar was shut off like a train going into a
tunnel. That night at Dalkey[8] the train had roared like that and
then, when it went into the tunnel, the roar stopped. He closed
his eyes and the train went on, roaring and then stopping;   230
roaring again, stopping. It was nice to hear it roar and stop and
then roar out of the tunnel again and then stop.

Then the higher line fellows began to come down along the
matting in the middle of the refectory, Paddy Rath and Jimmy
Magee and the Spaniard who was allowed to smoke cigars and   235
the little Portuguese who wore the woolly cap. And then the
lower line tables and the tables of the third line. And every
single fellow had a different way of walking.

He sat in a corner of the playroom pretending to watch a
game of dominos and once or twice he was able to hear for an   240
instant the little song of the gas. The prefect was at the door
with some boys and Simon Moonan was knotting his false
sleeves. He was telling them something about Tullabeg.[9]

Then he went away from the door and Wells came over to
Stephen and said: 245

—Tell us, Dedalus, do you kiss your mother every night before
you go to bed?

246 every night] ABSENT Eg–64; CF 251

8. Village on the coast south of Dublin.
9. Location of another Jesuit boys' school.

Stephen answered:

—I do.

Wells turned to the other fellows and said: 250

—O, I say, here's a fellow says he kisses his mother every night
before he goes to bed.

The other fellows stopped their game and turned round,
laughing. Stephen blushed under their eyes and said:

—I do not.   255

Wells said:

—O, I say, here's a fellow says he doesn't kiss his mother
before he goes to bed.

They all laughed again. Stephen tried to laugh with them.
He felt his whole body hot and confused in a moment. What   260
was the right answer to the question? He had given two and
still Wells laughed. But Wells must know the right answer for
he was in third of grammar. He tried to think of Wells's mother
but he did not dare to raise his eyes to Wells's face. He did not
like Wells's face. It was Wells who had shouldered him into the 265
square ditch the day before because he would not swop his
little snuffbox for Wells's seasoned hacking chestnut, the con=
queror of forty. It was a mean thing to do; all the fellows said it
was. And how cold and slimy the water had been! And a fellow
had once seen a big rat jump plop into the scum.   270

The cold slime of the ditch covered his whole body; and,
when the bell rang for study and the lines filed out of the
playrooms, he felt the cold air of the corridor and staircase
inside his clothes. He still tried to think what was the right
answer. Was it right to kiss his mother or wrong to kiss his   275
mother? What did that mean, to kiss? You put your face up like
that to say goodnight and then his mother put her face down.
That was to kiss. His mother put her lips on his cheek; her lips
were soft and they wetted his cheek; and they made a tiny little
noise: kiss. Why did people do that with their two faces?   280

Sitting in the studyhall he opened the lid of his desk and
changed the number pasted up inside from seventyseven to
seventysix.[1] But the Christmas vacation was very far away: but
one time it would come because the earth moved round always.

There was a picture of the earth on the first page of his   285
geography: a big ball in the middle of clouds. Fleming had a
box of crayons and one night during free study he had coloured
the earth green and the clouds maroon. That was like the two

---

282 seventyseven] aEg; ⁻ˡ⟨thir◇⟩ seventy-ˡ⸢ seven MS; seventy-seven Eg   283 seventysix.]
aEg; ⁻ˡ⟨◇⟩ seventy-ˡ⸢ six. MS; seventy-six. Eg

1. On Joyce's changes to the manuscript here, see pp. xxv–xxvi.

brushes in Dante's press, the brush with the green velvet back for Parnell and the brush with the maroon velvet back for 290 Michael Davitt. But he had not told Fleming to colour them those colours. Fleming had done it himself.

He opened the geography to study the lesson; but he could not learn the names of places in America. Still they were all different places that had those different names. They were all in 295 different countries and the countries were in continents and the continents were in the world and the world was in the universe.

He turned to the flyleaf of the geography and read what he had written there: himself, his name and where he was.

Stephen Dedalus 300
Class of Elements
Clongowes Wood College
Sallins
County Kildare
Ireland 305
Europe
The World
The Universe

That was in his writing: and Fleming one night for a cod[2] had written on the opposite page: 310

Stephen Dedalus is my name,
Ireland is my nation.
Clongowes is my dwellingplace
And heaven my expectation.

He read the verses backwards but then they were not poetry. 315 Then he read the flyleaf from the bottom to the top till he came to his own name. That was he: and he read down the page again. What was after the universe? Nothing. But was there anything round the universe to show where it stopped before the nothing place began? It could not be a wall but there could 320 be a thin thin line there all round everything. It was very big to think about everything and everywhere. Only God could do that. He tried to think what a big thought that must be but he could think only of God. God was God's name just as his name was Stephen. *Dieu* was the French for God and that was God's 325 name too; and when anyone prayed to God and said *Dieu* then God knew at once that it was a French person that was pray= ing. But though there were different names for God in all the different languages in the world and God understood what all

2. As a prank.

the people who prayed said in their different languages still   330
God remained always the same God and God's real name was
God.

It made him very tired to think that way. It made him feel
his head very big. He turned over the flyleaf and looked wearily
at the green round earth in the middle of the maroon clouds.   335
He wondered which was right, to be for the green or for the
maroon, because Dante had ripped the green velvet back off
the brush that was for Parnell one day with her scissors and
had told him that Parnell was a bad man. He wondered if they
were arguing at home about that. That was called politics.   340
There were two sides in it: Dante was on one side and his
father and Mr Casey were on the other side but his mother and
uncle Charles were on no side. Every day there was something
in the paper about it.[3]

It pained him that he did not know well what politics meant   345
and that he did not know where the universe ended. He felt
small and weak. When would he be like the fellows in poetry
and rhetoric?[4] They had big voices and big boots and they
studied trigonometry. That was very far away. First came the
vacation and then the next term and then vacation again and   350
then again another term and then again the vacation. It was
like a train going in and out of tunnels and that was like the
noise of the boys eating in the refectory when you opened and
closed the flaps of the ears. Term, vacation; tunnel, out; noise,
stop. How far away it was! It was better to go to bed to sleep.   355
Only prayers in the chapel and then bed. He shivered and
yawned. It would be lovely in bed after the sheets got a bit hot.
First they were so cold to get into. He shivered to think how
cold they were first. But then they got hot and then he could
sleep. It was lovely to be tired. He yawned again. Night prayers   360
and then bed: he shivered and wanted to yawn. It would be
lovely in a few minutes. He felt a warm glow creeping up from
the cold shivering sheets, warmer and warmer till he felt warm
all over, ever so warm; ever so warm and yet he shivered a little
and still wanted to yawn.   365

The bell rang for night prayers and he filed out of the study=
hall after the others and down the staircase and along the
corridors to the chapel. The corridors were darkly lit and the

---

3. Newspaper coverage, often biased and sensational, began when Captain William O'Shea
made public in 1889 the adulterous relationship between Parnell and O'Shea's wife, Katherine. The scandal divided the country and led to Parnell's being replaced in 1891 as leader of
the Irish Parliamentary Party.
4. The two divisions of the higher line, the oldest group of boys.

chapel was darkly lit. Soon all would be dark and sleeping.
There was cold night air in the chapel and the marbles[5] were the   370
colour the sea was at night. The sea was cold day and night:
but it was colder at night. It was cold and dark under the
seawall beside his father's house. But the kettle would be on the
hob to make punch.

The prefect of the chapel prayed above his head and his   375
memory knew the responses:

> *O Lord, open our lips*
> *And our mouth shall announce Thy praise.*
> *Incline unto our aid, O God!*
> *O Lord, make haste to help us!*   380

There was a cold night smell in the chapel. But it was a holy
smell. It was not like the smell of the old peasants who knelt at
the back of the chapel at Sunday mass. That was a smell of air
and rain and turf and corduroy. But they were very holy peas=
ants. They breathed behind him on his neck and sighed as they   385
prayed. They lived in Clane,[6] a fellow said: there were little
cottages there and he had seen a woman standing at the half=
door of a cottage with a child in her arms as the cars had come
past from Sallins. It would be lovely to sleep for one night in
that cottage before the fire of smoking turf, in the dark lit by   390
the fire, in the warm dark, breathing the smell of the peasants,
air and rain and turf and corduroy. But, O, the road there
between the trees was dark! You would be lost in the dark. It
made him afraid to think of how it was.

He heard the voice of the prefect of the chapel saying the last   395
prayer. He prayed it too against the dark outside under the
trees.

> *Visit, we beseech Thee, O Lord, this habitation and*
> *drive away from it all the snares of the enemy. May*
> *Thy holy angels dwell herein to preserve us in peace*   400
> *and may Thy blessing be always upon us through*
> *Christ, Our Lord. Amen.*

His fingers trembled as he undressed himself in the dormi=
tory. He told his fingers to hurry up. He had to undress and
then kneel and say his own prayers and be in bed before the gas   405
was lowered so that he might not go to hell when he died. He
rolled his stockings off and put on his nightshirt quickly and

---

369 sleeping.] TS BEGINS

5. Pillars painted to look like marble (Anderson).
6. Village near Clongowes, whose chapel served as the parish church.

knelt trembling at his bedside and repeated his prayers quickly quickly fearing that the gas would go down. He felt his shoul= ders shaking as he murmured: 410

> *God bless my father and my mother and spare them to me!*
> *God bless my little brothers and sisters and spare them to me!*
> *God bless Dante and uncle Charles and spare them to*   415
> *me!*

He blessed himself and climbed quickly into bed and, tuck= ing the end of the nightshirt under his feet, curled himself to= gether under the cold white sheets, shaking and trembling. But he would not go to hell when he died; and the shaking would   420 stop. A voice bade the boys in the dormitory goodnight. He peered out for an instant over the coverlet and saw the yellow curtains round and before his bed that shut him off on all sides. The light was lowered quietly.

The prefect's shoes went away. Where? Down the staircase   425 and along the corridors or to his room at the end? He saw the dark. Was it true about the black dog that walked there at night with eyes as big as carriagelamps? They said it was the ghost of a murderer. A long shiver of fear flowed over his body. He saw the dark entrance hall of the castle. Old servants in old dress   430 were in the ironingroom above the staircase. It was long ago. The old servants were quiet. There was a fire there but the hall was still dark. A figure came up the staircase from the hall. He wore the white cloak of a marshal; his face was pale and strange; he held his hand pressed to his side. He looked out of   435 strange eyes at the old servants. They looked at him and saw their master's face and cloak and knew that he had received his deathwound. But only the dark was where they looked: only dark silent air. Their master had received his deathwound on the battlefield of Prague far away over the sea. He was standing   440 on the field; his hand was pressed to his side; his face was pale and strange and he wore the white cloak of a marshal.

O how cold and strange it was to think of that! All the dark was cold and strange. There were pale strange faces there, great eyes like carriagelamps. They were the ghosts of murderers, the   445 figures of marshals who had received their deathwound on battlefields far away over the sea. What did they wish to say that their faces were so strange?

Visit, we beseech Thee, O Lord, this habitation and drive away from it all   450

408–409 quickly quickly] quickly Eg; quickly, 16–24; quickly quickly, 64

Going home for the holidays! That would be lovely: the fellows had told him. Getting up on the cars[7] in the early wintry morning outside the door of the castle. The cars were rolling on the gravel. Cheers for the rector!

Hurray! Hurray! Hurray!   455

The cars drove past the chapel and all caps were raised. They drove merrily along the country roads. The drivers pointed with their whips to Bodenstown. The fellows cheered. They passed the farmhouse of the Jolly Farmer. Cheer after cheer after cheer. Through Clane they drove, cheering and   460 cheered. The peasant women stood at the halfdoors, the men stood here and there. The lovely smell there was in the wintry air: the smell of Clane: rain and wintry air and turf smoulder= ing and corduroy.

The train was full of fellows: a long long chocolate train   465 with cream facings. The guards went to and fro opening, closing, locking, unlocking the doors. They were men in dark blue and silver; they had silvery whistles and their keys made a quick music: click, click: click, click.

And the train raced on over the flat lands and past the Hill   470 of Allen. The telegraphpoles were passing, passing. The train went on and on. It knew. There were coloured lanterns in the hall of his father's house and ropes of green branches. There were holly and ivy round the pierglass and holly and ivy, green and red, twined round the chandeliers. There were red holly   475 and green ivy round the old portraits on the walls. Holly and ivy for him and for Christmas.

Lovely . . . . . .

All the people. Welcome home, Stephen! Noises of welcome. His mother kissed him. Was that right? His father was a mar=   480 shal now: higher than a magistrate. Welcome home, Stephen!

Noises . . . . .

There was a noise of curtainrings running back along the rods, of water being splashed in the basins. There was a noise of rising and dressing and washing in the dormitory: a noise of   485 clapping of hands as the prefect went up and down telling the fellows to look sharp. A pale sunlight showed the yellow cur= tains drawn back, the tossed beds. His bed was very hot and his face and body were very hot.

He got up and sat on the side of his bed. He was weak. He   490 tried to pull on his stocking. It had a horrid rough feel. The sunlight was queer and cold.

Fleming said:

7. Horse-drawn transportation.

—Are you not well?

He did not know; and Fleming said:
    495
—Get back into bed. I'll tell McGlade you're not well.

—He's sick.

—Who is?

—Tell McGlade.

—Get back into bed.
    500
—Is he sick?

A fellow held his arms while he loosened the stocking cling=
ing to his foot and climbed back into the hot bed.

He crouched down between the sheets, glad of their tepid
glow. He heard the fellows talk among themselves about him   505
as they dressed for mass. It was a mean thing to do, to shoulder
him into the square ditch, they were saying.

Then their voices ceased; they had gone. A voice at his bed
said:

—Dedalus, don't spy on us,[8] sure you won't?   510

Wells's face was there. He looked at it and saw that Wells
was afraid.

—I didn't mean to. Sure you won't?

His father had told him, whatever he did, never to peach on
a fellow. He shook his head and answered no and felt glad.   515
Wells said:

—I didn't mean to, honour bright. It was only for cod. I'm
sorry.

The face and the voice went away. Sorry because he was
afraid. Afraid that it was some disease. Canker was a disease of   520
plants and cancer one of animals: or another different. That
was a long time ago then out on the playgrounds in the evening
light, creeping from point to point on the fringe of his line, a
heavy bird flying low through the grey light. Leicester Abbey lit
up. Wolsey died there. The abbots buried him themselves.   525

It was not Wells's face, it was the prefect's. He was not
foxing.[9] No, no: he was sick really. He was not foxing. And he
felt the prefect's hand on his forehead; and he felt his forehead
warm and damp against the prefect's cold damp hand. That
was the way a rat felt, slimy and damp and cold. Every rat had   530
two eyes to look out of. Sleek slimy coats, little little feet
tucked up to jump, black shiny eyes to look out of. They could
understand how to jump. But the minds of rats could not
understand trigonometry. When they were dead they lay on

523 to] TS; of MS

8. Don't inform against me.
9. Pretending (slang; *OED*).

their sides. Their coats dried then. They were only dead things.   535

The prefect was there again and it was his voice that was saying that he was to get up, that Father Minister had said he was to get up and dress and go to the infirmary. And while he was dressing himself as quickly as he could the prefect said:

—We must pack off to Brother[1] Michael because we have the   540 collywobbles. Terrible thing to have the collywobbles! How we wobble when we have the collywobbles!

He was very decent to say that. That was all to make him laugh. But he could not laugh because his cheeks and lips were all shivery: and then the prefect had to laugh by himself.   545

The prefect cried:

—Quick march! Hayfoot! Strawfoot![2]

They went together down the staircase and along the corri= dor and past the bath. As he passed the door he remembered with a vague fear the warm turfcoloured bogwater, the warm   550 moist air, the noise of plunges, the smell of the towels, like medicine.

Brother Michael was standing at the door of the infirmary and from the door of the dark cabinet on his right came a smell like medicine. That came from the bottles on the shelves. The   555 prefect spoke to Brother Michael and Brother Michael answered and called the prefect sir. He had reddish hair mixed with grey and a queer look. It was queer that he would always be a brother. It was queer too that you could not call him sir because he was a brother and had a different kind of look. Was   560 he not holy enough or why could he not catch up on the others?

There were two beds in the room and in one bed there was a fellow: and when they went in he called out:

—Hello! It's young Dedalus! What's up?

—The sky is up, Brother Michael said.   565

He was a fellow out of third of grammar and, while Stephen was undressing, he asked Brother Michael to bring him a round of buttered toast.

—Ah, do! he said.

—Butter you up! said Brother Michael. You'll get your walking   570 papers in the morning when the doctor comes.

—Will I? the fellow said. I'm not well yet.

Brother Michael repeated:

541–542 Terrible--collywobbles! How--collywobbles!] MS; ABSENT TS–24   566 of(1)] of the Eg–64

1. Member of the Jesuit order who is part of the community but is not ordained.
2. Joking reference to using hay on the left foot and straw on the right to teach soldiers how to tell the difference between their feet when marching.

—You'll get your walking papers, I tell you.

He bent down to rake the fire. He had a long back like the long back of a tramhorse. He shook the poker gravely and nodded his head at the fellow out of third of grammar. 575

Then Brother Michael went away and after a while the fel=low out of third of grammar turned in towards the wall and fell asleep. 580

That was the infirmary. He was sick then. Had they written home to tell his mother and father? But it would be quicker for one of the priests to go himself to tell them. Or he would write a letter for the priest to bring.

Dear Mother 585
I am sick. I want to go home. Please come and take me home. I am in the infirmary.

Your fond son,
Stephen

How far away they were! There was cold sunlight outside the window. He wondered if he would die. You could die just the same on a sunny day. He might die before his mother came. Then he would have a dead mass in the chapel like the way the fellows had told him it was when Little had died. All the fel=lows would be at the mass, dressed in black, all with sad faces. Wells too would be there but no fellow would look at him. The rector would be there in a cope of black and gold and there would be tall yellow candles on the altar and round the cata=falque.[3] And they would carry the coffin out of the chapel slowly and he would be buried in the little graveyard of the community off the main avenue of limes. And Wells would be sorry then for what he had done. And the bell would toll slowly. 590 595 600

He could hear the tolling. He said over to himself the song that Brigid had taught him. 605

Dingdong! The castle bell!
Farewell, my mother!
Bury me in the old churchyard
Beside my eldest brother.
My coffin shall be black, 610
Six angels at my back,
Two to sing and two to pray
And two to carry my soul away.

601 limes.] Eg; chestnuts. MS–TS

3. Decorated structure that holds a coffin during funeral ceremonies (*OED*).

How beautiful and sad that was! How beautiful the words
were where they said *Bury me in the old churchyard*! A tremor   615
passed over his body. How sad and how beautiful! He wanted
to cry quietly but not for himself: for the words, so beautiful
and sad, like music. The bell! The bell! Farewell! O farewell!

The cold sunlight was weaker and Brother Michael was
standing at his bedside with a bowl of beeftea.[4] He was glad for   620
his mouth was hot and dry. He could hear them playing on the
playgrounds. It was after lunchtime. And the day was going on
in the college just as if he were there.

Then Brother Michael was going away and the fellow out of
third of grammar told him to be sure and come back and tell   625
him all the news in the paper. He told Stephen that his name
was Athy and that his father kept a lot of racehorses that were
spiffing jumpers and that his father would give a good tip to
Brother Michael any time he wanted it because Brother Mi=
chael was very decent and always told him the news out of the   630
paper they got every day up in the castle. There was every kind
of news in the paper: accidents, shipwrecks, sports and politics.
—Now it is all about politics in the paper, he said. Do your
people talk about that too?
—Yes, Stephen said.   635
—Mine too, he said.

Then he thought for a moment and said:
—You have a queer name, Dedalus, and I have a queer name
too, Athy. My name is the name of a town. Your name is like
Latin.   640

Then he asked:
—Are you good at riddles?

Stephen answered:
—Not very good.

Then he said: 645
—Can you answer me this one? Why is the county Kildare like
the leg of a fellow's breeches?

Stephen thought what could be the answer and then said:
—I give it up.
—Because there is a thigh in it, he said. Do you see the joke?   650
Athy is the town in the county Kildare and a thigh is the other
thigh.
—O, I see, Stephen said.
—That's an old riddle, he said.

---

622 It--lunchtime.] ABSENT TS—64

4. The juice of beef extracted by simmering (*OED*).

After a moment he said: 655
—I say!
—What? asked Stephen.
—You know, he said, you can ask that riddle another way?
—Can you? said Stephen.
—The same riddle, he said. Do you know the other way to ask   660
it?
—No, said Stephen.
—Can you not think of the other way? he said.

He looked at Stephen over the bedclothes as he spoke. Then
he lay back on the pillow and said: 665
—There is another way but I won't tell you what it is.

Why did he not tell it? His father, who kept the racehorses,
must be a magistrate too like Saurin's father and Nasty Roche's
father. He thought of his own father, of how he sang songs
while his mother played and of how he always gave him a   670
shilling when he asked for sixpence[5] and he felt sorry for him
that he was not a magistrate like the other boys' fathers. Then
why was he sent to that place with them? But his father had
told him that he would be no stranger there because his grand=
uncle had presented an address to the liberator[6] there fifty years   675
before. You could know the people of that time by their old
dress. It seemed to him a solemn time: and he wondered if that
was the time when the fellows in Clongowes wore blue coats
with brass buttons and yellow waistcoats and caps of rabbit=
skin and drank beer like grownup people and kept greyhounds   680
of their own to course the hares with.

He looked at the window and saw that the daylight had
grown weaker. There would be cloudy grey light over the play=
grounds. There was no noise on the playgrounds. The class
must be doing the themes or perhaps Father Arnall was reading   685
a legend[7] out of the book.

It was queer that they had not given him any medicine.
Perhaps Brother Michael would bring it back when he came.
They said you got stinking stuff to drink when you were in the
infirmary. But he felt better now than before. It would be nice   690
getting better slowly. You could get a book then. There was a

---

673 father] MS; uncle TS [BY INTERIM INSTRUCTION TO TYPIST? Eg REVERTS TO father]
674 he] TS; we MS

5. In the British currency system, then in effect in Ireland, one shilling was worth twelve
   pence.
6. Daniel O'Connell (1775–1847), Irish political leader who worked for repeal of the Union
   with England and for Catholic emancipation (granted in 1829), the right of Catholics to
   hold high public offices, from which they had been excluded.
7. Story of a saint's life (OED).

book in the library about Holland. There were lovely foreign names in it and pictures of strangelooking cities and ships. It made you feel so happy.

How pale the light was at the window! But that was nice. The fire rose and fell on the wall. It was like waves. Someone had put coal on and he heard voices. They were talking. It was the noise of the waves. Or the waves were talking among them= selves as they rose and fell.

He saw the sea of waves, long dark waves rising and falling, dark under the moonless night. A tiny light twinkled at the pierhead where the ship was entering: and he saw a multitude of people gathered by the waters' edge to see the ship that was entering their harbour. A tall man stood on the deck, looking out towards the flat dark land: and by the light at the pierhead he saw his face, the sorrowful face of Brother Michael.

He saw him lift his hand towards the people and heard him say in a loud voice of sorrow over the waters:

—He is dead. We saw him lying upon the catafalque.

A wail of sorrow went up from the people.

—Parnell! Parnell! He is dead![8]

They fell upon their knees, moaning in sorrow.

And he saw Dante in a maroon velvet dress and with a green velvet mantle hanging from her shoulders walking proudly and silently past the people who knelt by the waters' edge.

◆　◆　◆

A great fire, banked high and red, flamed in the grate and under the ivytwined branches of the chandelier the Christmas table was spread. They had come home a little late and still dinner was not ready: but it would be ready in a jiffy, his mother had said. They were waiting for the door to open and for the servants to come in, holding the big dishes covered with their heavy metal covers.

All were waiting: uncle Charles, who sat far away in the shadow of the window, Dante and Mr Casey, who sat in the easychairs at either side of the hearth, Stephen, seated on a chair between them, his feet resting on the toasted boss.[9] Mr Dedalus looked at himself in the pierglass above the mantel= piece, waxed out his moustache ends and then, parting his coattails, stood with his back to the glowing fire: and still, from time to time, he withdrew a hand from his coattail to wax out one of his moustache ends. Mr Casey leaned his head to one

8. Parnell died October 6, 1891. On October 11, his body was brought by ship to Kingstown.
9. A stuffed footstool without a wooden frame (*Letters* III, 129).

side and, smiling, tapped the gland of his neck with his fingers.
And Stephen smiled too for he knew now that it was not true
that Mr Casey had a purse of silver in his throat. He smiled to
think how the silvery noise which Mr Casey used to make had   735
deceived him. And when he had tried to open Mr Casey's hand
to see if the purse of silver was hidden there he had seen that
the fingers could not be straightened out: and Mr Casey had
told him that he had got those three cramped fingers making a
birthday present for Queen Victoria.[1]   740

Mr Casey tapped the gland of his neck and smiled at Ste=
phen with sleepy eyes: and Mr Dedalus said to him:

—Yes. Well now, that's all right. O, we had a good walk,
hadn't we, John? Yes . . . . . . I wonder if there's any likelihood of
dinner this evening. Yes . . . . . O, well now, we got a good breath   745
of ozone round the Head[2] today. Ay, bedad.

He turned to Dante and said:

—You didn't stir out at all, Mrs Riordan?

Dante frowned and said shortly:

—No.   750

Mr Dedalus dropped his coattails and went over to the side=
board. He brought forth a great stone jar of whisky from the
locker and filled the decanter slowly, bending now and then to
see how much he had poured in. Then replacing the jar in the
locker he poured out a little of the whisky into two glasses,   755
added a little water and came with them back to the fireplace.

—A thimbleful, John, he said. Just to whet your appetite.

Mr Casey took the glass, drank, and placed it near him on
the mantelpiece. Then he said:

—Well, I can't help thinking of our friend Christopher manu=   760
facturing . . . .

He broke into a fit of laughter and coughing and added:

— . . . manufacturing that champagne for those fellows.

Mr Dedalus laughed loudly.

—Is it Christy? he said. There's more cunning in one of those 765
warts on his bald head than in a pack of jack foxes.

He inclined his head, closed his eyes, and, licking his lips
profusely, began to speak with the voice of the hotel keeper.

—And he has such a soft mouth when he's speaking to you,
don't you know. He's very moist and watery about the dew=   770
laps, God bless him.

755–756 glasses,--water] glasses ⌐⌐, added a little water⌐⌐ MS   756 with--back] back with
the Eg–64

1. His hand has been crippled by forced labor during imprisonment for revolutionary activities.
2. Bray Head, a headland on the east coast, about twelve miles south of Dublin; near Bray,
   the village where Stephen's family resides.

Mr Casey was still struggling through his fit of coughing and laughter. Stephen, seeing and hearing the hotel keeper through his father's face and voice, laughed.

Mr Dedalus put up his eyeglass and, staring down at him,   775
said quietly and kindly:

—What are you laughing at, you little puppy, you?

The servants entered and placed the dishes on the table. Mrs Dedalus followed and the places were arranged.

—Sit over, she said.   780

Mr Dedalus went to the end of the table and said:

—Now, Mrs Riordan, sit over. John, sit you down, my hearty.

He looked round to where uncle Charles sat and said:

—Now then, sir, there's a bird here waiting for you.

When all had taken their seats he laid his hand on the cover   785
and then said quickly, withdrawing it:

—Now, Stephen.

Stephen stood up in his place to say the grace before meals:

> Bless us, O Lord, and these Thy gifts which through
> Thy bounty we are about to receive through Christ   790
> Our Lord. Amen.

All blessed themselves and Mr Dedalus with a sigh of pleas= ure lifted from the dish the heavy cover pearled around the edge with glistening drops.

Stephen looked at the plump turkey which had lain, trussed   795
and skewered, on the kitchen table. He knew that his father had paid a guinea for it in Dunn's of D'Olier Street[3] and that the man had prodded it often at the breastbone to show how good it was: and he remembered the man's voice when he had said:

—Take that one, sir. That's the real Ally Daly.[4]   800

Why did Mr Barrett in Clongowes call his pandybat[5] a tur= key? It was not like a turkey. But Clongowes was far away: and the warm heavy smell of turkey and ham and celery rose from the plates and dishes and the great fire was banked high and red in the grate and the green ivy and red holly made you feel   805
so happy and when dinner was ended the big plumpudding would be carried in, studded with peeled almonds and sprigs of holly, with bluish fire running around it and a little green flag flying from the top.

---

801 Mr] aTS; Father MS   802 It--turkey.] MS; ABSENT TS–64   808 a] a ⟨□⟩ MS

3. Expensive shop for food in central Dublin. A guinea was a gold coin worth twenty-one shillings or the equivalent, one pound and one shilling.
4. The real thing, the best (slang).
5. An instrument, often a reinforced leather strap, for punishing schoolboys with strokes on the open palm.

It was his first Christmas dinner and he thought of his little   810
brothers and sisters who were waiting in the nursery, as he had
often waited, till the pudding came. The deep low collar and
the Eton jacket made him feel queer and oldish: and that morn=
ing when his mother had brought him down to the parlour,
dressed for mass, his father had cried. That was because he was   815
thinking of his own father. And uncle Charles had said so too.

Mr Dedalus covered the dish and began to eat hungrily.
Then he said:

—Poor old Christy, he's nearly lopsided now with roguery.

—Simon, said Mrs Dedalus, you haven't given Mrs Riordan   820
any sauce.

Mr Dedalus seized the sauceboat.

—Haven't I? he cried. Mrs Riordan, pity the poor blind.

Dante covered her plate with her hands and said:

—No, thanks.   825

Mr Dedalus turned to uncle Charles.

—How are you off, sir?

—Right as the mail, Simon.

—You, John?

—I'm all right. Go on yourself.   830

—Mary? Here, Stephen, here's something to make your hair
curl.

He poured sauce freely over Stephen's plate and set the boat
again on the table. Then he asked uncle Charles was it tender.
Uncle Charles could not speak because his mouth was full but   835
he nodded that it was.

—That was a good answer our friend made to the canon.
What? said Mr Dedalus.

—I didn't think he had that much in him, said Mr Casey.

—*I'll pay you your dues, father, when you cease turning the*   840
house of God into a pollingbooth.

—A nice answer, said Dante, for any man calling himself a
catholic to give to his priest.

—They have only themselves to blame, said Mr Dedalus
suavely. If they took a fool's advice they would confine their   845
attention to religion.

—It is religion, Dante said. They are doing their duty in warn=
ing the people.

—We go to the house of God, Mr Casey said, in all humility to
pray to our Maker and not to hear election addresses.   850

—It is religion, Dante said again. They are right. They must
direct their flocks.

813 oldish:] old ⟨:⟩ ⌐ish:⌐ᵣ MS   840 *you*(1)] ⌐*you*⌐ᵣ MS; ABSENT 16–24

—And preach politics from the altar, is it? asked Mr Dedalus.

—Certainly, said Dante. It is a question of public morality. A priest would not be a priest if he did not tell his flock what is right and what is wrong.

Mrs Dedalus laid down her knife and fork, saying:

—For pity' sake and for pity' sake let us have no political discussion on this day of all days in the year.

—Quite right, ma'am, said uncle Charles. Now, Simon, that's quite enough now. Not another word now.

—Yes, yes, said Mr Dedalus quickly.

He uncovered the dish boldly and said:

—Now then, who's for more turkey?

Nobody answered. Dante said:

—Nice language for any catholic to use!

—Mrs Riordan, I appeal to you, said Mrs Dedalus, to let the matter drop now.

Dante turned on her and said:

—And am I to sit here and listen to the pastors of my church being flouted?

—Nobody is saying a word against them, said Mr Dedalus, so long as they don't meddle in politics.

—The bishops and priests of Ireland have spoken, said Dante, and they must be obeyed.

—Let them leave politics alone, said Mr Casey, or the people may leave their church alone.

—You hear? said Dante turning to Mrs Dedalus.

—Mr Casey! Simon! said Mrs Dedalus. Let it end now.

—Too bad! Too bad! said uncle Charles.

—What? cried Mr Dedalus. Were we to desert him at the bid=ding of the English people?[6]

—He was no longer worthy to lead, said Dante. He was a public sinner.

—We are all sinners and black sinners, said Mr Casey coldly.

—*Woe be to the man by whom the scandal cometh!* said Mrs Riordan. *It would be better for him that a millstone were tied about his neck and that he were cast into the depths of the sea rather than that he should scandalise one of these, my least little ones.* That is the language of the Holy Ghost.[7]

855

860

865

870

875

880

885

890

---

883 was] ⁻¹⟨is⟩ was¹ʳ [TWICE] MS

6. After the adultery scandal, the English prime minister, William Gladstone (1809–1898), leader of the Liberal Party, which had been allied with Parnell over Home Rule, pressed for Parnell's removal as head of the Irish Parliamentary Party.

7. In Christianity, the third person of the Holy Trinity (Father, Son, and Holy Ghost, or Holy Spirit) constituting a triune God (*OED*).

—And very bad language, if you ask me, said Mr Dedalus coolly.

—Simon! Simon! said uncle Charles. The boy.

—Yes, yes, said Mr Dedalus. I meant about the . . . . I was think= ing about the bad language of that railway porter. Well now, that's all right. Here, Stephen, show me your plate, old chap. Eat away now. Here.

He heaped up the food on Stephen's plate and served uncle Charles and Mr Casey to large pieces of turkey and splashes of sauce. Mrs Dedalus was eating little and Dante sat with her hands in her lap. She was red in the face. Mr Dedalus rooted with the carvers at the end of the dish and said:

—There's a tasty bit here we call the pope's nose.[8] If any lady or gentleman . . . . .

He held a piece of fowl up on the prong of the carvingfork. Nobody spoke. He put it on his own plate, saying:

—Well, you can't say but you were asked. I think I had better eat it myself because I'm not well in my health lately.

He winked at Stephen and, replacing the dishcover, began to eat again.

There was a silence while he ate. Then he said:

—Well now, the day kept up fine after all. There were plenty of strangers down too.

Nobody spoke. He said again:

—I think there were more strangers down than last Christmas.

He looked round at the others whose faces were bent to= wards their plates and, receiving no reply, waited for a moment and said bitterly:

—Well, my Christmas dinner has been spoiled anyhow.

—There could be neither luck nor grace, Dante said, in a house where there is no respect for the pastors of the church.

Mr Dedalus threw his knife and fork noisily on his plate.

—Respect! he said. Is it for Billy with the lip or for the tub of guts up in Armagh?[9] Respect!

—Princes of the church, said Mr Casey with slow scorn.

—Lord Leitrim's coachman,[1] yes, said Mr Dedalus.

895

900

905

910

915

920

925

---

898 plate] TS; table MS

8. The rump of the turkey.
9. William J. Walsh (1841–1921), archbishop of Dublin and primate of Ireland, and Michael Logue (1840–1924), archbishop of Armagh and primate of All Ireland, the top-ranking Irish prelates, denounced Parnell in a published statement (reprinted in this volume) signed by themselves and numerous bishops.
1. Any Irish person who collaborates with oppressors. In 1878, the earl of Leitrim, a land-lord with large holdings, hated for his treatment of tenants, was attacked and murdered; his Irish coachman attempted to protect him.

—They are the Lord's anointed, Dante said. They are an hon=
our to their country.

—Tub of guts, said Mr Dedalus coarsely. He has a handsome
face, mind you, in repose. You should see that fellow lapping 930
up his bacon and cabbage of a cold winter's day. O Johnny!

He twisted his features into a grimace of heavy bestiality and
made a lapping noise with his lips.

—Really, Simon, said Mrs Dedalus, you should not speak that
way before Stephen. It's not right. 935

—O, he'll remember all this when he grows up, said Dante
hotly, the language he heard against God and religion and
priests in his own home.

—Let him remember too, cried Mr Casey to her from across
the table, the language with which the priests and the priests' 940
pawns broke Parnell's heart and hounded him into his grave.
Let him remember that too when he grows up.

—Sons of bitches! cried Mr Dedalus. When he was down they
turned on him to betray him and rend him like rats in a sewer.
Lowlived dogs! And they look it! By Christ, they look it! 945

—They behaved rightly, cried Dante. They obeyed their
bishops and their priests. Honour to them!

—Well, it is perfectly dreadful to say that not even for one day
of the year, said Mrs Dedalus, can we be free from these dread=
ful disputes! 950

Uncle Charles raised his hands mildly and said:

—Come now, come now, come now! Can we not have our
opinions whatever they are without this bad temper and this
bad language? It is too bad surely.

Mrs Dedalus spoke to Dante in a low voice but Dante said 955
loudly:

—I will not say nothing. I will defend my church and my
religion when it is insulted and spit on by renegade catholics.

Mr Casey pushed his plate rudely into the middle of the
table and, resting his elbows before him, said in a harsh voice 960
to his host:

—Tell me, did I tell you that story about a very famous spit?

—You did not, John, said Mr Dedalus.

—Why then, said Mr Casey, it is a most instructive story. It
happened not long ago in the county Wicklow where we are 965
now.

He broke off and, turning towards Dante, said with quiet
indignation:

949 of] in TS–64   960 harsh] hoarse TS–64   961 to--host:] ⁊¹⟨:⟩ to his host:ᴵ⁀ MS

—And I may tell you, ma'am, that I, if you mean me, am no renegade catholic. I am a catholic as my father was and his father before him and his father before him again when we gave up our lives rather than sell our faith.   970

—The more shame to you now, Dante said, to speak as you do.

—The story, John, said Mr Dedalus smiling. Let us have the story anyhow.   975

—Catholic indeed! repeated Dante ironically. The blackest[2] protestant in the land would not speak the language I have heard this evening.

Mr Dedalus began to sway his head to and fro, crooning like a country singer.   980

—I am no protestant, I tell you again, said Mr Casey flushing.

Mr Dedalus, still crooning and swaying his head, began to sing in a grunting nasal tone:

> *O, come all you Roman catholics*   985
> *That never went to mass.*

He took up his knife and fork again in good humour and set to eating, saying to Mr Casey:

—Let us have the story, John. It will help us to digest.

Stephen looked with affection at Mr Casey's face which   990
stared across the table over his joined hands. He liked to sit near him at the fire, looking up at his dark fierce face. But his dark eyes were never fierce and his slow voice was good to listen to. But why was he then against the priests? Because Dante must be right then. But he had heard his father say that   995
she was a spoiled nun and that she had come out of the convent in the Alleghanies when her brothers had got the money from the savages for the trinkets and chainies.[3] Perhaps that made her severe against Parnell. And she did not like him to play with Eileen because Eileen was a protestant and when she was   1000
young she knew children that used to play with protestants and the protestants used to make fun of the litany of the Blessed Virgin. *Tower of Ivory*, they used to say, *House of Gold!*[4] How could a woman be a tower of ivory or a house of gold? Who was right then? And he remembered the evening in the infirm=   1005

---

977 Dante] ⌐⟨◇⟩ Dante⌐ MS   992 fierce] ⌐fierce⌐ TS; ABSENT MS   997 brothers] brother TS–64   998 and] and the TS–64

2. Most prejudiced against Catholics.
3. A spoiled nun would have renounced her vows or never completed her training. The Allegheny Mountains are in the eastern U.S. The brothers cheated African natives in their trading.
4. Phrases from the "Litany of Our Lady" (of Loreto) applied to the Virgin Mary.

ary in Clongowes, the dark waters, the light at the pierhead
and the moan of sorrow from the people when they had heard.

Eileen had long white hands. One evening when playing tig[5]
she had put her hands over his eyes: long and white and thin
and cold and soft. That was ivory: a cold white thing. That
was the meaning of *Tower of Ivory*.

—The story is very short and sweet, Mr Casey said. It was one
day down in Arklow, a cold bitter day, not long before the
chief[6] died. May God have mercy on him!

He closed his eyes wearily and paused. Mr Dedalus took a
bone from his plate and tore some meat from it with his teeth,
saying:

—Before he was killed, you mean.

Mr Casey opened his eyes, sighed and went on:

—It was down in Arklow one day. We were down there at a
meeting and after the meeting was over we had to make our
way to the railway station through the crowd. Such booing and
baaing, man, you never heard. They called us all the names in
the world. Well there was one old lady, and a drunken old
harridan she was surely, that paid all her attention to me. She
kept dancing along beside me in the mud bawling and scream=
ing into my face: *Priesthunter! The Paris Funds! Mr Fox! Kitty
O'Shea!*[7]

—And what did you do, John? asked Mr Dedalus.

—I let her bawl away, said Mr Casey. It was a cold day and to
keep up my heart I had (saving your presence, ma'am) a quid of
Tullamore[8] in my mouth and sure I couldn't say a word in any
case because my mouth was full of tobacco juice.

—Well, John?

—Well. I let her bawl away to her heart's content *Kitty O'Shea*
and the rest of it till at last she called that lady a name that I
won't sully this Christmas board nor your ears, ma'am, nor my
own lips by repeating.

He paused. Mr Dedalus, lifting his head from the bone,
asked:

—And what did you do, John?

—Do! said Mr Casey. She stuck her ugly old face up at me
when she said it and I had my mouth full of tobacco juice. I
bent down to her and *Phth!* says I to her like that.

---

5. Children's game also known as "tag" (*OED*).
6. Parnell.
7. Insults that refer to, respectively, the hunting down of priests during the time of the Penal
   Laws (first enacted 1695), the political funds that Parnell had private control of, a pseudonym he used during his affair with Mrs. O'Shea, and a nickname for Katherine O'Shea
   that has sexual connotations.
8. Chewing tobacco.

He turned aside and made the act of spitting.   1045
—*Phth!* says I to her like that, right into her eye.
He clapped a hand to his eye and gave a hoarse scream of
pain.
—*O Jesus, Mary and Joseph!* says she. *I'm blinded! I'm
blinded and drownded!*   1050
He stopped in a fit of coughing and laughter, repeating:
—*I'm blinded entirely!*
Mr Dedalus laughed loudly and lay back in his chair while
uncle Charles swayed his head to and fro.
Dante looked terribly angry and repeated while they   1055
laughed:
—Very nice! Ha! Very nice!
It was not nice about the spit in the woman's eye. But what
was the name the woman had called Kitty O'Shea that Mr
Casey would not repeat? He thought of Mr Casey walking   1060
through the crowds of people and making speeches from a
wagonette. That was what he had been in prison for and he
remembered that one night Sergeant O'Neill had come to the
house and had stood in the hall, talking in a low voice with his
father and chewing nervously at the chinstrap of his cap. And 1065
that night Mr Casey had not gone to Dublin by train but a car
had come to the door and he had heard his father say some=
thing about the Cabinteely road.[9]
He was for Ireland and Parnell and so was his father: and so
was Dante too for one night at the band on the esplanade she   1070
had hit a gentleman on the head with her umbrella because he
had taken off his hat when the band played *God save the
Queen* at the end.
Mr Dedalus gave a snort of contempt.
—Ah, John, he said. It is true for them. We are an unfortunate 1075
priestridden race and always were and always will be till the
end of the chapter.
Uncle Charles shook his head, saying:
—A bad business! A bad business!
Mr Dedalus repeated: 1080
—A priestridden Godforsaken race!
He pointed to the portrait of his grandfather on the wall to
his right.
—Do you see that old chap up there, John? he said. He was a
good Irishman when there was no money in the job. He was   1085

1066 not] ⁻¹not¹⁻ MS

9. A road to Dublin that was sparsely used.

condemned to death as a whiteboy.[1] But he had a saying about our clerical friends, that he would never let one of them put his two feet under his mahogany.

Dante broke in angrily:

—If we are a priestridden race we ought to be proud of it! They are the apple of God's eye. *Touch them not*, says Christ, *for they are the apple of My eye.*[2]

—And can we not love our country then? asked Mr Casey. Are we not to follow the man that was born to lead us?

—A traitor to his country! replied Dante. A traitor, an adul= terer! The priests were right to abandon him. The priests were always the true friends of Ireland.

—Were they, faith? said Mr Casey.

He threw his fist on the table and, frowning angrily, pro= truded one finger after another.

—Didn't the bishops of Ireland betray us in the time of the union when bishop Lanigan presented an address of loyalty to the marquess Cornwallis? Didn't the bishops and priests sell the aspirations of this country in 1829 in return for catholic emancipation? Didn't they denounce the fenian movement from the pulpit and in the confession box? And didn't they dishonour the ashes of Terence Bellew MacManus?[3]

His face was glowing with anger and Stephen felt the glow rise to his own cheek as the spoken words thrilled him. Mr Dedalus uttered a guffaw of coarse scorn.

—O, by God, he cried, I forgot little old Paul Cullen![4] Another apple of God's eye!

Dante bent across the table and cried to Mr Casey:

—Right! Right! They were always right! God and morality and religion come first.

Mrs Dedalus, seeing her excitement, said to her:

—Mrs Riordan, don't excite yourself answering them.

1102 to] TS; of MS   1103 Didn't] Didⁿˡn'tˡʳ MS   1104 this] MS; their TS—64

1. Name applied to violent protestors for tenants' rights who wore white shirts when they made their raids at night.
2. The phrase "apple of my eye" occurs in Zacharias 2.8, in the Old Testament; the words are not Christ's.
3. This paragraph refers to compromises made over a period of three decades after the Act of Union of 1800 on the way to achieving Catholic emancipation in 1829. James Lanigan was bishop of Ossory. Charles, Marquess Cornwallis, became viceroy and commander-in-chief of Ireland during the rebellion of 1798. The Fenian Brotherhood, also known as the Irish Republican Brotherhood, was a militant nationalist group active in Ireland and the U.S. beginning in the 1850s. When MacManus, a nationalist deported to Australia, was denied a state funeral in 1861, the Fenians organized their first significant public demonstration.
4. Archbishop of Dublin from 1852 to 1878; he condemned the Fenians and other forms of revolutionary nationalism.

—God and religion before everything! Dante cried. God and religion before the world!

Mr Casey raised his clenched fist and brought it down on the table with a crash.

—Very well, then, he shouted hoarsely, if it comes to that, no God for Ireland!

—John! John! cried Mr Dedalus, seizing his guest by the coat sleeve.

Dante stared across the table, her cheeks shaking. Mr Casey struggled up from his chair and bent across the table towards her, scraping the air from before his eyes with one hand as though he were tearing aside a cobweb.

—No God for Ireland! he cried. We have had too much God in Ireland. Away with God!

—Blasphemer! Devil! screamed Dante, starting to her feet and almost spitting in his face.

Uncle Charles and Mr Dedalus pulled Mr Casey back into his chair again, talking to him from both sides reasonably. He stared before him out of his dark flaming eyes, repeating:

—Away with God, I say!

Dante shoved her chair violently aside and left the table, upsetting her napkinring which rolled slowly along the carpet and came to rest against the foot of an easychair. Mrs Dedalus rose quickly and followed her towards the door. At the door Dante turned round violently and shouted down the room, her cheeks flushed and quivering with rage:

—Devil out of hell! We won! We crushed him to death! Fiend!

The door slammed behind her.

Mr Casey, freeing his arms from his holders, suddenly bowed his head on his hands with a sob of pain.

—Poor Parnell! he cried loudly. My dead king!

He sobbed loudly and bitterly.

Stephen, raising his terrorstricken face, saw that his father's eyes were full of tears.

◆   ◆   ◆

The fellows talked together in little groups.

One fellow said:

—They were caught near the Hill of Lyons.

—Who caught them?

—Mr Gleeson and the minister.[5] They were on a car.

The same fellow added:

—A fellow in the higher line told me.

5. Vice-rector.

Fleming asked:

—But why did they run away, tell us?   1160

—I know why, Cecil Thunder said. Because they had fecked[6]
cash out of the rector's room.

—Who fecked it?

—Kickham's brother. And they all went shares in it.

But that was stealing. How could they have done that?   1165

—A fat lot you know about it, Thunder! Wells said. I know
why they scut.[7]

—Tell us why.

—I was told not to, Wells said.

—O, go on, Wells, all said. You might tell us. We won't let it   1170
out.

Stephen bent forward his head to hear. Wells looked round
to see if anyone was coming. Then he said secretly:

—You know the altar wine they keep in the press in the sac=
risty?   1175

—Yes.

—Well, they drank that and it was found out who did it by the
smell. And that's why they ran away, if you want to know.

And the fellow who had spoken first said:

—Yes, that's what I heard too from the fellow in the higher   1180
line.

The fellows were all silent. Stephen stood among them,
afraid to speak, listening. A faint sickness of awe made him feel
weak. How could they have done that? He thought of the dark
silent sacristy. There were dark wooden presses there where the   1185
crimped surplices lay quietly folded.[8] It was not the chapel but
still you had to speak under your breath. It was a holy place.
He remembered the summer evening he had been there to be
dressed as boatbearer,[9] the evening of the procession to the little
altar in the wood. A strange and holy place. The boy that held   1190
the censer had swung it gently to and fro near the door with the
silvery cap lifted by the middle chain to keep the coals lighting.
That was called charcoal: and it had burned quietly as the
fellow had swung it gently and had given off a weak sour smell.

1191, 1193, 1194(1), 1196, 1197 had] ⌐had⌐ MS   1194 had given] ⌐⟨gave⟩ had
given⌐ MS

6. Stolen.
7. Ran away (from a word for the tail of a rabbit; *OED*).
8. The sacristy is the room of a church used for storing sacred vessels, valuable property, and
   vestments, the ritual robes worn by clergy and their assistants during rites and services.
   Surplices are loose-fitting, white gowns with wide sleeves (*OED*).
9. Person who carries the boat, the vessel containing the incense before it is put into the
   censer, or thurible, for burning during the mass (*OED*).

And then when all were vested he had stood holding out the   1195
boat to the rector and the rector had put a spoonful of incense
in and it had hissed on the red coals.

The fellows were talking together in little groups here and
there on the playground. The fellows seemed to him to have
grown smaller: that was because a sprinter[1] had knocked him   1200
down the day before, a fellow out of second of grammar. He
had been thrown by the fellow's machine lightly on the cinder=
path and his spectacles had been broken in three pieces and
some of the grit of the cinders had gone into his mouth.

That was why the fellows seemed to him smaller and farther   1205
away and the goalposts so thin and far and the soft grey sky so
high up. But there was no play on the football grounds for
cricket was coming: and some said that Barnes would be the
prof[2] and some said it would be Flowers. And all over the play=
grounds they were playing rounders and bowling twisters and   1210
lobs.[3] And from here and from there came the sounds of the
cricket bats through the soft grey air. They said: pick, pack,
pock, puck: like drops of water in a fountain slowly falling in
the brimming bowl.

Athy, who had been silent, said quietly: 1215
—You are all wrong.

All turned towards him eagerly.
—Why?
—Do you know?
—Who told you?   1220
—Tell us, Athy.

Athy pointed across the playground to where Simon
Moonan was walking by himself kicking a stone before him.
—Ask him, he said.

The fellows looked there and then said: 1225
—Why him?
—Is he in it?
—Tell us, Athy. Go on. You might if you know.

Athy lowered his voice and said:
—Do you know why those fellows scut? I will tell you but you   1230
must not let on you know.

He paused for a moment and then said mysteriously:

1197 in] in it 18–64

1. Bicyclist going full speed.
2. Probably the captain of the cricket team; cricket is a summer game.
3. Rounders is an English game resembling American baseball; twisters and lobs are ways of
bowling, or delivering the ball, in cricket.

—They were caught with Simon Moonan and Tusker Boyle in
the square one night.

The fellows looked at him and asked:

—Caught?

—What doing?

Athy said:

—Smugging.[4]

All the fellows were silent: and Athy said:

—And that's why.

Stephen looked at the faces of the fellows but they were all
looking across the playground. He wanted to ask somebody
about it. What did that mean about the smugging in the
square? Why did the five fellows out of the higher line run
away for that? It was a joke, he thought. Simon Moonan had
nice clothes and one night he had shown him a ball of creamy
sweets that the fellows of the football fifteen had rolled down
to him along the carpet in the middle of the refectory when he
was at the door. It was the night of the match against the
Bective Rangers and the ball was made just like a red and green
apple only it opened and it was full of the creamy sweets. And
one day Boyle had said that an elephant had two tuskers in=
stead of two tusks and that was why he was called Tusker
Boyle but some fellows called him Lady Boyle because he was
always at his nails, paring them.

Eileen had long thin cool white hands too because she was a
girl. They were like ivory; only soft. That was the meaning of
Tower of Ivory but protestants could not understand it and
made fun of it. One day he had stood beside her looking into
the hotel grounds. A waiter was running up a trail of bunting
on the flagstaff and a fox terrier was scampering to and fro on
the sunny lawn. She had put her hand into his pocket where his
hand was and he had felt how cool and thin and soft her hand
was. She had said that pockets were funny things to have: and
then all of a sudden she had broken away and had run laughing
down the sloping curve of the path. Her fair hair had streamed
out behind her like gold in the sun. *Tower of Ivory. House of
Gold.* By thinking about things you could understand them.

But why in the square? You went there when you wanted to
do something. It was all thick slabs of slate and water trickled
all day out of tiny pinholes and there was a queer smell of stale
water there. And behind the door of one of the closets there

1269 about] MS of TS–64

4. Probably homosexual contact but possibly masturbation (Mullin, 93).

was a drawing in red pencil of a bearded man in a Roman dress
with a brick in each hand and underneath was the name of the 1275
drawing:

Balbus was building a wall.[5]

Some fellow had drawn it there for a cod. It had a funny
face but it was very like a man with a beard. And on the wall of
another closet there was written in backhand in beautiful writ= 1280
ing:

Julius Caesar wrote The Calico Belly.[6]

Perhaps that was why they were there because it was a place
where some fellows wrote things for cod. But all the same it
was queer what Athy said and the way he said it. It was not a 1285
cod because they had run away. He looked with the others in
silence across the playground and began to feel afraid.

At last Fleming said:

—And we are all to be punished for what other fellows did?

—I won't come back, see if I do, Cecil Thunder said. Three 1290
days' silence in the refectory and sending us up for six and eight[7]
every minute.

—Yes, said Wells. And old Barrett has a new way of twisting
the note so that you can't open it and fold it again to see how
many ferulae[8] you are to get. I won't come back too. 1295

—Yes, said Cecil Thunder, and the prefect of studies[9] was in
second of grammar this morning.

—Let us get up a rebellion, Fleming said. Will we?

All the fellows were silent. The air was very silent and you
could hear the cricket bats but more slowly than before: pick, 1300
pock.

Wells asked:

—What is going to be done to them?

—Simon Moonan and Tusker are going to be flogged,[1] Athy
said, and the fellows in the higher line got their choice of 1305
flogging or being expelled.

—And which are they taking? asked the fellow who had
spoken first.

1278 fellow] fellows TS–18, 64   1283 there] aTS; in the square MS; there, Eg

5. A reference to the Latin classes. Balbus is mentioned in Cicero's *Letters to Atticus* 12.2 (Anderson).
6. A takeoff on the title of Caesar's *Commentaries on the Gallic War* (*Commentarii de Bello Gallico*).
7. The number of strokes (with an implement), first three on each hand, then four on each hand.
8. Strokes with a cane or rod, from *ferula,* meaning rod (*OED*).
9. In charge of maintaining order in the conduct of classes.
1. Beaten with a rod (*OED*), in this case on the buttocks.

—All are taking expulsion except Corrigan, Athy answered.
He's going to be flogged by Mr Gleeson.   1310
—Is it Corrigan that big fellow? said Fleming. Why, he'd be
able for two of Gleeson!
—I know why, Cecil Thunder said. He is right and the other
fellows are wrong because a flogging wears off after a bit but a
fellow that has been expelled from college is known all his life 1315
on account of it. Besides Gleeson won't flog him hard.
—It's best of his play not to, Fleming said.
—I wouldn't like to be Simon Moonan and Tusker, Cecil
Thunder said. But I don't believe they will be flogged. Perhaps
they will be sent up for twice nine.[2]   1320
—No, no, said Athy. They'll both get it on the vital spot.
     Wells rubbed himself and said in a crying voice:
—Please, sir, let me off!
     Athy grinned and turned up the sleeves of his jacket, saying:

> It can't be helped;   1325
> It must be done.
> So down with your breeches
> And out with your bum.

     The fellows laughed; but he felt that they were a little afraid.
In the silence of the soft grey air he heard the cricket bats from 1330
here and from there: pock. That was a sound to hear but if you
were hit then you would feel a pain. The pandybat made a
sound too but not like that. The fellows said it was made of
whalebone and leather with lead inside: and he wondered what
was the pain like. There were different kinds of pains for all the 1335
different kinds of sounds. A long thin cane would have a high
whistling sound and he wondered what was that pain like. It
made him shivery to think of it and cold: and what Athy said
too. But what was there to laugh at in it? It made him shivery:
but that was because you always felt like a shiver when you let 1340
down your trousers. It was the same in the bath when you
undressed yourself. He wondered who had to let them down,
the master or the boy himself. O how could they laugh about it
that way?
     He looked at Athy's rolledup sleeves and knuckly inky 1345
hands. He had rolled up his sleeves to show how Mr Gleeson
would roll up his sleeves. But Mr Gleeson had round shiny
cuffs and clean white wrists and fattish white hands and the

1332 would] ⌐would⌐ MS

2. Nine strokes per hand.

nails of them were long and pointed. Perhaps he pared them too like Lady Boyle. But they were terribly long and pointed 1350 nails. So long and cruel they were though the white fattish hands were not cruel but gentle. And though he trembled with cold and fright to think of the cruel long nails and of the high whistling sound of the cane and of the chill you felt at the end of your shirt when you undressed yourself yet he felt a feeling 1355 of queer quiet pleasure inside him to think of the white fattish hands, clean and strong and gentle. And he thought of what Cecil Thunder had said: that Mr Gleeson would not flog Cor= rigan hard. And Fleming had said he would not because it was best of his play not to. But that was not why.   1360

A voice from far out on the playgrounds cried:

—All in!

And other voices cried:

—All in! All in!

During the writing lesson he sat with his arms folded, listen= 1365 ing to the slow scraping of the pens. Mr Harford went to and fro making little signs in red pencil and sometimes sitting beside the boy to show him how to hold the pen. He had tried to spell out the headline for himself though he knew already what it was for it was the last in the book. *Zeal without* 1370 *prudence is like a ship adrift.* But the lines of the letters were like fine invisible threads and it was only by closing his right eye tight tight and staring out of the left eye that he could make out the full curves of the capital.

But Mr Harford was very decent and never got into a, wax. 1375 All the other masters got into dreadful waxes. But why were they to suffer for what fellows in the higher line did? Wells had said that they had drunk some of the altar wine out of the press in the sacristy and that it had been found out who had done it by the smell. Perhaps they had stolen a monstrance[3] to run away 1380 with it and sell it somewhere. That must have been a terrible sin, to go in quietly there at night, to open the dark press and steal the flashing gold thing into which God was put on the altar in the middle of flowers and candles at benediction[4] while the incense went up in clouds at both sides as the fellow swung 1385 the censer and Dominic Kelly sang the first part by himself in

---

1361 playgrounds] playground Eg–64   1370 in] of TS–64   1375 But] MARKED FOR PARAGRAPHING IN RUN-ON TEXT MS   1382 to(2)] ᵀˡtoˡʳ MS

3. Open or transparent vessel made of gold or silver for showing the consecrated wafer of the Eucharist (*OED*).
4. In this case the "Benediction of the Blessed Sacrament," during which the consecrated host is exposed to the congregation (*Cath. Enc.*).

the choir. But God was not in it of course when they stole it.
But still it was a strange and a great sin even to touch it. He
thought of it with deep awe; a terrible and strange sin: it
thrilled him to think of it in the silence when the pens scraped   1390
lightly. But to drink the altar wine out of the press and be
found out by the smell was a sin too: but it was not terrible
and strange. It only made you feel a little sickish on account
of the smell of the wine. Because on the day when he had
made his first holy communion in the chapel he had shut his   1395
eyes and opened his mouth and put out his tongue a little: and
when the rector had stooped down to give him the holy com=
munion he had smelt a faint winy smell off the rector's breath
after the wine of the mass. The word was beautiful: wine. It
made you think of dark purple because the grapes were dark   1400
purple that grew in Greece outside houses like white temples.
But the faint smell off the rector's breath had made him feel
a sick feeling on the morning of his first communion. The day
of your first communion was the happiest day of your life.
And once a lot of generals had asked Napoleon what was the   1405
happiest day of his life. They thought he would say the day
he won some great battle or the day he was made an emperor.
But he said:
—Gentlemen, the happiest day of my life was the day on which
I made my first holy communion.   1410

Father Arnall came in and the Latin lesson began and he
remained still, leaning on the desk with his arms folded. Father
Arnall gave out the themebooks and he said that they were
scandalous and that they were all to be written out again with
the corrections at once. But the worst of all was Fleming's   1415
theme because the pages were stuck together by a blot: and
Father Arnall held it up by a corner and said it was an insult to
any master to send him up such a theme. Then he asked Jack
Lawton to decline the noun *mare* and Jack Lawton stopped at
the ablative singular and could not go on with the plural.[5]   1420
—You should be ashamed of yourself, said Father Arnall
sternly. You, the leader of the class!

Then he asked the next boy and the next and the next.
Nobody knew. Father Arnall became very quiet, more and
more quiet as each boy tried to answer and could not. But his   1425
face was blacklooking and his eyes were staring though his
voice was so quiet. Then he asked Fleming and Fleming said

1414 were] ONE PAGE MISSING IN TS

5. Lawton can decline (state the six grammatical cases for) the Latin noun *mare*, meaning sea,
  through the ablative, the last of the six, in the singular, but he does not know the plural.

that that word had no plural. Father Arnall suddenly shut the
book and shouted at him:

—Kneel out there in the middle of the class. You are one of the 1430
idlest boys I ever met. Copy out your themes again the rest of
you.

Fleming moved heavily out of his place and knelt between
the two last benches. The other boys bent over their theme=
books and began to write. A silence filled the classroom and 1435
Stephen, glancing timidly at Father Arnall's dark face, saw that
it was a little red from the wax he was in.

Was that a sin for Father Arnall to be in a wax or was he
allowed to get into a wax when the boys were idle because that
made them study better or was he only letting on to be in a 1440
wax? It was because he was allowed because a priest would
know what a sin was and would not do it. But if he did it one
time by mistake what would he do to go to confession? Perhaps
he would go to confession to the minister. And if the minister
did it he would go to the rector: and the rector to the provin= 1445
cial: and the provincial to the general of the jesuits.[6] That was
called the order: and he had heard his father say that they were
all clever men. They could all have become highup people in
the world if they had not become jesuits. And he wondered
what Father Arnall and Paddy Barrett would have become and 1450
what Mr McGlade and Mr Gleeson would have become if they
had not become jesuits. It was hard to think what because you
would have to think of them in a different way with different
coloured coats and trousers and with beards and moustaches
and different kinds of hats. 1455

The door opened quietly and closed. A quick whisper ran
through the class: the prefect of studies. There was an instant
of dead silence and then the loud crack of a pandybat on the
last desk. Stephen's heart leapt up in fear.

—Any boys want flogging here, Father Arnall? cried the pre= 1460
fect of studies. Any lazy idle loafers that want flogging in this
class?

He came to the middle of the class and saw Fleming on his
knees.

—Hoho! he cried. Who is this boy? Why is he on his knees? 1465
What is your name, boy?

—Fleming, sir.

1434 other] others 64   1442 one] TS RESUMES

6. Stephen reproduces the hierarchy of positions within the Jesuits, but confession need not
be addressed to a priest of higher rank. The general, or head, of the Jesuits has beneath
him provincials, who are in charge of the Jesuits in provinces (such as Ireland), within
which there are schools, such as Clongowes, run by a rector, in charge of the community.

—Hoho, Fleming! An idler of course. I can see it in your eye.
Why is he on his knees, Father Arnall?
—He wrote a bad Latin theme, Father Arnall said, and he   1470
missed all the questions in grammar.
—Of course he did! cried the prefect of studies. Of course he
did! A born idler! I can see it in the corner of his eye.
    He banged his pandybat down on the desk and cried:
—Up, Fleming! Up, my boy!   1475
    Fleming stood up slowly.
—Hold out! cried the prefect of studies.
    Fleming held out his hand. The pandybat came down on it
with a loud smacking sound: one, two, three, four, five, six.
—Other hand!   1480
    The pandybat came down again in six loud quick smacks.
—Kneel down! cried the prefect of studies.
    Fleming knelt down squeezing his hands under his armpits,
his face contorted with pain, but Stephen knew how hard his
hands were because Fleming was always rubbing rosin into   1485
them. But perhaps he was in great pain for the noise of the
pandies was terrible. Stephen's heart was beating and flutter=
ing.
—At your work, all of you! shouted the prefect of studies. We
want no lazy idle loafers here, lazy idle little schemers. At your   1490
work, I tell you. Father Dolan will be in to see you every day.
Father Dolan will be in tomorrow.
    He poked one of the boys in the side with the pandybat,
saying:
—You, boy! When will Father Dolan be in again?   1495
—Tomorrow, sir, said Tom Furlong's voice.
—Tomorrow and tomorrow and tomorrow,[7] said the prefect of
studies. Make up your minds for that. Every day Father Dolan.
Write away. You, boy, who are you?
    Stephen's heart jumped suddenly.   1500
—Dedalus, sir.
—Why are you not writing like the others?
—I . . . . . my . . .
    He could not speak with fright.
—Why is he not writing, Father Arnall?   1505
—He broke his glasses, said Father Arnall, and I exempted him
from work.
—Broke? What is this I hear? What is this your name is? said
the prefect of studies.
—Dedalus, sir.   1510

7. Part of Macbeth's response to the death of his wife (Shakespeare, *Macbeth* 5.5.18).

—Out here, Dedalus. Lazy little schemer. I see schemer in your face. Where did you break your glasses?

Stephen stumbled into the middle of the class, blinded by fear and haste.

—Where did you break your glasses? repeated the prefect of studies.

—The cinderpath, sir.

—Hoho! The cinderpath! cried the prefect of studies. I know that trick.

Stephen lifted his eyes in wonder and saw for a moment Father Dolan's whitegrey not young face, his baldy whitegrey head with fluff at the sides of it, the steel rims of his spectacles and his nocoloured eyes looking through the glasses. Why did he say that he knew that trick?

—Lazy idle little loafer! cried the prefect of studies. Broke my glasses! An old schoolboy trick! Out with your hand this moment!

Stephen closed his eyes and held out in the air his trembling hand with the palm upwards. He felt the prefect of studies touch it for a moment at the fingers to straighten it and then the swish of the sleeve of the soutane as the pandybat was lifted to strike. A hot burning stinging tingling blow like the loud crack of a broken stick made his trembling hand crumple together like a leaf in the fire: and at the sound and the pain scalding tears were driven into his eyes. His whole body was shaking with fright, his arm was shaking and his crumpled burning livid hand shook like a loose leaf in the air. A cry sprang to his lips, a prayer to be let off. But though the tears scalded his eyes and his limbs quivered with pain and fright he held back the hot tears and the cry that scalded his throat.

—Other hand! shouted the prefect of studies.

Stephen drew back his maimed and quivering right arm and held out his left hand. The soutane sleeve swished again as the pandybat was lifted and a loud crashing sound and a fierce maddening tingling burning pain made his hand shrink together with the palms and fingers in a livid quivering mass. The scalding water burst forth from his eyes and, burning with shame and agony and fear, he drew back his shaking arm in terror and burst out into a whine of pain. His body shook with a palsy of fright and in shame and rage he felt the scalding cry come from his throat and the scalding tears falling out of his eyes and down his flaming cheeks.

—Kneel down! cried the prefect of studies.

1524 that(1)] absent TS–64

Stephen knelt down quickly pressing his beaten hands to his
sides. To think of them beaten and swollen with pain all in a   1555
moment made him feel so sorry for them as if they were not his
own but someone else's that he felt so sorry for. And as he
knelt, calming the last sobs in his throat and feeling the burning
tingling pain pressed in to his sides, he thought of the hands
which he had held out in the air with the palms up and of the   1560
firm touch of the prefect of studies when he had steadied the
shaking fingers and of the beaten swollen reddened mass of
palm and fingers that shook helplessly in the air.
—Get at your work, all of you, cried the prefect of studies
from the door. Father Dolan will be in every day to see if any   1565
boy, any lazy idle little loafer wants flogging. Every day. Every
day.
The door closed behind him.
The hushed class continued to copy out the themes. Father
Arnall rose from his seat and went among them, helping the   1570
boys with gentle words and telling them the mistakes they had
made. His voice was very gentle and soft. Then he returned to
his seat and said to Fleming and Stephen:
—You may return to your places, you two.
Fleming and Stephen rose and, walking to their seats, sat   1575
down. Stephen, scarlet with shame, opened a book quickly
with one weak hand and bent down upon it, his face close to
the page.
It was unfair and cruel: because the doctor had told him not
to read without glasses and he had written home to his father   1580
that morning to send him a new pair. And Father Arnall had
said that he need not study till the new glasses came. Then to
be called a schemer before the class and to be pandied when he
always got the card for first or second and was the leader of the
Yorkists! How could the prefect of studies know that it was a   1585
trick? He felt the touch of the prefect's fingers as they had
steadied his hand and at first he had thought that he was going
to shake hands with him because the fingers were soft and firm:
but then in an instant he had heard the swish of the soutane
sleeve and the crash. It was cruel and unfair to make him kneel   1590
in the middle of the class then: and Father Arnall had told them
both that they might return to their places without making any
difference between them. He listened to Father Arnall's low
and gentle voice as he corrected the themes. Perhaps he was
sorry now and wanted to be decent. But it was unfair and cruel.   1595

1557 own] TS; hands MS   1557 so] ABSENT Eg–64   1575 and,--seats,] and⁻ˡ, walking--
seats,ˡʳ MS   1587 had] ONE PAGE MISSING IN TS   1587 that] ABSENT Eg–64

The prefect of studies was a priest but that was cruel and unfair. And his whitegrey face and the nocoloured eyes behind the steelrimmed spectacles were cruel looking because he had steadied the hand first with his firm soft fingers and that was to hit it better and louder.   1600

—It's a stinking mean thing, that's what it is, said Fleming in the corridor as the classes were passing out in file to the refec= tory, to pandy a fellow for what is not his fault.

—You really broke your glasses by accident, didn't you? Nasty Roche asked.   1605

Stephen felt his heart filled by Fleming's words and did not answer.

—Of course he did! said Fleming. I wouldn't stand it. I'd go up and tell the rector on him.

—Yes, said Cecil Thunder eagerly, and I saw him lift the   1610
pandybat over his shoulder and he's not allowed to do that.

—Did they hurt much? Nasty Roche asked.

—Very much, Stephen said.

—I wouldn't stand it, Fleming repeated, from Baldyhead or any other Baldyhead. It's a stinking mean low trick, that's what 1615
it is. I'd go up straight up to the rector and tell him about it after dinner.

—Yes, do. Yes, do, said Cecil Thunder.

—Yes, do. Yes, go up and tell the rector on him, Dedalus, said Nasty Roche, because he said that he'd come in tomorrow 1620
again to pandy you.

—Yes, yes. Tell the rector, all said.

And there were some fellows out of second of grammar lis= tening and one of them said:

—The senate and the Roman people declared that Dedalus had 1625
been wrongly punished.[8]

It was wrong; it was unfair and cruel: and, as he sat in the refectory, he suffered time after time in memory the same hu= miliation until he began to wonder whether it might not really be that there was something in his face which made him look 1630
like a schemer and he wished he had a little mirror to see. But there could not be; and it was unjust and cruel and unfair.

He could not eat the blackish fish fritters they got on Wednesdays in lent[9] and one of his potatoes had the mark of the spade in it. Yes, he would do what the fellows had told him. He 1635

1614 or] TS RESUMES   1616 up(1)] ABSENT Eg–64

8. A statement modeled on decrees by the Roman Senate.
9. The period of forty days of penitence before Easter, during which dietary restrictions apply involving abstinence and fasting; in this case, fish has been substituted for meat.

would go up and tell the rector that he had been wrongly
punished. A thing like that had been done before by somebody
in history, by some great person whose head was in the books
of history. And the rector would declare that he had been
wrongly punished because the senate and the Roman people 1640
always declared that the man who did that had been wrongly
punished. Those were the great men whose names were in
Richmal Magnall's Questions.[1] History was all about those men
and what they did and that was what Peter Parley's Tales about
Greece and Rome were all about.[2] Peter Parley himself was on 1645
the first page in a picture. There was a road over a heath with
grass at the side and little bushes: and Peter Parley had a broad
hat like a protestant minister and a big stick and he was walk=
ing fast along the road to Greece and Rome.

It was easy what he had to do. All he had to do was when 1650
the dinner was over and he came out in his turn to go on
walking but not out to the corridor but up the staircase on the
right that led to the castle. He had nothing to do but that: to
turn to the right and walk fast up the staircase and in half a
minute he would be in the low dark narrow corridor that led 1655
through the castle to the rector's room. And every fellow had
said that it was unfair, even the fellow out of second of gram=
mar who had said that about the senate and the Roman people.

What would happen? He heard the fellows of the higher line
stand up at the top of the refectory and heard their steps as 1660
they came down the matting: Paddy Rath and Jimmy Magee
and the Spaniard and the Portuguese and the fifth was big
Corrigan who was going to be flogged by Mr Gleeson. That
was why the prefect of studies had called him a schemer and
pandied him for nothing: and, straining his weak eyes, tired 1665
with the tears, he watched big Corrigan's broad shoulders and
big hanging black head passing in the file. But he had done
something and besides Mr Gleeson would not flog him hard:
and he remembered how big Corrigan looked in the bath. He
had skin the same colour as the turfcoloured bogwater in the 1670
shallow end of the bath and when he walked along the side his
feet slapped loudly on the wet tiles and at every step his thighs
shook a little because he was fat.

1641 man] men TS—64   1656 had] ⌐had⌐ᵣ MS

1. *Historical and Miscellaneous Questions for the Use of Young People* (1800), a textbook,
   widely reprinted throughout the nineteenth century, concerning mythology, astronomy,
   architecture, and other topics, by Richmal Mangnall (1769–1820), whose name is mis-
   spelled (*Enc. Brit.* 17.572).
2. "Peter Parley" was the pseudonym of Samuel Goodrich (1793–1860), author of *Peter Parley's Tales about Ancient Rome* (1833) and many other books for the young with similar
   titles (*Enc. Brit.* 12.238).

The refectory was half empty and the fellows were still passing out in file. He could go up the staircase because there was never a priest or a prefect outside the refectory door. But he could not go. The rector would side with the prefect of studies and think it was a schoolboy trick and then the prefect of studies would come in every day the same only it would be worse because he would be dreadfully waxy at any fellow going up to the rector about him. The fellows had told him to go but they would not go themselves. They had forgotten all about it. No, it was best to forget all about it: and perhaps the prefect of studies had only said he would come in. No, it was best to hide out of the way because when you were small and young you could often escape that way.

The fellows at his table stood up. He stood up and passed out among them in the file. He had to decide. He was coming near the door. If he went on with the fellows he could never go up to the rector because he could not leave the playground for that. And if he went and was pandied all the same all the fellows would make fun and talk about young Dedalus going up to the rector to tell on the prefect of studies.

He was walking down along the matting and he saw the door before him. It was impossible: he could not. He thought of the baldy head of the prefect of studies with the cruel no= coloured eyes looking at him and he heard the voice of the prefect of studies asking him twice what his name was. Why could he not remember the name when he was told the first time? Was he not listening the first time or was it to make fun out of the name? The great men in the history had names like that and nobody made fun of them. It was his own name that he should have made fun of if he wanted to make fun. Dolan: it was like the name of a woman that washed clothes.

He had reached the door and, turning quickly to the right, walked up the stairs: and, before he could make up his mind to come back, he had entered the low dark narrow corridor that led to the castle. And as he crossed the threshold of the door of the corridor he saw, without turning his head to look, that all the fellows were looking after him as they went filing by.

He passed along the narrow dark corridor, passing little doors that were the doors of the rooms of the community. He peered in front of him and right and left through the gloom and thought that those must be portraits. It was dark and silent and his eyes were weak and tired with tears so that he could not see. But he thought they were the portraits of the saints and

1684 had] ⌐¹had¹ʳ MS   1694 He] MARKED FOR PARAGRAPHING IN RUN-ON TEXT MS

great men of the order who were looking down on him silently as he passed: saint Ignatius Loyola holding an open book and pointing to the words *Ad Majorem Dei Gloriam* in it, saint Francis Xavier pointing to his chest, Lorenzo Ricci with his 1720 berretta on his head like one of the prefects of the lines, the three patrons of holy youth, saint Stanislaus Kostka, saint Aloysius Gonzaga and blessed John Berchmans, all with young faces because they died when they were young, and Father Peter Kenny sitting in a chair wrapped in a big cloak.[3]   1725

He came out on the landing above the entrance hall and looked about him. That was where Hamilton Rowan had passed and the marks of the soldiers' slugs were there. And it was there that the old servants had seen the ghost in the white cloak of a marshal.   1730

An old servant was sweeping at the end of the landing. He asked him where was the rector's room and the old servant pointed to the door at the far end and looked after him as he went on to it and knocked.

There was no answer. He knocked again more loudly and 1735 his heart jumped when he heard a muffled voice say:

—Come in!

He turned the handle and opened the door and fumbled for the handle of the green baize door inside. He found it and pushed it open and went in.   1740

He saw the rector sitting at a desk writing. There was a skull on the desk and a strange solemn smell in the room like the old leather of chairs.

His heart was beating fast on account of the solemn place he was in and the silence of the room: and he looked at the skull 1745 and at the rector's kindlooking face.

—Well, my little man, said the rector. What is it?

Stephen swallowed down the thing in his throat and said:

—I broke my glasses, sir.

The rector opened his mouth and said: 1750

—O!

Then he smiled and said:

—Well, if we broke our glasses we must write home for a new pair.

—I wrote home, sir, said Stephen, and Father Arnall said I am 1755 not to study till they come.

3. Saint Ignatius of Loyola (1491–1556), a Spanish priest, founded the Society of Jesus, recognized by the Roman Catholic Church in 1540. The Latin motto of the Jesuits means "To the greater glory of God." Francis Xavier (1506–1552) was Loyola's most important disciple. Ricci (1703–1775) was a general of the Jesuits. The three patrons were all youthful Jesuit saints of the sixteenth and seventeenth centuries. Peter Kenney, S.J. (1779–1841), whose name is here spelled Kenny, founded Clongowes Wood College, dedicated to Gonzaga.

—Quite right! said the rector.

Stephen swallowed down the thing again and tried to keep his legs and his voice from shaking.

—But, sir . . . .

—Yes?

—Father Dolan came in today and pandied me because I was not writing my theme.

The rector looked at him in silence and he could feel the blood rising to his face and the tears about to rise to his eyes.

The rector said:

—Your name is Dedalus, isn't it?

—Yes, sir.

—And where did you break your glasses?

—On the cinderpath, sir. A fellow was coming out of the bicycle house and I fell and they got broken. I don't know the fellow's name.

The rector looked at him again in silence. Then he smiled and said:

—O, well, it was a mistake. I am sure Father Dolan did not know.

—But I told him I broke them, sir, and he pandied me.

—Did you tell him that you had written home for a new pair? the rector asked.

—No, sir.

—O, well then, said the rector, Father Dolan did not under= stand. You can say that I excuse you from your lessons for a few days.

Stephen said quickly for fear his trembling would prevent him:

—Yes, sir, but Father Dolan said he will come in tomorrow to pandy me again for it.

—Very well, the rector said. It is a mistake and I shall speak to Father Dolan myself. Will that do now?

Stephen felt the tears wetting his eyes and murmured:

—O yes, sir, thanks.

The rector held his hand across the side of the desk where the skull was and Stephen, placing his hand in it for a moment, felt a cool moist palm.

—Good day now, said the rector, withdrawing his hand and bowing.

—Good day, sir, said Stephen.

He bowed and walked quietly out of the room, closing the doors carefully and slowly.

But when he had passed the old servant on the landing and was again in the low narrow dark corridor he began to walk faster and faster. Faster and faster he hurried on through the gloom, excitedly. He bumped his elbow against the door at the end and, hurrying down the staircase, walked quickly through the two corridors and out into the air.   1805

He could hear the cries of the fellows on the playgrounds. He broke into a run and, running quicker and quicker, ran across the cinderpath and reached the third line playground, panting.

The fellows had seen him running. They closed round him in 1810 a ring, pushing one against another to hear.

—Tell us! Tell us!

—What did he say?

—Did you go in?

—What did he say?   1815

—Tell us! Tell us!

He told them what he had said and what the rector had said and, when he had told them, all the fellows flung their caps spinning up into the air and cried:

—Hurroo!   1820

They caught their caps and sent them up again spinning skyhigh and cried again:

—Hurroo! Hurroo!

They made a cradle of their locked hands and hoisted him up among them and carried him along till he struggled to get 1825 free. And when he had escaped from them they broke away in all directions, flinging their caps again into the air and whis= tling as they went spinning up and crying:

—Hurroo!

And they gave three groans for Baldyhead Dolan and three 1830 cheers for Conmee and they said he was the decentest rector that was ever in Clongowes.

The cheers died away in the soft grey air. He was alone. He was happy and free: but he would not be anyway proud with Father Dolan. He would be very quiet and obedient: and he 1835 wished that he could do something kind for him to show him that he was not proud.

The air was soft and grey and mild and evening was coming. There was the smell of evening in the air, the smell of the fields in the country where they digged up turnips to peel them and 1840 eat them when they went out for a walk to Major Barton's, the smell there was in the little wood beyond the pavilion where the gallnuts[4] were.

---

4. A gallnut is a growth on a tree caused by insects (*OED*).

The fellows were practising long shies and bowling lobs and
slow twisters.[5] In the soft grey silence he could hear the bump of   1845
the balls: and from here and from there through the quiet air
the sound of the cricket bats: pick, pack, pock, puck: like drops
of water in a fountain falling softly in the brimming bowl.

II

Uncle Charles smoked such black twist[1] that at last his out=   1
spoken nephew suggested to him to enjoy his morning smoke
in a little outhouse[2] at the end of the garden.
—Very good, Simon. All serene, Simon, said the old man tran=
quilly. Anywhere you like. The outhouse will do me nicely: it   5
will be more salubrious.
—Damn me, said Mr Dedalus frankly, if I know how you can
smoke such villainous awful tobacco. It's like gunpowder, by
God.
—It's very nice, Simon, replied the old man. Very cool and   10
mollifying.
Every morning, therefore, uncle Charles repaired to his out=
house but not before he had creased and brushed scrupulously
his back hair and brushed and put on his tall hat. While he
smoked the brim of his tall hat and the bowl of his pipe were   15
just visible beyond the jambs of the outhouse door. His arbour,
as he called the reeking outhouse which he shared with the cat
and the garden tools, served him also as a soundingbox: and
every morning he hummed contentedly one of his favourite
songs: O, twine me a bower or Blue eyes and golden hair or   20
The Groves of Blarney while the grey and blue coils of smoke
rose slowly from his pipe and vanished in the pure air.
During the first part of the summer in Blackrock[3] uncle
Charles was Stephen's constant companion. Uncle Charles was
a hale old man with a well tanned skin, rugged features and   25
white side whiskers. On week days he did messages between
the house in Carysfort Avenue and those shops in the main
street of the town with which the family dealt. Stephen was

1–2 outspoken] MS; ABSENT TS–64 MS   8 such] ⁻¹such¹ʳ TS

5. In cricket, a shy is a throw (OED), while lobs and twisters are ways of bowling, that is,
   delivering the ball to the batsman (Enc. Brit. 7.439–40).
1. Dark, that is, strong tobacco.
2. A shed, such as a toolhouse (OED), not in this case a privy (as American usage could
   suggest).
3. Located five miles south of Dublin on Dublin Bay.

glad to go with him on these errands for uncle Charles helped
him very liberally to handfuls of whatever was exposed in open   30
boxes and barrels outside the counter. He would seize a hand=
ful of grapes and sawdust or three or four American apples and
thrust them generously into his grandnephew's hand while the
shopman smiled uneasily; and on Stephen's feigning reluctance
to take them, he would frown and say: 35
—Take them, sir. Do you hear me, sir? They're good for your
bowels.

When the order list had been booked the two would go on
to the park where an old friend of Stephen's father, Mike
Flynn, would be found seated on a bench, waiting for them.   40
Then would begin Stephen's run round the park. Mike Flynn
would stand at the gate near the railway station, watch in
hand, while Stephen ran round the track in the style Mike
Flynn favoured, his head high lifted, his knees well lifted and
his hands held straight down by his sides. When the morning   45
practice was over the trainer would make his comments and
sometimes illustrate them by shuffling along for a yard or so
comically in an old pair of blue canvas shoes. A small ring of
wonderstruck children and nursemaids would gather to watch
him and linger even when he and uncle Charles had sat down   50
again and were talking athletics and politics. Though he had
heard his father say that Mike Flynn had put some of the best
runners of modern times through his hands Stephen often
glanced with mistrust at his trainer's flabby stubblecovered
face, as it bent over the long stained fingers through which he   55
rolled his cigarette, and with pity at the mild lustreless blue
eyes which would look up suddenly from the task and gaze
vaguely into the bluer distance while the long swollen fingers
ceased their rolling and grains and fibres of tobacco fell back
into the pouch.   60

On the way home uncle Charles would often pay a visit to
the chapel and, as the font was above Stephen's reach, the old
man would dip his hand and then sprinkle the water briskly
about Stephen's clothes and on the floor of the porch. While he
prayed he knelt on his red handkerchief and read above his   65
breath from a thumbblackened prayerbook wherein catch=
words were printed at the foot of every page. Stephen knelt at
his side respecting, though he did not share, his piety. He often
wondered what his granduncle prayed for so seriously. Perhaps
he prayed for the souls in purgatory or for the grace of a happy   70

death: or perhaps he prayed that God might send him back a
part of the big fortune he had squandered in Cork.[4]

On Sundays Stephen with his father and his granduncle took
their constitutional. The old man was a nimble walker in spite
of his corns and often ten or twelve miles of the road were   75
covered. The little village of Stillorgan was the parting of the
ways. Either they went to the left towards the Dublin moun=
tains or along the Goatstown road and thence into Dundrum,
coming home by Sandyford. Trudging along the road or
standing in some grimy wayside publichouse his elders spoke   80
constantly of the subjects nearest their hearts, of Irish politics,
of Munster and of the legends of their own family, to all of
which Stephen lent an avid ear. Words which he did not under=
stand he said over and over to himself till he had learned them
by heart: and through them he had glimpses of the real world   85
about him. The hour when he too would take his part in the
life of that world seemed drawing near and in secret he began
to make ready for the great part which he felt awaited him the
nature of which he only dimly apprehended.

His evenings were his own; and he pored over a ragged   90
translation of *The Count of Monte Cristo*.[5] The figure of that
dark avenger stood forth in his mind for whatever he had heard
or divined in childhood of the strange and terrible. At night he
built up on the parlour table an image of the wonderful island
cave out of transfers and paper flowers and coloured tissue   95
paper and strips of the silver and golden paper in which choc=
olate is wrapped. When he had broken up this scenery, weary
of its tinsel, there would come to his mind the bright picture of
Marseilles, of sunny trellisses and of Mercedes. Outside Black=
rock, on the road that led to the mountains, stood a small   100
whitewashed house in the garden of which grew many rose=
bushes: and in this house, he told himself, another Mercedes
lived. Both on the outward and on the homeward journey he
measured distance by this landmark: and in his imagination he
lived through a long train of adventures, marvellous as those in   105
the book itself, towards the close of which there appeared an
image of himself, grown older and sadder, standing in a
moonlit garden with Mercedes who had so many years before

81 nearest] nearer TS–64   86 his] ABSENT Eg–64

4. The main city of County Cork, which is located in Munster, the southern province, one of
the four traditional geographical areas of Ireland.

5. A French novel of betrayal, escape, and revenge, by Alexandre Dumas *père* (1802–1870),
in which the hero, Edmond Dantès, escapes from prison and returns to Marseilles, a
French port on the Mediterranean, to avenge the deception that led his betrothed, Mercedes, to marry another man in the belief that Dantès was dead.

slighted his love, and with a sadly proud gesture of refusal,
saying: 110
—Madam, I never eat muscatel grapes.

He became the ally of a boy named Aubrey Mills and
founded with him a gang of adventurers in the avenue. Aubrey
carried a whistle dangling from his buttonhole and a bicycle
lamp attached to his belt while the others had short sticks   115
thrust daggerwise through theirs. Stephen, who had read of
Napoleon's plain style of dress, chose to remain unadorned and
thereby heightened for himself the pleasure of taking counsel
with his lieutenant before giving orders. The gang made forays
into the gardens of old maids or went down to the castle[6] and   120
fought a battle on the shaggy weedgrown rocks, coming home
after it weary stragglers with the stale odours of the foreshore
in their nostrils and the rank oils of the seawrack upon their
hands and in their hair.

Aubrey and Stephen had a common milkman and often they   125
drove out in the milkcar to Carrickmines[7] where the cows were
at grass. While the men were milking the boys would take turns
in riding the tractable mare round the field. But when autumn
came the cows were driven home from the grass: and the first
sight of the filthy cowyard at Stradbrook[8] with its foul green   130
puddles and clots of liquid dung and steaming brantroughs
sickened Stephen's heart. The cattle which had seemed so beau=
tiful in the country on sunny days revolted him and he could
not even look at the milk they yielded.

The coming of September did not trouble him this year for   135
he knew he was not to be sent back to Clongowes. The practice
in the park came to an end when Mike Flynn went into hospi=
tal. Aubrey was at school and had only an hour or two free in
the evening. The gang fell asunder and there were no more
nightly forays or battles on the rocks. Stephen sometimes went   140
round with the car which delivered the evening milk: and these
chilly drives blew away his memory of the filth of the cowyard
and he felt no repugnance at seeing the cowhairs and hayseeds
on the milkman's coat. Whenever the car drew up before a
house he waited to catch a glimpse of a well scrubbed kitchen   145
or of a softly lighted hall and to see how the servant would
hold the jug and how she would close the door. He thought it

---

6. A Martello tower, one of the defensive fortifications built on Ireland's east coast during
   the Napoleonic Wars (1803–06) in case of invasion.
7. A village located inland three miles south of Blackrock.
8. A locale one mile southeast of Blackrock.

should be a pleasant life enough, driving along the roads every evening to deliver milk, if he had warm gloves and a fat bag of gingernuts in his pocket to eat from. But the same foreknowl= edge which had sickened his heart and made his limbs sag suddenly as he raced round the park, the same intuition which had made him glance with mistrust at his trainer's flabby stubblecovered face as it bent heavily over his long stained fingers, dissipated any vision of the future. In a vague way he understood that his father was in trouble and that this was the reason why he himself had not been sent back to Clongowes. For some time he had felt the slight changes in his house; and these changes in what he had deemed unchangeable were so many slight shocks to his boyish conception of the world. The ambition which he felt astir at times in the darkness of his soul sought no outlet. A dusk like that of the outer world obscured his mind as he heard the mare's hoofs clattering along the tramtrack on the Rock Road and the great can swaying and rattling behind him.

He returned to Mercedes and, as he brooded upon her im= age, a strange unrest crept into his blood. Sometimes a fever gathered within him and led him to rove alone in the evening along the quiet avenues. The peace of the gardens and the kindly lights in the windows poured a tender influence into his restless heart. The noise of children at play annoyed him and their silly voices made him feel, even more keenly than he had felt at Clongowes, that he was different from others. He did not want to play. He wanted to meet in the real world the unsubstantial image which his soul so constantly beheld. He did not know where to seek it or how: but a premonition which led him on told him that this image would, without any overt act of his, encounter him. They would meet quietly as if they had known each other and had made their tryst, perhaps at one of the gates or in some more secret place. They would be alone, surrounded by darkness and silence: and in that moment of supreme tenderness he would be transfigured. He would fade into something impalpable under her eyes and then, in a mo= ment, he would be transfigured.[9] Weakness and timidity and inexperience would fall from him in that magic moment.

◆   ◆   ◆

151 limbs] legs Eg–64   169 avenues.] avenue. TS–64

9. Transformed, but "transfigured" would carry a religious overtone for Stephen. The Trans-figuration is the high point of Jesus's public life, the moment in which his divinity is rav-ishingly revealed to some of his disciples. The manifestation of the divine glory is celebrated by Catholics annually as the Feast of the Transfiguration.

Two great yellow caravans[1] had halted one morning before
the door and men had come tramping into the house to dis=
mantle it. The furniture had been hustled out through the front
garden which was strewn with wisps of straw and rope ends
and into the huge vans at the gate. When all had been safely   190
stowed the vans had set off noisily down the avenue: and from
the window of the railway carriage, in which he had sat with
his redeyed mother, Stephen had seen them lumbering heavily
along the Merrion Road.

The parlour fire would not draw that evening and Mr Deda=   195
lus rested the poker against the bars of the grate to attract the
flame. Uncle Charles dozed in a corner of the half furnished
uncarpeted room and near him the family portraits leaned
against the wall. The lamp on the table shed a weak light over
the boarded floor, muddied by the feet of the vanmen. Stephen   200
sat on a footstool beside his father listening to a long and
incoherent monologue. He understood little or nothing of it at
first but he became slowly aware that his father had enemies
and that some fight was going to take place. He felt, too, that
he was being enlisted for the fight, that some duty was being   205
laid upon his shoulders. The sudden flight from the comfort
and revery of Blackrock, the passage through the gloomy foggy
city, the thought of the bare cheerless house in which they were
now to live made his heart heavy: and again an intuition or
foreknowledge of the future came to him. He understood also   210
why the servants had often whispered together in the hall and
why his father had often stood on the hearthrug, with his back
to the fire, talking loudly to uncle Charles who urged him to sit
down and eat his dinner.

—There's a crack of the whip left in me yet, Stephen, old chap,   215
said Mr Dedalus, poking at the dull fire with fierce energy.
We're not dead yet, sonny. No, by the Lord Jesus (God forgive
me) nor half dead.

Dublin was a new and complex sensation. Uncle Charles
had grown so witless that he could no longer be sent out on   220
errands and the disorder in settling in the new house left Ste=
phen freer than he had been in Blackrock. In the beginning he
contented himself with circling timidly round the neighbouring
square or, at most, going half way down one of the side streets:
but when he had made a skeleton map of the city in his mind he   225
followed boldly one of its central lines until he reached the

1. Covered carts, or vans (*OED*), in this case for moving household goods; the word was frequently associated with gypsies and traveling performers.

customhouse.[2] He passed unchallenged among the docks and along the quays wondering at the multitude of corks that lay bobbing on the surface of the water in a thick yellow scum, at the crowds of quay porters and the rumbling carts and the illdressed bearded policeman. The vastness and strangeness of the life suggested to him by the bales of merchandise stacked along the walls or swung aloft out of the holds of steamers wakened again in him the unrest which had sent him wan= dering in the evening from garden to garden in search of Mercedes. And amid this new bustling life he might have fancied himself in another Marseilles but that he missed the bright sky and the sunwarmed trellisses of the wineshops. A vague dissatisfaction grew up within him as he looked on the quays and on the river and on the lowering skies and yet he continued to wander up and down day after day as if he really sought someone that eluded him.

He went once or twice with his mother to visit their rela= tives: and, though they passed a jovial array of shops lit up and adorned for Christmas, his mood of embittered silence did not leave him. The causes of his embitterment were many, remote and near. He was angry with himself for being young and the prey of restless foolish impulses, angry also with the change of fortune which was reshaping the world about him into a vision of squalor and insincerity. Yet his anger lent nothing to the vision. He chronicled with patience what he saw, detaching himself from it and tasting its mortifying flavour in secret.

He was sitting on the backless chair in his aunt's kitchen. A lamp with a reflector hung on the japanned wall[3] of the fire= place and by its light his aunt was reading the evening paper that lay on her knees. She looked a long time at a smiling picture that was set in it and said musingly:

—The beautiful Mabel Hunter![4]

A ringletted girl stood on tiptoe to peer at the picture and said softly:

—What is she in, mud?

—In the pantomime, love.

230

235

240

245

250

255

260

---

228 wondering] ⌐Awondering⌐r aTS; ABSENT MS   232 stacked] stocked TS–64   252 tasting] testing 16–18, 64   252 secret.] FIVE TO SIX LINES, PLUS TWO PAGES MISSING IN TS

2. The central line would be Gardiner Street, which runs along one side of Mountjoy Square, in the neighborhood where the family now lives, about 1.5 miles north of the River Liffey in Dublin. Gardiner Street leads to the Custom House (1791), a large governmental building on the river.
3. A wall finished with a black, glossy varnish (OED).
4. Probably a stage performer in pantomimes, dramatic performances of tales loosely linking singing, dancing, and jokes (OED).

The child leaned her ringletted head against her mother's sleeve, gazing on the picture and murmured, as if fascinated:

—The beautiful Mabel Hunter!   265

As if fascinated, her eyes rested long upon those demurely taunting eyes and she murmured again devotedly:

—Isn't she an exquisite creature?

And the boy who came in from the street, stamping crook=edly under his stone[5] of coal, heard her words. He dropped his   270
load promptly on the floor and hurried to her side to see. But she did not raise her easeful head to let him see. He mauled the edges of the paper with his reddened and blackened hands, shouldering her aside and complaining that he could not see.

He was sitting in the narrow breakfast room high up in the   275
old darkwindowed house. The firelight flickered on the wall and beyond the window a spectral dusk was gathering upon the river. Before the fire an old woman was busy making tea and, as she bustled at her task, she told in a low voice of what the priest and the doctor had said. She told too of certain changes   280
that she had seen in her of late and of her odd ways and sayings. He sat listening to the words and following the ways of adventure that lay open in the coals, arches and vaults and winding galleries and jagged caverns.

Suddenly he became aware of something in the doorway. A   285
skull appeared suspended in the gloom of the doorway. A feeble creature like a monkey was there, drawn thither by the sound of voices at the fire. A whining voice came from the door, asking:

—Is that Josephine?   290

The old bustling woman answered cheerily from the fire=place:

—No, Ellen. It's Stephen.

—O . . . . O, good evening, Stephen.

He answered the greeting and saw a silly smile break out   295
over the face in the doorway.

—Do you want anything, Ellen? asked the old woman at the fire.

But she did not answer the question and said:

—I thought it was Josephine. I thought you were Josephine,   300
Stephen.

And, repeating this several times, she fell to laughing feebly.

---

281 that--seen] that she seen Eg; they had seen 16–24; she had seen 64   295 out] ABSENT
Eg–64

5. A unit of measure weighing fourteen pounds (*OED*).

He was sitting in the midst of a children's party at Harold's Cross.[6] His silent watchful manner had grown upon him and he took little part in the games. The children, wearing the spoils of their crackers, danced and romped noisily and, though he tried to share their merriment, he felt himself a gloomy figure amid the gay cocked hats and sunbonnets.

But when he had sung his song and withdrawn into a snug corner of the room he began to taste the joy of his loneliness. The mirth, which in the beginning of the evening had seemed to him false and trivial, was like a soothing air to him, passing gaily by his senses, hiding from other eyes the feverish agitation of his blood while through the circling of the dancers and amid the music and laughter her glances travelled to his corner, flattering, taunting, searching, exciting his heart.

In the hall the children who had stayed latest were putting on their things: the party was over. She had thrown a shawl about her and, as they went together towards the tram, sprays of her fresh warm breath flew gaily above her cowled head and her shoes tapped blithely on the glassy road.

It was the last tram. The lank brown horses knew it and shook their bells to the clear night in admonition. The conduc= tor talked with the driver, both nodding often in the green light of the lamp. On the empty seats of the tram were scattered a few coloured tickets. No sound of footsteps came up or down the road. No sound broke the peace of the night save when the lank brown horses rubbed their noses together and shook their bells.

They seemed to listen, he on the upper step and she on the lower. She came up to his step many times and went down to hers again between their phrases and once or twice stood close beside him for some moments on the upper step, forgetting to go down, and then went down. His heart danced upon her movements like a cork upon a tide. He heard what her eyes said to him from beneath their cowl and knew that in some dim past, whether in life or in revery, he had heard their tale before. He saw her urge her vanities, her fine dress and sash and long black stockings, and knew that he had yielded to them a thou= sand times. Yet a voice within him spoke above the noise of his dancing heart, asking him would he take her gift to which he had only to stretch out his hand. And he remembered the day when he and Eileen had stood looking into the hotel grounds,

315 glances] glance Eg–64   340 above] Eg; ABSENT MS

6. A suburb of Dublin, just beyond the Grand Canal to the southwest.

watching the waiters running up a trail of bunting on the
flagstaff and the foxterrier scampering to and fro on the sunny   345
lawn, and how, all of a sudden, she had broken out into a peal
of laughter and had run down the sloping curve of the path.
Now, as then, he stood listlessly in his place, seemingly a
tranquil watcher of the scene before him.

—She too wants me to catch hold of her, he thought. That's   350
why she came with me to the tram. I could easily catch hold of
her when she comes up to my step: nobody is looking. I could
hold her and kiss her.

But he did neither: and, when he was sitting alone in the
deserted tram, he tore his ticket into shreds and stared gloomily   355
at the corrugated footboard.

The next day he sat at his table in the bare upper room for
many hours. Before him lay a new pen, a new bottle of ink and
a new emerald exercise.[7] From force of habit he had written at
the top of the first page the initial letters of the jesuit motto: 360
A. M. D. G.[8] On the first line of the page appeared the title of
the verses he was trying to write: To E— C—. He knew it was
right to begin so for he had seen similar titles in the collected
poems of Lord Byron.[9] When he had written this title and
drawn an ornamental line underneath he fell into a daydream   365
and began to draw diagrams on the cover of the book. He saw
himself sitting at his table in Bray the morning after the dis=
cussion at the Christmas dinnertable, trying to write a poem
about Parnell on the back of one of his father's second moiety
notices.[1] But his brain had then refused to grapple with the   370
theme and, desisting, he had covered the page with the names
and addresses of certain of his classmates:

> Roderick Kickham
> John Lawton
> Anthony MacSwiney   375
> Simon Moonan

Now it seemed as if he would fail again but, by dint of
brooding on the incident, he thought himself into confidence.
During this process all those elements which he deemed com=
mon and insignificant fell out of the scene. There remained no   380

---

379 those] these 64

7. A composition book for school assignments, in this case with an emerald-green cover.
8. Abbreviation of the Jesuit motto, *Ad Majorem Dei Gloriam* (Latin; "To the greater glory of
   God"), which students were required to write at the top of assignments.
9. George Gordon, Lord Byron (1788–1824), English Romantic poet.
1. Legal notices for payments due on the second half (moiety, *OED*) of a bill.

trace of the tram itself nor of the trammen nor of the horses: nor did he and she appear vividly. The verses told only of the night and the balmy breeze and the maiden lustre of the moon. Some undefined sorrow was hidden in the hearts of the protag= onists as they stood in silence beneath the leafless trees and 385 when the moment of farewell had come the kiss, which had been withheld by one, was given by both. After this the letters L. D. S.[2] were written at the foot of the page and, having hidden the book, he went into his mother's bedroom and gazed at his face for a long time in the mirror of her dressingtable. 390

But his long spell of leisure and liberty was drawing to its end. One evening his father came home full of news which kept his tongue busy all through dinner. Stephen had been awaiting his father's return for there had been mutton hash that day and he knew that his father would make him dip his bread in the 395 gravy. But he did not relish the hash for the mention of Clon= gowes had coated his palate with a scum of disgust.

—I walked bang into him, said Mr Dedalus for the fourth time, just at the corner of the square.

—Then I suppose, said Mrs Dedalus, he will be able to arrange 400 it. I mean, about Belvedere.[3]

—Of course he will, said Mr Dedalus. Don't I tell you he's provincial of the order[4] now?

—I never liked the idea of sending him to the christian brothers[5] myself, said Mrs Dedalus. 405

—Christian brothers be damned! said Mr Dedalus. Is it with Paddy Stink and Mickey Mud? No, let him stick to the jesuits in God's name since he began with them. They'll be of service to him in after years. Those are the fellows that can get you a position. 410

—And they're a very rich order, aren't they, Simon?

—Rather. They live well, I tell you. You saw their table at Clongowes. Fed up, by God, like gamecocks.

Mr Dedalus pushed his plate over to Stephen and bade him finish what was on it. 415

—Now then, Stephen, he said. You must put your shoulder to the wheel, old chap. You've had a fine long holiday.

—O, I'm sure he'll work very hard now, said Mrs Dedalus. Especially when he has Maurice with him.

—O, Holy Paul, I forgot about Maurice, said Mr Dedalus. 420

2. *Laus Deo Semper* (Latin; "Praise to God Always"), a Jesuit motto, often written at the end of assignments.
3. Belvedere College, a day school run by the Jesuits, close to Mountjoy Square.
4. High-ranking member of the Jesuit order, in charge of the province, Ireland.
5. The Irish Christian Brothers, a lay order of the Catholic Church, ran schools for students unable to pay the fees charged by the Jesuits.

Here, Maurice! Come here, you thickheaded ruffian! Do you
know I'm going to send you to a college where they'll teach you
to spell c.a.t: cat. And I'll buy you a nice little penny handker=
chief to keep your nose dry. Won't that be grand fun?

Maurice grinned at his father and then at his brother. Mr   425
Dedalus screwed his glass into his eye and stared hard at both
his sons. Stephen mumbled his bread[6] without answering his
father's gaze.

—By the bye, said Mr Dedalus at length, the rector, or provin=
cial, rather, was telling me that story about you and Father   430
Dolan. You're an impudent thief, he said.

—O, he didn't, Simon!

—Not he! said Mr Dedalus. But he gave me a great account of
the whole affair. We were chatting, you know, and one word
borrowed another. And, by the way, who do you think he told   435
me will get that job in the corporation?[7] But I'll tell you that
after. Well, as I was saying, we were chatting away quite
friendly and he asked me did our friend here wear glasses still
and then he told me the whole story.

—And was he annoyed, Simon?   440

—Annoyed! Not he! *Manly little chap!* he said.

Mr Dedalus imitated the mincing nasal tone of the provin=
cial.

—Father Dolan and I, when I told them all at dinner about it,
Father Dolan and I had a great laugh over it. *You better mind*   445
yourself, Father Dolan, said I, *or young Dedalus will send you*
up for twice nine. We had a famous laugh together over it. Ha!
Ha! Ha!

Mr Dedalus turned to his wife and interjected in his natural
voice: 450

—Shows you the spirit in which they take the boys there. O, a
jesuit for your life, for diplomacy!

He reassumed the provincial's voice and repeated:

—*I told them all at dinner about it and Father Dolan and I and*
all of us we all had a hearty laugh together over it. Ha! Ha! Ha! 455

◆　◆　◆

The night of the Whitsuntide[8] play had come and Stephen
from the window of the dressingroom looked out on the small

---

426 both] a16; both of MS, Eg–16   455 *all* (2)] all MS, Eg–18; ABSENT 64   456 The]
TS RESUMES

6. Tore his bread into small pieces (*OED*).
7. Dublin Corporation, the government bureaucracy in Dublin.
8. The week that includes the seventh Sunday following Easter, Whitsunday (or Pentecost),
   which marks the Holy Spirit's descent on the apostles. On the Holy Spirit, see note 7, p. 27.

grassplot across which lines of Chinese lanterns were stretched.
He watched the visitors come down the steps from the house
and pass into the theatre. Stewards in evening dress, old Belve=   460
dereans, loitered in groups about the entrance to the theatre
and ushered in the visitors with ceremony. Under the sudden
glow of a lantern he could recognize the smiling face of a priest.

The Blessed Sacrament had been removed from the taber=
nacle[9] and the first benches had been driven back so as to leave   465
the dais of the altar and the space before it free. Against the
walls stood companies of barbells and Indian clubs; the dumb=
bells were piled in one corner: and in the midst of countless
hillocks of gymnasium shoes and sweaters and singlets in
untidy brown parcels there stood the stout leatherjacketed   470
vaulting horse waiting its turn to be carried up on to the stage.
A large bronze shield, tipped with silver, leaned against the
panel of the altar also waiting its turn to be carried up on to the
stage and set in the middle of the winning team at the end of
the gymnastic display.   475

Stephen, though in deference to his reputation for essay=
writing he had been elected secretary to the gymnasium, had no
part in the first section of the programme: but in the play
which formed the second section he had the chief part, that of a
farcical pedagogue. He had been cast for it on account of his   480
stature and grave manners for he was now at the end of his
second year at Belvedere and in number two.[1]

A score of the younger boys in white knickers and singlets
came pattering down from the stage, through the vestry[2] and
into the chapel. The vestry and chapel were peopled with eager   485
masters and boys. The plump bald sergeantmajor was testing
with his foot the springboard of the vaulting horse. The lean
young man in a long overcoat, who was to give a special
display of intricate club swinging, stood near watching with
interest, his silvercoated clubs peeping out of his deep side=   490
pockets. The hollow rattle of the wooden dumbbells was heard
as another team made ready to go up on the stage: and in
another moment the excited prefect was hustling the boys
through the vestry like a flock of geese, flapping the wings of
his soutane nervously and crying to the laggards to make haste.   495
A little troop of Neapolitan peasants were practising their steps

465 back] ABSENT 64   471 on to] on TS–64   473 on to] on 64   477 had(2)] had had
TS–64   488 to] TS; ABSENT MS

9. The consecrated bread, or Host, has been removed from its container, the tabernacle, to
    prevent any accidents to it during the play.
1. The designation for students in their second-to-last year of study.
2. Room adjoining the chapel in which ritual robes are kept (OED).

at the end of the chapel, some arching their arms above their heads, some swaying their baskets of paper violets and curtsey= ing. In a dark corner of the chapel at the gospel side of the altar[3] a stout old lady knelt amid her copious black skirts. When she   500 stood up a pinkdressed figure, wearing a curly golden wig and an oldfashioned straw sunbonnet, with black pencilled eye= brows and cheeks delicately rouged and powdered, was dis= covered. A low murmur of curiosity ran round the chapel at the discovery of this girlish figure. One of the prefects, smiling and   505 nodding his head, approached the dark corner and, having bowed to the stout old lady, said pleasantly:

—Is this a beautiful young lady or a doll that you have here, Mrs Tallon?

Then, bending down to peer at the smiling painted face un=   510 der the leaf of the bonnet, he exclaimed:

—No! Upon my word I believe it's little Bertie Tallon after all!

Stephen at his post by the window heard the old lady and the priest laugh together and heard the boys' murmur of ad= miration behind him as they pressed forward to see the little   515 boy who had to dance the sunbonnet dance by himself. A movement of impatience escaped him. He let the edge of the blind fall and, stepping down from the bench on which he had been standing, walked out of the chapel.

He passed out of the schoolhouse and halted under the shed   520 that flanked the garden. From the theatre opposite came the muffled noise of the audience and sudden brazen clashes of the soldiers' band. The light spread upwards from the glass roof making the theatre seem a festive ark, anchored amid the hulks of houses, her frail cables of lanterns looping her to her moor=   525 ings. A sidedoor of the theatre opened suddenly and a shaft of light flew across the grassplots. A sudden burst of music issued from the ark, the prelude of a waltz: and when the sidedoor closed again the listener could hear the faint rhythm of the music. The sentiment of the opening bars, their languor and   530 supple movement, evoked the incommunicable emotion which had been the cause of all his day's unrest and of his impatient movement of a moment before. His unrest issued from him like a wave of sound: and on the tide of flowing music the ark was journeying, trailing her cables of lanterns in her wake. Then a   535

3. To the left of the altar, as the congregation sees it, where the priest reads the Gospels (the first four books of the New Testament), but not the Epistles (the letters from apostles included as books of the New Testament), which are read from the right side of the altar.

noise like dwarf artillery broke the movement. It was the clapping that greeted the entry of the dumbbell team on the stage.

At the far end of the shed near the street a speck of pink light showed in the darkness and as he walked towards it he 540 became aware of a faint aromatic odour. Two boys were standing in the shelter of the doorway, smoking, and before he reached them he had recognised Heron by his voice.

—Here comes the noble Dedalus! cried a high throaty voice. Welcome to our trusty friend! 545

This welcome ended in a soft peal of mirthless laughter as Heron salaamed and then began to poke the ground with his cane.

—Here I am, said Stephen, halting and glancing from Heron to his friend. 550

The latter was a stranger to him but in the darkness, by the aid of the glowing cigarette tips, he could make out a pale dandyish face, over which a smile was travelling slowly, a tall overcoated figure and a hard hat. Heron did not trouble him= self about an introduction but said instead: 555

—I was just telling my friend Wallis what a lark it would be tonight if you took off the rector in the part of the school= master. It would be a ripping good joke.

Heron made a poor attempt to imitate for his friend Wallis the rector's pedantic bass and then, laughing at his failure, 560 asked Stephen to do it.

—Go on, Dedalus, he urged. You can take him off rippingly. *He that will not hear the churcha let him be to theea as the heathena and the publicana.*[4]

The imitation was prevented by a mild expression of anger 565 from Wallis in whose mouthpiece the cigarette had become too tightly wedged.

—Damn this blankety blank holder, he said, taking it from his mouth and smiling and frowning upon it tolerantly. It's always getting stuck like that. Do you use a holder? 570

—I don't smoke, answered Stephen.

—No, said Heron, Dedalus is a model youth. He doesn't smoke and he doesn't go to bazaars and he doesn't flirt and he doesn't damn anything or damn all.

Stephen shook his head and smiled in his rival's flushed and 575

542 the(2)] a TS–64

4. A send-up of the rector repeating Jesus's words from Matthew 18:17: "And if he refuse to hear them, appeal to the Church, but if he refuse to hear even the Church, let him be to thee as the heathen and the publican."

mobile face, beaked like a bird's. He had often thought it
strange that Vincent Heron had a bird's face as well as a bird's
name. A shock of pale hair lay on the forehead like a ruffled
crest: the forehead was narrow and bony and a thin hooked
nose stood out between the closeset prominent eyes which were   580
light and inexpressive. The rivals were school friends. They sat
together in class, knelt together in the chapel, talked together
after beads[5] over their lunches. As the fellows in number one[6]
were undistinguished dullards Stephen and Heron had been
during the year the virtual heads of the school. It was they who   585
went up to the rector together to ask for a free day or to get a
fellow off.

—O, by the way, said Heron suddenly, I saw your governor
going in.

The smile waned on Stephen's face. Any allusion made to his   590
father by a fellow or by a master put his calm to rout in a
moment. He waited in timorous silence to hear what Heron
might say next. Heron, however, nudged him expressively with
his elbow and said:

—You're a sly dog, Dedalus!   595

—Why so? said Stephen.

—You'd think butter wouldn't melt in your mouth, said
Heron. But I'm afraid you're a sly dog.

—Might I ask you what you are talking about? said Stephen
urbanely.   600

—Indeed you might, answered Heron. We saw her, Wallis,
didn't we? And deucedly pretty she is too. And so inquisitive!
*And what part does Stephen take, Mr Dedalus? And will
Stephen not sing, Mr Dedalus?* Your governor was staring at
her through that eyeglass of his for all he was worth so that I   605
think the old man has found you out too. I wouldn't care a bit,
by Jove. She's ripping, isn't she, Wallis?

—Not half bad, answered Wallis quietly as he placed his
holder once more in a corner of his mouth.

A shaft of momentary anger flew through Stephen's mind at   610
these indelicate allusions in the hearing of a stranger. For him
there was nothing amusing in a girl's interest and regard. All
day he had thought of nothing but their leavetaking on the
steps of the tram at Harold's Cross, the stream of moody
emotions it had made to course through him and the poem he   615
had written about it. All day he had imagined a new meeting

608 —Not] TS; —Hot MS   609 a] the 64

5. After saying prayers using rosary beads.
6. The final year of study.

with her for he knew that she was to come to the play. The old
restless moodiness had again filled his heart as it had done on
the night of the party but had not found an outlet in verse. The
growth and knowledge of two years of boyhood stood between   620
then and now, forbidding such an outlet: and all day the stream
of gloomy tenderness within him had started forth and re=
turned upon itself in dark courses and eddies, wearying him in
the end until the pleasantry of the prefect and the painted little
boy had drawn from him a movement of impatience.   625

—So you may as well admit, Heron went on, that we've fairly
found you out this time. You can't play the saint on me any
more, that's one sure five.[7]

A soft peal of mirthless laughter escaped from his lips and,
bending down as before, he struck Stephen lightly across the   630
calf of the leg with his cane, as if in jesting reproof.

Stephen's moment of anger had already passed. He was nei=
ther flattered nor confused but simply wished the banter to
end. He scarcely resented what had seemed to him at first a
silly indelicateness for he knew that the adventure in his mind   635
stood in no danger from their words: and his face mirrored his
rival's false smile.

—Admit! repeated Heron, striking him again with his cane
across the calf of the leg.

The stroke was playful but not so lightly given as the first   640
one had been. Stephen felt the skin tingle and glow slightly and
almost painlessly; and bowing submissively, as if to meet his
companion's jesting mood, began to recite the *Confiteor*.[8] The
episode ended well for both Heron and Wallis laughed indul=
gently at the irreverence.   645

The confession came only from Stephen's lips and, while
they spoke the words, a sudden memory had carried him to
another scene called up, as if by magic, at the moment when he
had noted the faint cruel dimples at the corners of Heron's
smiling lips and had felt the familiar stroke of the cane against 650
his calf and had heard the familiar word of admonition:
—Admit!

It was towards the close of his first term in the college when
he was in number six.[9] His sensitive nature was still smarting
under the lashes of an undivined and squalid way of life. His   655

618 heart] breast TS [MISREADING]–64   632 moment] 24 [CF 610, NOT 625]; movement
MS–18

7. That's something guaranteed.
8. The prayer said at the beginning of confession, which opens with this Latin word meaning "I confess."
9. The group of students six years from finishing.

soul was still disquieted and cast down by the dull phenom=
enon of Dublin. He had emerged from a two years' spell of
revery to find himself in the midst of a new scene, every event
and figure of which affected him intimately, disheartened him
or allured him and, whether alluring or disheartening, filled   660
him always with unrest and bitter thoughts. All the leisure that
his school life left him was passed in the company of subversive
writers whose gibes and violence of speech set up a ferment in
his brain before they passed out of it into his crude writings.

The essay was for him the chief labour of his week and every   665
Tuesday, as he marched from home to the school, he read his
fate in the incidents of the way, pitting himself against some
figure ahead of him and quickening his pace to outstrip it be=
fore a certain goal was reached or planting his steps scrupu=
lously in the spaces of the patchwork of the footpath and   670
telling himself that he would be first and not first in the weekly
essay.

On a certain Tuesday the course of his triumphs was rudely
broken. Mr Tate, the English master, pointed his finger at him
and said bluntly: 675
—This fellow has heresy in his essay.

A hush fell on the class. Mr Tate did not break it but dug
with his hand between his crossed thighs while his heavily
starched linen creaked about his neck and wrists. Stephen did
not look up. It was a raw spring morning and his eyes were still   680
smarting and weak. He was conscious of failure and of detec=
tion, of the squalor of his own mind and home, and felt against
his neck the raw edge of his turned and jagged collar.

A short loud laugh from Mr Tate set the class more at ease.
—Perhaps you didn't know that, he said.   685
—Where? asked Stephen.

Mr Tate withdrew his delving hand and spread out the es=
say.
—Here. It's about the Creator and the soul. Rrm . . . rrm . . . . .
rrm . . . Ah! *without a possibility of ever approaching nearer.*   690
That's heresy.

Stephen murmured:
—I meant *without a possibility of ever reaching.*

It was a submission and Mr Tate, appeased, folded up the
essay and passed it across to him, saying: 695
—O . . . Ah! *ever reaching.* That's another story.

But the class was not so soon appeased. Though nobody

spoke to him of the affair after class he could feel about him a
vague general malignant joy.

A few nights after this public chiding he was walking with a   700
letter along the Drumcondra Road when he heard a voice cry:
—Halt!

He turned and saw three boys of his own class coming to=
wards him in the dusk. It was Heron who had called out and,
as he marched forward between his two attendants, he cleft the   705
air before him with a thin cane, in time to their steps. Boland,
his friend, marched beside him, a large grin on his face, while
Nash came on a few steps behind, blowing from the pace and
wagging his great red head.

As soon as the boys had turned into Clonliffe Road together   710
they began to speak about books and writers, saying what
books they were reading and how many books there were in
their fathers' bookcases at home. Stephen listened to them in
some wonderment for Boland was the dunce and Nash the idler
of the class. In fact after some talk about their favourite writers   715
Nash declared for Captain Marryat[1] who, he said, was the
greatest writer.

—Fudge! said Heron. Ask Dedalus. Who is the greatest writer,
Dedalus?

Stephen noted the mockery in the question and said: 720
—Of prose, do you mean?
—Yes.
—Newman,[2] I think.
—Is it Cardinal Newman? asked Boland.
—Yes, answered Stephen.   725

The grin broadened on Nash's freckled face as he turned to
Stephen and said:
—And do you like Cardinal Newman, Dedalus?
—O, many people say that Newman has the best prose style,
Heron said to the other two in explanation. Of course, he's not   730
a poet.
—And who is the best poet, Heron? asked Boland.
—Lord Tennyson,[3] of course, answered Heron.
—O, yes, Lord Tennyson, said Nash. We have all his poetry at
home in a book.   735

At this Stephen forgot the silent vows he had been making
and burst out:

729 people] MS; absent TS–64

1. Captain Frederick Marryat (1792–1848), English naval officer, who wrote adventure
   stories.
2. John Henry, Cardinal Newman (1801–1890), a prominent English Protestant clergyman,
   who converted to Catholicism, became a cardinal, and defended his faith in writings that
   were widely admired.
3. Alfred, Lord Tennyson (1809–1892), poet laureate of England.

—Tennyson a poet! Why, he's only a rhymester!

—O, get out! said Heron. Everyone knows that Tennyson is the greatest poet.   740

—And who do you think is the greatest poet? asked Boland, nudging his neighbour.

—Byron, of course, answered Stephen.

Heron gave the lead and all three joined in a scornful laugh.

—What are you laughing at? asked Stephen.   745

—You, said Heron. Byron the greatest poet! He's only a poet for uneducated people.

—He must be a fine poet! said Boland.

—You may keep your mouth shut, said Stephen, turning on him boldly. All you know about poetry is what you wrote up   750 on the slates in the yard and were going to be sent to the loft for.

Boland, in fact, was said to have written on the slates in the yard a couplet about a classmate of his who often rode home from the college on a pony: 755

> As Tyson was riding into Jerusalem
> He fell and hurt his Alec Kafoozelum.

This thrust put the two lieutenants to silence but Heron went on:

—In any case Byron was a heretic and immoral too.   760

—I don't care what he was, cried Stephen hotly.

—You don't care whether he was a heretic or not? said Nash.

—What do you know about it? shouted Stephen. You never read a line of anything in your life except a trans[4] or Boland either.   765

—I know that Byron was a bad man, said Boland.

—Here. Catch hold of this heretic, Heron called out.

In a moment Stephen was a prisoner.

—Tate made you buck up the other day, Heron went on, about the heresy in your essay.   770

—I'll tell him tomorrow, said Boland.

—Will you? said Stephen. You'd be afraid to open your lips.

—Afraid?

—Ay. Afraid of your life.

—Behave yourself! cried Heron, cutting at Stephen's legs with   775 his cane.

It was the signal for their onset. Nash pinioned his arms

761 hotly.] TS; ˥ˡHotly.ˡ˥ MS   762 don't] aEg; ABSENT MS–Eg

4. A translation, used as a shortcut by students instead of the text in the original language.

behind while Boland seized a long cabbage stump which was
lying in the gutter. Struggling and kicking under the cuts of the
cane and the blows of the knotty stump Stephen was borne   780
back against a barbed wire fence.

—Admit that Byron was no good.

—No.

—Admit.

—No.   785

—Admit.

—No. No.

At last after a fury of plunges he wrenched himself free. His
tormentors set off towards Jones's Road, laughing and jeering
at him, while he, half blinded with tears, stumbled on, clench=   790
ing his fists madly and sobbing.

While he was still repeating the *Confiteor* amid the indul=
gent laughter of his hearers and while the scenes of that
malignant episode were still passing sharply and swiftly before
his mind he wondered why he bore no malice now to those   795
who had tormented him. He had not forgotten a whit of their
cowardice and cruelty but the memory of it called forth no
anger from him. All the descriptions of fierce love and hatred
which he had met in books had seemed to him therefore unreal.
Even that night as he stumbled homewards along Jones's Road   800
he had felt that some power was divesting him of that sudden=
woven anger as easily as a fruit is divested of her soft ripe peel.

He remained standing with his two companions at the end
of the shed, listening idly to their talk or to the bursts of
applause in the theatre. She was sitting there among the others,   805
perhaps waiting for him to appear. He tried to recall her ap=
pearance but could not. He could remember only that she had
worn a shawl about her head like a cowl and that her dark eyes
had invited and unnerved him. He wondered had he been in her
thoughts as she had been in his. Then in the dark and unseen   810
by the other two he rested the tips of the fingers of one hand
upon the palm of the other hand, scarcely touching it and yet
pressing upon it lightly. But the pressure of her fingers had
been lighter and steadier: and suddenly the memory of their
touch traversed his brain and body like an invisible warm   815
wave.

A boy came towards them, running along under the shed.
He was excited and breathless.

790 half--on,] aEg; torn and flushed and panting, stumbled after them, half blinded with
tears, MS; half blinded with tears, TS-Eg; torn and flushed and panting, stumbled after
them half blinded with tears, 64   791 sobbing.] TS ENDS   802 her] its Eg–64

—O, Dedalus, he cried, Doyle is in a great bake[5] about you.
You're to go in at once and get dressed for the play. Hurry up,   820
you better.
—He's coming now, said Heron to the messenger with a
haughty drawl, when he wants to.
   The boy turned to Heron and repeated:
—But Doyle is in an awful bake.   825
—Will you tell Doyle with my best compliments that I damned
his eyes? answered Heron.
—Well, I must go now, said Stephen who cared little for such
points of honour.
—I wouldn't, said Heron, damn me if I would. That's no way   830
to send for one of the senior boys. In a bake, indeed! I think it's
quite enough that you're taking a part in his bally old play.

   This spirit of quarrelsome comradeship which he had ob=
served lately in his rival had not seduced Stephen from his
habits of quiet obedience. He mistrusted the turbulence and   835
doubted the sincerity of such comradeship which seemed to
him a sorry anticipation of manhood. The question of honour
here raised was, like all such questions, trivial to him. While his
mind had been pursuing its intangible phantoms and turning in
irresolution from such pursuit he had heard about him the   840
constant voices of his father and of his masters, urging him to
be a gentleman above all things and urging him to be a good
catholic above all things. These voices had now come to be
hollowsounding in his ears. When the gymnasium had been
opened he had heard another voice urging him to be strong and   845
manly and healthy and when the movement towards national
revival had begun to be felt in the college yet another voice had
bidden him be true to his country and help to raise up her
fallen language and tradition.[6] In the profane world, as he
foresaw, a wordly voice would bid him raise up his father's   850
fallen state by his labours and, meanwhile, the voice of his
schoolcomrades urged him to be a decent fellow, to shield
others from blame or to beg them off and to do his best to get
free days for the school. And it was the din of all these hollow=
sounding voices that made him halt irresolutely in the pursuit   855
of phantoms. He gave them ear only for a time but he was
happy only when he was far from them, beyond their call,
alone or in the company of phantasmal comrades.

839–840 turning--irresolution] Eg–64; turning back in irresoluteness MS

5. In an angry state of mind.
6. The opening of the gymnasium suggests the work of the Gaelic Athletic Association,
   while "national revival" refers to the Gaelic League (founded 1893), which advocated use
   of the Irish language instead of English.

In the vestry a plump freshfaced jesuit and an elderly man, in shabby blue clothes, were dabbling in a case of paints and chalks. The boys who had been painted walked about or stood still awkwardly, touching their faces in a gingerly fashion with their furtive fingertips. In the middle of the vestry a young jesuit, who was then on a visit to the college, stood rocking himself rhythmically from the tips of his toes to his heels and back again, his hands thrust well forward into his sidepockets. His small head set off with glossy red curls and his newly shaven face agreed well with the spotless decency of his soutane and with his spotless shoes.

As he watched this swaying form and tried to read for him= self the legend of the priest's mocking smile there came into Stephen's memory a saying which he had heard from his father before he had been sent to Clongowes, that you could always tell a jesuit by the style of his clothes. At the same moment he thought he saw a likeness between his father's mind and that of this smiling welldressed priest: and he was aware of some des= ecration of the priest's office or of the vestry itself, whose si= lence was now routed by loud talk and joking and its air pungent with the smells of the gasjets and the grease.

While his forehead was being wrinkled and his jaws painted black and blue by the elderly man he listened distractedly to the voice of the plump young jesuit which bade him speak up and make his points clearly. He could hear the band playing *The Lily of Killarney*[7] and knew that in a few moments the curtain would go up. He felt no stage fright but the thought of the part he had to play humiliated him. A remembrance of some of his lines made a sudden flush rise to his painted cheeks. He saw her serious alluring eyes watching him from among the audience and their image at once swept away his scruples, leaving his will compact. Another nature seemed to have been lent him: the infection of the excitement and youth about him entered into and transformed his moody mistrustfulness. For one rare moment he seemed to be clothed in the real apparel of boy= hood: and, as he stood in the wings among the other players, he shared the common mirth amid which the drop scene was hauled upwards by two ablebodied priests with violent jerks and all awry.

A few moments after he found himself on the stage amid the garish gas and the dim scenery, acting before the innumerable faces of the void. It surprised him to see that the play which he

7. The overture to the opera of that name (first performed in 1862); composed by Julius Benedict (1804–1885), German-born composer who worked primarily in England.

had known at rehearsals for a disjointed lifeless thing had suddenly assumed a life of its own. It seemed now to play itself, he and his fellow actors aiding it with their parts. When the curtain fell on the last scene he heard the void filled with applause and, through a rift in the side scene, saw the simple body before which he had acted magically deformed, the void of faces breaking at all points and falling asunder into busy groups.

He left the stage quickly and rid himself of his mummery[8] and passed out through the chapel into the college garden. Now that the play was over his nerves cried for some further adventure. He hurried onwards as if to overtake it. The doors of the theatre were all open and the audience had emptied out. On the lines which he had fancied the moorings of an ark a few lanterns swung in the night breeze, flickering cheerlessly. He mounted the steps from the garden in haste, eager that some prey should not elude him, and forced his way through the crowd in the hall and past the two jesuits who stood watching the exodus and bowing and shaking hands with the visitors. He pushed onward nervously, feigning a still greater haste and faintly conscious of the smiles and stares and nudges which his powdered head left in its wake.

When he came out on the steps he saw his family waiting for him at the first lamp. In a glance he noted that every figure of the group was familiar and ran down the steps angrily.

—I have to leave a message down in George's Street,[9] he said to his father quickly. I'll be home after you.

Without waiting for his father's questions he ran across the road and began to walk at breakneck speed down the hill. He hardly knew where he was walking. Pride and hope and desire like crushed herbs in his heart sent up vapours of maddening incense before the eyes of his mind. He strode down the hill amid the tumult of suddenrisen vapours of wounded pride and fallen hope and baffled desire. They streamed upwards before his anguished eyes in dense and maddening fumes and passed away above him till at last the air was clear and cold again.

A film still veiled his eyes but they burned no longer. A power, akin to that which had often made anger or resentment fall from him, brought his steps to rest. He stood still and gazed up at the sombre porch of the morgue and from that to the dark cobbled laneway at its side. He saw the word *Lotts* on the wall of the lane and breathed slowly the rank heavy air.

8. Literally his costume, but also the mood of the performance.
9. Name of a lane near the Liffey, 1.5 miles from the College.

—That is horse piss and rotted straw, he thought. It is a good odour to breathe. It will calm my heart. My heart is quite calm now. I will go back.   945

◆   ◆   ◆

Stephen was once again seated beside his father in the corner of a railway carriage at Kingsbridge.[1] He was travelling with his father by the night mail to Cork. As the train steamed out of the station he recalled his childish wonder of years before and every event of his first day in Clongowes. But he felt no wonder 950 now. He saw the darkening lands slipping past him, the silent telegraphpoles passing his window swiftly every four seconds, the little glimmering stations, manned by a few silent sentries, flung by the mail behind her and twinkling for a moment in the darkness like fiery grains flung backwards by a runner.   955

He listened without sympathy to his father's evocation of Cork and of scenes of his youth, a tale broken by sighs or draughts from his pocket flask whenever the image of some dead friend appeared in it or whenever the evoker remembered suddenly the purpose of his actual visit. Stephen heard but 960 could feel no pity. The images of the dead were all strange to him save that of uncle Charles, an image which had lately been fading out of memory. He knew, however, that his father's property was going to be sold by auction and in the manner of his own dispossession he felt the world give the lie rudely to his 965 phantasy.

At Maryborough he fell asleep. When he awoke the train had passed out of Mallow and his father was stretched asleep on the other seat. The cold light of the dawn lay over the country, over the unpeopled fields and the closed cottages. The 970 terror of sleep fascinated his mind as he watched the silent country or heard from time to time his father's deep breath or sudden sleepy movement. The neighbourhood of unseen sleepers filled him with strange dread as though they could harm him; and he prayed that the day might come quickly. His 975 prayer, addressed neither to God nor saint, began with a shiver, as the chilly morning breeze crept through the chink of the carriage door to his feet, and ended in a trail of foolish words which he made to fit the insistent rhythm of the train: and silently, at intervals of four seconds, the telegraphpoles held the 980 galloping notes of the music between punctual bars. This furi=

---

950 in] at Eg–64   959 evoker] Eg; evoked MS

1. Dublin railway station (now Heuston station) for trains going west and south.

ous music allayed his dread and, leaning against the window=
ledge, he let his eyelids close again.

They drove in a jingle[2] across Cork while it was still early
morning and Stephen finished his sleep in a bedroom of the   985
Victoria Hotel.[3] The bright warm sunlight was streaming
through the window and he could hear the din of traffic. His
father was standing before the dressingtable, examining his
hair and face and moustache with great care, craning his neck
across the waterjug and drawing it back sideways to see the   990
better. While he did so he sang softly to himself with quaint
accent and phrasing:

> 'Tis youth and folly
> Makes young men marry,
> So here, my love, I'll   995
> No longer stay.
> What can't be cured, sure,
> Must be injured, sure,
> So I'll go to
> Amerikay.   1000
>
> My love she's handsome,
> My love she's boney:
> She's like good whisky
> When it is new;
> But when 'tis old   1005
> And growing cold
> It fades and dies like
> The mountain dew.

The consciousness of the warm sunny city outside his win=
dow and the tender tremors with which his father's voice   1010
festooned the strange sad happy air drove off all the mists of
the night's ill humour from Stephen's brain. He got up quickly
to dress and, when the song had ended, said:
—That's much prettier than any of your other *come-all-yous*.[4]
—Do you think so? asked Mr Dedalus.   1015
—I like it, said Stephen.
—It's a pretty old air, said Mr Dedalus, twirling the points of
his moustache. Ah, but you should have heard Mick Lacy sing
it! Poor Mick Lacy! He had little turns for it, grace notes he

984 drove--across] ⌐¹⟨reached⟩ drove--across¹⌐ MS   1002 *boney:*] e:64; boney: MS, Eg;
bony: aEg–24; *bonny:* 64

2. A covered two-wheeled, horse-drawn car (*OED*).
3. The most expensive hotel in Cork at the time.
4. Irish ballads, many of which begin "Come all you."

used to put in that I haven't got. That was the boy could sing a 1020
come-all-you, if you like.

Mr Dedalus had ordered drisheens[5] for breakfast and during
the meal he crossexamined the waiter for local news. For the
most part they spoke at cross purposes when a name was
mentioned, the waiter having in mind its present holder and Mr 1025
Dedalus his father or perhaps his grandfather.

—Well, I hope they haven't moved the Queen's College[6] any=
how, said Mr Dedalus, for I want to show it to this youngster
of mine.

Along the Mardyke[7] the trees were in bloom. They entered 1030
the grounds of the college and were led by the garrulous porter
across the quadrangle. But their progress across the gravel was
brought to a halt after every dozen or so paces by some reply of
the porter's.

—Ah, do you tell me so? And is poor Pottlebelly dead? 1035
—Yes, sir. Dead, sir.

During these halts Stephen stood awkwardly behind the two
men, weary of the subject and waiting restlessly for the slow
march to begin again. By the time they had crossed the quad=
rangle his restlessness had risen to fever. He wondered how his 1040
father, whom he knew for a shrewd suspicious man, could be
duped by the servile manners of the porter: and the lively
southern speech which had entertained him all the morning
now irritated his ears.

They passed into the anatomy theatre where Mr Dedalus, 1045
the porter aiding him, searched the desks for his initials. Ste=
phen remained in the background, depressed more than ever by
the darkness and silence of the theatre and by the air it wore of
jaded and formal study. On the desk before him he read the
word *Foetus* cut several times in the dark stained wood. The 1050
sudden legend startled his blood: he seemed to feel the absent
students of the college about him and to shrink from their
company. A vision of their life, which his father's words had
been powerless to evoke, sprang up before him out of the word
cut in the desk. A broadshouldered student with a moustache 1055
was cutting in the letters with a jackknife, seriously. Other
students stood or sat near him laughing at his handiwork. One
jogged his elbow. The big student turned on him, frowning. He
was dressed in loose grey clothes and had tan boots.

1020 boy] boy who Eg–64   1025 its] the Eg–64

5. Blood sausages (P. W. Joyce, 251).
6. One of the three nonsectarian institutions of that name, located in Cork, Belfast, and
   Galway, at which Catholics could pursue higher education.
7. A promenade in the western part of Cork city.

Stephen's name was called. He hurried down the steps of the 1060
theatre so as to be as far away from the vision as he could be
and, peering closely at his father's initials, hid his flushed face.

But the word and the vision capered before his eyes as he
walked back across the quadrangle and towards the college
gate. It shocked him to find in the outer world a trace of what 1065
he had deemed till then a brutish and individual malady of his
own mind. His recent monstrous reveries came thronging into
his memory. They too had sprung up before him, suddenly and
furiously, out of mere words. He had soon given in to them and
allowed them to sweep across and abase his intellect, wonder= 1070
ing always where they came from, from what den of monstrous
images, and always weak and humble towards others, restless
and sickened of himself when they had swept over him.

—Ay, bedad! And there's the Groceries[8] sure enough! cried Mr
Dedalus. You often heard me speak of the Groceries, didn't 1075
you, Stephen. Many's the time we went down there when our
names had been marked, a crowd of us, Harry Peard and little
Jack Mountain and Bob Dyas and Maurice Moriarty, the
Frenchman, and Tom O'Grady and Mick Lacy that I told you
of this morning and Joey Corbet and poor little goodhearted 1080
Johnny Keevers of the Tantiles.

The leaves of the trees along the Mardyke were astir and
whispering in the sunlight. A team of cricketers passed, agile
young men in flannels and blazers, one of them carrying the
long green wicketbag. In a quiet bystreet a German band of five 1085
players in faded uniforms and with battered brass instruments
was playing to an audience of street arabs[9] and leisurely mess=
enger boys. A maid in a white cap and apron was watering a
box of plants on a sill which shone like a slab of limestone in
the warm glare. From another window open to the air came the 1090
sound of a piano, scale after scale rising into the treble.

Stephen walked on at his father's side, listening to stories he
had heard before, hearing again the names of the scattered and
dead revellers who had been the companions of his father's
youth. And a faint sickness sighed in his heart. He recalled his 1095
own equivocal position in Belvedere, a free boy,[1] a leader afraid
of his own authority, proud and sensitive and suspicious, bat=
tling against the squalor of his life and against the riot of his
mind. The letters cut in the stained wood of the desk stared
upon him, mocking his bodily weakness and futile enthusiasms 1100

8. A pub that also sold household items and nonperishable food.
9. Street urchins, children from the slums.
1. Student on scholarship, who pays no fees.

and making him loathe himself for his own mad and filthy orgies. The spittle in his throat grew bitter and foul to swallow and the faint sickness climbed to his brain so that for a moment he closed his eyes and walked on in darkness.

He could still hear his father's voice.   1105

—When you kick out for yourself, Stephen, (as I daresay you will one of those days) remember, whatever you do, to mix with gentlemen. When I was a young fellow I tell you I enjoyed myself. I mixed with fine decent fellows. Everyone of us could do something. One fellow had a good voice, another fellow   1110 was a good actor, another could sing a good comic song, an= other was a good oarsman or a good racketplayer, another could tell a good story and so on. We kept the ball rolling anyhow and enjoyed ourselves and saw a bit of life and we were none the worse of it either. But we were all gentlemen,   1115 Stephen, (at least I hope we were) and bloody good honest Irishmen too. That's the kind of fellows I want you to associate with, fellows of the right kidney. I'm talking to you as a friend, Stephen. I don't believe in playing the stern father. I don't believe a son should be afraid of his father. No, I treat you as   1120 your grandfather treated me when I was a young chap. We were more like brothers than father and son. I'll never forget the first day he caught me smoking. I was standing at the end of the South Terrace one day with some maneens[2] like myself and sure we thought we were grand fellows because we had   1125 pipes stuck in the corners of our mouths. Suddenly the gov= ernor passed. He didn't say a word or stop even. But the next day, Sunday, we were out for a walk together and when we were coming home he took out his cigar case and said: *By the bye, Simon, I didn't know you smoked:* or something like that.   1130 –Of course I tried to carry it off as best I could. *If you want a good smoke,* he said, *try one of these cigars. An American captain made me a present of them last night in Queenstown.*[3]

Stephen heard his father's voice break into a laugh which was almost a sob.   1135

—He was the handsomest man in Cork at that time, by God he was! The women used to stand to look after him in the street.

He heard the sob passing loudly down his father's throat and opened his eyes with a nervous impulse. The sunlight breaking suddenly on his sight turned the sky and clouds into a   1140 fantastic world of sombre masses with lakelike spaces of dark

2. "Little man," used derisively (Irish dialect).
3. A port (now known as Cobh) on the southern coast of County Cork from which many Irish emigrated for America and elsewhere.

rosy light. His very brain was sick and powerless. He could scarcely interpret the letters of the signboards of the shops. By his monstrous way of life he seemed to have put himself be= yond the limits of reality. Nothing moved him or spoke to him from the real world unless he heard in it an echo of the infuriated cries within him. He could respond to no earthly or human appeal, dumb and insensible to the call of summer and gladness and companionship, wearied and dejected by his fa= ther's voice. He could scarcely recognise as his his own thoughts, and repeated slowly to himself:

—I am Stephen Dedalus. I am walking beside my father whose name is Simon Dedalus. We are in Cork, in Ireland. Cork is a city. Our room is in the Victoria Hotel. Victoria and Stephen and Simon. Simon and Stephen and Victoria. Names.

The memory of his childhood suddenly grew dim. He tried to call forth some of its vivid moments but could not. He recalled only names: Dante, Parnell, Clane, Clongowes. A little boy had been taught geography by an old woman who kept two brushes in her wardrobe. Then he had been sent away from home to a college. In the college he had made his first communion and eaten slim jim[4] out of his cricket cap and watched the firelight leaping and dancing on the wall of a little bedroom in the infirmary and dreamed of being dead, of mass being said for him by the rector in a black and gold cope, of being buried then in the little graveyard of the community off the main avenue of limes. But he had not died then. Parnell had died. There had been no mass for the dead in the chapel and no procession. He had not died but he had faded out like a film in the sun. He had been lost or had wandered out of existence for he no longer existed. How strange to think of him passing out of existence in such a way, not by death but by fading out in the sun or by being lost and forgotten somewhere in the uni= verse! It was strange to see his small body appear again for a moment: a little boy in a grey belted suit. His hands were in his sidepockets and his trousers were tucked in at the knees by elastic bands.

On the evening of the day on which the property was sold Stephen followed his father meekly about the city from bar to bar. To the sellers in the market, to the barmen and barmaids, to the beggars who importuned him for a lob[5] Mr Dedalus told the same tale, that he was an old Corkonian, that he had been

1167 limes.] Eg; chestnuts. MS

4. A sugar-coated sweet that was sold in long strips (*Letters* III, 129).
5. Money (Irish dialect).

trying for thirty years to get rid of his Cork accent up in Dublin and that Peter Pickackafox beside him was his eldest son but that he was only a Dublin jackeen.[6]   1185

They had set out early in the morning from Newcombe's coffeehouse where Mr Dedalus' cup had rattled noisily against its saucer and Stephen had tried to cover that shameful sign of his father's drinkingbout of the night before by moving his chair and coughing. One humiliation had succeeded another: 1190 the false smiles of the market sellers, the curvettings and oglings of the barmaids with whom his father flirted, the com= pliments and encouraging words of his father's friends. They had told him that he had a great look of his grandfather and Mr Dedalus had agreed that he was an ugly likeness. They had 1195 unearthed traces of a Cork accent in his speech and made him admit that the Lee was a much finer river than the Liffey. One of them in order to put his Latin to the proof had made him translate short passages from Dilectus[7] and asked him whether it was correct to say: *Tempora mutantur nos et mutamur in illis* 1200 or *Tempora mutantur et nos mutamur in illis.*[8] Another, a brisk old man, whom Mr Dedalus called Johnny Cashman, had covered him with confusion by asking him to say which were prettier, the Dublin girls or the Cork girls.

—He's not that way built, said Mr Dedalus. Leave him alone. 1205 He's a levelheaded thinking boy who doesn't bother his head about that kind of nonsense.

—Then he's not his father's son, said the little old man.

—I don't know, I'm sure, said Mr Dedalus, smiling com= placently.   1210

—Your father, said the little old man to Stephen, was the boldest flirt in the city of Cork in his day. Do you know that?

Stephen looked down and studied the tiled floor of the bar into which they had drifted.

—Now don't be putting ideas into his head, said Mr Dedalus. 1215 Leave him to his Maker.

—Yerra, sure I wouldn't put any ideas into his head. I'm old enough to be his grandfather. And I am a grandfather, said the little old man to Stephen. Do you know that?

1184 Pickackafox] MS; Pickackafax Eg–64   1200 *Tempora--illis*] e:Eg, 18; Tempora mutantur et nos cum illis mutamur MS   1201 *Tempora--illis.*] Eg; Tempora mutantur et nos
mutamur cum illis. MS   1201 *in*] Eg; cum MS

6. A conceited lower-class person (Irish dialect).
7. A misspelling for *Delectus,* from the title, *Delectus Sententiarum,* of an early nineteenth-
   century anthology of Latin sentences by Richard Valpy (1754–1836), to accompany his
   grammar, both widely used for teaching Latin in schools.
8. Two metrically different ways of expressing the sentiment that times change and that we
   change with them, or because of them (Latin).

—Are you? asked Stephen.   1220
—Bedad I am, said the little old man. I have two bouncing
grandchildren out at Sunday's Well.[9] Now then! What age do
you think I am? And I remember seeing your grandfather in his
red coat riding out to hounds. That was before you were born.
—Ay, or thought of, said Mr Dedalus.   1225
—Bedad I did! repeated the little old man. And, more than
that, I can remember even your greatgrandfather, old John Ste=
phen Dedalus, and a fierce old fireeater he was. Now then!
There's a memory for you!
—That's three generations–four generations, said another of   1230
the company. Why, Johnny Cashman, you must be nearing the
century.
—Well, I'll tell you the truth, said the little old man. I'm just
twentyseven years of age.
—We're as old as we feel, Johnny, said Mr Dedalus. And just   1235
finish what you have there and we'll have another. Here, Tim
or Tom or whatever your name is, give us the same again here.
By God, I don't feel more than eighteen myself. There's that
son of mine there not half my age and I'm a better man than he
is any day of the week.   1240
—Draw it mild now, Dedalus. I think it's about time for you to
take a back seat, said the gentleman who had spoken before.
—No, by God! asserted Mr Dedalus. I'll sing a tenor song
against him or I'll vault a fivebarred gate against him or I'll run
with him after the hounds across the country as I did thirty   1245
years ago along with the Kerry Boy and the best man for it.
—But he'll beat you here, said the little old man, tapping his
forehead and raising his glass to drain it.
—Well, I hope he'll be as good a man as his father. That's all I
can say, said Mr Dedalus.   1250
—If he is, he'll do, said the little old man.
—And thanks be to God, Johnny, said Mr Dedalus, that we
lived so long and did so little harm.
—But did so much good, Simon, said the little old man
gravely. Thanks be to God we lived so long and did so much   1255
good.
    Stephen watched the three glasses being raised from the
counter as his father and his two cronies drank to the memory
of their past. An abyss of fortune or of temperament sundered
him from them. His mind seemed older than theirs: it shone   1260

1241 about] ABSENT Eg–64

9. A suburb of Cork city, just over a mile from the center.

coldly on their strifes and happiness and regrets like a moon
upon a younger earth. No life or youth stirred in him as it had
stirred in them. He had known neither the pleasure of compan=
ionship with others nor the vigour of rude male health nor filial
piety. Nothing stirred within his soul but a cold and cruel and   1265
loveless lust. His childhood was dead or lost and with it his
soul capable of simple joys: and he was drifting amid life like
the barren shell of the moon.

> Art thou pale for weariness
> Of climbing heaven and gazing on the earth   1270
> Wandering companionless . . . . ?[1]

He repeated to himself the lines of Shelley's fragment. Its
alternation of sad human ineffectiveness with vast inhuman
cycles of activity chilled him: and he forgot his own human and
ineffectual grieving.   1275

◆   ◆   ◆

Stephen's mother and his brother and one of his cousins
waited at the corner of quiet Foster Place while he and his
father went up the steps and along the colonnade where the
highland sentry was parading. When they had passed into the
great hall and stood at the counter Stephen drew forth his   1280
orders on the governor of the bank of Ireland for thirty and
three pounds; and these sums, the moneys of his exhibition[2] and
essay prize, were paid over to him rapidly by the teller in notes
and in coin respectively. He bestowed them in his pockets with
feigned composure and suffered the friendly teller, to whom his   1285
father chatted, to take his hand across the broad counter and
wish him a brilliant career in after life. He was impatient of
their voices and could not keep his feet at rest. But the teller
still deferred the serving of others to say that he was living in
changed times and that there was nothing like giving a boy the   1290
best education that money could buy. Mr Dedalus lingered in
the hall gazing about him and up at the roof and telling Ste=
phen, who urged him to come out, that they were standing in
the house of commons of the old Irish parliament.

—God help us! he said piously. To think of the men of those   1295

1273 ineffectiveness] a16 [cf unpublished letter to Harriet Shaw Weaver, c. 20 Nov.
1917, British Library]; ineffectualness MS–16   1289 that] absent Eg–64

1. Opening of "To the Moon," by the English Romantic poet Percy Bysshe Shelley
   (1792–1822).
2. Award made because of his performance on the annual competitive, national school
   examinations.

times, Stephen, Hely Hutchinson and Flood and Henry Grattan and Charles Kendal Bushe,[3] and the noblemen we have now, leaders of the Irish people at home and abroad. Why, by God, they wouldn't be seen dead in a ten acre field with them. No, Stephen, old chap, I'm sorry to say that they are only as I roved out one fine May morning in the merry month of sweet July.[4]

A keen October wind was blowing round the bank. The three figures standing at the edge of the muddy path had pinched cheeks and watery eyes. Stephen looked at his thinly clad mother and remembered that a few days before he had seen a mantle priced at twenty guineas in the window of Bar= nardo's.

—Well, that's done, said Mr Dedalus.

—We had better go to dinner, said Stephen. Where?

—Dinner? said Mr Dedalus. Well, I suppose we had better, what?

—Some place that's not too dear, said Mrs Dedalus.

—Underdone's?[5]

—Yes. Some quiet place.

—Come along, said Stephen quickly. It doesn't matter about the dearness.

He walked on before them with short nervous steps, smiling. They tried to keep up with him, smiling also at his eagerness.

—Take it easy like a good young fellow, said his father. We're not out for the half mile, are we?

For a swift season of merrymaking the money of his prizes ran through Stephen's fingers. Great parcels of groceries and delicacies and dried fruits arrived from the city. Every day he drew up a bill of fare for the family and every night led a party of three or four to the theatre to see *Ingomar* or *The Lady of Lyons*.[6] In his coat pockets he carried squares of Vienna choc= olate for his guests while his trousers' pockets bulged with masses of silver and copper coins. He bought presents for everyone, overhauled his room, wrote out resolutions, marshal= led his books up and down their shelves, pored upon all kinds

1300
1305
1310
1315
1320
1325
1330

1306 window] windows Eg–64

3. Irish statesmen and orators of the late eighteenth and early nineteenth centuries: John Hely-Hutchinson (1724–1794), Henry Flood (1732–1791), Henry Grattan (1746–1820), and Charles Kendal Bushe (1767–1843).
4. Mr. Dedalus's joking transformation of the opening line of the ballad "The Bonny Labour-ing Boy" expresses his skepticism about the leaders of the day.
5. The family's joking nickname for some expensive restaurant.
6. Two plays with happy endings for the young male heroes, Ingomar in *Ingomar the Bar-barian* (1851), by the English actress and dramatist Maria Lovell (1803–1877), and Claude Melnotte in *The Lady of Lyons* (1838), by the English novelist and playwright Edward Bulwer-Lytton (1803–1873).

of price lists, drew up a form of commonwealth for the household by which every member of it held some office, opened a loan bank for his family and pressed loans on willing borrowers so that he might have the pleasure of making out receipts and reckoning the interests on the sums lent. When he could do no more he drove up and down the city in trams. Then the season of pleasure came to an end. The pot of pink enamel paint gave out and the wainscot of his bedroom re= mained with its unfinished and illplastered coat.

His household returned to its usual way of life. His mother had no further occasion to upbraid him for squandering his money. He too returned to his old life at school and all his novel enterprises fell to pieces. The commonwealth fell, the loan bank closed its coffers and its books on a sensible loss,[7] the rules of life which he had drawn about himself fell into desue= tude.

How foolish his aim had been! He had tried to build a breakwater of order and elegance against the sordid tide of life without him and to dam up, by rules of conduct and active interests and new filial relations, the powerful recurrence of the tides within him. Useless. From without as from within the waters had flowed over his barriers: their tides began once more to jostle fiercely above the crumbled mole.[8]

He saw clearly too his own futile isolation. He had not gone one step nearer the lives he had sought to approach nor bridged the restless shame and rancour that divided him from father and mother and brother and sister. He felt that he was hardly of the one blood with them but stood to them rather in the mystical kinship of fosterage, fosterchild and fosterbrother.

He burned to appease the fierce longings of his heart before which everything else was idle and alien. He cared little that he was in mortal sin,[9] that his life had grown to be a tissue of subterfuges and falsehood. Beside the savage desire within him to realise the enormities which he brooded on nothing was sacred. He bore cynically with the shameful details of his secret riots in which he exulted to defile with patience whatever im= age had attracted his eyes. By day and by night he moved among distorted images of the outer world. A figure that had seemed to him by day demure and innocent came towards him

1344 loan] Eg [cf 1333]; loans MS   1352 waters] water Eg–18, 64

7. Perceptible, that is, substantial, loss.
8. "A massive structure, esp. of stone, serving as a pier or breakwater" (OED).
9. Sin that causes spiritual death; by contrast with venial sin, which is pardonable because not grave (OED).

by night through the winding darkness of sleep, her face trans= 1370
figured by a lecherous cunning, her eyes bright with brutish
joy. Only the morning pained him with its dim memory of dark
orgiastic riot, its keen and humiliating sense of transgression.

He returned to his wanderings. The veiled autumnal even=
ings led him from street to street as they had led him years 1375
before along the quiet avenues of Blackrock. But no vision of
trim front gardens or of kindly lights in the windows poured a
tender influence upon him now. Only at times, in the pauses of
his desire, when the luxury that was wasting him gave room to
a softer languor, the image of Mercedes traversed the back= 1380
ground of his memory. He saw again the small white house and
the garden of rosebushes on the road that led to the mountains
and he remembered the sadly proud gesture of refusal which he
was to make there, standing with her in the moonlit garden
after years of estrangement and adventure. At those moments 1385
the soft speeches of Claude Melnotte rose to his lips and eased
his unrest. A tender premonition touched him of the tryst he
had then looked forward to and, in spite of the horrible reality
which lay between his hope of then and now, of the holy
encounter he had then imagined at which weakness and timid= 1390
ity and inexperience were to fall from him.

Such moments passed and the wasting fires of lust sprang up
again. The verses passed from his lips and the inarticulate cries
and the unspoken brutal words rushed forth from his brain to
force a passage. His blood was in revolt. He wandered up and 1395
down the dark slimy streets peering into the gloom of lanes and
doorways, listening eagerly for any sound. He moaned to him=
self like some baffled prowling beast. He wanted to sin with
another of his kind, to force another being to sin with him and
to exult with her in sin. He felt some dark presence moving 1400
irresistibly upon him from the darkness, a presence subtle and
murmurous as a flood filling him wholly with itself. Its mur=
mur besieged his ears like the murmur of some multitude in
sleep; its subtle streams penetrated his being. His hands
clenched convulsively and his teeth set together as he suffered 1405
the agony of its penetration. He stretched out his arms in the
street to hold fast the frail swooning form that eluded him and
incited him: and the cry that he had strangled for so long in his
throat issued from his lips. It broke from him like a wail of
despair from a hell of sufferers and died in a wail of furious 1410
entreaty, a cry for an iniquitous abandonment, a cry which was

1379 him] Eg; ABSENT MS

but the echo of an obscene scrawl which he had read on the
oozing wall of a urinal.

He had wandered into a maze of narrow and dirty streets.
From the foul laneways he heard bursts of hoarse riot and   1415
wrangling and the drawling of drunken singers. He walked
onward, undismayed, wondering whether he had strayed into
the quarter of the jews. Women and girls dressed in long vivid
gowns traversed the street from house to house. They were
leisurely and perfumed. A trembling seized him and his eyes   1420
grew dim. The yellow gasflames arose before his troubled vi=
sion against the vapoury sky, burning as if before an altar.
Before the doors and in the lighted halls groups were gathered,
arrayed as for some rite. He was in another world: he had
awakened from a slumber of centuries.   1425

He stood still in the middle of the roadway, his heart clam=
ouring against his bosom in a tumult. A young woman dressed
in a long pink gown laid her hand on his arm to detain him and
gazed into his face. She said gaily:
—Good night, Willie dear!   1430

Her room was warm and lightsome. A huge doll sat with her
legs apart in the copious easychair beside the bed. He tried to
bid his tongue speak that he might seem at ease, watching her
as she undid her gown, noting the proud conscious movements
of her perfumed head.   1435

As he stood silent in the middle of the room she came over
to him and embraced him gaily and gravely. Her round arms
held him firmly to her and he, seeing her face lifted to him in
serious calm and feeling the warm calm rise and fall of her
breast, all but burst into hysterical weeping. Tears of joy and 1440
relief shone in his delighted eyes and his lips parted though they
would not speak.

She passed her tinkling hand through his hair, calling him a
little rascal.
—Give me a kiss, she said.   1445

His lips would not bend to kiss her. He wanted to be held
firmly in her arms, to be caressed slowly, slowly, slowly. In her
arms he felt that he had suddenly become strong and fearless
and sure of himself. But his lips would not bend to kiss her.

With a sudden movement she bowed his head and joined her   1450
lips to his and he read the meaning of her movements in her
frank uplifted eyes. It was too much for him. He closed his
eyes, surrendering himself to her, body and mind, conscious of

1434 she] Eg; he MS

nothing in the world but the dark pressure of her softly parting
lips. They pressed upon his brain as upon his lips as though   1455
they were the vehicle of a vague speech; and between them he
felt an unknown and timid pressure, darker than the swoon of
sin, softer than sound or odour.

III

The swift December dusk had come tumbling clownishly after
its dull day and as he stared through the dull square of the
window of the schoolroom he felt his belly crave for its food.
He hoped there would be stew for dinner, turnips and carrots
and bruised potatoes and fat mutton pieces to be ladled out in   5
thick peppered flourfattened sauce. Stuff it into you, his belly
counselled him.

   It would be a gloomy secret night. After early nightfall the
yellow lamps would light up here and there the squalid quarter
of the brothels. He would follow a devious course up and down   10
the streets, circling always nearer and nearer in a tremor of fear
and joy, until his feet led him suddenly round a dark corner.
The whores would be just coming out of their houses making
ready for the night, yawning lazily after their sleep and settling
the hairpins in their clusters of hair. He would pass by them   15
calmly waiting for a sudden movement of his own will or a
sudden call to his sinloving soul from their soft perfumed flesh.
Yet as he prowled in quest of that call his senses, stultified only
by his desire, would note keenly all that wounded and shamed
them, his eyes a ring of porter froth on a clothless table or a   20
photograph of two soldiers standing to attention or a gaudy
playbill, his ears the drawling jargon of greeting:
—Hello, Bertie, any good in your mind?
—Is that you, pigeon?
—Number ten. Fresh Nelly is waiting on you.   25
—Good night, husband! Coming in to have a short time?
   The equation on the page of his scribbler began to spread
out a widening tail, eyed and starred like a peacock's: and
when the eyes and stars of its indices had been eliminated be=
gan slowly to fold itself together again. The indices appearing   30
and disappearing were eyes opening and closing; the eyes
opening and closing were stars being born and being quenched.
The vast cycle of starry life bore his weary mind outward to its

1456 vehicle] Eg; vehicles MS   19 and] or 16–64

verge and inward to its centre, a distant music accompanying
him outward and inward. What music? The music came nearer   35
and he recalled the words, the words of Shelley's fragment
upon the moon wandering companionless, pale for weariness.[1]
The stars began to crumble and a cloud of fine stardust fell
through space.

The dull light fell more faintly upon the page whereon an=   40
other equation began to unfold itself slowly and to spread
abroad its widening tail. It was his own soul going forth to
experience, unfolding itself sin by sin, spreading abroad the
balefire[2] of its burning stars and folding back upon itself, fading
slowly, quenching its own lights and fires. They were   45
quenched: and the cold darkness filled chaos.

A cold lucid indifference reigned in his soul. At his first
violent sin he had felt a wave of vitality pass out of him and
had feared to find his body or his soul maimed by the excess.
Instead the vital wave had carried him on its bosom out of   50
himself and back again when it receded: and no part of body or
soul had been maimed but a dark peace had been established
between them. The chaos in which his ardour extinguished
itself was a cold indifferent knowledge of himself. He had
sinned mortally not once but many times and he knew that,   55
while he stood in danger of eternal damnation for the first sin
alone, by every succeeding sin he multiplied his guilt and his
punishment. His days and works and thoughts could make no
atonement for him, the fountains of sanctifying grace having
ceased to refresh his soul. At most by an alms given to a   60
beggar, whose blessing he fled from, he might hope wearily to
win for himself some measure of actual grace.[3] Devotion had
gone by the board. What did it avail to pray when he knew that
his soul lusted after its own destruction? A certain pride, a
certain awe, withheld him from offering to God even one   65
prayer at night though he knew it was in God's power to take
away his life while he slept and hurl his soul hellward ere he
could beg for mercy. His pride in his own sin, his loveless awe
of God told him that his offence was too grievous to be atoned
for in whole or in part by a false homage to the Allseeing and   70
Allknowing.

—Well now, Ennis, I declare you have a head and so has my

1. See II.1269–71 and note 1, p. 84.
2. Bonfire (*OED*).
3. According to Catholic doctrine, God's grace can manifest itself in the individual as a permanent state of habitual grace, or sanctifying grace, which can be lost because of mortal
sin, that is, sin that deadens the soul. Impulsive moral acts constitute a second contrasting form, actual grace, which lasts only during the act (*Cath. Enc.*).

stick! Do you mean to say that you are not able to tell me what a surd[4] is?

The blundering answer stirred the embers of his contempt of his fellows. Towards others he felt neither shame nor fear. On Sunday mornings as he passed the churchdoor he glanced coldly at the worshippers who stood bareheaded, four deep, outside the church, morally present at the mass which they could neither see nor hear. Their dull piety and the sickly smell of the cheap hairoil with which they had anointed their heads repelled him from the altar they prayed at. He stooped to the evil of hypocrisy with others, sceptical of their innocence which he could cajole so easily.

On the wall of his bedroom hung an illuminated scroll, the certificate of his prefecture in the college of the sodality of the Blessed Virgin Mary.[5] On Saturday mornings when the sodality met in the chapel to recite the little office[6] his place was a cushioned kneelingdesk at the right of the altar from which he led his wing of boys through the responses. The falsehood of his position did not pain him. If at moments he felt an impulse to rise from his post of honour and, confessing before them all his unworthiness, to leave the chapel, a glance at their faces restrained him. The imagery of the psalms of prophecy soothed his barren pride. The glories of Mary held his soul captive: spikenard and myrrh and frankincense, symbolising the preciousness of God's gifts to her soul, rich garments, symbol= ising her royal lineage, her emblems, the lateflowering plant and lateblossoming tree, symbolising the agelong gradual growth of her cultus among men. When it fell to him to read the lesson towards the close of the office he read it in a veiled voice, lulling his conscience to its music:

> *Quasi cedrus exaltata sum in Libanon et quasi cu=*
> *pressus in monte Sion. Quasi palma exaltata sum in*
> *Gades et quasi plantatio rosae in Jericho. Quasi uliva*
> *speciosa in campis et quasi platanus exaltata sum juxta*
> *aquam in plateis. Sicut cinnamomum et balsamum aro=*
> *matizans odorem dedi et quasi myrrha electa dedi*
> *suavitatem odoris.*[7]

84 easily.] Eg; lightly. MS

4. An irrational number.
5. His leadership of the devotional group dedicated to the Virgin Mary.
6. Readings drawn from the Bible to honor the Virgin Mary.
7. Latin version of a passage from Ecclesiasticus (not Ecclesiastes), a book in the Old Testament canon, not accepted by Protestants. In English: "I was exalted like a cedar in Libanus, and as a cypress tree on mount Sion. I was exalted like a palm tree in Cades, and as a rose plant in Jericho: As a fair olive tree in the plains, and as a plane tree by the water in the streets, was I exalted. I gave a sweet smell like cinnamon, and aromatical balm: I yielded a sweet odour like the best myrrh" (24:17–20).

His sin, which had covered him from the sight of God, had   110
led him nearer to the refuge of sinners. Her eyes seemed to
regard him with mild pity; her holiness, a strange light glowing
faintly upon her frail flesh, did not humiliate the sinner who
approached her. If ever he was impelled to cast sin from him
and to repent the impulse that moved him was the wish to be   115
her knight. If ever his soul, reentering her dwelling shyly after
the frenzy of his body's lust had spent itself, was turned to=
wards her whose emblem is the morning star, *bright and
musical, telling of heaven and infusing peace*,[8] it was when her
names were murmured softly by lips whereon there still lin=   120
gered foul and shameful words, the savour itself of a lewd kiss.

That was strange. He tried to think how it could be but the
dusk, deepening in the schoolroom, covered over his thought.
The bell rang. The master marked the sums and cuts[9] to be done
for the next lesson and went out. Heron, beside Stephen, began   125
to hum tunelessly:

My excellent friend Bombados.[1]

Ennis, who had gone to the yard, came back, saying:
—The boy from the house is coming up for the rector.
A tall boy behind Stephen rubbed his hands and said: 130
—That's game ball.[2] We can scut the whole hour. He won't be
in till after half two. Then you can ask him questions on the
catechism,[3] Dedalus.

Stephen, leaning back and drawing idly on his scribbler,
listened to the talk about him which Heron checked from time   135
to time by saying:
—Shut up, will you. Don't make such a bally racket!

It was strange too that he found an arid pleasure in follow=
ing up to the end the rigid lines of the doctrines of the church
and penetrating into obscure silences only to hear and feel the   140
more deeply his own condemnation. The sentence of saint
James which says that he who offends against one command=

---

123 thought.] MS; thoughts. Eg–64   127 *Bombados.*] e:Eg, aEg; *Pompados| My dearest
and best Patake* MS; *Pompados.* Eg

8. The Virgin Mary is associated with the morning star in the "Litany of Our Lady" (of
Loreto), alluded to in Part I (p. 30); the italicized language is quoted from John Henry
Cardinal Newman's "The Glories of Mary for the Sake of Her Son," in his *Discourses to
Mixed Congregations* (1849).
9. Mathematics schoolwork to be done from material in a text of Euclid's *Geometry* (*Letters*
III, 129).
1. A line probably from a music-hall pantomime.
2. The final ball, the deciding factor.
3. An instructional treatise concerning a religion's principles in the form of questions and
answers (*OED*).

ment becomes guilty of all[4] had seemed to him first a swollen
phrase until he had begun to grope in the darkness of his own
state. From the evil seed of lust all other deadly sins[5] had sprung   145
forth: pride in himself and contempt of others, covetousness in
using money for the purchase of unlawful pleasure, envy of
those whose vices he could not reach to and calumnious
murmuring against the pious, gluttonous enjoyment of food,
the dull glowering anger amid which he brooded upon his   150
longing, the swamp of spiritual and bodily sloth in which his
whole being had sunk.

As he sat in his bench gazing calmly at the rector's shrewd
harsh face his mind wound itself in and out of the curious
questions proposed to it. If a man had stolen a pound in his   155
youth and had used that pound to amass a huge fortune how
much was he obliged to give back, the pound he had stolen
only or the pound together with the compound interest accru=
ing upon it or all his huge fortune? If a layman in giving
baptism pour the water before saying the words is the child   160
baptised? Is baptism with a mineral water valid? How comes it
that while the first beatitude[6] promises the kingdom of heaven
to the poor of heart the second beatitude promises also to the
meek that they shall possess the land? Why was the sacrament
of the eucharist[7] instituted under the two species of bread and   165
wine if Jesus Christ be present body and blood, soul and divin=
ity, in the bread alone and in the wine alone? Does a tiny
particle of the consecrated bread contain all the body and
blood of Jesus Christ or a part only of the body and blood? If
the wine change into vinegar and the host crumble into cor=   170
ruption after they have been consecrated is Jesus Christ still
present under their species as God and as man?
—Here he is! Here he is!

A boy from his post at the window had seen the rector come
from the house. All the catechisms were opened and all heads   175
bent upon them silently. The rector entered and took his seat
on the dais. A gentle kick from the tall boy in the bench behind
urged Stephen to ask a difficult question.

168 bread] Eg; ABSENT MS

4. In the New Testament, James 2:10: "For whoever keeps the whole law, but offends in one
point, has become guilty in all."
5. All seven sins deadly to the soul are mentioned: lust, pride, covetousness, envy, gluttony,
anger, and sloth.
6. A declaration of blessedness. Stephen is thinking about Jesus's statements in Matthew
3–11 concerning the blessed.
7. The Christian sacrament, or religious rite, in which consecrated bread and wine are consumed.

The rector did not ask for a catechism to hear the lesson from. He clasped his hands on the desk and said: 180
—The retreat will begin on Wednesday afternoon in honour of saint Francis Xavier whose feast day is Saturday. The retreat will go on from Wednesday to Friday. On Friday confessions will be heard all the afternoon after beads. If any boys have special confessors perhaps it will be better for them not to 185 change. Mass will be on Saturday morning at nine o'clock and general communion for the whole college. Saturday will be a free day. Sunday of course. But Saturday and Sunday being free days some boys might be inclined to think that Monday is a free day also. Beware of making that mistake. I think you, 190 Lawless, are likely to make that mistake.
—I, sir? Why, sir?

A little wave of quiet mirth broke forth over the class of boys from the rector's grim smile. Stephen's heart began slowly to fold and fade with fear like a withering flower. 195

The rector went on gravely:
—You are all familiar with the story of the life of saint Francis Xavier, I suppose, the patron of your college. He came of an old and illustrious Spanish family and you remember that he was one of the first followers of saint Ignatius. They met in 200 Paris where Francis Xavier was professor of philosophy at the university. This young and brilliant nobleman and man of let= ters entered heart and soul into the ideas of our glorious founder and you know that he, at his own desire, was sent by saint Ignatius to preach to the Indians. He is called, as you 205 know, the apostle of the Indies. He went from country to country in the east, from Africa to India, from India to Japan, baptising the people. He is said to have baptised as many as ten thousand idolaters in one month. It is said that his right arm had grown powerless from having been raised so often over the 210 heads of those whom he baptised. He wished then to go to China to win still more souls for God but he died of fever on the island of Sancian.[8] A great saint, saint Francis Xavier! A great soldier of God!

The rector paused and then, shaking his clasped hands be= 215 fore him, went on:
—He had the faith in him that moves mountains. Ten thou= sand souls won for God in a single month! That is a true conqueror, true to the motto of our order *ad majorem Dei*

183 Friday] Eg; Fridays MS   183 confessions] MS; confession Eg–64

8. Off the Chinese coast.

gloriam! A saint who has great power in heaven, remember: 220
power to intercede for us in our grief, power to obtain what=
ever we pray for if it be for the good of our souls, power above
all to obtain for us the grace to repent if we be in sin. A great
saint, saint Francis Xavier! A great fisher of souls![9]

He ceased to shake his clasped hands and, resting them 225
against his forehead, looked right and left of them keenly at his
listeners out of his dark stern eyes.

In the silence their dark fire kindled the dusk into a tawny
glow. Stephen's heart had withered up like a flower of the
desert that feels the simoom[1] coming from afar. 230

◆   ◆   ◆

—*Remember only thy last things and thou shalt not sin for
ever*—words taken, my dear little brothers in Christ, from the
book of Ecclesiastes, seventh chapter, fortieth verse.[2] In the
name of the Father and of the Son and of the Holy Ghost.
Amen. 235

Stephen sat in the front bench of the chapel. Father Arnall
sat at a table to the left of the altar. He wore about his shoul=
ders a heavy cloak; his pale face was drawn and his voice
broken with rheum. The figure of his old master, so strangely
rearisen, brought back to Stephen's mind his life at Clongowes: 240
the wide playgrounds, swarming with boys, the square ditch,
the little cemetery off the main avenue of limes where he had
dreamed of being buried, the firelight on the wall of the infirm=
ary where he lay sick, the sorrowful face of Brother Michael.
His soul, as these memories came back to him, became again a 245
child's soul.

—We are assembled here today, my dear little brothers in
Christ, for one brief moment far away from the busy bustle of
the outer world to celebrate and to honour one of the greatest
of saints, the apostle of the Indies, the patron saint also of your 250
college, saint Francis Xavier. Year after year for much longer
than any of you, my dear little boys, can remember or than I
can remember the boys of this college have met in this very
chapel to make their annual retreat before the feast day of their
patron saint. Time has gone on and brought with it its changes. 255
Even in the last few years what changes can most of you not

242 limes] Eg; chestnuts MS

9. The implied comparison is to Jesus's disciples Peter and Andrew, to whom Jesus said, "Come, follow me, and I will make you fishers of men" (Matthew 4:19).
1. A hot, dry wind carrying dust (*OED*).
2. From Ecclesiasticus (see note 7, p. 91): "In all thy works remember thy last end, and thou shalt never sin" (7:40).

remember? Many of the boys who sat in those front benches a
few short years ago are perhaps now in distant lands, in the
burning tropics or immersed in professional duties or in sem=
inaries or voyaging over the vast expanse of the deep or, it may   260
be, already called by the great God to another life and to the
rendering up of their stewardship. And still as the years roll by,
bringing with them changes for good and bad, the memory of
the great saint is honoured by the boys of his college who make
every year their annual retreat on the days preceding the feast   265
day set apart by our holy mother the church to transmit to all
the ages the name and fame of one of the greatest sons of
catholic Spain.

Now what is the meaning of this word *retreat* and why is it
allowed on all hands to be a most salutary practice for all who   270
desire to lead before God and in the eyes of men a truly chris=
tian life? A retreat, my dear boys, signifies a withdrawal for a
while from the cares of our life, the cares of this workaday
world, in order to examine the state of our conscience, to
reflect on the mysteries of holy religion and to understand   275
better why we are here in this world. During these few days I
intend to put before you some thoughts concerning the four
last things. They are, as you know from your catechism, death,
judgment, hell and heaven. We shall try to understand them
fully during these few days so that we may derive from the   280
understanding of them a lasting benefit to our souls. And re=
member, my dear boys, that we have been sent into this world
for one thing and for one thing alone: to do God's holy will
and to save our immortal souls. All else is worthless. One thing
alone is needful, the salvation of one's soul. What doth it profit   285
a man to gain the whole world if he suffer the loss of his
immortal soul?[3] Ah, my dear boys, believe me there is nothing in
this wretched world that can make up for such a loss.

I will ask you therefore, my dear boys, to put away from
your minds during these few days all worldly thoughts,   290
whether of study or pleasure or ambition, and to give all your
attention to the state of your souls. I need hardly remind you
that during the days of the retreat all boys are expected to
preserve a quiet and pious demeanour and to shun all loud
unseemly pleasure. The elder boys, of course, will see that this   295
custom is not infringed and I look especially to the prefects and

258 short] MS; ABSENT Eg–64   269 Now] PARAGRAPH INDENT MS; DIALOGUE DASH 16–64:
HERE AND THROUGHOUT SERMONS

3. Based on Matthew 16:26: "For what doth it profit a man, if he gain the whole world, and
   suffer the loss of his own soul?"

officers of the sodality of Our Blessed Lady and of the sodality
of the holy angels to set a good example to their fellowstu=
dents.

Let us try therefore to make this retreat in honour of saint   300
Francis with our whole heart and our whole mind. God's bless=
ing will then be upon all your year's studies. But, above and
beyond all, let this retreat be one to which you can look back in
after years when maybe you are far from this college and
among very different surroundings, to which you can look back   305
with joy and thankfulness and give thanks to God for having
granted you this occasion of laying the first foundation of a
pious honourable zealous christian life. And if, as may so
happen, there be at this moment in these benches any poor soul
which has had the unutterable misfortune to lose God's holy   310
grace and to fall into grievous sin I fervently trust and pray that
this retreat may be the turningpoint in the life of that soul. I
pray to God through the merits of His zealous servant Francis
Xavier that such a soul may be led to sincere repentance and
that the holy communion on saint Francis' day of this year may 315
be a lasting covenant between God and that soul. For just and
unjust, for saint and sinner alike, may this retreat be a mem=
orable one.

Help me, my dear little brothers in Christ. Help me by your
pious attention, by your own devotion, by your outward de=   320
meanour. Banish from your minds all worldly thoughts and
think only of the last things, death, judgment, hell and heaven.
He who remembers these things, says Ecclesiastes, shall not sin
for ever. He who remembers the last things will act and think
with them always before his eyes. He will live a good life and   325
die a good death, believing and knowing that, if he has sacri=
ficed much in this earthly life, it will be given to him a
hundredfold and a thousandfold more in the life to come, in the
kingdom without end—a blessing, my dear boys, which I wish
you from my heart; one and all, in the name of the Father and   330
of the Son and of the Holy Ghost. Amen.

As he walked home with silent companions a thick fog
seemed to compass his mind. He waited in stupor of mind till it
should lift and reveal what it had hidden. He ate his dinner
with surly appetite and, when the meal was over and the   335
greasestrewn plates lay abandoned on the table, he rose and
went to the window, clearing the thick scum from his mouth
with his tongue and licking it from his lips. So he had sunk to
the state of a beast that licks his chaps after meat. This was the

310 which] who Eg–64   313 His] Eg; its MS

end: and a faint glimmer of fear began to pierce the fog of his   340
mind. He pressed his face against the pane of the window and
gazed out into the darkening street. Forms passed this way and
that way through the dull light. And that was life. The letters
of the name of Dublin lay heavily upon his mind, pushing one
another surlily hither and thither with slow boorish insistence.   345
His soul was fattening and congealing into a gross grease,
plunging ever deeper in its dull fear into a sombre threatening
dusk, while the body that was his stood, listless and dishon=
oured, gazing out of darkened eyes, helpless, perturbed and
human for a bovine god to stare upon.   350

The next day brought death and judgment, stirring his soul
slowly from its listless despair. The faint glimmer of fear be=
came a terror of spirit as the hoarse voice of the preacher blew
death into his soul. He suffered its agony. He felt the deathchill
touch the extremities and creep onward towards the heart, the   355
film of death veiling the eyes, the bright centres of the brain
extinguished one by one like lamps, the last sweat oozing upon
the skin, the powerlessness of the dying limbs, the speech
thickening and wandering and failing, the heart throbbing
faintly and more faintly, all but vanquished, the breath, the   360
poor timid breath, the poor helpless human spirit, sobbing and
sighing, gurgling and rattling in the throat. No help! No help!
He, he himself, his body to which he had yielded was dying.
Into the grave with it! Nail it down into a wooden box, the
corpse. Carry it out of the house on the shoulders of hirelings.   365
Thrust it out of men's sight into a long hole in the ground, into
the grave, to rot, to feed the mass of its creeping worms and to
be devoured by scuttling plumpbellied rats.

And while the friends were still standing in tears by the
bedside the soul of the sinner was judged. At the last moment   370
of consciousness the whole earthly life passed before the vision
of the soul and, ere it had time to reflect, the body had died and
the soul stood terrified before the judgmentseat. God, who had
long been merciful, would then be just. He had long been
patient, pleading with the sinful soul, giving it time to repent,   375
sparing it yet awhile. But that time had gone. Time was to sin
and to enjoy, time was to scoff at God and at the warnings of
His holy church, time was to defy His majesty, to disobey His
commands, to hoodwink one's fellow men, to commit sin after
sin and sin after sin and to hide one's corruption from the sight   380
of men. But that time was over. Now it was God's turn: and He
was not to be hoodwinked or deceived. Every sin would then

343 way] MS; ABSENT Eg–64 MS   361 timid] MS; ABSENT Eg–64

come forth from its lurkingplace, the most rebellious against
the divine will and the most degrading to our poor corrupt
nature, the tiniest imperfection and the most heinous atrocity. 385
What did it avail then to have been a great emperor, a great
general, a marvellous inventor, the most learned of the learned?
All were as one before the judgmentseat of God. He would
reward the good and punish the wicked. One single instant was
enough for the trial of a man's soul. One single instant after the 390
body's death, the soul had been weighed in the balance. The
particular judgment was over and the soul had passed to the
abode of bliss or to the prison of purgatory or had been hurled
howling into hell.

    Nor was that all. God's justice had still to be vindicated 395
before men: after the particular there still remained the general
judgment. The last day had come. The doomsday was at hand.
The stars of heaven were falling upon the earth like the figs
cast by the figtree which the wind has shaken. The sun, the
great luminary of the universe, had become as sackcloth of 400
hair. The moon was bloodred. The firmament was as a scroll
rolled away. The archangel Michael, the prince of the heavenly
host, appeared glorious and terrible against the sky. With one
foot on the sea and one foot on the land he blew from the
archangelical trumpet the brazen death of time. The three 405
blasts of the angel filled all the universe. Time is, time was but
time shall be no more. At the last blast the souls of universal
humanity throng towards the valley of Jehoshaphat, rich and
poor, gentle and simple, wise and foolish, good and wicked.
The soul of every human being that has ever existed, the souls 410
of all those who shall yet be born, all the sons and daughters of
Adam, all are assembled on that supreme day. And lo the
supreme judge is coming! No longer the lowly Lamb of God,
no longer the meek Jesus of Nazareth, no longer the Man of
Sorrows, no longer the Good Shepherd, He is seen now coming 415
upon the clouds, in great power and majesty, attended by nine
choirs of angels, angels and archangels, principalities, powers
and virtues, thrones and dominations, cherubim and seraphim,
God Omnipotent, God Everlasting. He speaks: and His voice is
heard even at the farthest limits of space, even in the bottom= 420
less abyss. Supreme Judge, from His sentence there will be and
can be no appeal. He calls the just to His side bidding them
enter into the kingdom, the eternity of bliss prepared for them.
The unjust He casts from Him, crying in His offended majesty:
Depart from me, ye cursed, into everlasting fire which was 425

397 The doomsday] 24 [REVERTS TO MS]; Doomsday a16–18

prepared for the devil and his angels.[4] O what agony then for the miserable sinners! Friend is torn apart from friend, children from their parents, husbands from their wives. The poor sinner holds out his arms to those who were dear and near to him in this earthly world, to those whose simple piety perhaps he made a mock of, to those who counselled him and tried to lead him on the right path, to a kind brother, to a loving sister, to the mother and father who loved him so dearly. But it is too late: the just turn away from the wretched damned souls which now appear before the eyes of all in their hideous and evil character. O you hypocrites, O you whited sepulchres, O you who present a smooth smiling face to the world while your soul within is a foul swamp of sin, how will it fare with you in that terrible day?

And this day will come, shall come, must come: the day of death and the day of judgment. It is appointed unto man to die and after death the judgment. Death is certain. The time and manner are uncertain, whether from long disease or from some unexpected accident: the Son of God cometh at an hour when you little expect Him. Be therefore ready every moment, seeing that you may die at any moment. Death is the end of us all. Death and judgment, brought into the world by the sin of our first parents, are the dark portals that close our earthly exist= ence, the portals that open into the unknown and the unseen, portals through which every soul must pass, alone, unaided save by its good works, without friend or brother or parents or master to help it, alone and trembling. Let that thought be ever before our minds and then we cannot sin. Death, a cause of terror to the sinner, is a blessed moment for him who has walked in the right path, fulfilling the duties of his station in life, attending to his morning and evening prayers, approaching the holy sacrament frequently and performing good and mer= ciful works. For the pious and believing catholic, for the just man, death is no cause of terror. Was it not Addison, the great English writer, who, when on his deathbed, sent for the wicked young earl of Warwick to let him see how a christian can meet his end? He it is and he alone, the pious and believing christian, who can say in his heart:

430

435

440

445

450

455

460

---

427 children] MS; children are torn Eg–64 MS   429 and near] MS; ABSENT Eg–64 MS
451 parents] MS; parent Eg–64

4. According to Jesus, this will be said to the damned, or goats, when they are separated from the sheep at the Last Judgment (Matthew 24:41).

> *O grave, where is thy victory?*
> *O death, where is thy sting?*[5]   465

Every word of it was for him. Against his sin, foul and
secret, the whole wrath of God was aimed. The preacher's
knife had probed deeply into his diseased conscience and he felt
now that his soul was festering in sin. Yes, the preacher was
right. God's turn had come. Like a beast in its lair his soul had   470
lain down in its own filth but the blasts of the angel's trumpet
had driven him forth from the darkness of sin into the light.
The words of doom cried by the angel shattered in an instant
his presumptuous peace. The wind of the last day blew through
his mind; his sins, the jeweleyed harlots of his imagination, fled   475
before the hurricane, squeaking like mice in their terror and
huddled under a mane of hair.

As he crossed the square, walking homeward, the light
laughter of a girl reached his burning ears. The frail gay sound
smote his heart more strongly than a trumpetblast, and, not   480
daring to lift his eyes, he turned aside and gazed, as he walked,
into the shadow of the tangled shrubs. Shame rose from his
smitten heart and flooded his whole being. The image of Emma
appeared before him and, under her eyes, the flood of shame
rushed forth anew from his heart. If she knew to what his mind   485
had subjected her or how his brutelike lust had torn and
trampled upon her innocence! Was that boyish love? Was that
chivalry? Was that poetry? The sordid details of his orgies stank
under his very nostrils: the sootcoated packet of pictures which
he had hidden in the flue of the fireplace and in the presence of   490
whose shameless or bashful wantonness he lay for hours sin=
ning in thought and deed: his monstrous dreams, peopled by
apelike creatures and by harlots with gleaming jewel eyes: the
foul long letters he had written in the joy of guilty confession
and carried secretly for days and days only to throw them   495
under cover of night among the grass in the corner of a field or
beneath some hingeless door or in some niche in the hedges
where a girl might come upon them as she walked by and read
them secretly. Mad! Mad! Was it possible he had done these

---

474 peace.] Eg; piece. MS   479 ears.] ear. Eg–64   482 shadow] Eg; shadows MS

5. "The Dying Christian to His soul," lines 17–18, by the English poet Alexander Pope
(1688–1744). Joseph Addison (1672–1719) collaborated with the Irish writer Sir Richard
Steele (1672–1729) and served as chief secretary for Ireland (1708–10, 1714–15), the
number two position in the English administration of the island. Although Pope is quoted
in this passage as if in harmony with Addison, the estrangement between the writers was
clear during their lives and in Pope's derision of Addison as "Atticus" in "An Epistle to Dr.
Arbuthnot" (1735).

things? A cold sweat broke out upon his forehead as the foul   500
memories condensed within his brain.

When the agony of shame had passed from him he tried to
raise his soul from its abject powerlessness. God and the
Blessed Virgin were too far from him: God was too great and
stern and the Blessed Virgin too pure and holy. But he imagined   505
that he stood near Emma in a wide land and, humbly and in
tears, bent and kissed the elbow of her sleeve.

In a wide land under a tender lucid evening sky, a cloud
drifting westward amid a pale green sea of heaven, they stood
together, children that had erred. Their error had offended   510
deeply God's majesty, though it was the error of two children,
but it had not offended her whose beauty *is not like earthly
beauty, dangerous to look upon, but like the morning star
which is its emblem, bright and musical.*[6] The eyes were not
offended which she turned upon them nor reproachful. She   515
placed their hands together, hand in hand, and said, speaking
to their hearts:

—Take hands, Stephen and Emma. It is a beautiful evening
now in heaven. You have erred but you are always my children.
It is one heart that loves another heart. Take hands together,   520
my dear children, and you will be happy together and your
hearts will love each other.

The chapel was flooded by the dull scarlet light that filtered
through the lowered blinds: and through the fissure between
the last blind and the sash a shaft of wan light entered like a   525
spear and touched the embossed brasses of the candlesticks
upon the altar that gleamed like the battleworn mail armour of
angels.

Rain was falling on the chapel, on the garden, on the college.
It would rain for ever, noiselessly. The water would rise inch   530
by inch, covering the grass and shrubs, covering the trees and
houses, covering the monuments and the mountain tops. All
life would be choked off, noiselessly: birds, men, elephants,
pigs, children: noiselessly floating corpses amid the litter of the
wreckage of the world. Forty days and forty nights the rain   535
would fall till the waters covered the face of the earth.

It might be. Why not?

—*Hell has enlarged its soul and opened its mouth without any
limits*—words taken, my dear little brothers in Christ Jesus,
from the book of Isaias, fifth chapter, fourteenth verse. In the   540

508 a(1)] the Eg—64   536 covered] Eg; had covered MS

6. From Newman's "The Glories of Mary for the Sake of Her Son" in *Discourses to Mixed Congregations,* quoted on p. 92.

name of the Father and of the Son and of the Holy Ghost.
Amen.

The preacher took a chainless watch from a pocket within
his soutane and, having considered its dial for a moment in
silence, placed it silently before him on the table.   545

He began to speak in a quiet tone.

—Adam and Eve, my dear boys, were, as you know, our first
parents and you will remember that they were created by God
in order that the seats in heaven left vacant by the fall of
Lucifer and his rebellious angels might be filled again. Lucifer,   550
we are told, was a son of the morning, a radiant and mighty
angel; yet he fell: he fell and there fell with him a third part of
the host of heaven: he fell and was hurled with his rebellious
angels into hell. What his sin was we cannot say. Theologians
consider that it was the sin of pride, the sinful thought con=   555
ceived in an instant: *non serviam: I will not serve.*[7] That instant
was his ruin. He offended the majesty of God by the sinful
thought of one instant and God cast him out of heaven into hell
for ever.

Adam and Eve were then created by God and placed in   560
Eden, that lovely garden in the plain of Damascus resplendent
with sunlight and colour, teeming with luxuriant vegetation.
The fruitful earth gave them her bounty: beasts and birds were
their willing servants: they knew not the ills our flesh is heir to,
disease and poverty and death: all that a great and generous   565
God could do for them was done. But there was one condition
imposed on them by God: obedience to His word. They were
not to eat of the fruit of the forbidden tree.

Alas, my dear little boys, they too fell. The devil, once a
shining angel, a son of the morning, now a foul fiend came to   570
them in the shape of a serpent, the subtlest of all the beasts of
the field. He envied them. He, the fallen great one, could not
bear to think that man, a being of clay, should possess the
inheritance which he by his sin had forfeited for ever. He came
to the woman, the weaker vessel, and poured the poison of his   575
eloquence into her ear, promising her (O, the blasphemy of that
promise!) that if she and Adam ate of the forbidden fruit they
would become as gods, nay as God Himself. Eve yielded to the
wiles of the archtempter. She ate the apple and gave it also to

561 that--Damascus] that lovely garden ⌐in the plain of Damascus⌐ MS; in the plain of
Damascus, that lovely garden Eg–64   563 and] Eg; are MS   570–571 to them] MS; AB-
SENT Eg–64

7. Based on Jeremias 2:20. See also note 2, p. 211.

Adam who had not the moral courage to resist her. The poison   580
tongue of Satan had done its work. They fell.

And then the voice of God was heard in that garden, calling
His creature man to account: and Michael, prince of the heav=
enly host, with a sword of flame in his hand appeared before
the guilty pair and drove them forth from Eden into the world,   585
the world of sickness and striving, of cruelty and disappoint=
ment, of labour and hardship, to earn their bread in the sweat
of their brow. But even then how merciful was God! He took
pity on our poor degraded first parents and promised that in
the fulness of time He would send down from heaven One who   590
would redeem them, make them once more children of God
and heirs to the kingdom of heaven: and that One, that
Redeemer of fallen man, was to be God's onlybegotten Son, the
Second Person of the Most Blessed Trinity, the Eternal Word.

He came. He was born of a virgin pure, Mary the virgin   595
mother. He was born in a poor cowhouse in Judea and lived as
a humble carpenter for thirty years until the hour of His
mission had come. And then, filled with love for men, He went
forth and called to men to hear the new gospel.

Did they listen? Yes, they listened but would not hear. He   600
was seized and bound like a common criminal, mocked at as a
fool, set aside to give place to a public robber, scourged with
five thousand lashes, crowned with a crown of thorns, hustled
through the streets by the jewish rabble and the Roman sol=
diery, stripped of His garments and hanged upon a gibbet and   605
His side was pierced with a lance and from the wounded body
of Our Lord water and blood issued continually.

Yet even then, in that hour of supreme agony, Our Merciful
Redeemer had pity for mankind. Yet even there, on the hill of
Calvary, He founded the holy catholic church against which, it   610
is promised, the gates of hell shall not prevail. He founded it
upon the rock of ages[8] and endowed it with His grace, with
sacraments and sacrifice, and promised that if men would obey
the word of His church they would still enter into eternal life
but if, after all that had been done for them, they still persisted   615
in their wickedness there remained for them an eternity of
torment: hell.

The preacher's voice sank. He paused, joined his palms for
an instant, parted them. Then he resumed:

—Now let us try for a moment to realise, as far as we can, the   620
nature of that abode of the damned which the justice of an

589 pity] Eg; ABSENT MS   589 first] MS; ABSENT Eg–64 MS   612 it] Eg; ABSENT MS

8. That is, Peter, referred to as "this rock" in Matthew 16:18.

offended God has called into existence for the eternal punish=
ment of sinners. Hell is a strait and dark and foulsmelling
prison, an abode of demons and lost souls, filled with fire and
smoke. The straitness of this prison house is expressly designed   625
by God to punish those who refused to be bound by His laws.
In earthly prisons the poor captive has at least some liberty of
movement, were it only within the four walls of his cell or in
the gloomy yard of his prison. Not so in hell. There, by reason
of the great number of the damned, the prisoners are heaped   630
together in their awful prison the walls of which are said to be
four thousand miles thick: and the damned are so utterly
bound and helpless that, as a blessed saint, saint Anselm, writes
in his book on similitudes,[9] they are not even able to remove
from the eye a worm that gnaws it.   635

They lie in exterior darkness. For, remember, the fire of hell
gives forth no light. As, at the command of God, the fire of the
Babylonian furnace lost its heat but not its light so, at the
command of God, the fire of hell, while retaining the intensity
of its heat, burns eternally in darkness. It is a neverending   640
storm of darkness, dark flames and dark smoke of burning
brimstone, amid which the bodies are heaped one upon another
without even a glimpse of air. Of all the plagues with which the
land of the Pharaohs was smitten one plague alone, that of
darkness, was called horrible. What name, then, shall we give   645
to the darkness of hell which is to last not for three days alone
but for all eternity?

The horror of this strait and dark prison is increased by its
awful stench. All the filth of the world, all the offal and scum
of the world, we are told, shall run there as to a vast reeking   650
sewer when the terrible conflagration of the last day has purged
the world. The brimstone too which burns there in such pro=
digious quantity fills all hell with its intolerable stench: and the
bodies of the damned themselves exhale such a pestilential
odour that, as saint Bonaventure says, one of them alone would   655
suffice to infect the whole world. The very air of this world,
that pure element, becomes foul and unbreathable when it has
been long enclosed. Consider then what must be the foulness of
the air of hell. Imagine some foul and putrid corpse that has
lain rotting and decomposing in the grave, a jellylike mass of   660
liquid corruption. Imagine such a corpse a prey to flames,
devoured by the fire of burning brimstone and giving off dense

623 a] aEg; ABSENT MS–Eg

9. Saint Anselm of Canterbury (1033–1109), a Benedictine theologian, wrote important
   treatises but not one on similitudes.

choking fumes of nauseous loathsome decomposition. And then imagine this sickening stench, multiplied a millionfold and a millionfold again from the millions upon millions of fetid carcases massed together in the reeking darkness, a huge and rotting human fungus. Imagine all this and you will have some idea of the horror of the stench of hell.

But this stench is not, horrible though it is, the greatest physical torment to which the damned are subjected. The torment of fire is the greatest torment to which the tyrant has ever subjected his fellowcreatures. Place your finger for a mo= ment in the flame of a candle and you will feel the pain of fire. But our earthly fire was created by God for the benefit of man, to maintain in him the spark of life and to help him in the useful arts whereas the fire of hell is of another quality and was created by God to torture and punish the unrepentant sinner. Our earthly fire also consumes more or less rapidly according as the object which it attacks is more or less combustible so that human ingenuity has even succeeded in inventing chemical preparations to check or frustrate its action. But the sulphu= reous brimstone which burns in hell is a substance which is specially designed to burn for ever and for ever with unspeak= able fury. Moreover our earthly fire destroys at the same time as it burns so that the more intense it is the shorter is its dur= ation: but the fire of hell has this property that it preserves that which it burns and though it rages with incredible intensity it rages for ever.

Our earthly fire again, no matter how fierce or widespread it may be, is always of a limited extent: but the lake of fire in hell is boundless, shoreless and bottomless. It is on record that the devil himself, when asked the question by a certain soldier, was obliged to confess that if a whole mountain were thrown into the burning ocean of hell it would be burned up in an instant like a piece of wax. And this terrible fire will not afflict the bodies of the damned only from without but each lost soul will be a hell unto itself, the boundless fire raging in its very vitals. O, how terrible is the lot of those wretched beings! The blood seethes and boils in the veins, the brains are boiling in the skull, the heart in the breast glowing and bursting, the bowels a redhot mass of burning pulp, the tender eyes flaming like mol= ten balls.

And yet what I have said as to the strength and quality and boundlessness of this fire is as nothing when compared to its intensity, an intensity which it has as being the instrument chosen by divine design for the punishment of soul and body alike. It is a fire which proceeds directly from the ire of God,

working not of its own activity but as an instrument of divine
vengeance. As the waters of baptism cleanse the soul with the
body so do the fires of punishment torture the spirit with the   710
flesh. Every sense of the flesh is tortured and every faculty of
the soul therewith: the eyes with impenetrable utter darkness,
the nose with noisome odours, the ears with yells and howls
and execrations, the taste with foul matter, leprous corruption,
nameless suffocating filth, the touch with redhot goads and   715
spikes, with cruel tongues of flame. And through the several
torments of the senses the immortal soul is tortured eternally in
its very essence amid the leagues upon leagues of glowing fires
kindled in the abyss by the offended majesty of the Omnipotent
God and fanned into everlasting and ever increasing fury by the   720
breath of the anger of the Godhead.
   Consider finally that the torment of this infernal prison is
increased by the company of the damned themselves. Evil com=
pany on earth is so noxious that even the plants, as if by
instinct, withdraw from the company of whatsoever is deadly   725
or hurtful to them. In hell all laws are overturned: there is no
thought of family or country, of ties or relationship. The
damned howl and scream at one another, their torture and rage
intensified by the presence of beings tortured and raging like
themselves. All sense of humanity is forgotten. The yells of the   730
suffering sinners fill the remotest corners of the vast abyss. The
mouths of the damned are full of blasphemies against God and
of hatred for their fellow sufferers and of curses against those
souls which were their accomplices in sin. In olden times it was
the custom to punish the parricide, the man who had raised his   735
murderous hand against his father, by casting him into the
depths of the sea in a sack in which were placed a cock, a
monkey and a serpent. The intention of those lawgivers who
framed such a law, which seems cruel in our times, was to
punish the criminal by the company of hateful and hurtful   740
beasts. But what is the fury of those dumb beasts compared
with the fury of execration which bursts from the parched lips
and aching throats of the damned in hell when they behold in
their companions in misery those who aided and abetted them
in sin, those whose words sowed the first seeds of evil thinking   745
and evil living in their minds, those whose immodest sugges=
tions led them on to sin, those whose eyes tempted and allured
them from the path of virtue. They turn upon those accom=

718 leagues(2)] Eg; ABSENT MS   727 or relationship.] of relationship. Eg; of relationships. 16–64

plices and upbraid them and curse them. But they are helpless
and hopeless: it is too late now for repentance.	750

Last of all consider the frightful torment to those damned
souls, tempters and tempted alike, of the company of the devils.
These devils will afflict the damned in two ways, by their pres=
ence and by their reproaches. We can have no idea of how
horrible these devils are. Saint Catherine of Siena once saw a	755
devil and she has written that, rather than look again for one
single instant on such a frightful monster, she would prefer to
walk until the end of her life along a track of red coals. These
devils, who were once beautiful angels, have become as hideous
and ugly as they once were beautiful. They mock and jeer at	760
the lost souls whom they dragged down to ruin. It is they, the
foul demons, who are made in hell the voices of conscience.
Why did you sin? Why did you lend an ear to the temptings of
fiends? Why did you turn aside from your pious practices and
good works? Why did you not shun the occasions of sin? Why	765
did you not leave that evil companion? Why did you not give
up that lewd habit, that impure habit? Why did you not listen
to the counsels of your confessor? Why did you not, even after
you had fallen the first or the second or the third or the fourth
or the hundredth time, repent of your evil ways and turn to	770
God who only waited for your repentance to absolve you of
your sins? Now the time for repentance has gone by. Time is,
time was but time shall be no more! Time was to sin in secrecy,
to indulge in that sloth and pride, to covet the unlawful, to
yield to the promptings of your lower nature, to live like the	775
beasts of the field, nay worse than the beasts of the field for
they, at least, are but brutes and have not reason to guide them:
time was but time shall be no more. God spoke to you by so
many voices but you would not hear. You would not crush out
that pride and anger in your heart, you would not restore those	780
illgotten goods, you would not obey the precepts of your holy
church nor attend to your religious duties, you would not
abandon those wicked companions, you would not avoid those
dangerous temptations. Such is the language of those fiendish
tormentors, words of taunting and of reproach, of hatred and	785
of disgust. Of disgust, yes! For even they, the very devils, when
they sinned sinned by such a sin as alone was compatible with
such angelical natures, a rebellion of the intellect: and they,
even they, the foul devils must turn away, revolted and dis=
gusted, from the contemplation of those unspeakable sins by	790
which degraded man outrages and defiles the temple of the
Holy Ghost, defiles and pollutes himself.[1]

1. The body is referred to as the temple of the Holy Spirit in 1 Corinthians 6:18–19.

O, my dear little brothers in Christ, may it never be our lot
to hear that language! May it never be our lot, I say! In the last
day of terrible reckoning I pray fervently to God that not a   795
single soul of those who are in this chapel today may be found
among those miserable beings whom the Great Judge shall
command to depart for ever from His sight, that not one of us
may ever hear ringing in his ears the awful sentence of rejec=
tion: *Depart from me, ye cursed, into everlasting fire which*   800
was prepared for the devil and his angels![2]

He came down the aisle of the chapel, his legs shaking and
the scalp of his head trembling as though it had been touched
by ghostly fingers. He passed up the staircase and into the
corridor along the walls of which the overcoats and water=   805
proofs hung like gibbeted malefactors, headless and dripping
and shapeless. And at every step he feared that he had already
died, that his soul had been wrenched forth of the sheath of his
body, that he was plunging headlong through space.

He could not grip the floor with his feet and sat heavily at   810
his desk, opening one of his books at random and poring over
it. Every word for him! It was true. God was almighty. God
could call him now, call him as he sat at his desk, before he had
time to be conscious of the summons. God had called him. Yes?
What? Yes? His flesh shrank together as it felt the approach of   815
the ravenous tongues of flames, dried up as it felt about it the
swirl of stifling air. He had died. Yes. He was judged. A wave
of fire swept through his body: the first. Again a wave. His
brain began to glow. Another. His brain was simmering and
bubbling within the cracking tenement of the skull. Flames   820
burst forth from his skull like a corolla,[3] shrieking like voices:

—Hell! Hell! Hell! Hell! Hell!

Voices spoke near him:

—On hell.

—I suppose he rubbed it into you well.   825

—You bet he did. He put us all into a blue funk.[4]

—That's what you fellows want: and plenty of it to make you
work.

He leaned back weakly in his desk. He had not died. God
had spared him still. He was still in the familiar world of the   830
school. Mr Tate and Vincent Heron stood at the window,

2. The separation of the damned from the saved at the Last Judgment (Matthew 24:41);
   quoted on pp. 99–100.
3. Crown (*OED*).
4. Ill humor (*OED*).

talking, jesting, gazing out at the bleak rain, moving their heads.

—I wish it would clear up. I had arranged to go for a spin on the bike with some fellows out by Malahide.[5] But the roads must be kneedeep.

—It might clear up, sir.

The voices that he knew so well, the common words, the quiet of the classroom when the voices paused and the silence was filled by the sound of softly browsing cattle as the other boys munched their lunches tranquilly, lulled his aching soul.

There was still time. O Mary, refuge of sinners, intercede for him! O Virgin Undefiled, save him from the gulf of death!

The English lesson began with the hearing of the history. Royal persons, favourites, intriguers, bishops passed like mute phantoms behind their veil of names. All had died: all had been judged. What did it profit a man to gain the whole world if he lost his soul? At last he had understood: and human life lay around him, a plain of peace whereon antlike men laboured in brotherhood, their dead sleeping under quiet mounds. The el= bow of his companion touched him and his heart was touched: and when he spoke to answer a question of his master he heard his own voice full of the quietude of humility and contrition.

His soul sank back deeper into depths of contrite peace, no longer able to suffer the pain of dread and sending forth, as she sank, a faint prayer. Ah yes, he would still be spared; he would repent in his heart and be forgiven: and then those above, those in heaven, would see what he would do to make up for the past: a whole life, every hour of life. Only wait.

—All, God! All, all!

A messenger came to the door to say that confessions were being heard in the chapel. Four boys left the room; and he heard others passing down the corridor. A tremulous chill blew round his heart, no stronger than a little wind, and yet, listen= ing and suffering silently, he seemed to have laid an ear against the muscle of his own heart, feeling it close and quail, listening to the flutter of its ventricles.

No escape. He had to confess, to speak out in words what he had done and thought, sin after sin. How? How?

—Father, I . . .

The thought slid like a cold shining rapier into his tender flesh: confession. But not there in the chapel of the college. He would confess all, every sin of deed and thought, sincerely: but not there among his school companions. Far away from there

5. Fishing village north of Dublin.

in some dark place he would murmur out his own shame: and   875
he besought God humbly not to be offended with him if he did
not dare to confess in the college chapel: and in utter abjection
of spirit he craved forgiveness mutely of the boyish hearts
about him.

Time passed.   880

He sat again in the front bench of the chapel. The daylight
without was already failing and, as it fell slowly through the
dull red blinds, it seemed that the sun of the last day was going
down and that all souls were being gathered for the judgment.

—*I am cast away from the sight of Thine eyes*: words taken,   885
my dear little brothers in Christ, from the Book of Psalms,
thirtieth chapter, twentythird verse. In the name of the Father
and of the Son and of the Holy Ghost. Amen.

The preacher began to speak in a quiet friendly tone. His
face was kind and he joined gently the fingers of each hand,   890
forming a frail cage by the union of their tips.

—This morning we endeavoured, in our reflection upon hell,
to make what our holy founder calls in his book of spiritual
exercises, the composition of place.[6] We endeavoured, that is, to
imagine with the senses of the mind, in our imagination, the   895
material character of that awful place and of the physical tor=
ments which all who are in hell endure. This evening we shall
consider for a few moments the nature of the spiritual torments
of hell.

Sin, remember, is a twofold enormity. It is a base consent to   900
the promptings of our corrupt nature, to the lower instincts, to
that which is gross and beastlike; and it is also a turning away
from the counsel of our higher nature, from all that is pure and
holy, from the Holy God Himself. For this reason mortal sin is
punished in hell by two different forms of punishment, physical 905
and spiritual.

Now of all these spiritual pains by far the greatest is the pain
of loss, so great, in fact, that in itself it is a torment greater
than all the others. Saint Thomas,[7] the greatest doctor of the
church, the angelic doctor, as he is called, says that the worst   910
damnation consists in this that the understanding of man is
totally deprived of divine light and his affection obstinately
turned away from the goodness of God. God, remember, is a
being infinitely good and therefore the loss of such a being

6. Saint Ignatius of Loyola's *Spiritual Exercises* stresses the efficacy in meditation of visual-
   izing the actual place being contemplated.
7. Saint Thomas Aquinas (1224 or 1225–1274), Dominican theologian, whose *Summa Theologica* eventually became central in Catholic thought.

must be a loss infinitely painful. In this life we have not a very   915
clear idea of what such a loss must be but the damned in hell,
for their greater torment, have a full understanding of that
which they have lost and understand that they have lost it
through their own sins and have lost it for ever. At the very
instant of death the bonds of the flesh are broken asunder and   920
the soul at once flies towards God. The soul tends towards
God as towards the center of her existence. Remember, my
dear little boys, our souls long to be with God. We come from
God, we live by God, we belong to God: we are His, inalien=
ably His. God loves with a divine love every human soul and   925
every human soul lives in that love. How could it be otherwise?
Every breath that we draw, every thought of our brain, every
instant of life proceed from God's inexhaustible goodness. And
if it be pain for a mother to be parted from her child, for a man
to be exiled from hearth and home, for friend to be sundered   930
from friend, O think what pain, what anguish it must be for
the poor soul to be spurned from the presence of the supremely
good and loving Creator Who has called that soul into exist=
ence from nothingness and sustained it in life and loved it with
an immeasurable love. This, then, to be separated for ever from   935
its greatest good, from God, and to feel the anguish of that
separation, knowing full well that it is unchangeable, this is the
greatest torment which the created soul is capable of bearing,
poena damni, the pain of loss.

The second pain which will afflict the souls of the damned in   940
hell is the pain of conscience. Just as in dead bodies worms are
engendered by putrefaction so in the souls of the lost there
arises a perpetual remorse from the putrefaction of sin, the
sting of conscience, the worm, as Pope Innocent the Third calls
it, of the triple sting. The first sting inflicted by this cruel worm   945
will be the memory of past pleasures. O what a dreadful mem=
ory will that be! In the lake of alldevouring flame the proud
king will remember the pomps of his court, the wise but wicked
man his libraries and instruments of research, the lover of ar=
tistic pleasures his marbles and pictures and other art treasures,   950
he who delighted in the pleasures of the table his gorgeous
feasts, his dishes prepared with such delicacy, his choice wines;
the miser will remember his hoard of gold, the robber his
illgotten wealth, the angry and revengeful and merciless mur=
derers their deeds of blood and violence in which they revelled,   955
the impure and adulterous the unspeakable and filthy pleasures
in which they delighted. They will remember all this and loathe
themselves and their sins. For how miserable will all those
pleasures seem to the soul condemned to suffer in hellfire for

ages and ages. How they will rage and fume to think that they   960
have lost the bliss of heaven for the dross of earth, for a few
pieces of metal, for vain honours, for bodily comforts, for a
tingling of the nerves. They will repent indeed: and this is the
second sting of the worm of conscience, a late and fruitless
sorrow for sins committed. Divine justice insists that the under=   965
standing of those miserable wretches be fixed continually on
the sins of which they were guilty and, moreover, as saint
Augustine[8] points out, God will impart to them His own
knowledge of sin so that sin will appear to them in all its
hideous malice as it appears to the eyes of God Himself. They   970
will behold their sins in all their foulness and repent but it will
be too late and then they will bewail the good occasions which
they neglected. This is the last and deepest and most cruel sting
of the worm of conscience. The conscience will say: You had
time and opportunity to repent and would not. You were   975
brought up religiously by your parents. You had the sacraments
and graces and indulgences[9] of the church to aid you. You had
the minister of God to preach to you, to call you back when
you had strayed, to forgive you your sins, no matter how many,
how abominable, if only you had confessed and repented. No.   980
You would not. You flouted the ministers of holy religion, you
turned your back on the confessional, you wallowed deeper
and deeper in the mire of sin. God appealed to you, threatened
you, entreated you to return to Him. O what shame, what
misery! The ruler of the universe entreated you, a creature   985
of clay, to love Him Who made you and to keep His law.
No. You would not. And now, though you were to flood all
hell with your tears if you could still weep, all that sea of
repentance would not gain for you what a single tear of true
repentance shed during your mortal life would have gained for   990
you. You implore now a moment of earthly life wherein to
repent: in vain. That time is gone: gone for ever.

    Such is the threefold sting of conscience, the viper which
gnaws the very heart's core of the wretches in hell so that filled
with hellish fury they curse themselves for their folly and curse   995
the evil companions who have brought them to such ruin and
curse the devils who tempted them in life and now mock them
and torture them in eternity and even revile and curse the
Supreme Being Whose goodness and patience they scorned and
slighted but Whose justice and power they cannot evade.   1000

8. Early Church father (354–430), who wrote the *Confessions* and the *City of God*.
9. The seven Catholic sacraments are baptism, confirmation, the Eucharist, penance, matrimony, ordination, and extreme unction. An indulgence is the remission of punishment for
   a sin (*OED*).

The next spiritual pain to which the damned are subjected is the pain of extension. Man, in this earthly life, though he be capable of many evils, is not capable of them all at once inas= much as one evil corrects and counteracts another just as one poison frequently corrects another. In hell on the contrary one torment, instead of counteracting another, lends it still greater force: and moreover as the internal faculties are more perfect than the external senses so are they more capable of suffering. Just as every sense is afflicted with a fitting torment so is every spiritual faculty; the fancy with horrible images, the sensitive faculty with alternate longing and rage, the mind and under= standing with an interior darkness more terrible even than the exterior darkness which reigns in that dreadful prison. The malice, impotent though it be, which possesses these demon souls is an evil of boundless extension, of limitless duration, a frightful state of wickedness which we can scarcely realise unless we bear in mind the enormity of sin and the hatred God bears to it.

Opposed to this pain of extension and yet coexistent with it we have the pain of intensity. Hell is the center of all evils and, as you know, things are more intense at their centers than at their remotest points. There are no contraries or admixtures of any kind to temper or soften in the least the pains of hell. Nay, things which are good in themselves become evil in hell. Com= pany, elsewhere a source of comfort to the afflicted, will be there a continual torment: knowledge, so much longed for as the chief good of the intellect, will there be hated worse than ignorance: light, so much coveted by all creatures from the lord of creation down to the humblest plant in the forest, will be loathed intensely. In this life our sorrows are either not very long or not very great because nature either overcomes them by habits or puts an end to them by sinking under their weight. But in hell the torments cannot be overcome by habit for while they are of terrible intensity they are at the same time of con= tinual variety, each pain, so to speak, taking fire from another and reendowing that which has enkindled it with a still fiercer flame. Nor can nature escape from these intense and various tortures by succumbing to them for the soul in hell is sustained and maintained in evil so that its suffering may be the greater. Boundless extension of torment, incredible intensity of suffer= ing, unceasing variety of torture—this is what the divine majesty, so outraged by sinners, demands, this is what the holiness of heaven, slighted and set aside for the lustful and low

1005

1010

1015

1020

1025

1030

1035

1040

1020 all] MS; absent Eg–64   1038 in hell] absent Eg–64

pleasures of the corrupt flesh, requires, this is what the blood
of the innocent Lamb of God, shed for the redemption of 1045
sinners, trampled upon by the vilest of the vile, insists upon.

Last and crowning torture of all the tortures of that awful
place is the eternity of hell. Eternity! O dread and dire word.
Eternity! What mind of man can understand it? And, remem=
ber, it is an eternity of pain. Even though the pains of hell were 1050
not so terrible as they are yet they would become infinite as
they are destined to last for ever. But while they are everlasting
they are at the same time, as you know, intolerably intense,
unbearably extensive. To bear even the sting of an insect for all
eternity would be a dreadful torment. What must it be then to 1055
bear the manifold tortures of hell for ever. For ever! For all
eternity! Not for a year or for an age but for ever. Try to
imagine the awful meaning of this. You have often seen the
sand on the seashore. How fine are its tiny grains! And how
many of those tiny little grains go to make up the small handful 1060
which a child grasps in its play. Now imagine a mountain of
that sand, a million miles high, reaching from the earth to the
farthest heavens, and a million miles broad, extending to re=
motest space, and a million miles in thickness: and imagine
such an enormous mass of countless particles of sand multi= 1065
plied as often as there are leaves in the forest, drops of water in
the mighty ocean, feathers on birds, scales on fish, hairs on
animals, atoms in the vast expanse of the air: and imagine that
at the end of every million years a little bird came to that
mountain and carried away in its beak a tiny grain of that sand. 1070
How many millions upon millions of centuries would pass be=
fore that bird had carried away even a square foot of that
mountain, how many eons upon eons of ages before it had
carried away all. Yet at the end of that immense stretch of time
not even one instant of eternity could be said to have ended. At 1075
the end of all those billions and trillions of years eternity would
have scarcely begun. And if that mountain rose again after it
had been all carried away and if the bird came again and
carried it all away again grain by grain: and if it so rose and
sank as many times as there are stars in the sky, atoms in the 1080
air, drops of water in the sea, leaves on the trees, feathers upon
birds, scales upon fish, hairs upon animals, at the end of all
those innumerable risings and sinkings of that immeasurably
vast mountain not one single instant of eternity could be said to
have ended: even then, at the end of such a period, after that 1085
eon of time the mere thought of which makes our very brain
reel dizzily, eternity would have scarcely begun.

A holy saint (one of our own fathers I believe it was) was

once vouchsafed a vision of hell. It seemed to him that he stood in the midst of a great hall, dark and silent save for the ticking of a great clock. The ticking went on unceasingly; and it seemed to this saint that the sound of the ticking was the ceaseless repetition of the words: ever, never; ever, never. Ever to be in hell, never to be in heaven; ever to be shut off from the presence of God, never to enjoy the beatific vision;[1] ever to be eaten with flames, gnawed by vermin, goaded with burning spikes, never to be free from those pains; ever to have the conscience upbraid one, the memory enrage, the mind filled with darkness and despair, never to escape; ever to curse and revile the foul demons who gloat fiendishly over the misery of their dupes, never to behold the shining raiment of the blessed spirits; ever to cry out of the abyss of fire to God for an instant, a single instant, of respite from such awful agony, never to receive, even for an instant, God's pardon; ever to suffer, never to enjoy; ever to be damned, never to be saved; ever, never; ever, never. O what a dreadful punishment! An eternity of endless agony, of endless bodily and spiritual torment, without one ray of hope, without one moment of cessation, of agony limitless in extent, limitless in intensity, of torment infinitely lasting, infinitely varied, of torture that sustains eternally that which it eternally devours, of anguish that everlastingly preys upon the spirit while it racks the flesh, an eternity, every instant of which is itself an eternity, and that eternity an eternity of woe. Such is the terrible punishment decreed for those who die in mortal sin by an almighty and a just God.

Yes, a just God! Men, reasoning always as men, are aston= ished that God should mete out an everlasting and infinite pun= ishment in the fires of hell for a single grievous sin. They reason thus because, blinded by the gross illusion of the flesh and the darkness of human understanding, they are unable to comprehend the hideous malice of mortal sin. They reason thus because they are unable to comprehend that even venial sin[2] is of such a foul and hideous nature that even if the omnipotent Creator could end all the evil and misery in the world, the wars, the diseases, the robberies, the crimes, the deaths, the murders, on condition that He allowed a single venial sin to pass unpunished, a single venial sin, a lie, an angry look, a moment of wilful sloth, He, the great omnipotent God could not do so because sin, be it in thought or deed, is a trans=

---

1. Direct apprehension of God, reserved for the blessed in heaven.
2. A thought, word, or deed at odds with God's law but that is, by contrast with a mortal sin, pardonable (*Cath. Enc.*).

gression of His law and God would not be God if He did not 1130
punish the transgressor.

A sin, an instant of rebellious pride of the intellect, made
Lucifer and a third part of the cohorts of angels fall from their
glory. A sin, an instant of folly and weakness, drove Adam and
Eve out of Eden and brought death and suffering into the 1135
world. To retrieve the consequences of that sin the onlybegot=
ten Son of God came down to earth, lived and suffered and
died a most painful death, hanging for three hours on the cross.

O, my dear little brethren in Christ Jesus, will we then
offend that good Redeemer and provoke His anger? Will we 1140
trample again upon that torn and mangled corpse? Will we spit
upon that face so full of sorrow and love? Will we too, like the
cruel jews and the brutal soldiers, mock that gentle and com=
passionate Saviour Who trod alone for our sakes the awful
winepress of sorrow? Every word of sin is a wound in His 1145
tender side. Every sinful act is a thorn piercing His head. Every
impure thought, deliberately yielded to, is a keen lance trans=
fixing that sacred and loving heart. No, no. It is impossible for
any human being to do that which offends so deeply the divine
majesty, that which is punished by an eternity of agony, that 1150
which crucifies again the Son of God and makes a mockery of
Him.

I pray to God that my poor words may have availed today to
confirm in holiness those who are in a state of grace, to
strengthen the wavering, to lead back to the state of grace the 1155
poor soul that has strayed if any such be among you. I pray to
God, and do you pray with me, that we may repent of our sins.
I will ask you now, all of you, to repeat after me the act of
contrition, kneeling here in this humble chapel in the presence
of God. He is there in the tabernacle burning with love for 1160
mankind, ready to comfort the afflicted. Be not afraid. No
matter how many or how foul the sins if only you repent of
them they will be forgiven you. Let no worldly shame hold you
back. God is still the merciful Lord Who wishes not the eternal
death of the sinner but rather that he be converted and live.   1165

He calls you to Him. You are His. He made you out of
nothing. He loved you as only a God can love. His arms are
open to receive you even though you have sinned against Him.
Come to Him, poor sinner, poor vain and erring sinner. Now is
the acceptable time. Now is the hour.   1170

The priest rose and turning towards the altar knelt upon the
step before the tabernacle in the fallen gloom. He waited till all

1144 Who] ⟨w⟩ Who MS   1144 sakes] sake Eg–64

in the chapel had knelt and every least noise was still. Then
raising his head he repeated the act of contrition,[3] phrase by
phrase, with fervour. The boys answered him phrase by phrase. 1175
Stephen, his tongue cleaving to his palate, bowed his head,
praying with his heart.

> —*O my God!*—
> —*O my God!*—
> —*I am heartily sorry*—   1180
> —*I am heartily sorry*—
> —*for having offended Thee*—
> —*for having offended Thee*—
> —*and I detest my sins*—
> —*and I detest my sins*—   1185
> —*above every other evil*—
> —*above every other evil*—
> —*because they displease Thee, my God*—
> —*because they displease Thee, my God*—
> —*Who art so deserving*—   1190
> —*Who art so deserving*—
> —*of all my love*—
> —*of all my love*—
> —*and I firmly purpose*—
> —*and I firmly purpose*—   1195
> —*by Thy holy grace*—
> —*by Thy holy grace*—
> —*never more to offend Thee*—
> —*never more to offend Thee*—
> —*and to amend my life*—   1200
> —*and to amend my life*—

◆   ◆   ◆

He went up to his room after dinner in order to be alone
with his soul: and at every step his soul seemed to sigh: at every
step his soul mounted with his feet, sighing in the ascent,
through a region of viscid[4] gloom.   1205

He halted on the landing before the door and then, grasping
the porcelain knob, opened the door quickly. He waited in fear,
his soul pining within him, praying silently that death might
not touch his brow as he passed over the threshold, that the
fiends that inhabit darkness might not be given power over 1210
him. He waited still at the threshold as at the entrance to some
dark cave. Faces were there; eyes: they waited and watched.

3. Formal prayer expressing sorrow for having sinned; the specific prayer spoken in this instance follows.
4. Thick and adhesive, sticky.

—We knew perfectly well of course that though it was bound
to come to the light he would find considerable difficulty in
endeavouring to try to induce himself to try to endeavour to 1215
ascertain the spiritual plenipotentiary[5] and so we knew of
course perfectly well—

Murmuring faces waited and watched; murmurous voices
filled the dark shell of the cave. He feared intensely in spirit
and in flesh but, raising his head bravely, he strode into the 1220
room firmly. A doorway, a room, the same room, same win=
dow. He told himself calmly that those words had absolutely
no sense which had seemed to rise murmurously from the dark.
He told himself that it was simply his room with the door
open.   1225

He closed the door and, walking swiftly to the bed, knelt
beside it and covered his face with his hands. His hands were
cold and damp and his limbs ached with chill. Bodily unrest
and chill and weariness beset him, routing his thoughts. Why
was he kneeling there like a child saying his evening prayers? 1230
To be alone with his soul, to examine his conscience, to meet
his sins face to face, to recall their times and manners and
circumstances, to weep over them. He could not weep. He
could not summon them to his memory. He felt only an ache of
soul and body, his whole being, memory, will, understanding, 1235
flesh, benumbed and weary.

That was the work of devils, to scatter his thoughts and
overcloud his conscience, assailing him at the gates of the cow=
ardly and sincorrupted flesh: and, praying God timidly to
forgive him his weakness, he crawled up on to the bed and,   1240
wrapping the blankets closely about him, covered his face again
with his hands. He had sinned. He had sinned so deeply against
heaven and before God that he was not worthy to be called
God's child.

Could it be that he, Stephen Dedalus, had done those things? 1245
His conscience sighed in answer. Yes, he had done them, se=
cretly, filthily, time after time, and, hardened in sinful impeni=
tence, he had dared to wear the mask of holiness before the
tabernacle itself while his soul within was a living mass of
corruption. How came it that God had not struck him dead?   1250
The leprous company of his sins closed about him, breathing
upon him, bending over him from all sides. He strove to forget

1213 though] a16; although MS–16, 64   1247 time,] MS, a16; time aEg

5. An inflated way to refer to a priest or some other individual empowered to deal with
   spiritual difficulties, including sin; a spiritual ambassador, with full powers.

them in an act of prayer, huddling his limbs closer together and
binding down his eyelids: but the senses of the soul would not
be bound and, though his eyes were shut fast, he saw the places 1255
where he had sinned and, though his ears were tightly covered,
he heard. He desired with all his will not to hear or see. He
desired till his frame shook under the strain of his desire and
until the senses of his soul closed. They closed for an instant
and then opened. He saw. 1260

A field of stiff weeds and thistles and tufted nettlebunches.
Thick among the tufts of rank stiff growth lay battered canis=
ters and clots and coils of solid excrement. A faint marshlight
struggled upwards from all the ordure through the bristling
greygreen weeds. An evil smell, faint and foul as the light, 1265
curled upwards sluggishly out of the canisters and from the
stale crusted dung.

Creatures were in the field; one, three, six: creatures were
moving in the field, hither and thither. Goatish creatures with
human faces, hornybrowed, lightly bearded and grey as india= 1270
rubber. The malice of evil glittered in their hard eyes, as they
moved hither and thither, trailing their long tails behind them.
A rictus of cruel malignity lit up greyly their old bony faces.
One was clasping about his ribs a torn flannel waistcoat, an=
other complained monotonously as his beard stuck in the 1275
tufted weeds. Soft language issued from their spittleless lips as
they swished in slow circles round and round the field, winding
hither and thither through the weeds, dragging their long tails
amid the rattling canisters. They moved in slow circles, circling
closer and closer, to enclose, to enclose, soft language issuing 1280
from their lips, their long swishing tails besmeared with stale
shite, thrusting upwards their terrific faces . . . . .

Help!

He flung the blankets from him madly to free his face and
neck. That was his hell. God had allowed him to see the hell 1285
reserved for his sins: stinking, bestial, malignant, a hell of lech=
erous goatish fiends. For him! For him!

He sprang from the bed, the reeking odour pouring down
his throat, clogging and revolting his entrails. Air! The air of
heaven! He stumbled towards the window, groaning and al= 1290
most fainting with sickness. At the washstand a convulsion
seized him within: and, clasping his cold forehead wildly, he
vomited profusely in agony.

When the fit had spent itself he walked weakly to the win=

dow and, lifting the sash, sat in a corner of the embrasure and 1295
leaned his elbow upon the sill. The rain had drawn off; and
amid the moving vapours from point to point of light the city
was spinning about herself a soft cocoon of yellowish haze.
Heaven was still and faintly luminous and the air sweet to
breathe, as in a thicket drenched with showers: and amid peace 1300
and shimmering lights and quiet fragrances he made a covenant
with his heart.

He prayed:

—*He once had meant to come on earth in heavenly glory but
we sinned: and then He could not safely visit us but with a* 1305
shrouded majesty and a bedimmed radiance for He was God.
So He came Himself in weakness not in power and He sent
thee, a creature in His stead, with a creature's comeliness and
lustre suited to our state. And now thy very face and form, dear
mother, speak to us of the Eternal; not like earthly beauty, 1310
dangerous to look upon, but like the morning star which is thy
emblem, bright and musical, breathing purity, telling of heaven
and infusing peace. O harbinger of day! O light of the pilgrim!
Lead us still as thou hast led. In the dark night, across the bleak
wilderness guide us on to our Lord Jesus, guide us home.[6] 1315

His eyes were dimmed with tears and, looking humbly up to
heaven, he wept for the innocence he had lost.

When evening had fallen he left the house and the first touch
of the damp dark air and the noise of the door as it closed
behind him made ache again his conscience, lulled by prayer 1320
and tears. Confess! Confess! It was not enough to lull the con=
science with a tear and a prayer. He had to kneel before the
minister of the Holy Ghost and tell over his hidden sins truly
and repentantly. Before he heard again the footboard of the
housedoor trail over the threshold as it opened to let him in, 1325
before he saw again the table in the kitchen set for supper he
would have knelt and confessed. It was quite simple.

The ache of conscience ceased and he walked onward swiftly
through the dark streets. There were so many flagstones on the
footpath of that street and so many streets in that city and so 1330
many cities in the world. Yet eternity had no end. He was in
mortal sin. Even once was a mortal sin. It could happen in an
instant. But how so quickly? By seeing or by thinking of seeing.
The eyes see the thing, without having wished first to see. Then
in an instant it happens. But does that part of the body under= 1335

1301 fragrances] fragrance Eg–64

6. The passage is nearly identical to one in Newman's "The Glories of Mary," quoted on
pp. 92 and 102.

stand or what? The serpent, the most subtle beast of the field.
It must understand when it desires in one instant and then
prolongs its own desire instant after instant, sinfully. It feels
and understands and desires. What a horrible thing! Who made
it to be like that, a bestial part of the body able to understand   1340
bestially and desire bestially? Was that then he or an inhuman
thing moved by a lower soul than his soul? His soul sickened at
the thought of a torpid snaky life feeding itself out of the tender
marrow of his life and fattening upon the slime of lust. O why
was that so? O why?   1345

He cowered in the shadow of the thought, abasing himself in
the awe of God Who had made all things and all men. Mad=
ness. Who could think such a thought? And, cowering in
darkness and abject, he prayed mutely to his angel guardian to
drive away with his sword the demon that was whispering to   1350
his brain.

The whisper ceased and he knew then clearly that his own
soul had sinned in thought and word and deed wilfully through
his own body. Confess! He had to confess every sin. How could
he utter in words to the priest what he had done? Must, must.   1355
Or how could he explain without dying of shame? Or how
could he have done such things without shame? A madman, a
loathsome madman! Confess! O he would indeed to be free and
sinless again! Perhaps the priest would know. O dear God!

He walked on and on through illlit streets, fearing to stand   1360
still for a moment lest it might seem that he held back from
what awaited him, fearing to arrive at that towards which he
still turned with longing. How beautiful must be a soul in the
state of grace when God looked upon it with love!

Frowsy girls sat along the curbstones before their baskets.   1365
Their dank hair hung trailed over their brows. They were not
beautiful to see as they crouched in the mire. But their souls
were seen by God; and if their souls were in a state of grace
they were radiant to see: and God loved them, seeing them.

A wasting breath of humiliation blew bleakly over his soul   1370
to think of how he had fallen, to feel that those souls were
dearer to God than his. The wind blew over him and passed on
to the myriads and myriads of other souls on whom God's
favour shone now more and now less, stars now brighter and
now dimmer, sustained and failing. And the glimmering souls   1375
passed away, sustained and failing, merged in a moving breath.
One soul was lost; a tiny soul: his. It flickered once and went
out, forgotten, lost. The end: black cold void waste.

1365 baskets.] aEg; baskets of herrings. MS–Eg

Consciousness of place came ebbing back to him slowly over
a vast tract of time unlit, unfelt, unlived. The squalid scene 1380
composed itself around him; the common accents, the burning
gasjets in the shops, odours of fish and spirits and wet sawdust,
moving men and women. An old woman was about to cross
the street, an oilcan in her hand. He bent down and asked her
was there a chapel near.   1385
—A chapel, sir? Yes, sir. Church Street chapel.
—Church?
She shifted the can to her other hand and directed him: and,
as she held out her reeking withered right hand under its fringe
of shawl, he bent lower towards her, saddened and soothed by 1390
her voice.
—Thank you.
—You are quite welcome, sir.
The candles on the high altar had been extinguished but the
fragrance of incense still floated down the dim nave. Bearded 1395
workmen with pious faces were guiding a canopy out through
a sidedoor, the sacristan aiding them with quiet gestures and
words. A few of the faithful still lingered, praying before one of
the sidealtars or kneeling in the benches near the confessionals.
He approached timidly and knelt at the last bench in the body, 1400
thankful for the peace and silence and fragrant shadow of the
church. The board on which he knelt was narrow and worn
and those who knelt near him were humble followers of Jesus.
Jesus too had been born in poverty and had worked in the shop
of a carpenter, cutting boards and planing them, and had first 1405
spoken of the kingdom of God to poor fishermen, teaching all
men to be meek and humble of heart.
He bowed his head upon his hands, bidding his heart be
meek and humble that he might be like those who knelt beside
him and his prayer as acceptable as theirs. He prayed beside 1410
them but it was hard. His soul was foul with sin and he dared
not ask forgiveness with the simple trust of those whom Jesus,
in the mysterious ways of God, had called first to His side, the
carpenters, the fishermen, poor and simple people following a
lowly trade, handling and shaping the wood of trees, mending 1415
their nets with patience.
A tall figure came down the aisle and the penitents stirred:
and, at the last moment glancing up swiftly, he saw a long grey
beard and the brown habit of a capuchin.[7] The priest entered
the box and was hidden. Two penitents rose and entered the 1420

---

7. The Capuchin monks, a division of the Franciscans, are named for the cowl (Italian,
  cappucio) that is part of their brown, white-belted habits (*OED*).

confessional at either side. The wooden slide was drawn back and the faint murmur of a voice troubled the silence.

His blood began to murmur in his veins, murmuring like a sinful city summoned from its sleep to hear its doom. Little flakes of fire fell and powdery ashes fell softly, alighting on the houses of men. They stirred, waking from sleep, troubled by the heated air.

The slide was shot back. The penitent emerged from the side of the box. The farther slide was drawn. A woman entered quietly and deftly where the first penitent had knelt. The faint murmur began again.

He could still leave the chapel. He could stand up, put one foot before the other and walk out softly and then run, run, run swiftly through the dark streets. He could still escape from the shame. O what shame! His face was burning with shame. Had it been any terrible crime but that one sin! Had it been murder! Little fiery flakes fell and touched him at all points, shameful thoughts, shameful words, shameful acts. Shame covered him wholly like fine glowing ashes falling continually. To say it in words! His soul, stifling and helpless, would cease to be.

The slide was shot back. A penitent emerged from the far= ther side of the box. The near slide was drawn. A penitent entered where the other penitent had come out. A soft whisper= ing noise floated in vaporous cloudlets out of the box. It was the woman: soft whispering cloudlets, soft whispering vapour, whispering and vanishing.

He beat his breast with his fist humbly, secretly under cover of the wooden armrest. He would be at one with others and with God. He would love his neighbour. He would love God Who had made and loved him. He would kneel and pray with others and be happy. God would look down on him and on them and would love them all.

It was easy to be good. God's yoke was sweet and light. It was better never to have sinned, to have remained always a child, for God loved little children and suffered them to come to Him. It was a terrible and a sad thing to sin. But God was merciful to poor sinners who were truly sorry. How true that was! That was indeed goodness.

The slide was shot to suddenly. The penitent came out. He was next. He stood up in terror and walked blindly into the box.

At last it had come. He knelt in the silent gloom and raised his eyes to the white crucifix suspended above him. God could see that he was sorry. He would tell all his sins. His confession would be long, long. Everybody in the chapel would know then what a sinner he had been. Let them know. It was true. But God had promised to forgive him if he was sorry. He was sorry. He clasped his hands and raised them towards the white form, praying with his darkened eyes, praying with all his trembling body, swaying his head to and fro like a lost crea= ture, praying with whimpering lips.

—Sorry! Sorry! O sorry!

The slide clicked back and his heart bounded in his breast. The face of an old priest was at the grating, averted from him, leaning upon a hand. He made the sign of the cross and prayed of the priest to bless him for he had sinned. Then, bowing his head, he repeated the *Confiteor*[8] in fright. At the words *my most grievous fault* he ceased, breathless.

—How long is it since your last confession, my child?

—A long time, father.

—A month, my child?

—Longer, father.

—Three months, my child?

—Longer, father.

—Six months?

—Eight months, father.

He had begun. The priest asked:

—And what do you remember since that time?

He began to confess his sins: masses missed, prayers not said, lies.

—Anything else, my child?

Sins of anger, envy of others, gluttony, vanity, disobedience.

—Anything else, my child?

Sloth.

—Anything else, my child?

There was no help. He murmured:

—I . . . . committed sins of impurity, father.

The priest did not turn his head.

—With yourself, my child?

—And . . . with others.

—With women, my child?

—Yes, father.

—Were they married women, my child?

8. The prayer said at the beginning of confession.

He did not know. His sins trickled from his lips, one by one, trickled in shameful drops from his soul festering and oozing like a sore, a squalid stream of vice. The last sins oozed forth, sluggish, filthy. There was no more to tell. He bowed his head, overcome. 1505

The priest was silent. Then he asked:

—How old are you, my child? 1510

—Sixteen, father.

The priest passed his hand several times over his face. Then, resting his forehead against his hand, he leaned towards the grating and, with eyes still averted, spoke slowly. His voice was weary and old. 1515

—You are very young, my child, he said, and let me implore of you to give up that sin. It is a terrible sin. It kills the body and it kills the soul. It is the cause of many crimes and misfortunes. Give it up, my child, for God' sake. It is dishonourable and unmanly. You cannot know where that wretched habit will 1520 lead you or where it will come against you. As long as you commit that sin, my poor child, you will never be worth one farthing to God. Pray to our mother Mary to help you. She will help you, my child. Pray to Our Blessed Lady when that sin comes into your mind. I am sure you will do that, will you not? 1525 You repent of all those sins. I am sure you do. And you will promise God now that by His holy grace you will never offend Him any more by that wicked sin. You will make that solemn promise to God, will you not?

—Yes, father. 1530

The old and weary voice fell like sweet rain upon his quak= ing parching heart. How sweet and sad!

—Do so, my poor child. The devil has led you astray. Drive him back to hell when he tempts you to dishonour your body in that way–the foul spirit who hates Our Lord. Promise God 1535 now that you will give up that sin, that wretched wretched sin.

Blinded by his tears and by the light of God's mercifulness he bent his head and heard the grave words of absolution spoken and saw the priest's hand raised above him in token of forgiveness.[9] 1540

—God bless you, my child. Pray for me.

He knelt to say his penance, praying in a corner of the dark nave: and his prayers ascended to heaven from his purified heart like perfume streaming upwards from a heart of white rose. 1545

9. That is, making the sign of the cross.

The muddy streets were gay. He strode homeward, con=
scious of an invisible grace pervading and making light his
limbs. In spite of all he had done it. He had confessed and God
had pardoned him. His soul was made fair and holy once more,
holy and happy.   1550

It would be beautiful to die if God so willed. It was beautiful
to live if God so willed, to live in grace a life of peace and
virtue and forbearance with others.

He sat by the fire in the kitchen, not daring to speak for
happiness. Till that moment he had not known how beautiful   1555
and peaceful life could be. The green square of paper pinned
round the lamp cast down a tender shade. On the dresser was a
plate of sausages and white pudding and on the shelf there were
eggs. They would be for the breakfast in the morning after the
communion in the college chapel. White pudding and eggs and   1560
sausages and cups of tea. How simple and beautiful was life
after all! And life lay all before him.

In a dream he fell asleep. In a dream he rose and saw that it
was morning. In a waking dream he went through the quiet
morning towards the college.   1565

The boys were all there, kneeling in their places. He knelt
among them, happy and shy. The altar was heaped with fra=
grant masses of white flowers: and in the morning light the pale
flames of the candles among the white flowers were clear and
silent as his own soul.   1570

He knelt before the altar with his classmates, holding the
altar cloth with them over a living rail of hands. His hands
were trembling: and his soul trembled as he heard the priest
pass with the ciborium[1] from communicant to communicant.
—*Corpus Domini nostri.*   1575

Could it be? He knelt there sinless and timid: and he would
hold upon his tongue the host and God would enter his purified
body.

—*In vitam eternam. Amen.*

Another life! A life of grace and virtue and happiness! It was   1580
true. It was not a dream from which he would wake. The past
was past.

—*Corpus Domini nostri.*[2]

The ciborium had come to him.

---

1. Covered receptacle for the consecrated wafers of the Eucharist.
2. Latin phrases, meaning "Unto life eternal," "Amen," and "The body of our Lord," spoken
   by priests during administration of the Eucharist.

IV

Sunday was dedicated to the mystery of the Holy Trinity,[1]
Monday to the Holy Ghost, Tuesday to the Guardian Angels,
Wednesday to saint Joseph, Thursday to the Most Blessed Sac=
rament of the Altar, Friday to the Suffering Jesus, Saturday to
the Blessed Virgin Mary.   5

Every morning he hallowed himself anew in the presence of
some holy image or mystery. His day began with an heroic
offering of its every moment of thought or action for the inten=
tions of the sovereign pontiff[2] and with an early mass. The raw
morning air whetted his resolute piety; and often as he knelt   10
among the few worshippers at the sidealtar, following with his
interleaved prayerbook[3] the murmur of the priest, he glanced up
for an instant towards the vested figure standing in the gloom
between the two candles which were the old and the new
testaments and imagined that he was kneeling at mass in the   15
catacombs.[4]

His daily life was laid out in devotional areas. By means of
ejaculations[5] and prayers he stored up ungrudgingly for the
souls in purgatory centuries of days and quarantines[6] and years;
yet the spiritual triumph which he felt in achieving with ease so 20
many fabulous ages of canonical penances did not wholly re=
ward his zeal of prayer since he could never know how much
temporal punishment he had remitted by way of suffrage for
the agonising souls: and, fearful lest in the midst of the purga=
torial fire, which differed from the infernal only in that it was   25
not everlasting, his penance might avail no more than a drop of
moisture, he drove his soul daily through an increasing circle of
works of supererogation.[7]

Every part of his day, divided by what he regarded now as
the duties of his station in life, circled about its own centre of   30
spiritual energy. His life seemed to have drawn near to eternity;
every thought, word and deed, every instance of consciousness

---

23 by--suffrage] ⌐¹by--suffrage¹⌐ MS   32 instance] 16; instant MS–Eg

1. In Catholic doctrine, a mystery is something incomprehensible to human intelligence,
   such as the infinite, eternal nature of God (*Cath. Enc.*). On the Holy Trinity, see note 7, p.
   27.
2. A heroic offering is a vow to donate all of one's good deeds to the spiritual well-being of
   another person, in this case the pope (*Cath. Enc.*).
3. Prayerbook supplemented with devotional material placed between the pages out of piety
   by the person using the book.
4. Subterranean tombs used by early Christians to hide their worship services from the
   Romans.
5. Short prayers emotionally performed.
6. Periods of forty days of strict ecclesiastical penance (*Cath. Enc.*).
7. Works that go beyond duty in an attempt to reach perfection (*Cath. Enc.*).

could be made to revibrate radiantly in heaven: and at times his
sense of such immediate repercussion was so lively that he
seemed to feel his soul in devotion pressing like fingers the   35
keyboard of a great cash register and to see the amount of his
purchase start forth immediately in heaven not as a number but
as a frail column of incense or as a slender flower.

The rosaries too which he said constantly (for he carried his
beads loose in his trousers' pockets that he might tell them as   40
he walked the streets) transformed themselves into coronals of
flowers of such vague unearthly texture that they seemed to
him as hueless and odourless as they were nameless. He offered
up each of his three daily chaplets[8] that his soul might grow
strong in each of the three theological virtues, in faith in the   45
Father Who had created him, in hope in the Son Who had
redeemed him and in love of the Holy Ghost Who had sanc=
tified him: and this thrice triple prayer he offered to the Three
Persons through Mary in the name of her joyful and sorrowful
and glorious mysteries.   50

On each of the seven days of the week he further prayed that
one of the seven gifts of the Holy Ghost[9] might descend upon
his soul and drive out of it day by day the seven deadly sins
which had defiled it in the past: and he prayed for each gift on
its appointed day, confident that it would descend upon him,   55
though it seemed to him strange at times that wisdom and
understanding and knowledge were so distinct in their nature
that each should be prayed for apart from the others. Yet he
believed that at some future stage of his spiritual progress this
difficulty would be removed when his sinful soul had been   60
raised up from its weakness and enlightened by the Third Per=
son of the Most Blessed Trinity. He believed this all the more
and with trepidation because of the divine gloom and silence
wherein dwelt the unseen Paraclete,[1] Whose symbols were a
dove and a mighty wind, to sin against Whom was a sin be=   65
yond forgiveness, the eternal, mysterious, secret Being to
Whom, as God, the priests offered up mass once a year, robed
in the scarlet of the tongues of fire.[2]

---

43 as(1)] ⌐¹as¹⌐ MS   45–48 the(2)--offered] Eg, aEg; the Father, in hope in the Son, in
charity in the Holy Ghost, and as daily offerings of thanksgiving MS   56 seemed]
⌐ˢseemedˢ⌐ MS   56 to--strange] strange to him Eg–64   68 the(1)] ⌐¹the¹⌐ MS   68 of--
fire.] ⌐¹of the tongues of fire¹⌐. MS

8. Three groups of fifty-five beads, each representing a prayer, that make up the rosary (*OED*).
9. Wisdom, understanding, counsel, fortitude, knowledge, piety, and fear of the Lord (Isaias
   11:2–3).
1. The Holy Spirit, the third person of the Trinity.
2. At Pentecost, the seventh Sunday after Easter (Whitsunday), the priests' red robes represent the descent of the Holy Spirit as tongues of fire (Acts 2:3).

The imagery through which the nature and kinship of the Three Persons of the Trinity were darkly shadowed forth in the books of devotion which he read (the Father contemplating from all eternity as in a mirror His Divine Perfections and thereby begetting eternally the Eternal Son and the Holy Spirit proceeding out of Father and Son from all eternity) were easier of acceptance by his mind by reason of their august incompre= hensibility than was the simple fact that God had loved his soul from all eternity, for ages before he had been born into the world, for ages before the world itself had existed. He had heard the names of the passions of love and hate pronounced solemnly on the stage and in the pulpit, had found them set forth solemnly in books, and had wondered why his soul was unable to harbour them for any time or to force his lips to utter their names with conviction. A brief anger had often invested him but he had never been able to make it an abiding passion and had always felt himself passing out of it as if his very body were being divested with ease of some outer skin or peel. He had felt a subtle, dark and murmurous presence penetrate his being and fire him with a brief iniquitous lust: it too had slipped beyond his grasp leaving his mind lucid and indifferent. This, it seemed, was the only love and that the only hate his soul would harbour.

But he could no longer disbelieve in the reality of love since God Himself had loved his individual soul with divine love from all eternity. Gradually, as his soul was enriched with spiritual knowledge, he saw the whole world forming one vast symmetrical expression of God's power and love. Life became a divine gift for every moment and sensation of which, were it even the sight of a single leaf hanging on the twig of a tree, his soul should praise and thank the Giver. The world for all its solid substance and complexity no longer existed for his soul save as a theorem of divine power and love and universality. So entire and unquestionable was this sense of the divine meaning in all nature granted to his soul that he could scarcely under= stand why it was in any way necessary that he should continue to live. Yet that also was part of the divine purpose and he dared not question its use, he above all others who had sinned so deeply and so foully against the divine purpose. Meek and abased by this consciousness of the one eternal omnipresent perfect reality his soul took up again her burden of pieties, masses and prayers and sacraments and mortifications: and

only then for the first time since he had brooded on the great
mystery of love did he feel within him a warm movement like
that of some newly born life or virtue of the soul itself. The
attitude of rapture in sacred art, the raised and parted hands,
the parted lips and eyes as of one about to swoon, became for   115
him an image of the soul in prayer, humiliated and faint before
her Creator.

But he had been forewarned of the dangers of spiritual exal=
tation and did not allow himself to desist from even the least or
lowliest devotion, striving also by constant mortification to   120
undo the sinful past rather than to achieve a saintliness fraught
with peril. Each of his senses was brought under a rigorous
discipline. In order to mortify the sense of sight he made it his
rule to walk in the street with downcast eyes, glancing neither
to right nor left and never behind him. His eyes shunned every   125
encounter with the eyes of women. From time to time also he
balked them by a sudden effort of the will, as by lifting them
suddenly in the middle of an unfinished sentence and closing
the book. To mortify his hearing he exerted no control over his
voice which was then breaking, neither sang nor whistled and   130
made no attempt to flee from noises which caused him painful
nervous irritation such as the sharpening of knives on the
knifeboard, the gathering of cinders on the fireshovel and the
twigging[3] of the carpet. To mortify his smell was more difficult
as he found in himself no instinctive repugnance to bad odours,   135
whether they were the odours of the outdoor world such as
those of dung and tar or the odours of his own person among
which he had made many curious comparisons and experi=
ments. He found in the end that the only odour against which
his sense of smell revolted was a certain stale fishy stink like   140
that of longstanding urine: and whenever it was possible he
subjected himself to this unpleasant odour. To mortify the taste
he practised strict habits at table, observed to the letter all the
fasts of the church and sought by distraction to divert his mind
from the savours of different foods. But it was to the mortifi=   145
cation of touch that he brought the most assiduous ingenuity of
inventiveness. He never consciously changed his position in
bed, sat in the most uncomfortable positions, suffered patiently
every itch and pain, kept away from the fire, remained on his
knees all through the mass except at the gospels,[4] left parts of   150

3. Beating (*OED*) or, possibly, brushing vigorously with a broom.
4. Rather than sitting part of the time, he remained on his knees except when everyone was
   expected to stand.

his neck and face undried so that the air might sting them and, whenever he was not saying his beads, carried his arms stiffly at his sides like a runner and never in his pockets or clasped behind him.

He had no temptations to sin mortally. It surprised him however to find that at the end of his course of intricate piety and selfrestraint he was so easily at the mercy of childish and unworthy imperfections. His prayers and fasts availed him little for the suppression of anger at hearing his mother sneeze or at being disturbed in his devotions. It needed an immense effort of his will to master the impulse which urged him to give outlet to such irritation. Images of the outbursts of trivial anger which he had often noted among his masters, their twitching mouths, closeshut lips and flushed cheeks, recurred to his memory, dis= couraging him, for all his practice of humility, by the compari= son. To merge his life in the common tide of other lives was harder for him than any fasting or prayer and it was his constant failure to do this to his own satisfaction which caused in his soul at last a sensation of spiritual dryness together with a growth of doubts and scruples. His soul traversed a period of desolation in which the sacraments themselves seemed to have turned into dried up sources. His confession became a channel for the escape of scrupulous and unrepented imperfections. His actual reception of the eucharist did not bring him the same dissolving moments of virginal selfsurrender as did those spiri= tual communions made by him sometimes at the close of some visit to the Blessed Sacrament.[5] The book which he used for these visits was an old neglected book written by saint Alphon= sus Liguori with fading characters and sere foxpapered leaves.[6] A faded world of fervent love and virginal responses seemed to be evoked for his soul by the reading of its pages in which the imagery of the canticles[7] was interwoven with the communi= cant's prayers. An inaudible voice seemed to caress the soul, telling her names and glories, bidding her arise as for espousal and come away, bidding her look forth, a spouse, from Amana and from the mountains of the leopards; and the soul seemed to answer with the same inaudible voice, surrendering herself:

155

160

165

170

175

180

185

---

151 the] ABSENT Eg–64   151–152 and, whenever--beads,] and ⁊₁, whenever--beads,ᴵʳ MS

5. Visits alone to the church, between masses, to pray.
6. Saint Alphonsus Liguori (1696–1787) wrote various books, including *The Visits to the Most Holy Sacrament,* the one probably meant here, whose pages have become foxed, or discolored by decay (*OED*).
7. The Old Testament book known as the Canticle of Canticles in the Catholic tradition and as the Song of Solomon (or Song of Songs) in the Protestant tradition. The Canticle pres- ents an allegory of the soul as the bride and lover of God.

Inter ubera mea commorabitur.[8]

This idea of surrender had a perilous attraction for his mind now that he felt his soul beset once again by the insistent voices of the flesh which began to murmur to him again during his prayers and meditations. It gave him an intense sense of power to know that he could, by a single act of consent, in a moment of thought, undo all that he had done. He seemed to feel a flood slowly advancing towards his naked feet and to be wait= ing for the first faint timid noiseless wavelet to touch his fevered skin. Then, almost at the instant of that touch, almost at the verge of sinful consent, he found himself standing far away from the flood upon a dry shore, saved by a sudden act of the will or a sudden ejaculation: and, seeing the silver line of the flood far away and beginning again its slow advance to= wards his feet, a new thrill of power and satisfaction shook his soul to know that he had not yielded nor undone all.

When he had eluded the flood of temptation many times in this way he grew troubled and wondered whether the grace which he had refused to lose was not being filched from him little by little. The clear certitude of his own immunity grew dim and to it succeeded a vague fear that his soul had really fallen unawares. It was with difficulty that he won back his old consciousness of his state of grace by telling himself that he had prayed to God at every temptation and that the grace which he had prayed for must have been given to him inasmuch as God was obliged to give it. The very frequency and violence of temptations showed him at last the truth of what he had heard about the trials of the saints. Frequent and violent temptations were a proof that the citadel of the soul had not fallen and that the devil raged to make it fall.

Often when he had confessed his doubts and scruples, some momentary inattention at prayer, a movement of trivial anger in his soul or a subtle wilfulness in speech or act, he was bidden by his confessor to name some sin of his past life before absol= ution was given him. He named it with humility and shame and repented of it once more. It humiliated and shamed him to think that he would never be freed from it wholly, however holily he might live or whatever virtues or perfections he might attain. A restless feeling of guilt would always be present with him: he would confess and repent and be absolved, confess and repent again and be absolved again, fruitlessly. Perhaps that

190

195

200

205

210

215

220

225

214 heard] Eg; ABSENT MS   227 would] ⁿ¹would¹ʳ MS

8. "He shall abide between my breasts" (Latin; Canticle 1:12).

first hasty confession wrung from him by the fear of hell had
not been good? Perhaps, concerned only for his imminent   230
doom, he had not had sincere sorrow for his sin? But the surest
sign that his confession had been good and that he had had
sincere sorrow for his sin was, he knew, the amendment of his
life.

—I have amended my life, have I not? he asked himself.   235

◆   ◆   ◆

The director stood in the embrasure of the window, his back
to the light, leaning an elbow on the brown crossblind and, as
he spoke and smiled, slowly dangling and looping the cord of
the other blind. Stephen stood before him, following for a mo=
ment with his eyes the waning of the long summer daylight   240
above the roofs or the slow deft movements of the priestly
fingers. The priest's face was in total shadow but the waning
daylight from behind him touched the deeply grooved temples
and the curves of the skull. Stephen followed also with his ears
the accents and intervals of the priest's voice as he spoke   245
gravely and cordially of indifferent themes, the vacation which
had just ended, the colleges of the order abroad, the transfer=
ence of masters. The grave and cordial voice went on easily
with its tale and in the pauses Stephen felt bound to set it on
again with respectful questions. He knew that the tale was a   250
prelude and his mind waited for the sequel. Ever since the
message of summons had come for him from the director his
mind had struggled to find the meaning of the message: and
during the long restless time he had sat in the college parlour
waiting for the director to come in his eyes had wandered from   255
one sober picture to another around the walls and his mind had
wandered from one guess to another until the meaning of the
summons had almost become clear. Then just as he was wish=
ing that some unforeseen cause might prevent the director from
coming he had heard the handle of the door turning and the   260
swish of a soutane.

The director had begun to speak of the dominican and fran=
ciscan orders and of the friendship between saint Thomas and
saint Bonaventure.[9] The capuchin dress, he thought, was rather
too   265

Stephen's face gave back the priest's indulgent smile and, not

---

256 had] ABSENT Eg–64

9. Saint Thomas Aquinas (see note 7, p. 111), and Saint Bonaventure (1221–1274), a Franciscan, would have known each other at the University of Paris.

being anxious to give an opinion, he made a slight dubitative
movement with his lips.

—I believe, continued the director, that there is some talk now
among the capuchins themselves of doing away with it and   270
following the example of the other franciscans.

—I suppose they would retain it in the cloister, said Stephen.

—O certainly, said the director. For the cloister it is all right
but for the street I really think it would be better to do away
with it, don't you?   275

—It must be troublesome, I imagine.

—Of course it is: of course. Just imagine, when I was in Bel=
gium I used to see them out cycling in all kinds of weather with
this thing up about their knees! It was really ridiculous. *Les
jupes*,[1] they call them in Belgium.   280

The vowel was so modified as to be indistinct.

—What do they call them?

—*Les jupes*.

—O.

Stephen smiled again in answer to the smile which he could   285
not see on the priest's shadowed face, its image or spectre only
passing rapidly across his mind as the low discreet accent fell
upon his ear. He gazed calmly before him at the waning sky,
glad of the cool of the evening and of the faint yellow glow
which hid the tiny flame kindling upon his cheek.   290

The names of articles of dress worn by women or of certain
soft and delicate stuffs used in their making brought always to
his mind a delicate and sinful perfume. As a boy he had imag=
ined the reins by which horses are driven as slender silken
bands and it had shocked him to feel at Stradbrooke the greasy   295
leather of harness. It had shocked him too when he had felt for
the first time beneath his tremulous fingers the brittle texture of
a woman's stocking for, retaining nothing of all he read save
that which seemed to him an echo or a prophecy of his own
state, it was only amid softworded phrases or within rosesoft   300
stuffs that he dared to conceive of the soul or body of a woman
moving with tender life.

But the phrase on the priest's lips was disingenuous for he
knew that a priest should not speak lightly on that theme. The
phrase had been spoken lightly with design and he felt that his   305
face was being searched by the eyes in the shadow. Whatever
he had heard or read of the craft of jesuits he had put aside

275 with it,] with, Eg–16, 64   281 was] ⌐was⌐ MS   289 of(3)] a16; ABSENT MS–16,
64   295 had] ABSENT Eg–64

1. "The skirts" (French).

frankly as not borne out by his own experience. His masters, even when they had not attracted him, had seemed to him always intelligent and serious priests, athletic and highspirited prefects. He thought of them as men who washed their bodies briskly with cold water and wore clean cold linen. During all the years he had lived among them in Clongowes and in Bel= vedere he had received only two pandies and, though these had been dealt him in the wrong, he knew that he had often escaped punishment. During all those years he had never heard from any of his masters a flippant word: it was they who had taught him christian doctrine and urged him to live a good life and, when he had fallen into grievous sin, it was they who had led him back to grace. Their presence had made him diffident of himself when he was a muff[2] in Clongowes and it had made him diffident of himself also while he had held his equivocal position in Belvedere. A constant sense of this had remained with him up to the last year of his school life. He had never once disobeyed or allowed turbulent companions to seduce him from his habit of quiet obedience: and, even when he doubted some statement of a master, he had never presumed to doubt openly. Lately some of their judgments had sounded a little childish in his ears and had made him feel a regret and pity as though he were slowly passing out of an accustomed world and were hearing its language for the last time. One day when some boys had gathered round a priest under the shed near the chapel he had heard the priest say:

—I believe that Lord Macaulay[3] was a man who probably never committed a mortal sin in his life, that is to say, a deliberate mortal sin.[4]

Some of the boys had then asked the priest if Victor Hugo were not the greatest French writer. The priest had answered that Victor Hugo had never written half so well when he had turned against the church as he had written when he was a catholic.

—But there are many eminent French critics, said the priest, who consider that even Victor Hugo, great as he certainly was, had not so pure a French style as Louis Veuillot.[5]

340 had written] aEg; wrote MS–Eg

2. Someone without skill, a beginner (colloquial; *OED*).
3. Thomas Babington Macaulay, 1st Baron Macaulay (1800–1859), English essayist and historian.
4. A mortal sin is by definition deliberate, that is, intended.
5. The contrast drawn between these two Frenchmen, Victor Hugo (1802–1885), a famous writer, and Louis Veuillot (1813–1883), a journalist who openly supported the Catholic Church, is unwarranted.

The tiny flame which the priest's allusion had kindled upon 345
Stephen's cheek had sunk down again and his eyes were still
fixed calmly on the colourless sky. But an unresting doubt flew
hither and thither before his mind. Masked memories passed
quickly before him: he recognized scenes and persons yet he
was conscious that he had failed to perceive some vital circum= 350
stance in them. He saw himself walking about the grounds
watching the sports in Clongowes and eating slim jim out of his
cricketcap. Some jesuits were walking round the cycletrack in
the company of ladies. The echoes of certain expressions used
in Clongowes sounded in remote caves of his mind. 355

His ears were listening to these distant echoes amid the si=
lence of the parlour when he became aware that the priest was
addressing him in a different voice.

—I sent for you today, Stephen, because I wished to speak to
you on a very important subject. 360
—Yes, sir.
—Have you ever felt that you had a vocation?

Stephen parted his lips to answer yes and then withheld the
word suddenly. The priest waited for the answer and added:
—I mean have you ever felt within yourself, in your soul, a 365
desire to join the order. Think.
—I have sometimes thought of it, said Stephen.

The priest let the blindcord fall to one side and, uniting his
hands, leaned his chin gravely upon them, communing with
himself. 370
—In a college like this, he said at length, there is one boy or
perhaps two or three boys whom God calls to the religious life.
Such a boy is marked off from his companions by his piety, by
the good example he shows to others. He is looked up to by
them; he is chosen perhaps as prefect by his fellow sodalists. 375
And you, Stephen, have been such a boy in this college, prefect
of Our Blessed Lady's sodality. Perhaps you are the boy in this
college whom God designs to call to Himself.

A strong note of pride reinforcing the gravity of the priest's
voice made Stephen's heart quicken in response. 380
—To receive that call, Stephen, said the priest, is the greatest
honour that the Almighty God can bestow upon a man. No
king or emperor on this earth has the power of the priest
of God. No angel or archangel in heaven, no saint, not even

the Blessed Virgin herself has the power of a priest of God: the   385
power of the keys, the power to bind and to loose from sin,[6] the
power of exorcism, the power to cast out from the creatures of
God the evil spirits that have power over them, the power, the
authority, to make the great God of Heaven come down upon
the altar and take the form of bread and wine. What an awful   390
power, Stephen!

A flame began to flutter again on Stephen's cheek as he
heard in this proud address an echo of his own proud musings.
How often had he seen himself as a priest wielding calmly and
humbly the awful power of which angels and saints stood in   395
reverence! His soul had loved to muse in secret on this desire.
He had seen himself, a young and silentmannered priest, en=
tering a confessional swiftly, ascending the altarsteps, in=
censing, genuflecting, accomplishing the vague acts of the
priesthood which pleased him by reason of their semblance of   400
reality and of their distance from it. In that dim life which he
had lived through in his musings he had assumed the voices and
gestures which he had noted with various priests. He had bent
his knee sideways like such a one, he had shaken the thurible[7]
only slightly like such a one, his chasuble[8] had swung open like   405
that of such another as he had turned to the altar again after
having blessed the people. And above all it had pleased him to
fill the second place in those dim scenes of his imagining. He
shrank from the dignity of celebrant because it displeased him
to imagine that all the vague pomp should end in his own   410
person or that the ritual should assign to him so clear and final
an office. He longed for the minor sacred offices, to be vested
with the tunicle of subdeacon[9] at high mass, to stand aloof from
the altar, forgotten by the people, his shoulders covered with a
humeral veil, holding the paten within its folds,[1] or when the   415
sacrifice had been accomplished, to stand as deacon in a dal=
matic of cloth of gold[2] on the step below the celebrant, his

385–386 the–keys,] ⁷¹the–keys¹ʳ MS   386–388 the (3)–them,] ⁷¹the–them,¹ʳ MS   406
had] ⁷¹had¹ʳ MS   407 him] ⁷¹him¹ʳ MS   412 minor sacred] ⁷¹minor sacrded¹ʳ MS
412–413 offices, to–tunicle] offices ⁷¹, to–tunicle¹ʳ MS   413 subdeacon] aEg; ⁷¹sub-|¹ʳ
deacon MS; sub-deacon Eg   415 holding–folds,] ⁷¹holding–folds,¹ʳ MS   415 or] ⁷¹⟨and
then⟩ or¹ʳ MS   416 accomplished,] accomplish⟨ing⟩ed, MS   416 as deacon] ⁷¹⟨once
again⟩ as deacon¹ʳ MS

6. The power of entry to heaven by acting as confessor and giving absolution (Matthew
   16:19).
7. The container for burning incense during the mass.
8. Sleeveless outer vestment worn by a priest during the mass.
9. The short tunic worn by the assistant to the deacon; the deacon assists the priest.
1. The veil is a cloth that the subdeacon wears on his shoulder during mass to wrap sacred
   vessels when he touches them; these vessels include the paten, the plate for the consecrated Host.
2. The wide-sleeved vestment, open at the sides, that deacons wear during mass, of a fabric
   woven wholly or partially from gold.

hands joined and his face towards the people, and sing the
chant *Ite, missa est*.[3] If ever he had seen himself celebrant it was
as in the pictures of the mass in his child's massbook, in a   420
church without worshippers, save for the angel of the sacrifice,
at a bare altar and served by an acolyte scarcely more boyish
than himself. In vague sacrificial or sacramental acts alone his
will seemed drawn to go forth to encounter reality: and it was
partly the absence of an appointed rite which had always con=   425
strained him to inaction whether he had allowed silence to
cover his anger or pride or had suffered only an embrace he
longed to give.

He listened in reverent silence now to the priest's appeal and
through the words he heard even more distinctly a voice bid=   430
ding him approach, offering him secret knowledge and secret
power. He would know then what was the sin of Simon Magus[4]
and what the sin against the Holy Ghost[5] for which there was
no forgiveness. He would know obscure things, hidden from
others, from those who were conceived and born children of   435
wrath. He would know the sins, the sinful longings and sinful
thoughts and sinful acts, of others, hearing them murmured
into his ear in the confessional under the shame of a darkened
chapel by the lips of women and of girls: but rendered immune
mysteriously at his ordination by the imposition of hands his   440
soul would pass again uncontaminated to the white peace of
the altar. No touch of sin would linger upon the hands with
which he would elevate and break the host; no touch of sin
would linger on his lips in prayer to make him eat and drink
damnation to himself, not discerning the body of the Lord.[6] He   445
would hold his secret knowledge and secret power, being as
sinless as the innocent: and he would be a priest for ever
according to the order of Melchisedech.[7]

—I will offer up my mass tomorrow morning, said the direc=
tor, that Almighty God may reveal to you His holy will. And   450
let you, Stephen, make a novena to your patron saint, the first

---

421 worshippers, save--sacrifice,] worshippers ⁷ˡ, save--sacrifice,ˡʳ MS   425 an appointed]
⁷ˡ⟨a⟩ an appointedˡʳ MS   438 ear] MS; ears Eg–64   451 patron] MS; holy patron Eg
[SETTING ERROR]–64

3. Latin words, meaning "Go, the mass is finished," spoken to release the congregation at
   the end of the mass.
4. The sin of simony, from Simon, known as "Magus" because he was considered a "sor-
   cerer" or "magician" (Latin), who tried to buy their spiritual powers from the apostles.
5. To sin against the Holy Ghost is to confound him with evil, to deny maliciously the divine
   character of divine works (*Cath. Enc.*); but the theological debates about the precise
   character of this sin may make it particularly mysterious for Stephen.
6. Without recognizing Christ's divine presence in the Host.
7. A priest mentioned in the Old Testament (Genesis 14:18) who is treated in the New Testament (Hebrews 5:6) as a precursor of Jesus; by implication a forerunner of Catholic priests.

martyr,[8] who is very powerful with God, that God may en=
lighten your mind. But you must be quite sure, Stephen, that
you have a vocation because it would be terrible if you found
afterwards that you had none. Once a priest always a priest,   455
remember. Your catechism tells you that the sacrament of Holy
Orders is one of those which can be received only once because
it imprints on the soul an indelible spiritual mark which can
never be effaced. It is before you must weigh well, not after. It
is a solemn question, Stephen, because on it may depend the   460
salvation of your eternal soul. But we will pray to God to=
gether.

He held open the heavy halldoor and gave his hand as if
already to a companion in the spiritual life. Stephen passed out
on to the wide platform above the steps and was conscious of   465
the caress of mild evening air. Towards Findlater's church a
quartet of young men were striding along with linked arms,
swaying their heads and stepping to the agile melody of their
leader's concertina. The music passed in an instant, as the first
bars of sudden music always did, over the fantastic fabrics of   470
his mind, dissolving them painlessly and noiselessly as a sudden
wave dissolves the sandbuilt turrets of children. Smiling at the
trivial air he raised his eyes to the priest's face and, seeing in it
a mirthless reflection of the sunken day, detached his hand
slowly which had acquiesced faintly in that companionship.   475

As he descended the steps the impression which effaced his
troubled selfcommunion was that of a mirthless mask reflecting
a sunken day from the threshold of the college. The shadow,
then, of the life of the college passed gravely over his conscious=
ness. It was a grave and ordered and passionless life that   480
awaited him, a life without material cares. He wondered how
he would pass the first night in the novitiate[9] and with what
dismay he would wake the first morning in the dormitory. The
troubling odour of the long corridors of Clongowes came back
to him and he heard the discreet murmur of the burning   485
gasflames. At once from every part of his being unrest began to
irradiate. A feverish quickening of his pulses followed and a din
of meaningless words drove his reasoned thoughts hither and
thither confusedly. His lungs dilated and sank as if he were
inhaling a warm moist unsustaining air and he smelt again the   490

8. That is, make a devotion lasting nine days, dedicated to Saint Stephen, the first Christian
   martyr, who was stoned for blasphemy.
9. The probationary period before an aspiring priest can formally enter a religious order;
   also the residence for aspirants during that period.

warm moist air which hung in the bath in Clongowes above the
sluggish turfcoloured water.

Some instinct, waking at these memories, stronger than edu=
cation or piety, quickened within him at every near approach
to that life, an instinct subtle and hostile, and armed him   495
against acquiescence. The chill and order of the life repelled
him. He saw himself rising in the cold of the morning and filing
down with the others to early mass and trying vainly to
struggle with his prayers against the fainting sickness of his
stomach. He saw himself sitting at dinner with the community   500
of a college. What then had come of that deeprooted shyness of
his which had made him loth to eat or drink under a strange
roof? What had come of the pride of his spirit which had
always made him conceive himself as a being apart in every
order?   505

The Reverend Stephen Dedalus, S. J.[1]

His name in that new life leaped into characters before his
eyes and to it there followed a mental sensation of an unde=
fined face or colour of a face. The colour faded and became
strong like a changing glow of pallid brick red. Was it the raw   510
reddish glow he had so often seen on wintry mornings on the
shaven gills of the priests? The face was eyeless and sourfa=
voured and devout, shot with pink tinges of suffocated anger.
Was it not a mental spectre of the face of one of the jesuits
whom some of the boys called Lantern Jaws and others Foxy   515
Campbell?

He was passing at that moment before the jesuit house in
Gardiner Street and wondered vaguely which window would
be his if he ever joined the order. Then he wondered at the
vagueness of his wonder, at the remoteness of his own soul   520
from what he had hitherto imagined her sanctuary, at the frail
hold which so many years of order and obedience had of him
when once a definite and irrevocable act of his threatened to
end for ever, in time and in eternity, his freedom. The voice of
the director urging upon him the proud claims of the church   525
and the mystery and power of the priestly office repeated itself
idly in his memory. His soul was not there to hear and greet it
and he knew now that the exhortation he had listened to had
already fallen into an idle formal tale. He would never swing
the thurible before the tabernacle as priest. His destiny was to 530
be elusive of social or religious orders. The wisdom of the

501 come] MS; become Eg–64   513 pink] ⁻ˡpinkˡʳ MS   520 own] ABSENT 16, 64

1. Society of Jesus, that is, a member of the Jesuits.

priest's appeal did not touch him to the quick. He was destined
to learn his own wisdom apart from others or to learn the
wisdom of others himself wandering among the snares of the
world.   535

The snares of the world were its ways of sin. He would fall.
He had not yet fallen but he would fall silently, in an instant.
Not to fall was too hard, too hard: and he felt the silent lapse
of his soul, as it would be at some instant to come, falling,
falling but not yet fallen, still unfallen but about to fall.   540

He crossed the bridge over the stream of the Tolka[2] and
turned his eyes coldly for an instant towards the faded blue
shrine of the Blessed Virgin which stood fowlwise on a pole in
the middle of a hamshaped encampment of poor cottages.
Then, bending to the left, he followed the lane which led up to   545
his house. The faint sour stink of rotted cabbages came to=
wards him from the kitchen gardens on the rising ground above
the river. He smiled to think that it was this disorder, the
misrule and confusion of his father's house and the stagnation
of vegetable life, which was to win the day in his soul. Then a   550
short laugh broke from his lips as he thought of that solitary
farmhand in the kitchen gardens behind their house whom they
had nicknamed the man with the hat. A second laugh, taking
rise from the first after a pause, broke from him involuntarily
as he thought of how the man with the hat worked, considering   555
in turn the four points of the sky and then regretfully plunging
his spade in the earth.

He pushed open the latchless door of the porch and passed
through the naked hallway into the kitchen. A group of his
brothers and sisters was sitting round the table. Tea was nearly   560
over and only the last of the second watered tea[3] remained in
the bottoms of the small glassjars and jampots which did ser=
vice for teacups. Discarded crusts and lumps of sugared bread,
turned brown by the tea which had been poured over them, lay
scattered on the table. Little wells of tea lay here and there on   565
the board and a knife with a broken ivory handle was stuck
through the pith of a ravaged turnover.

The sad quiet greyblue glow of the dying day came through
the window and the open door, covering over and allaying
quietly a sudden instinct of remorse in Stephen's heart. All that   570
had been denied them had been freely given to him, the eldest:

563 sugared] ⁿlsugaredlⁿ MS

2. Ballybough Bridge, over the Tolka River in north Dublin.
3. Weak tea, either watered to make it go further or brewed by using the tea leaves a second
time, here because of financial difficulties.

but the quiet glow of evening showed him in their faces no sign
of rancour.

He sat near them at the table and asked where his father and
mother were. One answered: 575
—Goneboro toboro lookboro atboro aboro houseboro.

Still another removal! A boy named Fallon in Belvedere had
often asked him with a silly laugh why they moved so often. A
frown of scorn darkened quickly his forehead as he heard again
the silly laugh of the questioner.   580

He asked:
—Why are we on the move again, if it's a fair question?

The same sister answered:
—Becauseboro theboro landboro lordboro willboro putboro
usboro outboro.   585

The voice of his youngest brother from the farther side of
the fireplace began to sing the air *Oft in the Stilly Night*.[4] One
by one the others took up the air until a full choir of voices was
singing. They would sing so for hours, melody after melody,
glee after glee, till the last pale light died down on the horizon, 590
till the first dark nightclouds came forth and night fell.

He waited for some moments, listening, before he too took
up the air with them. He was listening with pain of spirit to the
overtone of weariness behind their frail fresh innocent voices.
Even before they set out on life's journey they seemed weary   595
already of the way.

He heard the choir of voices in the kitchen echoed and mul=
tiplied through an endless reverberation of the choirs of endless
generations of children: and heard in all the echoes an echo also
of the recurring note of weariness and pain. All seemed weary   600
of life even before entering upon it. And he remembered that
Newman had heard this note also in the broken lines of Virgil
*giving utterance, like the voice of Nature herself, to that pain
and weariness yet hope of better things which has been the
experience of her children in every time*.[5]   605

◆   ◆   ◆

He could wait no longer.

From the door of Byron's publichouse to the gate of Clon=
tarf[6] chapel, from the gate of Clontarf chapel to the door of
Byron's publichouse and then back again to the chapel and
then back again to the publichouse he had paced slowly at first 610

578 silly] ⌐¹silly¹⌐ MS

4. First, and identifying, line of a popular song from *National Airs*, by the Irish poet Thomas
   Moore (1779–1852).
5. From Cardinal Newman's *An Essay in Aid of a Grammar of Assent* (1870).
6. Clontarf is east of Dublin on Dublin Bay.

planting his steps scrupulously in the spaces of the patchwork of the footpath, then timing their fall to the fall of verses. A full hour had passed since his father had gone in with Dan Crosby, the tutor, to find out from him something about the university.[7] For a full hour he had paced up and down, waiting: but he could wait no longer. 615

He set off abruptly for the Bull,[8] walking rapidly lest his father's shrill whistle might call him back; and in a few mo= ments he had rounded the curve at the police barrack and was safe. 620

Yes, his mother was hostile to the idea as he had read from her listless silence. Yet her mistrust pricked him more keenly than his father's pride and he thought coldly how he had watched the faith which was fading down in his soul aging and strengthening in her eyes. A dim antagonism gathered force 625 within him and darkened his mind as a cloud against her dis= loyalty: and when it passed cloudlike leaving his mind serene and dutiful towards her again he was made aware dimly and without regret of a first noiseless sundering of their lives.

The university! So he had passed beyond the challenge of the 630 sentries who had stood as guardians of his boyhood and had sought to keep him among them, that he might be subject to them and serve their ends. Pride after satisfaction uplifted him like long slow waves. The end he had been born to serve yet did not see had led him to escape by an unseen path: and now it 635 beckoned to him once more and a new adventure was about to be opened to him. It seemed to him that he heard notes of fitful music leaping upwards a tone and downwards a diminished fourth, upwards a tone and downwards a major third, like triplebranching flames leaping fitfully, flame after flame, out of 640 a midnight wood. It was an elfin prelude, endless and formless: and, as it grew wilder and faster, the flames leaping out of time, he seemed to hear from under the boughs and grasses wild creatures racing, their feet pattering like rain upon the leaves. Their feet passed in pattering tumult over his mind, the 645 feet of hares and rabbits, the feet of harts and hinds and ante= lopes, until he heard them no more and remembered only a proud cadence from Newman: *Whose feet are as the feet of harts and underneath the everlasting arms.*[9]

614 from] MS; for Eg–64   646 harts--hinds] Eg; hinds and harts MS

7. This teacher could give advice and information about University College, Dublin, a Catholic institution founded in 1854 with Newman as rector and affiliated with the Jesuits from 1883 to 1908.
8. The seawall from Clontarf into Dublin Bay.
9. From Newman's *The Idea of the University Defined and Illustrated* (1852).

The pride of that dim image brought back to his mind the 650
dignity of the office he had refused. All through his boyhood he
had mused upon that which he had so often thought to be his
destiny and when the moment had come for him to obey the
call he had turned aside, obeying a wayward instinct. Now
time lay between: the oils of ordination would never anoint his 655
body. He had refused. Why?

He turned seaward from the road at Dollymount[1] and as he
passed on to the thin wooden bridge he felt the planks shaking
with the tramp of heavily shod feet. A squad of christian
brothers was on its way back from the Bull and had begun to 660
pass, two by two, across the bridge. Soon the whole bridge was
trembling and resounding. The uncouth faces passed him two
by two, stained yellow or red or livid by the sea and, as he
strove to look at them with ease and indifference, a faint stain
of personal shame and commiseration rose to his own face. 665
Angry with himself he tried to hide his face from their eyes by
gazing down sideways into the shallow swirling water under
the bridge but he still saw a reflection therein of their topheavy
silk hats and humble tapelike collars and loosely hanging cleri=
cal clothes.   670

—Brother Hickey.
  Brother Quaid.
  Brother MacArdle.
  Brother Keogh.

Their piety would be like their names, like their faces, like 675
their clothes: and it was idle for him to tell himself that their
humble and contrite hearts, it might be, paid a far richer tribute
of devotion than his had ever been, a gift tenfold more accept=
able than his elaborate adoration. It was idle for him to move
himself to be generous towards them, to tell himself that if he 680
ever came to their gates, stripped of his pride, beaten and in
beggar's weeds, that they would be generous towards him,
loving him as themselves. Idle and embittering, finally, to ar=
gue, against his own dispassionate certitude, that the com=
mandment of love bade us not to love our neighbour as 685
ourselves with the same amount and intensity of love but to
love him as ourselves with the same kind of love.

He drew forth a phrase from his treasure and spoke it softly
to himself:

—A day of dappled seaborne clouds.[2]   690

The phrase and the day and the scene harmonised in a chord. Words. Was it their colours?[3] He allowed them to glow and fade, hue after hue: sunrise gold, the russet and green of apple orchards, azure of waves, the greyfringed fleece of clouds. No, it was not their colours: it was the poise and   695 balance of the period itself. Did he then love the rhythmic rise and fall of words better than their associations of legend and colour? Or was it that, being as weak of sight as he was shy of mind, he drew less pleasure from the reflection of the glowing sensible world through the prism of a language manycoloured   700 and richly storied than from the contemplation of an inner world of individual emotions mirrored perfectly in a lucid supple periodic prose?[4]

He passed from the trembling bridge on to firm land again. At that instant, as it seemed to him, the air was chilled; and   705 looking askance towards the water he saw a flying squall dark= ening and crisping suddenly the tide. A faint click at his heart, a faint throb in his throat told him once more of how his flesh dreaded the cold infrahuman odour of the sea: yet he did not strike across the downs on his left but held straight on along   710 the spine of rocks that pointed against the river's mouth.

A veiled sunlight lit up faintly the grey sheet of water where the river was embayed.[5] In the distance along the course of the slowflowing Liffey slender masts flecked the sky and, more distant still, the dim fabric of the city lay prone in haze. Like a   715 scene on some vague arras,[6] old as man's weariness, the image of the seventh city of christendom was visible to him across the timeless air, no older nor more weary nor less patient of subjec= tion than in the days of the thingmote.[7]

Disheartened, he raised his eyes towards the slowdrifting   720 clouds, dappled and seaborne. They were voyaging across the deserts of the sky, a host of nomads on the march, voyaging high over Ireland, westward bound. The Europe they had come from lay out there beyond the Irish Sea, Europe of strange tongues and valleyed and woodbegirt and citadelled and of   725 entrenched and marshalled races. He heard a confused music

---

2. Remembered from Hugh Miller's *The Testimony of the Rocks* (1857), a theological tract, where Miller has "breeze-borne," rather than seaborne.
3. "Rhetorical modes or figures; ornaments of style or diction, embellishments" (*OED*).
4. Prose characterized by periodic sentences, in which the main clause or its verb is post- poned until the end.
5. Formed into a bay.
6. Tapestry.
7. A mound, removed in the seventeenth century, where public councils were held during the Scandinavian occupation of Dublin from the ninth to the eleventh centuries.

within him as of memories and names which he was almost
conscious of but could not capture even for an instant; then the
music seemed to recede, to recede, to recede: and from each
receding trail of nebulous music there fell always one long= 730
drawn calling note, piercing like a star the dusk of silence.
Again! Again! Again! Again! A voice from beyond the world
was calling.

—Hello, Stephanos![8]

—Here comes The Dedalus! 735

—Ao! . . . Eh, give it over, Dwyer, I'm telling you or I'll give you
a stuff in the kisser[9] for yourself . . . . Ao!

—Good man, Towser! Duck him!

—Come along, Dedalus! Bous Stephanoumenos! Bous Steph=
aneforos![1] 740

—Duck him! Guzzle him now, Towser!

—Help! Help! . . . Ao!

He recognised their speech collectively before he distin=
guished their faces. The mere sight of that medley of wet
nakedness chilled him to the bone. Their bodies, corpsewhite 745
or suffused with a pallid golden light or rawly tanned by the
sun, gleamed with the wet of the sea. Their divingstone, poised
on its rude supports and rocking under their plunges, and the
roughhewn stones of the sloping breakwater over which they
scrambled in their horseplay gleamed with cold wet lustre. The 750
towels with which they smacked their bodies were heavy with
cold seawater: and drenched with cold brine was their matted
hair.

He stood still in deference to their calls and parried their
banter with easy words. How characterless they looked: Shuley 755
without his deep unbuttoned collar, Ennis without his scarlet
belt with the snaky clasp and Connolly without his Norfolk
coat with the flapless sidepockets! It was a pain to see them and
a swordlike pain to see the signs of adolescence that made
repellent their pitiable nakedness. Perhaps they had taken ref= 760
uge in number and noise from the secret dread in their souls.
But he, apart from them and in silence, remembered in what
dread he stood of the mystery of his own body.

—Stephanos Dedalos! Bous Stephanoumenos! Bous Stephane=
foros! 765

---

732 Again!(4)] MS; ABSENT Eg–64   747 sun,] 18; suns, MS–16, 64

8. "Wreath," "crown" (Greek).
9. A hit in the mouth (colloquial).
1. "Ox as wreath-bearer for the sacrifice," with a play on Stephen's name that suggests "ox as Stephen's soul" (Greek).

Their banter was not new to him and now, as always, it flattered his mild proud sovereignty. Now, as never before, his strange name seemed to him a prophecy. So timeless seemed the grey warm air, so fluid and impersonal his own mood, that all ages were as one to him. A moment before the ghost of the ancient kingdom of the Danes had looked forth through the vesture of the hazewrapped city. Now, at the name of the fabulous artificer,[2] he seemed to hear the noise of dim waves and to see a winged form flying above the waves and slowly climbing the air. What did it mean? Was it a quaint device opening a page of some medieval book of prophecies and sym= bols, a hawklike man flying sunward above the sea, a prophecy of the end he had been born to serve and had been following through the mists of childhood and boyhood, a symbol of the artist forging anew in his workshop out of the sluggish matter of the earth a new soaring impalpable imperishable being?

His heart trembled; his breath came faster and a wild spirit passed over his limbs as though he were soaring sunward. His heart trembled in an ecstasy of fear and his soul was in flight. His soul was soaring in an air beyond the world and the body he knew was purified in a breath and delivered of incertitude and made radiant and commingled with the element of the spirit. An ecstasy of flight made radiant his eyes and wild his breath and tremulous and wild and radiant his windswept limbs.

—One! Two! . . . Look out!

—O, Cripes, I'm drownded!

—One! Two! Three and away!

—Me next! Me next!

—One! . . . Uk!

—Stephaneforos!

His throat ached with a desire to cry aloud, the cry of a hawk or eagle on high, to cry piercingly of his deliverance to the winds. This was the call of life to his soul not the dull gross voice of the world of duties and despair, not the inhuman voice that had called him to the pale service of the altar. An instant of wild flight had delivered him and the cry of triumph which his lips withheld cleft his brain.

—Stephaneforos!

766 now,--always,] now Eg–64   792 Cripes,] cripes, 64

2. Daedalus, the inventor (see note 1, p. 3).

What were they now but cerements[3] shaken from the body of   805
death–the fear he had walked in night and day, the incertitude
that had ringed him round, the shame that had abased him
within and without–cerements, the linens of the grave?

His soul had arisen from the grave of boyhood, spurning her
graveclothes. Yes! Yes! Yes! He would create proudly out of the   810
freedom and power of his soul, as the great artificer whose
name he bore, a living thing, new and soaring and beautiful,
impalpable, imperishable.

He started up nervously from the stoneblock for he could no
longer quench the flame in his blood. He felt his cheeks aflame   815
and his throat throbbing with song. There was a lust of wan=
dering in his feet that burned to set out for the ends of the
earth. On! On! his heart seemed to cry. Evening would deepen
above the sea, night fall upon the plains, dawn glimmer before
the wanderer and show him strange fields and hills and faces.   820
Where?

He looked northward towards Howth.[4] The sea had fallen
below the line of seawrack on the shallow side of the break=
water and already the tide was running out fast along the
foreshore. Already one long oval bank of sand lay warm and   825
dry amid the wavelets. Here and there warm isles of sand
gleamed above the shallow tide: and about the isles and around
the long bank and amid the shallow currents of the beach were
lightclad gayclad figures wading and delving.

In a few moments he was barefoot, his stockings folded in   830
his pockets and his canvas shoes dangling by their knotted laces
over his shoulders: and, picking a pointed salteaten stick out of
the jetsam among the rocks, he clambered down the slope of
the breakwater.

There was a long rivulet in the strand: and, as he waded   835
slowly up its course, he wondered at the endless drift of sea=
weed. Emerald and black and russet and olive, it moved
beneath the current, swaying and turning. The water of the
rivulet was dark with endless drift and mirrored the highdrift=
ing clouds. The clouds were drifting above him silently and   840
silently the seatangle was drifting below him; and the grey
warm air was still: and a new wild life was singing in his veins.

Where was his boyhood now? Where was the soul that had
hung back from her destiny, to brood alone upon the shame of
her wounds and in her house of squalor and subterfuge to   845

805 cerements] a16; the cerements MS–16

3. Graveclothes.
4. Headland on Dublin Bay's northeast coast.

queen it in faded cerements and in wreaths that withered at the touch? Or where was he?

He was alone. He was unheeded, happy and near to the wild heart of life. He was alone and young and wilful and wild= hearted, alone amid a waste of wild air and brackish waters and the seaharvest of shells and tangle and veiled grey sunlight and gayclad lightclad figures of children and girls and voices childish and girlish in the air.

A girl stood before him in midstream: alone and still, gazing out to sea. She seemed like one whom magic had changed into the likeness of a strange and beautiful seabird. Her long slender bare legs were delicate as a crane's and pure save where an emerald trail of seaweed had fashioned itself as a sign upon the flesh. Her thighs, fuller and softhued as ivory, were bared al= most to the hips where the white fringes of her drawers were like featherings of soft white down. Her slateblue skirts were kilted boldly about her waist and dovetailed behind her. Her bosom was as a bird's, soft and slight; slight and soft as the breast of some darkplumaged dove. But her long fair hair was girlish; and girlish, and touched with the wonder of mortal beauty, her face.

She was alone and still, gazing out to sea; and when she felt his presence and the worship of his eyes her eyes turned to him in quiet sufferance of his gaze, without shame or wantonness. Long, long she suffered his gaze and then quietly withdrew her eyes from his and bent them towards the stream, gently stirring the water with her foot hither and thither. The first faint noise of gently moving water broke the silence, low and faint and whispering, faint as the bells of sleep; hither and thither, hither and thither: and a faint flame trembled on her cheek.

—Heavenly God! cried Stephen's soul in an outburst of pro= fane joy.

He turned away from her suddenly and set off across the strand. His cheeks were aflame; his body was aglow; his limbs were trembling. On and on and on and on he strode, far out over the sands, singing wildly to the sea, crying to greet the advent of the life that had cried to him.

Her image had passed into his soul for ever and no word had broken the holy silence of his ecstasy. Her eyes had called him and his soul had leaped at the call. To live, to err, to fall, to triumph, to recreate life out of life! A wild angel had appeared to him, the angel of mortal youth and beauty, an envoy from the fair courts of life, to throw open before him in an instant of ecstasy the gates of all the ways of error and glory. On and on and on and on!

He halted suddenly and heard his heart in the silence. How far had he walked? What hour was it?

There was no human figure near him nor any sound borne to him over the air. But the tide was near the turn and already the day was on the wane. He turned landward and ran towards   895
the shore and, running up the sloping beach, reckless of the sharp shingle, found a sandy nook amid a ring of tufted sand= knolls and lay down there that the peace and silence of the evening might still the riot of his blood.

He felt above him the vast indifferent dome and the calm   900
processes of the heavenly bodies: and the earth beneath him, the earth that had borne him, had taken him to her breast.

He closed his eyes in the languor of sleep. His eyelids trembled as if they felt the vast cyclic movement of the earth and her watchers, trembled as if they felt the strange light of   905
some new world. His soul was swooning into some new world, fantastic, dim, uncertain as under sea, traversed by cloudy shapes and beings. A world, a glimmer or a flower? Glimmer= ing and trembling, trembling and unfolding, a breaking light, an opening flower, it spread in endless succession to itself,   910
breaking in full crimson and unfolding and fading to palest rose, leaf by leaf and wave of light by wave of light, flooding all the heavens with its soft flushes, every flush deeper than other.

Evening had fallen when he woke and the sand and arid grasses of his bed glowed no longer. He rose slowly and, re=   915
calling the rapture of his sleep, sighed at its joy.

He climbed to the crest of the sandhill and gazed about him. Evening had fallen. A rim of the young moon cleft the pale waste of sky like the rim of a silver hoop embedded in grey sand: and the tide was flowing in fast to the land with a low   920
whisper of her waves, islanding a few last figures in distant pools.

V

He drained his third cup of watery tea to the dregs and set to chewing the crusts of fried bread that were scattered near him, staring into the dark pool of the jar. The yellow dripping had been scooped out like a boghole and the pool under it brought   5
back to his memory the dark turfcoloured water of the bath in Clongowes. The box of pawntickets at his elbow had just been

rifled and he took up idly one after another in his greasy fingers
the blue and white dockets, scrawled and sanded and creased
and bearing the name of the pledger as Daly or MacEvoy.[1]
—1 Pair Buskins
   1 D. Coat
   3 Articles and White
   1 Man's Pants
Then he put them aside and gazed thoughtfully at the lid of
the box, speckled with lousemarks, and asked vaguely:
—How much is the clock fast now?
His mother straightened the battered alarmclock that was
lying on its side in the middle of the kitchen mantelpiece until
its dial showed a quarter to twelve and then laid it once more
on its side.
—An hour and twentyfive minutes, she said. The right time
now is twenty past ten. The dear knows[2] you might try to be in
time for your lectures.
—Fill out the place for me to wash, said Stephen.
—Katey, fill out the place for Stephen to wash.
—Boody, fill out the place for Stephen to wash.
—I can't. I'm going for blue. Fill it out, you, Maggie.
When the enamelled basin had been fitted into the well of
the sink and the old washingglove flung on the side of it he
allowed his mother to scrub his neck and root into the folds of
his ears and into the interstices at the wings of his nose.
—Well, it's a poor case, she said, when a university student is
so dirty that his mother has to wash him.
—But it gives you pleasure, said Stephen calmly.
An earsplitting whistle was heard from upstairs and his
mother thrust a damp overall into his hands, saying:
—Dry yourself and hurry out for the love of goodness.
A second shrill whistle, prolonged angrily, brought one of
the girls to the foot of the staircase.
—Yes, father?
—Is your lazy bitch of a brother gone out yet?
—Yes, father.
—Sure?
—Yes, father.
—Hm!

---

10 —1] NO DIALOGUE DASH TO INDICATE THE LIST AS AUDIBLY SPOKEN Eg–64

1. Aliases used when items were pawned.
2. "God knows" (polite anglicized form of a Gaelic expression; P. W. Joyce).

The girl came back making signs to him to be quick and go
out quietly by the back. Stephen laughed and said:

—He has a curious idea of genders if he thinks a bitch is
masculine.

—Ah, it's a scandalous shame for you, Stephen, said his
mother, and you'll live to rue the day you set your foot in that
place. I know how it has changed you.

—Good morning, everybody, said Stephen smiling and kissing
the tips of his fingers in adieu.

The lane behind the terrace was waterlogged and as he went
down it slowly, choosing his steps amid heaps of wet rubbish,
he heard a mad nun screeching in the nuns' madhouse beyond
the wall:[3]

—Jesus! O Jesus! Jesus!

He shook the sound out of his ears by an angry toss of his
head and hurried on, stumbling through the mouldering offal,
his heart already bitten by an ache of loathing and bitterness.
His father's whistle, his mother's mutterings, the screech of an
unseen maniac were to him now so many voices offending and
threatening to humble the pride of his youth. He drove their
echoes even out of his heart with an execration: but as he
walked down the avenue and felt the grey morning light falling
about him through the dripping trees and smelt the strange
wild smell of the wet leaves and bark his soul was loosed of her
miseries.

The rainladen trees of the avenue evoked in him, as always,
memories of the girls and women in the plays of Gerhart
Hauptmann:[4] and the memory of their pale sorrows and the
fragrance falling from the wet branches mingled in a mood of
quiet joy. His morning walk across the city had begun: and he
foreknew that as he passed the sloblands of Fairview[5] he would
think of the cloistral silverveined prose of Newman, that as he
walked along the North Strand Road, glancing idly at the win=
dows of the provision shops, he would recall the dark humour
of Guido Cavalcanti[6] and smile, that as he went by Baird's
stonecutting works in Talbot Place the spirit of Ibsen[7] would
blow through him like a keen wind, a spirit of wayward boyish
beauty, and that passing a grimy marine dealer's shop beyond

3. St. Vincent's Lunatic Asylum, run by the Sisters of Charity and located in Fairview, just
   across the Tolka River in northeast Dublin, where the Dedalus family lives, on Royal Terrace (now Inverness Road).
4. Gerhardt Hauptmann (1862–1946), German writer.
5. Tidal flatlands where the Tolka enters Dublin Bay.
6. Italian poet (c. 1255–1300).
7. Henrik Ibsen (1828–1906), Norwegian dramatist.

the Liffey he would repeat the song by Ben Jonson which
begins: 85

I was not wearier where I lay.[8]

His mind when wearied of its search for the essence of
beauty amid the spectral words of Aristotle or Aquinas turned
often for its pleasure to the dainty songs of the Elizabethans.
His mind, in the vesture of a doubting monk, stood often in   90
shadow under the windows of that age, to hear the grave and
mocking music of the lutenists or the frank laughter of waist=
coateers[9] until a laugh too low, a phrase, tarnished by time, of
chambering[1] and false honour stung his monkish pride and
drove him on from his lurkingplace.   95
    The lore which he was believed to pass his days brooding
upon so that it had rapt him from the companionships of youth
was only a garner of slender sentences from Aristotle's poetics
and psychology and a Synopsis Philosophiae Scholasticae ad
mentem divi Thomae.[2] His thinking was a dusk of doubt and   100
selfmistrust lit up at moments by the lightnings of intuition, but
lightnings of so clear a splendour that in those moments the
world perished about his feet as if it had been fireconsumed:
and thereafter his tongue grew heavy and he met the eyes of
others with unanswering eyes for he felt that the spirit of   105
beauty had folded him round like a mantle and that in revery at
least he had been acquainted with nobility. But when this brief
pride of silence upheld him no longer he was glad to find him=
self still in the midst of common lives, passing on his way amid
the squalor and noise and sloth of the city fearlessly and with a   110
light heart.
    Near the hoardings[3] on the canal he met the consumptive
man with the doll's face and the brimless hat coming towards
him down the slope of the bridge with little steps, tightly but=
toned into his chocolate overcoat and holding his furled um=   115
brella a span or two from him like a diviningrod. It must be
eleven, he thought, and peered into a dairy to see the time. The
clock in the dairy told him that it was five minutes to five but,
as he turned away, he heard a clock somewhere near him but
unseen beating eleven strokes in swift precision. He laughed as   120

8. From The Vision of Delight (1617), by the English poet and dramatist Ben Jonson
   (1572–1637).
9. Low-class prostitutes (OED).
1. Sexual indulgences, lewdness (OED).
2. Selections from Aristotle's writings pertaining to literature, the Poetics, and to the mind,
   De Sensu (Of the Senses) and De Anima (Of the Soul), and a book whose Latin title in English would be A Synopsis of Scholastic Philosophy for the Understanding of Saint Thomas.
3. Fence made of boards, where bills are posted (OED).

he heard it for it made him think of MacCann; and he saw him
a squat figure in a shooting jacket and breeches and with a fair
goatee standing in the wind at Hopkins' corner and heard him
say:
—Dedalus, you're an antisocial being, wrapped up in yourself. 125
I'm not. I'm a democrat: and I'll work and act for social liberty
and equality among all classes and sexes in the United States of
the Europe of the future.
  Eleven! Then he was late for that lecture too. What day of
the week was it? He stopped at a newsagent's to read the 130
headline of a placard. Thursday. Ten to eleven; English: eleven
to twelve; French: twelve to one; physics. He fancied to himself
the English lecture and felt, even at that distance, restless and
helpless. He saw the heads of his classmates meekly bent as
they wrote in their notebooks the points they were bidden to 135
note, nominal definitions, essential definitions[4] and examples or
dates of birth and death, chief works, a favourable and an
unfavourable criticism side by side. His own head was unbent
for his thoughts wandered abroad and whether he looked
around the little class of students or out of the window across 140
the desolate gardens of the green an odour assailed him of
cheerless cellardamp and decay. Another head than his, right
before him in the first benches, was poised squarely above its
bending fellows like the head of a priest appealing without
humility to the tabernacle for the humble worshippers about 145
him. Why was it that when he thought of Cranly he could
never raise before his mind the entire image of his body but
only the image of the head and face? Even now against the grey
curtain of the morning he saw it before him like the phantom
of a dream, the face of a severed head or deathmask, crowned 150
on the brows by its stiff black upright hair as by an iron crown.
It was a priestlike face, priestlike in its pallor, in the wide=
winged nose, in the shadowings below the eyes and along the
jaws, priestlike in the lips that were long and bloodless and
faintly smiling: and Stephen, remembering swiftly how he had 155
told Cranly of all the tumults and unrest and longings in his
soul, day after day and night by night only to be answered by
his friend's listening silence, would have told himself that it
was the face of a guilty priest who heard confessions of those
whom he had not power to absolve but that he felt again in 160
memory the gaze of its dark womanish eyes.

137 and(1)] or Eg–64   159–160 of--whom] Eg; ABSENT MS

4. For Aristotle in the *Posterior Analytics*, definitions that focus on effects produced are
nominal, while those that focus on cause, or "essence," are essential.

Through this image he had a glimpse of a strange dark cavern of speculation but at once turned away from it feeling that it was not yet the hour to enter it. But the nightshade of his friend's listlessness seemed to be diffusing in the air around him   165
a tenuous and deadly exhalation: and he found himself glancing from one casual word to another on his right or left in stolid wonder that they had been so silently emptied of instan=taneous sense until every mean shop legend bound his mind like the words of a spell and his soul shrivelled up sighing with   170
age as he walked on in a lane among heaps of dead language. His own consciousness of language was ebbing from his brain and trickling into the very words themselves which set to band and disband themselves in wayward rhythms:

> The ivy whines upon the wall   175
> And whines and twines upon the wall
> The ivy whines upon the wall
> The yellow ivy on the wall
> Ivy, ivy up the wall.

Did any one ever hear such drivel? Lord Almighty! Who ever   180
heard of ivy whining on a wall? Yellow ivy: that was all right. Yellow ivory also. And what about ivory ivy?

The word now shone in his brain, clearer and brighter than any ivory sawn from the mottled tusks of elephants. *Ivory, ivoire, avorio, ebur.*[5] One of the first examples that he had   185
learnt in Latin had run: *India mittit ebur:*[6] and he recalled the shrewd northern face of the rector who had taught him to construe the Metamorphoses of Ovid[7] in a courtly English, made whimsical by the mention of porkers and potsherds and chines of bacon. He had learnt what little he knew of the laws   190
of Latin verse from a ragged book written by a Portuguese priest:

Contrahit orator, variant in carmine vates.[8]

The crises and victories and secessions in Roman history were handed on to him in the trite words *in tanto discrimine*[9]   195
and he had tried to peer into the social life of the city of cities through the words *implere ollam denariorum* which the rector had rendered sonorously as the filling of a pot with denaries.[1]

---

5. Words for ivory in English, French, Italian, and Latin.
6. "India sends ivory."
7. A series of mythological narratives about transformations among humans, animals, and plants, by the Roman poet Ovid (Publius Ovidius Naso, 43 BCE–17 CE).
8. Literally, "the orator summarizes; the poet amplifies in song" (Latin), but in the *Prosodia,* by the Portuguese Jesuit Emmanuel Alvarez (1562–1582), the subject is prose rhythm.
9. "In such a great crisis" (Latin).
1. The phrase translates the Latin of the preceding line; "denaries" were Roman coins.

The pages of his timeworn Horace[2] never felt cold to the touch
even when his own fingers were cold: they were human pages: 200
and fifty years before they had been turned by the human
fingers of John Duncan Inverarity and by his brother William
Malcolm Inverarity. Yes, those were noble names on the dusky
flyleaf and, even for so poor a Latinist as he, the dusky verses
were as fragrant as though they had lain all those years in   205
myrtle and lavender and vervain: but yet it wounded him to
think that he would never be but a shy guest at the feast of the
world's culture and that the monkish learning, in terms of
which he was striving to forge out an esthetic philosophy, was
held no higher by the age he lived in than the subtle and   210
curious jargons of heraldry and falconry.

The grey block of Trinity[3] on his left, set heavily in the city's
ignorance like a great dull stone set in a cumbrous ring, pulled
his mind downward: and while he was striving this way and
that to free his feet from the fetters of the reformed conscience[4]   215
he came upon the droll statue of the national poet of Ireland.[5]

He looked at it without anger: for, though sloth of the body
and of the soul crept over it like unseen vermin, over the
shuffling feet and up the folds of the cloak and around the
servile head, it seemed humbly conscious of its indignity. It   220
was a Firbolg in the borrowed cloak of a Milesian;[6] and he
thought of his friend Davin, the peasant student. It was a
jesting name between them but the young peasant bore with it
lightly, saying:

—Go on, Stevie. I have a hard head, you tell me. Call me what   225
you will.

The homely version of his christian name on the lips of his
friend had touched Stephen pleasantly when first heard for he
was as formal in speech with others as they were with him.
Often, as he sat in Davin's rooms in Grantham Street, wonder=   230
ing at his friend's wellmade boots that flanked the wall pair by
pair and repeating for his friend's simple ear the verses and
cadences of others which were the veils of his own longing and

---

228 had] ⌐had⌐r MS

2. Quintus Horatius Flaccus (65–8 BCE), Roman poet.
3. Trinity College, a Protestant, Anglo-Irish institution that Catholics did not attend, first because they were barred from admission and later because the Catholic establishment forbade enrollment.
4. The post-Reformation, that is, Protestant, English attitudes represented by Trinity College.
5. The statue of Thomas Moore outside the gates of Trinity College is "droll," or amusing, because it presents him in a toga. Not officially Ireland's national poet, Moore was popular for his sentimentally Irish writing.
6. An early inhabitant of Ireland, a Firbolg, trying to dress up like one of the more civilized invaders, the Milesians.

dejection, the rude Firbolg mind of his listener had drawn his
mind towards it and flung it back again, drawing it by a quiet   235
inbred courtesy of attention or by a quaint turn of old English
speech or by the force of its delight in rude bodily skill (for
Davin had sat at the feet of Michael Cusack, the Gael),[7]
repelling swiftly and suddenly by a grossness of intelligence or
by a bluntness of feeling or by a dull stare of terror in the eyes   240
the terror of soul of a starving Irish village in which the curfew[8]
was still a nightly fear.

Side by side with his memory of the deeds of prowess of his
uncle Mat Davin, the athlete,[9] the young peasant worshipped
the sorrowful legend of Ireland. The gossip of his fellowstu=   245
dents which strove to render the flat life of the college signifi=
cant at any cost loved to think of him as a young fenian.[1] His
nurse had taught him Irish and shaped the rude imagination by
the broken lights of Irish myth. He stood towards this myth
upon which no individual mind had ever drawn out a line of   250
beauty and to its unwieldy tales that divided against themselves
as they moved down the cycles[2] in the same attitude as towards
the Roman catholic religion, the attitude of a dullwitted loyal
serf. Whatsoever of thought or of feeling came to him from
England or by way of English culture his mind stood armed   255
against in obedience to a password: and of the world that lay
beyond England he knew only the foreign legion of France in
which he spoke of serving.

Coupling this ambition with the young man's diffident hu=
mour Stephen had often called him one of the tame geese:[3] and   260
there was even a point of irritation in the name pointed against
that very reluctance of speech and deed in his friend which
seemed so often to stand between Stephen's mind, eager of
speculation, and the hidden ways of Irish life.

One night the young peasant, his spirit stung by the violent   265
or luxurious language in which Stephen escaped from the cold
silence of intellectual revolt, had called up before Stephen's
mind a strange vision. The two were walking slowly towards

248 the] MS; his Eg–64   251 against] ABSENT Eg–18, 64   259   diffident] MS; ABSENT
Eg–64

7. Cusack (1847–1906) was involved in founding the Gaelic Athletic Association (1884).
8. Curfew, including the extinguishing of lights, was imposed by the English early in the
   eighteenth century and again as part of the Coercion Acts from 1800 to 1921.
9. Maurice Davin (1864–1927), a founder of the Gaelic Athletic Association, held international athletic records.
1. Militant Irish nationalist.
2. Ancient Irish heroic legends, grouped into "cycles," such as the Fenian Cycle, which focused on Finn Mac Cumhaill.
3. A play on the "wild geese," Irish Catholic soldiers who, after William III reconquered Ireland, fled to the Continent in 1691 and served in foreign armies.

Davin's rooms through the dark narrow streets of the poorer
jews.   270
—A thing happened to myself, Stevie, last autumn coming on
winter and I never told it to a living soul and you are the first
person now I ever told it to. I disremember if it was October or
November. It was October because it was before I came up
here to join the matriculation class.   275

    Stephen had turned his smiling eyes towards his friend's
face, flattered by his confidence and won over to sympathy by
the speaker's simple accent.
—I was away all that day from my own place, over in Butte=
vant (I don't know if you know where that is) at a hurling   280
match[4] between the Croke's Own Boys and the Fearless Thurles
and by God, Stevie, that was the hard fight. My first cousin
Fonsy Davin was stripped to his buff that day minding cool[5] for
the Limericks but he was up with the forwards half the time
and shouting like mad. I never will forget that day. One of the 285
Crokes made a woful wipe at him one time with his camaun
and I declare to God he was within an aim's ace of getting it at
the side of the temple. O, honest to God, if the crook of it
caught him that time he was done for.
—I am glad he escaped, Stephen had said with a laugh, but   290
surely that's not the strange thing that happened you?
—Well, I suppose that doesn't interest you but leastways there
was such noise after the match that I missed the train home and
I couldn't get any kind of a yoke[6] to give me a lift for, as luck
would have it, there was a mass meeting that same day over in   295
Castletownroche[7] and all the cars in the country were there. So
there was nothing for it only to stay the night or to foot it out.
Well, I started to walk and on I went and it was coming on
night when I got into the Ballyhoura hills, that's better than ten
miles from Kilmallock and there's a long lonely road after that. 300
You wouldn't see the sign of a christian house along the road or
hear a sound. It was pitch dark almost. Once or twice I stopped
by the way under a bush to redden my pipe and only for the
dew was thick I'd have stretched out there and slept. At last
after a bend of the road I spied a little cottage with a light in   305
the window. I went up and knocked at the door. A voice asked

269 rooms] room 64

4. The match to be played in a town in County Cork involves hurling, a traditional game
resembling both lacrosse and hockey played with a bladed stick known as a *camaun* or
camann.
5. Played shirtless minding the goal. "Cool" is anglicized from the Irish *cúl,* meaning goal.
6. Conveyance, transportation.
7. A political meeting in a town five miles from Buttevant.

who was there and I answered I was over at the match in
Buttevant and was walking back and that I'd be thankful for a
glass of water. After a while a young woman opened the door
and brought me out a big mug of milk. She was half undressed   310
as if she was going to bed when I knocked and she had her hair
hanging: and I thought by her figure and by something in the
look of her eyes that she must be carrying a child. She kept me
in talk a long while at the door and I thought it strange because
her breast and her shoulders were bare. She asked me was I   315
tired and would I like to stop the night there. She said she was
all alone in the house and that her husband had gone that
morning to Queenstown with his sister to see her off. And all
the time she was talking, Stevie, she had her eyes fixed on my
face and she stood so close to me I could hear her breathing.   320
When I handed her back the mug at last she took my hand to
draw me in over the threshold and said: *Come in and stay the
night here. You've no call to be frightened. There's no-one in it
but ourselves* . . . . I didn't go in, Stevie. I thanked her and
went on my way again, all in a fever. At the first bend of the   325
road I looked back and she was standing in the door.

The last words of Davin's story sang in his memory and the
figure of the woman in the story stood forth reflected in other
figures of the peasant women whom he had seen standing in
the doorways at Clane[8] as the college cars drove by, as a type of   330
her race and his own, a batlike soul waking to the conscious=
ness of itself in darkness and secrecy and loneliness and,
through the eyes and voice and gesture of a woman without
guile, calling the stranger to her bed.

A hand was laid on his arm and a young voice cried: 335
—Ah, gentleman, your own girl, sir! The first handsel[9] today,
gentleman. Buy that lovely bunch. Will you, gentleman?

The blue flowers which she lifted towards him and her
young blue eyes seemed to him at that instant images of guile=
lessness: and he halted till the image had vanished and he saw   340
only her ragged dress and damp coarse hair and hoydenish
face.

—Do, gentleman! Don't forget your own girl, sir!
—I have no money, said Stephen.
—Buy them lovely ones, will you, sir? Only a penny.   345
—Did you hear what I said? asked Stephen, bending towards
her. I told you I had no money. I tell you again now.

326 in] MS; at Eg—64

8. A village near Clongowes.
9. "First money taken by a trader in the morning" (*OED*).

—Well, sure, you will some day, sir, please God, the girl
answered after an instant.
—Possibly, said Stephen, but I don't think it likely.   350

He left her quickly, fearing that her intimacy might turn to
gibing and wishing to be out of the way before she offered her
ware to another, a tourist from England or a student of Trinity.
Grafton Street along which he walked prolonged that moment
of discouraged poverty. In the roadway at the head of the street   355
a slab was set to the memory of Wolfe Tone[1] and he remem=
bered having been present with his father at its laying. He re=
membered with bitterness that scene of tawdry tribute. There
were four French delegates in a brake and one, a plump smiling
young man, held, wedged on a stick, a card on which were   360
printed the words: *Vive l'Irlande!*[2]

But the trees in Stephen's Green were fragrant of rain and
the rainsodden earth gave forth its moral odour, a faint in=
cense rising upward through the mould from many hearts. The
soul of the gallant venal city which his elders had told him of   365
had shrunk with time to a faint mortal odour rising from the
earth and he knew that in a moment when he entered the
sombre college he would be conscious of a corruption other
than that of Buck Egan and Burnchapel Whaley.[3]

It was too late to go upstairs to the French class. He crossed   370
the hall and took the corridor to the left which led to the
physics theatre. The corridor was dark and silent but not un=
watchful. Why did he feel that it was not unwatchful? Was it
because he had heard that in Buck Whaley's time there was a
secret staircase there? Or was the jesuit house extraterritorial[4]   375
and was he walking among aliens? The Ireland of Tone and of
Parnell[5] seemed to have receded in space.

He opened the door of the theatre and halted in the chilly
grey light that struggled through the dusty windows. A figure
was crouching before the large grate and by its leanness and   380
greyness he knew that it was the dean of studies lighting the

---

1. A memorial placed at one corner of Stephen's Green in 1898, the centenary of the Insurrection of 1798 against the English, to honor (Theobald) Wolfe Tone (1763–1798), who,
after accompanying French forces into Ireland to fight for independence, was captured
and died by his own hand during his imprisonment.
2. This sign, held by French representatives in a carriage, reads "Long live Ireland!" (French).
3. Confused reference, probably not to John "Bully" Egan (c. 1750–1810) but to Thomas
"Buck" Whaley (1766–1800), son of Richard "Burnchapel" Whaley (c. 1700–1769). All
had reputations for extreme behavior, but the Whaleys were noted for corruption, including involvement with the Hellfire Club, a licentious group of rakes reputed to practice Satanism. Stephen associates the Whaleys with the college because Whaley's house, 86
Stephen's Green, became part of University College.
4. Not a part of Ireland, presumably because of the tie to the Vatican, an independent state,
and because of the attitudes Stephen associates with the Jesuit house.
5. Heroic figures associated with sacrifice and Irish independence.

fire. Stephen closed the door quietly and approached the fire=
place.

—Good morning, sir! Can I help you?

The priest looked up quickly and said: 385

—One moment now, Mr Dedalus, and you will see. There is
an art in lighting a fire. We have the liberal arts and we have
the useful arts. This is one of the useful arts.

—I will try to learn it, said Stephen.

—Not too much coal, said the dean, working briskly at his   390
task, that is one of the secrets.

He produced four candle butts from the sidepockets of his
soutane and placed them deftly among the coals and twisted
papers. Stephen watched him in silence. Kneeling thus on the
flagstone to kindle the fire and busied with the disposition of   395
his wisps of paper and candle butts he seemed more than ever a
humble server making ready the place of sacrifice in an empty
temple, a levite of the Lord. Like a levite's robe of plain linen
the faded worn soutane draped the kneeling figure of one
whom the canonicals or the bellbordered ephod[6] would irk and   400
trouble. His very body had waxed old in lowly service of the
Lord—in tending the fire upon the altar, in bearing tidings se=
cretly, in waiting upon worldlings, in striking swiftly when
bidden—and yet had remained ungraced by aught of saintly or
of prelatic beauty. Nay, his very soul had waxed old in that   405
service without growing towards light and beauty or spreading
abroad a sweet odour of her sanctity—a mortified will no more
responsive to the thrill of its obedience than was to the thrill of
love or combat his aging body, spare and sinewy, greyed with a
silverpointed down.   410

The dean rested back on his hunkers[7] and watched the sticks
catch. Stephen, to fill the silence, said:

—I am sure I could not light a fire.

—You are an artist, are you not, Mr Dedalus? said the dean,
glancing up and blinking his pale eyes. The object of the artist   415
is the creation of the beautiful. What the beautiful is is another
question.

He rubbed his hands slowly and drily over the difficulty.

—Can you solve that question now? he asked.

—Aquinas, answered Stephen, says *Pulcra sunt quae visa*   420
placent.[8]

---

6. The robe of an assistant, or levite, by contrast with the more splendid garments.
7. On his heels (P. W. Joyce).
8. "Those things are beautiful that please the eye" (Latin), an adaptation of Aquinas's statement in *Summa Theologica* (I.5.4), "*Pulchra enim dicuntur quae visa placent*" ("Those
things are called beautiful that please the eye").

—This fire before us, said the dean, will be pleasing to the eye. Will it therefore be beautiful?

—In so far as it is apprehended by the sight, which I suppose means here esthetic intellection, it will be beautiful. But Aqui= nas also says *Bonum est in quod tendit appetitus.*[9] In so far as it satisfies the animal craving for warmth fire is a good. In hell however it is an evil.

—Quite so, said the dean, you have certainly hit the nail on the head.

He rose nimbly and went towards the door, set it ajar and said:

—A draught is said to be a help in these matters.

As he came back to the hearth, limping slightly but with a brisk step, Stephen saw the silent soul of a jesuit look out at him from the pale loveless eyes. Like Ignatius he was lame but in his eyes burned no spark of Ignatius' enthusiasm. Even the legendary craft of the company,[1] a craft subtler and more secret than its fabled books of secret subtle wisdom, had not fired his soul with the energy of apostleship. It seemed as if he used the shifts and lore and cunning of the world, as bidden to do, for the greater glory of God, without joy in their handling or hatred of that in them which was evil but turning them, with a firm gesture of obedience, back upon themselves: and for all this silent service it seemed as if he loved not at all the master and little, if at all, the ends he served. *Similiter atque senis baculus,*[2] he was, as the founder would have had him, like a staff in an old man's hand, to be left in a corner, to be leaned on in the road at nightfall or in stress of weather, to lie with a lady's nosegay on a garden seat, to be raised in menace.

The dean returned to the hearth and began to stroke his chin.

—When may we expect to have something from you on the esthetic question? he asked.

—From me! said Stephen in astonishment. I stumble on an idea once a fortnight if I am lucky.

—These questions are very profound, Mr Dedalus, said the dean. It is like looking down from the cliffs of Moher[3] into the depths. Many go down into the depths and never come up. Only the trained diver can go down into those depths and explore them and come to the surface again.

9. "The good inheres in what is desired" (Latin), another adaptation of Aquinas from the same passage.
1. The Jesuits.
2. Stephen translates this comparison, quoted in Latin, from Ignatius Loyola's constitution of the Society of Jesus.
3. Steep coastal cliffs in County Clare, on Ireland's west coast.

—If you mean speculation, sir, said Stephen, I also am sure
that there is no such thing as free thinking inasmuch as all
thinking must be bound by its own laws.

—Ha!   465

—For my purpose I can work on at present by the light of one
or two ideas of Aristotle and Aquinas.

—I see. I quite see your point.

—I need them only for my own use and guidance until I have
done something for myself by their light. If the lamp smokes or   470
smells I shall try to trim it. If it does not give light enough I
shall sell it and buy or borrow another.

—Epictetus[4] also had a lamp, said the dean, which was sold for
a fancy price after his death. It was the lamp he wrote his
philosophical dissertations by. You know Epictetus?   475

—An old gentleman, said Stephen coarsely, who said that the
soul is very like a bucketful of water.

—He tells us in his homely way, the dean went on, that he put
an iron lamp before a statue of one of the gods and that a thief
stole the lamp. What did the philosopher do? He reflected that   480
it was in the character of a thief to steal and determined to buy
an earthen lamp next day instead of the iron lamp.

A smell of molten tallow came up from the dean's candle
butts and fused itself in Stephen's consciousness with the jingle of the words, bucket and lamp and lamp and bucket. The   485
priest's voice too had a hard jingling tone. Stephen's mind
halted by instinct, checked by the strange tone and the imagery
and by the priest's face which seemed like an unlit lamp or a
reflector hung in a false focus. What lay behind it or within it?
A dull torpor of the soul or the dullness of the thundercloud,   490
charged with intellection and capable of the gloom of God?

—I meant a different kind of lamp, sir, said Stephen.

—Undoubtedly, said the dean.

—One difficulty, said Stephen, in esthetic discussion is to
know whether words are being used according to the literary   495
tradition or according to the tradition of the marketplace. I
remember a sentence of Newman's in which he says of the
Blessed Virgin that she was detained in the full company of the
saints. The use of the word in the marketplace is quite differ=
ent. *I hope I am not detaining you.*   500

—Not in the least, said the dean politely.

---

472 or borrow] ABSENT Eg–64   479 one of] Eg; ABSENT MS   481 in] Eg; ABSENT MS

4. Greek Stoic philosopher (c. 55–c. 135), whose *Discourses* include the comparison of the
   soul to a container of water and the story of the lamps mentioned below.

—No, no, said Stephen smiling, I mean . . . .

—Yes, yes: I see, said the dean quickly, I quite catch the point: *detain*.

He thrust forward his under jaw and uttered a dry short 505 cough.

—To return to the lamp, he said, the feeding of it is also a nice problem. You must choose the pure oil and you must be careful when you pour it in not to overflow it, not to pour in more than the funnel can hold.   510

—What funnel? asked Stephen.

—The funnel through which you pour the oil into your lamp.

—That? said Stephen. Is that called a funnel? Is it not a tun= dish?[5]

—What is a tundish?   515

—That. The . . . the funnel.

—Is that called a tundish in Ireland? asked the dean. I never heard the word in my life.

—It is called a tundish in Lower Drumcondra,[6] said Stephen laughing, where they speak the best English.   520

—A tundish! said the dean reflectively. That is a most interest= ing word. I must look that word up. Upon my word I must.

His courtesy of manner rang a little false and Stephen looked at the English convert with the same eyes as the elder brother in the parable may have turned on the prodigal.[7] A humble fol= 525 lower in the wake of clamorous conversions, a poor English= man in Ireland, he seemed to have entered on the stage of jesuit history when that strange play of intrigue and suffering and envy and struggle and indignity had been all but given through —a latecomer, a tardy spirit.[8] From what had he set out? Per= 530 haps he had been born and bred among serious dissenters,[9] seeing salvation in Jesus only and abhorring the vain pomps of the establishment. Had he felt the need of an implicit faith amid the welter of sectarianism and the jargon of its turbulent schisms, six principle men, peculiar people, seed and snake 535 baptists, supralapsarian dogmatists?[1] Had he found the true church all of a sudden in winding up to the end like a reel of cotton some finespun line of reasoning upon insufflation or the

---

519 Lower] Eg; ABSENT MS

5. An English word, found in Shakespeare, now little used, but not Irish in origin.
6. Northern suburb of Dublin.
7. The story of the obedient son and his prodigal younger brother is told in Luke 15:11–32.
8. Late convert, long after the highly publicized conversions, including Newman's, which occurred in 1845.
9. Protestants who were not members of the Anglican Church, the established church in England.
1. Dissenting sects, all Baptist, with distinctive beliefs.

imposition of hands or the procession of the Holy Ghost?[2] Or
had Lord Christ touched him and bidden him follow, like that   540
disciple who had sat at the receipt of custom,[3] as he sat by the
door of some zincroofed chapel,[4] yawning and telling over his
church pence?

The dean repeated the word yet again.

—Tundish! Well now, that is interesting!   545

—The question you asked me a moment ago seems to me more
interesting. What is that beauty which the artist struggles to
express from lumps of earth, said Stephen coldly.

The little word seemed to have turned a rapier point of his
sensitiveness against this courteous and vigilant foe. He felt   550
with a smart of dejection that the man to whom he was speak=
ing was a countryman of Ben Jonson. He thought:

—The language in which we are speaking is his before it is
mine. How different are the words *home, Christ, ale, master* on
his lips and on mine! I cannot speak or write these words with=   555
out unrest of spirit. His language, so familiar and so foreign,
will always be for me an acquired speech. I have not made or
accepted its words. My voice holds them at bay. My soul frets
in the shadow of his language.

—And to distinguish between the beautiful and the sublime,   560
the dean added. To distinguish between moral beauty and ma=
terial beauty. And to inquire what kind of beauty is proper to
each of the various arts. These are some interesting points we
might take up.

Stephen, disheartened suddenly by the dean's firm dry tone,   565
was silent. The dean also was silent: and through the silence a
distant noise of many boots and confused voices came up the
staircase.

—In pursuing these speculations, said the dean conclusively,
there is however the danger of perishing of inanition. First you   570
must take your degree. Set that before you as your first aim.
Then, little by little, you will see your way. I mean in every
sense, your way in life and in thinking. It may be uphill pedal=
ling at first. Take Mr Moonan. He was a long time before he
got to the top. But he got there.   575

—I may not have his talent, said Stephen quietly.

---

2. Aspects of Catholic beliefs that are implicitly being compared to the idiosyncratic views
   of the dissenting sects. Insufflation involves breathing on someone to represent the coming of the Holy Ghost. The imposition, or laying on, of hands can pass on authority or expel evil. The doctrine of the Trinity (see note 7, p. 27) involves the Holy Ghost's
   proceeding from the Father and the Son together.
3. Matthew, who was collecting taxes when Jesus called him (Matthew 9:9).
4. In England, a freestanding place of worship for a dissenting sect is called a chapel rather
   than a church.

—You never know, said the dean brightly. We never can say
what is in us. I most certainly should not be despondent. *Per
aspera ad astra.*[5]

He left the hearth quickly and went towards the landing to   580
oversee the arrival of the first arts' class.

Leaning against the fireplace Stephen heard him greet briskly
and impartially every student of the class and could almost see
the frank smiles of the coarser students. A desolating pity be=
gan to fall like a dew upon his easily embittered heart for this   585
faithful servingman of the knightly Loyola, for this halfbrother
of the clergy, more venal than they in speech, more steadfast of
soul than they, one whom he would never call his ghostly fa=
ther: and he thought how this man and his companions had
earned the name of worldlings at the hands not of the un=   590
worldly only but of the worldly also for having pleaded, during
all their history, at the bar of God's justice for the souls of the
lax and the lukewarm and the prudent.

The entry of the professor was signalled by a few rounds of
Kentish fire[6] from the heavy boots of those students who sat on 595
the highest tier of the gloomy theatre under the grey cob=
webbed windows. The calling of the roll began and the re=
sponses to the names were given out in all tones until the name
of Peter Byrne was reached.

—Here!   600

A deep bass note in response came from the upper tier,
followed by coughs of protest along the other benches.

The professor paused in his reading and called the next
name:

—Cranly!   605

No answer.

—Mr Cranly!

A smile flew across Stephen's face as he thought of his
friend's studies.

—Try Leopardstown![7] said a voice from the bench behind.   610

Stephen glanced up quickly but Moynihan's snoutish face
outlined on the grey light was impassive. A formula was given
out. Amid the rustling of the notebooks Stephen turned back
again and said:

—Give me some paper for God' sake.   615

615 God'] MS; God's Eg—64

5. "Through difficulties to the stars" (Latin).
6. Extended hand clapping or, in this case, foot stamping; the expression is "said to have
   originated in reference to meetings held in Kent in 1828–1829" in opposition to proposed
   Catholic Emancipation (*OED*).
7. A track for horseracing, six miles south of central Dublin.

—Are you as bad as that? asked Moynihan with a broad grin.

He tore a sheet from his scribbler and passed it down, whis=
pering:

—In case of necessity any layman or woman can do it.

The formula which he wrote obediently on the sheet of   620
paper, the coiling and uncoiling calculations of the professor,
the spectrelike symbols of force and velocity fascinated and
jaded Stephen's mind. He had heard some say that the old
professor was an atheist freemason.[8] O the grey dull day! It
seemed a limbo of painless patient consciousness through   625
which souls of mathematicians might wander, projecting long
slender fabrics from plane to plane of ever rarer and paler
twilight, radiating swift eddies to the last verges of a universe
ever vaster, farther and more impalpable.

—So we must distinguish between elliptical and ellipsoidal.   630
Perhaps some of you gentlemen may be familiar with the works
of Mr W. S. Gilbert. In one of his songs he speaks of the
billiard sharp who is condemned to play:

> On a cloth untrue
> With a twisted cue   635
> And elliptical billiard balls.[9]

He means a ball having the form of the ellipsoid of the princi=
pal axes of which I spoke a moment ago.

Moynihan leaned down towards Stephen's ear and mur=
mured: 640

—What price ellipsoidal balls! Chase me, ladies, I'm in the
cavalry!

His fellowstudent's rude humour ran like a gust through the
cloister of Stephen's mind, shaking into gay life limp priestly
vestments that hung upon the walls, setting them to sway and 645
caper in a sabbath of misrule. The forms of the community
emerged from the gustblown vestments, the dean of studies,
the portly florid bursar with his cap of grey hair, the president,
the little priest with feathery hair who wrote devout verses, the
squat peasant form of the professor of economics, the tall form 650
of the young professor of mental science discussing on the
landing a case of conscience with his class like a giraffe crop=
ping high leafage among a herd of antelopes, the grave troubled
prefect of the sodality, the plump roundheaded professor of

---

634 *untrue*] ⌐⟨*that's new*⟩ *untrue*⌐ MS

8. A contradiction in terms, because Freemasonry requires belief in God.
9. From the last act of the light opera *The Mikado* (1885), by W. S. Gilbert (1836–1911)
and Arthur Sullivan (1842–1900).

Italian with his rogue's eyes. They came ambling and stum= 655
bling, tumbling and capering, kilting their gowns for leap frog,
holding one another back, shaken with deep false laughter,
smacking one another behind and laughing at their rude mal=
ice, calling to one another by familiar nicknames, protesting
with sudden dignity at some rough usage, whispering two and 660
two behind their hands.

The professor had gone to the glass cases on the sidewall
from a shelf of which he took down a set of coils, blew away
the dust from many points and, bearing it carefully to the table,
held a finger on it while he proceeded with his lecture. He 665
explained that the wires in modern coils were of a compound
called platinoid lately discovered by F. W. Martino.[1]

He spoke clearly the initials and surname of the discoverer.
Moynihan whispered from behind:
—Good old Fresh Water Martin! 670
—Ask him, Stephen whispered back with weary humour, if he
wants a subject for electrocution. He can have me.

Moynihan, seeing the professor bend over the coils, rose in
his bench and, clacking noiselessly the fingers of his right hand,
began to call with the voice of a slobbering urchin: 675
—Please, teacher! Please, teacher! This boy is after saying a
bad word, teacher.
—Platinoid, the professor said solemnly, is preferred to Ger=
man silver because it has a lower coefficient of resistance
variation by changes of temperature. The platinoid wire is in= 680
sulated and the covering of silk that insulates it is wound
double on the ebonite bobbins just where my finger is. If it
were wound single an extra current would be induced in the
coils. The bobbins are saturated in hot paraffinwax . . .

A sharp Ulster[2] voice said from the bench below Stephen: 685
—Are we likely to be asked questions on applied science?

The professor began to juggle gravely with the terms pure
science and applied science. A heavybuilt student wearing gold
spectacles stared with some wonder at the questioner. Moyni=
han murmured from behind in his natural voice: 690
—Isn't MacAlister a devil for his pound of flesh?

Stephen looked down coldly on the oblong skull beneath

657 false] fast 64   682 double] MS; ABSENT Eg–64

1. Fernando Wood Martin (1863–1933), American chemist, may be meant. *Encyclopedia Britannica* mentions "Martino" as having introduced platinoid but gives no identifying information (*Enc. Brit.* 6:857n.2).
2. One of the four traditional provinces of Ireland, located in the northeast portion of the island, where Protestants are in the majority.

him overgrown with tangled twinecoloured hair. The voice, the
accent, the mind of the questioner offended him and he allowed
the offence to carry him towards wilful unkindness, bidding his   695
mind think that the student's father would have done better
had he sent his son to Belfast[3] to study and have saved some=
thing on the trainfare by so doing.

The oblong skull beneath did not turn to meet this shaft of
thought and yet the shaft came back to its bowstring: for he   700
saw in a moment the student's wheypale face.

—That thought is not mine, he said to himself quickly. It came
from the comic Irishman in the bench behind. Patience. Can
you say with certitude by whom the soul of your race was
bartered and its elect betrayed—by the questioner or by the   705
mocker? Patience. Remember Epictetus. It is probably in his
character to ask such a question at such a moment in such a
tone and to pronounce the word *science* as a monosyllable.

The droning voice of the professor continued to wind itself
slowly round and round the coils it spoke of, doubling,   710
trebling, quadrupling its somnolent energy as the coil multi=
plied its ohms of resistance.

Moynihan's voice called from behind in echo to a distant
bell:

—Closing time, gents!   715

The entrance hall was crowded and loud with talk. On a
table near the door were two photographs in frames and be=
tween them a long roll of paper bearing an irregular tail of
signatures. MacCann went briskly to and fro among the stu=
dents, talking rapidly, answering rebuffs and leading one after   720
another to the table. In the inner hall the dean of studies stood
talking to a young professor, stroking his chin gravely and nod=
ding his head.

Stephen, checked by the crowd at the door, halted irresol=
utely. From under the wide falling leaf of a soft hat Cranly's   725
dark eyes were watching him.

—Have you signed? Stephen asked.

Cranly closed his long thinlipped mouth, communed with
himself an instant and answered:

—*Ego habeo.*[4]   730

—What is it for?

—*Quod?*[5]

—What is it for?

---

3. Largest city in Ulster and the location of Queen's University.
4. "I have." The first in a series of joking statements in simplified Latin.
5. "What?"

Cranly turned his pale face to Stephen and said blandly and
bitterly: 735
—*Per pax universalis.*[6]
Stephen pointed to the Czar's photograph[7] and said:
—He has the face of a besotted Christ.
The scorn and anger in his voice brought Cranly's eyes back
from a calm survey of the walls of the hall.   740
—Are you annoyed? he asked.
—No, answered Stephen.
—Are you in bad humour?
—No.
—*Credo ut vos sanguinarius mendax estis*, said Cranly, *quia*   745
facies vostra monstrat ut vos in damno malo humore estis.[8]
Moynihan, on his way to the table, said in Stephen's ear:
—MacCann is in tiptop form. Ready to shed the last drop.
Brandnew world. No stimulants and votes for the bitches.
Stephen smiled at the manner of this confidence and, when   750
Moynihan had passed, turned again to meet Cranly's eyes.
—Perhaps you can tell me, he said, why he pours his soul so
freely into my ear. Can you?
A dull scowl appeared on Cranly's forehead. He stared at
the table where Moynihan had bent to write his name on the   755
roll, and then said flatly:
—A sugar![9]
—*Quis est in malo humore*, said Stephen, *ego aut vos?*[1]
Cranly did not take up the taunt. He brooded sourly on his
judgment and repeated with the same flat force: 760
—A flaming bloody sugar, that's what he is!
It was his epitaph for all dead friendships and Stephen won=
dered whether it would ever be spoken in the same tone over
his memory. The heavy lumpish phrase sank slowly out of
hearing like a stone through a quagmire. Stephen saw it sink as   765
he had seen many an other, feeling its heaviness depress his
heart. Cranly's speech, unlike that of Davin, had neither rare
phrases of Elizabethan English nor quaintly turned versions of
Irish idioms. Its drawl was an echo of the quays of Dublin
given back by a bleak decaying seaport, its energy an echo of   770

766 an other,] MS; another, Eg–64

6. "For universal peace."
7. Photograph of Czar Nicholas II (1868–1918) of Russia, on display with one of his wife,
   Czarina Alexandra Feodorovna (1872–1918).
8. "I believe that you are a bloody liar and from the expression on your face that you are in a
   damned bad mood."
9. A euphemistic play on the word *shit*, with which *sugar* shares an initial sound (*Letters* III,
   129–30).
1. "Who is in a bad mood, me or you?"

the sacred eloquence of Dublin given back flatly by a Wicklow pulpit.[2]

The heavy scowl faded from Cranly's face as MacCann marched briskly towards them from the other side of the hall.

—Here you are! said MacCann cheerily.   775

—Here I am! said Stephen.

—Late as usual. Can you not combine the progressive tendency[3] with a respect for punctuality?

—That question is out of order, said Stephen. Next business.

His smiling eyes were fixed on a silverwrapped tablet of milk   780 chocolate which peeped out of the propagandist's breastpocket. A little ring of listeners closed round to hear the war of wits. A lean student with olive skin and lank black hair thrust his face between the two, glancing from one to the other at each phrase and seeming to try to catch each flying phrase in his open moist   785 mouth. Cranly took a small grey handball from his pocket and began to examine it closely, turning it over and over.

—Next business? said MacCann. Hom!

He gave a loud cough of laughter, smiled broadly and tugged twice at the strawcoloured goatee which hung from his   790 blunt chin.

—The next business is to sign the testimonial.

—Will you pay me anything if I sign? asked Stephen.

—I thought you were an idealist, said MacCann.

The gipsylike student looked about him and addressed the   795 onlookers in an indistinct bleating voice.

—By hell, that's a queer notion. I consider that notion to be a mercenary notion.

His voice faded into silence. No heed was paid to his words. He turned his olive face, equine in expression, towards Ste=   800 phen, inviting him to speak again.

MacCann began to speak with fluent energy of the Czar's rescript,[4] of Stead,[5] of general disarmament, arbitration in cases of international disputes, of the signs of the times, of the new humanity and the new gospel of life which would make it the   805 business of the community to secure as cheaply as possible the greatest possible happiness of the greatest possible number.

---

2. Davin, who grew up on the land, retains in his speaking the influence of Elizabethan English combined with Irish turns of phrase. By contrast, Cranly's speech is a degenerated version of eighteenth-century Irish orators' eloquence.
3. Progressive political beliefs, that is, socialistic attitudes.
4. Nicholas II's "Peace Rescript" (1898), which led to a peace conference in the Hague in 1899 and to discussions involving the people, issues, and attitudes mentioned in the paragraph.
5. William Thomas Stead (1849–1912), English journalist, who actively opposed war and published The United States of Europe (1899).

The gipsy student responded to the close of the period by crying:
—Three cheers for universal brotherhood!   810
—Go on, Temple, said a stout ruddy student near him. I'll stand you a pint after.
—I'm a believer in universal brotherhood, said Temple, glancing about him out of his dark oval eyes. Marx is only a bloody cod.[6]   815

Cranly gripped his arm tightly to check his tongue, smiling uneasily, and repeated:
—Easy, easy, easy!

Temple struggled to free his arm but continued, his mouth flecked by a thin foam: 820
—Socialism was founded by an Irishman and the first man in Europe who preached the freedom of thought was Collins.[7] Two hundred years ago. He denounced priestcraft. The philosopher of Middlesex. Three cheers for John Anthony Collins!

A thin voice from the verge of the ring replied: 825
—Pip! pip!

Moynihan murmured beside Stephen's ear:
—And what about John Anthony's poor little sister:

> Lottie Collins lost her drawers;
> Won't you kindly lend her yours?[8]   830

Stephen laughed and Moynihan, pleased with the result, murmured again:
—We'll have five bob each way on John Anthony Collins.[9]
—I am waiting for your answer, said MacCann briefly.
—The affair doesn't interest me in the least, said Stephen   835
wearily. You knew that well. Why do you make a scene about it?
—Good! said MacCann, smacking his lips. You are a reaction=ary then?
—Do you think you impress me, Stephen asked, when you   840
flourish your wooden sword?
—Metaphors! said MacCann bluntly. Come to facts.

Stephen blushed and turned aside. MacCann stood his ground and said with hostile humour:

---

823 priestcraft. The] priestcraft, the Eg–64   836 knew] know Eg–64

6. Fool.
7. Anthony Collins (1676–1729), English theologian, author of *A Discourse of Free-thinking* (1713), that is, thinking free of institutionalized religion and its dogma.
8. The joking rhyme refers to an English music-hall performer of the 1890s.
9. Five shillings to place and five to show, as though Collins were a race horse (*Letters* III, 130).

—Minor poets, I suppose, are above such trivial questions as   845
the question of universal peace.

Cranly raised his head and held the handball between the
two students by way of a peaceoffering, saying:

—*Pax super totum sanguinarium globum.*[1]

Stephen, moving away the bystanders, jerked his shoulder   850
angrily in the direction of the Czar's image, saying:

—Keep your icon. If we must have a Jesus let us have a legit=
imate Jesus.

—By hell, that's a good one! said the gipsy student to those
about him. That's a fine expression. I like that expression   855
immensely.

He gulped down the spittle in his throat as if he were gulp=
ing down the phrase and, fumbling at the peak of his tweed
cap, turned to Stephen, saying:

—Excuse me, sir, what do you mean by that expression you   860
uttered just now?

Feeling himself jostled by the students near him, he said to
them:

—I am curious to know now what he meant by that ex=
pression.   865

He turned again to Stephen and said in a whisper:

—Do you believe in Jesus? I believe in man. Of course, I don't
know if you believe in man. I admire you, sir. I admire the
mind of man independent of all religions. Is that your opinion
about the mind of Jesus?   870

—Go on, Temple, said the stout ruddy student returning, as
was his wont, to his first idea, that pint is waiting for you.

—He thinks I'm an imbecile, Temple explained to Stephen,
because I'm a believer in the power of mind.

Cranly linked his arms into those of Stephen and his admirer   875
and said:

—*Nos ad manum ballum jocabimus.*[2]

Stephen, in the act of being led away, caught sight of
MacCann's flushed bluntfeatured face.

—My signature is of no account, he said politely. You are right   880
to go your way. Leave me to go mine.

—Dedalus, said MacCann crisply, I believe you're a good fel=
low but you have yet to learn the dignity of altruism and the
responsibility of the human individual.

A voice said: 885

881 your] Eg; your own MS

1. More joking Latin: "Peace over the entire bloody globe."
2. Modified Latin: "Let's go play handball."

—Intellectual crankery is better out of this movement than in it.

Stephen, recognising the harsh tone of MacAlister's voice, did not turn in the direction of the voice. Cranly pushed sol= emnly through the throng of students, linking Stephen and Temple like a celebrant attended by his ministers on his way to the altar.

Temple bent eagerly across Cranly's breast and said:

—Did you hear MacAlister what he said? That youth is jealous of you. Did you see that? I bet Cranly didn't see that. By hell, I saw that at once.

As they crossed the inner hall the dean of studies was in the act of escaping from the student with whom he had been con= versing. He stood at the foot of the staircase, a foot on the lowest step, his threadbare soutane gathered about him for the ascent with womanish care, nodding his head often and repeating:

—Not a doubt of it, Mr Hackett! Very true! Not a doubt of it!

In the middle of the hall the prefect of the college sodality was speaking earnestly, in a soft querulous voice, with a boarder. As he spoke he wrinkled a little his freckled brow and bit, between his phrases, at a tiny bone pencil.

—I hope the matric men will all come. The first arts men are pretty sure. Second arts too. We must make sure of the new= comers.[3]

Temple bent again across Cranly, as they were passing through the doorway, and said in a swift whisper:

—Do you know that he is a married man? He was a married man before they converted him. He has a wife and children somewhere. By hell, I think that's the queerest notion I ever heard! Eh?

His whisper trailed off into sly cackling laughter. The mo= ment they were through the doorway Cranly seized him rudely by the neck and shook him, saying:

—You flaming floundering fool! I'll take my dying bible there isn't a bigger bloody ape, do you know, than you in the whole flaming bloody world!

Temple wriggled in his grip, laughing still with sly content, while Cranly repeated flatly at every rude shake:

—A flaming flaring bloody idiot!

890

895

900

905

910

915

920

925

903 true!] fine! Eg–64

3. First-, second-, and third-year students, called by the names of the examinations they were required to take at the end of each year; "matric": short for matriculation.

They crossed the weedy garden together. The president, wrapped in a heavy loose cloak, was coming towards them along one of the walks, reading his office. At the end of the walk he halted before turning and raised his eyes. The students saluted, Temple fumbling as before at the peak of his cap. They walked forward in silence. As they neared the alley Stephen could hear the thuds of the players' hands and the wet smacks of the ball and Davin's voice crying out excitedly at each stroke.

The three students halted round the box on which Davin sat to follow the game. Temple, after a few moments, sidled across to Stephen and said:

—Excuse me, I wanted to ask you do you believe that Jean Jacques Rousseau[4] was a sincere man?

Stephen laughed outright. Cranly, picking up the broken stave of a cask from the grass at his foot, turned swiftly and said sternly:

—Temple, I declare to the living God if you say another word, do you know, to anybody on any subject I'll kill you *super spottum*.[5]

—He was like you, I fancy, said Stephen, an emotional man.

—Blast him, curse him! said Cranly broadly. Don't talk to him at all. Sure you might as well be talking, do you know, to a flaming chamberpot as talking to Temple. Go home, Temple. For God' sake go home.

—I don't care a damn about you, Cranly, answered Temple, moving out of reach of the uplifted stave and pointing at Ste= phen. He's the only man I see in this institution that has an individual mind.

—Institution! Individual! cried Cranly. Go home, blast you, for you're a hopeless bloody man.

—I'm an emotional man, said Temple. That's quite rightly expressed. And I'm proud that I'm an emotionalist.

He sidled out of the alley, smiling slily. Cranly watched him with a blank expressionless face.

—Look at him! he said. Did you ever see such a go-by-the-wall?

His phrase was greeted by a strange laugh from a student who lounged against the wall, his peaked cap down on his eyes. The laugh, pitched in a high key and coming from a so muscu=

950 God'] God's Eg–64

4. Swiss thinker (1712–1778), whose writings about the contractual responsibilities of governments to the people anticipated the French Revolution.
5. "On the spot" (simplified Latin).

lar frame, seemed like the whinny of an elephant. The student's body shook all over and, to ease his mirth, he rubbed both his hands delightedly over his groins.

—Lynch is awake, said Cranly.

Lynch, for answer, straightened himself and thrust forward 970 his chest.

—Lynch puts out his chest, said Stephen, as a criticism of life.

Lynch smote himself sonorously on the chest and said:

—Who has anything to say about my girth?

Cranly took him at the word and the two began to tussle. 975 When their faces had flushed with the struggle they drew apart, panting. Stephen bent down towards Davin who, intent on the game, had paid no heed to the talk of the others.

—And how is my little tame goose? he asked. Did he sign too?

Davin nodded and said: 980

—And you, Stevie?

Stephen shook his head.

—You're a terrible man, Stevie, said Davin, taking the short pipe from his mouth. Always alone.

—Now that you have signed the petition for universal peace, 985 said Stephen, I suppose you will burn that little copybook I saw in your room.

As Davin did not answer Stephen began to quote:

—Long pace, fianna! Right incline, fianna! Fianna, by num= bers, salute, one, two![6] 990

—That's a different question, said Davin. I'm an Irish nation= alist, first and foremost. But that's you all out. You're a born sneerer, Stevie.

—When you make the next rebellion with hurleysticks,[7] said Stephen, and want the indispensable informer, tell me. I can 995 find you a few in this college.

—I can't understand you, said Davin. One time I hear you talk against English literature. Now you talk against the Irish in= formers. What with your name and your ideas. . . . Are you Irish at all? 1000

—Come with me now to the office of arms[8] and I will show you the tree of my family, said Stephen.

—Then be one of us, said Davin. Why don't you learn Irish? Why did you drop out of the league class[9] after the first lesson?

---

967 body] aEg; trunk MS–Eg

6. Military drill instructions from Davin's Fenian handbook. "Fianna" means warriors (Gaelic).
7. The bladed sticks used in the traditional Irish game of hurling.
8. Coats of arms, that is, genealogies.
9. Gaelic League class to learn Irish.

—You know one reason why, answered Stephen.   1005
  Davin tossed his head and laughed.
—O, come now, he said. Is it on account of that certain young
lady and Father Moran? But that's all in your own mind,
Stevie. They were only talking and laughing.
  Stephen paused and laid a friendly hand upon Davin's 1010
shoulder.
—Do you remember, he said, when we knew each other first.
The first morning we met you asked me to show you the
way to the matriculation class, putting a very strong stress on
the first syllable. You remember? Then you used to address the 1015
jesuits as father,[1] you remember? I ask myself about you: *Is
he as innocent as his speech?*
—I'm a simple person, said Davin. You know that. When you
told me that night in Harcourt Street those things about your
private life, honest to God, Stevie, I was not able to eat my 1020
dinner. I was quite bad. I was awake a long time that night.
Why did you tell me those things?
—Thanks, said Stephen. You mean I am a monster.
—No, said Davin, but I wish you had not told me.
  A tide began to surge beneath the calm surface of Stephen's 1025
friendliness.
—This race and this country and this life produced me, he
said. I shall express myself as I am.
—Try to be one of us, repeated Davin. In your heart you are an
Irishman but your pride is too powerful.   1030
—My ancestors threw off their language and took on another,
Stephen said. They allowed a handful of foreigners to subject
them. Do you fancy I am going to pay in my own life and
person debts they made? What for?
—For our freedom, said Davin.   1035
—No honourable and sincere man, said Stephen, has given up
to you his life and his youth and his affections from the days of
Tone to those of Parnell but you sold him to the enemy or
failed him in need or reviled him and left him for another. And
you invite me to be one of you. I'd see you damned first.   1040
—They died for their ideals, Stevie, said Davin. Our day will
come yet,[2] believe me.
  Stephen, following his own thought, was silent for an in=
stant.

1031 on] MS; ABSENT Eg–64

1. A form of address that Davin brings from the country. More worldly city dwellers address
Jesuits as "sir."
2. Fenian slogan.

—The soul is born, he said vaguely, first in those moments I 1045
told you of. It has a slow and dark birth, more mysterious than
the birth of the body. When the soul of a man is born in this
country there are nets flung at it to hold it back from flight.
You talk to me of nationality, language, religion. I shall try to
fly by those nets.   1050
    Davin knocked the ashes from his pipe.
—Too deep for me, Stevie, he said. But a man's country comes
first. Ireland first, Stevie. You can be a poet or a mystic after.
—Do you know what Ireland is? asked Stephen with cold
violence. Ireland is the old sow that eats her farrow.   1055
    Davin rose from his box and went towards the players,
shaking his head sadly. But in a moment his sadness left him
and he was hotly disputing with Cranly and the two players
who had finished their game. A match of four was arranged,
Cranly insisting, however, that his ball should be used. He let it 1060
rebound twice or thrice to his hand and then struck it strongly
and swiftly towards the base of the alley, exclaiming in answer
to its thud:
—Your soul!
    Stephen stood with Lynch till the score began to rise. Then 1065
he plucked him by the sleeve to come away. Lynch obeyed,
saying:
—Let us eke[3] go, as Cranly has it.
    Stephen smiled at this sidethrust. They passed back through
the garden and out through the hall where the doddering porter 1070
was pinning up a notice in the frame. At the foot of the steps
they halted and Stephen took a packet of cigarettes from his
pocket and offered it to his companion.
—I know you are poor, he said.
—Damn your yellow insolence, answered Lynch.   1075
    This second proof of Lynch's culture made Stephen smile
again.
—It was a great day for European culture, he said, when you
made up your mind to swear in yellow.[4]
    They lit their cigarettes and turned to the right. After a 1080
pause Stephen began:
—Aristotle has not defined pity and terror.[5] I have. I say . . .

1053 a(2)] a16; ABSENT MS–16, 64   1061 then] ABSENT Eg–64

3. Lynch echoes Cranly's habitual speech, in which he misuses the archaic word "eke,"
   meaning also (Letters III, 130).
4. Lynch jokingly transforms the conventional use of bloody as a swear by his substitution
   (Letters III, 130).
5. Terms that Aristotle uses in his Poetics to describe the achievement of catharsis in tragedy.

Lynch halted and said bluntly:

—Stop! I won't listen! I am sick. I was out last night on a yellow drunk with Horan and Goggins.   1085

Stephen went on:

—Pity is the feeling which arrests the mind in the presence of whatsoever is grave and constant in human sufferings and unites it with the human sufferer. Terror is the feeling which arrests the mind in the presence of whatsoever is grave and   1090 constant in human sufferings and unites it with the secret cause.

—Repeat, said Lynch.

Stephen repeated the definitions slowly.

—A girl got into a hansom a few days ago, he went on, in   1095 London. She was on her way to meet her mother whom she had not seen for many years. At the corner of a street the shaft of a lorry shivered the window of the hansom in the shape of a star. A long fine needle of the shivered glass pierced her heart. She died on the instant. The reporter called it a tragic death. It   1100 is not. It is remote from terror and pity according to the terms of my definitions.

The tragic emotion, in fact, is a face looking two ways, towards terror and towards pity, both of which are phases of it. You see I use the word *arrest*. I mean that the tragic emotion   1105 is static. Or rather the dramatic emotion is. The feelings ex= cited by improper art are kinetic, desire or loathing. Desire urges us to possess, to go to something, loathing urges us to abandon, to go from something. These are kinetic emotions. The arts which excite them, pornographical or didactic, are   1110 therefore improper arts. The esthetic emotion (I use the general term) is therefore static. The mind is arrested and raised above desire and loathing.

—You say that art must not excite desire, said Lynch. I told you that one day I wrote my name in pencil on the backside of   1115 the Venus of Praxiteles in the Museum.[6] Was that not desire?

—I speak of normal natures, said Stephen. You also told me that when you were a boy in that charming carmelite school[7] you ate pieces of dried cowdung.

Lynch broke again into a whinny of laughter and again   1120 rubbed both his hands over his groins but without taking them from his pockets.

—O, I did! I did! he cried.

6. Plaster cast of a nude Venus by the Greek sculptor Praxiteles (4th century BCE), which stood in the National Museum.
7. Run by the Carmelites, the order of Our Lady of Mount Carmel.

Stephen turned towards his companion and looked at him
for a moment boldly in the eyes. Lynch, recovering from his   1125
laughter, answered his look from his humbled eyes. The long
slender flattened skull beneath the long pointed cap brought
before Stephen's mind the image of a hooded reptile. The eyes,
too, were reptilelike in glint and gaze. Yet at that instant,
humbled and alert in their look, they were lit by one tiny   1130
human point, the window of a shrivelled soul, poignant and
selfembittered.

—As for that, Stephen said in polite parenthesis, we are all
animals. I also am an animal.

—You are, said Lynch.   1135

—But we are just now in a mental world, Stephen continued.
The desire and loathing excited by improper esthetic means are
really not esthetic emotions not only because they are kinetic
in character but also because they are not more than physical.
Our flesh shrinks from what it dreads and responds to the   1140
stimulus of what it desires by a purely reflex action of the nerv=
ous system. Our eyelid closes before we are aware that the fly is
about to enter our eye.

—Not always, said Lynch critically.

—In the same way, said Stephen, your flesh responded to the   1145
stimulus of a naked statue but it was, I say, simply a reflex
action of the nerves. Beauty expressed by the artist cannot
awaken in us an emotion which is kinetic or a sensation which
is purely physical. It awakens, or ought to awaken, or induces,
or ought to induce, an esthetic stasis, an ideal pity or an ideal 1150
terror, a stasis called forth, prolonged and at last dissolved by
what I call the rhythm of beauty.

—What is that exactly? asked Lynch.

—Rhythm, said Stephen, is the first formal esthetic relation of
part to part in any esthetic whole or of an esthetic whole to its 1155
part or parts or of any part to the esthetic whole of which it is a
part.

—If that is rhythm, said Lynch, let me hear what you call
beauty: and, please remember, though I did eat a cake of cow=
dung once, that I admire only beauty.   1160

Stephen raised his cap as if in greeting. Then, blushing
slightly, he laid his hand on Lynch's thick tweed sleeve.

—We are right, he said, and the others are wrong. To speak of
these things and to try to understand their nature and, having
understood it, to try slowly and humbly and constantly to   1165

express, to press out again, from the gross earth or what it brings forth, from sound and shape and colour which are the prison gates of our soul, an image of the beauty we have come to understand–that is art.

They had reached the canal bridge[8] and, turning from their course, went on by the trees. A crude grey light, mirrored in the sluggish water, and a smell of wet branches over their heads seemed to war against the course of Stephen's thought. 1170

—But you have not answered my question, said Lynch. What is art? What is the beauty it expresses? 1175

—That was the first definition I gave you, you sleepyheaded wretch, said Stephen, when I began to try to think out the matter for myself. Do you remember the night? Cranly lost his temper and began to talk about Wicklow bacon.

—I remember, said Lynch. He told us about them flaming fat devils of pigs. 1180

—Art, said Stephen, is the human disposition of sensible or intelligible matter for an esthetic end. You remember the pigs and forget that. You are a distressing pair, you and Cranly.

Lynch made a grimace at the raw grey sky and said: 1185

—If I am to listen to your esthetic philosophy give me at least another cigarette. I don't care about it. I don't even care about women. Damn you and damn everything. I want a job of five hundred a year. You can't get me one.

Stephen handed him the packet of cigarettes. Lynch took the last one that remained, saying simply: 1190

—Proceed!

—Aquinas, said Stephen, says that is beautiful the apprehen= sion of which pleases.

Lynch nodded. 1195

—I remember that, he said. *Pulcra sunt quae visa placent.*

—He uses the word *visa*, said Stephen, to cover esthetic appre= hension of all kinds, whether through sight or hearing or through any other avenue of apprehension. This word, though it is vague, is clear enough to keep away good and evil which excite desire and loathing. It means certainly a stasis and not a kinesis. How about the true? It produces also a stasis of the mind. You would not write your name in pencil across the hypothenuse of a rightangled triangle. 1200

—No, said Lynch. Give me the hypothenuse of the Venus of Praxiteles. 1205

1197–98   apprehension] MS; apprehensions Eg–64

8. Over the Grand Canal in south Dublin.

—Static therefore, said Stephen. Plato, I believe, said that
beauty is the splendour of truth.[9] I don't think that it has a
meaning but the true and the beautiful are akin. Truth is beheld
by the intellect which is appeased by the most satisfying   1210
relations of the intelligible: beauty is beheld by the imagination
which is appeased by the most satisfying relations of the sen=
sible. The first step in the direction of truth is to understand the
frame and scope of the intellect itself, to comprehend the act
itself of intellection. Aristotle's entire system of philosophy   1215
rests upon his book of psychology and that, I think, rests on his
statement that the same attribute cannot at the same time and
in the same connection belong to and not belong to the same
subject.[1] The first step in the direction of beauty is to under=
stand the frame and scope of the imagination, to comprehend   1220
the act itself of esthetic apprehension. Is that clear?
—But what is beauty? asked Lynch impatiently. Out with an=
other definition. Something we see and like! Is that the best you
and Aquinas can do?
—Let us take woman, said Stephen.   1225
—Let us take her! said Lynch fervently.
—The Greek, the Turk, the Chinese, the Copt, the Hottentot,
said Stephen, all admire a different type of female beauty. That
seems to be a maze out of which we cannot escape. I see
however two ways out. One is this hypothesis: that every physi=   1230
cal quality admired by men in women is in direct connection
with the manifold functions of women for the propagation of
the species. It may be so. The world, it seems, is drearier than
even you, Lynch, imagined. For my part I dislike that way out.
It leads to eugenics rather than to esthetic. It leads you out of   1235
the maze into a new gaudy lectureroom where MacCann, with
one hand on *The Origin of Species*[2] and the other hand on the
new testament, tells you that you admired the great flanks of
Venus because you felt that she would bear you burly offspring
and admired her great breasts because you felt that she would   1240
give good milk to her children and yours.
—Then MacCann is a sulphuryellow liar, said Lynch energeti=
cally.
—There remains another way out, said Stephen laughing.
—To wit? said Lynch.   1245

9. Plato comments on truth and beauty in his dialogues that concern art, the *Symposium* and the *Phaedrus*.
1. Aristotle wrote about the mind, but he never produced a book narrowly about psychology. Stephen correctly claims that Aristotle's prohibition against contradiction is central to his thinking about identity.
2. Published in 1859 by the English naturalist Charles Darwin (1809–1882), whose claims about evolution posed challenges to Christian beliefs.

—This hypothesis, Stephen began.

A long dray laden with old iron came round the corner of sir Patrick Dun's hospital covering the end of Stephen's speech with the harsh roar of jangled and rattling metal. Lynch closed his ears and gave out oath after oath till the dray had passed. 1250 Then he turned on his heel rudely. Stephen turned also and waited for a few moments till his companion's illhumour had had its vent.

—This hypothesis, Stephen repeated, is the other way out: that, though the same object may not seem beautiful to all 1255 people, all people who admire a beautiful object find in it certain relations which satisfy and coincide with the stages themselves of all esthetic apprehension. These relations of the sensible, visible to you through one form and to me through another, must be therefore the necessary qualities of beauty. 1260 Now, we can return to our old friend saint Thomas for another pennyworth of wisdom.

Lynch laughed.

—It amuses me vastly, he said, to hear you quoting him time after time like a jolly round friar. Are you laughing in your 1265 sleeve?

—MacAlister, answered Stephen, would call my esthetic the= ory applied Aquinas. So far as this side of esthetic philosophy extends Aquinas will carry me all along the line. When we come to the phenomenon of artistic conception, artistic gesta= 1270 tion and artistic reproduction I require a new terminology and a new personal experience.

—Of course, said Lynch. After all Aquinas, in spite of his intellect, was exactly a good round friar. But you will tell me about the new personal experience and new terminology some 1275 other day. Hurry up and finish the first part.

—Who knows? said Stephen smiling. Perhaps Aquinas would understand me better than you. He was a poet himself. He wrote a hymn for Maundy Thursday. It begins with the words *Pange lingua gloriosi*.[3] They say it is the highest glory of the 1280 hymnal. It is an intricate and soothing hymn. I like it: but there is no hymn that can be put beside that mournful and majestic processional song, the *Vexilla Regis* of Venantius Fortunatus.[4]

1270 phenomenon] MS; phenomena Eg–64

3. Partial Latin title of a hymn, sung on Maundy Thursday, the day before Good Friday, *Pange Lingua Gloriosi Corporis Mysterium* ("Tell, My Tongue, of the Mystery of Christ's Glorious Body"). The hymn is by Fortunatus (6th century), not Aquinas (*Cath. Enc.*).
4. Partial Latin title of another hymn sung on Maundy Thursday, *Vexilla Regis Prodeunt* ("The Banners of the King Advance").

Lynch began to sing softly and solemnly in a deep bass
voice: 1285

> Impleta sunt quae concinit
> David fideli carmine
> Dicendo nationibus
> Regnavit a ligno Deus.[5]

—That's great! he said, well pleased. Great music!   1290
They turned into Lower Mount Street. A few steps from the
corner a fat young man, wearing a silk neckcloth, saluted them
and stopped.
—Did you hear the results of the exams? he asked. Griffin was
plucked. Halpin and O'Flynn are through the home civil.   1295
Moonan got fifth place in the Indian. O'Shaughenessy got four=
teenth.[6] The Irish fellows in Clarke's gave them a feed last night.
They all ate curry.
His pallid bloated face expressed benevolent malice and, as
he had advanced through his tidings of success, his small   1300
fatencircled eyes vanished out of sight and his weak wheezing
voice out of hearing.
In reply to a question of Stephen's his eyes and his voice
came forth again from their lurkingplaces.
—Yes. MacCullagh and I, he said. He's taking pure mathemat=   1305
ics and I'm taking constitutional history. There are twenty
subjects. I'm taking botany too. You know I'm a member of the
field club.
He drew back from the other two in a stately fashion and
placed a plump woollengloved hand on his breast from which   1310
muttered wheezing laughter at once broke forth.
—Bring us a few turnips and onions the next time you go out
said Stephen drily, to make a stew.
The fat student laughed indulgently and said:
—We are all highly respectable people in the field club. Last   1315
Saturday we went out to Glenmalure,[7] seven of us.
—With women, Donovan? said Lynch.
Donovan again laid his hand on his chest and said:
—Our end is the acquisition of knowledge.
Then he said quickly: 1320

1289 *Regnavit*] Eg; *Regnavi* MS   1299 malice] Eg, 16; mirth MS; malice, Eg

5. The second stanza of *Pange Lingua,* these lines concern David's having foretold in his
   songs that God would rule the nations from a tree, that is, a cross.
6. The exam results pertain to gaining a place in the British civil service, the government administration at home and abroad. "Plucked" means failed. "Through" means success, in
   this case for posts in the United Kingdom. Doing well on the "Indian" exams enables serving in the British Empire's administration of India.
7. Valley in County Wicklow.

—I hear you are writing some essay about esthetics.

Stephen made a vague gesture of denial.

—Goethe and Lessing,[8] said Donovan, have written a lot on that subject, the classical school and the romantic school and all that. The *Laocoon*[9] interested me very much when I read it. 1325 Of course it is idealistic, German, ultraprofound.

Neither of the others spoke. Donovan took leave of them urbanely.

—I must go, he said softly and benevolently. I have a strong suspicion, amounting almost to a conviction, that my sister 1330 intended to make pancakes today for the dinner of the Don= ovan family.

—Goodbye, Stephen said in his wake. Don't forget the turnips for me and my mate.

Lynch gazed after him, his lip curling in slow scorn till his 1335 face resembled a devil's mask:

—To think that that yellow pancakeeating excrement can get a good job, he said at length, and I have to smoke cheap ciga= rettes!

They turned their faces towards Merrion Square and went 1340 on for a little in silence.

—To finish what I was saying about beauty, said Stephen, the most satisfying relations of the sensible must therefore corre= spond to the necessary phases of artistic apprehension. Find these and you find the qualities of universal beauty. Aquinas 1345 says: *ad pulcritudinem tria requiruntur, integritas, consonantia, claritas*. I translate it so: *Three things are needed for beauty, wholeness, harmony and radiance*. Do these correspond to the phases of apprehension? Are you following?

—Of course, I am, said Lynch. If you think I have an excre= 1350 mentitious intelligence run after Donovan and ask him to listen to you.

Stephen pointed to a basket which a butcher's boy had slung inverted on his head.

—Look at that basket, he said.   1355

—I see it, said Lynch.

—In order to see that basket, said Stephen, your mind first of all separates the basket from the rest of the visible universe which is not the basket. The first phase of apprehension is a bounding line drawn about the object to be apprehended. An 1360

8. Johann Wolfgang von Goethe (1749–1832) and Gotthold Ephraim Lessing (1729–1781), German writers.

9. Lessing's book of that title (1766), on the differences in character and value between lit- erature as a temporal art and sculpture as a spatial art, involves centrally the large Greek sculpture of Laocoön and his two sons struggling with serpents.

esthetic image is presented to us either in space or in time.
What is audible is presented in time, what is visible is presented
in space. But temporal or spatial the esthetic image is first
luminously apprehended as selfbounded and selfcontained
upon the immeasurable background of space or time which is   1365
not it. You apprehend it as *one* thing. You see it as one whole.
You apprehend its wholeness. That is *integritas*.
—Bull's eye! said Lynch laughing. Go on.
—Then, said Stephen, you pass from point to point, led by its
formal lines; you apprehend it as balanced part against part   1370
within its limits; you feel the rhythm of its structure. In other
words the synthesis of immediate perception is followed by the
analysis of apprehension. Having first felt that it is *one* thing
you feel now that it is a *thing*. You apprehend it as complex,
multiple, divisible, separable, made up of its parts, the result of   1375
its parts and their sum, harmonious. That is *consonantia*.
—Bull's eye again! said Lynch wittily. Tell me now what is
claritas and you win the cigar.
—The connotation of the word, Stephen said, is rather vague.
Aquinas uses a term which seems to be inexact. It baffled me   1380
for a long time. It would lead you to believe that he had in
mind symbolism or idealism, the supreme quality of beauty
being a light from some other world, the idea of which the
matter is but the shadow, the reality of which it is but the
symbol. I thought he might mean that *claritas* is the artistic   1385
discovery and representation of the divine purpose in anything
or a force of generalisation which would make the esthetic
image a universal one, make it outshine its proper conditions.
But that is literary talk. I understand it so. When you have
apprehended that basket as one thing and have then analysed it   1390
according to its form and apprehended it as a thing you make
the only synthesis which is logically and esthetically permiss=
ible. You see that it is that thing which it is and no other thing.
The radiance of which he speaks is the scholastic *quidditas*, the
whatness of a thing. This supreme quality is felt by the artist   1395
when the esthetic image is first conceived in his imagination.
The mind in that mysterious instant Shelley likened beautifully
to a fading coal.[1] The instant wherein that supreme quality of
beauty, the clear radiance of the esthetic image, is apprehended
luminously by the mind which has been arrested by its whole=   1400
ness and fascinated by its harmony is the luminous silent stasis

1384–85 is] a16; was MS–16 [THREE TIMES]

1. The comparison, in "A Defence of Poetry" (1821), suggests that some invisible power, like
a wind, from within causes a fleeting glow.

of esthetic pleasure, a spiritual state very like to that cardiac condition which the Italian physiologist Luigi Galvani, using a phrase almost as beautiful as Shelley's, called the enchantment of the heart.[2]

1405

Stephen paused and, though his companion did not speak, felt that his words had called up around them a thoughten= chanted silence.

—What I have said, he began again, refers to beauty in the wider sense of the word, in the sense which the word has in the 1410 literary tradition. In the marketplace it has another sense. When we speak of beauty in the second sense of the term our judgment is influenced in the first place by the art itself and by the form of that art. The image, it is clear, must be set between the mind or senses of the artist himself and the mind or senses 1415 of others. If you bear this in memory you will see that art necessarily divides itself into three forms progressing from one to the next. These forms are: the lyrical form, the form wherein the artist presents his image in immediate relation to himself; the epical form, the form wherein he presents his image in 1420 mediate relation to himself and to others; the dramatic form, the form wherein he presents his image in immediate relation to others.

—That you told me a few nights ago, said Lynch, and we began the famous discussion.

1425

—I have a book at home, said Stephen, in which I have written down questions which are more amusing than yours were. In finding the answers to them I found the theory of esthetic which I am trying to explain. Here are some questions I set myself: *Is a chair finely made tragic or comic? Is the portrait of* 1430 *Mona Lisa good if I desire to see it? Is the bust of sir Philip Crampton[3] lyrical, epical or dramatic? Can excrement or a child or a louse be a work of art? If not, why not?*

—Why not, indeed? said Lynch laughing.

—*If a man hacking in fury at a block of wood*, Stephen con= 1435 tinued, *make there an image of a cow is that image a work of art? If not, why not?*

—That's a lovely one, said Lynch laughing again. That has the true scholastic stink.

—Lessing, said Stephen, should not have taken a group of 1440 statues to write of. The art, being inferior, does not present the

2. Galvani (1737–1798), an Italian scientist, described the pause in a frog's heartbeat when the frog's heart was pierced with a needle.
3. A grotesque bust of Crampton (1777–1858), a famous surgeon, once stood near Trinity College on a drinking fountain.

forms I spoke of distinguished clearly one from another. Even
in literature, the highest and most spiritual art, the forms are
often confused. The lyrical form is in fact the simplest verbal
vesture of an instant of emotion, a rhythmical cry such as ages   1445
ago cheered on the man who pulled at the oar or dragged
stones up a slope. He who utters it is more conscious of the
instant of emotion than of himself as feeling emotion. The
simplest epical form is seen emerging out of lyrical literature
when the artist prolongs and broods upon himself as the centre   1450
of an epical event and this form progresses till the centre of
emotional gravity is equidistant from the artist himself and
from others. The narrative is no longer purely personal. The
personality of the artist passes into the narration itself, flowing
round and round the persons and the action like a vital sea.   1455
This progress you will see easily in that old English ballad
Turpin Hero which begins in the first person and ends in the
third person.[4] The dramatic form is reached when the vitality
which has flowed and eddied round each person fills every
person with such vital force that he or she assumes a proper   1460
and intangible esthetic life. The personality of the artist at first
a cry or a cadence or a mood and then a fluid and lambent
narrative finally refines itself out of existence, impersonalises
itself, so to speak. The esthetic image in the dramatic form is
life purified in and reprojected from the human imagination.   1465
The mystery of esthetic like that of material creation is accom=
plished. The artist, like the God of the creation, remains within
or behind or beyond or above his handiwork, invisible, refined
out of existence, indifferent, paring his fingernails.[5]
—Trying to refine them also out of existence, said Lynch.   1470
   A fine rain began to fall from the high veiled sky and they
turned into the duke's lawn to reach the national library[6] before
the shower came.
—What do you mean, Lynch asked surlily, by prating about
beauty and the imagination in this miserable Godforsaken is=   1475
land? No wonder the artist retired within or behind his handi=
work after having perpetrated this country.
   The rain fell faster. When they passed through the passage

---

4. Some versions of this ballad about the eighteenth-century highwayman Dick Turpin include the shift in person.
5. This statement resembles one made by the French novelist Gustave Flaubert
   (1821–1880) in a famous letter of 1857, where he asserts that the artist in the work must
   be like God in the created world, invisible, all powerful, felt everywhere but not seen.
6. The Duke of Leinster's residence, called Leinster House (originally Kildare House), and
   its small lawn are in the same complex of buildings as the National Library.

beside Kildare house they found many students sheltering un=
der the arcade of the library. Cranly leaning against a pillar ₁₄₈₀
was picking his teeth with a sharpened match, listening to some
companions. Some girls stood near the entrance door. Lynch
whispered to Stephen:

—Your beloved is here.

Stephen took his place silently on the step below the group ₁₄₈₅
of students, heedless of the rain which fell fast, turning his eyes
towards her from time to time. She too stood silently among
her companions. She has no priest to flirt with, he thought with
conscious bitterness, remembering how he had seen her last.
Lynch was right. His mind, emptied of theory and courage, ₁₄₉₀
lapsed back into a listless peace.

He heard the students talking among themselves. They
spoke of two friends who had passed the final medical exam=
ination, of the chances of getting places on ocean liners, of
poor and rich practices.   ₁₄₉₅

—That's all a bubble. An Irish country practice is better.

—Hynes was two years in Liverpool and he says the same. A
frightful hole he said it was. Nothing but midwifery cases. Half
a crown cases.[7]

—Do you mean to say it is better to have a job here in the ₁₅₀₀
country than in a rich city like that? I know a fellow . . . .

—Hynes has no brains. He got through by stewing, pure
stewing.[8]

—Don't mind him. There's plenty of money to be made in a
big commercial city.   ₁₅₀₅

—Depends on the practice.

—*Ego credo ut vita pauperum est simpliciter atrox, simpliciter
sanguinarius atrox, in Liverpoolio.*[9]

Their voices reached his ears as if from a distance in inter=
rupted pulsation. She was preparing to go away with her ₁₅₁₀
companions.

The quick light shower had drawn off, tarrying in clusters of
diamonds among the shrubs of the quadrangle where an exha=
lation was breathed forth by the blackened earth. Their trim
boots prattled as they stood on the steps of the colonnade ₁₅₁₅
talking quietly and gaily, glancing at the clouds, holding their

---

1479 Kildare house] a16 [cf UNPUBLISHED LETTER TO HARRIET SHAW WEAVER, *c.* 20 Nov.
1917, BRITISH LIBRARY]; the Royal Irish Academy MS–16, 64

7. Poor Irish inhabitants of this large English city across the Irish Channel could not afford
    medical care.
8. Hard study rather than natural ability.
9. Joke Latin: "I believe that the life of the poor is simply frightful, simply bloody frightful,
    in Liverpool."

umbrellas at cunning angles against the few last raindrops, closing them again, holding their skirts demurely.

And if he had judged her harshly? If her life were a simple rosary of hours, her life simple and strange as a bird's life, gay 1520 in the morning, restless all day, tired at sundown? Her heart simple and wilful as a bird's heart?

◆ ◆ ◆

Towards dawn he awoke. O what sweet music! His soul was all dewy wet. Over his limbs in sleep pale cool waves of light had passed. He lay still, as if his soul lay amid cool waters, 1525 conscious of faint sweet music. His mind was waking slowly to a tremulous morning knowledge, a morning inspiration. A spirit filled him, pure as the purest water, sweet as dew, moving as music. But how faintly it was inbreathed, how passionlessly as if the seraphim themselves were breathing upon him! His 1530 soul was waking slowly, fearing to awake wholly. It was that windless hour of dawn when madness wakes and strange plants open to the light and the moth flies forth silently.

An enchantment of the heart! The night had been enchanted. In dream or vision he had known the ecstasy of seraphic life.[1] 1535 Was it an instant of enchantment only or long hours and days and years and ages?

The instant of inspiration seemed now to be reflected from all sides at once from a multitude of cloudy circumstance of what had happened or of what might have happened. The in= 1540 stant flashed forth like a point of light and now from cloud on cloud of vague circumstance confused form was veiling softly its afterglow. O! In the virgin womb of the imagination the word was made flesh. Gabriel the seraph had come to the virgin's chamber.[2] An afterglow deepened within his spirit, 1545 whence the white flame had passed, deepening to a rose and ardent light. That rose and ardent light was her strange wilful heart, strange that no man had known or would know, wilful from before the beginning of the world: and lured by that ardent roselike glow the choirs of the seraphim were falling 1550 from heaven.

> *Are you not weary of ardent ways,*
> *Lure of the fallen seraphim?*
> *Tell no more of enchanted days.*

1. The life of the seraphs, the highest ranking angels.
2. The passage echoes New Testament passages concerning the future birth of Jesus. At the moment "the Word was made flesh" (John 1:14), Gabriel, an archangel, not a seraph, announces to Mary the character of her pregnancy (Luke 1:26–38).

The verses passed from his mind to his lips and, murmuring 1555
them over, he felt the rhythmic movement of a villanelle[3] pass
through them. The roselike glow sent forth its rays of rhyme;
ways, days, blaze, praise, raise. Its rays burned up the world,
consumed the hearts of men and angels: the rays from the rose
that was her wilful heart. 1560

> Your eyes have set man's heart ablaze
> And you have had your will of him.
> Are you not weary of ardent ways?

And then? The rhythm died away, ceased, began again to
move and beat. And then? Smoke, incense ascending from the 1565
altar of the world.

> Above the flame the smoke of praise
> Goes up from ocean rim to rim.
> Tell no more of enchanted days.

Smoke went up from the whole earth, from the vapoury 1570
oceans, smoke of her praise. The earth was like a swinging
swaying smoking censer, a ball of incense, an ellipsoidal ball.
The rhythm died out at once; the cry of his heart was broken.
His lips began to murmur the first verses over and over; then
went on stumbling through half verses, stammering and 1575
baffled; then stopped. The heart's cry was broken.

The veiled windless hour had passed and behind the panes
of the naked window the morning light was gathering. A bell
beat faintly very far away. A bird twittered; two birds, three.
The bell and the birds ceased: and the dull white light spread 1580
itself east and west, covering the world, covering the roselight
in his heart.

Fearing to lose all he raised himself suddenly on his elbow to
look for paper and pencil. There was neither on the table; only
the soup plate he had eaten the rice from for supper and the 1585
candlestick with its tendrils of tallow and its paper socket,
singed by the last flame. He stretched his arm wearily towards
the foot of the bed, groping with his hand in the pockets of the
coat that hung there. His fingers found a pencil and then a
cigarette packet. He lay back and, tearing open the packet, 1590
placed the last cigarette on the window ledge and began to
write out the stanzas of the villanelle in small neat letters on the
rough cardboard surface.

1572 swaying smoking] swaying Eg–24; smoking swaying 64   1580 birds] bird Eg–64

3. Complex French poetic form using only two rhymes and requiring specific repetitions of
   rhymes and lines.

Having written them out he lay back on the lumpy pillow, murmuring them again. The lumps of knotted flock under his head reminded him of the lumps of knotted horsehair in the sofa of her parlour on which he used to sit, smiling or serious, asking himself why he had come, displeased with her and with himself, confounded by the print of the Sacred Heart[4] above the untenanted sideboard. He saw her approach him in a lull of the talk and beg him to sing one of his curious songs. Then he saw himself sitting at the old piano, striking chords softly from its speckled keys and singing, amid the talk which had risen again in the room, to her who leaned beside the mantelpiece a dainty song of the Elizabethans, a sad and sweet loth to depart, the victory chant of Agincourt,[5] the happy air of Greensleeves.[6] While he sang and she listened, or feigned to listen, his heart was at rest but when the quaint old songs had ended and he heard again the voices in the room he remembered his own sarcasm: the house where young men are called by their chris= tian names a little too soon.

At certain instants her eyes seemed about to trust him but he had waited in vain. She passed now dancing lightly across his memory as she had been that night at the carnival ball. Her white dress a little lifted, a white spray nodding in her hair. She danced lightly in the round. She was dancing towards him and, as she came, her eyes were a little averted and a faint glow was on her cheek. At the pause in the chain of hands her hand had lain in his an instant, a soft merchandise.

—You are a great stranger now.

—Yes. I was born to be a monk.

—I am afraid you are a heretic.

—Are you much afraid?

For answer she had danced away from him along the chain of hands, dancing lightly and discreetly, giving herself to none. The white spray nodded to her dancing and when she was in shadow the glow was deeper on her cheek.

A monk! His own image started forth a profaner of the cloister, a heretic franciscan, willing and willing not to serve, spinning like Gherardino da Borgo San Donnino[7] a lithe web of sophistry and whispering in her ear.

1595 · 1600 · 1605 · 1610 · 1615 · 1620 · 1625 · 1630

1624 him] aEg; ABSENT MS–Eg

4. A representation of Jesus, frequently hung on the walls of Irish Catholic homes, with his heart showing to indicate his love.
5. Where the English defeated the French (1415).
6. A sixteenth-century English ballad in which the singer complains to the lady Greensleeves about her disdaining him.
7. Thirteenth-century Franciscan who was condemned for heresy because of his efforts to return the order to stricter practices.

No, it was not his image. It was the image of the young priest in whose company he had seen her last, looking at him out of dove's eyes, toying with the pages of her Irish phrase= book. 1635

—Yes, yes, the ladies are coming round to us. I can see it every day. The ladies are with us. The best helpers the language has.

—And the church, Father Moran?

—The church too. Coming round too. The work is going ahead there too. Don't fret about the church. 1640

Bah! he had done well to leave the room in disdain. He had done well not to salute her on the steps of the library. He had done well to leave her to flirt with her priest, to toy with a church which was the scullerymaid of christendom.

Rude brutal anger routed the last lingering instant of ecstasy 1645 from his soul. It broke up violently her fair image and flung the fragments on all sides. On all sides distorted reflections of her image started from his memory: the flowergirl in the ragged dress with damp coarse hair and a hoyden's face who had called herself his own girl and begged his handsel, the kitchen= 1650 girl in the next house who sang over the clatter of her plates with the drawl of a country singer the first bars of *By Killarney's Lakes and Fells*,[8] a girl who had laughed gaily to see him stumble when the iron grating in the footpath near Cork Hill had caught the broken sole of his shoe, a girl he had 1655 glanced at, attracted by her small ripe mouth as she passed out of Jacob's biscuit factory, who had cried to him over her shoul= der:

—Do you like what you seen of me, straight hair and curly eyebrows? 1660

And yet he felt that, however he might revile and mock her image, his anger was also a form of homage. He had left the classroom in disdain that was not wholly sincere, feeling that perhaps the secret of her race lay behind those dark eyes upon which her long lashes flung a quick shadow. He had told him= 1665 self bitterly as he walked through the streets that she was a figure of the womanhood of her country, a batlike soul waking to the consciousness of itself in darkness and secrecy and lone= liness, tarrying a while, loveless and sinless, with her mild lover and leaving him to whisper of innocent transgressions in the 1670 latticed ear of a priest.[9] His anger against her found vent in

1632 was(2)] was like Eg–64   1643 well] Eg; ABSENT MS   1659 seen] aEg; saw MS–Eg   1669 a while,] awhile, Eg–64

8. Ballad from the opera *Inisfallen,* by the Irish composer Michael Balfe (1808–1870).
9. "Latticed" from being pressed up against the separating grid in the confessional.

coarse railing at her paramour, whose name and voice and
features offended his baffled pride: a priested peasant, with a
brother a policeman in Dublin and a brother a potboy in
Moycullen.[1] To him she would unveil her soul's shy nakedness,   1675
to one who was but schooled in the discharging of a formal rite
rather than to him, a priest of the eternal imagination, trans=
muting the daily bread of experience into the radiant body of
everliving life.[2]

The radiant image of the eucharist united again in an instant   1680
his bitter and despairing thoughts, their cries arising unbroken
in a hymn of thanksgiving.

> *Our broken cries and mournful lays*
> *Rise in one eucharistic hymn.*
> *Are you not weary of ardent ways?*   1685

> *While sacrificing hands upraise*
> *The chalice flowing to the brim.*
> *Tell no more of enchanted days.*

He spoke the verses aloud from the first lines till the music
and rhythm suffused his mind, turning it to quiet indulgence;   1690
then copied them painfully to feel them the better by seeing
them; then lay back on his bolster.

The full morning light had come. No sound was to be heard:
but he knew that all around him life was about to awaken in
common noises, hoarse voices, sleepy prayers. Shrinking from   1695
that life he turned towards the wall, making a cowl of the
blanket and staring at the great overblown scarlet flowers of
the tattered wallpaper. He tried to warm his perishing joy in
their scarlet glow, imagining a roseway from where he lay
upwards to heaven all strewn with scarlet flowers. Weary!   1700
Weary! He too was weary of ardent ways.

A gradual warmth, a languorous weariness passed over him
descending along his spine from his closely cowled head. He
felt it descend and, seeing himself as he lay, smiled. Soon he
would sleep.   1705

He had written verses for her again after ten years. Ten years
before she had worn her shawl cowlwise about her head, send=
ing sprays of her warm breath into the night air, tapping her
foot upon the glassy road. It was the last tram; the lank brown
horses knew it and shook their bells to the clear night in   1710

1675 Moycullen.] aEg; Athenry. MS–Eg   1676 in] Eg; to MS   1677 the] MS; ABSENT 64

1. Someone serving pots of drinks in a pub in Moycullen, a village in County Galway.
2. Stephen understands his role as artist as essentially similar to that of a Catholic priest,
   who transforms bread into the consecrated Host.

admonition. The conductor talked with the driver, both nod=
ding often in the green light of the lamp. They stood on the
steps of the tram, he on the upper, she on the lower. She came
up to his step many times between their phrases and went
down again and once or twice remained beside him forgetting   1715
to go down and then went down. Let be! Let be!

Ten years from that wisdom of children to his folly. If he
sent her the verses? They would be read out at breakfast amid
the tapping of eggshells. Folly indeed! The brothers would
laugh and try to wrest the page from each other with their   1720
strong hard fingers. The suave priest, her uncle, seated in his
armchair, would hold the page at arm's length, read it smiling
and approve of the literary form.

No, no: that was folly. Even if he sent her the verses she
would not show them to others. No, no: she could not.   1725

He began to feel that he had wronged her. A sense of her
innocence moved him almost to pity her, an innocence he had
never understood till he had come to the knowledge of it
through sin, an innocence which she too had not understood
while she was innocent or before the strange humiliation of her   1730
nature[3] had first come upon her. Then first her soul had begun
to live as his soul had when he had first sinned: and a tender
compassion filled his heart as he remembered her frail pallor
and her eyes, humbled and saddened by the dark shame of
womanhood.   1735

While his soul had passed from ecstasy to languor where had
she been? Might it be, in the mysterious ways of spiritual life,
that her soul at those same moments had been conscious of his
homage? It might be.

A glow of desire kindled again his soul and fired and ful=   1740
filled all his body. Conscious of his desire she was waking from
odorous sleep, the temptress of his villanelle. Her eyes, dark
and with a look of languor, were opening to his eyes. Her
nakedness yielded to him, radiant, warm, odorous and lavish=
limbed, enfolded him like a shining cloud, enfolded him like   1745
water with a liquid life: and like a cloud of vapour or like
waters circumfluent in space the liquid letters of speech, sym=
bols of the element of mystery, flowed forth over his brain.

> *Are you not weary of ardent ways?*
> *Lure of the fallen seraphim.*   1750
> *Tell no more of enchanted days.*

1749 *ways?*] e:MS; *ways,* Eg–64

3. Her menstrual period.

V   197

Your eyes have set man's heart ablaze
And you have had your will of him.
Are you not weary of ardent ways?

Above the flame the smoke of praise   1755
Goes up from ocean rim to rim.
Tell no more of enchanted days.

Our broken cries and mournful lays
Rise in one eucharistic hymn.
Are you not weary of ardent ways?   1760

While sacrificing hands upraise
The chalice flowing to the brim.
Tell no more of enchanted days.

And still you hold our longing gaze
With languorous look and lavish limb.   1765
Are you not weary of ardent ways?
Tell no more of enchanted days.

◆   ◆   ◆

What birds were they?

He stood on the steps of the library to look at them, leaning
wearily on his ashplant.[4] They flew round and round the jutting   1770
shoulder of a house in Molesworth Street.[5] The air of the late
March evening made clear their flight, their dark darting
quivering bodies flying clearly against the sky as against a
limphung cloth of smoky tenuous blue.

He watched their flight: bird after bird: a dark flash, a   1775
swerve, a flash again, a dart aside, a curve, a flutter of wings.
He tried to count them before all their darting quivering bodies
passed: six, ten, eleven: and wondered were they odd or even in
number. Twelve, thirteen: for two came wheeling down from
the upper sky. They were flying high and low but ever round   1780
and round in straight and curving lines and ever flying from left
to right, circling about a temple of air.

He listened to their cries: like the squeak of mice behind the
wainscot: a shrill twofold note. But the notes were long and
shrill and whirring, unlike the cry of vermin, falling a third or a 1785
fourth and trilled as the flying beaks clove the air. Their cry
was shrill and clear and fine and falling like threads of silken
light unwound from whirring spools.

1765 *limb.*] e:MS, Eg; limb. MS; *limb!* Eg–64   1769 He NEW PARAGRAPH] NO PARAGRAPH
Eg–64   1783 their] the Eg–64

4. Sapling of the ash tree used as a walking stick (*OED*).
5. Off Kildare Street at the National Library and the National Museum.

The inhuman clamour soothed his ears in which his
mother's sobs and reproaches murmured insistently and the 1790
dark frail quivering bodies wheeling and fluttering and swerv=
ing round an airy temple of the tenuous sky soothed his eyes
which still saw the image of his mother's face.

Why was he gazing upwards from the steps of the porch,
hearing their shrill twofold cry, watching their flight? For an 1795
augury of good or evil? A phrase of Cornelius Agrippa[6] flew
through his mind and then there flew hither and thither shape=
less thoughts from Swedenborg[7] on the correspondence of birds
to things of the intellect and of how the creatures of the air
have their knowledge and know their times and seasons be= 1800
cause they, unlike man, are in the order of their life and have
not perverted that order by reason.

And for ages men had gazed upward as he was gazing at
birds in flight. The colonnade above him made him think
vaguely of an ancient temple and the ashplant on which he 1805
leaned wearily of the curved stick of an augur. A sense of fear
of the unknown moved in the heart of his weariness, a fear of
symbols and portents, of the hawklike man whose name he
bore soaring out of his captivity on osierwoven wings, of
Thoth, the god of writers, writing with a reed upon a tablet 1810
and bearing on his narrow ibis head the cusped moon.[8]

He smiled as he thought of the god's image for it made him
think of a bottlenosed judge in a wig, putting commas into a
document which he held at arm's length and he knew that he
would not have remembered the god's name but that it was like 1815
an Irish oath. It was folly. But was it for this folly that he was
about to leave for ever the house of prayer and prudence into
which he had been born and the order of life out of which he
had come?

They came back with shrill cries over the jutting shoulder of 1820
the house, flying darkly against the fading air. What birds were
they? He thought that they must be swallows who had come
back from the south. Then he was to go away? for they were
birds ever going and coming, building ever an unlasting home
under the eaves of men's houses and ever leaving the homes 1825
they had built to wander.

1823 away?] away 18–64

6. Heinrich Cornelius Agrippa von Nettesheim (1486–1535), German occult philosopher,
who discusses augury (divination by means of birds) in his *De Occulta Philosophia*
(1531).
7. Emmanuel Swedenborg (1688–1772), Swedish mystical philosopher and scientist.
8. Thoth, the ancient Egyptian god of wisdom and writing, was frequently depicted in human form with an ibis head crowned by the moon's horns.

> *Bend down your faces, Oona and Aleel.*
> *I gaze upon them as the swallow gazes*
> *Upon the nest under the eave before*
> *He wander the loud waters.*[9]   1830

A soft liquid joy like the noise of many waters flowed over
his memory and he felt in his heart the soft peace of silent
spaces of fading tenuous sky above the waters, of oceanic si=
lence, of swallows flying through the seadusk over the flowing
waters.   1835

A soft liquid joy flowed through the words where the soft
long vowels hurtled noiselessly and fell away, lapping and
flowing back and ever shaking the white bells of their waves in
mute chime and mute peal and soft low swooning cry: and he
felt that the augury he had sought in the wheeling darting birds   1840
and in the pale space of sky above him had come forth from his
heart like a bird from a turret quietly and swiftly.

Symbol of departure or of loneliness? The verses crooned in
the ear of his memory composed slowly before his remember=
ing eyes the scene of the hall on the night of the opening of the 1845
national theatre.[1] He was alone at the side of the balcony,
looking out of jaded eyes at the culture of Dublin in the stalls
and at the tawdry scenecloths and human dolls framed by the
garish lamps of the stage. A burly policeman sweated behind
him and seemed at every moment about to act. The catcalls   1850
and hisses and mocking cries ran in rude gusts round the hall
from his scattered fellowstudents.

—A libel on Ireland!

—Made in Germany![2]

—Blasphemy!   1855

—We never sold our faith!

—No Irish woman ever did it!

—We want no amateur atheists.

—We want no budding buddhists.[3]

A sudden soft hiss fell from the windows above him and he   1860

1837 noiselessly] noiselessly⟨,⟩ MS   1839 mute] ⁻|mute|ʳ MS [TWICE]   1841–42 from--
heart] ⁻|from--heart|ʳ MS   1844 the--of] ⁻|the--of|ʳ MS   1845 the opening of] ⁻|the
opening of|ʳ MS   1860 soft] e; brief MS; swift Eg–64 [REVISION MISREAD? CF 2071, 2076]
1860 fell--him] ⁻|⟨was heard⟩ fell--him|ʳ MS

9. Opening of Cathleen's dying farewell in the play *The Countess Cathleen* (1892), by the
   Irish poet and dramatist W. B. Yeats (1865–1939).
1. May 8, 1899, when *The Countess Cathleen,* the first production of the Irish Literary Theatre, drew protests because Cathleen gives up her soul to feed her people.
2. At the time, Germany would have been thought of as largely Protestant and Jewish, by
   contrast with Catholic Ireland.
3. Yeats and others involved in the nationalist literary revival held occult beliefs, participated
   in séances, and explored Eastern religions and thought.

knew that the electric lamps had been switched on in the readers' room. He turned into the pillared hall, now calmly lit, went up the staircase and passed in through the clicking turn=stile.

Cranly was sitting over near the dictionaries. A thick book, opened at the frontispiece, lay before him on the wooden rest. He leaned back in his chair, inclining his ear like that of a confessor to the face of the medical student who was reading to him a problem from the chess page of a journal. Stephen sat down at his right and the priest at the other side of the table closed his copy of *The Tablet*[4] with an angry snap and stood up.

Cranly gazed after him blandly and vaguely. The medical student went on in a softer voice:

—Pawn to king's fourth.[5]

—We had better go, Dixon, said Stephen in warning. He has gone to complain.

Dixon folded the journal and rose with dignity, saying:

—Our men retired in good order.

—With guns and cattle, added Stephen, pointing to the title=page of Cranly's book on which was printed *Diseases of the Ox*.

As they passed through a lane of the tables Stephen said:

—Cranly, I want to speak to you.

Cranly did not answer or turn. He laid his book on the counter and passed out, his wellshod feet sounding flatly on the floor. On the staircase he paused and gazing absently at Dixon repeated:

—Pawn to king's bloody fourth.

—Put it that way if you like, Dixon said.

He had a quiet toneless voice and urbane manners and on a finger of his plump clean hand he displayed at moments a signet ring.

As they crossed the hall a man of dwarfish stature came towards them. Under the dome of his tiny hat his unshaven face began to smile with pleasure and he was heard to murmur. The eyes were melancholy as those of a monkey.

—Good evening, captain, said Cranly, halting.

—Good evening, gentlemen, said the stubblegrown monkeyish face.

1862 readers'] reader's 16–64   1863 went] ⌐(and going) went⌐ MS   1880 printed]
a16; written MS–16   1890 toneless] Eg; ringless MS

4. A conservative Catholic weekly.
5. A typical opening move in chess.

—Warm weather for March, said Cranly. They have the win= 1900
dows open upstairs.

Dixon smiled and turned his ring. The blackish monkey=
puckered face pursed its human mouth with gentle pleasure
and its voice purred:

—Delightful weather for March. Simply delightful.   1905

—There are two nice young ladies upstairs, captain, tired of
waiting, Dixon said.

Cranly smiled and said kindly:

—The captain has only one love: sir Walter Scott. Isn't that so,
captain?   1910

—What are you reading now, captain? Dixon asked. *The Bride
of Lammermoor?*[6]

—I love old Scott, the flexible lips said. I think he writes some=
thing lovely. There is no writer can touch sir Walter Scott.

He moved a thin shrunken brown hand gently in the air in 1915
time to his praise and his thin quick eyelids beat often over his
sad eyes.

Sadder to Stephen's ear was his speech: a genteel accent, low
and moist, marred by errors:[7] and listening to it he wondered
was the story true and was the thin blood that flowed in his 1920
shrunken frame noble and come of an incestuous love?

The park trees were heavy with rain and rain fell still and
ever in the lake, lying grey like a shield. A game of swans[8] flew
there and the water and the shore beneath were fouled with
their greenwhite slime. They embraced softly impelled by the 1925
grey rainy light, the wet silent trees, the shieldlike witnessing
lake, the swans. They embraced without joy or passion, his
arm about his sister's neck. A grey woollen cloak was wrapped
athwart from her shoulder to her waist: and her fair head was
bent in willing shame. He had loose redbrown hair and tender 1930
shapely strong freckled hands. Face? There was no face seen.
The brother's face was bent upon her fair rainfragrant hair.
The hand freckled and strong and shapely and caressing was
Davin's hand.

He frowned angrily upon his thought and on the shrivelled 1935
mannikin who had called it forth. His father's gibes at the

1902 blackish] black⌐ish⌐ MS   1906 of] Eg; ABSENT MS   1921 noble and] ⌐noble
and⌐ MS   1921 of an] ⌐of an⌐ MS   1923 A--of] Eg; Old MS   1929 athwart] MS;
athwart her Eg–64

6. Novel (1819) by the Scottish writer Sir Walter Scott (1771–1832).
7. A combination of upper-class pronunciation and grammatical mistakes.
8. A flock kept for pleasure (*OED*).

Bantry gang[9] leaped out of his memory. He held them at a distance and brooded uneasily on his own thought again. Why were they not Cranly's hands? Had Davin's simplicity and in= nocence stung him more secretly?   1940

He walked on across the hall with Dixon, leaving Cranly to take leave elaborately of the dwarf.

Under the colonnade Temple was standing in the midst of a little group of students. One of them cried:

—Dixon, come over till you hear. Temple is in grand form.   1945

Temple turned on him his dark gipsy eyes.

—You're a hypocrite, O'Keeffe, he said. And Dixon's a smiler. By hell, I think that's a good literary expression.

He laughed slily, looking in Stephen's face, repeating:

—By hell, I'm delighted with that name. A smiler.   1950

A stout student who stood below them on the steps said:

—Come back to the mistress, Temple. We want to hear about that.

—He had, faith, Temple said. And he was a married man too. And all the priests used to be dining there. By hell, I think they 1955 all had a touch.[1]

—We shall call it riding a hack to spare the hunter,[2] said Dixon.

—Tell us, Temple, O'Keeffe said. How many quarts of porter have you in you?

—All your intellectual soul is in that phrase, O'Keeffe, said 1960 Temple with open scorn.

He moved with a shambling gait round the group and spoke to Stephen.

—Did you know that the Forsters are the kings of Belgium?[3] he asked.   1965

Cranly came out through the door of the entrance hall, his hat thrust back on the nape of his neck and picking his teeth with care.

—And here's the wiseacre, said Temple. Do you know that about the Forsters?   1970

He paused for an answer. Cranly dislodged a figseed from his teeth on the point of his rude toothpick and gazed at it intently.

1958 How] how Eg–64   1972 rude] Eg; ABSENT MS

9. A group of politicians from the town of Bantry, in County Cork, who were considered Parnell's betrayers, including Timothy Healy (1855–1931), who led the opposition to Parnell
  within the Irish Parliamentary Party after the adultery scandal.
1. Sexual contact.
2. Riding a workhorse instead of a more valuable, better-looking one.
3. A drunken claim, perhaps made jokingly as a play on the tendency to see Irish origins in
  unlikely places.

—The Forster family, Temple said, is descended from Baldwin the First, king of Flanders. He was called the Forester. Forester 1975 and Forster are the same name. A descendant of Baldwin the First, captain Francis Forster, settled in Ireland and married the daughter of the last chieftain of Clanbrassil. Then there are the Blake Forsters. That's a different branch.[4]

—From Baldhead, king of Flanders, Cranly repeated, rooting 1980 again deliberately at his gleaming uncovered teeth.

—Where did you pick up all that history? O'Keeffe asked.

—I know all the history of your family too, Temple said, turning to Stephen. Do you know what Giraldus Cambrensis[5] says about your family?   1985

—Is he descended from Baldwin too? asked a tall consumptive student with dark eyes.

—Baldhead, Cranly repeated, sucking at a crevice in his teeth.

—*Pernobilis et pervetusta familia,*[6] Temple said to Stephen.

The stout student who stood below them on the steps farted 1990 briefly. Dixon turned towards him saying in a soft voice:

—Did an angel speak?

Cranly turned also and said vehemently but without anger:

—Goggins, you're the flamingest dirty devil I ever met, do you know.   1995

—I had it on my mind to say that, Goggins answered firmly. It did no-one any harm, did it?

—We hope, Dixon said suavely, that it was not of the kind known to science as a *paulo post futurum.*[7]

—Didn't I tell you he was a smiler? said Temple, turning right 2000 and left. Didn't I give him that name?

—You did. We're not deaf, said the tall consumptive.

Cranly still frowned at the stout student below him. Then, with a snort of disgust, he shoved him violently down the steps.

—Go away from here, he said rudely. Go away, you stinkpot. 2005 And you are a stinkpot.

Goggins skipped down on to the gravel and at once returned to his place with good humour. Temple turned back to Stephen and asked:

—Do you believe in the law of heredity?   2010

—Are you drunk or what are you or what are you trying to say? asked Cranly, facing round on him with an expression of wonder.

---

4. More drunken claims parodying the enthusiasm for Irish genealogies.
5. Twelfth-century Welsh historian who wrote about Ireland.
6. "From a noble and venerable family" (Latin).
7. Latin name of a Greek verb tense for an event that will happen soon, jokingly used to express the hope that Goggins's fart has no future aspect.

—The most profound sentence ever written, Temple said with enthusiasm, is the sentence at the end of the zoology. Repro= 2015 duction is the beginning of death.

He touched Stephen timidly at the elbow and said eagerly:

—Do you feel how profound that is because you are a poet?

Cranly pointed his long forefinger.

—Look at him! he said with scorn to the others. Look at 2020 Ireland's hope!

They laughed at his words and gesture. Temple turned on him bravely, saying:

—Cranly, you're always sneering at me. I can see that. But I am as good as you are any day. Do you know what I think 2025 about you now as compared with myself?

—My dear man, said Cranly urbanely, you are incapable, do you know, absolutely incapable of thinking.

—But do you know, Temple went on, what I think of you and of myself compared together? 2030

—Out with it, Temple! the stout student cried from the steps. Get it out in bits!

Temple turned right and left, making sudden feeble gestures as he spoke.

—I'm a ballocks,[8] he said, shaking his head in despair. I am. 2035 And I know I am. And I admit it that I am.

Dixon patted him lightly on the shoulder and said mildly:

—And it does you every credit, Temple.

—But he, Temple said, pointing to Cranly. He is a ballocks too like me. Only he doesn't know it. And that's the only difference 2040 I see.

A burst of laughter covered his words. But he turned again to Stephen and said with a sudden eagerness:

—That word is a most interesting word. That's the only Eng= lish dual number.[9] Did you know? 2045

—Is it? Stephen said vaguely.

He was watching Cranly's firmfeatured suffering face, lit up now by a smile of false patience. The gross name had passed over it like foul water poured over an old stone image, patient of injuries: and, as he watched him, he saw him raise his hat in 2050 salute and uncover the black hair that stood up stiffly from his forehead like an iron crown.

She passed out from the porch of the library and bowed across Stephen in reply to Cranly's greeting. He also? Was there

---

2025 are] MS; ABSENT Eg–64   2051 up] ABSENT 18–24

8. Literally, a testicle; figuratively, a clumsy person.
9. Grammatical form that expresses a pair.

not a slight flush on Cranly's cheek? Or had it come forth at 2055
Temple's words? The light had waned. He could not see.

Did that explain his friend's listless silence, his harsh com=
ments, the sudden intrusions of rude speech with which he had
shattered so often Stephen's ardent wayward confessions? Ste=
phen had forgiven freely for he had found this rudeness also in 2060
himself towards himself. And he remembered an evening when
he had dismounted from a borrowed creaking bicycle to pray
to God in a wood near Malahide.[1] He had lifted up his arms
and spoken in ecstasy to the sombre nave of the trees, knowing
that he stood on holy ground and in a holy hour. And when 2065
two constabularymen had come into sight round a bend in the
gloomy road he had broken off his prayer to whistle loudly an
air from the last pantomime.

He began to beat the frayed end of his ashplant against the
base of a pillar. Had Cranly not heard him? Yet he could wait. 2070
The talk about him ceased for a moment: and a soft hiss fell
again from a window above. But no other sound was in the air
and the swallows whose flight he had followed with idle eyes
were sleeping.

She had passed through the dusk. And therefore the air was 2075
silent save for one soft hiss that fell. And therefore the tongues
about him had ceased their babble. Darkness was falling.

Darkness falls from the air.[2]

A trembling joy, lambent as a faint light, played like a fairy
host around him. But why? Her passage through the darkening 2080
air or the verse with its black vowels and its opening sound,
rich and lutelike?

He walked away slowly towards the deeper shadows at the
end of the colonnade, beating the stone softly with his stick to
hide his revery from the students whom he had left: and 2085
allowed his mind to summon back to itself the age of Dowland
and Byrd and Nash.[3]

Eyes, opening from the darkness of desire, eyes that dimmed
the breaking east. What was their languid grace but the soft=
ness of chambering? And what was their shimmer but the 2090
shimmer of the scum that mantled the cesspool of the court of a

2076 soft] Eg; brief MS   2089 grace] Eg; ABSENT MS

1. Coastal village north of Dublin.
2. Misrecollection of the line, which concerns brightness falling, from "A Litany in Time of
   Plague" (1592), by the English poet and dramatist Thomas Nashe (1567–1601).
3. The Elizabethan and Jacobean era in England. Elizabeth I reigned 1558–1603. James I
   reigned 1603–25. John Dowland (c. 1563–1626) and William Byrd (1543–1623) were
   composers. "Nash" is a variation of "Nashe" (see previous note).

slobbering Stuart.[4] And he tasted in the language of memory
ambered wines,[5] dying fallings of sweet airs, the proud pavan:[6]
and saw with the eyes of memory kind gentlewomen in Covent
Garden[7] wooing from their balconies with sucking mouths and   2095
the poxfouled wenches of the taverns and young wives that,
gaily yielding to their ravishers, clipped[8] and clipped again.

The images he had summoned gave him no pleasure. They
were secret and enflaming but her image was not entangled by
them. That was not the way to think of her. It was not even the   2100
way in which he thought of her. Could his mind then not trust
itself? Old phrases, sweet only with a disinterred sweetness like
the figseeds Cranly rooted out of his gleaming teeth.

It was not thought nor vision though he knew vaguely that
her figure was passing homeward through the city. Vaguely   2105
first and then more sharply he smelt her body. A conscious
unrest seethed in his blood. Yes, it was her body that he smelt:
a wild and languid smell: the tepid limbs over which his music
had flowed desirously and the secret soft linen upon which her
flesh distilled odour and a dew.   2110

A louse crawled over the nape of his neck and, putting his
thumb and forefinger deftly beneath his loose collar, he caught
it. He rolled its body, tender yet brittle as a grain of rice, be=
tween thumb and finger for an instant before he let it fall from
him and wondered would it live or die. There came to his mind   2115
a curious phrase from Cornelius a Lapide[9] which said that the
lice born of human sweat were not created by God with the
other animals on the sixth day. But the tickling of the skin of
his neck made his mind raw and red. The life of his body,
illclad, illfed, louseeaten, made him close his eyelids in a sud=   2120
den spasm of despair: and in the darkness he saw the brittle
bright bodies of lice falling from the air and turning often as
they fell. Yes: and it was not darkness that fell from the air. It
was brightness.

2096 wenches] Eg–64; wenchers MS, 93   2107 that] ABSENT Eg–64   2119 red. The]
red⟨,⟩. ⟨t⟩ The MS

4. James I of England, who has often been compared unfavorably with his predecessor,
    Elizabeth I.
5. Perfumed with ambergris (*OED*).
6. An Elizabethan dance.
7. An area in the eastern part of central London that developed in the 1630s under the guid-
    ance of the English architect and stage designer Inigo Jones (1573–1652), who incorpo-
    rated what had been primarily a market for flowers, fruits, and vegetables into a piazza.
    When Charles II (1630–1685) let theaters reopen after eighteen years of Puritan repres-
    sion and allowed women to act in public for the first time, the first theater was in Covent
    Garden. Stephen's imagined memories have moved forward half a century from Dowland,
    Byrd, and Nash.
8. Embraced.
9. Flemish Jesuit (1567–1637), who made the following claim.

> *Brightness falls from the air.*   2125

He had not even remembered rightly Nash's line. All the
images it had awakened were false. His mind bred vermin. His
thoughts were lice born of the sweat of sloth.

He came back quickly along the colonnade towards the
group of students. Well then let her go and be damned to her.   2130
She could love some clean athlete who washed himself every
morning to the waist and had black hair on his chest. Let her.

Cranly had taken another dried fig from the supply in his
pocket and was eating it slowly and noisily. Temple sat on the
pediment of a pillar, leaning back, his cap pulled down on his   2135
sleepy eyes. A squat young man came out of the porch, a
leather portfolio tucked under his armpit. He marched towards
the group, striking the flags[1] with the heels of his boots and
with the ferrule[2] of his heavy umbrella. Then, raising the um=
brella in salute, he said to all: 2140

—Good evening, sirs.

He struck the flags again and tittered while his head
trembled with a slight nervous movement. The tall consump=
tive student and Dixon and O'Keeffe were speaking in Irish and
did not answer him. Then, turning to Cranly, he said: 2145

—Good evening, particularly to you.

He moved the umbrella in indication and tittered again.
Cranly, who was still chewing the fig, answered with loud
movements of his jaws.

—Good? Yes. It is a good evening.   2150

The squat student looked at him seriously and shook his
umbrella gently and reprovingly.

—I can see, he said, that you are about to make obvious
remarks.

—Um, Cranly answered, holding out what remained of the   2155
halfchewed fig and jerking it towards the squat student's
mouth in sign that he should eat.

The squat student did not eat it but, indulging his special
humour, said gravely, still tittering and prodding his phrase
with his umbrella: 2160

—Do you intend that . . .

He broke off, pointed bluntly to the munched pulp of the fig
and said loudly:

—I allude to that.

—Um, Cranly said as before.   2165

2133 dried] ⌐dried⌐ MS

1. Flagstones (*OED*).
2. Metal ring or cap to protect the end of a stick.

—Do you intend that now, the squat student said, as *ipso facto*[3] or, let us say, as so to speak?

Dixon turned aside from his group, saying:

—Goggins was waiting for you, Glynn. He has gone round to the Adelphi[4] to look for you and Moynihan. What have you there? he asked, tapping the portfolio under Glynn's arm.

—Examination papers, Glynn answered. I give them monthly examinations to see that they are profiting by my tuition.

He also tapped the portfolio and coughed gently and smiled.

—Tuition! said Cranly rudely. I suppose you mean the bare= footed children that are taught by a bloody ape like you. God help them!

He bit off the rest of the fig and flung away the butt.

—I suffer little children to come unto me,[5] Glynn said amiably.

—A bloody ape, Cranly repeated with emphasis, and a blas= phemous bloody ape!

Temple stood up and, pushing past Cranly, addressed Glynn:

—That phrase you said now, he said, is from the new testa= ment about suffer the children to come to me.

—Go to sleep again, Temple, said O'Keeffe.

—Very well, then, Temple continued, still addressing Glynn, and if Jesus suffered the children to come why does the church send them all to hell if they die unbaptised? Why is that?

—Were you baptised yourself, Temple? the consumptive stu= dent asked.

—But why are they sent to hell if Jesus said they were all to come? Temple said, his eyes searching in Glynn's eyes.

Glynn coughed and said gently, holding back with difficulty the nervous titter in his voice and moving his umbrella at every word:

—And, as you remark, if it is thus I ask emphatically whence comes this thusness.

—Because the church is cruel like all old sinners, Temple said.

—Are you quite orthodox on that point, Temple? Dixon said suavely.

—Saint Augustine says that about unbaptised children going to hell, Temple answered, because he was a cruel old sinner too.

—I bow to you, Dixon said, but I had the impression that limbo existed for such cases.

2170
2175
2180
2185
2190
2195
2200
2205

2193 in] ⁿˡinˡʳ MS

3. "By that very fact" (Latin); part of the meaningless babble of the conversation (*Letters* III, 130).
4. Adelphi Hotel, near the National Library.
5. Alludes to Mark 10:14.

—Don't argue with him, Dixon, Cranly said brutally. Don't talk to him or look at him. Lead him home with a sugan[6] the way you'd lead a bleating goat.

—Limbo! Temple cried. That's a fine invention too. Like hell.

—But with the unpleasantness left out, Dixon said.

He turned smiling to the others and said:

—I think I am voicing the opinions of all present in saying so much.

—You are, Glynn said in a firm tone. On that point Ireland is united.

He struck the ferrule of his umbrella on the stone floor of the colonnade.

—Hell, Temple said. I can respect that invention of the grey spouse of Satan.[7] Hell is Roman, like the walls of the Romans, strong and ugly. But what is limbo?

—Put him back into the perambulator, Cranly, O'Keeffe called out.

Cranly made a swift step towards Temple, halted, stamping his foot and crying as if to a fowl:

—Hoosh!

Temple moved away nimbly.

—Do you know what limbo is? he cried. Do you know what we call a notion like that in Roscommon?[8]

—Hoosh! Blast you! Cranly cried, clapping his hands.

—Neither my arse nor my elbow! Temple cried out scornfully. And that's what I call limbo.

—Give us that stick here, Cranly said.

He snatched the ashplant roughly from Stephen's hand and sprang down the steps: but Temple, hearing him move in pur= suit, fled through the dusk like a wild creature, nimble and fleetfooted. Cranly's heavy boots were heard loudly charging across the quadrangle and then returning heavily, foiled and spurning the gravel at each step.

His step was angry and with an angry abrupt gesture he thrust the stick back into Stephen's hand. Stephen felt that his anger had another cause but, feigning patience, touched his arm slightly and said quietly:

—Cranly, I told you I wanted to speak to you. Come away.

Cranly looked at him for a few moments and asked:

—Now?

2224 and] MS; ABSENT Eg–64   2236 heard] heard ⟨in⟩ MS

6. A straw or hay rope (Gaelic; P. W. Joyce).
7. Sin, in *Paradise Lost* (book two), by the English poet John Milton (1608–1674).
8. In the west of Ireland, both a town and a county.

—Yes, now, Stephen said. We can't speak here. Come away.

They crossed the quadrangle together without speaking. The birdcall from *Siegfried*[9] whistled softly followed them from the steps of the porch. Cranly turned: and Dixon, who had whistled, called out: 2250

—Where are you fellows off to? What about that game, Cranly?

They parleyed in shouts across the still air about a game of billiards to be played in the Adelphi hotel. Stephen walked on alone and out into the quiet of Kildare Street. Opposite 2255 Maple's hotel he stood to wait, patient again. The name of the hotel, a colourless polished wood, and its colourless quiet front stung him like a glance of polite disdain. He stared angrily back at the softly lit drawingroom of the hotel in which he imagined the sleek lives of the patricians of Ireland housed in calm. They 2260 thought of army commissions and land agents: peasants greeted them along the roads in the country: they knew the names of certain French dishes and gave orders to jarvies[1] in highpitched provincial voices which pierced through their skintight accents.

How could he hit their conscience or how cast his shadow 2265 over the imagination of their daughters, before their squires begat upon them, that they might breed a race less ignoble than their own? And under the deepened dusk he felt the thoughts and desires of the race to which he belonged flitting like bats across the dark country lanes, under trees by the edges of 2270 streams and near the poolmottled bogs. A woman had waited in the doorway as Davin had passed by at night and, offering him a cup of milk, had all but wooed him to her bed: for Davin had the mild eyes of one that could be secret. But him no woman's eyes had wooed.   2275

His arm was taken in a strong grip and Cranly's voice said:

—Let us eke go.

They walked southward in silence. Then Cranly said:

—That blithering idiot Temple! I swear to Moses, do you know, that I'll be the death of that fellow one time.   2280

But his voice was no longer angry and Stephen wondered was he thinking of her greeting to him under the porch.

They turned to the left and walked on as before. When they had gone on so for some time Stephen said:

—Cranly, I had an unpleasant quarrel this evening.   2285

2266 imagination] imaginations 16–64   2274 that] who Eg–64   2278 southward] Eg; northward MS

9. Musical passage from the opera *Siegfried* (1876), by the German composer Richard Wagner (1813–1883).
1. Hackney coachmen (*OED*).

—With your people? Cranly asked.

—With my mother.

—About religion?

—Yes, Stephen answered.

After a pause Cranly asked: 2290

—What age is your mother?

—Not old, Stephen said. She wishes me to make my easter duty.

—And will you?

—I will not, Stephen said.   2295

—Why not? Cranly said.

—I will not serve, answered Stephen.

—That remark was made before,[2] Cranly said calmly.

—It is made behind now, said Stephen hotly.

Cranly pressed Stephen's arm, saying: 2300

—Go easy, my dear man. You're an excitable bloody man, do you know.

He laughed nervously as he spoke and, looking up into Ste= phen's face with moved and friendly eyes, said:

—Do you know that you are an excitable man?   2305

—I daresay I am, said Stephen, laughing also.

Their minds, lately estranged, seemed suddenly to have been drawn closer, one to the other.

—Do you believe in the eucharist?[3] Cranly asked.

—I do not, Stephen said.   2310

—Do you disbelieve then?

—I neither believe in it nor disbelieve in it, Stephen answered.

—Many persons have doubts, even religious persons, yet they overcome them or put them aside, Cranly said. Are your doubts on that point too strong?   2315

—I do not wish to overcome them, Stephen answered.

Cranly, embarrassed for a moment, took another fig from his pocket and was about to eat it when Stephen said:

—Don't, please. You cannot discuss this question with your mouth full of chewed fig.   2320

Cranly examined the fig by the light of a lamp under which he halted. Then he smelt it with both nostrils, bit a tiny piece, spat it out and threw the fig rudely into the gutter. Addressing it as it lay, he said:

2. Made before by Satan, who according to tradition said *"non serviam"* when he fell. This Latin phrase occurs and is translated into English in one of the sermons of Part III (line 556), where it is attributed to Lucifer, another name for Satan. Joyce could have encoun= tered the Latin in the Vulgate Bible, the early fifth-century translation from Greek and Hebrew attributed primarily to St. Jerome (347–420). In Jeremias 2:20, it applies to Israel's rejection of God, not Satan's.

3. Believe that the consecrated bread and wine are the body and blood of Christ.

—Depart from me, ye cursed, into everlasting fire!   2325

Taking Stephen's arm he went on again and said:

—Do you not fear that those words may be spoken to you on the day of judgment?

—What is offered me on the other hand? Stephen asked. An eternity of bliss in the company of the dean of studies?   2330

—Remember, Cranly said, that he would be glorified.

—Ay, Stephen said somewhat bitterly. Bright, agile, impassible and, above all, subtle.

—It is a curious thing, do you know, Cranly said dispassion= ately, how your mind is supersaturated with the religion in   2335 which you say you disbelieve. Did you believe in it when you were at school? I bet you did.

—I did, Stephen answered.

—And were you happier then? Cranly asked softly. Happier than you are now, for instance?   2340

—Often happy, Stephen said, and often unhappy. I was some= one else then.

—How someone else? What do you mean by that statement?

—I mean, said Stephen, that I was not myself as I am now, as I had to become.   2345

—Not as you are now, not as you had to become, Cranly repeated. Let me ask you a question. Do you love your mother?

Stephen shook his head slowly.

—I don't know what your words mean, he said simply.

—Have you never loved anyone? Cranly asked.   2350

—Do you mean women?

—I am not speaking of that, Cranly said in a colder tone. I ask you if you ever felt love towards anyone or anything.

Stephen walked on beside his friend, staring gloomily at the footpath.   2355

—I tried to love God, he said at length. It seems now I failed. It is very difficult. I tried to unite my will with the will of God instant by instant. In that I did not always fail. I could perhaps do that still . . . . .

Cranly cut him short by asking: 2360

—Has your mother had a happy life?

—How do I know? Stephen said.

—How many children had she?

—Nine or ten, Stephen answered. Some died.

—Was your father . . . . Cranly interrupted himself for an in=   2365 stant: and then said: I don't want to pry into your family affairs. But was your father what is called well-to-do? I mean when you were growing up?

—Yes, Stephen said.

—What was he? Cranly asked after a pause.   2370
     Stephen began to enumerate glibly his father's attributes.
—A medical student, an oarsman, a tenor, an amateur actor, a
shouting politician, a small landlord, a small investor, a
drinker, a good fellow, a storyteller, somebody's secretary,
something in a distillery, a taxgatherer, a bankrupt and at   2375
present a praiser of his own past.
     Cranly laughed, tightening his grip on Stephen's arm, and
said:
—The distillery is damn good.
—Is there anything else you want to know? Stephen asked.   2380
—Are you in good circumstances at present?
—Do I look it? Stephen asked bluntly.
—So then, Cranly went on musingly, you were born in the lap
of luxury.
     He used the phrase broadly and loudly as he often used   2385
technical expressions as if he wished his hearer to understand
that they were used by him without conviction.
—Your mother must have gone through a good deal of suffer=
ing, he said then. Would you not try to save her from suffering
more even if . . . . or would you?   2390
—If I could, Stephen said. That would cost me very little.
—Then do so, Cranly said. Do as she wishes you to do. What
is it for you? You disbelieve in it. It is a form: nothing else. And
you will set her mind at rest.
     He ceased and, as Stephen did not reply, remained silent.   2395
Then, as if giving utterance to the process of his own thought,
he said:
—Whatever else is unsure in this stinking dunghill of a world a
mother's love is not. Your mother brings you into the world,
carries you first in her body. What do we know about what she   2400
feels? But whatever she feels, it, at least, must be real. It must
be. What are our ideas or ambitions? Play. Ideas! Why, that
bloody bleating goat Temple has ideas. MacCann has ideas too.
Every jackass going the roads thinks he has ideas.
     Stephen, who had been listening to the unspoken speech   2405
behind the words, said with assumed carelessness:
—Pascal, if I remember rightly, would not suffer his mother to
kiss him as he feared the contact of her sex.[4]
—Pascal was a pig, said Cranly.

4. An unconfirmed story but in line with the extreme, conservative Catholicism of the
   French philosopher Blaise Pascal (1623–1662).

—Aloysius Gonzaga,[5] I think, was of the same mind, Stephen   2410
said.

—And he was another pig then, said Cranly.

—The church calls him a saint, Stephen objected.

—I don't care a flaming damn what anyone calls him, Cranly
said rudely and flatly. I call him a pig.   2415

Stephen, preparing the words neatly in his mind, continued:

—Jesus too seems to have treated his mother with scant cour=
tesy in public but Suarez,[6] a jesuit theologian and Spanish
gentleman, has apologised for him.

—Did the idea ever occur to you, Cranly asked, that Jesus was   2420
not what he pretended to be?

—The first person to whom that idea occurred, Stephen
answered, was Jesus himself.

—I mean, Cranly said, hardening in his speech, did the idea
ever occur to you that he was himself a conscious hypocrite,   2425
what he called the jews of his time, a whited sepulchre?[7] Or, to
put it more plainly, that he was a blackguard?

—That idea never occurred to me, Stephen answered. But I am
curious to know are you trying to make a convert of me or a
pervert[8] of yourself?   2430

He turned towards his friend's face and saw there a raw
smile which some force of will strove to make finely significant.

Cranly asked suddenly in a plain sensible tone:

—Tell me the truth. Were you at all shocked by what I said?

—Somewhat, Stephen said.   2435

—And why were you shocked, Cranly pressed on in the same
tone, if you feel sure that our religion is false and that Jesus
was not the son of God?

—I am not at all sure of it, Stephen said. He is more like a son
of God than a son of Mary.   2440

—And is that why you will not communicate,[9] Cranly asked,
because you are not sure of that too, because you feel that the
host too may be the body and blood of the son of God and not
a wafer of bread? And because you fear that it may be?

—Yes, Stephen said quietly. I feel that and I also fear it.   2445

—I see, Cranly said.

---

5. A young saint (1568–1591), patron of youth and of Clongowes Wood College, who is reputed to have held attitudes about the body similar to Pascal's.

6. Francisco Suarez (1548–1617).

7. Jesus denounced the hypocrisy of the scribes and Pharisees, a self-righteous ancient Jewish sect, by comparing them to "whited sepulchres, which outwardly appear to men beautiful, but within are full of dead men's bones, and of all uncleanness" (Matthew 23:27).

8. In a religious context, someone who turns away from a faith, the opposite of a convert,
who turns toward it (OED).

9. Receive Holy Communion (OED).

Stephen, struck by his tone of closure, reopened the dis=
cussion at once by saying:
—I fear many things: dogs, horses, firearms, the sea, thunder=
storms, machinery, the country roads at night.   2450
—But why do you fear a bit of bread?
—I imagine, Stephen said, that there is a malevolent reality
behind those things I say I fear.
—Do you fear then, Cranly asked, that the God of the Roman
catholics would strike you dead and damn you if you made a   2455
sacrilegious communion?
—The God of the Roman catholics could do that now, Stephen
said. I fear more than that the chemical action which would be
set up in my soul by a false homage to a symbol behind which
are massed twenty centuries of authority and veneration.   2460
—Would you, Cranly asked, in extreme danger commit that
particular sacrilege? For instance, if you lived in the penal days?[1]
—I cannot answer for the past, Stephen replied. Possibly not.
—Then, said Cranly, you do not intend to become a protes=
tant?   2465
—I said that I had lost the faith, Stephen answered, but not
that I had lost selfrespect. What kind of liberation would that
be to forsake an absurdity which is logical and coherent and to
embrace one which is illogical and incoherent?

They had walked on towards the township of Pembroke[2] and   2470
now, as they went on slowly along the avenues, the trees and
the scattered lights in the villas soothed their minds. The air of
wealth and repose diffused about them seemed to comfort their
neediness. Behind a hedge of laurel a light glimmered in the
window of a kitchen and the voice of a servant was heard   2475
singing as she sharpened knives. She sang in short broken bars
Rosie O'Grady.[3]
Cranly stopped to listen, saying:
—*Mulier cantat*.[4]
The soft beauty of the Latin word touched with an enchant=   2480
ing touch the dark of the evening, with a touch fainter and
more persuading than the touch of music or of a woman's
hand. The strife of their minds was quelled. The figure of

1. The period from 1697 until Catholic Emancipation in 1829, when laws prohibited
   Catholics in Ireland from practicing their religion and denied them civil rights.
2. Township (1863–1930) comprised of Donnybrook, Ballsbridge, Sandymount, and
   Ringsend, east and south of central Dublin.
3. "Sweet Rosie O'Grady" was a popular song credited to the music-hall singer Maude Nugent
   (1877–1958), also known as Maude Jerome. Cranly remembers the well-known refrain.
4. "A woman is singing" (Latin).

woman as she appears in the liturgy of the church passed si=
lently through the darkness: a whiterobed figure, small and   2485
slender as a boy and with a falling girdle. Her voice, frail and
high as a boy's, was heard intoning from a distant choir the
first words of a woman which pierce the gloom and clamour of
the first chanting of the passion:

—*Et tu cum Jesu Galilaeo eras.*[5]   2490

And all hearts were touched and turned to her voice, shining
like a young star, shining clearer as the voice intoned the pro=
paroxyton[6] and more faintly as the cadence died.

The singing ceased. They went on together, Cranly repeating
in strongly stressed rhythm the end of the refrain: 2495

> *And when we are married*
> *O, how happy we'll be*
> *For I love sweet Rosie O'Grady*
> *And Rosie O'Grady loves me.*

—There's real poetry for you, he said. There's real love.   2500

He glanced sideways at Stephen with a strange smile and
said:

—Do you consider that poetry? Or do you know what the
words mean?

—I want to see Rosie first, said Stephen.   2505

—She's easy to find, Cranly said.

His hat had come down on his forehead. He shoved it back:
and in the shadow of the trees Stephen saw his pale face,
framed by the dark, and his large dark eyes. Yes. His face was
handsome: and his body was strong and hard. He had spoken   2510
of a mother's love. He felt then the sufferings of women, the
weaknesses of their bodies and souls: and would shield them
with a strong and resolute arm and bow his mind to them.

Away then: it is time to go. A voice spoke softly to Stephen's
lonely heart, bidding him go and telling him that his friendship   2515
was coming to an end. Yes: he would go. He could not strive
against another. He knew his part.

—Probably I shall go away, he said.

—Where? Cranly asked.

—Where I can, Stephen said.   2520

—Yes, Cranly said. It might be difficult for you to live here
now. But is it that that makes you go?

2484 liturgy--the] ⁿliturgy--theⁱ⸍ MS

5. "Thou also wast with Jesus the Galilean" (Matthew 26:69), spoken to Peter just before he
   denies knowing Jesus. In Latin here as part of the mass sung on Palm Sunday, the Sunday
   before Easter.
6. A word accented on the third to last syllable, as in the word itself.

—I have to go, Stephen answered.

—Because, Cranly continued, you need not look upon yourself
as driven away if you do not wish to go or as a heretic or an 2525
outlaw. There are many good believers who think as you do.
Would that surprise you? The church is not the stone building
nor even the clergy and their dogmas. It is the whole mass of
those born into it. I don't know what you wish to do in life. Is
it what you told me the night we were standing outside Har= 2530
court Street station?[7]

—Yes, Stephen said, smiling in spite of himself at Cranly's way
of remembering thoughts in connection with places. The night
you spent half an hour wrangling with Doherty about the
shortest way from Sallygap to Larras.[8]   2535

—Pothead! Cranly said with calm contempt. What does he
know about the way from Sallygap to Larras? Or what does he
know about anything for that matter? And the big slobbering
washingpot head of him!

He broke out into a loud long laugh.   2540

—Well? Stephen said. Do you remember the rest?

—What you said, is it? Cranly asked. Yes, I remember it. To
discover the mode of life or of art whereby your spirit could
express itself in unfettered freedom.

Stephen raised his hat in acknowledgment.   2545

—Freedom! Cranly repeated. But you are not free enough yet
to commit a sacrilege. Tell me, would you rob?

—I would beg first, Stephen said.

—And if you got nothing would you rob?

—You wish me to say, Stephen answered, that the rights of 2550
property are provisional and that in certain circumstances it is
not unlawful to rob. Everyone would act in that belief. So I will
not make you that answer. Apply to the jesuit theologian Juan
Mariana de Talavera[9] who will also explain to you in what
circumstances you may lawfully kill your king and whether you 2555
had better hand him his poison in a goblet or smear it for him
upon his robe or his saddlebow. Ask me rather would I suffer
others to rob me or, if they did, would I call down upon them
what I believe is called the chastisement of the secular arm.

—And would you?   2560

—I think, Stephen said, it would pain me as much to do so as
to be robbed.

2544 itself] aEg; it MS–Eg

7. Rail station (functioning until 1959) south of the west side of Stephen's Green.
8. In the Wicklow Mountains, south of Dublin; where Cranly's family lives.
9. Spanish Jesuit (1536–1623).

—I see, Cranly said.

He produced his match and began to clean the crevice be= tween two teeth. Then he said carelessly: 2565

—Tell me, for example, would you deflower a virgin?

—Excuse me, Stephen said politely. Is that not the ambition of most young gentlemen?

—What then is your point of view? Cranly asked.

His last phrase, soursmelling as the smoke of charcoal and   2570 disheartening, excited Stephen's brain over which its fumes seemed to brood.

—Look here, Cranly, he said. You have asked me what I would do and what I would not do. I will tell you what I will do and what I will not do. I will not serve that in which I no longer   2575 believe whether it call itself my home, my fatherland or my church: and I will try to express myself in some mode of life or art as freely as I can and as wholly as I can, using for my defence the only arms I allow myself to use, silence, exile and cunning.   2580

Cranly seized his arm and steered him round so as to lead him back towards Leeson Park.[1] He laughed almost slily and pressed Stephen's arm with an elder's affection.

—Cunning indeed! he said. Is it you? You poor poet, you!

—And you made me confess to you, Stephen said, thrilled by   2585 his touch, as I have confessed to you so many other things, have I not?

—Yes, my child,[2] Cranly said, still gaily.

—You made me confess the fears that I have. But I will tell you also what I do not fear. I do not fear to be alone or to be   2590 spurned for another or to leave whatever I have to leave. And I am not afraid to make a mistake, even a great mistake, a lifelong mistake and perhaps as long as eternity too.

Cranly, now grave again, slowed his pace and said:

—Alone, quite alone. You have no fear of that. And you know   2595 what that word means? Not only to be separate from all others but to have not even one friend.

—I will take the risk, said Stephen.

—And not to have any one person, Cranly said, who would be more than a friend, more even than the noblest and truest   2600 friend a man ever had.

2564 his match] ⌐his match⌐ MS   2581–82 lead him] a16; head MS; lead Eg–16; head 64
2596 word] Eg; words MS

1. Leading to the Leeson Street Bridge over the Grand Canal and back toward Stephen's Green.
2. Words a priest would speak in the confessional to someone confessing.

His words seemed to have struck some deep chord in his own nature. Had he spoken of himself, of himself as he was or wished to be? Stephen watched his face for some moments in silence. A cold sadness was there. He had spoken of himself, of 2605 his own loneliness which he feared.

—Of whom are you speaking? Stephen asked at length.

Cranly did not answer.

◆   ◆   ◆

20 March: Long talk with Cranly on the subject of my re= volt. He had his grand manner on. I supple and suave. Attacked 2610 me on the score of love for one's mother. Tried to imagine his mother: cannot. Told me once, in a moment of thoughtlessness, his father was sixtyone when he was born. Can see him. Strong farmer type. Pepper and salt suit. Square feet. Unkempt grizzled beard. Probably attends coursing matches.[3] Pays his 2615 dues regularly but not plentifully to Father Dwyer of Larras. Sometimes talks to girls after nightfall. But his mother? Very young or very old? Hardly the first. If so, Cranly would not have spoken as he did. Old then. Probably: and neglected. Hence Cranly's despair of soul: the child of exhausted loins. 2620

21 March, morning: Thought this in bed last night but was too lazy and free to add it. Free, yes. The exhausted loins are those of Elizabeth and Zachary. Then is he the precursor. Item: he eats chiefly belly bacon and dried figs. Read locusts and wild honey. Also, when thinking of him, saw always a stern severed 2625 head or deathmask as if outlined on a grey curtain or veronica. Decollation they call it in the fold. Puzzled for the moment by saint John at the Latin gate. What do I see? A decollated precursor trying to pick the lock.[4]

21 March, night: Free. Soulfree and fancyfree. Let the dead 2630 bury the dead. Ay. And let the dead marry the dead.[5]

2623 Elizabeth] ⁻|⟨Anna⟩ Elizabeth|ʳ MS   2623 Zachary.] ⁻|⟨Joachim⟩ Zachary|ʳ. MS
2623 is he] he is Eg–64

3. Matches in which greyhounds pursue hares (*OED*).
4. The details of the entry link Cranly to John the Baptist, whose parents, Elizabeth and Zachary, were old. When he was a hermit, John lived on locusts and wild honey. He suffered decollation, or beheading, when Salomé tricked her stepfather, Herod, into granting her wish. Stephen compares the severed head to a deathmask and to a veronica, a cloth bearing the image of Jesus's face, after the cloth used by Saint Veronica to wipe his face on his way to the cross. John the Baptist was the precursor of Jesus, but Saint John "at the Latin gate" is John the Apostle. They are linked by their names but also by the fact that the Lateran Church (at the Latin gate in Rome), where John the Apostle miraculously escaped from the Romans, is consecrated to John the Baptist. John the Baptist figuratively opened the door for Jesus and figuratively picked the lock of the Latin gate for John the Apostle.
5. Stephen cites and then transforms Luke 9:60, "Let the dead bury their dead."

22 *March:* In company with Lynch followed a sizable hos=
pital nurse. Lynch's idea. Dislike it. Two lean hungry grey=
hounds walking after a heifer.

23 *March:* Have not seen her since that night. Unwell? Sits at   2635
the fire perhaps with mamma's shawl on her shoulders. But not
peevish. A nice bowl of gruel? Won't you now?

24 *March:* Began with a discussion with my mother. Subject:
B. V. M.[6] Handicapped by my sex and youth. To escape held up
relations between Jesus and Papa against those between Mary   2640
and her son. Said religion is not a lying-in hospital.[7] Mother
indulgent. Said I have a queer mind and have read too much.
Not true. Have read little and understood less. Then she said I
would come back to faith because I had a restless mind. This
means to leave church by backdoor of sin and reenter through   2645
the skylight of repentance. Cannot repent. Told her so and
asked for sixpence. Got threepence.

Then went to college. Other wrangle with little roundhead
rogue's eye Ghezzi.[8] This time about Bruno the Nolan.[9] Began in
Italian and ended in pidgin English. He said Bruno was a ter=   2650
rible heretic. I said he was terribly burned. He agreed to this
with some sorrow. Then gave me recipe for what he calls
risotto alla bergamasca.[1] When he pronounces a soft *o* he pro=
trudes his full carnal lips as if he kissed the vowel. Has he? And
could he repent? Yes, he could: and cry two round rogue's   2655
tears, one from each eye.

Crossing Stephen's, that is, my green, remembered that his
countrymen and not mine had invented what Cranly the other
night called our religion. A quartet of them, soldiers of the
ninetyseventh infantry regiment, sat at the foot of the cross and   2660
tossed up dice for the overcoat of the crucified.

Went to library. Tried to read three reviews. Useless. She is
not out yet. Am I alarmed? About what? That she will never be
out again. Blake wrote:

> *I wonder if William Bond will die.*   2665
> *For assuredly he is very ill.*

Alas, poor William!

2641 is] was Eg–64   2664 Blake NO PARAGRAPH] NEW PARAGRAPH Eg–64

6. The Blessed Virgin Mary.
7. Maternity hospital.
8. Italian teacher at University College.
9. Giordano Bruno (1548–1600), Italian Dominican and philosopher, was born in Nola; he
   was burned at the stake as a heretic.
1. "Risotto as prepared in Bergamo" (Italian), ostensibly a rice dish typical of northern Italy,
   but a dish known by that name has never been identified.

I was once at a diorama in Rotunda.[2] At the end were pic=
tures of big nobs. Among them William Ewart Gladstone, just
then dead. Orchestra played O *Willie, we have missed you.*[3]   2670
    A race of clodhoppers.
    25 *March, morning*: A troubled night of dreams. Want to get
them off my chest.
    A long curving gallery. From the floor ascend pillars of dark
vapours. It is peopled by the images of fabulous kings, set in   2675
stone. Their hands are folded upon their knees in token of
weariness and their eyes are darkened for the errors of men go
up before them for ever as dark vapours.
    Strange figures advance from a cave. They are not as tall as
men. One does not seem to stand quite apart from another.   2680
Their faces are phosphorescent, with darker streaks. They peer
at me and their eyes seem to ask me something. They do not
speak.
    30 *March*: This evening Cranly was in the porch of the
library, proposing a problem to Dixon and her brother. A   2685
mother let her child fall into the Nile. Still harping on the
mother. A crocodile seized the child. Mother asked it back.
Crocodile said all right if she told him what he was going to do
with the child, eat it or not eat it.
    This mentality, Lepidus would say, is indeed bred out of   2690
your mud by the operation of your sun.[4]
    And mine? Is it not too? Then into Nilemud with it!
    1 *April*: Disapprove of this last phrase.
    2 *April*: Saw her drinking tea and eating cakes in Johnston,
Mooney and O'Brien's. Rather, lynxeyed Lynch saw her as we   2695
passed. He tells me Cranly was invited there by brother. Did he
bring his crocodile? Is he the shining light now? Well, I dis=
covered him. I protest I did. Shining quietly behind a bushel of
Wicklow bran.
    3 *April*: Met Davin at the cigar shop opposite Findlater's   2700
church.[5] He was in a black sweater and had a hurleystick.
Asked me was it true I was going away and why. Told him the

2668 Rotunda.] ⌐¹⟨Leinster Hall⟩ Rotunda¹ʳ. MS   2679 from] as from Eg–24

2. A group of buildings used for various public purposes, at the end of Sackville (now
   O'Connell) Street at Rutland (now Parnell) Square. "Diorama": a forerunner of the
   cinema.
3. The passage evokes various Williams, starting with the English Romantic poet William
   Blake (1757–1827), whose poem "William Bond" is cited, and ending with the line from
   the song "Willie, We Have Missed You" (1854), by the American songwriter Stephen
   Collins Foster (1826–1864). On Gladstone, see note 6, p. 27.
4. In Shakespeare's *Antony and Cleopatra,* Lepidus says drunkenly, "Your serpent of Egypt is
   bred now of your mud by the operation of your sun; so is your crocodile" (2.7.25–26).
5. Presbyterian church in Rutland (now Parnell) Square.

shortest way to Tara was via Holyhead.[6] Just then my father
came up. Introduction. Father polite and observant. Asked
Davin if he might offer him some refreshment. Davin could   2705
not, was going to a meeting. When we came away father told
me he had a good honest eye. Asked me why I did not join a
rowing club. I pretended to think it over. Told me then how he
broke Pennyfeather's heart.[7] Wants me to read law. Says I was
cut out for that. More mud, more crocodiles.   2710

5 *April:* Wild spring. Scudding clouds. O life! Dark stream of
swirling bogwater on which appletrees have cast down their
delicate flowers. Eyes of girls among the leaves. Girls demure
and romping. All fair or auburn: no dark ones. They blush
better. Houp-la!   2715

6 *April:* Certainly she remembers the past. Lynch says all
women do. Then she remembers the time of her childhood—
and mine if I was ever a child. The past is consumed in the
present and the present is living only because it brings forth the
future. Statues of women, if Lynch be right, should always be   2720
fully draped, one hand of the woman feeling regretfully her
own hinder parts.

6 *April: later:* Michael Robartes remembers forgotten beauty
and, when his arms wrap her round, he presses in his arms the
loveliness which has long faded from the world. Not this. Not   2725
at all. I desire to press in my arms the loveliness which has not
yet come into the world.[8]

10 *April:* Faintly, under the heavy night, through the silence
of the city which has turned from dreams to dreamless sleep as
a weary lover whom no caresses move, the sound of hoofs   2730
upon the road. Not so faintly now as they come near the
bridge; and in a moment as they pass the darkened windows
the silence is cloven by alarm as by an arrow. They are heard
now far away, hoofs that shine amid the heavy night as gems,
hurrying beyond the sleeping fields to what journey's end—   2735
what heart?—bearing what tidings?

11 *April:* Read what I wrote last night. Vague words for a
vague emotion. Would she like it? I think so. Then I should
have to like it also.

13 *April:* That tundish has been on my mind for a long time.   2740
I looked it up and find it is English and good old blunt English

2741 is] MS; ABSENT Eg–64

6. Taking the ferry to Holyhead, the Welsh port across the Irish Channel, is the most direct
   route to Tara, the seat of the ancient kings of Ireland.
7. A stock phrase suggesting with a touch of irony disappointed love (*Letters* III, 130).
8. Stephen rejects the sentiment expressed in Yeats's poem "Michael Robartes Remembers
   Forgotten Beauty" (1899), later retitled "He Remembers Forgotten Beauty."

too. Damn the dean of studies and his funnel! What did he
come here for to teach us his own language or to learn it from
us. Damn him one way or the other!

14 April: John Alphonsus Mulrennan has just returned from 2745
the west of Ireland (European and Asiatic papers please copy).
He told us he met an old man there in a mountain cabin. Old
man had red eyes and short pipe. Old man spoke Irish.
Mulrennan spoke Irish. Then old man and Mulrennan spoke
English. Mulrennan spoke to him about universe and stars. Old 2750
man sat, listened, smoked, spat. Then said:

—Ah, there must be terrible queer creatures at the latter end of
the world.

I fear him. I fear his redrimmed horny eyes. It is with him I
must struggle all through this night till day come, till he or I lie 2755
dead, gripping him by the sinewy throat till . . . . Till what? Till
he yield to me? No. I mean him no harm.

15 April: Met her today pointblank in Grafton Street. The
crowd brought us together. We both stopped. She asked me
why I never came, said she had heard all sorts of stories about 2760
me. This was only to gain time. Asked me was I writing poems.
About whom? I asked her. This confused her more and I felt
sorry and mean. Turned off that valve at once and opened the
spiritual-heroic refrigerating apparatus, invented and patented
in all countries by Dante Alighieri.[9] Talked rapidly of myself 2765
and my plans. In the midst of it unluckily I made a sudden
gesture of a revolutionary nature. I must have looked like a
fellow throwing a handful of peas up into the air. People began
to look at us. She shook hands a moment after and, in going
away, said she hoped I would do what I said. 2770

Now I call that friendly, don't you?

Yes. I liked her today. A little or much? Don't know. I liked
her—and it seems a new feeling to me. Then, in that case, all
the rest, all that I thought I thought and all that I felt I felt, all
the rest before now, in fact . . . . . . O, give it up, old chap! Sleep it 2775
off!

16 April: Away! Away!

The spell of arms and voices: the white arms of roads, their
promise of close embraces and the black arms of tall ships that
stand against the moon, their tale of distant nations. They are 2780
held out to say: We are alone. Come. And the voices say with

2768 up] ABSENT 18–64

9. In *La Vita Nuova* (*The New Life*), Dante (1265–1321) presents his idealized adoration,
free of physical desire, for Beatrice Portinari, whom he first met as a child. Beatrice appears later as a guide to spiritual salvation in Dante's *Divine Comedy.*

them: We are your kinsmen. And the air is thick with their company as they call to me, their kinsman, making ready to go, shaking the wings of their exultant and terrible youth.

26 April: Mother is putting my new secondhand clothes in order. She prays now, she says, that I may learn in my own life and away from home and friends what the heart is and what it feels. Amen. So be it. Welcome, O life! I go to encounter for the millionth time the reality of experience and to forge in the smithy of my soul the uncreated conscience of my race.[1]

27 April: Old father, old artificer, stand me now and ever in good stead.

Dublin 1904
Trieste 1914

2792 stead.] stead. RECTANGLE BLOT BELOW MS   2793 Dublin] ⟨Cabra⟩, Dublin MS
2794 Trieste] Trieste, ⟨Austria⟩ MS

1. Can be understood as biologically based, but can also mean, more broadly, "tribe, nation, or people" (*OED*), and was often used with that meaning in Joyce's youth. "Uncreated": can mean "not brought into being," but also means "self-existent or eternal" as an attribute of something divine (*OED*).

BACKGROUNDS
AND CONTEXTS

Political Nationalism:
Irish History, 1798–1916

KEY DATES, EVENTS, AND FIGURES

1798   **Insurrection of 1798,** led by the radical **Society of United Irishmen;** the unsuccessful rebellion, inspired in part by the French and American revolutions, resulted in possibly thirty thousand deaths. United Irish leaders included **(Theobald) Wolfe Tone** (1763–1798), founder of the modern Irish republican movement, who committed suicide before he could be executed.

1801   **United Kingdom of Great Britain and Ireland** established as a response to the Insurrection by an **Act of Union** (1800) passed under English pressure by both Irish and English parliaments. Irish Parliament dissolved, with Irish representatives then elected to the House of Commons in Westminster. Under the Union, the English government intervened frequently in Irish public affairs (education, public health) and exercised centralized control.

1803   **Rebellion of 1803,** an unsuccessful uprising in Dublin by remnants of the United Irishmen led by **Robert Emmet** (1778–1803), who was captured, hanged, and beheaded.

1828   Election of **Daniel O'Connell** (1775–1847), "The Liberator," to Parliament, despite prohibition against Catholic representatives; election led to Catholic Emancipation in 1829. O'Connell then worked for repeal of the Union.

1842–48   **Young Ireland Movement,** made up of nationalists dissatisfied with O'Connell's moderate political directions and willing to use force; leaders included

227

Charles Gavin Duffy, Thomas Davis, and John Blake Dillon.

1845–49   **The Great Famine,** involving repeated failures of the potato crop due to a fungus, resulted in a **population loss** from death and emigration of 20–25 percent (possibly two million of eight million). **Insufficiency of English aid** resulted in bitterness that fueled future separatist activities in Ireland and among Irish who had emigrated. **John Mitchel** (1815–1875), a Young Irelander, memorably captured the post-famine Irish view when he wrote, "The Almighty, indeed, sent the potato blight, but the English created the famine."

1848   **Rebellion of 1848,** led by Young Ireland in the same year as violent revolutionary activity in France and other European countries; the unsuccessful action put an end to the Young Ireland Movement.

1858   **Fenian Brotherhood,** also known as the **Irish Republican Brotherhood,** a militant nationalist group, established in Dublin by James Stephens (1824–1901) soon after a parallel organization sprang up in America.

1867   **Rising of 1867,** led by the Fenians at scattered locations around Ireland, quickly put down by the forces of the Crown. Attempt to break a Fenian prisoner out of Clerkenwell Prison, London, later in the year involved an explosion that killed several people.

1870   **Disestablishment of the Church of Ireland** (Anglican), which had been the state church, under the English monarch, since 1537.

1879   Irish National **Land League** founded in Dublin by **Michael Davitt** (1846–1906) to advocate peasant ownership of the land. **Charles Stewart Parnell** (1846–1891) named president.

1881   **Land League** leaders, including Parnell, **imprisoned in Kilmainham Jail** near Dublin; **League outlawed** for advocating nonpayment of rent.

1882   **Kilmainham "treaty,"** an agreement between Parnell and the English government, that made some land reforms possible and resulted in the release of Land League leaders from jail. The agreement was a step toward negotiations for Home Rule.

Lord Frederick Cavendish, the new Irish chief secretary (English official in charge of administering Ireland), and the undersecretary, T. H. Burke, assassinated in the **Phoenix Park murders,** by the **Invincibles,** an extremist nationalist group. The horrific murders, involving surgical knives, undermined the immediate chances for Home Rule. Already existing **Coercion Acts,** meant to keep Irish unrest under tight control, were renewed and strengthened.

Parnell established the **National League** to replace the suppressed Land League and to focus on establishing home rule constitutionally rather than on land reform.

1884   **Gaelic Athletic Association** founded—an openly nationalist, at times actively political organization that fostered traditional Irish sports, such as hurling and Gaelic football, and discouraged foreign sports. In 1890–91, the GAA supported Parnell's attempt to retain his leadership.

1886   **Home Rule Bill defeated.** Introduced by the English prime minister, William Gladstone (1809–1898), leader of the Liberals, in cooperation with Parnell, the bill would have given partial autonomy to Ireland.

1891   **Parnell removed** as leader of the Irish Parliamentary Party after he is denounced by Michael Davitt and the Catholic clergy following his involvement in a divorce trial and adultery scandal.

1893   Second **Home Rule Bill defeated**.

            Gaelic League founded, with **Douglas Hyde** (1860–1949) as president, to revive the Irish language, both spoken and literary.

1914   Third **Home Rule Bill passed,** but never implemented because of the outbreak of **World War I** that year and Irish demands for separation from England after the Rising of 1916.

1916   **Easter Rising** and **Proclamation of the Irish Republic** by elements of the Irish Republican Brotherhood and the smaller Irish Citizens Army in Dublin, with scattered supporting events elsewhere. Harsh British response, including the quick execution of the leaders and the imposition of martial law, led to widespread support for

the separatist movement and eventually to a con-
tested treaty with England (1922) that partitioned
the island into Northern Ireland (six counties) and
the Irish Free State (twenty-six counties). The
Anglo-Irish Treaty triggered the Irish Civil War
(1922–23). The partition persists between Northern Ireland, under English dominion, and the
country often called "The Republic of Ireland,"
whose official name is Éire/Ireland, as established
in the 1937 Constitution of Ireland.

JOHN MITCHEL

[On the Great Famine, 1845–49:
English Intentions]†

Preface

TO THE IRISH EDITION
[OF *THE LAST CONQUEST OF IRELAND (PERHAPS)*]

These letters were first published two years ago in the United States;
and with the purpose professed in the letters themselves;—namely,
to give information to Americans, on Irish authority and from an
Irish point of view, concerning a series of events in Ireland, which
have been studiously presented to all mankind by the British Press
from precisely the *opposite* point of view.

In this volume Irish readers have the Letters slightly revised and corrected. There has not been, to my knowledge, any other attempt to
give a connected narrative of the Decline and Fall of "Repeal,"—of the
English Famine policy, and its complete success,—and of the steady
progress of demoralization and de-nationalization, which have brought
Ireland into her present abject state.

* * *

† John Mitchel (1815–1875), Irish political writer, responded to the Great Famine
(1845–49) by advocating revolution to create an independent Ireland. Mitchel's castiga-
tion of the English for not doing enough to help the Irish strongly influenced later nationalist thinking. He was reacting to the pervasive suffering in Ireland because of the famine,
reflected in a 20–25 percent decline in the population, including excess mortality that has
been reasonably estimated at over one million (Connolly 361, 228–29).
   From *The Last Conquest of Ireland (Perhaps)*. Dublin: The Irishman Office, 1861, iii,
1–4, 165–66, 310–11, 321–25. One of Mitchel's footnotes has been omitted.

Letter I

* * *

TO THE HON A. STEPHENS (OF GEORGIA)

Sir—

To be the historiographer of defeat and humiliation is not a task to be coveted, especially by one of the defeated. Neither can the world bring itself to take much interest in that side of human affairs. It sympathizes with success; it lends an ear to the successful; and inclines to believe what they affirm. Nevertheless, I have undertaken to narrate, for especial behoof of American readers, the last Conquest of Ireland; meaning by the word "last," not the final conquest, but the last up to this date: for it is probable that the island will need to be conquered again.

I have chosen the form of letters, and have asked permission to address them to you; for two reasons—first, that I may never forget I am writing for the information of Americans, and must explain many things which to Irish readers would need no explanation—and next, that having my correspondent always present to my mind, and personifying in him the rather select American audience whom one would especially desire to address, I may be more completely withheld from all declamation, exaggeration and vituperation—may eschew adjectives, cleave unto substantives, and in short come to the point.

* * *

* * * there are some circumstances which perplex an inquirer who derives his information from the English periodical press. That an island which is said to be an integral part of the richest empire on the globe—and the most fertile portion of that empire—with British Constitution, *Habeas Corpus*, Members of Parliament, and Trial by Jury—should in five years lose two and a half millions of its people (more than one-fourth) by hunger and fever, the consequence of hunger, and flight beyond sea to escape from hunger—while that empire of which it is said to be a part, was all the while advancing in wealth, prosperity and comfort, at a faster pace than ever before—is a matter that seems to ask elucidation. In the year 1841, Ireland, a country precisely half the size of your State of Georgia, had a population of 8,175,124. The natural increase of population in Ireland, through all her former troubles, would have given upwards of nine millions in 1851; but in 1851 the Census Commissioners find in Ireland but 6,515,794 living souls. (*Thom's Official Directory.*)[1]

---

1. *Thom's Irish Almanac and Official Directory,* published in Dublin by Alexander Thom beginning in 1844.

Another thing, which to a spectator must appear anomalous, is that during each of those five years of "famine," from '46 to '51— that famine-struck land produced more than double the needful sustenance for all her own people; and of the best and choicest kind. Governor Wise, of Virginia, was in Brazil while the ends of the earth were resounding with the cry of Irish starvation; and was surprised to see unloaded at Rio abundance of the best quality of packed beef from Ireland. He surmised that the superiority of this Irish beef in all markets, depended on the greater care in its packing, and recommended attention to that matter in his own country. That the people who were dying of hunger did, in each year of their agony, produce upon Irish ground, of wheat and other grain, and of cattle and poultry, more than double the amount that they could all by any gluttony devour, is a fact that must be not only asserted, but in another letter proved beyond doubt.

*   *   *

From *Letter XIII*

*   *   *

This is the estate of a certain Marquis of Conyngham: and for him those desolate people, while health lasts, and they may still keep body and soul together, outside the Poorhouse, are for ever employed in making up a *subsidy,* called rent; which that district sends half-yearly to be consumed in England, or wherever else it may please their noble proprietor to devour their hearts' blood and the marrow of their bones.

So it is; and so it was, even before Famine, with almost the whole of that coast region. The landlords were all absentees. All the grain and cattle the people could raise were never enough to make up the rent: it all went away, of course; it was all consumed in England; but Ireland received in exchange stamped rent receipts. Of course there were no improvements,—because *they* would have only raised the rent; and in ordinary years many thousands of those poor people lived mainly on sea-weed some months of every year. But this was trespass and robbery; for the sea-weed belonged to the lord of the manor, who frequently made examples of the depredators.[2]

Can you picture in your mind a race of white men reduced to this condition? White men! Yes of the highest and purest blood and breed of men. The very region I have described to you was

---

2. I have defended poor devils on charges of trespass by gathering sea-weed below high-water mark, and remember one case in which a large number of farmers near the sea were indicted *for robbery*, on the charge of taking limestone from a rock uncovered at low water only—to burn it for spreading on their fields [Author].

once—before British civilization overtook us—the abode of the strongest and richest clans in Ireland; the Scotic MacCauras; the Norman Clan-Gerralt, (or Geraldin or Fitzgerald)—the Norman MacWilliams (or De Burgo, or Burke)—the princely and munificent O'Briens and O'Donnells, founders of many monasteries, chiefs of glittering hosts, generous patrons of Ollamh, Bard, and Brehon; sea-roving Macnamaras and O'Malleys, whose ships brought from Spain wine and horses,—from England fair-haired, white-armed Saxon slaves, "tall, handsome women," as the chroniclers call them, fit to weave wool or embroider mantles in the house of a king.

After a struggle of six or seven centuries, after many bloody wars and sweeping confiscations, English "civilization" prevailed,—and had brought the clans to the condition I have related. The ultimate idea of English civilization being that "the sole *nexus* between man and man is cash payment,"—and the "Union" having finally determined the course and current of that payment, out of Ireland into England,—it had come to pass that the chiefs were exchanged for landlords, and the clansman had sunk into able-bodied paupers.

The details of this frightful famine, as it ravaged those Western districts, I need not narrate;—they are sufficiently known. It is enough to say that in this year, 1846, not less than 300,000 perished, either of mere hunger, or of typhus-fever caused by hunger. But as it has ever since been a main object of the British Government to conceal the amount of the carnage (which, indeed, they ought to do if they can) I find that the Census Commissioners, in their Report for 1851, admit only 2,041 "registered" deaths by famine alone.

* * *

Letter XXIV

* * *

The Conquest, as I said, was now consummated—England, great, populous, and wealthy, with all the resources and vast patronage of an existing government in her hands—with a magnificent army and navy—with the established course and current of commerce steadily flowing in the precise direction that suited her interests—with a powerful party on her side in Ireland itself, bound to her by lineage and by interest—and, above all, with her vast brute mass lying between us and the rest of Europe, enabling her to intercept the natural sympathies of other struggling nations, to interpret between us and the rest of mankind, and represent the troublesome sister island, exactly in the light that she wished us to be regarded—England prosperous, potent, and at peace with all the earth besides—had succeeded (to her immortal honour and glory) in anticipating and crushing out of sight the last agonies of resistance in a small, poor and divided island, which she had herself made poor and divided, carefully disarmed, almost totally disfranchised, and almost totally deprived of the benefits of that very British "law" against which we revolted with such loathing and horror. England had done this; and whatsoever credit and prestige, whatsoever profit and power could be gained by such a feat, she has them all. "Now, for the first time these six hundred years," said the London *Times*, "England has Ireland at her mercy, and can deal with her as she pleases."

It was an opportunity not to be lost, for the interests of British civilization. Parliament met late in January, 1849. The Queen, in her "speech," lamented that "*another* failure of the potato crop had caused severe distress in Ireland: and thereupon asked Parliament to continue, "for a limited period," the extraordinary power; that is the power of proclaiming any district under martial law, and of throwing suspected persons into prison, without any charge against them. The act was passed, of course.

*   *   *

* * * Whenever Irishmen grow numerous again, as they surely will, and whenever "that ancient swelling and desire of liberty," as Lord Mountjoy expressed it, shall once more stir their souls—as once more it certainly will—why, the British Government can crush them again, with greater ease than ever; for the small farmers are destroyed; the middle-classes are extensively corrupted; and neither stipendiary officials nor able-bodied paupers ever make revolutions.

This very dismal and humiliating narrative draws to a close. It is the story of an ancient Nation stricken down by a war more ruthless and sanguinary than any seven years' war, or thirty years' war, that Europe ever saw. No sack of Magdeburg, or ravage of the Palatinate, ever approached in horror and desolation to the slaughters done in Ireland by mere official red-tape and stationery, and the principles of Political Economy. A few statistics may fitly conclude this dreary subject.

The Census of Ireland in 1841, gave a population of 8,175,125. At the usual rate of increase, there must have been, in 1846, when the Famine commenced, at least eight and a half millions; at the same rate of increase, there ought to have been, in 1851, (according to the estimate of the Census Commissioners) 9,018,799. But in that year, after five seasons of artificial famine, there were found alive only 6,552,385—a deficit of about two millions and a half. Now, what became of those two millions and a half?

The "government" Census Commissioners, and compilers of returns of all sorts, whose principal duty it has been, since that fatal time, to conceal the amount of the havoc, attempt to account for nearly the whole deficiency by emigration. In Thom's Official Almanac,[3] I find set down on one side, the actual decrease from 1841 to 1851, (that is without taking into account the increase by births in that period) 1,623,154. Against this, they place their own estimate of the emigration during those same ten years, which they put down at 1,589,133. But in the first place the decrease did not *begin* till 1846—there had been till then a rapid increase in the population: the government returns, then, not only ignore the increase, but set the emigration of *ten* years against the depopulation of *five*. This will not do: we must reduce their emigrants by one-half, say to six hundred thousand—and add to the depopulation the estimated increase *up* to 1846, say half a million. This will give upwards of two millions whose disappearance is to be accounted for—and six hundred thousand emigrants in the other column. Balance unaccounted for, *a million and a half*.

This is without computing those who were born in the five famine years; whom we may leave to be balanced by the deaths from *natural* causes in the same period.

Now, that million and a half of men, women, and children, were carefully, prudently, and peacefully *slain* by the English Government. They died of hunger in the midst of abundance, which their own hands created; and it is quite immaterial to distinguish those who perished in the agonies of famine itself from those who died of typhus fever, which in Ireland is always caused by famine.

Further, I have called it an artificial famine: that is to say, it was a famine which desolated a rich and fertile island, that produced every year abundance and superabundance to sustain all her people and many more. The English, indeed, call that famine a dispensation of Providence; and ascribe it entirely to the blight of the potatoes. But potatoes failed in like manner all over Europe, yet there was no famine save in Ireland. The British account of the matter, then, is first, a fraud—second, a blasphemy. The Almighty, indeed, sent the potato blight, but the English created the famine.

* * *

3. See note 1, p. 231.

MICHAEL DAVITT

The Phoenix Park Murders†

* * *

* * * The manifesto was written by a few of us in the hotel * * * as a declaration absolutely necessary to imparting a sentiment of un-equivocal sincerity to the terms in which the crime was looked upon and condemned by the Irish people and their leaders. It was sent at once to the press agencies in Great Britain, cabled to John Boyle O'Reilly, of Boston, for the widest publication in America, and wired to Mr. Alfred Webb, of Dublin, to be printed as a placard, and despatched by Sunday night's last train to every city and town in Ireland, so as to be posted on the walls of the country on Monday morning.

The facts relating to the murders were few, but they created a world-wide sensation. Earl Spencer, the new Lord Lieutenant, made his entry into Dublin on Saturday, May 6th. He was accompanied by Lord Frederick Cavendish, the successor to Mr. Forster in the chief-secretaryship. After the official ceremonies in Dublin Castle were concluded, Lord Frederick Cavendish set out to walk to his offi-cial residence in Phoenix Park, about a mile distant. On entering the park gate he was joined by Mr. Burke, the permanent under-secretary for Ireland and recognized head of "The Castle." Both men continued walking in the direction of the chief secretary's lodge. On nearing a spot on the wide roadway, almost exactly oppo-site the viceregal residence, and distant in a direct line about four hundred yards therefrom, four or five men sprang upon Burke and attacked him with knives. Lord Cavendish attempted to defend the assailed under-secretary, and was himself stabbed and also killed. The time was between half-past six and seven o'clock in the evening. It was still daylight, and the park had its ordinary number of visitors in the usual places of resort. The assailants made off in the direction of Chapelizod, mounting a car which apparently awaited them in

---

† Michael Davitt (1846–1906), Irish nationalist political leader, worked in sometimes uneasy alliance with Charles Stewart Parnell (1846–1891), the leader of the Irish Parliamentary Party in the 1880s during campaigns for land tenants' rights and Home Rule (limited autonomy) for Ireland. Davitt opposed Parnell's attempt to retain his political leadership after Parnell was involved in an adultery scandal. A copy of Davitt's book is listed in the inventory of Joyce's library in Trieste, where he lived while he was writing *A Portrait of the Artist as a Young Man.*

From chapter XIX, "The Phoenix Park Murders," *The Fall of Feudalism in Ireland or The Story of the Land League Revolution.* London and New York: Harper & Brothers, 1904, 359–64.

that direction, and got clear away before any effort could be made to capture or to track them in their flight. Their subsequent arrest, six months later, their trial and execution for the crime, are now matters of common history.

The motive of the attack on Mr. Burke, who alone was singled out for vengeance, was entirely political. He personified the Castle system of rule, being an Irishman and Catholic who became, on both these grounds, in the view of those who conspired to kill him, the worst type of anti-national official and the strongest prop of alien power. He was credited with being the arch-coercionist of the administration, the employer of informers, and active antagonist of all revolutionary movements. Those who had resolved to kill him were not animated by any purpose friendly to the Land League in their deadly design. It transpired that the chief instigators of the deed of vengeance were inimical to the league movement. But Mr. Burke typified to them the embodiment of English dominance and oppression. He had, they believed, been Mr. Forster's evil adviser, and he had imprisoned men and women of his own race and creed in a despotic manner, his coercionist policy and measures being applied against many men suspected of being Fenians as well as against Land-Leaguers and others. He alone was the object of attack on that fatal Saturday evening. Lord Cavendish's murder was accidental to his presence with and attempted defence of his companion.

*   *   *

[The Kilmainham "Treaty"]

The sensational anti-climax to the bright anticipations of the journey from Portland to London created by the tragedy in Dublin did not prevent Mr. Parnell fulfilling his promise on the following day to explain the policy which had led to Forster's downfall and to our release. The explanation in substance was this: The no-rent manifesto had failed. The tenants, instead of working his plan of testing the land act in the manner suggested by the Land-League convention broke away and entered the courts. They thereby contracted obligations for a term of fifteen years. All other tenants not weighted down with arrears would follow suit. The ruined tenants, mostly those of small holdings, would be sacrificed unless an arrears act could be obtained which would wipe out most of their indebtedness and give them a clear road into the land court, too. To accomplish this a "parley" with the government became necessary. But the reason by which he was chiefly influenced in the negotiations through O'Shea was the growing power of "secret societies" and the alarming growth of outrages. By "secret societies" he did not necessarily mean Fenian bodies. He believed the obnoxious societies to be more or less local, like those that had sprung up in past periods of agrarian warfare in the wake of evictions and coercion. He saw in this development, and in the growth of the revolutionary feeling inside the movement, a menace to the existence of the constitutional agitation and a peril to the country which could only be successfully resisted and arrested by the release of those who could wield a counter influence and who could calm down popular feeling. Then it was evident that Mr. Chamberlain and his friends in the ministry were equally anxious for other—that was, cabinet—reasons to abandon coercion, and to face the larger question of self-government, which could not be done while Ireland continued in a condition of semi-anarchy.

* * * In this explanation he made no mention of his own letters from Kilmainham, nor of the undertaking given by him in one of those, that "the agitation would be slowed down," and that the Irish party could then see its way to co-operate with the English Liberal party in passing measures of common necessity or advantage to both countries. These parts of the treaty only leaked out months afterwards.

The situation created by the Kilmainham treaty was still further complicated by the Phoenix Park tragedy, inasmuch as coercion, instead of being modified, as agreed to by Mr. Gladstone, would probably become more stringent, while the deep anti-Irish feeling aroused in Great Britain by the killing of Lord Cavendish would render all present thought of concessions in the direction of Home Rule an impossible task for any ministry.

Probably no political leader ever found himself in so dangerous a position as Mr. Parnell occupied at this time. The "treaty" had done him great harm in Ireland. Almost all the "suspects" repudiated its rumored terms. It was "a deal" with the government, and under the circumstances that condemned it in their eyes. In America it was denounced as "the sale of the Land League." On the face of it, it wore the appearance of a bargain with the defeated coercionists to get out of Kilmainham, and as a virtual surrender of the movement to its enemies. On this state of things the park murders came as a cyclonic sensation, sweeping everything else out of the path of a tragic event fraught with disastrous consequences to a movement which had a few hours previously reached almost to the goal of success. In fact, the Phoenix Park murders saved Mr. Parnell from the perils which lurked in the terms of the compact, while both events snatched from the Land League the guerdon of triumph, and literally smote it to the death which the treaty had planned for it by other means.

Apart from the effect made upon his mind by the act of the Invincibles, Mr. Parnell left prison resolved to have no more semi-revolutionary Land Leagues and no more relations with men or movements which could involve him or any party under his lead in any conflict, open or secret, with law and order in Ireland. The event of May 6th having almost driven him from public life, necessarily increased his resolve never again to engage in any fight like that of the Land League. And this resolve he never deviated from afterwards for a single hour.

* * *

The motive and the making of the Kilmainham treaty appealed to diverging views for support and disapproval. To conservative nationalists and to the large element of Mr. Parnell's personal following the treaty was an adroit political manoeuvre and a notable triumph of party leadership. It appeared to turn the flank of his enemy's position, while it procured at the same time the fall from power of his chief adversary. There was also the release of all the suspects secured, together with the promise of a concession which would relieve a large number of small tenants from the risk of immediate eviction. In addition, there was the prestige of a victorious compromise obtained out of what was felt to be a most dangerous situation, and it was reasoned that the leader who had accomplished all this, while he was still a prisoner in the hands of his enemy, had gained a tactical and decided victory for himself along with very good terms for the people whom he represented.

[Davitt's Differences with Parnell]

On the other hand, these concessions were obtained on the condition that the forces which compelled Mr. Gladstone to change his policy were to be disbanded, while the movement that had given Mr. Parnell his position and power was to disappear. This was virtually the other side of the bargain. The price was too great, and the terms were so obnoxious to the league sentiment in Ireland and America that had not the Phoenix Park catastrophe intervened as a stroke of Ireland's unfriendly destiny, Mr. Parnell's leadership would have trembled in the balance, even should it survive the shock of such a surrender. English rule in Ireland had never been so shaken and demoralized since 1798 as it was in 1881–82, nor had Castle rule ever been so fiercely and effectively assaulted in the century. The country was absolutely ungovernable, while an organization having nearly a million members throughout the world stood behind Mr. Parnell's lead, with abundant friends and ample power to keep

the struggle going until the whole system of anti-national administration would fall to pieces and necessitate a radical and fundamental change.

*   *   *

* * * Looked at, therefore, from the point of view of the policy and
purpose of the Land League, to destroy landlordism and to demoral-
ize Dublin-Castle rule so as to force a settlement of the agrarian and
national problems on radical but rational lines, the Kilmainham
treaty was a victory for these menaced institutions and a political
defeat of the forces led by Mr. Parnell.

ENGLISH POLITICAL CARTOON AFTER THE PHOENIX PARK MURDERS

PUNCH, OR THE LONDON CHARIVARI.—MAY 20, 1882.

THE IRISH FRANKENSTEIN.

"The baneful and blood-stained Monster * * * yet was it not my Master to the very extent that it was my Creature ? * * * Had I not breathed into it my own spirit ?" * * * (*Extract from the Works of* C. S. P-RN-LL, M.P.)

In small print under the title in the cartoon is the following extract from Mary Shelley's narrative *Frankenstein*, attributed to Charles Stewart Parnell: "'The baneful and blood-stained Monster * * * yet was it not my Master to the very extent that it was my Creature? * * * Had I not breathed into it my own spirit?' * * * (*Extract from the Works of* C. S. P-RN-LL, M.P." The document at the monster's feet has a death's head and is signed "Cap\[t\] Moonlight," the alias of Andrew Scott (1842 or 1845–1880), an Irishman who became a notorious criminal in Australia, where he was involved in daring and violent crimes. His execution in Australia in 1880 for the shooting death of a senior constable had been widely publicized not long before the Phoenix Park murders.

ENGLISH POLITICAL CARTOON AFTER THE DIVORCE SCANDAL

Fun (December 10, 1890)

THE TWO PARNELLS; OR, THE MAN BESIDE HIMSELF.
PARNELL THE PATRIOT AND PARNELL THE TRAITOR.

In the pocket of the Parnell with Satanic wings is a document entitled "Manifesto." At the end of November 1890, Parnell had issued his final political manifesto, a self-serving document that was damaging to Gladstone, his English political ally concerning Home Rule. He apparently thought, erroneously, that the manifesto would distract attention from the divorce scandal.

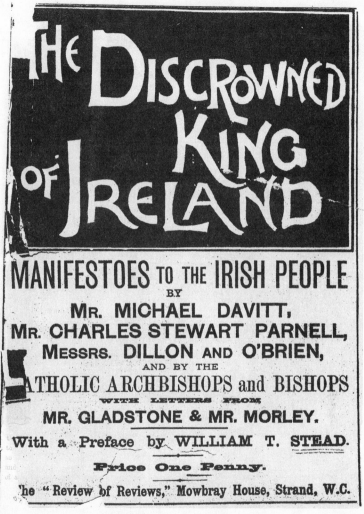

Pages 243–51 are from *The Discrowned King of Ireland*, ed. William J. Stead. Dublin: Review of Reviews, 1890: front cover (above), back cover (244), inside front cover ("Address"), pp. 16–17 ("An Appeal"), inside back cover ("Protest"). The pamphlet's title plays on the popular view before the divorce scandal that Charles Stewart Parnell was the "uncrowned King of Ireland."

IF YOU SUPPORT MR. PARNELL,

REMEMBER!

WILLIAM O'BRIEN says :

"Mr. Parnell's continued Leadership means destruction."

JOHN DILLON adds :

"All the success of the last few years will result in final failure."

MICHAEL DAVITT says :

"The Cause of Home Rule is not only dead but damned for years."

PATRICK FORD says :

"It is his imperative duty to retire."

And the IRISH BISHOPS :

"Surely Catholic Ireland will not accept as its leader a man thus dishonoured, and wholly unworthy of Christian confidence ?"

ADDRESS
BY THE
BISHOPS OF IRELAND

At Dublin, on December 3rd

A Meeting of the Standing Committee of the Archbishops and Bishops of Ireland was held at the Archbishop's House, Dublin.

THE COMMITTEE CONSISTS OF FOUR ARCHBISHOPS AND SIX BISHOPS ELECTED TO REPRESENT FOUR ECCLESIASTICAL PROVINCES OF IRELAND.

The following Address was unanimously adopted:—

The Standing Committee communicated by telegraph with their absent brethren of the Episcopacy, and have received the adhesion of the Bishops, whose names, with their own, are signed to the address:—

Address of the Standing Committee of the Archbishops and Bishops of Ireland to the clergy and laity of their flock.

Very Rev. and Rev. Fathers and Fellow-countrymen:—The Bishops of Ireland can no longer keep silent in the presence of the all-engrossing question which agitates, not Ireland and England alone, but every spot where Irishmen have found a home. That question is—Who is to be in future the leader of the Irish people, or, rather, who is not to be their leader?

Without hesitation or doubt, and in the plainest possible terms, we give it as our unanimous judgment that, whoever else is fit to fill that highly-responsible post, *Mr. Parnell* decidedly is not.

As pastors of this Catholic nation we do not base this our judgment and solemn declaration on political grounds, but simply and solely on the facts and circumstances revealed in the London Divorce Court. After the verdict given in that Court we cannot regard Mr. Parnell in any other light than as a man convicted of one of the greatest offences known to religion and society, aggravated as it is in his case by almost every circumstance that could possibly attach to it so as to give to it a scandalous pre-eminence in guilt and shame.

Surely Catholic Ireland, so eminently conspicuous for its virtue and the purity of its social life, will not accept as its leader a man who is dishonoured and wholly unworthy of Christian confidence.

Furthermore, as Irishmen devoted to our country, eager for its elevation, and earnestly intent on securing for it the benefits of domestic legislation, we cannot but be influenced by the conviction that the continuance of Mr. Parnell as leader of even a section of the Irish party must have the effect of disorganizing our ranks, and ranging as in hostile camps the hitherto united forces of our country. Confronted with the prospect of contingencies disastrous, we see nothing but inevitable defeat at the approaching general election, and, as a result, Home Rule indefinitely postponed, coercion perpetuated, the hands of the evictor strengthened, and the tenants already evicted left without the shadow of a hope of ever being restored to their homes.

"Your devoted servants in Christ,

"X Michael Logue, Archbishop of Armagh and Primate of All Ireland.

"X Wm. J. Walsh, Archbishop of Dublin and Primate of Ireland.

"X T. W. Croke, Archbishop of Cashel.

"X Jno. MacEvilly, Archbishop of Tuam.

"X Jas. Donnelly, Bishop of Clogher.

"X James Lynch, Bishop of Kildare and Leighlin.

"X Francis J. MacCormack, Bishop of Galway and Kilmaeduagh.

"X John MacCarthy, Bishop of Cloyne.

"X Wm. Fitzgerald, Bishop of Ross.

"X Bartholomew Woodlock, Bishop of Ardagh and Clonmaenoise.

"X Thomas Alphonsus O'Callaghan, Bishop of Cork.

"X James Browne, Bishop of Ferns.

"X Abraham Brownrigg, Bishop of Ossory.

"X Patrick M'Allister, Bishop of Down and Connor.

"X Patrick O'Donnell, Bishop of Raphoe.

"X John Lyster, Bishop of Achonry.

"X Edward Magennis, Bishop of Kilmore.

"X Thomas MacGivern, Bishop of Dromore.

"X John K. O'Doherty, Bishop of Derry.

"X Michael Comerford Coadjutor Bishop of Kildare and Leighlin.

"X Thomas M'Redmond, Coadjutor Bishop of Killaloe.

"X Nicholas Donnelly, Bishop of Canea.

"Dublin, Dec. 3, 1890

AN APPEAL TO THE IRISH PEOPLE
BY MR. MICHAEL DAVITT

In the Labour World *of November 27th, Mr. Davitt published the following editorial, entitled "An appeal to the Irish people":—*

The issue which has to be decided by the Irish Parliamentary party on Monday next is plain and unmistakable. That party has to consider one thing, and one thing only—What is best for Home Rule? In our judgment there is no room now for a moment's hesitation, whatever may have been the case a few days ago.

Mr. Parnell has, it is true, claims upon the allegiance and friendship of his colleagues which appeal most strongly to their sense of loyalty and comradeship. They would not be Irishmen, warm-hearted, impulsive, and generous, if they did not exhibit these distinguishing qualities of their race when compelled to sit in judgment upon the man under whose banner they have marched and fought for their country during the last ten years; and it cannot be denied that in unanimously re-electing him as their leader, under circumstances which demanded from him the tendering of his resignation, they have given abundant proof of their gratitude for his past services to Ireland and of personal attachment to himself. They are now called upon to weigh the consequences of retaining him in the position which he appears resolved to maintain, at whatever cost to the interests of the cause of which he has been the chief exponent. They cannot be blind to the result which must follow the carrying out of Mr. Gladstone's expressed resolution to retire from politics if Mr. Parnell retains the Irish leadership. Every sane politician in the country knows that without the co-operation of the party led by Mr. Gladstone Home Rule is impossible for years to come.

Will Mr. Parnell allow the hopes which the Irish people have centred in the Liberal alliance to be shattered rather than relinquish even for a time the headship of the Irish party? At the moment it seems as if this were so, and from the report of the proceedings of the meeting of his party it appears he carries with him a majority of Ireland's national representatives. This, then, is the situation which confronts us at the present moment. It is in all conscience grave enough.

Mr. Gladstone's letter puts before the Irish Parliamentary party and the Irish people the clearest and most momentous issue ever submitted to political allies. There can be no possible mistake as to its meaning, or doubt as to the consequences that must ensue if the proposition of the Liberal leader be not accepted. Will Irish members and Mr. Parnell be deaf to the touching appeal which Mr. Sheehy is reported to have addressed to them in behalf of the evicted tenants of Ireland? Do they forget the thousands of homes that have been torn from the peasantry of Ireland during the last ten years—the thousands of evicted tenants who have patiently lived in the hope that Mr. Gladstone and his followers in Great Britain would carry the next general election and be able to give to Ireland a system of domestic government under which the victims of Irish landlordism would be restored to their hearthstones, and Ireland relieved of agrarian and other agitation? Will Mr. W. O'Brien's words, which we print elsewhere, help them to arrive at a salutary decision on Monday?

We are loth to recriminate at this terrible moment, but there is no blinking the fact that the speeches delivered in Dublin, and the action of the Irish party in unanimously re-electing Mr. Parnell, have lost the Irish cause thousands of friends, who it is to be feared will not return, while they have tended to place Ireland in a humiliating position before the nations. In this last respect there are more than the Irish party to blame for a silence that can be construed into tacit condonation of conduct which ought to be more repellent to a nation of Ireland's acknowledged high moral standard than to the English people. Yet the bishops and priests of Ireland have left it to the sturdy Dissenters of Great Britain to make the protest which was called for in the interests of public morality as well as of Home Rule.

However, regrettable as this temporary loss of moral prestige is to the Irish cause, the situation, desperate though it be, may yet be retrieved. If the Irish party, reinforced by an outspoken expression of Irish popular opinion, decide on Monday next to prefer Home Rule to Mr. Parnell, victory may yet be ours. There is no other choice. Last week we made an appeal to Mr. Parnell to save Home Rule and give one more proof of his patriotism and statesmanship. Our appeal has passed unheeded. In some quarters it was for a time even misunderstood. That is so no longer. What we urged a week ago has since been repeated by friends of Ireland everywhere.

Irish members and Irish newspapers have, in the face of the present terrible crisis, besought Mr. Parnell to place country before pride and love of power. They have been treated with a silence bordering on contempt. The friends of Home Rule in Great Britain, beginning with the venerable leader of the Liberal party, have been unanimous in their views. Mr. Parnell declines to yield to prayers or requests. The promptings of duty, of patriotism, of honour, are stifled, and in their place we see the workings of hidden influences which, if permitted free rein, will ruin for a generation the chances of Home Rule for Ireland. * * *

* * *

We need say little more. We implore the Irish race at home and abroad to rise and show themselves equal to this emergency. There may be those who believe that Mr. Parnell can be retained and yet Ireland's cause be saved. We have no such hope. We believe that in the Irish party there is more than one man who can lead it to victory. We believe that there is sufficient patriotism in that party to follow a leader chosen from its own ranks by a majority of its members. Let the Irish race consider these points. We urge them in all earnestness to do this, and with hope and confidence we await a decision. Whatever that decision may be, the Irish cause remains imperishable. It may be thwarted for a time, but not for ever. Of its victory in the end we have no doubt. Monday's decision will postpone it for a generation or retrieve all that is now endangered. May wisdom and courage guide those in whom Ireland's hopes are centred.

PROTEST FROM A CATHOLIC PRIEST

Canon Doyle on the Parnell Scandal

The Rev. Canon Doyle, of Ramsgrange, Arthurstown, has addressed a vigorous letter to the Editor of the *Freeman's Journal* on the subject of Mr. Parnell's position. I take the following extracts from this manly appeal by an Irish priest to be the conscience of the Irish people:—

One of the most shocking scandals I remember to have occurred in my time is the futile attempt made by you and others to whitewash unfortunate Charles Stewart Parnell. Now that all the resolutions on this nasty subject have been passed, and that the country has been swamped under a deluge of feeble fustian, what do they all come to? Why, this, and only this, that Parnell, yet "essential" to Ireland, "can not be done without." I feel it my duty to enter my feeble but solemn protest against this degradation of our just and imperishable cause and of our dear old country. I had to perform many painful duties in the course of my ministry and in my conflicts for our suffering people, but that which devolves on me, now in the advanced evening of a long life, is the most painful of all. Until this divorce case turned up, I entertained for Mr. Parnell the most sincere esteem and profound respect. In the infancy of his political career I went to his assistance with decisive effect, as he was good enough to publicly acknowledge.

How deep must be the guilt of this crime committed in the midday light of the Gospel, and how black the criminal who sacrilegiously tramples under foot the holy bonds of matrimony—the very foundation of civilized society! Yet without one word of repentance, he crawls, reeking from ten years' adulterous concubinage, to claim the leadership of holy Ireland, whose banner, though rent and torn in many a hard-fought battle, is till now as stainless as the driven snow. Until this dark, disgraceful hour no one ever dared to trail it in the mire.

We have now strong reason to suspect why the Vatican is so prompt to visit us with its displeasure. It seems this horrid scandal was well known in what is called "Society" in England, though we heard nothing of it. Our numerous enemies there had abundance of material to send to Rome. * * *

You boast that you and your jerrymandered meetings represent the feeling of Ireland regarding Parnell's leadership. I say you do not. I assert the honest opinion of the country is dead against this infamous man. I venture, further, to prophesy that no Irish constituency will, at the next General Election, accept a candidate at the declaration of the self-convicted, audacious adulterer of One Ash Lodge.[1]

* * * Should any evil befall the Irish cause at this supreme crisis, the blame will rest solely and entirely on those gentlemen of the party who dishonourably and dishonestly have attempted to whitewash Parnell by a snatch vote of jerrymandered meetings in Dublin, falsely declared to represent the feelings of the country. I deliberately assert they do not represent the feelings or the wishes of either priests or people. Did the Parnell *claquers*[2] even condescend to consult the people? Whom did they consult on this most important and vital subject? Did they consult the Catholic clergy? No. Did they consult the people and the leaders of the people throughout Ireland? No, emphatically no. And if ever there were a subject on which the honest, calm, and deliberate opinion of the country was necessary, it is whether they can accept and follow Parnell as a leader after his ten years' adulterous profligacy.

Have you, as a Catholic journalist or a Christian gentleman, and your platform friends, reflected for a moment on the step you have taken? Have you resolved to banish clergymen of every denomination from your movement? It would seem that you have, and to banish with them tens of thousands of honest upright laymen who have been horrified at the *dénouement* of the O'Shea Divorce suit. * * * You have not expelled us by a direct vote, but just as effectually by a side wind. I would respectfully ask you, or any gentleman who attended your late meetings, how could a clergyman of any denomination stand on a platform from which Parnell is cheered, and then stand in his pulpit on the following Sunday, except in a white sheet? How could such a clergyman denounce vice of a similar kind in one of his humble parishioners? Would not the poor man naturally and justly say—"It is because I am poor I am treated after this fashion. If I had an esquire after my name, or an M.P.,[3] I might do what I liked. His reverence denounced me to-day till the dogs would not eat my flesh; yet only last week he was at a great meeting for Parnell, and there he was on the platform cheering him and saying no other man should be our leader, though he is one of the most awful sinners the

---

1. A mistake for, or else an intentional play on, Wonersh Lodge near Eltham in Kent, where Katherine O'Shea, who became Parnell's mistress and eventually his wife, lived when they met and during their affair.
2. Those who clap (French); fawning admirers.
3. Member of Parliament. "Esquire": title added to the name of a gentleman because of birth, status, or education.

world ever produced. God help the poor. The rich can do as they like, and we never hear a world about it." That is the position in which you place us, and which no clergyman can on a moment's reflection retain. The masses don't understand your metaphysical distinctions condemning him as an adulterer and admiring him as a politician. If you retain the politician you must retain the adulterer. If you expel the adulterer the politician must go. You say the party will break up. Well, if they are only kept together by so rotten a bond the sooner the better. The lust of M'Murrogh brought us the English invasion and all its evil consequences.[4] It would seem by the infatuation of a few headlong enthusiasts and the cunning of a few scheming barristers the lust of Parnell is about to rivet our chains anew. Where now is the holy zeal that only a few years back cleaned out the Augean Stable[5] of Dublin Castle? * * *

I call upon the faithful fathers and husbands of Ireland, upon the virtuous and loving wives and mothers, upon our modest and chaste young girls, and upon our chivalrous young men, to put an immediate end to this infamy—to call with one voice for the retirement of this unfortunate man from the position he has disgraced, and to insist in the most unequivocal manner on the appointment of a new leader. Thus, and thus only, can peace be restored, and the cause now ripe for settlement be brought to a happy consummation. * * *

4. After taking Dervorgilla, the wife of the rival chieftain Tiernan O'Rourke, Dermot Mac-Murrough (1110–1171), king of Leinster, asked for help from King Henry II of England, who subsequently became lord of Ireland and initiated eight centuries of English dominance.
5. In Greek mythology, as one of the labors imposed on him as penance for murdering his family, Hercules cleaned the immense, filthy stables of King Augeas of Elis in a single day.

MICHAEL DAVITT

Death of Parnell—Appreciation[†]

Mr. Parnell continued the combat against great odds, with characteristic tenacity, during the summer and autumn of 1891. He addressed demonstrations in various parts of the country each Sunday for months, travelling from Brighton, in the south of England, to Ireland on a Saturday, and returning again direct to his home from the place of meeting. He lost ground steadily in his desperate campaign, but never lost courage. Doggedly, if hopelessly, he persisted in the struggle until his strength gave way. The end came with startling suddenness. There had been no tidings of serious illness, though it was known that his health was breaking down from the physical strain of weekly journeys from England to meetings in Ireland. He died at Brighton on October 6, 1891. He was only in his forty-sixth year, and but ten short months had rolled by since he broke with the majority of his following in refusing to adopt the course which his wisest friends pressed in vain upon him. * * *

Parnell's claim to greatness no Irish nationalist, and few Irishmen, will ever deny. To do so would be like ignoring the existence of a mountain or some other objective fact in nature. His work was great, and would of itself make the political fame of any man with a similar record. Like all the world's historic characters, there were marked limitations to his greatness, not counting the final weakness which precipitated his fall.

His immense popularity with the Irish people was not due to any Celtic qualities. Of these he had not even a trace. There was no racial affinity between him and them. He was far less like O'Connell than even Mr. Gladstone. The great Englishman inherited a Scottish kinship with the Irish nation through his maternal ancestors, and had some traits of character more Celtic than Saxon. Mr. Parnell was born in Ireland. Beyond this and his descent from English ancestors of the Pale,[1] there was nothing in habits, temperament, or individuality that would establish relationship between him and those whose boundless confidence he had won, except in the common purpose of the national movement which he led.

He was a Protestant, leading a nation chiefly Catholic; a landlord, commanding tenants in a war against his own class; a cold, reserved

† On Davitt, see p. 236.

  From chapter LIII, "Death of Parnell—Appreciation," *The Fall of Feudalism in Ireland or The Story of the Land League Revolution*. London and New York: Harper & Brothers, 1904, 651–57. Davitt's footnote has been omitted.

1. The English Pale was an area of twenty miles in radius around Dublin fortified with a ditch and rampart by the English to protect them from attack by the native Irish until the island could be conquered.

man, at the head of one of the most warmhearted and impulsive of races; a sober, unemotional speaker, who never quoted an Irish poet but once, and did it wrong, in a country remarkable for passion and ornate oratory; a public man and leader who treated his party with icy aloofness for years, who lived away from Ireland most of his time; and who appeared in his conduct towards the Irish people to be absolutely unconcerned as to what they thought of him until the personal issue involved in the unhappy event of 1890 roused him into a fierce contest with those who questioned his right to lead only when the leadership headed directly for disaster.

He was unlike all the leaders who had preceded him in his accomplishments, traits of character, and personal idiosyncrasies. He had neither wit nor humor, eloquence or the passion of conviction, academical distinction of any kind, scholarship or profession, Irish accent, appearance, or mannerism. In fact, he was a paradox in Irish leadership, and will stand unique in his niche in Irish history as bearing no resemblance of any kind to those who handed down to his time the fight for Irish nationhood.

What, then, was the secret of his immense influence and popularity? He was above and before everything else a splendid fighter. He had attacked and beaten the enemies of Ireland in the citadel of their power—the British Parliament. It was here where he loomed great and powerful in Irish imagination. As Wendell Phillips put it on one occasion, Parnell was the Irishman who had compelled John Bull to listen to what he in behalf of Ireland had to say in the House of Commons; and the personal force which had done this, and had flung the Irish question and representatives across the plans and purposes of English parties, in a battle for the Irish people, appealed instinctively to the admiration of those in whose name this work was accomplished.

He was fortunate, too, in being heir to the ripening fruits of his predecessors' labors—the Daniel O'Connells, Fintan Lalors, Gavan Duffys, James Stephenses, and Isaac Butts, who had sown the seed in less propitious days and under darker skies. * * *

* * *

* * * Parnell's prestige and triumphs sprang from a unique kind of blended character, endowed with a magnetic power which made him more formidable than mental culture or oratorical abilities could do. He derived nothing from the profession of political opinions, but everything from an insurrection of social forces led by him in revolt against a system which was the very basis of English government in Ireland, and of aristocratic and class privilege in England—land monopoly. The English classes looked at him as a desperate revolutionist—which, unfortunately, he was not—because he had the courage and capacity to strike at what was the weakest point in

the foreign rule of his country, and also at the very foundations of England's own supremacy—the House of Commons and the land-owning power of those who filled and owned the House of Lords. Political opinions had little or nothing to do with Parnell's work in the days when he won his fame. He was armed with a reformer's crow-bar and not with a politician's note-book. His work was to undermine and pull down what had been chiefly responsible for Ireland's oppression * * *.

* * *

Mr. Gladstone diagnosed Mr. Parnell's political character and purpose clearly during and after the events of 1885–86. He recognized in him a man of great practical capacity, with conservative tendencies scarcely hidden behind the controlling head of a semi-revolutionary agitation. He knew that a successful reformer would be the likeliest personal influence to accept the responsibility of guiding and directing the forces he had led in the revolt against Dublin Castle and landlordism, when once a rational concession of alternatives to these systems would appeal to his sense of patriotic statesmanship. No one more sincerely regretted Mr. Parnell's fall than Mr. Gladstone. "An invaluable man," was his summary of the power and potential qualities of his one-time ally. Not so Lord Salisbury.[2] He took *The Times* estimate of the great Irishman, and persuaded himself that he was a revolutionist, a radical, and an incarnate enemy of the English connection. This was the judgment of prejudice, and not the true estimate of either a penetrating or generous mind.

* * *

[Ireland in 1904 and in the Future][†]

Why should not the Irish people make a persistent demand, inside and out of Parliament, for the fullest measure of freedom to which, as a separate nationality among civilized peoples, we are in every sense, and on every rational ground, entitled? Why should Ireland not be a state in the freest and fullest sense in which Holland, Denmark, Belgium, Switzerland, Bulgaria, Servia, and Greece are nations? On the grounds of abstract justice, of historic claim, or racial right—or on that of England's failure in Ireland—our demands could not, in reason, be

2. Robert Gascoyne-Cecil (1830–1903), 3rd Marquess of Salisbury, Conservative member of the House of Lords who was prime minister at the time of Parnell's death.
† From chapter LX, "A Future Racial Programme," *The Fall of Feudalism in Ireland or The Story of the Land League Revolution.* London and New York: Harper & Brothers, 1904, 717, 721–22, 724.

disputed. England has not alone failed to win our assent to her selfish dominion over us; she has shown her incapacity to rule Ireland either for its contentment or prosperity, or for her own advantage and peace. The present condition and prospects of a depopulated country, after centuries of English lordship, and a hundred years of direct rule over us, is alone a full condemnation of the system of government which has reduced it to the level of the poorest country in Europe, and made it the only civilized land on earth in which a hardy and prolific race is persistently diminishing in numbers.

*   *   *

What has been the general result to Ireland of the enforced partnership of 1801—that is, of British imperialism? I can reply to this question best by the test of comparison with other countries. When the act of union was passed Ireland had one-half the population of Great Britain, three-and-a-quarter times that of Scotland, ten times that of Wales, and five times that of London. To-day our population is about one-eighth of that of Great Britain, twenty thousand less than Scotland, two and a half times that of Wales, and about two millions less than that of greater London.

Going beyond the bounds of the United Kingdom, we find a similar progress in population in all the small nations of Europe, without a single exception. Holland, Belgium, Norway, Sweden, Switzerland, Bavaria, Portugal, Greece, have added more than fifty per cent. to their respective populations during the last fifty years. While these small states have thus increased their populations, through the guardian care of national liberty, Ireland, under the evil influence of an alien rule, has lost a hundred per cent. of her people. In this respect she stands in a unique position among civilized lands, there being, in fact, no parallel in the history of Christian nations for the steady and deadly drain of population away from a country blessed by nature with resources capable of sustaining three times the present number of inhabitants of Belgium.

This, however, is only half the indictment of this alien rule. As a direct result of this fatal weakening of Ireland's vital energies, both the birth-rate and the marriage-rate of the country are now near the lowest of any nation in Europe. There is, likewise, an alarming increase of insanity among the diminishing numbers; a fact also due to the emigration of the more virile of the people, leaving the physically impoverished behind to carry on the racial functions of human development. As a further comment upon all this decay and retrogression, a combined national and local taxation, which amounted to a total of £2,000,000 a year under an Irish parliament, with a population equal to that of to-day, is now, as a result of a hundred years of England's government, over £12,000,000 annually, an increase of six hundred per cent. On the top of all this, there is the fact that we have far more pauperism in the country to-day than there was thirty years ago, when Ireland had two millions more of people. Add to this the humiliating admission that our population is the worst educated in these islands, and my readers have a brief summary of what we owe to English rule in Ireland.

There is no hope for Ireland under such government—absolutely none—any more than there is for a person into whose blood an insidious poison has been infused and who is denied the effective remedy which would counteract the deadly fluid. We must, therefore, demand the remedy that can alone save our country from national death. Nationhood, and that only—the full, free, and unfettered right of our people to rule and govern themselves in everything concerning the domestic laws, peace, and welfare of Ireland—is what we must demand and work for henceforth, if England's callous selfishness is not to be allowed to carry out and to complete the ruin it has already all but consummated.

*   *   *

The Irish race have a place in the world's affairs of to-day that is incompatible with the position which Ireland occupies as a kind of vegetable-patch for selfish imperial purposes. We are fully twenty millions of the world's population, and though four-fifths of these reside out of Ireland, they are potential factors, nevertheless, in the political fate and fortunes of the country from which a rule of stupidity and race-hatred drove their progenitors away. Moreover, Ireland and its race have a mission in the world, have national characteristics, a distinctive individuality and ideas, greatly differing from Anglo-Saxonism, with its purely materialistic spirit and aims. These alone entitle our country to a recognized and separate place in the ranks of civilized states.

P. H. PEARSE

Theobald Wolfe Tone[†]

*An Address Delivered at the Grave of Wolfe Tone
in Bodenstown Churchyard, 22nd June, 1913*

We have come to the holiest place in Ireland; holier to us even than the place where Patrick[1] sleeps in Down. Patrick brought us life, but this man died for us. And though many before him and some since

† Patrick Pearse (1879–1916), Irish educator, writer, and revolutionary, shifted from advocating cultural nationalism to urging violent action in order to free Ireland from English

have died in testimony of the truth of Ireland's claim to nationhood, Wolfe Tone was the greatest of all that have made that testimony, the greatest of all that have died for Ireland whether in old time or in new. He was the greatest of Irish Nationalists; I believe he was the greatest of Irish men. And if I am right in this I am right in saying that we stand in the holiest place in Ireland, for it must be that the holiest sod of a nation's soil is the sod where the greatest of her dead lies buried.

* * *

We have come here not merely to salute this noble dust and to pay our homage to the noble spirit of Tone. We have come to renew our adhesion to the faith of Tone; to express once more our full acceptance of the gospel of Irish Nationalism which he was the first to formulate in worthy terms, giving clear definition and plenary meaning to all that had been thought and taught before him by Irish-speaking or English-speaking men; uttered half articulately by a Shane O'Neill in some defiance flung at the Englishry, expressed under some passionate metaphor by a Geoffrey Keating, hinted at by a Swift in some biting gibe, but clearly and greatly stated by Wolfe Tone, and not needing now ever to be stated anew for any new generation.[2] He has spoken for all time, and his voice resounds throughout Ireland, calling to us from this grave when we wander astray following other voices that ring less true.

This, then, is the first part of Wolfe Tone's achievement—he made articulate the dumb voices of the centuries, he gave Ireland a clear and precise and worthy concept of Nationality. But he did more than this: not only did he define Irish Nationalism, but he armed his generation in defence of it. Thinker and doer, dreamer of the immortal dream and doer of the immortal deed—we owe to this dead man more than we can ever repay him by making pilgrimages to his grave or by rearing to him the stateliest monument in the streets of his city. To his teaching we owe it that there is such a thing as Irish Nationalism, and

---

rule. As a student at University College, Dublin, Joyce took Irish lessons from Pearse, who later became the leader of the Rising of 1916. As commander-in-chief of the Irish Volunteers, Pearse signed the surrender when the British put down the Rising and was executed, along with other leaders.

Tone (1763–1798), the founder of modern Irish republicanism, is commemorated annually at his grave in Bodenstown, County Kildare. See the 1798 entry in "Key Dates, Events, and Figures," p. 227.

From *How Does She Stand? Three Addresses*. Second Ed. The Bodenstown Series, No. 1. Dublin: "Irish Freedom" Office, 1915, 3–4, 6–7.

1. Patron saint of Ireland, active in the fifth century.
2. O'Neill (c. 1530–1567), an early Irish leader in Ulster, was murdered. Keating (c. 1580–c. 1644) wrote religious political tracts, including a history of Ireland that defended the Irish nation against foreign misrepresentations. Jonathan Swift (1667–1745), dean of St. Patrick's Cathedral (Anglican), Dublin, was a satirist and political writer who produced biting indictments of England's treatment of Ireland.

to the memory of the deed he nerved his generation to do, to the
memory of '98, we owe it that there is any manhood left in Ireland.

*   *   *

And let us make no mistake as to what Tone sought to do, what it
remains for us to do. We need not re-state our programme; Tone has
stated it for us:

"To break the connection with England, the never-failing source
of all our political evils, and to assert the independence of my
country—these were my objects. To unite the whole people of Ireland, to abolish the memory of all past dissensions, and to substitute
the common name of Irishmen in place of the dominations of
Protestant, Catholic, and Dissenter—these were my means."

I find here implicit all the philosophy of Irish Nationalism, all the
teaching of the Gaelic League and the later prophets. Ireland one
and Ireland free—is not this the definition of Ireland a Nation? To
that definition and to that programme we declare our adhesion
anew; pledging ourselves as Tone pledged himself—and in this sacred
place, by this graveside, let us not pledge ourselves unless we mean
to keep our pledge—we pledge ourselves to follow in the steps of
Tone, never to rest, either by day or by night, until his work be accomplished, deeming it the proudest of all privileges to fight for freedom,
to fight, not in despondency, but in great joy, hoping for the victory
in our day, but fighting on whether victory seem near or far, never
lowering our ideal, never bartering one jot or tittle of our birthright,
holding faith to the memory and the inspiration of Tone, and account-
ing ourselves base as long as we endure the evil thing against which
he testified with his blood.

Robert Emmet and the Ireland of To-day[†]

*An Address Delivered at the Emmet Commemoration in the
Academy of Music, Brooklyn, New York, 2nd March, 1914*

You ask me to speak of the Ireland of to-day. What can I tell you of
it that is worthy of commemoration where we commemorate heroic
faith and the splendour of death? *   *   *

Be assured that such a death always means a redemption. Emmet
redeemed Ireland from acquiescence in the Union. His attempt was
not a failure, but a triumph for that deathless thing we call Irish

---

† Emmet (1778–1803) was a leader of United Irishmen after the failed Rebellion of 1798.
  See the 1798 entry in "Key Dates, Events, and Figures," p. 227.
     From *How Does She Stand? Three Addresses*. Second Ed. The Bodenstown Series, No. 1.
  Dublin: "Irish Freedom" Office, 1915, 10–12.

Nationality. It was by Emmet that men remembered Ireland until Davis and Mitchel took up his work again, and '48 handed on the tradition to '67, and from '67 we receive the tradition unbroken.

You ask me to speak of the Ireland of to-day. What need I say but that to-day Ireland is turning her face once more to the old path? Nothing seems more definitely to emerge when one looks at the movements that are stirring both above the surface and beneath the surface in men's minds at home than the fact that the new generation is re-affirming the Fenian faith, the faith of Emmet. It is because we know that this is so that we can suffer in patience the things that are said and done in the name of Irish Nationality by some of our leaders. What one may call the Westminster phase is passing: the National movement is swinging back again into its proper channel.[1] A new junction has been made with the past: into the movement that has never wholly died since '67 have come the young men of the Gaelic League. Having renewed communion with its origins, Irish Nationalism is to-day a more virile thing than ever before in our time. Of that be sure.

I have said again and again that when the Gaelic League was founded in 1893 the Irish Revolution began. The Gaelic League brought it a certain distance upon its way; but the Gaelic League could not accomplish the Revolution. For five or six years a new phase has been due, and lo! it is with us now. To-day Ireland is once more organising, once more learning the noble trade of arms. In our towns and country places Volunteer companies are springing up. Dublin pointed the way, Galway has followed Dublin, Cork has followed Galway, Wexford has followed Cork, Limerick has followed Wexford, Monaghan has followed Limerick, Sligo has followed Monaghan, Donegal has followed Sligo. There is again in Ireland the murmur of a marching, and talk of guns and tactics. What this movement may mean for our country no man can say. But it is plain to all that the existence on Irish soil of an Irish army is the most portentous fact that has appeared in Ireland for over a hundred years: a fact which marks definitely the beginning of the second stage of the Revolution which was commenced when the Gaelic League was founded. The inner significance of the movement lies in this, that men of every rank and class, of every section of Nationalist opinion, of every shade of religious belief, have discovered that they share a common patriotism, that their faith is one and that there is one service in which they can come together at last: the service of their country in arms. We are realising now how proud a thing it is to serve, and in the comradeship and joy of the new service we are forgetting many ancient misunderstandings. * * *

1. "Westminster phase": political phase. Westminster is the seat of the English Parliament, which included Irish representatives at the time of this speech.

After all, there are in Ireland but two parties: those who stand for the English connection and those who stand against it. On what side, think you, stand the Irish Volunteers? I cannot speak for the Volunteers; I am not authorised to say when they will use their arms or where or how. I can speak only for myself; and it is strictly a personal perception that I am recording, but a perception that to me is very clear, when I say that before this generation has passed the Volunteers will draw the sword of Ireland. There is no truth but the old truth and no way but the old way. Home Rule may come or may not come, but under Home Rule or in its absence there remains for the Volunteers and for Ireland the substantial business of achieving Irish nationhood. And I do not know how nationhood is achieved except by armed men; I do not know how nationhood is guarded except by armed men.

I ask you, then, to salute with me the Irish Volunteers. I ask you to mark their advent as an augury that, no matter what pledges may be given by men who do not know Ireland—the stubborn soul of Ireland—that nation of ancient faith will never sell her birthright of freedom for a mess of pottage: a mess of dubious pottage, at that. Ireland has been guilty of many meannesses, of many shrinkings back when she should have marched forward; but she will never be guilty of that immense infidelity.

PROCLAMATION

POBLACHT NA H EIREANN.

THE PROVISIONAL GOVERNMENT
OF THE
IRISH REPUBLIC
TO THE PEOPLE OF IRELAND.

IRISHMEN AND IRISHWOMEN : In the name of God and of the dead generations from which she receives her old tradition of nationhood, Ireland, through us, summons her children to her flag and strikes for her freedom.

Having organised and trained her manhood through her secret revolutionary organisation, the Irish Republican Brotherhood, and through her open military organisations, the Irish Volunteers and the Irish Citizen Army, having patiently perfected her discipline, having resolutely waited for the right moment to reveal itself, she now seizes that moment, and, supported by her exiled children in America and by gallant allies in Europe, but relying in the first on her own strength, she strikes in full confidence of victory.

We declare the right of the people of Ireland to the ownership of Ireland, and to the unfettered control of Irish destinies, to be sovereign and indefeasible. The long usurpation of that right by a foreign people and government has not extinguished the right, nor can it ever be extinguished except by the destruction of the Irish people. In every generation the Irish people have asserted their right to national freedom and sovereignty ; six times during the past three hundred years they have asserted it in arms. Standing on that fundamental right and again asserting it in arms in the face of the world, we hereby proclaim the Irish Republic as a Sovereign Independent State, and we pledge our lives and the lives of our comrades-in-arms to the cause of its freedom, of its welfare, and of its exaltation among the nations.

The Irish Republic is entitled to, and hereby claims, the allegiance of every Irishman and Irishwoman. The Republic guarantees religious and civil liberty, equal rights and equal opportunities to all its citizens, and declares its resolve to pursue the happiness and prosperity of the whole nation and of all its parts, cherishing all the children of the nation equally, and oblivious of the differences carefully fostered by an alien government, which have divided a minority from the majority in the past.

Until our arms have brought the opportune moment for the establishment of a permanent National Government, representative of the whole people of Ireland and elected by the suffrages of all her men and women, the Provisional Government, hereby constituted, will administer the civil and military affairs of the Republic in trust for the people.

We place the cause of the Irish Republic under the protection of the Most High God, Whose blessing we invoke upon our arms, and we pray that no one who serves that cause will dishonour it by cowardice, inhumanity, or rapine. In this supreme hour the Irish nation must, by its valour and discipline and by the readiness of its children to sacrifice themselves for the common good, prove itself worthy of the august destiny to which it is called.

Signed on Behalf of the Provisional Government,

THOMAS J. CLARKE.

SEAN Mac DIARMADA.   THOMAS MacDONAGH.
P. H. PEARSE,   EAMONN CEANNT,
JAMES CONNOLLY.   JOSEPH PLUNKETT,

The image of the Proclamation of the Irish Republic is reprinted with permission of the National Library of Ireland. On Easter Sunday, April 23, 1916, the day before the Rising began, a thousand copies of the

Proclamation were printed in Liberty Hall (destroyed by English artillery during the fighting), the headquarters of the Irish Citizen Army, where the newspaper *The Irish Worker* was published. Constance Markiewicz, a commandant in the Irish Citizen Army, read it to a group on the Hall's steps; P. H. Pearse read it formally in front of the General Post Office the next day, when the rebels seized that building. The English executed all seven who signed the document, among others, by firing squad.

The Irish Literary and Cultural Revival

DOUGLAS HYDE

The Necessity for De-Anglicising Ireland[†]

When we speak of "The Necessity for De-Anglicising the Irish Nation," we mean it, not as a protest against imitating what is *best* in the English people, for that would be absurd, but rather to show the folly of neglecting what is Irish, and hastening to adopt, pell-mell, and indiscriminately, everything that is English, simply because it *is* English.

This is a question which most Irishmen will naturally look at from a National point of view, but it is one which ought also to claim the sympathies of every intelligent Unionist,[1] and which, as I know, does claim the sympathy of many.

If we take a bird's-eye view of our island to-day, and compare it with what it used to be, we must be struck by the extraordinary fact that the nation which was once, as every one admits, one of the most classically learned and cultured nations in Europe, is now one of the least so; how one of the most reading and literary peoples has become one of the *least* studious and most *un*-literary, and how the present art products of one of the quickest, most sensitive, and most artistic races on earth are now only distinguished for their hideousness.

[†] Douglas Hyde (1860–1949), Irish scholar and outspoken advocate of Irish cultural revival, delivered the address from which these selections are taken at his inauguration as president of the National Literary Society (1892). He was the first president of the Gaelic League (1893) and later became professor of Irish at University College, Dublin (1909–32), an Irish senator (1925 and 1938), and the first president of Ireland (1938–45).
   From Charles Gavan Duffy, George Sigerson, and Douglas Hyde, *The Revival of Irish Literature*. London: T. F. Unwin, 1994, 115–61. The author's notes have been omitted.

1. Supporter of the Union between Ireland and England as the United Kingdom of Great Britain and Ireland, which was created by the Act of Union (1800) passed by the British and Irish parliaments. The Home Rule movement, important after 1870, was an effort to modify the Union by giving Ireland limited autonomy. See the 1801 entry in "Key Dates, Events, and Figures," p. 227.

I shall endeavour to show that this failure of the Irish people in recent times has been largely brought about by the race diverging during this century from the right path, and ceasing to be Irish without becoming English. I shall attempt to show that with the bulk of the people this change took place quite recently, much more recently than most people imagine, and is, in fact, still going on. I should also like to call attention to the illogical position of men who drop their own language to speak English, of men who translate their euphonious Irish names into English monosyllables, of men who read English books, and know nothing about Gaelic literature, nevertheless protesting as a matter of sentiment that they hate the country which at every hand's turn they rush to imitate.

*   *   *

* * * Such movements as Young Irelandism, Fenianism, Land Leagueism, and Parliamentary obstruction seem always to gain their sympathy and support.[2] It is just because there appears no earthly chance of their becoming good members of the Empire that I urge that they should not remain in the anomalous position they are in, but since they absolutely refuse to become the one thing, that they become the other; cultivate what they have rejected, and build up an Irish nation on Irish lines.

*   *   *

And yet this awful idea of complete Anglicisation, which I have here put before you in all its crudity, is, and has been, making silent inroads upon us for nearly a century.

*   *   *

What we must endeavour to never forget is this, that the Ireland of to-day is the descendant of the Ireland of the seventh century, then the school of Europe and the torch of learning. It is true that Northmen made some minor settlements in it in the ninth and tenth centuries, it is true that the Normans made extensive settlements during the succeeding centuries, but none of those broke the continuity of the social life of the island. Dane and Norman drawn to the kindly Irish breast issued forth in a generation or two fully Irishised, and more Hibernian than the Hibernians themselves, and even after

2. Young Ireland, a prominent nationalist group in the 1840s, encouraged national literature, the revival of Gaelic, and repeal of the Union; the Fenian Brotherhood was a revolutionary movement advocating the use of force that began in the 1850s among Irish in both Ireland and the U.S.; the Irish National Land League, founded by Michael Davitt in 1879, demanded peasant proprietorship of the land; Parliamentary obstruction was a technique used by Charles Stuart Parnell and other Irish Members of Parliament to press for action on issues affecting the Irish people.

the Cromwellian plantation the children of numbers of the English soldiers who settled in the south and midlands, were, after forty years' residence, and after marrying Irish wives, turned into good Irishmen, and unable to speak a word of English, while several Gaelic poets of the last century have, like Father English, the most unmistakably English names. In two points only was the continuity of the Irishism of Ireland damaged. First, in the north-east of Ulster, where the Gaelic race was expelled and the land planted with aliens, whom our dear mother Erin, assimilative as she is, has hitherto found it difficult to absorb, and in the ownership of the land, eight-ninths of which belongs to people many of whom always lived, or live, abroad, and not half of whom Ireland can be said to have assimilated.

*   *   *

The bulk of the Irish race really lived in the closest contact with the traditions of the past and the national life of nearly eighteen hundred years, until the beginning of this century. Not only so, but during the whole of the dark Penal times[3] they produced amongst themselves a most vigorous literary development. Their schoolmasters and wealthy farmers, unwearied scribes, produced innumerable manuscripts in beautiful writing, each letter separated from another as in Greek, transcripts both of the ancient literature of their sires and of the more modern literature produced by themselves. Until the beginning of the present century there was no county, no barony, and, I may almost say, no townland which did not boast of an Irish poet, the people's representative of those ancient bards who died out with the extirpation of the great Milesian families.[4] * * * This training, however, nearly every one of fair education during the Penal times possessed, nor did they begin to lose their Irish training and knowledge until after the establishment of Maynooth and the rise of O'Connell.[5] * * *

Thomas Davis and his brilliant band of Young Irelanders came just at the dividing of the line, and tried to give to Ireland a new literature in English to replace the literature which was just being discarded. It succeeded and it did not succeed. It was a most brilliant effort, but the old bark had been too recently stripped off the Irish

---

3. A period of nearly a century, which began in the 1690s with the introduction of anti-Catholic penal laws that limited or took away rights, including voting and property ownership.
4. The Milesians were the Gaels, that is, the ancestors of the Irish, who were held to be the descendants of the legendary warrior Mil.
5. St. Patrick's College, Maynooth, authorized in 1795, was the main seminary producing Irish Catholic priests, many of whom had earlier been trained on the Continent. Daniel O'Connell (1775–1847) was a moderate nationalist political leader who opposed the Act of Union (1800) and urged its repeal.

tree, and the trunk could not take as it might have done to a fresh
one. It was a new departure, and at first produced a violent effect.
Yet in the long run it failed to properly leaven our peasantry who
might, perhaps, have been reached upon other lines. I say they
might have been reached upon other lines because it is quite certain that even well on into the beginning of this century, Irish poor
scholars and schoolmasters used to gain the greatest favour and
applause by reading out manuscripts in the people's houses at
night, some of which manuscripts had an antiquity of a couple of
hundred years or more behind them, and which, when they got
illegible from age, were always recopied. The Irish peasantry at
that time were all to some extent cultured men, and many of the
better off ones were scholars and poets. What have we now left of
all that? Scarcely a trace. Many of them read newspapers indeed,
but who reads, much less recites, an epic poem, or chants an ele-
giac or even a hymn?

Wherever Irish throughout Ireland continued to be spoken, there
the ancient MSS. continued to be read, there the epics of Cuchul-
lain, Conor MacNessa, Déirdre, Finn, Oscar, and Ossian continued
to be told, and there poetry and music held sway. * * * In fact, I may
venture to say that, up to the beginning of the present century, neither man, woman, nor child of the Gaelic race, either of high blood
or low blood, existed in Ireland who did not either speak Irish or
understand it. But within the last ninety years we have, with an
unparalleled frivolity, deliberately thrown away our birthright and
Anglicised ourselves. None of the children of those people of whom
I have spoken know Irish, and the race will from henceforth be
changed; for as Monsieur Jubainville[6] says of the influence of Rome
upon Gaul, England "has definitely conquered us, she has even
imposed upon us her language, that is to say, the form of our
thoughts during every instant of our existence." It is curious that
those who most fear West Britainism[7] have so eagerly consented to
imposing upon the Irish race what, according to Jubainville, who in
common with all the great scholars of the continent, seems to regret
it very much, is "the form of our thoughts during every instant of our
existence."

* * *

I have no hesitation at all in saying that every Irish-feeling Irishman, who hates the reproach of West-Britonism, should set himself

---

6. Marie Henri d'Arbois de Jubainville (1827–1910), French historian and philologist, who
   held the chair of Celtic at the Collège de France.
7. Also West-Britonism; the turning of Ireland into the westernmost province of England.

to encourage the efforts which are being made to keep alive our once great national tongue. The losing of it is our greatest blow, and the sorest stroke that the rapid Anglicisation of Ireland has inflicted upon us. In order to de-Anglicise ourselves we must at once arrest the decay of the language. * * *

We can, however, insist, and we *shall* insist if Home Rule be carried, that the Irish language, which so many foreign scholars of the first calibre find so worthy of study, shall be placed on a par with—or even above—Greek, Latin, and modern languages, in all examinations held under the Irish Government. We can also insist, and we *shall* insist, that in those baronies where the children speak Irish, Irish shall be taught, and that Irish-speaking schoolmasters, petty sessions clerks, and even magistrates be appointed in Irish-speaking districts. If all this were done, it should not be very difficult, with the aid of the foremost foreign scholars, to bring about a tone of thought which would make it disgraceful for an educated Irishman—especially of the old Celtic race, MacDermotts, O'Conors, O'Sullivans, MacCarthys, O'Neills—to be ignorant of his own language—would make it at least as disgraceful as for an educated Jew to be quite ignorant of Hebrew.

We find the decay of our language faithfully reflected in the decay of our surnames. In Celtic times a great proof of the powers of assimilation which the Irish nation possessed, was the fact that so many of the great Norman and English nobles lived like the native chiefs and took Irish names. In this way the De Bourgos of Connacht became MacWilliams, of which clan again some minor branches became MacPhilpins, MacGibbons, and MacRaymonds. * * * Roughly speaking, it may be said that most of the English and Norman families outside of the Pale[8] were Irish in name and manners from the beginning of the fourteenth to the middle of the seventeenth century.

In 1465 an Act was passed by the Parliament of the English Pale that all Irishmen inside the Pale should take an English name "of one towne as Sutton, Chester, Trym, Skryne, Corke, Kinsale; or colour, as white, black, brown; or art or science, as smith or carpenter; or office, as cooke, butler; and that he and his issue shall use this name" or forfeit all his goods. A great number of the lesser families complied with this typically English ordiance; but the greater ones—the MacMurroghs, O'Tooles, O'Byrnes, O'Nolans, O'Mores, O'Ryans, O'Conor Falys, O'Kellys, &c.—refused, and never did change their

8. The area of Dublin within the fortified perimeter that designated English rule.

names. A hundred and thirty years later we find Spenser, the poet, advocating the renewal of this statute.[9] By doing this, says Spenser, "they shall in time learne quite to forget the Irish nation. And herewithal," he says, "would I also wish the O's and Macs which the heads of septs have taken to their names to be utterly forbidden and extinguished, for that the same being an ordinance (as some say) first made by O'Brien * * * for the strengthening of the Irish, the abrogation thereof will as much enfeeble them." It was, however, only after Aughrim and the Boyne[1] that Irish names began to be changed in great numbers, and O'Conors to become "Conyers," O'Reillys "Ridleys," O'Donnells "Daniels," O'Sullivans "Silvans," MacCarthys "Carters," and so on.

*   *   *

Numbers of people, again, like Mr. Davitt or Mr. Hennessy, drop the O and Mac which properly belong to their names; others, without actually changing them, metamorphose their names, as we have seen, into every possible form. * * *

With our Irish Christian names the case is nearly as bad. Where are now all the fine old Irish Christian names of both men and women which were in vogue even a hundred years ago? They have been discarded as unclean things, not because they were ugly in themselves or inharmonious, but simply because they were not English. No man is now christened by a Gaelic name, "nor no woman neither." Such common Irish Christian names as Conn, Cairbre, Farfeasa, Teig, Diarmuid, Kian, Cuan, Ae, Art, Mahon, Eochaidh, Fearflatha, Cathan, Rory, Coll, Lochlainn, Cathal, Lughaidh, Turlough, Eamon, Randal, Niall, Sorley, and Conor, are now extinct or nearly so. * * * In fact, of the great wealth of Gaelic Christian names in use a century or two ago, only Owen, Brian, Cormac, and Patrick seem to have survived in general use.

Nor have our female names fared one bit better; we have discarded them even more ruthlessly than those of our men. Surely Sadhbh (Sive) is a prettier name than Sabina or Sibby, and Nóra than Onny, Honny, or Honour (so translated simply because Nóra sounds like onóir, the Irish for "honour"); surely Una is prettier than Winny, which it becomes when West-Britonised. Mève, the great name of the Queen of Connacht who led the famous cattle spoiling of Cuailgne, celebrated in the greatest Irish epic, is at least as pretty as Maud, which it becomes when Anglicised, and Eibhlin (Eileen) is prettier than Ellen or Elinor. * * *

9. Edmund Spenser (1552–1599), English poet and colonist in Ireland, argued for the destruction of the Irish language and customs by any means, including violence.
1. The Battles of Aughrim (1691) and the Boyne (1690), both lost by the supporters of James II to the forces of William III. James's defeat confirmed Protestant dominance of Ireland.

Our topographical nomenclature too—as we may now be prepared to expect—has been also shamefully corrupted to suit English
ears * * * . Suffice it to say, that many of the best-known names in
our history and annals have become almost wholly unrecognisable,
through the ignorant West-Britonising of them. The unfortunate
natives of the eighteenth century allowed all kinds of havoc to be
played with even their best-known names. For example the river
Feóir they allowed to be turned permanently into the Nore, which
happened this way. Some Englishman, asking the name of the river,
was told that it was *An Fheóir,* pronounced In n'yore, because the F
when preceded by the definite article *an* is not sounded, so that in his
ignorance he mistook the word Feóir for Neóir, and the name has
been thus perpetuated. In the same way the great Connacht lake,
Loch Corrib, is really Loch Orrib, or rather Loch Orbsen, some
Englishman having mistaken the C at the end of loch for the beginning of the next word. Sometimes the Ordnance Survey people make
a rough guess at the Irish name and jot down certain English letters
almost on chance. Sometimes again they make an Irish word resemble an English one, as in the celebrated Tailtin in Meath, where the
great gathering of the nation was held, and, which, to make sure that
no national memories should stick to it, has been West-Britonised
Telltown. On the whole, our place names have been treated with
about the same respect as if they were the names of a savage tribe
which had never before been reduced to writing, and with about the
same intelligence and contempt as vulgar English squatters treat
the topographical nomenclature of the Red Indians. These things
are now to a certain extent stereotyped, and are difficult at this hour
to change, especially where Irish names have been translated into
English, like Swinford and Strokestown, or ignored as in Charleville
or Midleton. But though it would take the strength and goodwill of
an united nation to put our topographical nomenclature on a rational
basis like that of Wales and the Scotch Highlands, there is one thing
which our Society can do, and that is to insist upon pronouncing
our Irish names properly. Why will a certain class of people insist
upon getting as far away from the pronunciation of the natives as
possible? * * *
  * * * I hope and trust that where it may be done without any great
inconvenience a native Irish Government will be induced to provide
for the restoration of our place-names on something like a rational
basis.

Our music, too, has become Anglicised to an alarming extent. Not
only has the national instrument, the harp—which efforts are now
being made to revive in the Highlands—become extinct, but even
the Irish pipes are threatened with the same fate. In place of the

pipers and fiddlers who, even twenty years ago, were comparatively common, we are now in many places menaced by the German band and the barrel organ. * * * A few years ago all our travelling fiddlers and pipers could play the old airs which were then constantly called for, the *Cúis d'á pléidh, Drinaun Dunn, Roseen Dubh, Gamhan Geal Bán, Eileen-a-roon, Shawn O'Dwyer in Glanna*, and the rest, whether gay or plaintive, which have for so many centuries entranced the Gael. But now English music-hall ballads and Scotch songs have gained an enormous place in the repertoire of the wandering minstrel, and the minstrels themselves are becoming fewer and fewer, and I fear worse and worse. * * *

Our games, too, were in a most grievous condition until the brave and patriotic men who started the Gaelic Athletic Association took in hand their revival. I confess that the instantaneous and extraordinary success which attended their efforts when working upon national lines has filled me with more hope for the future of Ireland than everything else put together. I consider the work of the association in reviving our ancient national game of caman, or hurling, and Gaelic football, has done more for Ireland than all the speeches of politicians for the last five years. And it is not alone that that splendid association revived for a time with vigour our national sports, but it revived also our national recollections, and the names of the various clubs through the country have perpetuated the memory of the great and good men and martyrs of Ireland. The physique of our youth has been improved in many of our counties; they have been taught self-restraint, and how to obey their captains; they have been, in many places, weaned from standing idle in their own roads or street corners; and not least, they have been introduced to the use of a thoroughly good and Irish garb. Wherever the warm striped green jersey of the Gaelic Athletic Association was seen, there Irish manhood and Irish memories were rapidly reviving. There torn collars and ugly neckties hanging awry and far better not there at all, and dirty shirts of bad linen were banished, and our young hurlers were clad like men and Irishmen, and not in the shoddy second-hand suits of Manchester and London shop-boys. * * *

I have now mentioned a few of the principal points on which it would be desirable for us to move, with a view to de-Anglicising ourselves; but perhaps the principal point of all I have taken for granted. That is the necessity for encouraging the use of Anglo-Irish literature instead of English books, especially instead of English periodicals. We must set our face sternly against penny dreadfuls, shilling shockers, and still more, the garbage of vulgar English weeklies like *Bow Bells* and the *Police Intelligence*. Every house should have a copy of Moore and Davis.[2] * * * I knew fifteen Irish workmen who were working in a haggard[3] in England give up talking Irish amongst themselves because the English farmer laughed at them. And yet O'Connell used to call us the "finest peasantry in Europe." Unfortunately, he took little care that we should remain so. We must teach ourselves to be less sensitive, we must teach ourselves not to be ashamed of ourselves, because the Gaelic people can never produce its best before the world as long as it remains tied to the apron-strings of another race and another island, waiting for *it* to move before it will venture to take any step itself.

In conclusion, I would earnestly appeal to every one, whether Unionist or Nationalist, who wishes to see the Irish nation produce its best—and surely whatever our politics are we all wish that—to set his face against this constant running to England for our books, literature, music, games, fashions, and ideas. I appeal to every one whatever his politics—for this is no political matter—to do his best to help the Irish race to develop in future upon Irish lines, even at the risk of encouraging national aspirations, because upon Irish lines alone can the Irish race once more become what it was of yore— one of the most original, artistic, literary, and charming peoples of Europe.

JOHN MILLINGTON SYNGE[†]

[The Birdgirl on the Shore]

* * *

The drought is also causing a scarcity of water. * * * The water for washing is also coming short, and as I walk round the edges of

2. Thomas Moore (1779–1852), poet, whose *Irish Melodies* (1808–34) became immensely popular as songs. Thomas Davis (1814–1845), nationalist and poet, famous for leading the Young Ireland movement and for ballads such as "A Nation Once Again."
3. In Irish usage, an area on a farm, set aside for stacking agricultural products such as corn and hay.
† J. M. Synge (1871–1909) was a central figure in the Irish Literary Revival, which was in progress when Joyce was a university student and while he was writing *A Portrait of the Artist as a Young Man*. Synge cofounded the Abbey Theatre with Lady Augusta Gregory (1852–1932) and W. B. Yeats (1865–1939), and his one-act play *The Shadow of the Glen* formed part of the Abbey's opening bill in 1904. When Synge's masterpiece, *The Playboy of the Western World,* premiered there in 1907, it triggered riots by nationalists who claimed that the play demeaned the Irish. Even living in Italy beginning in 1904, Joyce would have known Synge's writings and been aware of these events, which were central to the developing literary life of Ireland. Among the books in Joyce's library in Trieste is a first edition of Synge's book *The Aran Islands,* published in 1907 with illustrations by Jack B. Yeats (1871–1957), W. B. Yeats's brother. Joyce also would have known Synge's earlier, brief account of traditional life on the isolated, rugged islands off the west coast of Ireland, published in 1898 in the *New Ireland Review*.

the sea I often come on a girl[1] with her petticoats tucked up round her, standing in a pool left by the tide and washing her flannels among the sea-anemones and crabs. Their red bodices and white tapering legs make them as beautiful as tropical sea-birds, as they stand in a frame of seaweeds against the brink of the Atlantic. Michael, however, is a little uneasy when they are in sight, and I cannot pause to watch them. * * *

                              *   *   *

[Girls Wreathed with Seaweed; Trembling and Exultation]

                              *   *   *

At the south-west corner of the island I came upon a number of people gathering the seaweed that is now thick on the rocks. It was raked from the surf by the men, and then carried up to the brow of the cliff by a party of young girls.

In addition to their ordinary clothing these girls wore a raw sheep-skin on their shoulders, to catch the oozing sea-water, and they looked strangely wild and seal-like with the salt caked upon their lips and wreaths of seaweed in their hair.

For the rest of my walk I saw no living thing but one flock of curlews, and a few pipits hiding among the stones.

About the sunset the clouds broke and the storm turned to a hurricane. Bars of purple cloud stretched across the sound where immense waves were rolling from the west, wreathed with snowy phantasies of spray. * * *

The suggestion from this world of inarticulate power was immense, and now at midnight, when the wind is abating, I am still trembling and flushed with exultation.

The following excerpts from *The Aran Islands,* which is based on Synge's experiences living among the people of the islands, bear direct, frequently contrasting relation to aspects of Joyce's narrative, especially Stephen's encounter with the birdlike girl on the shore, Davin's story about meeting in the countryside a wife who wanted to be unfaithful, Stephen's journal entry of 14 April about an encounter with an Irish peasant, and his conversation with the dean of studies, who gives him advice about lighting a fire. At the end of the narrative Stephen is on the verge of leaving Ireland, heading east, presumably for Europe. *The Aran Islands,* by contrast, presents a powerful attraction to the west, to a world that is native rather than cosmopolitan.

From *The Aran Islands.* Dublin: Maunsel & Co., Ltd., 1907, 54–55, 112–13, 42–46, 120–22, 177–78. The text drawn on here is the 1910 reprinting by Maunsel as vol. 3 of *The Works of John M. Synge.*

1. In the idiom of the time, "coming short" means running low, and to "come on a girl" is to happen upon her.

[The Tale of the Unfaithful Wife]

Pat told me a story of an unfaithful wife * * * .
Here is his story:—

One day I was travelling on foot from Galway to Dublin, and the darkness came on me and I ten miles from the town I was wanting to pass the night in. Then a hard rain began to fall and I was tired walking, so when I saw a sort of a house with no roof on it up against the road, I got in the way the walls would give me shelter.

As I was looking round I saw a light in some trees two perches off, and thinking any sort of a house would be better than where I was, I got over a wall and went up to the house to look in at the window.

I saw a dead man laid on a table, and candles lighted, and a woman watching him. I was frightened when I saw him, but it was raining hard, and I said to myself, if he was dead he couldn't hurt me. Then I knocked on the door and the woman came and opened it.

'Good evening, ma'am,' says I.

'Good evening kindly, stranger,' says she. 'Come in out of the rain.'

Then she took me in and told me her husband was after dying on her, and she was watching him that night.

'But it's thirsty you'll be, stranger,' says she. 'Come into the parlour.'

Then she took me into the parlour—and it was a fine clean house—and she put a cup, with a saucer under it, on the table before me, with fine sugar and bread.

When I'd had a cup of tea I went back into the kitchen where the dead man was lying, and she gave me a fine new pipe off the table with a drop of spirits.

'Stranger,' says she, 'would you be afeard to be alone with himself?'

'Not a bit in the world, ma'am,' says I; 'he that's dead can do no hurt.'

Then she said she wanted to go over and tell the neighbours the way her husband was after dying on her, and she went out and locked the door behind her.

I smoked one pipe, and I leaned out and took another off the table. I was smoking it with my hand on the back of my chair—the way you are yourself this minute, God bless you—and I looking on the dead man, when he opened his eyes as wide as myself and looked at me.

'Don't be afeard, stranger,' said the dead man; 'I'm not dead at all in the world. Come here and help me up, and I'll tell you all about it.'

Well, I went up and took the sheet off of him, and I saw that he had a fine clean shirt on his body, and fine flannel drawers.

He sat up then, and says he—

'I've got a bad wife, stranger, and I let on to be dead the way I'd catch her goings on.'

Then he got two fine sticks he had to keep down his wife, and he put them at each side of his body, and he laid himself out again as if he was dead.

In half an hour his wife came back, and a young man along with her. Well, she gave him his tea, and she told him he was tired, and he would do right to go and lie down in the bedroom.

The young man went in, and the woman sat down to watch by the dead man. A while after she got up, and 'Stranger,' says she, 'I'm going in to get the candle out of the room; I'm thinking the young man will be asleep by this time.' She went into the bedroom, but the divil a bit of her came back.[2]

Then the dead man got up, and he took one stick, and he gave the other to myself. We went in and we saw them lying together with her head on his arm.

The dead man hit him a blow with the stick so that the blood out of him leapt up and hit the gallery.

That is my story.

[Queer Places and People; Lighting a Fire]

* * *

In the evenings I sometimes meet with a girl who is not yet half through her 'teens, yet seems in some ways more consciously developed[3] than any one else that I have met here. She has passed part of her life on the mainland, and the disillusion she found in Galway has coloured her imagination.

As we sit on stools on either side of the fire I hear her voice going backwards and forwards in the same sentence from the gaiety of a child to the plaintive intonation of an old race that is worn with sorrow. At one moment she is a simple peasant, at another she seems to be looking out at the world with a sense of prehistoric disillusion and to sum up in the expression of her grey-blue eyes the whole external despondency of the clouds and sea.

Our conversation is usually disjointed. One evening we talked of a town on the mainland.

'Ah, it's a queer place,' she said; 'I wouldn't choose to live in it. It's a queer place, and indeed I don't know the place that isn't.'

---

2. But she never came back.
3. Developed in her mental abilities.

Another evening we talked of the people who live on the island or come to visit it.

'Father——is gone,' she said; 'he was a kind man but a queer man. Priests is queer people, and I don't know who isn't.'

*   *   *

One evening I found her trying to light a fire in the little side room of her cottage, where there is an ordinary fireplace. I went in to help her and showed her how to hold up a paper before the mouth of the chimney to make a draught, a method she had never seen. Then I told her of men who live alone in Paris and make their own fires that they may have no one to bother them. She was sitting in a heap on the floor staring into the turf, and as I finished she looked up with surprise.

'They're like me so,' she said; 'would any one have thought that!'

Below the sympathy we feel there is still a chasm between us.

'Musha,' she muttered as I was leaving her this evening, 'I think it's to hell you'll be going by and by.'

*   *   *

[Rejecting Paris; Choosing Ancient Simplicity]

*   *   *

Even after the people of the south island, these men of the Inishmaan[4] seemed to be moved by strange archaic sympathies with the world. Their mood accorded itself with wonderful fineness to the suggestions of the day, and their ancient Gaelic seemed so full of divine simplicity that I would have liked to turn the prow to the west and row with them for ever.

I told them I was going back to Paris in a few days to sell my books and my bed, and that then I was coming back to grow as strong and simple as they were among the islands of the west.

4. The middle island of the three Aran Islands, only slightly larger than Inishere to the south.

Religion

ST. IGNATIUS OF LOYOLA

From *The Spiritual Exercises*[†]

Annotations

TO GIVE SOME UNDERSTANDING OF THE SPIRITUAL
EXERCISES WHICH FOLLOW, AND TO ENABLE HIM
WHO IS TO GIVE AND HIM WHO IS TO RECEIVE
THEM TO HELP THEMSELVES

First Annotation. The first Annotation is that by this name of Spiritual Exercises is meant every way of examining one's conscience, of meditating, of contemplating, of praying vocally and mentally, and of performing other spiritual actions, as will be said later. For as strolling, walking and running are bodily exercises, so every way of preparing and disposing the soul to rid itself of all the disordered tendencies, and, after it is rid, to seek and find the Divine Will as to the management of one's life for the salvation of the soul, is called a Spiritual Exercise.

* * *

Fourth Annotation. The fourth: The following Exercises are divided into four parts:

First, the consideration and contemplation on the sins;
Second, the life of Christ our Lord up to Palm Sunday inclusively;
Third, the Passion of Christ our Lord;

---

† Saint Ignatius of Loyola (1491–1556) founded the Society of Jesus, also known as the Jesuits, the order within the Roman Catholic Church that established and ran Clongowes Wood College and Belvedere College. Although he probably first drafted *The Spiritual Exercises* in the 1520s, the earliest copy known is from 1541. This immensely influential book consists largely of highly structured meditations to be pursued intently by people in search of spiritual direction. The exercises are meant to strengthen faith and to enhance the experience of faith. Frequently they are undertaken during religious retreats, such as the one Stephen experiences in Part III, and as a result of such retreats. Pinamonti's *Hell Opened to Christians* provides a supplement to the fifth exercise (meditation on hell) during the first week of *The Spiritual Exercises*. A portion from the fourth week has also been included because, rather than emphasizing discipline and abstinence, as do most of the exercises, it projects a positive recognition related to Stephen's experience at the close of Part III.

Fourth, the Resurrection and Ascension, with the three Methods of Prayer.

*   *   *

[*From* "First Week"]
Fifth Exercise

IT IS A MEDITATION ON HELL

It contains in it, after the Preparatory Prayer and two Preludes, five Points and one Colloquy:

Prayer. Let the Preparatory Prayer be the usual one.[1]

First Prelude. The first Prelude is the composition, which is here to see with the sight of the imagination the length, breadth and depth of Hell.

Second Prelude. The second, to ask for what I want: it will be here to ask for interior sense of the pain which the damned suffer, in order that, if, through my faults, I should forget the love of the Eternal Lord, at least the fear of the pains may help me not to come into sin.

First Point. The first Point will be to see with the sight of the imagination the great fires, and the souls as in bodies of fire.

Second Point. The second, to hear with the ears wailings, howlings, cries, blasphemies against Christ our Lord and against all His Saints.

Third Point. The third, to smell with the smell smoke, sulphur, dregs and putrid things.

Fourth Point. The fourth, to taste with the taste bitter things, like tears, sadness and the worm of conscience.

Fifth Point. The fifth, to touch with the touch; that is to say, how the fires touch and burn the souls.

Colloquy. Making a Colloquy to Christ our Lord, I will bring to memory the souls that are in Hell, some because they did not believe the Coming, others because, believing, they did not act according to His Commandments; making three divisions:

First, Second, and Third Divisions. The first, before the Coming; the second, during His life; the third, after His life in this world; and

Trans. Father Elder Mullan, S.J. New York: P. J. Kenedy & Sons, 1914. For this reprinting, the translator's notes have been omitted. The entire text is available online as a .pdf document: http://www.jesuit.org/images/docs/915dWg.pdf. The selections are taken from .pdf pages 12, 29–33, 64–69.

1. As stated in the First Exercise, "The Preparatory Prayer is to ask grace of God our Lord that all my intentions, actions and operations may be directed purely to the service and praise of His Divine Majesty" (.pdf p. 26).

with this I will give Him thanks that He has not let me fall into any of these divisions, ending my life.

Likewise, I will consider how up to now He has always had so great pity and mercy on me.

I will end with an OUR FATHER.

Note. The first Exercise will be made at midnight; the second immediately on rising in the morning; the third, before or after Mass; in any case, before dinner; the fourth at the hour of Vespers; the fifth, an hour before supper.

This arrangement of hours, more or less, I always mean in all the four Weeks, according as his age, disposition and physical condition help the person who is exercising himself to make five Exercises or fewer.

Additions

TO MAKE THE EXERCISES BETTER AND TO FIND BETTER WHAT ONE DESIRES

First Addition. The first Addition is, after going to bed, just when I want to go asleep, to think, for the space of a HAIL MARY, of the hour that I have to rise and for what, making a resume of the Exercise which I have to make.

* * *

Fourth Addition. The fourth: To enter on the contemplation now on my knees, now prostrate on the earth, now lying face upwards, now seated, now standing, always intent on seeking what I want.

We will attend to two things. The first is, that if I find what I want kneeling, I will not pass on; and if prostrate, likewise, etc. The second; in the Point in which I find what I want, there I will rest, without being anxious to pass on, until I content myself.

* * *

Sixth Addition. The sixth: Not to want to think on things of pleasure or joy, such as heavenly glory, the Resurrection, etc. Because whatever consideration of joy and gladness hinders our feeling pain and grief and shedding tears for our sins: but to keep before me that I want to grieve and feel pain, bringing to memory rather Death and Judgment.

Seventh Addition. The seventh: For the same end, to deprive myself of all light, closing the blinds and doors while I am in the room, if it be not to recite prayers, to read and eat.

Eighth Addition. The eighth: Not to laugh nor say a thing provocative of laughter.

Ninth Addition. The ninth: To restrain my sight, except in receiving or dismissing the person with whom I have spoken.

Tenth Addition. The tenth Addition is penance.

This is divided into interior and exterior. The interior is to grieve for one's sins, with a firm purpose of not committing them nor any others. The exterior, or fruit of the first, is chastisement for the sins committed, and is chiefly taken in three ways.

First Way. The first is as to eating. That is to say, when we leave off the superfluous, it is not penance, but temperance. It is penance when we leave off from the suitable; and the more and more, the greater and better—provided that the person does not injure himself, and that no notable illness follows.

Second Way. The second, as to the manner of sleeping. Here too it is not penance to leave off the superfluous of delicate or soft things, but it is penance when one leaves off from the suitable in the manner: and the more and more, the better—provided that the person does not injure himself and no notable illness follows. Besides, let not anything of the suitable sleep be left off, unless in order to come to the mean, if one has a bad habit of sleeping too much.

Third Way. The third, to chastise the flesh, that is, giving it sensible pain, which is given by wearing haircloth or cords or iron chains next to the flesh, by scourging or wounding oneself, and by other kinds of austerity.

Note. What appears most suitable and most secure with regard to penance is that the pain should be sensible in the flesh and not enter within the bones, so that it give pain and not illness. For this it appears to be more suitable to scourge oneself with thin cords, which give pain exteriorly, rather than in another way which would cause notable illness within.

First Note. The first Note is that the exterior penances are done chiefly for three ends: First, as satisfaction for the sins committed;

Second, to conquer oneself—that is, to make sensuality obey reason and all inferior parts be more subject to the superior;

Third, to seek and find some grace or gift which the person wants and desires; as, for instance, if he desires to have interior contrition for his sins, or to weep much over them, or over the pains and sufferings which Christ our Lord suffered in His Passion, or to settle some doubt in which the person finds himself.

* * *

[*From* "Fourth Week"]
Contemplation to Gain Love

Prayer. The usual Prayer.

First Prelude. The first Prelude is a composition, which is here to see how I am standing before God our Lord, and of the Angels and of the Saints interceding for me.

Second Prelude. The second, to ask for what I want. It will be here to ask for interior knowledge of so great good received, in order that being entirely grateful, I may be able in all to love and serve His Divine Majesty.

First Point. The First Point is, to bring to memory the benefits received, of Creation, Redemption and particular gifts, pondering with much feeling how much God our Lord has done for me, and how much He has given me of what He has, and then the same Lord desires to give me Himself as much as He can, according to His Divine ordination.

And with this to reflect on myself, considering with much reason and justice, what I ought on my side to offer and give to His Divine Majesty, that is to say, everything that is mine, and myself with it, as one who makes an offering with much feeling:

Take, Lord, and receive all my liberty, my memory, my intellect, and all my will—all that I have and possess. Thou gavest it to me: to Thee, Lord, I return it! All is Thine, dispose of it according to all Thy will. Give me Thy love and grace, for this is enough for me.

Second Point. The second, to look how God dwells in creatures, in the elements, giving them being, in the plants vegetating, in the animals feeling in them, in men giving them to understand: and so in me, giving me being, animating me, giving me sensation and making me to understand; likewise making a temple of me, being created to the likeness and image of His Divine Majesty; reflecting as much on myself in the way which is said in the first Point, or in another which I feel to be better. In the same manner will be done on each Point which follows.

Third Point. The third, to consider how God works and labors for me in all things created on the face of the earth—that is, behaves like one who labors—as in the heavens, elements, plants, fruits, cattle, etc., giving them being, preserving them, giving them vegetation and sensation, etc.

Then to reflect on myself.

Fourth Point. The fourth, to look how all the good things and gifts descend from above, as my poor power from the supreme and infinite power from above; and so justice, goodness, pity, mercy, etc.; as from the sun descend the rays, from the fountain the waters, etc.

Then to finish reflecting on myself, as has been said.

I will end with a Colloquy and an OUR FATHER.

From the Rev. Father Giovanni Pietro Pinamonti, S.J., *Hell Opened to Christians, To Caution Them from Entering into It*. Dublin: G. P. Warren, n.d. That Joyce drew on the English translation of Pinamonti's text (published originally in Italian in 1688) in Part III has been established by James R. Thrane in "Joyce's Sermon on Hell: Its Source and Its Backgrounds," *Modern Philology* 57 (February 1960): 172–98. The pamphlet used for reprinting the eight woodcuts that accompany Pinamonti's text is in the collection of the National Library of Ireland. It would have been used as a supplement to St. Ignatius's *Spiritual Exercises*, specifically to the meditation on hell from the fifth exercise of the first week, reprinted above. Such a pamphlet might have played a role at religious retreats, such as the one Stephen participates in during Part III.

The image above is the frontispiece.

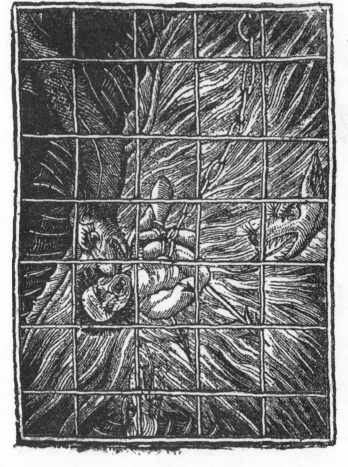

The Straightness of the Prison of Hell. The First Consideration, For Sunday.

The Fire. The Second Consideration, For Monday.
[Best available image]

The Company of the Damned. The Third Consideration, For Tuesday.
[Best available image]

The Pain of Loss. The Fourth Consideration, For Wednesday. [Best available image]

The Sting of Conscience. The Fifth Consideration, For Thursday.
[Best available image]

Despair. The Sixth Consideration, For Friday.

The Eternity of Pain. The Seventh Consideration, For Saturday.

Aesthetic Backgrounds

LAOCOÖN

The following image of the *Laocoön* sculpture group is reproduced from Plate I of Percy Gardner's entry on Greek art, *Encyclopaedia Britannica*, Eleventh Ed. London and New York: Encyclopaedia Britannica, 1910, 12.472bis. This edition represents the state of knowledge in the English-speaking world at the time Joyce wrote *A Portrait*. Gardner comments that this work, "signed by Rhodian sculptors of the 1st century B.C., . . . has been perhaps more discussed than any work of the Greek chisel, and served as a peg for the aesthetic theories of Lessing and Goethe" (491–92; on Lessing and Goethe, see note 8, p. 186). Stephen Dedalus's comments about aesthetics in Part V respond to Lessing's meditations on the character of art, in which the sculpture group plays a central role. The photograph shows the group as Joyce and his contemporaries would have known it, but not as we know it today. The statue was found in Michelangelo's day in Rome, broken, without the complete right arm of the central figure. It was mistakenly restored to the form shown in the photograph. Around 1960, it was restored again with significant changes to the handling of the broken arms and the missing one. The image of figures held involuntarily and tormented by a serpent is matched by the woodcuts in Pinamonti's *Hell Opened to Christians*, which Stephen, like his author, would have encountered during his education.

WALTER PATER

The Renaissance[†]

Pico della Mirandola

No account of the Renaissance can be complete without some notice of the attempt made by certain Italian scholars of the fifteenth century to reconcile Christianity with the religion of ancient Greece. To reconcile forms of sentiment which at first sight seem incompatible, to adjust the various products of the human mind to each other in one many-sided type of intellectual culture, to give humanity, for heart and imagination to feed upon, as much as it could possibly receive, belonged to the generous instincts of that age. * * *

* * *

It was after many wanderings, wanderings of the intellect as well as physical journeys, that Pico came to rest at Florence. He was then about twenty years old, having been born in 1463. He was called Giovanni at baptism; Pico, like all his ancestors, from Picus, nephew of the Emperor Constantine, from whom they claimed to be descended; and Mirandola, from the place of his birth, a little town afterwards part of the duchy of Modena, of which small territory his family had long been the feudal lords. Pico was the youngest of the family, and his mother, delighting in his wonderful memory, sent him at the age of fourteen to the famous school of law at Bologna. From the first, indeed, she seems to have had some presentiment of his future fame, for, with a faith in omens characteristic of her time, she believed that a strange circumstance had happened at the time of Pico's birth—the appearance of a circular flame which suddenly vanished away, on the wall of the chamber where she lay. He

† Walter Pater (1839–1894), whose ideas inspired the British Aesthetic movement of the last quarter of the nineteenth century, is most famous for his writings on literature and art. Emphasizing the importance of experiencing beauty in art intensely, those writings were well known to Joyce and to Joyce's older contemporaries Oscar Wilde (see p. 301) and W. B. Yeats (see note 9, p. 199). *Studies in the History of the Renaissance*, whose title was eventually shortened to *The Renaissance*, appeared in four editions during Pater's lifetime. The first edition (1873) drew criticism from religious authorities on the grounds that the attitudes expressed in the "Conclusion" placed art above religion. Pater removed the conclusion from the second edition (1877), then restored it in revised form in the third edition (1888). The excerpts come from a reprinting of the fourth edition (1893), the current edition when Joyce was a student. The inventory of Joyce's library in Trieste lists a slightly later reprinting (1912) by the same publisher. The revised "Conclusion" and the description of the *Mona Lisa* from the essay on Leonardo were famous passages of prose among English-speaking artists and intellectuals during Joyce's youth. Early in *Ulysses* (1922), Stephen Dedalus's thinking about Pico della Mirandola makes clear that Joyce knew this essay, in which Pater emphasizes the attempt to reconcile ancient Greek culture with European culture of a later time.
From *The Renaissance*. London: Macmillan, 1906, 30, 38–49, 122–26, 233–39. One of Pater's footnotes has been omitted.

remained two years at Bologna; and then, with an inexhaustible, unrivalled thirst for knowledge, the strange, confused, uncritical learning of that age, passed through the principal schools of Italy and France, penetrating, as he thought, into the secrets of all ancient philosophies, and many eastern languages. And with this flood of erudition came the generous hope, so often disabused, of reconciling the philosophers with each other, and all alike with the Church. At last he came to Rome. There, like some knight-errant of philosophy, he offered to defend nine hundred bold paradoxes, drawn from the most opposite sources, against all comers. But the pontifical court was led to suspect the orthodoxy of some of these propositions, and even the reading of the book which contained them was forbidden by the Pope. It was not until 1493 that Pico was finally absolved, by a brief of Alexander the Sixth. Ten years before that date he had arrived at Florence; an early instance of those who, after following the vain hope of an impossible reconciliation from system to system, have at last fallen back unsatisfied on the simplicities of their childhood's belief.

The oration which Pico composed for the opening of this philosophical tournament still remains; its subject is the dignity of human nature, the greatness of man. * * * For this high dignity of man, thus bringing the dust under his feet into sensible communion with the thoughts and affections of the angels, was supposed to belong to him, not as renewed by a religious system, but by his own natural right. The proclamation of it was a counterpoise to the increasing tendency of medieval religion to depreciate man's nature, to sacrifice this or that element in it, to make it ashamed of itself, to keep the degrading or painful accidents of it always in view. It helped man onward to that reassertion of himself, that rehabilitation of human nature, the body, the senses, the heart, the intelligence, which the Renaissance fulfils. And yet to read a page of one of Pico's forgotten books is like a glance into one of those ancient sepulchres, upon which the wanderer in classical lands has sometimes stumbled, with the old disused ornaments and furniture of a world wholly unlike ours still fresh in them. * * *

He was already almost wearied out when he came to Florence. He had loved much and been beloved by women, "wandering over the crooked hills of delicious pleasure"; but their reign over him was over, and long before Savonarola's famous "bonfire of vanities,"[1] he had destroyed those love-songs in the vulgar tongue, which would have been such a relief to us, after the scholastic prolixity of his Latin writings. It was in another spirit that he composed a Platonic

---

1. The burning in Florence, Italy, in 1497 of books, artworks, mirrors, and other items considered immoral by the Italian priest and Florentine ruler Girolamo Savonarola (1452–1498) and his followers.

commentary, the only work of his in Italian which has come down to us, on the "Song of Divine Love"—*secondo la mente ed opinione dei Platonici*—"according to the mind and opinion of the Platonists," by his friend Hieronymo Beniveni, in which, with an ambitious array of every sort of learning, and a profusion of imagery borrowed indifferently from the astrologers, the Cabala, and Homer, and Scripture, and Dionysius the Areopagite, he attempts to define the stages by which the soul passes from the earthly to the unseen beauty.[2] * * *

Yet he who had this fine touch for spiritual things did not—and in this is the enduring interest of his story—even after his conversion, forget the old gods. He is one of the last who seriously and sincerely entertained the claims on men's faith of the pagan religions; he is anxious to ascertain the true significance of the obscurest legend, the lightest tradition concerning them. * * *

It is because the life of Pico, thus lying down to rest in the Dominican habit, yet amid thoughts of the older gods, himself like one of those comely divinities, reconciled indeed to the new religion, but still with a tenderness for the earlier life, and desirous literally to "bind the ages each to each by natural piety"—it is because this life is so perfect a parallel to the attempt made in his writings to reconcile Christianity with the ideas of paganism, that Pico, in spite of the scholastic character of those writings, is really interesting. * * *

In explaining the harmony between Plato and Moses, Pico lays hold on every sort of figure and analogy, on the double meanings of words, the symbols of the Jewish ritual, the secondary meanings of obscure stories in the later Greek mythologists. Everywhere there is an unbroken system of correspondences. Every object in the terrestrial world is an analogue, a symbol or counterpart, of some higher reality in the starry heavens, and this again of some law of the angelic life in the world beyond the stars. There is the element of fire in the material world; the sun is the fire of heaven; and in the super-celestial world there is the fire of the seraphic intelligence. "But behold how they differ! The elementary fire burns, the heavenly fire vivifies, the super-celestial fire loves." In this way, every natural object, every combination of natural forces, every accident in the lives of men, is filled with higher meanings. Omens, prophecies, supernatural coincidences, accompany Pico himself all through life. There are oracles in every tree and mountain-top, and a significance in every accidental combination of the events of life.

---

2. Platonic would mean not narrowly in the mode of the ancient Greek philosopher Plato (c. 427–c. 347 BCE) but Neoplatonic, that is, with a Platonic emphasis on the dominant reality of a nonmaterial realm supplemented by mystical thought, including astrology (based on the belief that celestial bodies influence human affairs), the Cabala (rabbinical mysticism derived from esoteric readings of Hebrew Scripture), and fifth-century mystical writings attributed to Dionysius the Areopagite, who is mentioned in the New Testament as a convert to Christianity (Acts 17:34).

This constant tendency to symbolism and imagery gives Pico's work a figured style, by which it has some real resemblance to Plato's, and he differs from other mystical writers of his time by a real desire to know his authorities at first hand. He reads Plato in Greek, Moses in Hebrew, and by this his work really belongs to the higher culture. Above all, we have a constant sense in reading him, that his thoughts, however little their positive value may be, are connected with springs beneath them of deep and passionate emotion; and when he explains the grades or steps by which the soul passes from the love of a physical object to the love of unseen beauty, and unfolds the analogies between this process and other movements upward of human thought, there is a glow and vehemence in his words which remind one of the manner in which his own brief existence flamed itself away.

I said that the Renaissance of the fifteenth century was in many things great, rather by what it designed or aspired to do, than by what it actually achieved. * * * When the ship-load of sacred earth from the soil of Jerusalem was mingled with the common clay in the *Campo Santo* at Pisa,[3] a new flower grew up from it, unlike any flower men had seen before, the anemone with its concentric rings of strangely blended colour, still to be found by those who search long enough for it, in the long grass of the Maremma.[4] Just such a strange flower was that mythology of the Italian Renaissance, which grew up from the mixture of two traditions, two sentiments, the sacred and the profane. * * *

It is because this picturesque union of contrasts, belonging properly to the art of the close of the fifteenth century, pervades, in Pico della Mirandola, an actual person, that the figure of Pico is so attractive. He will not let one go; he wins one on, in spite of oneself, to turn again to the pages of his forgotten books, although we know already that the actual solution proposed in them will satisfy us as little as perhaps it satisfied him. It is said that in his eagerness for mysterious learning he once paid a great sum for a collection of cabalistic manuscripts, which turned out to be forgeries; and the story might well stand as a parable of all he ever seemed to gain in the way of actual knowledge. He had sought knowledge, and passed from system to system, and hazarded much; but less for the sake of positive knowledge than because he believed there was a spirit of order and beauty in knowledge, which would come down and unite what men's ignorance had divided, and renew what time had made dim. * * *

3. Literally (in Italian and Spanish), the sacred field, or cemetery, at Pisa in Italy, traditionally thought to be on the site of an earlier burial ground, for which earth was brought from the place of Christ's crucifixion. The strange flower of mixed traditions also suggests the architectural character of the cemetery, which contained many pieces of classical sculpture.
4. Area in Italy that includes part of southern Tuscany and a portion of northern Latium.

From *Leonardo da Vinci*

[ON THE *MONA LISA* (*LA GIOCONDA*)]

* * *

The remaining years of Leonardo's life are more or less years of wandering. From his brilliant life at court he had saved nothing, and he returned to Florence a poor man. Perhaps necessity kept his spirit excited: the next four years are one prolonged rapture or ecstasy of invention. He painted the pictures of the Louvre, his most authentic works, which came there straight from the cabinet of Francis the First, at Fontainebleau. * * * But his work was less with the saints than with the living women of Florence; for he lived still in the polished society that he loved, and in the houses of Florence, left perhaps a little subject to light thoughts by the death of Savonarola[5]—the latest gossip (1869) is of an undraped Monna Lisa, found in some out-of-the-way corner of the late *Orleans* collection—he saw Ginevra di Benci, and Lisa, the young third wife of Francesco del Giocondo. As we have seen him using incidents of sacred story, not for their own sake, or as mere subjects for pictorial realisation, but as a symbolical language for fancies all his own, so now he found a vent for his thoughts in taking one of these languid women, and raising her, as Leda or Pomona, Modesty or Vanity, to the seventh heaven of symbolical expression.[6]

La Gioconda is, in the truest sense, Leonardo's masterpiece, the revealing instance of his mode of thought and work. In suggestiveness, only the *Melancholia* of Dürer is comparable to it; and no crude symbolism disturbs the effect of its subdued and graceful mystery. We all know the face and hands of the figure, set in its marble chair, in that cirque of fantastic rocks, as in some faint light under sea. Perhaps of all ancient pictures time has chilled it least. As often happens with works in which invention seems to reach its limits, there is an element in it given to, not invented by, the master. In that inestimable folio of drawings, once in the possession of Vasari, were certain designs by Verrocchio,[7] faces of such impressive beauty that Leonardo in his boyhood copied them many times. It is hard not to connect with these designs of the elder, by-past master, as with its germinal principle, the unfathomable smile, always

5. See note 1, p. 293.
6. Leonardo has elevated the young woman to the level of these mythological and allegorical figures, which were appropriate subjects for Renaissance painting. In Greek mythology, Leda was ravished by Zeus, who took the form of a swan. In Roman mythology, Pomona, goddess of fruit, was associated with amorous adventures. The mention of modesty and vanity together suggests the contradictory implications of her image.
7. Andrea del Verrocchio (1435–1488), Florentine sculptor and painter with whom Leonardo studied. Giorgio Vasari (1511–1574), Italian painter and architect best known for his biographies of Italian artists.

with a touch of something sinister in it, which plays over all Leonardo's work. Besides, the picture is a portrait. From childhood we see this image defining itself on the fabric of his dreams; and but for express historical testimony, we might fancy that this was but his ideal lady, embodied and beheld at last. What was the relationship of a living Florentine to this creature of his thought? By means of what strange affinities had the person and the dream grown up thus apart, and yet so closely together? Present from the first incorporeally in Leonardo's thought, dimly traced in the designs of Verrocchio, she is found present at last in *Il Giocondo*'s house. That there is much of mere portraiture in the picture is attested by the legend that by artificial means, the presence of mimes and flute-players, that subtle expression was protracted on the face. Again, was it in four years and by renewed labour never really completed, or in four months and as by stroke of magic, that the image was projected?

The presence that thus rose so strangely beside the waters, is expressive of what in the ways of a thousand years men had come to desire. Hers is the head upon which all "the ends of the world are come," and the eyelids are a little weary. It is a beauty wrought out from within upon the flesh, the deposit, little cell by cell, of strange thoughts and fantastic reveries and exquisite passions. Set it for a moment beside one of those white Greek goddesses or beautiful women of antiquity, and how would they be troubled by this beauty, into which the soul with all its maladies has passed! All the thoughts and experience of the world have etched and moulded there, in that which they have of power to refine and make expressive the outward form, the animalism of Greece, the lust of Rome, the reverie of the middle age with its spiritual ambition and imaginative loves, the return of the Pagan world, the sins of the Borgias.[8] She is older than the rocks among which she sits; like the vampire, she has been dead many times, and learned the secrets of the grave; and has been a diver in deep seas, and keeps their fallen day about her; and trafficked for strange webs with Eastern merchants: and, as Leda, was the mother of Helen of Troy, and, as Saint Anne, the mother of Mary; and all this has been to her but as the sound of lyres and flutes, and lives only in the delicacy with which it has moulded the changing lineaments, and tinged the eyelids and the hands. The fancy of a perpetual life, sweeping together ten thousand experiences, is an old one; and modern thought has conceived the idea of humanity as wrought upon by, and summing up in itself, all modes of thought and life.

8. Italian Renaissance family known primarily for corruption and for the use of violence in the pursuit of power.

Certainly Lady Lisa might stand as the embodiment of the old fancy, the symbol of the modern idea.

*   *   *

Conclusion[9]

[ART AS BURNING WITH A HARD, GEMLIKE FLAME]
Δέγει που Ἡράκλειτος ὅτι πάντα χωρεῖ καὶ οὐδὲν μένει[1]

To regard all things and principles of things as inconstant modes or fashions has more and more become the tendency of modern thought. Let us begin with that which is without—our physical life. Fix upon it in one of its more exquisite intervals, the moment, for instance, of delicious recoil from the flood of water in summer heat. What is the whole physical life in that moment but a combination of natural elements to which science gives their names? But these elements, phosphorus and lime and delicate fibres, are present not in the human body alone: we detect them in places most remote from it. Our physical life is a perpetual motion of them—the passage of the blood, the wasting and repairing of the lenses of the eye, the modification of the tissues of the brain by every ray of light and sound—processes which science reduces to simpler and more elementary forces. Like the elements of which we are composed, the action of these forces extends beyond us; it rusts iron and ripens corn. Far out on every side of us those elements are broadcast, driven by many forces; and birth and gesture and death and the springing of violets from the grave are but a few out of ten thousand resultant combinations. That clear, perpetual outline of face and limb is but an image of ours, under which we group them—a design in a web, the actual threads of which pass out beyond it. This at least of flamelike our life has, that it is but the concurrence, renewed from moment to moment, of forces parting sooner or later on their ways.

Or if we begin with the inward world of thought and feeling, the whirlpool is still more rapid, the flame more eager and devouring. There it is no longer the gradual darkening of the eye and fading of colour from the wall,—the movement of the shore-side, where the water flows down indeed, though in apparent rest,—but the race of the mid-stream, a drift of momentary acts of sight and passion and thought. At first sight experience seems to bury us under a flood of external objects, pressing upon us with a sharp and importunate

---

9. This brief "Conclusion" was omitted in the second edition of this book, as I conceived it might possibly mislead some of those young men into whose hands it might fall. On the whole, I have thought it best to reprint it here, with some slight changes which bring it closer to my original meaning. I have dealt more fully in *Marius the Epicurean* with the thoughts suggested by it [Pater's note].
1. "Heraclitus says, 'All things are in movement and nothing still'" (Greek).

reality, calling us out of ourselves in a thousand forms of action. But when reflexion begins to act upon those objects they are dissipated under its influence; the cohesive force seems suspended like a trick of magic; each object is loosed into a group of impressions—colour, odour, texture—in the mind of the observer. And if we continue to dwell in thought on this world, not of objects in the solidity with which language invests them, but of impressions unstable, flickering, inconsistent, which burn and are extinguished with our conscious-ness of them, it contracts still further; the whole scope of observa-tion is dwarfed to the narrow chamber of the individual mind. Experience, already reduced to a swarm of impressions, is ringed round for each one of us by that thick wall of personality through which no real voice has ever pierced on its way to us, or from us to that which we can only conjecture to be without. Every one of those impressions is the impression of the individual in his isolation, each mind keeping as a solitary prisoner its own dream of a world. Analy-sis goes a step farther still, and assures us that those impressions of the individual mind to which, for each one of us, experience dwindles down, are in perpetual flight; that each of them is limited by time, and that as time is infinitely divisible, each of them is infinitely divis-ible also; all that is actual in it being a single moment, gone while we try to apprehend it, of which it may ever be more truly said that it has ceased to be than that it is. To such a tremulous wisp constantly re-forming itself on the stream, to a single sharp impression, with a sense in it, a relic more or less fleeting, of such moments gone by, what is real in our life fines itself down. It is with this movement, with the passage and dissolution of impressions, images, sensations, that analysis leaves off—that continual vanishing away, that strange, perpetual weaving and unweaving of ourselves.

Philosophiren, says Novalis, *ist dephlegmatisiren vivificiren*.[2] The service of philosophy, of speculative culture, towards the human spirit is to rouse, to startle it into sharp and eager observation. Every moment some form grows perfect in hand or face; some tone on the hills or the sea is choicer than the rest; some mood of passion or in-sight or intellectual excitement is irresistibly real and attractive for us,—for that moment only. Not the fruit of experience, but experi-ence itself, is the end. A counted number of pulses only is given to us of a variegated, dramatic life. How may we see in them all that is to be seen in them by the finest senses? How shall we pass most swiftly from point to point, and be present always at the focus where the greatest number of vital forces unite in their purest energy?

To burn always with this hard, gemlike flame, to maintain this ecstasy, is success in life. In a sense it might even be said that our

2. "To philosophize is to dephlagmatize, to bring to life" (German).

failure is to form habits: for, after all, habit is relative to a stereotyped world, and meantime it is only the roughness of the eye that makes any two persons, things, situations, seem alike. While all melts under our feet, we may well catch at any exquisite passion, or any contribution to knowledge that seems by a lifted horizon to set the spirit free for a moment, or any stirring of the senses, strange dyes, strange colours, and curious odours, or work of the artist's hands, or the face of one's friend. Not to discriminate every moment some passionate attitude in those about us, and in the brilliancy of their gifts some tragic dividing of forces on their ways, is, on this short day of frost and sun, to sleep before evening. With this sense of the splendour of our experience and of its awful brevity, gathering all we are into one desperate effort to see and touch, we shall hardly have time to make theories about the things we see and touch. What we have to do is to be for ever curiously testing new opinions and courting new impressions, never acquiescing in a facile orthodoxy of Comte, or of Hegel,[3] or of our own. Philosophical theories or ideas, as points of view, instruments of criticism, may help us to gather up what might otherwise pass unregarded by us. "Philosophy is the microscope of thought." The theory or idea or system which requires of us the sacrifice of any part of this experience, in consideration of some interest into which we cannot enter, or some abstract theory we have not identified with ourselves, or what is only conventional, has no real claim upon us.

One of the most beautiful passages in the writings of Rousseau is that in the sixth book of the *Confessions*,[4] where he describes the awakening in him of the literary sense. An undefinable taint of death had always clung about him, and now in early manhood he believed himself smitten by mortal disease. He asked himself how he might make as much as possible of the interval that remained; and he was not biassed by anything in his previous life when he decided that it must be by intellectual excitement, which he found just then in the clear, fresh writings of Voltaire. Well! we are all *condamnés*, as Victor Hugo says:[5] we are all under sentence of death

3. Georg Wilhelm Friedrich Hegel (1770–1831), German philosopher who claimed that absolute knowledge involves deriving a higher unity from apparent contradictions. Auguste Comte (1798–1857), French thinker who developed the philosophy of positivism, which claims that only the scientific method, with its emphasis on observation, not on speculative thinking, yields authentic knowledge.
4. In his posthumously published *Confessions* (1782), the Swiss-born French philosopher Jean-Jacques Rousseau (1712–1778) focuses on the first fifty-three years of his life. In the sixth of the twelve main sections of this autobiography, Rousseau presents the illness that he suffered in 1736, which resulted in his undertaking extensive reading and study.
5. Pater is citing *Le Dernier Jour d'un Condamné* (*Last Days of a Condemned Man*; 1829), by the French writer Victor-Marie Hugo (1802–1885). Voltaire: the penname of the iconoclastic French writer and philosopher François-Marie Arouet (1694–1778), who wrote the satirical narrative *Candide, ou l'Optimisme* (*Candide, or Optimism*; 1759).

but with a sort of indefinite reprieve—*les hommes sont tous con-damnés à mort avec des sursis indéfinis:* we have an interval, and then our place knows us no more. Some spend this interval in list-lessness, some in high passions, the wisest, at least among "the children of this world," in art and song. For our one chance lies in expanding that interval, in getting as many pulsations as possible into the given time. Great passions may give us this quickened sense of life, ecstasy and sorrow of love, the various forms of en-thusiastic activity, disinterested or otherwise, which come natu-rally to many of us. Only be sure it is passion—that it does yield you this fruit of a quickened, multiplied consciousness. Of this wisdom, the poetic passion, the desire of beauty, the love of art for art's sake, has most; for art comes to you professing frankly to give nothing but the highest quality to your moments as they pass, and simply for those moments' sake.

OSCAR WILDE

The Picture of Dorian Gray[†]

[*Wilde and His Characters on the Artist*]

FROM THE PREFACE

The artist is the creator of beautiful things.
To reveal art and conceal the artist is art's aim.

* * *

FROM CHAPTER I

* * *

In the centre of the room, clamped to an upright easel, stood the full-length portrait of a young man of extraordinary personal beauty, and in front of it, some little distance away, was sitting the artist him-self, Basil Hallward, whose sudden disappearance some years ago

---

[†] Oscar Wilde (1854–1900) was the most successful Irish writer of the generation before Joyce's, until his career and fortunes were ruined when he was imprisoned in England after being convicted in 1895 for homosexual acts. Joyce, W. B. Yeats (see note 9, p. 199), and others who were Wilde's younger contemporaries were profoundly influenced by Wilde's life and his writings, which often meditate on art and the artist. The phrase "a por-trait of the artist" occurs in the excerpt from the opening chapter of *The Picture of Dorian Gray* (1891) that is reprinted below. Among the volumes that Joyce owned in Trieste is a continental edition of Wilde's book in English published by Tauchnitz (1908).

From *The Collected Edition of the Works of Oscar Wilde,* ed. Robert Ross. Vol. 12. *The Picture of Dorian Gray* (1891). Paris: Charles Carrington Publisher and Bookseller, 1908, ix, 2–7.

caused, at the time, such public excitement, and gave rise to so many strange conjectures.

As the painter looked at the gracious and comely form he had so skilfully mirrored in his art, a smile of pleasure passed across his face, and seemed about to linger there. But he suddenly started up, and, closing his eyes, placed his fingers upon the lids, as though he sought to imprison within his brain some curious dream from which he feared he might awake.

'It is your best work, Basil, the best thing you have ever done,' said Lord Henry languidly. 'You must certainly send it next year to the Grosvenor. The Academy is too large and too vulgar. Whenever I have gone there, there have been either so many people that I have not been able to see the pictures, which was dreadful, or so many pictures that I have not been able to see the people, which was worse. The Grosvenor is really the only place.'

'I don't think I shall send it anywhere,' he answered, tossing his head back in that odd way that used to make his friends laugh at him at Oxford. 'No: I won't send it anywhere.'

Lord Henry elevated his eyebrows, and looked at him in amazement through the thin blue wreaths of smoke that curled up in such fanciful whorls from his heavy opium-tainted cigarette. 'Not send it anywhere? My dear fellow, why? Have you any reason? What odd chaps you painters are! You do anything in the world to gain a reputation. As soon as you have one, you seem to want to throw it away. It is silly of you, for there is only one thing in the world worse than being talked about, and that is not being talked about. A portrait like this would set you far above all the young men in England, and make the old men quite jealous, if old men are ever capable of any emotion.'

'I know you will laugh at me,' he replied, 'but I really can't exhibit it. I have put too much of myself into it.'

Lord Henry stretched himself out on the divan and laughed.

'Yes, I knew you would; but it is quite true, all the same.'

'Too much of yourself in it! Upon my word, Basil, I didn't know you were so vain; and I really can't see any resemblance between you, with your rugged strong face and your coal-black hair, and this young Adonis, who looks as if he was made out of ivory and rose-leaves. Why, my dear Basil, he is a Narcissus, and you—well, of course you have an intellectual expression, and all that. But beauty, real beauty, ends where an intellectual expression begins. Intellect is in itself a mode of exaggeration, and destroys the harmony of any face. The moment one sits down to think, one becomes all nose, or all forehead, or something horrid. Look at the successful men in any of the learned professions. How perfectly hideous they are! Except, of course, in the Church. But then in the Church they don't think. A bishop keeps on saying at the age of eighty what he was told to say when he was a boy of eighteen, and as a natural consequence he always looks absolutely delightful. Your mysterious young friend, whose name you have never told me, but whose picture really fascinates me, never thinks. I feel quite sure of that. He is some brainless, beautiful creature, who should be always here in winter when we have no flowers to look at, and always here in summer when we want something to chill our intelligence. Don't flatter yourself, Basil: you are not in the least like him.'

'You don't understand me, Harry,' answered the artist. 'Of course I am not like him. I know that perfectly well. Indeed, I should be sorry to look like him. You shrug your shoulders? I am telling you the truth. There is a fatality about all physical and intellectual distinction, the sort of fatality that seems to dog through history the faltering steps of kings. It is better not to be different from one's fellows. * * * Your rank and wealth, Harry; my brains, such as they are—my art, whatever it may be worth; Dorian Gray's good looks—we shall all suffer for what the gods have given us, suffer terribly.'

'Dorian Gray? Is that his name?' asked Lord Henry, walking across the studio towards Basil Hallward.

'Yes, that is his name. I didn't intend to tell it to you.'

* * *

After a pause, Lord Henry pulled out his watch. 'I am afraid I must be going, Basil,' he murmured, 'and before I go, I insist on your answering a question I put to you some time ago.'

'What is that?' said the painter, keeping his eyes fixed on the ground.

'You know quite well.'

'I do not, Harry.'

'Well, I will tell you what it is. I want you to explain to me why you won't exhibit Dorian Gray's picture. I want the real reason.'

'I told you the real reason.'

'No, you did not. You said it was because there was too much of yourself in it. Now, that is childish.'

'Harry,' said Basil Hallward, looking him straight in the face, 'every portrait that is painted with feeling is a portrait of the artist, not of the sitter. The sitter is merely the accident, the occasion. It is not he who is revealed by the painter; it is rather the painter who, on the coloured canvas, reveals himself. The reason I will not exhibit this picture is that I am afraid that I have shown in it the secret of my own soul.'

* * *

CRITICISM

Structural Overview
of the Narrative

JOHN PAUL RIQUELME

The Parts and the Structural Rhythm
of *A Portrait*[†]

The Parts

Like *Ulysses* and *Finnegans Wake*, *A Portrait* consists of untitled, unnumbered segments grouped into several parts designated by roman numerals. While the conventions of referring to the episodes of *Ulysses* by Homeric titles and to the chapters of the *Wake* by part and chapter numbers were adopted long ago, no similar convention has developed for *A Portrait*. To facilitate reference to specific sections and to indicate their particular placement within the sectional arrangement of the part, I provide the following scheme. Adopting a convention like that for citing chapters of the *Wake*, in my discussion of *A Portrait* I refer to sections by part and section numbers.

Part and Section	Designation	Lines
Part I		
I.1	Prelude	1–41
I.2	Clongowes (playing field; classroom; infirmary)	42–715
I.3	Christmas Dinner	716–1151
I.4	Broken Glasses (smugging; writing lesson, pandybat; rector)	1152–1848
Part II		
II.1	Blackrock (Uncle Charles; *The Count of Monte Cristo*; Cowyard)	1–185

[†] Revised and elaborated from *Teller and Tale in Joyce's Fiction: Oscillating Perspectives*. Baltimore and London: Johns Hopkins UP, 1983, 232–34. Reprinted by permission of the publisher.

The Structural Rhythm

Besides giving brief numerical designations to the sections of *A Portrait,* this schema provides some evidence for a conjecture about the structural rhythm of Joyce's arrangement. A peculiar sort of unity of effect arises from the juxtaposing of fragmented narrative segments. Part of that unity can be traced to expansions and contractions of narrative focus that become a defining configuration for our experience of the text. My conjecture can be translated into structural terms simply by examining the lengths of the various parts and sections. From such an examination we can describe the narrative structure as made up of three units. The first consists of the first three parts, each of about the same length. The second unit is the climactic fourth part, by far the shortest one, about half the length of any of the three preceding parts. The final unit is the fifth part, by far the longest one, nearly twice as long as Part II, the briefest of the first three.

I emphasize these proportions because they are also the proportions of the narrative configuration of Part V. The unusually long

V.1 (longer even than Part II), with its heterogeneous mix of scenes, memories, and dialogues, is the equivalent for the first unit of the larger narrative. The writing of the villanelle, V.2, corresponds to the climactic second unit, Part IV. The talk with Cranly and the journal, V.3 and V.4, provide a denouement, as does all of Part V in the larger scheme. The narrative structure of V, then, duplicates the structure of the entire book. * * *

Joyce stresses this duplicated configuration, one structure nesting within the conclusion of the other, by the way he frames the climaxes of the book and of Part V. In both cases, the sections preceding and following the climactic segments are clearly linked. III.3 presents Stephen in the kitchen of his home idealizing and contemplating with anticipation the food that will be his breakfast after Communion the next morning. In V.1 he is again presented in the kitchen eating a greasy breakfast before leaving belatedly for his classes at the university. * * * V.1 ends and V.3 begins with Stephen on the steps in front of the library. In between the two similar scenes of V, he has decided to break with his past and to leave Ireland. Both climaxes act as intervening segments explaining the transformation that has occurred. * * *

Both the large arrangement of sections and the details framing the climactic portions of the narrative contribute to the structural rhythm and duplication. * * *

My division of the narrative into titled sections responds to Kenneth Burke's suggestion, in "Fact, Inference, and Proof in the Analysis of Literary Symbolism" (pp. 311–28) that the parts be treated as titled "substages" (p. 319). He asks what titles would be appropriate for the five numbered parts, suggesting as possibilities "Childhood Sensibility," "The Fall," "The Sermon," "The New Vocation" (or "Epiphany"), and "The New Doctrine." Burke also comments on the book's structural centers, its quantitative midpoint in the sermon, and its center of narrative reversal, which I call its climax, in Part IV.

Essays in Criticism

KENNETH BURKE

Fact, Inference, and Proof in the Analysis of Literary Symbolism[†]

This essay is part of a project called "Theory of the Index," concerned with the taking of preparatory notes for purposes of critical analysis. The hope is to make the analysis of literary symbolism as systematic as possible, while allowing for an experimental range required by the subtle and complex nature of the subject matter.

Fundamentally, the essay is built about the "principle of the concordance." But whereas concordances, listing all passages where a given word appears in a text, have been compiled for a few major works, obviously criticism cannot have the advantage of such scholarship when studying the terminology of most literary texts. And even where concordances are available, there must be grounds for paying more attention to some terms than to others.

Here, treating the individual words of a work as the basic "facts" of that work, and using for test case some problems in the "indexing" of James Joyce's *A Portrait of the Artist as a Young Man*, the essay asks how to operate with these "facts," how to use them as a means of keeping one's inferences under control, yet how to go beyond them, for purposes of inference, when seeking to characterize the motives and "salient traits" of the work, in its nature as a total symbolic structure.

I

Insofar as possible, we confine the realm of the "factual" to a low but necessary and unquestioned order of observations. Thus, it is a "fact" that the book proper begins, "Once upon a time and a very

† From *Terms for Order*, ed. Stanley Edgar Hyman. Bloomington: Indiana UP, 1964, 145–72. Reprinted with approval of the Kenneth Burke Literary Trust. Some of Burke's notes have been omitted. Page references have been replaced with part and line numbers of this Norton Critical Edition. Some cited passages might differ slightly from the equivalent passages in this volume.

good time it was . . ." etc., and ends: "Old father, old artificer, stand me now and ever in good stead." We say it is a fact that the "book proper" so begins and so ends. But it is also a "fact" that the text begins with a prior quotation from Ovid's *Metamorphoses* and ends on a reference to duality of scene: "Dublin, 1904/Trieste, 1914." We might get different results, depending upon which of these "facts" we worked from. But in either case, the existence of such "facts" is literally verifiable. "Facts" are what was said or done, as interpreted in the strictest possible sense.

The ideal "atomic fact" in literary symbolism is probably the individual word. We do not say that the literary work is "nothing but" words. We do say that it is "at least" words. True, a word is further reducible to smaller oral and visual particles (letters and phonemes); and such reducibility allows for special cases of "alchemic" transformation whereby the accident of a word's structure may surreptitiously relate it (punwise) to other words that happen to be similar in structure though "semantically" quite distinct from it. But the word is the first full "perfection" of a term. And we move from it either way as our base, either "back" to the dissolution of meaning that threatens it by reason of its accidental punwise associates, or "forward" to its dissolution through inclusion in a "higher meaning," which attains *its* perfection in the sentence.

Surprisingly enough, such a terministic approach to symbolism can be much more "factual" than is the case with reports about actual conditions or happenings in the extrasymbolic realm. In the extrasymbolic realm, there is usually a higher necessary percentage of "interpretation" or "inference" in a statement we call "factual." We can but infer what the diplomat did. But we can cite "factually" some report that says what he did. People usually think that the nonsymbolic realm is the clear one, while the symbolic realm is hazy. But if you agree that the words, or terms, in a book are its "facts," then by the same token you see there is a sense in which we get our view of *deeds* as facts from our sense of *words* as facts, rather than *vice versa*.

In this strict usage, many observations that might ordinarily be treated under the headings of "fact" fall on the side of "inference." For instance, when referring to the formula, "Dublin, 1904/Trieste, 1914," we described it as "a duality of scene." There is a slight tendentiousness here; for our characterization leans to the side of "Dublin *versus* Trieste" rather than to the side of "Dublin equals Trieste" (toward opposition rather than apposition). And when referring to the quotation from Ovid, we might rather have referred to the quoted words themselves, stressing perhaps the *original context* from which they were lifted. Thus quickly and spontaneously we smuggle inferences, or interpretations, into our report of the "factual."

Yet, insofar as there is a record, there is an underlying structure of "factuality" to which we can repeatedly repair, in the hopes of hermeneutic improvement.

"Proof," then, would be of two sorts. While grounding itself in reference to the textual "facts," it must seek to make clear all elements of inference or interpretation it adds to these facts; and it must offer a rationale for its selections and interpretations. Ideally, it might even begin from different orders of "facts," and show how they led in the end to the same interpretation. We should not have much difficulty, for instance, in showing how "Dublin *versus* Trieste" could still allow for "Dublin equals Trieste," for there are respects in which Joyce's (or Stephen's!) original motives are transformed, and there are respects in which they were continued.

At the point of greatest ideal distance, an attempt to ground the analysis of literary symbolism in "terministic factuality" is to be contrasted with the analysis of symbols in terms of "analogy." If, for instance, the *word* "tree" appears in two contexts, we would not begin by asking ourselves what rare "symbolic" meaning a tree might have, in either religious or psychoanalytic allegory. We would begin rather with the literal fact that this term bridges the two contexts.

Or let us go a step further. Suppose that you *did* begin with some pat meaning for tree, over and above its meaning as a positive concept. (In our hypothetical case, we are assuming that, whatever else "tree" may stand for, in these two contexts it *at least* refers to a tree in the primary dictionary sense, as it might not if one reference was to a "family tree.") Suppose you were prepared to say *in advance* exactly what recondite meaning the "image" of a tree might have, in its nature as a "symbol" enigmatically "emblematic" of esoteric meanings. (For instance, we could imagine a psychologist saying, "It's not just a 'tree'; it's a father-symbol, or a mother-symbol, or in general a parent-symbol.") Even if we granted that your "symbolic" or "analogical" meaning for "tree" was correct, *the fact would still remain* that the term had *one particular* set of associates in some particular work. This is the kind of interconnectedness we would watch, when studying the "facts" of an identical *word* that recurs in changing *contexts*. Such an investigation would be in contrast with the confining of one's interpretation to equivalences—"analogies"—already established even before one looks at the given text.

The "analogical" method is alluring, because by it you get these things settled once and for all. A good literature student, trained in the ways of indexing of "contexts," requires that each work be studied anew, "from scratch." Night, bird, sun, blood, tree, mountain, death? No matter, once the topic is introduced, analogy has the answer, without ever looking further.

Part of the trouble, to be sure, comes from the fact that often brief poems are the texts used. And the short lyric is the *most diffi-cult* form to explain, as its transformations are necessarily quick, while being concealed beneath the lyric's urgent need to establish intense unity of mood (a need so urgent that in most lyrics the transformations are negligible, though such is not the case with great lyrists like Keats). Long forms (epics, dramas, novels, or poetic *sequences*) afford the most viable material for the study of terms in changing contexts. And the principles we learn through this better documented analysis can then be applied, *mutatis mutandis*,[1] to the study of lyric "naturalness."

Three illustrations, before proceeding:

In I.1531–32 and I.1543–44, in connection with the episode of Stephen's unjust punishment, we read: ". . . the swish of the sleeve of the soutane as the pandybat was lifted to strike . . ." and "the soutane sleeve swished again as the pandybat was lifted . . ." In IV.258–61: "Then, just as he was wishing that some unforeseen cause might prevent the director from coming, he had heard the handle of the door turning and the swish of a soutane." Here the recurrence of the swish establishes a purely "factual" bond between the two passages; and this factual bond is to be noted first as such, in its sheer terminal identity, without reference to "symbolic" or "analogical" meanings. More remotely, the "swish" might be said to *subsist* punwise in "was wishing." Hence, if this iterative verb-form were noted elsewhere in the work, one might tentatively include its context, too, as part of this grouping (made by leaps and zigzags through the narrative).

Or one may isolate this concordance: II.1269, citing Shelley's "Art thou pale for weariness"; V.86, Ben Jonson's, "I was not wearier where I lay"; V.1552, in Stephen's villanelle, "Are you not weary of ardent ways?"; and in V.1769–70, V.1805–06, and V.1806–07, when Stephen is watching the birds as an augury, "leaning wearily on his ashplant . . . the ashplant on which he leaned wearily . . . a sense of fear of the unknown moved in the heart of his weariness." (Ordinarily, we take it that the various grammatical forms of a word can be treated as identical. But one must always be prepared for a case where this will not be so. One could imagine a work, for instance, in which "fly" and "flight" were so used that "fly" was found to appear only in contexts meaning "soar above" or "transcend," whereas "flight" was only in contexts meaning "flee." Ordinarily, "flight" would cover both meanings, as we believe the symbol of flight does in Joyce. Or should we say that in Stephen's ecstatic vision of artistic flight the "negative" sense of *fleeing* attains rather the "positive" sense of *flying*?)

1. With respective differences taken into account (Latin) [Editor].

Or again: in V.1467–69, Stephen's esthetic is stated doctrinally thus: "The artist, like the god of the creation, remains within or behind or beyond or above his handiwork, invisible, refined out of existence, indifferent, paring his fingernails." Without yet asking ourselves what such paring of the nails may "symbolize," we "factually" unite this passage with ". . . some fellows called him Lady Boyle because he was always at his nails, paring them" (I.1255–56); and (I.1347–50): "Mr. Gleason had round shiny cuffs and clean white wrists and fattish white hands and the nails of them were long and pointed. Perhaps he pared them too like Lady Boyle."

Such concordances are initially noted without inference or interpretation. For whereas purely terministic correlation can serve the ends of "analogical" or "symbolic" exegesis, it is far more tentative and empirical, with a constant demand for fresh inquiry. In fact, one may experimentally note many correlations of this sort without being able to fit them into an over-all scheme of interpretation.

But a grounding in the concordances of "terminal factuality" is by no means a solution to our problems.

2

If we are to begin with a "factual" index, what do we feature? Obviously, we cannot make a concordance of every book we read. And besides, even if we had a concordance before we began, we must find some principle of selection, since some terms are much more likely than others to yield good hermeneutical results. If a researcher is looking for *some particular topic,* of course, there is no problem of selection. But if the critic is attempting to characterize, in as well rounded a way as he can, the salient traits of the given work, trying to give an over-all interpretation of it as a unified symbolic act, he has a lot more to do than merely look for terminal correlations.

Almost without thinking, he will select certain *key terms.* For instance, every reader would spontaneously agree that "Stephen Dedalus" is a term to be featured. And at the very least, he would expand the name in the directions explicitly indicated by Joyce: Daedalus, Stephanoumenos, Stephaneforos.

Also, the title suggests that the critic might ask himself: "What will be the *operational* definition of 'artist' in this work?" One must be wary of titles, however. For often they were assigned or altered to meet real or imagined conditions of the market; and sometimes a work may be given a title purely for its sales value as a title, which was invented without reference to the work so entitled. In the case of the *Portrait,* of course, it would be generally agreed that the work is depicting the growth of an artist (*as so defined*) not only emotionally but in terms of a doctrine explicitly stated. For, ironically, although Stephen's doctrine denounces the "didactic" in art, it is itself as "didactic" as the Gospel; in fact it is an esthetic gospel.

But whereas the primary terms of a work operate by secondary connections, we can never be quite sure what secondary terms are likely to produce the best results. For instance, the first few lines of the book refer twice to "baby tuckoo." In a sense, this is Stephen's "real" name; for by the resources natural to narrative, an *essence* is stated in terms of *temporal* priority. Tentatively, then, we note it. And having done so, we find these possibly related entries: (I.417–18) "tucking the end of the nightshirt"; (I.531–32) "little feet tucked up"; (V.2136–37) "a leather portfolio tucked under his armpit." What, then, of "Tusker Boyle" (I.1233 and I.1254–55), the unsavory fellow whom we have already mentioned in connection with the paring of his fingernails, a reference also connected with reference to the artist's "handiwork" (V.1468)? But the reference to hands also radiates in another direction, including both the priest's painful paddling of Stephen's hands in the pandybat episode, and the episode in IV.472–75, where Stephen withdraws his hand from the priest as a sign that he is not to choose the religious vocation, but to become instead, in V.1677, a "priest of the imagination." (The scene was introduced by the already cited reference to the "swish of the soutane.") This and the four references in sixteen lines to the "pain" suffered in the pandybat episode have as counterpart in the later passage an assurance that the music which had distracted him from the priest's promises dissolved his thoughts "painlessly and noiselessly" (IV.471).

We could radiate in many other directions. In I.1254–57, for instance, the reference to Tusker (or Lady) Boyle had led immediately into talk of Eileen's hands, with the memory of the time when this Protestant girl had put her hand into his pocket. Her hands "were like ivory; only soft. That was the meaning of *Tower of Ivory*," etc., whereat we can radiate to "yellow ivory" and "mottled tusks of elephants," in I.1258–59, V.182, and V.184.

We could go on. But already we glimpse how, without our asking ourselves just what any of our bridging terms may mean "analogically" or "symbolically," a circle of terminal interrelationships is beginning to build up. And even though we might abandon some positions under pressure (as for instance the series "tuckoo-tucking-Tusker-tusks"), we find connections of similar import being established by many other routes, most of them not requiring us to do any punwise "joycing" of terms (though we might at least be justified in applying such tentatives to even early work by Joyce, in the likelihood that his later typical susceptibilities were already emerging).

But let us get back to our more immediate problem. What *should* have been indexed in the opening pages? There was a "moocow" ("symbolically" maternal?), there was a father with a "hairy face," there is a progression from "baby tuckoo" to "moocow" to "Betty Byrne" (beddy burn?!) to "lemon platt" (which puzzles us, except insofar as it may be yellow, anent[2] which more anon). There are some *childishly* distorted jingles; and these may so set the rules of this *adult* work that we can look tentatively for such distortion *as a principle*, operating perhaps over and above the examples explicitly given in the text. (Otherwise put: if these paragraphs are *under the sign of* such punwise distortion, might we not be justified in asking whether there could also be *displaced* distortion, such as would be there if *particular* distortions were taken to stand for more than themselves, indicating that a *principle* of distortion was operating *at this point*? We bring up the possibility, to suggest *methodological* reasons why we might experimentally so pun on "Betty Byrne" as we did. We would remind our reader, however, that *we are as yet committed to nothing*, so far as this text goes. *In advance,* we make allowance for a *latitudinarian* range—as contrasted with those who, in advance, have it *all sewed up*. But we need not yet make decisions.)

Should we have noted that "His mother had a nicer smell than his father" (I.15)? In any case, there are many other references to smell (I.131, I.381, I.382, I.383, and I.391, for instance); and the passage becomes doubly interesting when, in his stage of contrition (IV.134–35) Stephen has trouble mortifying his sense of smell: "To mortify his smell was more difficult as he found in himself no instinctive repugnance to bad odours," etc.

Where do we start? Where do we stop?

Let us admit: there must be a certain amount of waste motion here, particularly if one undertakes an index before having a fairly clear idea of a book's developments. One is threatened with a kind of methodic demoralization—for anything might pay off. Yet by an "index" we most decidedly do *not* mean such lists (by author or topic) as one finds in the back of a book. In fact, whereas an index is normally made by entries on a set of cards which are then rearranged alphabetically, we must allow our entries to remain "in the order of their appearance." For a purely alphabetical reordering makes it almost impossible to inspect a work in its *unfoldings*. And we must keep on the move, watching both for static interrelationships and for *principles of transformation* whereby a motive may progress from one combination through another to a third, etc.

Over and above whatever we may enter in our index, there will be the search for "stages." Methodologically, such a search implies a

theory of "substance." That is, in contrast with those "semantic"
theories which would banish from their vocabulary any term for
"substance," we must believe above all in the reasonableness of "enti-
tling." Confronting a complexity of details, we do not confine ourselves merely to the detailed tracing of interrelationships among
them, or among the ones that we consider outstanding. We must
also keep prodding ourselves to attempt answering this question:
"Suppose you were required to find an over-all title for this entire
batch of particulars. What would that be?"

The *Portrait* is in five parts, which are merely numbered. What,
then, should their titles be, if they had titles? We say that such a
question implies a grounding in the term "substance" or in the furtive
function indicated by that term, because it implies that all the disparate details included under one head are infused with a common
spirit, or purpose, *i.e.*, are *consubstantial*. We may be in varying
degrees right or wrong, as regards the substance that we impute to
a given set of details. But they are ultimately organized with relation
to one another by their joint participation in a unitary purpose, or
"idea." In brief, we must keep hypothetically shifting between the
particular and the general.

True: you can take it for granted that, once such a range is available, you can always attain *some* level of generalization in terms of
which disparate details might be substantially related. Ideally, one
seeks for terms that account for kinship not only with regard to tests
of consistency; one also wants to place *sequences, developments,*
showing why the parts are *in precisely that order and no other*; and if
one seeks to be overthorough here, the excess should be revealed by
trouble in finding cogent rationalizations.

Often, for instance, the critic may be overzealous in trying to show
how a whole plot may unfold from some original situation, somewhat
like an artificial Japanese flower unfolding in water. But an accurate
analysis would have to show how a series of *new steps* was needed, to
carry the work from its opening "germ" to its final "growth." Thus,
some opening imagery might be said to contain the later plot "in
germ." (We have seen this very *Portrait* so analyzed.) But on closer
analysis you will find that the opening imagery "pointed to" the ultimate destination of the plot only in the sense that, if one makes a
sweep of the hand from south-southwest to north-northwest, one
has thereby "implicitly" pointed due west. Critics who would analyze
a book as an unfolding from an all-inclusive implication will need to
use a different kind of dialectic[3] as well. They will need to show by
what successive stages a work is "narrowed down"; for its "unfolding"
will be rather like a definition that begins with too broad a category,

---

3. Process of determining the truth through the exchange of logical arguments [Editor].

and gradually imposes strictures until the subject is "pinpointed" (as with the game of Twenty Questions).

In the case of the *Portrait*, whatever difficulties we might have in deciding how we would specifically treat any of the details in Part I, we could "idealize" the problem in general terms thus: we note that this work leads up to the explicit propounding of an Esthetic (a doctrine, catechism, or "philosophy" of art). Then we ask how each of the parts might look, as seen from this point of view. The first part deals with rudimentary sensory perception, primary sensations of smell, touch, sight, sound, taste (basic bodily feelings that, at a later stage in the story, will be methodically "mortified"). And there is our answer. Lo! the *Esthetic* begins in simple *aisthesis*.[4] So, in this sense, the entire first chapter could be entitled "Childhood Sensibility." It will "render" the basic requirement for the artist, as defined by the terms (and their transformations) in this particular work. It depicts the kind of personality, or temperament, required of one who would take this course that leads to the Joycean diploma (to a chair spiritually endowed by Joycean Foundations). Family relations, religion, and even politics are thus "esthetically" experienced in this opening part—experienced not as mature "ideas," or even as adolescent "passions," but as "sensations," or "images."

But whereas we would thus entitle the first section of the *Portrait*, we do not want our whole argument to depend upon this one particular choice. We are here interested mainly in the attempt to illustrate the *principle* we are discussing. We might further note that, though "Childhood Sensibility" as a title fits *developmentally* into the story as a whole, it does *not* suggest a logic of development *within* the single chapter it is intended to sum up. It merely provides a term for describing *self-consistency* among the details of the chapter. It names them solely in terms of "repetitive" form, so far as their relation to one another is concerned. And only when treating them *en bloc*,[5] with relation to the entire five chapters, do we suggest a measure of "progressive" form here. Ideally, therefore, we should also ask ourselves into what substages (with appropriate titles) this chapter on "Childhood Sensibility" should in turn be divided. At least, when indexing, we keep thus resurveying, in quest of developments. (The thought also suggests why an index arranged alphabetically would conceal too much for our purposes.)

The very rigors of our stress upon "terminal factuality" as the ideal beginning quickly force us to become aware of this step from particulars to generalizings (a step the exact nature of which is often concealed beneath terms like "symbol" and "analogy"). Hypothetically,

4. Sense perception (Greek) [Editor].
5. All together (French) [Editor].

even in a long work there might be no significant literal repeating of
key terms. (We have heard tell of some ancient Chinese *tour de force*
in which, though it is a work of considerable length, no single character is repeated. And one would usually be hardpressed for a wide
range of literal repetitions in individual lyrics, though the quest of
"factually" joined contexts usually yields good results where we have
an opportunity to study a poet's terminology as maintained through
several poems.) And even with the Joyce *Portrait,* which abounds in
factually related contexts, we confront a notable place where we
would obviously accept suicidal restrictions if we refused to take the
generalizing or idealizing step from particulars to principles (or, in
this case, from particular *words* to the more general *themes* or *topics*
that these words signify).

We have in mind Stephen's formula for his artistic jesuitry, "silence,
exile, and cunning" (V.2579–80). "Silence" yields good results, even
factually. It is a word that appears at all notable moments along the
road of Stephen's development up to the pronouncing of his esthetic
creed. There are a few references to cunning, the most pointed
being this passage, V.435–46 (all italics ours, to indicate terms we
consider focal here):

> Stephen saw the *silent* soul of a jesuit look out at him from
> the pale loveless eyes. Like Ignatius he was lame but in his eyes
> burned no spark of Ignatius' enthusiasm. Even the legendary
> *craft* of the company, a *craft* subtler and more *secret* than its
> fabled books of *secret* subtle wisdom, had not fired his soul with
> the energy of apostleship. It seemed as if he used the shifts and
> lore and *cunning* of the world, as bidden to do, for the greater
> glory of God, without *joy* in their handling or hatred of that in
> them which was evil but turning them, with a firm gesture of
> obedience, back upon themselves; and for all this *silent service*
> it seemed as if he loved not at all the master and little if at all,
> the ends he *served.*

The references to "service" touch upon the *non serviam* theme
that emerged so startlingly in the sermon. And the silence-exile-
cunning formula (V.2580) had been immediately preceded by
Stephen's challenge, "I will not serve," etc. We here see "cunning"
and "silence" interwoven quite "factually." Also, we see the references to "craft" that could lead us into the final theme (patronymi-
cally punning) of the labyrinthine "artificer."

Yet "artificer" is not literally (thus not "factually") identical with
"craft." And as for "exile": unless we missed some entries (and we
may have!) the particular word does not appear elsewhere in this
text. However, even assuming that we are correct, a punctiliousness
bordering on "methodological suicide" would be required to keep us

from including, under the *principle* of "exile," Stephen's question, "Symbol of departure or loneliness?" (V.1843), when he is considering the augury of the birds that stand for his new vocation. And once we can equate "exile" with *aloneness* (and *its* kinds of secrecy, either guilty or gestatory) we open our inquiry almost to a frenzy of entries: For "alone," in this story of a renegade Catholic boy who "forges"[6] a vocation somehow also under the aegis of a Protestant girl's hands, is as typical as any adjective in the book. Whereupon we find reasons to question whether the *apparent* disjunction (departure *or* loneliness) is really a disjunction at all. Far from their being antitheses in this work, the difference between them is hardly that between a bursting bud and a newly opened blossom.

In sum, once you go from "factual" word to a theme or topic that would include *synonyms* of this word, you are on the way to including also what we might call "operational synonyms," words which are synonyms in this particular text though they would not be so listed in a dictionary. That is, not only would a word like "stillness" be included under the same head as "silence," but you might also include here a silent *gesture* that was called "the vehicle of a vague speech," particularly as it is a scene in which we are explicitly told that he "stood silent" (II.1456, II.1436). Or, otherwise put: similarly, variants of "loneliness" *and* "departure" (hence even the theme of the flying bird) might be classed with "exile." And "cunning" in being extended to cover the artistic "craft," might thus expand not only into Daedalian, labyrinthine artifice, "maze," etc., but also into that doctrinal circle the center of which is the term "imagination." We would then need some summarizing term, such as "the Joycean artist," or "the hawkman motive," to include under one head the "fact" that "silence," "exile," and "cunning" are *trinitarian* terms, which in turn are themselves linked sometimes dictionarywise (as synonyms), and sometimes "operationally" (in terms of contexts interconnected roundabout).[7]

Clearly, in the analysis of short lyrics where terms cannot be repeated in many contexts, one spontaneously looks for what the old rhetoric called "amplification," some theme or topic that is restated in many ways, no single one of which could be taken as a sufficient

---

6. (V.2789–90) "To forge in the smithy of my soul the uncreated conscience of my race"; (IV.777–81) "A hawklike man flying sunward above the sea, a prophecy of the end he had been born to serve . . . a symbol of the artist forging anew in his workshop out of the sluggish matter of the earth a new soaring impalpable imperishable being"; (V.208–09) "The monkish learning, in terms of which he was trying to forge out an esthetic philosophy." (Incidentally, we would watch a word like "force," on the chance that it may turn out to be a punwise, furtive variant of "forge.")

7. Any connection by synonyms should always be watched for the possibility of a lurking antithesis. That is, words on their face synonymous may really *function* as antitheses in a given symbol-system. Conversely, words *apparently* "as different as day and night" may be but operational concealments of a *single* motive. ° ° °

summing up. (Here again, ideally, we might try to find working subtitles for each stanza, as a way of aggressively asking ourselves whether
we can honestly say that the lyric really does get ahead, even while
pausing to summarize attitudinally.)

In essentializing by entitlement, one again confronts the usual
range of choices between some particular of plot or situation and
some wide generalization. Specifically, for instance, we might have
chosen to call the first chapter "The Pandybat," since the artist's
sensitivity is built plotwise about this as its crowning incident. The
second stage (marking the turn from childhood sensibility to youthful passion) is built about the logic of "The Fall," the incident in
which the chapter terminates. With this title, it so happens, there is
no need to decide whether we are being particular or general, or
even whether we are discussing content or form. (Ideally, working
titles are best when they simultaneously suggest both the gist of the
story as such and the developmental stage in the purely formal sense.)
We say the "logic" of the fall, as in this work the fall is a *necessary*
stage in the development of the esthetic. Thus, later, V.1045–46,
Stephen says, "The soul is born . . . first in those moments I told you
of." And we shall later try to indicate, indexwise, with what thor-
oughness the work interweaves its terms to this end.

Surely, the third chapter should be called "The Sermon." For that
ironic masterpiece of rhetorical amplification is clearly the turning
point of the chapter. To say as much, however, is to make a discovery
about the form of this novel. For though the culmination of the sermon is close even to the mathematical center of the book (in
III.1047–48 we come to the "last and crowning torture of all tortures . . . the eternity of hell"), there is a very important sense in
which the peripety[8] is reserved for Chapter IV, which we might call
"The New Vocation." We shall later try to show how thorough a crisis there may have been in Chapter III, in Stephen's emotions following the sermon, as revealed in the study of the Joycean esthetic.
Meanwhile, we may recall that, when the choice between religion
and art is finally made, it is a qualified choice, as art will be conceived in terms of theology secularized. Following Joycean theories
of the emblematic image, we might also have called Chapter IV
"Epiphany"; for in Stephen's vision of the bird-girl the symbol of his
new vocation is made manifest. Chapter V might then be called
"The New Doctrine," for we here get the catechistic equivalent of
the revelation that forms the ecstatic end of Chapter IV.

When an author himself provides subtitles (and thus threatens to
deprive the critic of certain delightful exercisings) at least the critic
can experimentally shuttle, in looking for particular equivalents

8. Synonym for *peripeteia*, meaning sudden change [Editor].

where the titles are general, and *vice versa*. But though all such essentializing by entitlement helps force us to decide what terms we should especially feature in our index, there are other procedures available.

3

First, let us consider a somewhat nondescript procedure. Some notations seem more likely than others to keep critical observation centrally directed. We list these at random:

Note all striking terms for acts, attitudes, ideas, images, relationships.

Note oppositions. In the *Portrait*, of course, we watch particularly anything bearing upon the distinction between art and religion. And as usual with such a dialectic, we watch for shifts whereby the oppositions become appositions. Stephen's secularizing of theology, for instance, could not be adequately interpreted either as a flat rejection of theological thought or as a continuation of it. Stephen has what Buck Mulligan in *Ulysses* calls "the cursed jesuit strain . . . only it's injected the wrong way." And it could be classed as another variant of the many literary tactics reflecting a shift from the religious passion to the romantic (or sexual) passion (the extremes being perhaps the varied imagery of self-crucifixion that characterizes much nineteenth-century literary Satanism).

Pay particular attention to beginnings and endings of sections or subsections. Note characteristics defining transitional moments. Note *breaks* (a point to which we shall return later, as we believe that, following the sermon, there is a notable stylistic break, a notable interruption of the continuity, even though Joyce's artistry keeps it from being felt as an outright violation of the reader's expectations already formed).

Watch names, as indicative of essence. (*Cf. numen, nomen, omen.*) In one's preparatory index, it is permissible to "joyce" them, for heuristic purposes, by even extreme punwise transformations. Not just from "dedalus" to "daedalus," for instance. But, why not even "dead louse," in view of the important part that the catching and rolling of the louse played (V.2111–28) in Stephen's correcting of a misremembered quotation that contained the strategic word, "fall"? (The context has, besides "falls" twice in the quoted line, "falling" twice, "dying falling" once, "fall" once, and "fell" twice. But though Stephen likens himself to a louse, it is the louse that falls this time. He himself is already imbued with the spirit of Daedalian flight, whereby his fall has become transformed into a rise.)

Experimental tinkering with names does not in itself provide *proof* of anything. (So keep it a secret between us and the index.) But it does suggest lines of inquiry, by bringing up new possibilities of internal relationship. * * *

While watching for the expressions that best name a given character's number, watch also for incidental properties of one character that are present in another. Such properties in common may provide insight into the ways whereby figures on their face disparate are to be treated as different manifestations of a common motive.

Note internal forms. While noting them in their particularity, try also to conceptualize them. For instance, here's a neat job for someone who believes as much in the discipline of literary analysis as a mathematician believes in his mathematics: in V.2078–128, conceptualize the steps from the misremembered line, "Darkness falls from the air," to the correction, "Brightness falls from the air." Of course, there are good memorizers who could reproduce the stages for you word for word. But there is a sense in which such accurate memory is itself "unprincipled," being not much more rational than a mechanical recording of the passage.

Watch for a point of *farthest internality*. We believe that in the *Portrait* this point occurs just after the sermon, most notably in the circular passage (III.1213–17) beginning, "We knew perfectly well of course," . . . and ending "We of course knew perfectly well," with its center in the expression, "endeavouring to try to induce himself to try to endeavour."

* * *

In particular, one should note expressions marking secrecy, privacy, mystery, marvel, power, silence, guilt. Such terms are likely to point in the direction of central concerns in all cultures. Here also we might include terms for *order*, since the pyramidal nature of order brings us close to relations of "superiority" and "inferiority," with the many kinds of tension "natural" to social inequality. Such observations lead us in turn to watch for the particular devices whereby the given work "states a policy" with regard to a society's typical "problems." Here we seek hints for characterizing the work as a "strategy."

* * *

We are even willing to look for ways whereby the artistic strategy that is a "solution" may serve to reestablish the very tension it is resolving. Or, if that way of stating the case seems too ironic, let us watch at least for cathartic devices whereby a rising (as seen from one angle) is a fall (as seen from another), whereby, lo! a "fall" can be a "rise." The possibility is of great importance in the case of the *Portrait,* the "factual" analysis of which *explicitly* depicts a *fall* in terms of a *soaring above.* Note, in particular, this passage:

He would fall. He had not yet fallen but he would fall silently,
in an instant. Not to fall was too hard, too hard; and he felt the
silent lapse of his soul, as it would be at some instant to come,
falling, falling, but not yet fallen, still unfallen, but about to
fall. (IV.536–40)

Recall that this passage marks, almost "sloganistically," the step
intermediate between Stephen's rejection of the religious vocation
and his ecstatic vision of the bird-girl who stands imaginally for his
artistic vocation.

*   *   *

4

By the "entelechial" test, we have in mind this principle: look for
moments at which, in your opinion, the work comes to *fruition*.
Imbue yourself with the terminology of these moments. And spin
from them. Thus, at the very least, you would have the "epiphany"
near the end of Chapter IV (IV.854–90) to guide you.

*   *   *

* * * You have seen the bird-girl, who is to stand for motives far
beyond her nature as sheer image. So, *at the very least,* with this
obvious fulfillment to guide you, you would put in your index the
first implicit announcements of the bird theme, in I.33, I.45–46:
"the eagles will come and pull out his eyes"; "the greasy leather orb
flew like a heavy bird through the grey light." You do not know just
how you will use these entries. You are not even sure that you will
use them at all. But you note them. You would note them because
of the fact that they are classed among things to do with birdness,
a category experimentally broad enough to include Stephen's
roommate Heron, the final reference to "old father, old artificer,"
the vision of the "hawklike man," and (V.1768–843) the augury of
the birds circling "from left to right," their emblematic nature defined by questionable disjunction as "symbol of departure or of
loneliness." Also, as we are trying ever to see *beyond* the symboliz-
ings in the given work even while trying to see as far as we can *into*
that work's purely internal consistency, we *especially* note all *eye*
terms with regard to Joyce, even beyond the eye-I pun natural to
the accidents of English. And having in mind the step from "dying
fallings of sweet airs" to "sucking mouths" in V.2093–95, we dare
think also of the "blind mouths" in Milton's "Lycidas," while the
reference to "scum" here throws us back to Stephen's childhood
baptism in rat-infested scum (V.2091; I.126–27, I.269–70), and

other incidences of this term (II.229, II.397, III.337, III.649). One should remember, for later use, that in II.229 this scum is called "yellow": yellow turns out to be a particularly notable color, because of its specific relation to Stephen's esthetic, as we shall explain later.

If (in this same passage of "epiphany") you have noted "soft," which appears six times in six lines (V.1831–39), surely a sufficient incidence to make it experimentally notable, then you would certainly note (III.1276–82) the "soft language" twice so called, and equated with "stale shite" and the horrors that were "circling closer and closer to enclose." Or you would note the words linking "sin" and softness that terminate Chapter II, the chapter we have entitled "The Fall."[9]

If you asked what the young moon meant, and took notes to find out, you would get the answer doubly, though ambiguously, in V.1810–16: "Thoth, the god of writers . . . bearing on his narrow ibis head the cusped moon. . . . He would not have remembered the god's name but that it was like an Irish oath." The reference to "profane joy" might admonish us to note the "tears of joy" and the "tremor of fear and joy" in the brothel scene (IV.876–77; II.1440, III.11–12). "Silence" we have already discussed. Meanwhile, beyond the sheer pattern of the turning tide (transitional scene for transitional act) we would note the further pattern in the fact that, upon seeing the girl who is henceforth to stand for his vocation, Stephen exaltedly turns *from her,* going "on and on and on" (IV.889–90).

Since the bird-girl is a "wild angel," whose presence sanctions his resolve "to live, to err, to fall" (IV.885–86), and since the word "wild" appears several times in this passage of "fulfillment," which we have been experimentally examining for cues as to the terms

---

9. The partially involuntary fall through sexual passion at the end of Chapter II might be distinguished from the deliberate fall of Chapter IV (the choice of a new vocation) somewhat as "passive" is distinguished from "active." It is the latter that Stephen equates with Luciferian pride, epitomized in his many variants of the formula "I will not serve." All told, the accountancy is somewhat like this: The earlier passionate fall prepared for the later vocational choice; the two were thus related as different species of a common genus (a genus also marked by such "operational synonyms" as "soft," "circling," "yellow," and "scum"). By the time the book is finished, the theme of falling has become translated into the theme of ecstatic elevation, even while retaining signs of its beginnings.

We might also note how music figures in this psychic bookkeeping. Music stands for the new motive. When turning from the Bible as doctrine, Stephen still loved it as music (III.100–02). When the jesuit was proposing that he become a priest, the sound of distant music snapped the continuity (IV.469–72). The themes of rising and falling are interwoven with the music theme and the bird theme as the music theme itself has this design: "It seemed to him that he heard notes of fitful music leaping upwards a tone and downwards a diminishing fourth, upwards a tone and downwards a major third" (IV.637–39); "But the notes were long and shrill and whirring, unlike the cry of vermin, falling a third or a fourth and trilled as the flying beaks clove the air. Their cry was shrill and clear and fine and falling like threads of silken light unwound from whirring spools" (V.1784–88). (And, of course, when considering this purely grammatical disjunction between vermin and the new vocation, we would note rather how, so far as sheer imagery is concerned, the two themes are *brought together,* being as it were "said in the same breath.")

that we might favor in our index, we watch "wild." It occurs in many notable contexts, including (III.1292–93) the passage where, in his terror, Stephen undergoes a purgation in the most literal, physical sense: "clasping his cold forehead wildly, he vomited profusely in agony."

But with that reference to Stephen's physical purgation, following the sermon and his almost cataleptic response to it (III.1202–25) as he pauses in terror outside the door of his room, our inquiry could well take another turn. For immediately after the physical cleansing, a new life begins. We read that "the city was spinning about herself a soft cocoon of yellowish haze" (III.1297–98). Yet in both II.1421 and III.9, the flames of the brothels were called "yellow." Later, when the esthetic doctrine is being spelled out, one of Stephen's companions who participates in the definition of the doctrine is Lynch, with his "excrementitious intellect" and his resolve "to swear in yellow" (V.1350–51, V.1079, etc.). Yellow is the first color we encounter (line two) in *Ulysses*. The passage somewhat sacrilegiously equates shaving with the ministry of the Mass. In the *Portrait*, we note how we again circle back to the theme of Lady Boyle, since Stephen at one point (as we already noted) ponders on "yellow ivory" and the "mottled tusks of elephants" (V.182–84). Nor should we forget that the bird-girl (IV.859) had thighs "softhued as ivory." And we can now discern how the *principle* of yellow, though not the *literal* term, is lurking (I.1258) in the turn from Lady Boyle paring his nails to the memory of Eileen, whose hands were "like ivory; only soft."

Admittedly, our work has hardly more than begun, so far as the study of this particular text is concerned. In particular, for instance, we would like to have talked at some length about the passage which we take to be the moment of farthest internality, the "circular" paragraph of III.1213–17. We have tried elsewhere to show that this "break" in the structure of the work (the sudden brief irruption of Joyce's later manner into a narrative style otherwise traditionally realistic) can be related to the principle of "arrest" that characterizes Stephen's esthetic, as proclaimed in Part V. For it is precisely here that Stephen, terrified by the sermon, pauses, unable to cross a threshold: precisely at this moment of arrest, there leaps forth the passage cryptically prophetic of the later manner:

> —We knew perfectly well of course that although it was bound to come to the light he would find considerable difficulty in endeavouring to try to induce himself to try to endeavour to ascertain the spiritual plenipotentiary and so we knew of course perfectly well— (III.1213–17).

We believe that much can be done with this "break," even beyond the confines of the one book. But in any case, for the time being we can note that it is another of those places where the book comes to a kind of *ad interim*[1] fulfillment; hence it would be another place from which our search could radiate. On the next page, for instance, it leads "factually" into talk of "circling." Stephen's doctrine itself, of course, would be another "entelechial moment"[2] to work from, particularly if one remembered that Stephen's interlocutors in the discussion are to be taken as part of the definition. We could add a few other spots (for instance, the formula "silence, exile, and cunning" is a splendid fulfillment, or culminating moment). There are eight or nine such in all.

Similarly, there are places where some one word flares up like a *nova*, as we saw with regard to the word "fall." These, too, would be watched as "fulfillments."

All told, one proceeds from such places, where the work comes to a temporary head. One radiates in search of labyrinthine internal consistency, while at the same time watching for progressions. One tries to be aware of one's shifts between "factuality" and "thematic" generalizing. One watches for over-all social tensions, and for the varying tactics of "purification" with regard to them. And one is thereby talking about "symbolism," willy-nilly.[3]

---

1. Temporary; literally "for the meantime" (Latin) [Editor].
2. A moment that indicates fulfillment [Editor].
3. Burke's use of the term *symbolism* needs to be understood in the context of the intellectual disagreements about the *symbol*, particularly in literary interpretation, in the early 1950s, when the essay was written. He puts the term in quotation marks because a central goal of his essay has been to establish a meaning for it that differs, for example, from its use in the work of the influential literary critic William York Tindall, author of *James Joyce: His Way of Interpreting the Modern World* (New York: Scribner, 1950). Tindall's interpretation of Joyce depends on identifying symbols, elements of the work to which he assigns speculative meanings that are not tied closely to the text by careful examination of its language. By contrast, Burke insists that the justification of any meaning, or "symbolism," in literary interpretation depends on deriving our hypotheses about themes from textual facts, that is, details of the language, and then revising our tentative conclusions about theme in light of more and different relevant textual facts. Burke's notion of "symbolism" is more closely tied to a work's language than is Tindall's [Editor].

UMBERTO ECO

[The Artist and Medieval Thought in the Early Joyce]†

"Steeled in the school of old Aquinas."
—James Joyce, "The Holy Office"[1]

The term "poetics" has acquired many meanings during the centuries. Aristotle's *Poetics* is an answer to both the questions "What is Art?" and "How does one make a work of art?" The modern philosophical tradition has preferred to define the theoretical answer to the first question as "aesthetics" and to utilize "poetics" in order to describe the program of a single artist or a particular artistic school. In this context, "poetics" addresses the question "How does one make a work of art according to a personal program and an idiosyncratic world view?"[2] * * *

Joyce * * * interweaves questions as to the concept of art, the nature of his personal artistic program, and the structural mechanisms of the texts themselves. In this respect all of Joyce's works might be understood as a continuous discussion of their own artistic procedures.

A Portrait is the story of a young artist who wants to write *A Portrait*; *Ulysses*, a little less explicit, is a book which is a model of itself; *Finnegans Wake* is, above all, a complete treatise on its own nature, a continuous definition of "the Book" as the *Ersatz*[3] of the universe. The reader, therefore, is continually tempted to isolate the poetics proposed by Joyce in order to define, in Joycean terms, the solutions that Joyce has adopted.

* * * Joyce's poetics cannot be separated from Joyce's texts. The poetics themselves form an intimate part of the artistic creation and are clarified in the various phases of the development of his opus. The entire Joycean project might thus be seen as the development of a poetics, or rather, as the dialectical movement[4] of various

---

† From "The Early Joyce," *The Aesthetics of Chaosmos: The Middle Ages of James Joyce,* trans. Ellen Esrock. Cambridge, Mass.: Harvard UP, 1989, 1–32. English trans. from *Le Poetiche di Joyce* (Milan: Bompiani, 1962) used by permission of the University of Tulsa. Some notes have been omitted. Page references for *A Portrait* have been replaced with part and line numbers of this Norton Critical Edition. Some cited passages might differ slightly from the equivalent passages in this volume.
1. *The Critical Writings,* ed. Ellsworth Mason and Richard Ellmann. New York: Viking Press, 1959, 152. Hereafter abbreviated *CW* [Editor].
2. Roman Jakobson, "Closing Statements: Linguistics and Poetics," in *Style in Language,* ed. T. A. Sebeok (Cambridge: MIT Press, 1960).
3. Substitute (German) [Editor].
4. Movement between opposing elements that results in a new blended view, as is sometimes possible through dialogue [Editor].

opposite and complementary poetics—the history of contemporary poetics in a game of oppositions and continuous implications.

Among the numerous cultural influences upon the young Joyce, we note three major lines which appear in all his works. On one count, we find the influence of Aquinas, thrown into crisis but not completely destroyed by the reading of Bruno and, on another, the influence of Ibsen, with a call for closer ties between art and life.[5] Finally, we note the influence of the symbolist poets,[6] with the aesthetic ideal of a life devoted to art and of art as a substitute for life, and with their stimulus to resolve the great problems of the spirit in the laboratory of language.[7] These contrasting influences from different centuries were assimilated within a framework that grew increasingly concerned with the problems of contemporary culture, from the psychology of the unconscious to the physics of relativity. The staggering quantity of Joyce's reading and the diversity of his interests opened the way to his discovery of new dimensions of the universe.

Approached in this way, our research needs a guiding thread, a line of investigation, an operative hypothesis. We take, therefore, the opposition between a classical conception of form and the need for a more pliable and "open" structure of the work and of the world. This can be identified as a dialectic of order and adventure, a contrast between the world of the medieval *summae*[8] and that of contemporary science and philosophy.

Joyce himself authorizes us to use this dialectical key. The Joycean detachment from the familiar clarity of the schoolmen and his choice of a more modern and uneasy problematic is actually based on the Brunian revelation of a dialectic of contraries, on the acceptance of the *coincidentia oppositorum* of Cusano.[9] Art and life, symbolism and realism, classical world and contemporary world, aesthetic life and daily life, Stephen Dedalus and Leopold Bloom, Shem and Shaun,[1] order and possibility are the continuous terms of a tension that has its

---

5. Aquinas: Saint Thomas Aquinas (1224 or 1225–1274), Dominican theologian. Bruno: Giordano Bruno (1548–1600), Italian Dominican and philosopher, burned at the stake as a heretic. Ibsen: Henrik Ibsen (1828–1906), Norwegian dramatist [Editor].

6. Late nineteenth-century French poets—including Paul Verlaine (1844–1896), Arthur Rimbaud (1854–1891), and Stéphane Mallarmé (1842–1898)—who reacted against realistic and naturalistic descriptions of external reality by producing poetry using subjective language and private symbols [Editor].

7. See "The Study of Languages" (*CW,* Chapter III), in which Joyce (1898–99, at the age of sixteen) already outlines his main lines of thought * * *.

8. Plural of *summa* (Latin), meaning literally "sum"; compilations of theological writings intended to represent the summation of important thinking on religious issues. The most famous *summa* is Aquinas's *Summa Theologica,* which eventually became central in Catholic thought [Editor].

9. Latin phrase for "coincidence of opposites," used by the German philosopher Nicholas of Cusa (1401–1464), who claimed that the principle of noncontradiction, which asserts that contradictory perspectives cannot be true simultaneously, was itself not true, especially with regard to God as infinite [Editor].

1. Brothers in Joyce's *Finnegans Wake* (1939) who are both at odds and hard to distinguish [Editor].

roots in this theoretical discovery. In Joyce's works the very crisis of late scholasticism is accelerated and therein a new cosmos is born.

But this dialectic is not perfectly articulated; it does not have the balance of those ideal triadic dances upon which more optimistic philosophies build legends. While Joyce's mind brings this elegant curve of oppositions and mediations to its limits, his unconscious agitates like the unexpressed memory of an ancestral trauma. Joyce departs from the *summa* to arrive at *Finnegans Wake,* from the ordered cosmos of scholasticism to the verbal image of an expanding universe. But his medieval heritage, from which his movements arise, will never be abandoned. Underneath the game of oppositions and resolutions in which the various cultural influences collide, on the deepest level, is the radical opposition between the medieval man, nostalgic for an ordered world of clear signs, and the modern man, seeking a new habitat but unable to find the elusive rules and thus burning continually in the nostalgia of a lost infancy.

We would like to demonstrate that the definitive choice is not made and that the Joycean dialectic, more than a mediation, offers us the development of a continuous polarity between Chaos and Cosmos, between disorder and order, liberty and rules, between the nostalgia of Middle Ages and the attempts to envisage a new order. Our analysis of the poetics of James Joyce will be the analysis of a moment of transition in contemporary culture.

The Catholicism of Joyce

* * *

It is * * * necessary to ask how much of the scholasticism of the young Joyce is substantial and how much is only superficial—a mischievous taste for contamination or an attempt to smuggle revolutionary ideas under the cape of Doctor Angelicus[2] (the technique that Stephen frequently utilizes with the college professors).

Stephen confesses to having read "only a garner of slender sentences from Aristotle's poetics and psychology and a *Synopsis Philosophiae Scholasticae ad mentem divi Thomae*" (V.98–100). The question that must be asked is whether or not Stephen is lying. It is of little help to discuss Joyce's reading material while he was in Paris. There is the confession to Valery Larbaud that "il passait plusieures heures chaque soir à la bibliothèque St. Geneviève lisant Aristote et St. Thomas d'Aquin."[3] But we know the Joycean ability in mystifying his friends. His "Paris Notebook" shows that he studied the Aris-

2. That is, Aquinas [Editor].
3. The French writer Valery Larbaud (1881–1957) said of Joyce that "he passed many hours each evening in the Library of St. Geneviève reading Aristotle and St. Thomas Aquinas" [Editor].

totelian definitions of pity and terror, rhythm, and imitation of nature by art. This would suggest that Joyce had probably read excerpts from the *Poetics*. Where St. Thomas is concerned, the quotations in the "Pola Notebook" ("Bonum est in quo tendit appetitum [*sic*]" and "Pulcera [*sic*] sunt quae visa placent") are both misquoted, and the definition of the three conditions of Beauty in *A Portrait* is linguistically correct but abridged (V.1357–88). From this we infer that Joyce had probably never read directly from the texts of Aquinas.[4]

The Medieval Model

What is meant by the affirmation that Joyce remained medievally minded from youth through maturity? In reading all of Joyce it is possible to single out thousands of situations in which he uses terms drawn from the medieval tradition, arguments accorded to a technique from medieval literature and philosophy. * * *

* * *

* * * We will attempt to follow the process of the young artist who conserves and repudiates the mental forms that preside over the ordered cosmos proposed by the medieval Christian tradition and who, still thinking as a medieval, dissolves the ordered Cosmos into the polyvalent form of the Chaosmos.

The Young Attempts

At the beginning of the century Joyce was about eighteen years old. The scholastic culture which he absorbed during high school was already facing a crisis. Joyce's contact with Giordano Bruno in these years provided him with what in fact Brunian philosophy provided for modern thought, a bridge from medievalism to the new naturalism. During this time, Joyce was cultivating the threefold refusal that would isolate him in exile until the end. He had settled his accounts with heresy: "He said Bruno was a terrible heretic. I said he was terribly burned" (V.2650–51).

Having shaken off the weight of orthodoxy, Joyce was open to new suggestions which came to him from the Irish literary polemics, from the great problems stirring world literature. On the one side he was influenced by the symbolists, the poets of the Celtic Renaissance, by Pater and Wilde; on the other side, by the realism of Flaubert (as well as Flaubert's love for *le mot juste*, the dedication to an aesthetic ideal).

---

4. As for Joyce's Aristotelian and Thomistic readings, see *Critical Writings*; Richard Ellmann, *James Joyce*, New and Rev. Ed. (New York: Viking, 1982); William T. Noon, *Joyce and Aquinas* (New Haven: Yale UP, 1957); John J. Slocum and Herbert Cahoon, *A Bibliography of James Joyce, 1882–1941* (New Haven: Yale UP, 1959) [Updated version of author's note. Editor].

Four fundamental texts mark those years—the conference [i.e., lecture] *Drama and Life* held in 1900, the essay "Ibsen's New Drama" published the same year in *Fortnightly Review,* the pamphlet *The Day of the Rabblement* published in 1901, and finally, in 1902, the essay "James Clarence Mangan."[5] Condensed in these four writings are all the contradictions that raged within the young artist.

In the first two essays, Joyce argues for close connections between theater and life. The theater must represent real life "as we see it before our eyes, men and women as we meet them in the real world, not as we apprehend them in the world of faery" (*CW* 45). This representation is not mere imitation, since the theater must manifest the great rules that govern human events through the action of performance. In this way, art proposes truth as the primary end. Not a didactic truth (for Joyce claims an absolute moral neutrality for the artistic representation) but pure and simple truth, reality. And beauty? The search for beauty itself has something that is spiritually anemic and brutally animal. Beauty does not go beyond the surface and appears, therefore, as a morbid result of art. Great art tends only towards the pursuit of truth. Against the symbolists' idea that "tout est bu, tout est mangé! Plus rien à dire!" (Verlaine),[6] Joyce stresses that

> Many feel like the Frenchman that they have been born too late in a world too old. . . . Still I think out of the dreary sameness of existence, a measure of dramatic life may be drawn. Even the most commonplace, the deadest among the living, may play a part in a great drama. (*CW* 44–45)

This apparent commitment to daily life makes even more discordant the position upheld in the *Day of the Rabblement,* a work which vibrates with disdain for compromise with the masses and projects an ascetic type of aspiration for the withdrawal and the absolute isolation of the artist. "No man, said the Nolan,[7] can be a lover of the true or the good unless he abhors the multitude" (*CW* 69). This withdrawal might be understood as a reserve on the level of practical contact, a refusal for commercial compromise rather than an aesthetic position, were it not for the essay on Mangan.[8]

Mangan was not a realist nor did he search for poetic truth in the representation of historical truth. He constitutes, instead, an example

---

5. All reprinted in *CW* [Editor].
6. "Everything is drunk, everything is eaten! Nothing more to say!" (French). On Verlaine and the symbolists, see note 6, p. 330 [Editor].
7. That is, Bruno [Editor].
8. James Clarence Mangan (1803–1849), Irish poet [Editor].

of the excited imagination on the border of prophecy, nourished by the exaltation of the senses, by drugs, and by an unruly and eccentric life. His poetry belongs in a romantic-symbolist line; his spiritual brothers are Nerval and Baudelaire.[9] It is this aspect that interested Joyce. In the conference on Mangan held in 1907 at Trieste, Joyce dwelt at length on this poetry:

> It is a wild world, a world of night in the orient. The mental activity that comes from opium has scattered this world of magnificent and terrible images, and all the orient that the poet recreated in his flaming dream, which is the paradise of the opium-eater, pulsates in these pages in Apocalyptic phrases and similes and landscapes. (CW 183)

These contradictions might seem to be the fruit of a pure, youthful intemperance, but in Joyce they appear as the germs of vast contradictions and opposing aspirations which are perpetuated through all his works. It is Joyce himself who offered the key in a conference [lecture] in 1907, with a phrase referring to Mangan but which perfectly fits the "Joyce case":

> There are certain poets who, in addition to the virtue of revealing to us some phase of the human conscience unknown until their time, also have the more doubtful virtue of summing up in themselves the thousand contrasting tendencies of their era, of being, so to speak, the storage batteries of new forces. (CW 175)

While Joyce provides an exact description of our daily humanity (in *Dubliners* as well as *Ulysses*), at the same time he discovers in Mangan an example of the revelatory function of poetry. Once again, the artist can succeed in possessing and communicating the truth, but only through beauty. Thus the situation is reversed. When Joyce speaks of beauty as the splendor of truth in the essay on Mangan, he no longer thinks of a truth that—*qua* truth—becomes beauty, but of a gratuitous beauty, born from the provocative strength of the imagination which, in fact, becomes the only possible truth.

Even when Joyce uses expressions analogous to those in the discourse on drama, he speaks unequivocally in the tone of the Mangan essay. The language is that of *fin de siècle*[1] decadentism. Traces of occultism also shine through the discourses and reflect what Joyce had assimilated in the Dublin circle of AE, George Russell.

---

9. Gérard de Nerval: pen name of Gérard Labrunie (1808–1855), French poet. Charles Baudelaire (1821–1867), French poet, critic, and translator [Editor].
1. French phrase, meaning "end of the century," often applied to the self-consciously decadent rejection by some artists of middle-class attitudes, especially concerning the moral and social function of art [Editor].

Without a doubt, Ibsen had left the post to the symbolist poets and mystics.

How could these divergent tendencies be fused in the thought of the early Joyce? At least we know how they merge in the thought of Stephen Dedalus and in what way Joyce sought to synthesize his own former attitudes when he was writing *Stephen Hero* between 1904 and 1906. The lecture "Art and Life" that Stephen reads in college before the Literary and Historical Society reunites "Drama and Life" and "J.C. Mangan." If the title recalls more the lecture on Ibsen, the subjects used—often the very expressions—are those of the essay on Mangan. Here Joyce defines the aesthetics of the young artist on purely symbolist grounds. But his scholastic formation leads him to retranslate his basic assumptions into Aristotelian and Thomistic terms,[2] a seemingly superficial change but one which recasts the entire perspective.

Stephen's lecture attempts to underline the importance of a new theater and of an art free from moral preoccupations. We see here the decision to break at last with the laws and conventions of a bourgeois society. This polemic, based on a conception of the poet as creator, as founder of a new reality, originates in the essay on Mangan and is supported by a clever use of Thomistic thought.

The aesthetics of *Stephen Hero* represent this point of fusion which, developed and nuanced, will be reproposed in *A Portrait*. Although the differences between the two drafts are considerable, together they establish the main lines of an aesthetics, not lacking in rigor, in which one witnesses the amazing convergence of three diverse attitudes—realism, decadence, and the scholastic *forma mentis*.[3]

Portrait of the Artist as a Young Thomist

The principal themes of Stephen's aesthetics are: 1) the subdivision of art into three genres—lyric, epic and dramatic; 2) the objectivity and impersonality of the work; 3) the autonomy of art; 4) the nature of the aesthetic emotion; 5) the criteria of beauty. From this last theme emerge 6) the doctrine of the epiphany[4] and 7) the pronouncements on the nature of poetic activity and the function of the poet.

The discussion of genres is somewhat academic.[5] In the lyrical genre the artist presents his image in immediate relationship with

---

2. Philosophical and theological vocabulary used by Aquinas and later thinkers who followed him, frequently called Thomists [Editor].
3. Ways of thinking; literally "forms of mind" (Latin) [Editor].
4. Joyce's view as a young writer that experiences could be epiphanies, or showings forth, which a writer could capture [Editor].
5. This distinction appears in Aristotle's *Poetics*, 1447 *a* and *b* to 1462 *a* and *b*. In Joyce references it appears in *Stephen Hero*, Chapter XIX, and *Portrait*, Chapter V. * * *

himself, while in the epic he presents it in an indirect relationship
with himself and others:

> The lyrical form is in fact the simplest verbal vesture of an
> instant of emotion, a rhythmical cry such as ages ago cheered
> on the man who pulled at the oar or dragged stones up a slope.
> He who utters it is more conscious of the instant of emotion
> than of himself as feeling emotion. (V.1444–48)

*   *   *

It is clear, at least theoretically, that the dramatic form represents
for Joyce the true and proper form of art. From such an assumption
the principle of the *impersonality* of the work of art, so typical of the
Joycean poetic, vigorously emerges. When he elaborated this theory,
Joyce had already come into contact with the analogous theories of
Mallarmé[6] * * *.

Undoubtedly, the problem of the impersonality of the artist had
already been proposed to Joyce by other youthful readings, for we
can easily recognize the ancestors of this concept in Baudelaire,
Flaubert, and Yeats. It is necessary to recognize how widely the idea
circulated throughout the Anglo-Saxon atmosphere of the epoch,
later finding its definitive arrangement in the writings of Pound and
Eliot.[7]

From this poetic objective, the reference to Aristotle's *Poetics*
comes spontaneously. Joyce was undoubtedly influenced by the traditional Anglo-Saxon critical method of considering art in Aristotelian terms. This is demonstrated in the diversity existing between
the text of *A Portrait* and the probable Mallarméan source * * *.
When Mallarmé speaks of the pure artistic work in which the poet
disappears, he has in mind a Platonic conception in which *l'Oeuvre*
aspires to become *Le Livre,* the impersonal reflection of Beauty as an
absolute essence expressed by the *Verbe.*[8] The Mallarméan work thus
tends to be an impersonal, evocative apparatus which goes beyond
itself towards a world of metaphysical archetypes.[9] On the contrary,
the impersonal work of Joyce appears as an object centered and resolved in itself. References are located inside the aesthetic object,
and the object aspires to be the surrogate of life and not the means
towards a subsequent and purer life. The Mallarméan suggestions

6. See note 6, p. 330 [Editor].
7. See, for instance, T. S. Eliot, "Tradition and the Individual Talent," *Selected Essays: New
   Edition* (New York: Harcourt, Brace and World, 1960), 3–11. [Expansion of author's note.
   Editor].
8. This sequence of French words suggests that the simple work, *l'Oeuvre,* becomes the
   Book, *Le Livre,* in a magnified sense, because of the ability of the word, *Verbe* [Editor].
9. Guy Delfel, *L'esthétique de Mallarmé* (Paris: Flammarion, 1951). Against Mallarmé's poetics of "absence," Joyce holds a poetics of "presence," in which the work does not send back
   outside itself but sends to itself, through the mediation of concrete events and characters.

have deep-rooted mystical ambitions while the Joycean ones aspire to be the triumph of a perfect mechanism which exhausts its own function.[1]

It is interesting to note how the Platonic conception of beauty came to Mallarmé from Baudelaire and to Baudelaire from Poe. But in Poe, the Platonic element develops according to the ways of an Aristotelian methodology which is attentive to the psychological relationship of work-reader and the constructive logic of the work (consider "The Philosophy of Composition"[2]). Thus, starting from an Anglo-Saxon environment and the Aristotelian tradition, passing through the filter of the French symbolist poets, these and other ferments returned to Anglo-Saxon territory and were reconverted by Joyce within the ambit of an Aristotelian sensitivity.

The aesthetic formulations of St. Thomas were also influential. The quotations that Joyce had within reach nowhere discuss a work capable of expressing the personality of the poet. Joyce then realized that even Aquinas upheld the impersonal and objective work. This was not a matter of drawing a convenient conclusion from lack of contrary documents. Demonstrating a keen understanding of medieval thought, integrating the few texts with which he was acquainted, Joyce understood that the Aristotelian and Thomist aesthetics were not at all concerned with the affirmation of the artist's self: the work is an object which expresses its own structural laws and not the person of the author. For this reason, Joyce was convinced that he would not be able to elaborate a theory of the creative process on the basis of Thomist thinking. Scholasticism undoubtedly had a theory of *ars*, but this did not shed light on the process of poetic creation. * * * Joyce reduces this to a concise formula: "Art . . . is the human disposition of sensible or intelligible matter for an esthetic end" (V.1182–83). By adding "for an esthetic end," a precision which is not considered in the medieval formula, he changes the meaning of the old definition, passing from the Greco-Latin idea of *"techne-ars"* to the modern one of "art" as exclusively "fine arts."[3] But Stephen is persuaded that his

1. One could claim that the notion of impersonality is denied by the continuous autobiographical procedure of Joyce himself. In the article "Mr. Mason's Novels" (CW 130) Joyce says that Leonardo "has noted the tendency of the mind to impress its own likeness upon that which it creates"; and the entire discussion of *Hamlet* in *Ulysses* deals with the concept of the work of poetry as the image of a personal situation of its author. But it must be stressed that impersonality does not imply that the author should avoid speaking of the emotions; rather, it implies that the author must escape from the emotion, that he should not be the slave of the emotion of which he is speaking. Even the autobiography must become an objective texture of rhythms and symbols.
2. An essay by the American writer Edgar Allan Poe (1809–1849) in which he describes the writing of literature as a premeditated act to achieve a desired effect, rather than as an act of inspiration [Editor].
3. See Noon (p. 28). Joyce meets the traditional definition of art by reading Aristotle and Aquinas in Paris ("Paris Notebook" and "Pola Notebook"—CW 143–48) [Author]. * * *

"applied Aquinas" can serve him only to a certain point: "When we come to the phenomena of artistic conception, artistic gestation and artistic reproduction I require a new terminology and a new personal experience" (V.1269–72). In fact, the sporadic affirmations concerning the nature of the poet and his function that we find in *Stephen Hero* are completely foreign to the Aristotelian-Thomist problematic, as are certain allusions to the creative process in *A Portrait*.

The discourse on the autonomy of art is completely typical. Here the young Stephen reveals the formal nature of his adhesion to scholasticism. The formulas of Aquinas boldly smuggle in a theory of *l'art pour l'art* that Stephen assimilated from other sources. Aquinas affirmed that *"pulchrae dicuntur quae visa placent,"*[4] noting furthermore that the artifex[5] must interest himself solely in the perfection of the artistic work that he creates and not in the exterior ends to which the work can be used. But medieval theory refers to *ars* understood in a rather large sense, as the construction of objects, as handicraft, in short, as more than just the formation of works of art in the modern sense of the term. For such *ars* it establishes a standard of artisan integrity. In effect, a work of art is a form, and the perfection of a form becomes established as much in terms of *perfectio prima* as in terms of *perfectio secunda*.[6] While the *perfectio prima* examines the formal quality of the object produced, the *perfectio secunda* considers the proper end of that object. In other words, an ax is beautiful if it is constructed according to the rules of formal harmony; but above all, it is beautiful if it is well-fitted for its final end, which is chopping wood. In the Thomist hierarchy of ends and means, the value of an object is established upon the relationship of means to ends: the entire thing is evaluated in terms of the supernatural ends to which man is oriented. Beauty, Goodness, and Truth are reciprocally implicated. Thus, a statue used for obscene or magical ends is intrinsically ugly, reflected in the sinister light of its distorted finality. To interpret the propositions of St. Thomas in a rigorously formalistic sense (as has been done by many zealous Neo-Thomists) is to misunderstand the substantially unified and hierarchial vision by which the medieval man confronted the world.[7] Therefore, when Stephen argues with the professors of the college in order to demonstrate that

---

Ars (Latin) means art, but medieval philosophers were not interested in poetic creation, or imagination, which is a modern conception. When Stephen includes the artistic end, he moves beyond the notion of art as technique or craft (*techne*) for a more modern one in which the artist's creative process produces not just objects but fine art [Editor].

4. "The beautiful is said to be that which pleases sight" (Latin) [Editor].

5. Maker of art [Editor].

6. The Latin terms for primary and secondary perfection distinguish between the object as an achievement of craft and the work as realizing a worthwhile effect [Editor].

7. On the autonomy of art see *Summa Theologiae*, I–II, 57, 3 *co*; on the distinction between *perfectio prima* and *perfectio secunda* see I, 73, 1 *co* and 3 *co*; II–III, 169, 2 and 4. ° ° °

Aquinas "is certainly on the side of the capable artist"[8] and when he claims not to find in Aquinas' definition of the beautiful any necessity for learning or moral elevation, Stephen conceals with casuist ability, under medieval garments, propositions like those of Wilde, for whom "all art is perfectly useless."[9] The most curious fact is that the Jesuits with whom Joyce spoke felt a certain dissatisfaction but were not in a position to object to his quotations. They were victims of their own traditional formalism in which the words of the Doctor Angelicus could not be discussed. Joyce, reversing the situation in his favor and profiting from the congenital weakness of a mental system, shows that he finds himself completely at ease with the Catholic sensitivity.

On these grounds Stephen carries forward the systematic arrangement of his aesthetics. In discussing the nature of the aesthetic emotion he is still following his conception of the autonomy of art. In aesthetic contemplation the pornographic moment is as extraneous as the didactic one. Stephen then renews ties with Aristotle, assuming the cathartic theory of poetry. He elaborates a definition of pity and terror, lamenting that Aristotle did not give a definition in the *Poetics* but ignoring it in the *Rhetoric*. Joyce defines the aesthetic emotion as a sort of stasis, the arrestment of a sensitivity before an ideal pity and terror, a stasis provoked, protracted and dissolved into what he calls the "rhythm of beauty" (V.1152).[1] This definition would appear to have its roots in certain modern conceptions, were it not that Stephen's definition of aesthetic rhythm is of clear Pythagorean[2] origin:

> Rhythm . . . is the first formal esthetic relation of part to part in any esthetic whole or of an esthetic whole to its part or parts or of any part to the esthetic whole of which it is a part. (V.1154–57)

Such a definition is compared by Stuart Gilbert with an analogous one from Coleridge:[3]

---

8. James Joyce, *Stephen Hero, A New Edition.* New York: New Directions, 1963, 96. Hereafter abbreviated *SH* [Editor].
9. The preface to Wilde's *The Picture of Dorian Gray* concludes with the statement *"All art is quite useless"* [Editor].
1. According to Stephen, "Pity is the feeling which arrests the mind in the presence of whatsoever is grave and constant in human sufferings and unites it with the human sufferer. Terror is the feeling which arrests the mind in the presence of whatsoever is grave and constant in human sufferings and unites it with the secret cause" (V.1087–92). According to Aristotle, "terror is a sorrow or a trouble produced by the imagining of an evil, that could arrive, bringing pain and destruction" (*Rhet.*, 1382 *a*) and "pity is a sorrow caused by a destructive and painful evil happening to an unmeriting person and that ourselves or somebody linked to us could expect to suffer" (*Rhet.*, 1485 *b*). Stephen's definitions do not differ so much from Aristotle's, except that in the place of "terror" Stephen speaks of a "secret cause" (adding a shade of romanticism to the notion of fear).
2. In the spirit of Pythagoras (c. 580–c. 500 BCE), the Greek philosopher, mathematician, and music theorist.
3. Samuel Taylor Coleridge (1772–1834), English poet and philosopher, who wrote influentially about imagination in his *Biographia Literaria* (1817) [Editor].

The sense of beauty subsists in simultaneous intuition of the relation of parts, each to each, and of all to the whole: exciting an immediate and absolute complacency, without intervenence, therefore, of any interest, sensual or intellectual.[4]

* * * There is a Platonic and Pythagorean background in which transcendentalist[5] organicism and scholasticism join hands and converge in the formula of the young Stephen. When forced to define the essential characteristics of beauty, Stephen returns to the analogous formulations and the famous three principles stated by Aquinas. * * *

We will try to follow this interpretive process step by step. Stephen's discussion with Lynch on this topic begins with an allusion concerning the identification of beauty and truth. Here Joyce approaches the scholastic tradition, even though the metaphysical implications of the concept do not interest him:

> Truth is beheld by the intellect which is appeased by the most satisfying relations of the intelligible: beauty is beheld by the imagination which is appeased by the most satisfying relations of the sensible. (V. 1209–13)

This definition has much in common with certain annotations added to the Thomist text, especially by commentators of the last century. The memory of certain remarks made by the professors of the college should not be excluded here. The only extraneous contribution, and in that sense curious, is the appearance of the term "imagination," absent from the medieval concept and typical of modern aesthetics. Coleridge and Poe speak of imagination; St. Thomas does not. * * *

The notion of imagination appears in the early writings of Joyce but is not highly developed in the aesthetics of Stephen Dedalus. Here imagination is only seen as a particular relation between mind and things. As in Aquinas, it is the way the mind looks at things in order to see them aesthetically. In fact, if "The first step in the direction of beauty is to understand the frame and scope of the imagination, to comprehend the act itself of esthetic apprehension" (V.1219–21), then for Stephen the frame and scope of the imagination become clarified only on the way: "all people who admire a beautiful object find in it certain relations which satisfy and coincide with the stages themselves of all esthetic apprehension" (V.1256–58). Instead of explaining what the imagination is, Stephen indicates the actual process undertaken by the mind in order to grasp the sensible relations

---

4. *On the Principles of Genial Criticism Concerning Fine Arts*; see Stuart Gilbert, *James Joyce's "Ulysses"* (London: Faber and Faber, 1930), 36 [Expansion of author's note. Editor].
5. In line with the philosophical movement transcendentalism, which claims the existence of a spiritual reality, knowable by intuition, that surpasses the ordinary world [Editor].

among the objects of perceptual experience. In fact, in *Stephen Hero* it is stated that "the apprehensive faculty must be scrutinised in action" (*SH* 212).[6]

The interesting fact is that while the nature of the imagination is defined in relation to the objective criteria of beauty, these criteria are defined in relation to the process undergone by the imagination in order to recognize them. This aspect of the question differentiates the Joycean attitude from that of Aquinas. In the modern author, the ontological[7] modes of beauty become the modes of the apprehension (or production) of beauty. We will see the importance of this in the discussion of the epiphany.

In *A Portrait*, Stephen must interpret the concepts of *integritas, proportio,* and *claritas* which he translates by "wholeness," "harmony," and "radiance."

"Look at the basket," Stephen says to Lynch; and explains:

> In order to see that basket . . . your mind first of all separates the basket from the rest of the visible universe which is not the basket. The first phase of apprehension is a bounding line drawn about the object to be apprehended. An esthetic image is presented to us either in space or in time. What is audible is presented in time, what is visible is presented in space. But, temporal or spatial, the esthetic image is first luminously apprehended as selfbounded and selfcontained upon the immeasurable background of space or time which is not it. You apprehend it as one thing. You see it as one whole. You apprehend its wholeness. That is integritas. (V.1357–67)

It is clear from these lines that the Thomist *integritas* is not the Joycean *integritas*. The former is a fact of substantial completion, the latter is a fact of spatial delimitation. The former is a problem of ontological volume, the latter is one of physical perimeter. The Joycean *integritas* is the result of a psychological focusing; it is the imagination that selects the thing.

Because the possibilities of deformation are fewer, the Joycean interpretation of the concept of *proportio* is more faithful to its Thomist counterpart than his interpretation of *integritas*:

> Then . . . you pass from point to point, led by its formal lines; you apprehend it as balanced part against part within its limits; you feel the rhythm of its structure. In other words the synthesis of immediate perception is followed by the analysis of apprehension. Having first felt that it is one thing you feel now that it is a thing. You apprehend it as complex, multiple, divisible, separable,

6. Ed. John J. Slocum and Herbert Cahoon. New York: New Directions, 1963 [Editor].
7. Pertaining to the nature of being; the word suggests here an aspect that cannot be reduced to the way beauty is perceived or created [Editor].

made up of its parts, the result of its parts and their sum, harmonious. That is consonantia. (V.1369–76)

The remarks concerning rhythm have been explained previously. The determination of *claritas* is longer and more difficult, and the Joycean texts that refer to it are more discordant. The final drafting of *A Portrait* reads like this:

> The connotation of the word . . . is rather vague. Aquinas uses a term which seems to be inexact. It baffled me for a long time. It would lead you to believe that he had in mind symbolism or idealism, the supreme quality of beauty being a light from some other world, the idea of which the matter is but the shadow, the reality of which it is but the symbol. I thought he might mean that claritas is the artistic discovery and representation of the divine purpose in anything or a force of generalisation which would make the esthetic image a universal one, make it outshine its proper conditions. But that is literary talk. I understand it so. When you have apprehended that basket as one thing and have then analysed it according to its form and apprehended it as a thing you make the only synthesis which is logically and esthetically permissible. You see that it is that thing which it is and no other thing. The radiance of which he speaks is the scholastic quidditas, the whatness of a thing. (V.1379–95)

The Joycean interpretation is quite subtle. He starts from the elementary and incomplete Thomist texts, uprooted from their widest context, and reaches an acuteness lacking in many authorized commentators. As for Aquinas, the *quidditas* is the substance in so far as it can be understood and defined. Consequently, to speak about *quidditas* is to speak about substance, about form as organism and structure. * * * Here Joyce gives us an explanation that is truly congenial with Thomist thinking, without yet having extended the formulation in a personal direction. By his clear refusal of Platonic interpretations of the concept of *claritas* (when he speaks of "literary talk"), Joyce also wants to clarify his own position. In so doing, Joyce strikes the center of the issue.

Only in the passages that follow this interpretation will Stephen's discourse assume inflections of greater autonomy and thereby reveal that his fidelity to Aquinas is only a formal means by which to support a freer development of personal themes. The text from *A Portrait* reads:

> This supreme quality is felt by the artist when the esthetic image is first conceived in his imagination. The mind in that mysterious instant Shelley likened beautifully to a fading coal. The instant wherein that supreme quality of beauty, the clear radiance of the esthetic image, is apprehended luminously by

the mind which has been arrested by its wholeness and fascinated by its harmony is the luminous silent stasis of esthetic
pleasure, a spiritual state very like to that cardiac condition
which the Italian physiologist Luigi Galvani, using a phrase almost as beautiful as Shelley's, called the enchantment of the
heart. (V.1395–1405)

In *Stephen Hero* the context is somewhat different. The moment
of *radiance* comes to be defined more specifically as the moment of
epiphany.

By an epiphany he meant a sudden spiritual manifestation,
whether in the vulgarity of speech or of a gesture or in a mem-
orable phase of the mind itself. He believed that it was for the
man of letters to record these epiphanies with extreme care,
seeing that they themselves are the most delicate and evanescent of moments. (*SH* 211)

The expression "fading coal" and "evanescent state of mind" are too
ambiguous to be adapted to a concept like that of Thomist *claritas*.
Claritas is the solid, clear, almost tangible display of formal harmony. Here Stephen avoids the suggestions of the medieval texts
and sketches a personal theory. In *Stephen Hero* epiphany is
expressly mentioned. Although the term itself does not appear in *A
Portrait* (as though Joyce were cautious of the theoretical approach
of his early years), the passage on the enchantment of the heart
deals precisely with epiphany. What happens to the old concept of
claritas when it is understood as "epiphany"?

Epiphany: from Scholasticism to Symbolism

The concept, not the term, "epiphany" reached Joyce from Walter
Pater or, more explicitly, from that "Conclusion" to the *Studies in
the History of the Renaissance* which had so great an influence on
English culture between the two centuries [i.e., at the end of the
nineteenth century; at the turn of the twentieth century]. Rereading
the pages of Pater, we realize that the analysis of the various
moments in the process of the epiphanization of reality proceeds in
a way that is analogous to the Joycean analysis of the three criteria
of beauty. In Joyce, however, the object of analysis is a stable and
objective given, while in Pater, it is the elusive flow of reality. It is
not by chance that the famous "Conclusion" begins with a quotation
from Heraclitus.[8]

For Pater, reality is the sum of forces and elements that fade away
as soon as they arise; they are made tangible and embodied in a

---

8. Heraclitus of Ephesus (c. 540–c. 480 BCE), pre-Socratic Greek philosopher. For Pater's
"Conclusion," see pp. 298–301 [Editor].

troublesome presence only by our superficial experience, but when subjected to deeper reflection, they dissolve and their cohesive force is instantly suspended. We are then in a world of incoherent, flashing, unstable impressions. Habit is broken, everyday life dissolves, and only singular moments remain, seizable for an instant then immediately vanishing. In every moment, the perfection of a form appears in a hand or in a face; some tonality on the hill or on the sea is more exquisite than the rest; some state of passion or vision or intellectual excitement is "irresistibly real and attractive for us—for that moment only." Afterwards the moment has vanished, but for that moment only life has taken on a value, a reality, a reason. Not the fruit of experience, but experience itself is the end. To maintain this ecstasy would be "the success of life."

In this portrait of Pater is the English *fin de siècle* aesthete and his day-by-day strain to capture the fugitive and exquisite instant. In Joyce this heredity is purified of such delicacy and languor; Stephen Dedalus is not Marius the Epicurean.[9] Nonetheless, the influence of the page cited above is quite vivid. Thus we realize that the entire scholastic framework that Stephen has erected to support his aesthetic perspective is used only to sustain a romantic idea of the poetic word as revelation and the poet as the only one who can give a reason to things, a meaning to life, a form to experience, a finality to the world.

Stephen's reasoning, crammed with Thomistic quotations, tends toward this resolution. In fact, only in the light of this resolution does one find real value in the various affirmations concerning the nature of the poet and the imagination that are found in Stephen's discussions and in the early writings of Joyce. * * *

The poet is thus the one who, in a moment of grace, discovers the profound soul of things, and he is the one who makes them *exist* solely through the poetic word. Epiphany is thus a way of discovering reality and, at the same time, a way of defining reality through discourse. This conception develops somewhat from *Stephen Hero* to *A Portrait*. In the first book, the epiphany is still a way of seeing the world and thus a type of intellectual and emotional experience. Such experiences are represented in the sketches that the young Joyce gathers in his notebook *Epiphanies*—pieces of conversation that serve to identify a character, a tic, a typical vice, an existential experience. They are the rapid and imponderable visions that are noted in *Stephen Hero*—a conversation between two lovers overheard by chance on a foggy evening that gives Stephen "an impression keen enough to afflict his sensitiveness" (*SH* 211), or the clock in the customs which is suddenly epiphanized and,

9. Title character of Pater's book-length narrative (1885) [Editor].

without apparent reason, becomes "important." But why, and for whom? Pater offers an answer—*for the aesthete,* at the very moment when he seizes the event at a level beyond its habitual evaluation. Various pages in *A Portrait* seem directly inspired by this idea:

> His thinking was a dusk of doubt and selfmistrust lit up at moments by the lightnings of intuition, but lightnings of so clear a splendour that in those moments the world perished about his feet as if it had been fireconsumed: and thereafter his tongue grew heavy and he met the eyes of others with unanswering eyes for he felt that the spirit of beauty had folded him round like a mantle and that in revery at least he had been acquainted with nobility. * * * (V. 100–07)

Sometimes the image is more rapid: the vision of the reverend Stephen Dedalus, the *Mulier cantat,*[1] an odor of rotten cabbage. The insignificant thing takes on importance. In *Stephen Hero* these are the cases in which there seems to be a tacit agreement between the aesthete and reality. These are also the cases in which *A Portrait* most clearly shows itself as the ironic and affectionate report of those inner experiences which, in *Stephen Hero,* were the unique moments, the central moments of the aesthetic experience as identified with the experience of life.

* * *

In *A Portrait* the epiphany is no longer an emotional moment that the artistic word helps to recall but an operative moment of art. It founds and institutes, not a way to perceive but a way to produce life. At this point Joyce abandons the word "epiphany" for it suggests a moment of vision in which *something shows itself;* what now interests him is the act of the *artist who shows something* by a strategic elaboration of the image. Stephen truly becomes "a priest of eternal imagination, transmuting the daily bread of experience into the radiant body of everliving life" (V.1677–79).

* * *

The paramount example of epiphany in *A Portrait* is that of the seabird girl. It is no longer a question of a fleeting experience that can be written down and communicated by brief hints. Here reality is epiphanized through the verbal suggestions of the poet. The vision, with all its potential for the revelation of a universe resolved in beauty, in the pure aesthetic emotion, acquires its full importance only in the total and unalterable structure of the page.

1. See V.2479 [Editor].

At this point the last suspicion of Thomism is radically discarded and the categories of Aquinas reveal themselves as they were understood by the young artist—as a useful launching pad, a stimulating interpretive exercise whose sole purpose is to serve as the departure point for another solution. Although the epiphanies in *Stephen Hero,* identified with a discovery of reality, still retain a connection with the scholastic concept of *quidditas,* the artist now builds his epiphanic vision from the objective context of events—by connecting isolated facts in new relationships through a completely arbitrary poetic catalysis. An object does not reveal itself because of its verifiable, objective structure but because it becomes the symbol of an interior moment in Stephen.

Why does it become a symbol? The object which is epiphanized has no reasons for its epiphany other than the fact that it has been epiphanized. Both before and after Joyce, contemporary literature offers examples of this type. We notice that the fact is never epiphanized because it is worthy of being epiphanized. On the contrary, it appears worthy of being epiphanized because, in fact, it *has been* epiphanized. * * * Only after it has become *gratuitously* important can an epiphanic fact overload itself with meaning and become a symbol.

This is not an example of the revelation of a thing itself in its objective essence, *quidditas,* but the revelation of what the thing means to us in that moment. It is the value bestowed on the thing at that moment which actually *makes* the thing. The epiphany confers upon the thing a value which it did not have before encountering the gaze of the artist. In this respect the doctrine of epiphany and *radiance* is clearly in opposition to the Thomist doctrine of *claritas.* Aquinas maintains a surrender to the object and its splendor. Joyce uproots the object from its usual context, subjecting it to new conditions and conferring upon it new splendor and value as the result of a creative vision.

In this light even the *integritas* can be understood as a type of choice, a perimeter, as we have said, not so much following the contours of the given object as conferring outlines upon the chosen object. The epiphany is now the result of an art that dismantles reality and reshapes it according to new means. The evolution from the early writings, still anchored to an Aristotelian principle, to those of *A Portrait* is now complete.

* * *

Although it appears unaltered in its surface form, the conception has radically changed from the early writings to *A Portrait.* In *A Portrait* the aesthetic joy and the stasis of passions become "the luminous silent stasis of esthetic pleasure" [V.1401–02]. The terminology charges the concept with new implications. This static pleasure is not the purity of rational contemplation but the thrill in the face of mystery, the tension of sensitivity at the limits of the ineffable. Walter Pater, the symbolists, and D'Annunzio[2] have replaced Aristotle.

In order to make this transition, Joyce needs to reconceptualize the mechanism of aesthetic perception and the nature of the perceived object. This happens in the theory of *claritas* and in the development of the idea of epiphany. Pleasure is no longer given by the fullness of an objective perception but by the subjective translation of an imponderable moment of experience. By a stylistic strategy, one thereby translates an actual experience into a linguistic equivalent of reality. The medieval artist was the servant of things and their laws, charged to create the work according to given rules. The Joycean artist, last inheritor of the romantic tradition, elicits meanings from a world that would otherwise be amorphous and, in so doing, masters the world of which he becomes the center.

Throughout *A Portrait*, Joyce thus debates a series of unresolved contradictions. Stephen, steeled in the school of the old Aquinas, rejects both the faith and the lessons of the master, modernizing the scholastic categories by instinct, without even realizing it. He does this by drawing upon an idea that is present in contemporary culture and that deeply influenced him. This is the romantic concept of the poetic act as the foundation and resolution of the world. Through this romanticism, the world is denied as a place of objective relationships and is conceived instead as a network of subjective connections established through the poetic act.

Could this poetic theory suffice one who has absorbed the lesson of Ibsen in order to find a way of clarifying, through art, the laws that govern human events? Could it suffice someone nourished by a scholastic way of thinking, a mode of thought which is a continuous invitation to order, to clear and qualifiable structure rather than lyrical and evanescent allusion?

In other words, Joyce, who began his career of aesthete with an essay titled "Art and Life" and who found in Ibsen a profound relationship between the artistic work and moral experience, seems to reject any link between art and life in *A Portrait*. As his heritage of decadentism, he recognizes the only livable life to be the one which lives on the pages of the artist. If Joyce had stopped with *A Portrait*, nothing in the aesthetic formulation of the book could have been criticized and the aesthetics of Stephen would have been identified with those of the author. But from the moment that Joyce proposes

2. Gabriele D'Annunzio (1863–1938), Italian writer, whose novel, *Il Fuoco* (*The Flame of Life*; 1900) is in the tradition of late nineteenth-century decadence and French symbolism [Editor].

to write *Ulysses,* he reveals the deep conviction that if art is a shaping activity, "the human disposition of sensible matter for an aesthetic end," then the exercise of shaping must be applied to a well-determined material, the tissue itself of the real events, psychological phenomena, moral relations, that is, to the whole of society and culture.[3] Thus Stephen's aesthetics will not entirely be the aesthetics of *Ulysses.* In fact, what Joyce states concerning *Ulysses* goes beyond the well-defined borders of the philosophical categories and the cultural choices of the young artist.

Joyce knew this and, in fact, *A Portrait* does not claim to be the aesthetic manifesto of Joyce but the portrait of *a* Joyce who no longer existed when the author had finished this ironic, autobiographical sketch and begun *Ulysses.* In the third chapter of the book [*Ulysses*], Stephen is walking along the beach and remembers his own youthful projects: "remember your epiphanies on green oval leaves. . . ."

Naturally, many of the major aesthetic pivots of the early Joyce remain valid in his successive works. But the aesthetics of the first two books [*Stephen Hero* and *A Portrait*] remain exemplary under another aspect; they propose, in all its significance, the conflict between a world thought *ad mentem divi Thomae*[4] and the need for a contemporary sensibility. This conflict will be fatally repeated in the two successive works in a different form. It is the conflict of a traditional order and a new vision of the world, the conflict of the artist who tries to give form to the chaos in which he moves yet finds in his hands the instruments of the old Order which he has not yet succeeded in replacing.

HUGH KENNER

Joyce's *Portrait*—A Reconsideration[†]

What you are about to read is a summary of conclusions, without a great deal of evidence. I assume that by now the evidence is pretty familiar. The Joyce canon is not very large, and certainly *A Portrait of the Artist as a Young Man* has been read by everyone not hopelessly given over to the supposition that the novel ceased with Bulwer-Lytton.[1]

I am coming back to it, as I do from time to time, because, fifteen years after I first wrote an essay about it, I still think it is the key to

---

3. See the chapter "Art and Life" in S. L. Goldberg, *The Classical Temper: A Study of James Joyce's "Ulysses"* (London: Chatto and Windus, 1961), 41–65 [Expansion of author's note. Editor].
4. According to the thinking of the divine Thomas [Editor].
† From *The University of Windsor Review* 1:1 (Spring 1965): 1–15. Reprinted by permission of *Windsor Review.*
1. Edward Bulwer-Lytton (1803–1873), English novelist and playwright.

the entire Joyce operation, though I hope I know more about it by now than I did when I wrote my essay. I am not going to deal in local explanations; what I have done along that line is in print, and whoever is interested can find it, while those who are not need not be disturbed.[2] I am simply going to try to describe, as fully and carefully as I can, what the *Portrait* seems to be.

It has been supposed from the beginning that about this at least there is no mystery; for does not the title tell us that it is the portrait of the artist as a young man? To which I think it relevant to answer, that if we are to take this title at its face value, then it is unique among Joyce titles; and since it is too long a title to be printed conveniently upon the spine of a shortish novel—the sort of detail to which Joyce could always be relied on to pay attention—he must have wanted all those words for a purpose, and we had better look at them pretty carefully.

The first thing to be noticed, I think, is that the title imposes a pictorial and spatial analogy, an expectation of static repose, on a book in which nothing except the spiritual life of Dublin stands still: a book of fluid transitions in which the central figure is growing older by the page. The book is a becoming, which the title tells us to apprehend as a being. I shall have more to say about this in a moment; let me first draw attention to two more things we may notice in the title. One of them is this, that it has the same grammatical form as "A Portrait of the Merchant as a Young Man" or "A Portrait of the Blacksmith as a Young Man." It succeeds in not wholly avowing that the Artist in question is the same being who painted the portrait; it permits us to suppose that he may be the generic artist, the artistic type, the sort of person who sets up as an artist, or acts the artist, or is even described by irreverent friends as The Artist. I do not press this theme, though I shall later extract a consequence or two from it. The third thing the title says is that we have before us a Portrait of the Artist *as a Young Man*. Now there is a clear analogy here, and the analogy is with Rembrandt, who painted self-portraits nearly every year of his life beginning in his early twenties. Like most Joycean analogies, however, it is an analogy with a difference, because the painter of self-portraits looks in a mirror, but the writer of such a novel as we have before us must look in the mirror of memory. A Rembrandt portrait of the artist at twenty-two shows the flesh of twenty-two and the features of twenty-two as portrayed by the hand of twenty-two and interpreted by the wisdom of twenty-two. Outlook and insight, subject and perception, feed one another in a little oscillating node of objectified introspection, all locked into an eternalized

2. The earlier essay, which has been widely reprinted, is "The *Portrait* in Perspective," in Kenner's *Dublin's Joyce*. Bloomington: Indiana UP, 1956, 109–33 [Editor].

present moment. What that face knows, that painter knows, and no
more. The canvas holds the mirror up to a mirror, and it is not surprising that this situation should have caught the attention of an
Irish genius, since the mirror facing a mirror, the book that contains
a book, the book (like *A Tale of a Tub*) which is about a book which
is itself, or the book (like *Malone Dies*) which is a history of the writing both of itself and of another book like itself, or the poem (like
"The Phases of the Moon")[3] which is about people who are debating
whether to tell the poet things he put into their heads when he created them, and are debating this, moreover, while he is in the very
act of writing the poem about their debate: this theme, "mirror on
mirror mirroring all the show," has been since at least Swift's time
the inescapable mode of the Irish literary imagination, which is happiest when it can subsume ethical notions into an epistemological
comedy. So far so good; but Joyce, as usual, has brooded on the theme
a great deal longer than is customary, and has not been arrested, like
Swift or Samuel Beckett or even Yeats, by the surface neatness of a
logical antinomy. For it inheres in his highly individual application
of Rembrandt's theme, that the Portrait of the Artist as a Young Man
can only be painted by an older man, if older only by the time it
takes to write the book. Joyce was careful to inform us at the bottom
of the last page of this book that it took ten years. We have a Portrait, then, the subject of which ages from birth to twenty years
within the picture space, while the artist has lived through ten more
years in the course of painting it.

There follows a conclusion of capital importance: that we shall
look in vain for analogies to the two principal conventions of a normal portrait, the static subject and the static viewpoint, those data
from which all Renaissance theories of painting derive. The one substantial revision I would want to make in the essay on this book I
wrote in 1947 is its title; I entitled it "The *Portrait* in Perspective,"
and the more I think about the matter now the more I see that the
analogies of perspective are simply inapplicable. The laws of perspective place painter and subject in an exact geometrical relation to
one another, in space and by analogy in time; but here they are both
of them moving, one twice as fast as the other. The *Portrait* may well
be the first piece of cubism in the history of art.

I have already hinted that a few of the topics on which we have
come already will require further development; so I am not really
through with the title yet. But let us open the book and see what we

---

3. Dialogue poem published in *The Wild Swans at Coole* (1919), by the Irish writer W. B.
Yeats (1865–1939). *A Tale of a Tub:* prose satire (published 1704) by the Irish writer
Jonathan Swift (1667–1745). *Malone Dies:* the middle work in a trilogy of novels by the
Irish writer Samuel Beckett (1906–1989); originally published in French as *Malone
Muert* (1951), then in the author's English translation in 1956 [Editor].

discover. We discover, behind and around the central figure, what Wyndham Lewis[4] described as a swept and tidied naturalism, and nowhere more completely than in the places, the accessory figures, the sights and sounds, the speeches and the names. Joyce is famous for his meticulous care with fact; "he is a bold man," he once wrote, "who will venture to alter what he has seen and heard." He used, in *Dubliners* and *Ulysses*, the names of real people, so often that their concerted determination to sue him the minute he should step off the boat became, I think, an implacable efficient cause for his long exile from Ireland, which commenced virtually on the eve of the publication of *Dubliners*. The BBC had an unfortunate experience a few years ago, when they broadcast in all innocence a radio transcription of the funeral episode in *Ulysses*, with its story about the pawnbroker Reuben J. Dodd, whose son was fished out of the Liffey by a boatman. Father rewarded the boatman with two shillings, and someone comments, "One and eightpence too much." A few days later there arrived at Broadcasting House a letter signed "Reuben J. Dodd, Jr." Since one does not receive letters from fictional characters, the BBC dismissed it as a joke, until they were persuaded, to their heavy cost, that it was no joke. It is clear that for Joyce authenticity of detail was of overriding moment. If actual names were artistically correct, he used them at whatever risk. If they were not, he supplied better ones, but always plausible ones. So far so good. And what stares us in the face wherever we open the first sustained narrative of this ferocious and uncompromising realist? Why, a name like a huge smudged fingerprint: the most implausible name that could conceivably be devised for an inhabitant of lower-class Catholic Dublin: a name that no accident of immigration, no freak of etymology, no canon of naturalism however stretched, can justify: the name of Stephen Dedalus.

It seems to me very odd that we accept this name without protest; it is given to no eccentric accessory figure, but to the central character himself, the subject of the *Portrait*. But I cannot see that it has ever had the sort of effect Joyce must have intended: he must have meant it to arrest speculation at the outset, detaching the central figure at once from the conventions of quiet naturalism. What has happened instead is instructive: for Joyce is the best case available of the principle that the history of the reception of a writer's works is one of the basic data of criticism. Joyce himself, as the Satanic antinomian,[5] attracted attention as soon as the book did, and far more strongly; it was at once assumed that the book was nothing

---

4. Percy Wyndam Lewis (1882–1957), Canadian-born writer and painter who spent his career mainly in England [Editor].
5. Adhering to the doctrine of antinomianism, which maintains that salvation comes through faith and divine grace, not through obedience to laws.

more than a thinly veiled autobiography. It was a natural assumption from this premise, that the author treated his early self with considerable indulgence, especially since the Stephen of the *Portrait* seemed clearly destined to turn into the man Joyce was supposed to be. So it seemed clear that the name of Stephen Dedalus should be scrutinized for a piece of indulgent symbolism: and indeed it yields this symbolism quite readily, the strange name a figure of prophecy, prophecy of light and escape, and fabulous artifice.

Now it is true that Joyce exploits the symbolism of the name, in the latter part of the book; but if we could somehow get Joyce himself out of our minds for a moment, and consider the early part of the book on the terms it seems to impose, we should see a central figure with a name so odd it seems a pseudonym. And indeed it seems to have been modelled on a pseudonym. It combines a Christian martyr with a fabulous artificer. I think it very likely that it was based on another name constructed in the same way, a name adopted by a famous Irishman which also combines a Christian martyr with a fabulous wanderer. The model, I think, is the name Sebastian Melmoth, which was adopted during the brief time of his continental exile by the most lurid Dubliner of them all, Oscar Wilde.

Wilde built his pseudonym of exile deliberately. Sebastian—Saint Sebastian—may be described as the fashionable martyr of 19th-century aestheticism. Melmoth—*Melmoth the Wanderer*—was the hero of a novel written 80 years before by yet another Irish romancer, Charles Maturin. The two names joined the Christian and the pagan, the sufferer and the exile; in combination they vibrate with a heavy mysterious exoticism, linking Wilde with the creed of beleaguered beauty and with the land of his ancestors, affirming at the same time something richer and stranger about this shuffling Irish scapegoat than would seem possible, in Wilde's view, to a countryman of people with names like Casey, Sullivan, and Moonan. It is a haunting homeless name, crying for exegesis, deliberately assumed by a haunted, homeless man. He was a man, futhermore, in whom Joyce did not fail to see enacted one of his own preoccupations, the artist as scapegoat for middle-class rectitude. And in modelling, as I believe he did, the name of the hero of his novel on the pseudonym of the fallen Wilde, Joyce was, I believe, deliberately invoking the Wildean parallel.

To give this remark a context, let me now say as plainly as possible what I think the *Portrait* is. The *Portrait* is a sort of Euclidean demonstration,[6] in five parts, of how a provincial capital—for instance

---

6. A logical proof involving deductive principles and clearly defined axioms, as in the geometric proofs by the Greek mathematician Euclid (c. 325–265 BCE) [Editor].

Dublin, though Toronto or Melbourne would do—goes about converting unusual talent into formlessly clever bohemanism. This demonstration is completed in *Ulysses*, when the bourgeois misfit *par excellence* turns out to be the bohemian's spiritual father. (The principle, by the way, that underlies the spiritual paternity of Bloom and Stephen is the simple and excellent scholastic maxim that opposites belong to the same species.) Now Dublin, by the time Joyce came to look back on the process to which he had barely escaped falling victim, had already extruded the arch-bohemian of a generation, Oscar Wilde, and Wilde had completed the Icarian myth by falling forever. If we are going to be consistent about the symbolism of names, it should be clear that Stephen is the son of Dedalus, and what the son of Dedalus did was fall. It seems clear that Joyce sees Stephen as a figure who is going to fall, not as a figure who is going to turn into the author himself. It is in *Ulysses*, of course, that we last see Stephen, aged twenty-two; and I think it significant that Joyce remarked one day to Frank Budgen,[7] while he was engaged on the figure of Leopold Bloom in *Ulysses*, that Stephen no longer interested him as Bloom did; for Stephen, he said, "has a shape that can't be changed." This seems decisive; but let us go back to Wilde a moment. It is, to put it plainly, possible if not sufficient to regard the *Portrait* as a lower-class Catholic parallel to Wilde's upper-class Protestant career.

This idea, for all the attention that has been devoted to Joyce's work, remains absurdly unfamiliar. Let me expand it. I am not arguing that Joyce hated Stephen, or could not bear Stephen, or was satirizing Stephen. I am merely pointing out that Joyce, though he used everything usable from his own experience, was creating all the time a character not himself, so little resembling himself that he may well have been suggested by the notoriety of a famous compatriot who had died only a few years before the first version of the book was begun. One of the incidents for which even the careful researches of Mr. Kevin Sullivan[8] have turned up no prototype whatever, the caning of Stephen by schoolfellows because he refuses to "admit that Byron was no good," may even have been contrived as an Irish parallel to the famous indignities Wilde suffered at Oxford.

I have said that Joyce used everything usable from his own experience to create a character not himself. Now the evidence multiplies, as biographical trivia come to light, that Joyce did this with all his characters; but the party line of Joyce exegesis is wonderfully accommodating. When we learn, as I learned recently from an eye-witness of the Paris years, that he liked grilled kidneys for breakfast, we at

---

7. English painter (1882–1971), who wrote *James Joyce and the Making of "Ulysses"* (1934), based on conversations with Joyce [Editor].
8. Kevin P. Sullivan, *Joyce among the Jesuits.* New York: Columbia UP, 1958 [Editor].

once remember the familiar opening lines of the second section of
Ulysses: "Mr. Leopold Bloom ate with relish the inner organs of
beasts and fowls. . . . Most of all he liked grilled mutton kidneys,
which gave to his palate a fine tang of faintly scented urine." This
would seem to be a clear example of Joyce's way of using any detail
that was handy, including, or especially, the most intimate trivia of
his own existence, in the process of building from the inside a fictional creation. But this is not what we are normally told. When such
details come to light the analogy of Stephen is trotted out. Stephen
shares many experiences and attitudes with his author, because
Stephen is Joyce. Now here is Bloom sharing characteristics with his
author, therefore Bloom is Joyce. Mr. Ellmann actually commits himself (p. 369) to the judgment that Bloom is Joyce's mature persona,
and avers (p. 309) that the movement of *Ulysses* "is to bring Stephen,
the young Joyce, into *rapport* with Bloom, the mature Joyce."[9]

It is surely wiser to work the analogy of Stephen the other way. If
Bloom shares characteristics with Joyce and is plainly not Joyce,
then Stephen, merely because he shares characteristics with Joyce,
is not necessarily Joyce either.

I sketch this argument because it seems to be called for, not because
I think it especially enlightening. If we want to know what Joyce is
doing with the character called Stephen, we shall arrive at nothing
conclusive by checking our impressions against the evidence of what
he does with Leopold Bloom, simply because Leopold Bloom is—
like Stephen himself, for that matter—a special case. He is a special
case because he is so greatly elaborated; one would expect a good
number of the author's own characteristics to find their way into the
portrait of Bloom simply because so many small characteristics are
needed for the presentation of a character on such a scale. The people who turn up in the short stories provide a much better control
group. Can we find in *Dubliners* any useful prototypes of Stephen
Dedalus, useful because formed in a similar way, but so controlled
by the smaller scale and the unchanging viewpoint that we may have
less trouble deciding what they are meant to signify? The answer is
that we can find a great many.

There is Mr. James Duffy, for instance, in "A Painful Case." Mr.
Duffy has been endowed with the author's Christian name, and a surname with just as many letters in it as there are in Joyce. (This is a tiny
point, to be sure, but Joyce was a great counter of letters.) He has
moved out of Dublin, though it is true that he has not moved far, only
as far as suburban Chapelizod. He elected Chapelizod because he
found all the other suburbs of Dublin "mean, modern and
pretentious." He is a man obsessed with ideas of order, with pattern,

---

9. Richard Ellmann, *James Joyce.* New York: Oxford UP, 1959 [Editor].

symmetry, classification: he expresses these impulses by, among other things, the care with which he arranges his books. Like his creator, who kept a notebook headed "Epiphanies," he keeps on his desk a sheaf of papers headed "Bile Beans," held together by a brass pin, and in these papers he inscribes from time to time a sorrowful or sardonic epigram. The woman with whom he attempts to strike up a relationship is named Mrs. Sinico, which was the name of a singing teacher Joyce frequented in Trieste. He has even translated *Michael Kramer*, as Joyce had done in the summer of 1901. The manuscript of his translation is exceptionally tidy: the stage directions are written in purple ink. And he listens, as did the author of *Exiles* and of the final pages of *Finnegans Wake*, to "the strange impersonal voice which he recognized as his own, insisting on the soul's incurable loneliness. We cannot give ourselves, it said: we are our own." "Ourselves, oursouls, alone," echoes Anna Livia across thirty years. Mr. Duffy, in short, is A Portrait of the Artist as Dublin Bank-clerk.

Or consider Jimmy Doyle, in "After the Race," whose name is Jimmy Joyce's with only two letters altered. Jimmy Doyle, who becomes infatuated with continental swish and hangs around racing drivers, owes detail after detail of his taste for the anti-Dublin to the life of Jimmy Joyce, who even made a few shillings during his first bleak winter in Paris by interviewing a French motor-racing driver for the *Irish Times*. Or consider Little Chandler in "A Little Cloud," with his taste for Byron, his yearning after a literary career, his poverty, his fascination with escape from Dublin, his wife and baby. Almost every detail of his story has its source in the author's life. Or consider finally Gabriel Conroy, in "The Dead."

Gabriel Conroy, who is sick of his own country and has "visited not a few places abroad," who writes book reviews, as did Joyce, for the *Daily Express*, teaches language, as did Joyce, parts his hair in the middle, as did Joyce, wears rimmed glasses, as did Joyce, clings to petty respectabilities, as did Joyce, has taken a wife from the savage bogs of the west counties, as did Joyce, snubs people unexpectedly, as did Joyce, and is eternally preoccupied, as was Joyce, with the notion that his wife has had earlier lovers: Gabriel Conroy, attending a festivity in a house that belonged to Joyce's great-aunts, and restive in his patent-leather cosmopolitanism among the provincials of the capital by the Liffey, is pretty clearly modelled on his author by rather the same sort of process that was later to produce Stephen Dedalus.

There is nothing original in these observations, and we have not by any means exhausted the list of Joycean shadow-selves who turn up in these strangely intimate stories. But when we find them in the stories, instead of in an equivocally autobiographical novel, we can see more clearly what they are. They are not the author, they are potentialities contained within the author. They are what he has not become.

The sharpest exegetical instrument to bring to the work of Joyce is Aristotle's great conception of potency and act. Joyce's awareness of it, his concern with it, is what distinguishes him from every other writer who has used the conventions of naturalism. Naturalist fiction as it was developed in France was based on scientific positivism, its conviction that realities are bounded by phenomena, persons by behaviour, that what seems is, and that what *is* must be. But Joyce is always concerned with multiple possibilities. For a Zola, a Maupassant, a Flaubert,[1] it is simply meaningless to consider what might have been; for since it was not, it is meaningless to *say* that it might have been. In the mind of Joyce, however, there hung a radiant field of potentialities: ways in which a man may go, and correspondingly selves he may become, bounding himself in one form or another while remaining the same person in the eyes of God. The events of history, Stephen considers in *Ulysses*, are branded by time and hung fettered "in the room of the infinite possibilities they have ousted." Pathos, the dominant or subdominant Joycean emotion, inheres in the inspection of such limits: men longing to become what they can never be, though it lies in them to be it, simply because they have become something else.

All potentiality is bounded by alien and circumstantial limits. The people in *Dubliners* are thwarted, all of them, by the limitation of potentiality the city imposes. They sense this, all of them, and yearn to remove themselves, but in their yearning they are subjected to another scholastic axiom, that we cannot desire what we do not know. If they have notions of what it would be like to live another way, in another place, they confect these notions out of what Dublin makes available. The story called "A Little Cloud" presents the counter-Dublin in what is unmistakeably Dublin's image, a roisterer and journalist named Ignatius Gallagher, who incarnates for Little Chandler the possibility of liberation. But Ignatius Gallagher himself is simply fulfilling Dublin appetites, and enacting Dublin tavern images of rebelliousness. The story called "Eveline" posits this theme still more sharply. Eveline's token of escape is a sailor called Frank, which is just the right name for him. Frank is "kindly, manly, open-hearted," like a stage sailor, and when Eveline's father says "I know these sailor chaps" he is probably right. There is nothing discernible in Frank that is not part of the stock-in-trade of the Dublin common dream, as enacted in the music-halls every night. Having said this, we should go on to say (1) that all our knowledge of Frank comes through Eveline, and (2) that we cannot really say that Eveline sees Frank at all; she sees a kind of approximation to Frank, assembled out of a list of characteristics—kindness, manliness,

1. The French novelists Émile Zola (1840–1902), Guy de Maupassant (1850–1893), and Gustave Flaubert (1821–1880). All were naturalists, in the sense that they presented everyday realities in believable ways [Editor].

openheartedness, etc.—with which Dublin has supplied her. So the Frank she considers fleeing with is a chimera of her own mind, and in refusing to decide to flee, in fearing Frank, she is refusing herself, fearing herself. "Eveline" is another of those Irish mirror-stories of which we were speaking. If Frank, or the image of Frank, is the counter-Dublin, he is the counter-Dublin made in her imagination out of pieces of Dublin, which is all her imagination has to work with. And opposites belong to the same species. That is why Stephen says, in *Ulysses*, that if Socrates step forth from his house today, it is to Socrates that his steps will tend.

I hope no one thinks that I am forgetting Stephen Dedalus all this time. I am supplying a context for all those people in *Dubliners* who resemble the author, so as to supply in turn a context for the ways in which Stephen Dedalus resembles the author. At every moment of his life, the author, like anyone else in Dublin or anywhere else, was confronted with decisions and choices, courses of conduct elected or not elected; and each of these in turn, branches, if he elects it, into a whole branching family of further courses, or if he does not elect it, branches into a whole different family of branching courses. If the nose on Cleopatra's face had been shorter, the destiny of the world would have altered; if the swan had not come to Leda, Troy would not have fallen, nor Homer educated Greece, nor Greece Rome, and we should none of us perhaps exist. So there lies before a man an indefinitely large potentiality of events he may set in motion, ways he may go, and selves he may become. But each way, each self, each branching upon a branch, is supplied by Dublin; so the field, however large, is closed. In Dublin one can only become a Dubliner; a Dubliner in exile, since the exile was elected from within Dublin and is situated along one of the many paths leading out of Dublin and so connected to Dublin, is a Dubliner still. Even refusing Dublin is a Dublin stratagem.

He contains, then, within him, multitudes. All the people in *Dubliners* are people he might have been, all imprisoned in devious ways by the city, all come to terms of some sort with it, all meeting or refusing shadow-selves who taunt them with the spectre of yet another course once possible but possible now no longer. *Dubliners* is a portrait of the artist as many men. And it foreruns the more famous *Portrait* in one other aspect also, that while it has one subject the subject does not stay still in time. The boy in the first story, "The Sisters," does not become Gabriel Conroy, but he might. Eveline does not become Maria in "Clay," but she might. Bob Doran in "The Boarding-House" does not become Little Chandler in "A Little Cloud," but he might. And none of the men becomes James Joyce, nor none of the women Nora Joyce, but they might: they contain those potentialities. It is only by a fantastic series of accidents that anyone becomes what he does become, and though he can be only what he is, he can look back along the way he has come, testing it for branching-points now obsolete.

So the subject of *Dubliners* is a single subject, metamorphosing along many lines of potentiality as the circle of light directed by the story-teller moves through time, picking out, successively, a small boy of the time when he was himself a small boy, or adolescents of the time when he was an adolescent. Each story obeys, or seems to obey, the pictorial convention of a fixed perspective, subject and viewer set in place until the work of portrayal is finished. The book, however, is a succession of such pictures; or better, it is the trace of a moving subject, seen from a moving viewpoint which is always very close to him.

And if we apply this account to *A Portrait of the Artist as a Young Man* we shall find that it applies exactly: the moving point of view, product not only of a book ten years in the writing but of a standpoint which remains close to the subject as he moves; the moving subject, passing from infancy forward for twenty years; and the subject himself a potentiality drawn from within the author, the most fully developed of the alternative selves he projected over a long life with such careful labor. If the differences between Stephen and Joyce seem small, all differences are small, and it is always small differences that are decisive. One has only to accept or refuse a causal opportunity, and the curve of one's life commences a long slow bending away from what it otherwise would have been. This line of argument is not only Aristotelian[2] but wholly familiar to a man brought up, like Joyce, in a climate of clerical exhortation. From the time he could first remember hearing human words, he must have listened to hundreds of homilies, ruminations, admonitions, developing the principle that it is the little sins that prepare the habit great sins will later gratify, or that the destiny of the soul is prepared in early youth, so that there is nothing that does not matter.

So Stephen is a perfectly normal Joyce character, not the intimate image of what Joyce in fact was, but a figure generated according to a way of working that came naturally to him in a hundred ways. Stephen, unlike a character in *Dubliners*, is followed with unflagging attention for twenty years instead of being exhibited as he was during the course of a few hours. But like the characters in *Dubliners*, who also do many things Joyce did, he also leaves undone many other things Joyce did, and does many things Joyce did not. And these, if you accept my account of Joyce's way of thinking on human destiny, are not trivial divergences, but precisely the many small points of decision that make him Stephen and not Joyce.

2. In accordance with the thinking of the Greek philosopher Aristotle (384–322 BCE), with regard to potential and act, mentioned earlier in the essay, and the logical relation of cause to effect [Editor].

And, to recapitulate further, Joyce was fascinated by the way Dublin contrives to maintain its life-long hold on its denizens. He himself made no pretence of having escaped the city, except in body; he remained so thoroughly a Dubliner that he kept in repair to the last his knowledge of the shops and streets, pressing visitors from the distant town for news of civic alterations, or carefully making note of the fact that such-and-such a place of business had changed hands. Stephen's talk of flying by nets of language, nationality, religion, remains— Stephen's talk. One does not fly by Dublin's nets, though the illusion that one may fly by them may be one of Dublin's sorts of birdlime.

Once we are in possession of the formula for Stephen, his many little points of divergence from his creator cease to point toward mysterious formal requirements. Stephen is a young man rather like Joyce, who imagines that he is going to put the city behind him; he is going to fly, like Shelley's skylark; and he is going to fall into cold water, like Icarus, or like Oscar Wilde. Given this formula, Joyce used everything he could find or remember that was relevant, all the time fabricating liberally in order to simplify and heighten a being whose entire emotional life is in fact an act of ruthless simplification. Consider the famous retreat, and the hell-fire sermon which scares Stephen into the only act of capitulation he is ever to make to a priesthood which rules by fear. Mr. Kevin Sullivan, in a very careful investigation of Joyce's time at Belvedere, has showed that if we try to fit the events of the book into the author's life the chronology is impossible. The retreat, for instance, is represented as occurring in 1898 (when December 3 fell on a Saturday), and in 1898 James Joyce was not a secondary schoolboy but a college freshman. Mr. Sullivan also notes that for James Joyce "a Jesuit retreat was neither a terrifying nor a unique experience," since during his Belvedere school years he made at least five of them. And the familiar notion of phrases from a scarifying sermon burning themselves on the appalled young Joyce's mind, to be reproduced years later by Joyce the artist in a paroxysm of stupefied recall, rather dies away when we are shown, with a table of parallel passages, Joyce the artist constructing the sermon in cold blood from the Sodality Manual, a book which would have been his *vade mecum*[3] during the two years when, on account of his intellectual and spiritual eminence, he served as prefect of the Sodality. And these are the years to which, if we insist on believing the *Portrait* (or for that matter the recollections of people who recalled the *Portrait* more vividly than they did their own half-century-old impressions) we must assign him a time of wallowing in brothels. Another

---

3. Guidebook that would be constantly available; literally "go with me" (Latin). "Sodality Manual": the manual of the devotional fellowship, or sodality, used at Belvedere College [Editor].

writer has since shown that while the passages Mr. Sullivan cites from the Sodality Manual are very close, a certain hell-fire pamphlet[4] that was circulating in Dublin at the turn of the century is even closer; the more reason, of course, to doubt that a set of rhetorical commonplaces would have affected Joyce as they are supposed to have affected Stephen.

I have a last observation to make, which concerns Joyce's tone. I am always a little surprised to find myself cited, from time to time, as the bellwether of the Stephen-hating school of critics. It is clear that Stephen is not hateful, though he is irritating when he is being put forth by the massed proprietors of the Joyce Legend as an authentic genius. Considered as a genius, he is a tedious cliché, weary, disdainful, sterile; he writes an exceedingly conventional poem in the idiom of the empurpled nineties, indeed a poem Wilde might well have admired, one which seems unlikely to pass beyond the nineties. He has, as Joyce said, a shape that can't be changed.

Or has by the end of the book. But when we were first considering the title of the book, we noticed that the title imposes a look of pictorial repose on a subject constantly changing. We noticed, too, the author's announcement, on the last line of the last page, that he had spent fully ten years revolving the subject and revising and re-revising the writing. As we observed that we had a Portrait with a difference, neither subject nor artist united in a normal geometrical relationship. This is the last thing I want to stress. What we normally call "tone" is the product of a fixed relationship between writer and material. It is the exact analogy of perspective in painting. Its two familiar modes are utter sympathy and sustained irony. Irony says, "I see very well what is going on here, and I know how to value it." But Joyce's view of Stephen is not ironic; it is not determined by a standpoint of immovable superiority. Sympathy says, "Withhold your judgment; if you undervalue this man you will offend *me*." Joyce's view of Stephen is not sympathetic either, by which I mean that it is not defensive, or self-defensive. Like a Chinese painter, or a mediaeval painter, Joyce expects our viewpoint to move as the subject moves. We are detached from Stephen, we comprehend his motions and emotions, we are not to reject him nor defend him, nor feel a kind of embarrassment on the writer's behalf. We have not "irony," we have simply the truth. This is so until the end. At the end, when Stephen's development ceases, when he passes into, or has very nearly passed into, the shape that can't be changed, then he is troubling; and we sense, I think, a little, Joyce deliberately withholding judgment.

It is a terrible, a shaking story; and it brings Stephen where so many other potential Joyces have been brought, into a fixed rôle, into

4. Pinamonti's *Hell Opened to Christians* (see p. 282 in this volume) [Editor].

nothing; into paralysis, frustration, or a sorry, endlessly painful, coming to terms: for the best of them, a meditating on restful symbols, as Gabriel Conroy, stretched out in living death beside his wife, turns to the snow, or as Leopold Bloom, in the room of his cuckolding, thinks on the intellectual pleasures of water. For all the potential selves we can imagine stop short of what we are, and this is true however little we may be satisfied with what we are. Dubliner after Dubliner suffers panic, thinks to escape, and accepts paralysis. It is the premise of the most sensitive of them, as it is for Stephen Dedalus, that the indispensable thing is to escape. It was Joyce's fortune that having carried through Stephen's resolve and having escaped, he saw the exile he accepted as the means of being more thoroughly a Dubliner, a citizen of the city that cannot be escaped but need not be obliterated from the mind. He celebrated it all his life, and projected the moods through which he had passed, and for which he retained an active sympathy, into fictional characters for each of whom the drab city by the Liffey, whatever else it is, is nothing at all to celebrate.

HÉLÈNE CIXOUS

[The Artist and the Law]†

*   *   *

I'll tell you a series of stories regarding the first story in the world, which is Genesis. I'll tell you something about how an artist is formed, about what actually makes an artist. The genesis of an artist is not unrelated to genesis generally speaking. There is a whole genre of literature which is concerned with that, the *Bildungsroman*, and this is what I am going to speak about—about *Bildung*, about the education, the formation of the artist: But what I am interested in is the libidinal education of the artist, that is, what in his/her libidinal structure, in his/her affective, in his/her psychic structure is going to be determined particularly by sexual difference.

Urszene or "Cènes Primitives"

I'll start with the opening of Joyce's *A Portrait of the Artist as a Young Man*. All the pieces I refer to deal with one scene which one

† From pages 1–7 of "Reaching the Point of Wheat, or A Portrait of the Artist as a Maturing Woman," *New Literary History* 19:1 (Autumn 1987): 1–21. Used by permission of the author. The portion of the essay not included deals with the Brazilian writer Clarice Lispector [Editor].

This paper was first presented as a lecture given at Portland State University in 1984 [Author].

could call a Primitive Scene, and when I use the expression "primitive scene," I use it in every possible way: that is, you'll think in Freudian terms of the primitive scene, and in some ways, the scene *is* a primitive scene, having to do with discovering a forbidden secret. But I'd like you also to consider the primitive scene in the way we would write the word *cène* in French without an "s"; without an "s," it means "the meal." "The primitive scene" is also "the primitive meal." The first scene, or the initiating scene of the artist, or of the artistic human being, is composed of the usual characters: the parents, father and mother, and so on. Of course, such a scene immediately brings into question the enigma of origins. The main character in this scene is somehow impersonal: it is the Law and its representative the Word— Words. Another very important character is the apple, the fruit, whichever you like, the meal. And then, usually, one finds the rest of creation—birds, hens, whatever.

During the first s-cene, there will emerge the questions that will be the essential questions of the life of the artist, particularly the question of knowing, of the desire for knowledge, of the means of knowing, and of the symbolic value of knowing. There are two types of knowledge: there is the knowledge we learn here in universities, which is the knowledge of knowing, which has to do with mastering; and there is another type of knowledge, which does not derive from higher education, but from the highest education, and that is knowing through pleasure—it is pleasure itself. In the first s-cene, there is a kind of struggle between the two types of knowing, the pleasurable and the symbolic. Which is going to win? That is the question.

The Taste of Knowledge

Now, I'll simply recall briefly the familiar story of Eve. She goes through the test of the apple. She is told by He who is called God that she must not eat the apple. She is told that she mustn't, because otherwise she is going to die. And this is a completely opaque message. It does not mean anything for her, since death does not exist in Paradise. This will give birth to Milton's *Paradise Lost* and even to all philosophy. So the message is: "Don't." That's all: "Don't." And there is the other message, that of the apple, which says: "Try me, I am beautiful." There is no reason why she should not try, because the death message is meaningless. So she tries, because she is a woman. That is what the Bible says, and it is probably true.

I think it is true that her decision must have been determined by something "feminine" in her structure, particularly her desire and her non-fear of *knowing what is inside*. So knowledge started for all of us with knowing with the mouth, by tasting. Taste is the first act of knowledge, for women and for all men who are women. And the price of it has been exile, death, but also work, art, creation.

It is very interesting to see when reading *Bildungsromane* that this primitive scene comes up immediately, of course with some variations. There is a very old primitive scene which is extremely interesting in a story I like, the story of *Percival the Welshman,* a medieval quest story. Percival is a kind of mixed being. Although he is supposed to be a man, he is a woman's son. His father has completely disappeared, and he has been brought up in a wild way. He is always called "wild" in the story. Percival has been living in a very happy way, in a forest, which of course is the mother figure, but since he is after all a boy and a man, he is going to become a real, proper man by going through a series of tests which make up the quest.

The first thing that happens to him is that he goes out of the forest and meets with real knights in full armor, with swords and helmets. And they are so brilliant and invisible in a way that he thinks they are angels, and he falls in love with them. Then starts his real, manly education. In the second episode he finds himself in a castle which belongs to a man called "The King Fisherman," and this man is paralyzed, that is, he is a figure of castration. Percival is invited to a huge meal, which is fantastic, and he enjoys it considerably and keeps eating. During the meal, he sees somebody crossing the hall, bearing all kinds of dishes to another room. This happens several times and every time with great ceremony. Now and then he also sees a long lance going through the room with blood dripping from it, and he keeps wondering: What is that? What does that mean? Where is it going? But he had been told, just before entering the castle, by a wise man who acts like a kind of teacher, that good men mustn't ask questions, that it is impolite and that one musn't do it. So he refrains from asking questions, although he really would like to know.

At this point the narrative starts threatening Percival. The narrative starts saying: You know, Percival, you are doing wrong. You *should* ask questions. Something horrible is going to happen if you *don't* ask questions. Ask questions! But the narrative speaks mutely in the book at the enunciation level. Percival does not understand, does not hear. And when the meal comes to an end, suddenly there is a huge explosion, and the narrative shouts: You see what you have done! You haven't asked questions, and so you'll be punished. Now you are a horrible sinner, and because of you the world has been lost a second time. The King Fisherman, who would have been saved by Percival if he had asked questions, will remain paralyzed for eternity.

When we read that, we are completely appalled. If we are innocent, as we are supposed to be, we do not understand what happened because Percival did what he was told to do. And then something in the narrative said that he should have done just the contrary, which is completely incomprehensible, illogical, and mysterious. But that is it. And the moral of the story is—this is exactly the mechanism of the law—that we *are* guilty. We have got to learn about guilt, and the best way to do that is to be completely innocent. The first stage in education is to come to know the law as it is, that is, as pure law, pure interdiction, pure "you mustn't," which makes for its power. The law is completely negative, it is absolute, and it gives no signs, except that kind of strange order. In fact, in the beginning, there was a "Not" or a "No." Whereas, in the beginning of the women's bible, there is the "Yes" of Molly Bloom.[1]

An illustration of the power of the law is a very famous little text by Kafka,[2] called *Before the Law (Vor dem Gesetz)*. It starts this way: "Before the law, there stands the doorkeeper." A man from the country asks for admittance to the law. The doorkeeper says: You can't come in. And the man says: When can I go into the law? And the doorkeeper says: I don't know, maybe later. The doorkeeper is a big man with a big beard, and he looks very fierce. So the little country-man just stands in front of the law and waits. And he waits all his life. By and by he changes, because time passes, and he becomes very, very small, bit-size, as small as a pea. In the meantime, the doorkeeper has grown very tall and the countryman looks up at the beard of the doorkeeper. He is about to die and suddenly he has an idea. He had been thinking all the time in front of the law, and he suddenly realizes that during all these years he has never seen anyone coming to the law and asking for entrance, as he has. So he asks the doorkeeper, How is it that no one has come and done as I did? And the doorkeeper shouts very loudly because the man is actually already dead, "Because this was your own door," and he shuts the door.

So the little countryman will never have known anything about the law? He will never have known whether the law had an inside. He didn't step in, he didn't go over the threshold, he stayed there all the time. So he did not know anything about the law, that is, he knew everything about the law. All his life he stayed in front of the law, just as the law wanted. So he was in the law without knowing it. And, of course, it was his own door, his own law; he made law to himself (which is called autonomy). We behave as country people when we read Kafka's fable. Because we read "Before the law stands the doorkeeper," and we go on reading and staying in the front of the door of the text, and go on and die. And suddenly we can ask, we can wonder, But what is the law? The text-as-law functions the moment

1. This affirmation occurs in the closing of *Ulysses* (1922), in the thoughts of Molly Bloom, the central female character [Editor].
2. Franz Kafka (1883–1924), German-language writer born in Prague, then part of the Austro-Hungarian Empire [Editor].

the sentence starts; we are in front of the sentence exactly as in front of a door, and we don't move. We don't even think about it.

In Front of the Pome: The Sound of the Law

Now to take the little text by Joyce, which is exemplary of what an artist, not a countryman, is going to do with the law when he is in front of the law. These pages tell us everything about the artist. They start like a kind of fairy tale, and we have everything that makes a human being: "a cow," as a mother, of course, and "a baby tuckoo." The first adult character who comes to the page is the father: "His father told him that story: his father looked at him through a glass: he had a hairy face." Who is "he"? We don't know. There is a confusion of personal subjects in all the text. "He was baby tuckoo." We don't know whether it is the father or the baby who is "he." But the father is hairy, exactly as the doorkeeper; that is, he is a real "man." Now, the little boy is going to get educated in two pages. On the first page, there are three very short poems. The first is:

> O, the wild rose blossoms
> On the little green place.

And the second:

> Tralala lala
> Tralala tralaladdy
> Tralala lala
> Tralala lala.

In these two pages, Stephen Dedalus becomes a boy, a son, and an artist, and this is the way it goes. First he has to face the father, who tells him the story. The father is his own storyteller. The mother, who is the classical anal mother—that is, she makes him clean, body and soul—has a very special role because she makes him dance on the piano. For Joyce, the mother is also a substitute for the church: she makes him move like a puppet, but she is second to the father. Then comes a series of little events, and the final and most important event comes on the next page: "The Vances lived in number seven." Exactly as in a nursery rhyme: They lived in a shoe.

> They had a different father and mother. They were Eileen's father and mother. When they were grown up he was going to marry Eileen. He hid under the table. His mother said:
> —O, Stephen will apologise.
> Dante said:
> —O, if not, the eagles will come and pull out his eyes.

And the chapter finishes this way:

> *Pull out his eyes,*
> *Apologise,*
> *Apologise,*
> *Pull out his eyes.*
>
> *Apologise,*
> *Pull out his eyes,*
> *Pull out his eyes,*
> *Apologise.*

This is the first work of art of Stephen the artist. How did it happen? It is exactly the story of Percival or of Eve. He has been threatened with a horrible chastisement, and doesn't know why, of course. Is it because he hid under the table? Or did he hide under the table because he was already threatened? We don't know anything about it and he doesn't either. The whole thing comes down to his mother saying that he is going to apologize—so he is guilty; then he can commit his sin. And his aunt says: "O, if not, the eagles will come and pull out his eyes." And he becomes Prometheus, Oedipus, and Stephen. And what does he do? He makes a poem out of it, a little poem with rhymes. He has picked up the word "apologize" and subverted it into a little poetry, which is his way of playing with the law. What he does—and this is already a big difference and all art goes through this difference—is that he accepts the law in order to transgress it. And he transgresses by being attentive to what is *inside* the words. He enjoys it, so what he will take care of is the sound of the law, not the message of the law. This is how he becomes an artist.

* * *

JOHN PAUL RIQUELME

[Dedalus and Joyce Writing the Book of Themselves]†

The genius in the act of creation . . . resembles the uncanny fairy tale image which is able to see itself by turning its eyes. He is at once subject and object, poet, actor, and audience.
                                    —Nietzsche, *The Birth of Tragedy*

† Abridged and slightly revised from *Teller and Tale in Joyce's Fiction: Oscillating Perspectives.* Baltimore and London: Johns Hopkins UP, 1983, 48–64, 250–52. Reprinted by permission of the publisher. Page references have been replaced with part and line numbers of this Norton Critical Edition. Some cited passages might differ slightly from the equivalent passages in this volume.

Oscillating Perspective

In my commentary on *Finnegans Wake*, I explain how Joyce provides the reader in various ways with the means for achieving an oscillating perspective. That perspective is a viewpoint for reading that vacillates between mutually defining poles, just as our perception of the relation between figure and ground in some optical illusions may shift. The vacillating viewpoint is available in Joyce's writing much earlier than the *Wake*, as early, in fact, as *A Portrait of the Artist as a Young Man*. Joyce creates it through style in the continuing refinement of his techniques for rendering consciousness that he develops during the writing of *Dubliners* and *Stephen Hero*. The subtle intermingling of third- and first-person perspectives that Joyce effects in *A Portrait* is the most significant change in the style of his autobiographical work, one that differentiates it clearly from *Stephen Hero*. The mixing of narrator's and character's views and voices in *A Portrait*, which is prepared for by aspects of *Dubliners*, will become the given of *Ulysses*, the stylistic element the later work starts with, deviates from, then returns to in "Penelope." It is also an early step toward the radical superimposing of voices in *Finnegans Wake*.

In addition, Joyce encourages the oscillating perspective in *A Portrait* by constructing his narrative to avoid the pretense that his narration is a transparent vehicle for plot. He eschews that pretense through subverting the conventions of realism. Generally speaking, in fiction those conventions, including a single telling voice or style and a coherent chronological presentation, are undercut when the narration includes apparently heterogeneous material: diagrams, documents, or stories-within-the-text. Joyce achieves some of his most arresting and puzzling effects in *A Portrait* by injecting heterogeneous elements into the narrative. By disrupting the semblance of a continuous flow of narrative, these elements draw attention to the book's artifice, to its status as art, and to themselves as relatively independent of the text containing them. * * * They set up counter-movements in the reading process that may engender an oscillating perspective on the totality of the work's details.

In this regard, Joyce's autobiographical fiction resembles another eccentric work, a fictional autobiography, Laurence Sterne's *Tristram Shandy* (1759–67). Sterne's book is one of the most famous heterogeneous instances in the history of fiction, in part because the narrator's divagations distract the reader repeatedly from any passive response to the text based on unquestioned assumptions about what a novel should be and what its implications may legitimately include. Sterne's book contains blank, black, and marbled pages, as well as ellipses, diagrams, and a musical score. * * *

*   *   *

Although Joyce's *A Portrait of the Artist as a Young Man* is neither as obviously idiosyncratic as *Tristram Shandy* nor as unusual as Joyce's later fictions, like them, it is only marginally a *novel,* if by that term we mean a prose narration that abides by the canons of realism. These works include elements of form revealing disequilibria in the conventions of the telling that are startling and, at times, disquieting. In *A Portrait* the disturbing elements that raise the question of the book's marginal status are most prominent at the beginning and the ending. These are the locations of the text's margins, its borders with a world not delimited by the language of the story. Title, epigraph, and journal are the gates into and out of Joyce's work. They provide for the reader portals of discovery, margins to be negotiated and filled during the reading process.

*   *   *

Many critics who have written on *A Portrait* interpret that work autobiographically, claiming that it is based on details of Joyce's youth. Generally, they adduce the title as evidence for the link between the life and the work of art: the portrait is of the artist who writes the book. Unquestionably, strong evidence supports this kind of autobiographical reading. But an autobiographical interpretation of a different sort is also possible, one that sees Stephen Dedalus as the teller of his own story. * * * Implicit in the story of Stephen Dedalus's growth to maturity is the process by which his book emerges from previously existing texts that Stephen knows, some of which he has written himself. *A Portrait* is both the author's autobiographical fiction and the autobiography of the fictional character. It provides the portrait of both artists.

Any interpretation that suggests Stephen may be the narrator will take exception to most readings that dwell on the problem of irony, or aesthetic distance, and on the impersonality of the narration.[1] By emphasizing the narrator's invisibility and the would-be dramatic or objective presentation of Stephen, those readings cannot account adequately for either the narrator's recurring presentation of Stephen's consciousness or the various paradoxes of the narration that make describing the details of the story and its form so difficult. Although there can still be disagreements concerning the precise

1. For a review of discussions of aesthetic distance in *A Portrait,* see James J. Sosnowski's "Reading Acts and Reading Warrants: Some Implications for Readers Responding to Joyce's Portrait of Stephen," *James Joyce Quarterly* 16 (Fall 1978/Winter 1979): 43–63. Thomas F. Staley provides a helpful overview of trends in the criticism of *A Portrait* in "Strings in the Labyrinth: Sixty Years with Joyce's *Portrait,*" in *Approaches to Joyce's "Portrait": Ten Essays,* ed. Thomas F. Staley and Bernard Benstock (Pittsburgh: University of Pittsburgh Press, 1976), pp. 3–24. * * *

mix of the narrator's attitudes toward the central character at any given moment in the story, if Stephen narrates, the large problem of his future as an artist can no longer be at issue. If he writes his own tale, the story itself as text provides the strongest possible indication that his choice of vocation will yield more valuable work than the writing he produces within the narrative. And the narration indicates exactly what kind of artist Stephen has become. The teller in *A Portrait,* like the purloined letter of Poe's story,[2] is well-hidden out in the open, where anyone who cares to look can find him.

Dislocations in Style and Story

A Portrait of the Artist contains displacements in both narrative and narration, story and telling. The literal displacements include the moves of the Dedalus family from one residence to the next always less attractive abode, compounded with Stephen's displacements from school to school, from Clongowes to Belvedere to University College. "Still another removal" (IV.577), Stephen exclaims to himself during the scene in the kitchen with his siblings at the end of IV.2. In Stephen's boyhood and adolescence, sex and religion replace one another in mutually modifying and mutually defining alternation, until their ultimate displacement through coalescence in Stephen's choice of art as vocation. In the future projected by the book's ending, this last development will be last in the sense of previous. That future may bring a series of further developments, each transforming the last from final to merely previous. Stephen's choice of vocation is accompanied by suggestions of the next physical displacement, his planned departure from Ireland, which will take him eventually not just to Paris, but to Trieste.

Displacements in *A Portrait* are temporal as well as spatial and stylistic as well as literal. The ending indicates that Stephen may be entering a period of more mature adulthood, which will replace his young adulthood, the most recent in a series of states stretching back through adolescence to childhood and infancy. The displacements of style are both those of Stephen as developing artist and of the narrator as mature artist. As William M. Schutte has pointed out, "*Portrait,* like *Ulysses* and *Finnegans Wake,* has no one style."[3] By entwining strands of language into a narrative, the teller of the story reaches back through the past to the origins of Stephen's development as an artist. * * *

---

2. "The Purloined Letter" (1845), by the American writer Edgar Allan Poe (1809–1849).
3. William M. Schutte, editor's introduction, in *Twentieth-Century Interpretations of "A Portrait of the Artist as a Young Man"* (Englewood Cliffs, N.J.: Prentice-Hall, 1968), p. 14. In the fourth section of his introduction to this volume of essays (pp. 10–14), Schutte provides what he calls a "summary account" of the styles that is quite helpful, though brief.

* * * In *A Portrait,* by shifting styles Joyce meets a special challenge: to present a wide variety of stylistic exercises that would simultaneously mark the development of a young character's aesthetic sensibilities and form the basis for the writer's exhibition of his own technical mastery. In the various styles of portraiture we have proof of both the character's aesthetic sensitivity and the narrator's virtuosity. The same language serves two purposes. From time to time Joyce directs his adventure in styles toward culminating passages of discovery and self-revelation in which the heightened language vividly calls attention to the relationship of narrator's skill to character's state of mind. The writing of the villanelle in Part V will be especially important in this regard for our consideration of the teller's merging with character in *A Portrait.*

During the displacing of earlier parts of the narrative by later parts, the teller modulates among his different styles of narration, including a "vague, nineteenth-century romanticism," "exalted, almost hysterical lyricism," "workaday prose," and the language of Pater and the decadents.[4] In general, the narration consists of anonymous representations of scene, action, and dialogue in the third person together with the report of Stephen's thoughts, also in the third person. The thoughts of other characters are not reported. This sort of presentation allows Joyce a great deal of flexibility. Modulation from one style to another can be smoothly executed as a shift in the character's thinking within the often relatively unobtrusive framework of third-person narration. Some of the more violent, jarring shifts of style occur at the breaks between typographically demarcated segments of the narrative, between the five parts, and between the nineteen smaller sections making up those parts.[5]

There are so many modulations of style in *A Portrait* that any endeavor to characterize generally the details of narration will prove inadequate in some respects. Part of the work's richness and appeal is a verbal texture so variable that it defeats all attempts at reduction to a simple pattern. But the fluctuations do develop in a general direction as the narrative proceeds. In broad terms, the style shifts from psycho-narration narrowly conceived toward narrated monologue; that is, it moves from the narrator's discourse concerning the character's mind to a presentation that also includes the character's mental discourse rendered as the narrator's language. Occasionally, the narrator employs the technique of quoted monologue, language that we understand as the character's supposedly unmediated mental discourse because it employs first person and present tense. The general distinctions between psycho-narration, quoted monologue,

4. All pointed out by Schutte in his introduction to *Twentieth-Century Interpretations of "A Portrait,"* pp. 13–14.
5. See "The Parts and the Structural Rhythm of *A Portrait,*" pp. 307–09 in this volume.

and narrated monologue will emerge as we examine specific passages in *A Portrait*.[6] Each technique affects our stance toward character and teller and our sense of the teller's relationship to the tale. All three occur in the context of third-person narration. While we may want to distinguish between them for the purposes of analysis, they hardly ever occur in complete isolation from one another.

Of the three, the most problematic is the narrated monologue, also known as *erlebte Rede* and as *le style indirect libre*, a technique Joyce would have found in Flaubert.[7] This device involves the rendering of the character's consciousness in the third person and the past tense. Although there may be no explicit announcement of mental process in the narrator's language, we understand the passages as thoughts occurring to the character in the first person and in the present tense. The present time of the action, as opposed to the past time indicated by the narration, is often emphasized by deictic adjectives and adverbs (ones that point to specific contexts of time or place, such as *here* and *now*) and by demonstrative pronouns, which create a sense of immediacy. Here arises the crucial complication that Joyce develops with such subtlety in both *A Portrait* and *Ulysses*. The reader translates the third person into "I" during the reading process. We speak the character's subjectivity, as do narrator and character in their different ways. The use of third person and past tense indicates a tendency toward a fusion of character's voice with teller's voice. The ambiguous merger of voices makes it difficult, even impossible, for the reader to distinguish between the cunningly combined voices of character and narrator. Because the technique requires the reader to translate third person into first and to attempt discriminations, however difficult, between the merged voices, it necessitates the reader's active recreative rendering of the narration. The reader *performs* the text of narrated monologue with a special kind of involvement because of the device's unusual nature.

Quite frequently, the narrator in *A Portrait* summarizes Stephen's thoughts as psycho-narration employing verbs of consiousness prominently either in the past tense or as infinitives. There are numerous examples from the book's early pages: "felt" (I.48), "wondered" (I.105), "to remember" (I.159), "knew" (I.376, I.733, I.796). Occasionally several verbs indicating thought are clustered together. In one paragraph early in I.2 (I.181–98), there are six instances of

---

6. I have adopted the terms *psycho-narration, quoted monologue,* and *narrated monologue* from the typology Dorrit Cohn presents in *Transparent Minds: Narrative Modes for Presenting Consciousness in Fiction* (Princeton: Princeton University Press, 1978). She draws extensively on Joyce for examples illustrating her categories. * * *

7. Gustave Flaubert (1821–1880), French novelist. *Erlebte Rede*: "experienced (in the sense of felt) speech" (German). *Le style indirect libre*: "free indirect style" (French).

such verbs. In general, in this portion of the narrative, there is little emphasis on the complex combination of voices that appears later.[8] The reader can easily distinguish the narrator's discourse about Stephen's thoughts from the presentation of scene and dialogue; for instance, in the alternation between these two complementary aspects of the narration in I.3, the Christmas dinner. As Stephen grows older, the narrator's techniques for presenting his thoughts change. Verbs denoting mental process still occur but less frequently, and other words connoting thought supplement them. Predicates less directly evocative of consciousness, often together with a prepositional phrase, become the reminders that we have access to Stephen's mind.

In II.2, when Stephen begins wandering the streets of Dublin alone, the passages describing his adventures contain just as many indicators of thought as do some earlier passages, but the indications are of a different order. Stephen makes a map of the city "in his mind." As he follows physically the routes of this internal map, the verb "to wonder," used before in the past tense, now occurs as a present participle, "wondering." While an explicit reference to mental process is still provided, the transformation of the verb denoting thought from a predicate to a modifier makes the reference less obtrusive. Instead of telling us that Stephen thought, felt, or remembered, the narrator presents Stephen's impressions as they "suggested to him," "wakened again in him," or "grew up within him" (II.232, II.234, II.239). As before, the references to thought are clustered together, though they are more muted now. These last three predicates and the two preceding quotations are all from a single paragraph. And the predications of thought, even these muted ones, begin to be supplemented or replaced by a new affective vocabulary presenting mood, as in the phrases "mood of embittered silence" and "angry with himself" (II.245, II.247). Or nouns and verbs not necessarily denoting mental activity, such as "vision" and "chronicled" (II.249, II.251), take on connotations that suggest consciousness because of their use in context.

There are two distinctions implicit in the alternation between scene and psyche that occurs in the work's first sections: the distinction between an external world and the character's mind and between narrator and character. Starting in Part II both begin to be blurred in various ways. The alternation becomes overlap when the narrator quotes Stephen's thoughts in II.2 using the same typographical indicator, the dash, that previously identified only direct discourse: "—She too wants me to catch hold of her, he thought.

---

8. Some exceptions to this general description are I.1 and such passages as the paragraph in I.3 beginning "Why did Mr. Barrett . . ." (I.801).

That's why she came with me to the tram. I could easily catch hold
of her when she comes up to my step: nobody is looking. I could
hold her and kiss her" (II.350–53). The character's interior speech
is utilized here as the equivalent of a stage monologue or aside in
drama. It has the form of direct discourse but a different effect. In
II.3 the narrator carries his modifications further during Stephen's
encounter with his schoolmate Heron just before the play. We are
given the narrative of Stephen's heretical essay and the drubbing it
leads to as scene, dialogue, and action (II.638–791). But this narrative occurs in Stephen's mind. His memory now is rendered in
nearly the same way as the narrator's presentation of the external
world. The growing resemblance between the two modes of narration prepares for the more radical alignment of teller and character
that occurs later.

   The more striking fusion of inner and outer and of character and
teller begins emerging in the next part, when the teller adopts the
narrated monologue while presenting the retreat in III.2. As in the
narration of the Christmas dinner, the telling alternates between
an external scene (the sermons) and Stephen's reaction to the
outer world. Although the narrator continues to employ techniques
introduced in previous sections, there are some crucial modifications. These changes suggest, among other things, the intensity of
Stephen's reaction to events. Section III.2 consists of an introduc-
tory talk and three sermons that take place on consecutive days. The
initial, prominent use of narrated monologue occurs in the passage
presenting Stephen's walk home the first evening after the introduc-
tory talk: "So he had sunk to the state of a beast that licks his chaps
after meat. This was the end; . . . And that was life" (III.338–43).
The device is especially manifest because Joyce uses demonstrative
pronouns in a paragraph otherwise relatively free of them. The
statements can be easily transformed into the character's speech to
himself in first person and present tense. In the paragraph that follows, the narrator presents the initial sermon, on death and judgment (III.351–465), in a curious way. He renders it not as direct
discourse, the technique he uses to report the two subsequent sermons on hell, but as speech mediated by Stephen's consciousness.
The brief passage of narrated monologue acts as the preparation for
this odd filtering of Father Arnall's words through Stephen's mind.
The narration of the sermon begins in the past tense with a series of
verbs and phrases indicating Stephen's consciousness is being rendered: "stirring his soul," "fear," "terror," "into his soul," "he suffered,"
"he felt" (III.351–54). In the middle of the sermon, although the
dashes of direct discourse are absent, the past tense is replaced with
a mixture of tenses, including present and future, much closer to
the quotation of the later sermons as speech.

After this lengthy report of Stephen's consciousness during the first sermon, the alternation of passages focusing on psyche with those focusing on scene is again established, but now the narrated monologue has become a recurring feature of the narration. The narrator employs it briefly but regularly throughout the remainder of III (instances occur in lines 466–77, 529–36, 812–21, 871–79, 1284–93, 1447–71, 1546–53).[9] In III.3 Stephen's thoughts are quoted directly, once with a dash indicating direct discourse when he hears voices (III.1213–17), but at other times without the dash as apparently unmediated interior exclamations: "Confess! Confess!" (III.1321). While this last exclamation can be read as a direct presentation of Stephen's thought, the similar one, "For him! For him!" (III.1287), that occurs only a page earlier is an instance of narrated monologue. We read "For him" as "For *me*," understanding the third person as applying to the character.

With a device as problematic as narrated monologue, there will almost certainly be some disagreement among readers concerning the application of the term to specific passages. Whatever the differing judgments about the particular passages I have identified as narrated monologue, the general point concerning the sudden, recurring appearance of the technique in the narration is irrefragable: these numerous possible instances of narrated monologue grouped together in Part III mark a significant shift in the style. The shift is increasingly toward renderings of Stephen's intensely felt thoughts that create an ambiguity concerning the relationship of the style to the character's language. In the two remaining parts the narrator freely employs in combination the various techniques he has used to present Stephen's mind. Once the reader has grown accustomed to the different modes for representing consciousnenss that have been introduced seriatim over the course of nearly 150 pages, the teller can rely on the reader's newly created capacity for responding to the salmagundi of techniques that will now be employed in the narration.

The narrator has been making a persona for the reader as well as for himself in his portrayal of Stephen. The reader has learned the conventions of the literary techniques that the author uses to compose his own self-representation as teller and to present Stephen's gradually developing sensibilities. Only after all the techniques have become thoroughly established as conventions of the fiction can the narrator begin to shift rapidly from one to another. The swift alternation of devices evoking the hard, gemlike flame of Stephen's mind occurs in the book's two climactic segments: at the end of IV.3 when

---

9. This and the following lists provided parenthetically are meant to be indicative only, not exhaustive.

Stephen is on the strand, and during Stephen's composing of his villanelle in V.2. At the end of IV.3, the narrator gives us Stephen's interior exclamations, "Yes! Yes! Yes!" (IV.810), combined with possible instances of narrated monologue, (IV.810–21, IV.883–90, IV.900–02) and with Stephen's thoughts quoted as if they were direct discourse: "—Heavenly God! cried Stephen's soul, in an outburst of profane joy" (IV.876–77). Near the end of my discussion of *A Portrait,* I shall deal with the implications of the similar combination in V.2

In V.1 and V.3 there are numerous instances of narrated monologue (V.129–61, V.175–211, V.1918–40, V.2047–82, V.2111–32, V.2507–17). The narrator also employs at great length the technique he used in II.3 by presenting Stephen's memories while he is walking to the university as scene, action, and dialogue (as in the long recollection of Davin's story about his walk in the country and his encounter with the peasant woman [V.265–334]). The ambiguity about the source of the narration's language is particularly pronounced throughout V. Repeatedly the narrator introduces long passages of Stephen's thoughts by asserting first that Stephen "watched" (V.394), "saw" (V.435), "looked at" (V.1124), or "had heard" (V.623) something, then that someone or something "seemed" (V.396, V.440, V.445, V.488, V.527, V.549, V.625) a certain way. These passages omit the phrase "to him" or "to Stephen," which would identify explicitly the language to follow as Stephen's rather than the narrator's. The narrator will introduce a long paragraph of revery with only a brief reference to "Stephen's mind" (V.643–44), which the reader may tend to forget, or he will conclude rather than introduce such a long paragraph with a phrase indicating the passage was Stephen's "thought" (V.1935). As in so many other late passages, the effect is to align the teller's voice and the character's, if only temporarily. The residual and cumulative sense of merger created by such alignments molds the reader's stance toward the narration with particular force. While *some* distinctions can be made between teller and character (this discussion would not have been possible without them), the passages ask us again and again to consider the relationship of the two voices that are so complexly mixed.

The subtly mingled but counterpointed language of teller and character emerges vividly in the book's second half, primarily because the narrated monologues together with the related techniques appear frequently beginning in III.2. Along with the seemingly intimate presentation of Stephen's thoughts, in Part V the reader encounters longer and more elaborate statements to his companions than Stephen has made earlier. His voices, both internal and public, are thrust to the foreground. At the book's ending, it is primarily these voices that determine the reader's overall judgment of Stephen's potential.

Journal and Epigraph:
Beginning and Homeward Glance

The representations of Stephen's consciousness that occur in Part V are particularly relevant for understanding the relationship of narrative to narration in *A Portrait*. The following paragraph, in which Stephen comments silently on Cranly's remark about a fellow student, is typical of the last section:

> It was his [Cranly's] epitaph for all dead friendships and Stephen wondered whether it would ever be spoken in the same tone over his memory. The heavy lumpish phrase sank slowly out of hearing like a stone through a quagmire. Stephen saw it sink as he had seen many another, feeling its heaviness depress his heart. Cranly's speech, unlike that of Davin, had neither rare phrases of Elizabethan English nor quaintly turned versions of Irish idioms. Its drawl was an echo of the quays of Dublin given back by a bleak decaying seaport, its energy an echo of the sacred eloquence of Dublin given back flatly by a Wicklow pulpit. (V.762–72)

Such insertions, made by the narrator during his report of conversations, amount to brief digressions. As part of a commentary on time in fiction, Jean Ricardou remarks on the effect passages like this one can have in a narrative. Because of their length, they disrupt any illusion of a continuous flow of time in the plot by calling attention to the time of the narration. As Ricardou says, they emphasize "the writing (habitually concealed by the story)."[1] When their prominence begins to define the mode of narration, as it does in *A Portrait*, in Ricardou's formulation the work "ceases to be the writing of a story to become the story of a writing."[2] The passage emphasizes writing in two senses, as process of narration and as style of language. The teller's activity of narrating is emphasized in ways it cannot be through the quotation of dialogue. And attention is drawn to the specific kind of language employed, particularly in this passage, in which Stephen explicitly makes contrasts between various styles.

As narration, *A Portrait* includes all the styles mentioned in the paragraph and many more. They are the literary styles the character has heard or read (and sometimes spoken) and that the narrator has adopted in his written mimicry of the character's mind and the

1. Jean Ricardou, "Time of the Narration, Time of the Fiction," trans. Joseph Kestner, *James Joyce Quarterly* 16 (Fall 1978/Winter 1979): 13.
2. Ricardou, p. 11.

character's world. At times we understand them primarily as styles within the narrative; at other times, as styles of the narration. When the styles characterize Stephen's thoughts intimately presented, distinguishing narrative from narration is often no longer possible. * * * The language of the narration is opaque. We see *it* as well as the story communicated, just as Stephen sees the phrase Cranly speaks. Stephen understands the semantic meaning of Cranly's words and the implication of Cranly's style. And the reader understands the implications of the narration, including the recurring reports of Stephen's thoughts.

Through an energetic echo that gives back Stephen's eloquence, the narrator fuses inextricably with character. There is no means for disentangling Stephen's attitudes from the voice of the narrator who speaks them. The two voices are linked by the author's act of writing, a mediating process we become aware of through the style of narration but can never experience directly. We know the product and its implications but not the process itself. Instead, we experience the analogous mediating process of the act of reading, which aligns *our* activities of mind with those of character and teller. As Wayne Booth has said, "any sustained inside view, of whatever depth, temporarily turns the character whose mind is shown into a narrator."[3] The narrator's reiterated shifts between internal and external views make *A Portrait* a work about the transforming of a character into an artist in which style regularly turns the character into a teller. When the style includes narrated monologue, the reader shares the role of teller with the character by speaking the character's mind.

The final style adopted by the narrator, one especially pertinent to the present inquiry, is that of the journal, from which the entries of 20 March through 27 April are apparently only an excerpt. In the narrative's fictive chronology, as distinct from the chronology of narration, the journal is the last example of Stephen's styles as well. The potential ambiguity of the word "last" is the crux of the difference between the narrative and the narration. The style of the journal displaces the villanelle, the aesthetic theory, and the other examples of Stephen's expression—written, spoken, and internal— that are either directly presented or alluded to earlier. In its turn, the styles of the entire book displace that of the journal. The dual, interlocking process of feedback points to the problem of the ending and the end toward which the narrative tends. Two styles, the teller's and the character's, not just one, are brought to conclusion, or at least partial closure, in the one document that can be read as

3. Wayne C. Booth, *The Rhetoric of Fiction* (Chicago: University of Chicago Press, 1961), p. 164.

two documents. The journal kept by a character is also a portion of a narrative reported by the teller.

There is an acute disequilibrium between process and product, between Stephen's activity of keeping a journal and the portion reproduced by the narrator through an act of quotation that resembles the reporting of dialogue. * * * The shifting focus becomes particularly evident for the reader of *A Portrait* who attempts to reconcile the journal in its fictional and textual contexts (of story and of narration) with the title and the epigraph of the title page and with the dates and places noted on the final page. All these parts of the book are relatively independent of what falls between them. Their implications do not appear at first to be wholly integrated with the remainder of the book as coherent aspects of style and story. This apparent failure of integration provides grounds for interpreting *A Portrait* as preposterous in that word's etymological sense.

Before and after, pre- and post-, are made to exchange places and to interact reciprocally. The exchange and interaction are manifest in the ending, from the perspective of which the reader revises the provisional interpretations generated up to that state of the reading. At the end of any narrative the reader engaged in an interpretive process experiences the preposterous aspect of reading. The reader's new perspective for scrutinizing the text's details allows a look backward that sees the text in retrospective arrangement. That arrangement modifies and displaces provisional readings, which are now seen anew in revision. The reading process flows temporally from the present to the past as the reader experiences portions of the text becoming parts of new contexts that are the bases for reinterpretations. Prospective and retrospective, provisional and revisionary judgments merge as the reader encounters and assimilates the conceptual implications of the narrative's form. The reader's experience of retrospective rearrangements shifting places through time duplicates the character's experience when he becomes the teller of his own tale in retrospect.

The closing of both book and journal with the notation of dates and places, "Dublin 1904/Trieste 1914," presents in small the problematic, preposterous quality of the entire work. The reader must decide whether the references are part of the story or part of the writing, whether they are appropriate to the product or to the process of creation. Like the title, they refer at once to both product and process, to both character and author as artists. The autobiographical bases of the dates and places are well known. They point to the time and locations at which the author initiates and completes the writing of the book. Joyce finished *A Portrait* in Trieste just over ten years after leaving Dublin. Serial publication began in

1914.[4] The authorial, autobiographical significance in no way diminishes the relevance the references possess for Stephen Dedalus's story. There is a complicated, uncanny doubling lurking within and behind the apparently innocent closing that is a *post scriptum*. This doubling that occurs through the telling of the story is more radical than most interpretations have allowed. * * *

The strange duplication becomes apparent once dates and times are both understood as referring to Joyce's process of writing *and* to the story of Stephen Dedalus as it appears to develop beyond the time of the excerpt printed from the journal. Although no exact dates are ever provided for Stephen's activities earlier in the narrative, Dublin is obviously the place appropriate to the journal and to much of the action, and 1904 is within the limits of probability suggested in the fiction. Nineteen fourteen would be the year and Trieste the place in which Stephen completes the transforming of the journal into a book that is the simulacrum of Joyce's. The last portion of *A Portrait* presents what comes first with respect to the remainder of the text. In Stephen Dedalus's fictional life, which includes his life as a writer of fiction, the keeping of the journal precedes the completing of the book. The last—that is, the most recent—stage of Stephen's development as an artist is presented through the narration, not in the narrative. The dates and places that stand both inside and outside the story are the signatures of author and character as writers, their superimposed self-portraits painted in the corner of the finished canvas. They are the equivalent of the closing that Stanislaus Joyce reports his brother intended to append to *Stephen Hero*, "the signature, *Stephanus Daedalus Pinxit*."[5]

In Ovid's *Metamorphoses* the line quoted as epigraph to *A Portrait* refers to the mythic artist Daedalus, the "old father, old artificer" (V.2791) mentioned at the end of Stephen's journal. Ovid presents Daedalus setting his mind to work upon unknown arts. As with the notations at the book's end, the question of the epigraph's meaning concerns its referent. Like the journal, the epigraph is presented as a fragment quoted out of its original context. For the epigraph, but not for the journal, the original context is available to be examined. There is no evidence that the fragmentary journal actually has an origin in the same way as the epigraph does. In the *Metamorphoses* the epigraph's context indicates Daedalus's longing for home:

4. For a discussion of the dates of composition see Schutte's introduction to *Twentieth-Century Interpretations of "A Portrait,"* pp. 5–7.
5. Stanislaus Joyce, *My Brother's Keeper: James Joyce's Early Years*, ed. Richard Ellmann (New York: Viking Press, 1958), p. 244.

Homesick for homeland, Daedalus hated Crete
And his long exile there, but the sea held him.
. . . He turned his thinking
Toward unknown arts, changing the laws of nature.[6]

In the case of Ovid's Daedalus, the act of turning the mind to work on obscure arts has an explicit cause and an explicit effect. Daedalus fashions wings for himself and for Icarus in order to escape from a prison and return home. Daedalus's work violates the laws of nature through the accomplishment of a feat seemingly beyond human possibility. The result also includes the death of Icarus, an apparently unavoidable concomitant of the mature artist's act of making in order to escape.

At the beginning of A Portrait as well as at its end, Joyce challenges the laws of conventional narrative by turning his own mind to intricate arts that result in a death and a doubling through the creation of a ghostly presence for the artist in a voice that repeats itself. Like the designations of place and time, the epigraph refers to the Dedalian character as well as to the Daedalian author. When the character's role as son is over after the final page, his fatherly role as teller is born phoenixlike to return home on the first page. Character transforms himself into artist as the son becomes his own father. Essential to the transformation is the importance of home in both Ovid's work and Joyce's. The act of producing the portrait combines the longing for home with the homecoming itself. * * *

* * *

In A Portrait, because Stephen exhibits the antithetical traits of Daedalus and Icarus in his two manifestations, the Daedalian narrator can present the young protagonist in the guise of an Icarus transforming himself into a Daedalus. Both Odysseus and Daedalus are homesick and homeward bound in their myths. At the end of A Portrait Stephen is outward bound, having determined to serve no longer. Stephen's decision to leave is necessarily connected for the reader to his act of keeping a journal, for the presentation of the journal signals Stephen's departure. But the keeping of the journal, which indicates the decision to write as well as to leave, is glossed by the epigraph. In order to write Stephen turns his mind to obscure arts, arts that lead him far from home, as Daedalus is lead far from home, but these arts inevitably bring him back to a home, not literally but literarily. The subject of the journal that ostensibly announces departure from home, like the subject of the book containing the journal, is home, as well as the displacements of wandering. For Joyce,

6. Ovid, Metamorphoses, trans. Rolfe Humphries (Bloomington: Indiana University Press, 1955), Book VIII, ll. 182–88, p. 187.

to turn the mind toward intricate arts is to look homeward. In the act of refusing to serve the home, the artist makes it possible for the home to serve him as the primary material for his art. Daedalus and Icarus, Sicily and Crete, Trieste and Dublin, 1914 and 1904, Stephen as teller and Stephen as character all merge in the book's oscillating focus. In *A Portrait* and later, the homeward look, no matter how intricately expressed in and as wanderings of style, involves a merging that occurs in the encounters of reader and teller and of reader and character. In Joyce's fiction the two encounters are not necessarily distinct.

The language of the one book casts two shadows, projects two images related by superimposition as in a palimpsest. The character who tells his own tale never writes on a tabula rasa. He always and inevitably displaces the past by erasing it and writing over the erasure, even when the writing constitutes a recapturing of the past as well as a displacing of it. Like Tristram Shandy and every other teller, Stephen Dedalus as writer can never capture himself or his own process of writing. He can only suggest the nature of the activity of writing as self-portrayal, as self-representation. The pretext for the narration given in the title, to portray a young, developing artist, precedes the reader's experience of the story. But the prior text for the character, the writing that precedes the text temporally in the character's experience, is the journal that is part of the book as well as prior to it. That journal allows the reader to redefine the narrative in a new frame of reference. By experiencing the earlier text as both behind the later one and within it, the reader can see through, as well as by means of, the story's pretense.

KAREN LAWRENCE

Gender and Narrative Voice in *Jacob's Room* and *A Portrait of the Artist as a Young Man*[†]

Both Virginia Woolf's *Jacob's Room* and James Joyce's *A Portrait of the Artist as a Young Man* are *Bildungsromane* that chronicle the development of young male protagonists and the effect of tradition upon them: Jacob Flanders and Stephen Dedalus struggle to find their place amid society's institutions. However, these novels of education

---

[†] From *James Joyce: The Centennial Symposium*, ed. Morris Beja et al. Urbana: U of Il P, 1986, 29–38. Copyright © 1986 by the Board of Trustees of the University of Illinois. Used with permission of the author and the University of Illinois Press. Information from the author's Works Cited list has been incorporated into her footnotes and combined with some of her parenthetical page references into new footnotes. Page references for *A Portrait* have been replaced with part and line numbers of this Norton Critical Edition. Some cited passages might differ slightly from the equivalent passages in this volume.

reveal something about not only the protagonist's relation to tradition, but the writer's as well, for the genre lends itself to treatment of the general problem of cultural inclusion and exclusion. The narrative strategies of the novels shed light on the writer's position in society and the effect of sex on that position.

In *A Room of One's Own*, Woolf comments on gender, tradition, and writing in a description of a fictitious visit to "Oxbridge" (her hybrid term for the two famous patriarchal academic institutions): "I thought how unpleasant it is to be locked out; and I thought how it is worse perhaps to be locked in; and, thinking of the safety and prosperity of the one sex and of the poverty and insecurity of the other and of the effect of tradition and of the lack of tradition upon the mind of a writer, I thought at last that it was time to roll up the crumpled skin of the day, with its arguments and its impressions and its anger and its laughter, and cast it into the hedge."[1] In *Jacob's Room*, Woolf thematizes the female artist's cultural exclusion by emphasizing the distance between the female narrator and male protagonist. Demonstrating that narrative authority is not a birthright, Woolf raises questions about legitimacy and authority as they pertain to the narrative act.

It should be acknowledged that in many ways both Joyce and Woolf eschew the traditional nineteenth-century form of the *Bildungsroman* in favor of a new kind of novel of education. To borrow Woolf's categories in her celebrated essay "Mr. Bennett and Mrs. Brown," both authors are "Georgian" rather than "Edwardian" writers.[2] They subvert certain thematic and formal conventions of the traditional nineteenth-century *Bildungsroman*. Both *A Portrait* and *Jacob's Room* end on a note of dispossession—the young sons of Ireland and England do not take up the mantles of their fathers. Stephen Dedalus renounces church and country; Jacob Flanders, who has lived in careless rather than rebellious relation to society's institutions, dies meaninglessly in World War I. Both novels, too, eschew the narrative continuity of traditional omniscience or first-person retrospection, providing instead a narrative with lacunae between the various experiences of the characters. Thus neither novel displays the epistemological security of the nineteenth-century form.

But despite the fact that in plot and style Joyce breaks with the traditional novel of education, he nevertheless accepts some of the premises of that form. First, he accepts what Edward Said has called the central element in the classical novel—the development of the "self " of the protagonist.[3] Joyce accepts the central notions of identity

---

1. Virginia Woolf, *A Room of One's Own* (New York: Harcourt Brace Jovanovich, 1929), 24.
2. Virginia Woolf, *Collected Essays* (London: Hogarth P, 1966), I: 319–37.
3. Edward Said, *Beginnings: Intention and Method* (New York: Basic Books, 1975), 141.

and vocation in the *Bildungsroman*: Stephen Dedalus has a calling. *A Portrait* moves in the direction of a goal (even if Stephen's aspirations are ironically deflated at times and we may question the greatness of his ultimate destination). Moments of revelation mark the stages of Stephen's journey toward identity, moments when he feels that the prophecy of his name coincides with events in the real world. The basic idea of growth and development, however problematic, is, nevertheless, ultimately accepted.[4]

Secondly, although Stephen rejects his biological father, he accepts the dynastic power of paternity. Stephen disowns Simon Dedalus only to invoke the power of the "old father, old artificer" Daedalus, whose legacy will in turn enable him to become the father of his race and "forge" its "uncreated conscience" (V.2789–91). Metaphors of paternity, inheritance, privilege, and authority are at the heart of the novel, charting Stephen's fundamental attempt to understand "himself, his name and where he was" (I.299). As Edmund Epstein says in his book *The Ordeal of Stephen Dedalus: The Conflict of Generations in James Joyce's "A Portrait of the Artist as a Young Man,"* the question of symbolic fatherhood is at the center of *A Portrait* and is related precisely to Stephen's destiny as an artist.[5] If paternity is a "legal fiction," as Stephen says in *Ulysses*, its power as fiction is not fundamentally doubted in *A Portrait*.

Such metaphors of authority and paternity pertain to the narrative as well as to the theme of the novel. As a recent critic has put it, *A Portrait* may be both the author's autobiographical fiction (the portrait of Joyce as a young man) and the autobiography of the fictional character, Stephen Dedalus. Either way, the relationship between narrator and protagonist can be described as paternal: the male narrator/author fathers forth the image of himself as a young man.[6] The close identification of narrator and protagonist is effected largely through the technique of free indirect discourse, which has certain important implications for the notion of narrative authority and privilege. As technically unobtrusive and withdrawn as he may appear, the narrator of *A Portrait* enjoys considerable authority: his

---

4. In their introduction to *The Voyage In: Fictions of Female Development*, ed. Elizabeth Abel et al. (Hanover, N.H.: UP of New England, 1983), the editors observe that although much modernist fiction has tended to call into question the primary assumptions underlying the traditional male *Bildungsroman*, the form is still perceived as viable for contemporary women writing about women (13). As I hope to show, in *Jacob's Room*, Woolf's unusual combination of male protagonist/female narrator radically subverts the underlying assumptions of the traditional form of the *Bildungsroman*.

5. (Carbondale: Southern Il UP, 1971), 7.

6. John Paul Riquelme, *Teller and Tale in Joyce's Fiction: Oscillating Perspectives* (Baltimore: Johns Hopkins UP, 1983), 51. Advancing the theory that Stephen is the narrator of *A Portrait*, Riquelme says that "Stephen fathers himself in language" (68). Whether one accepts this reading or the more traditional one that posits the work as Joyce's fictional autobiography, the paternal metaphor still applies.

voice is authorized to speak about Stephen; he claims, however implicitly, to have access to the thoughts, even the rhythms, of Stephen's mind. ("It was wrong; it was unfair and cruel: and, as he sat in the refectory, he suffered time after time in memory the same humiliation . . ." [I.1627–29].) What I speak of has less to do with questions of narrative attitude (e.g., ironic, sympathetic) than it concerns narrative privilege in relation to the main character. Although it may appear paradoxical to call such an unobtrusive narrator authoritative, as recent theorists have shown, narrative authority cannot be related simply to explicit intrusiveness; covert and unobtrusive narrators have their own style of power and authority. Like Stephen's "God of creation" who "remains within or behind or beyond or above his handiwork . . ." (V.1467–68), the narrator of *A Portrait* exercises power and privilege. He practices what Stephen himself only resolves to practice: "silence, exile, and cunning" (V.2579–80).[7]

In contrast to Joyce's treatment of the narrator/protagonist relationship, Woolf's narrative strategy and mode of characterization in *Jacob's Room* call into question the concepts of the male ego, patriarchal succession, and narrative power. Unlike Stephen Dedalus, Jacob Flanders is a mystery, in part because Woolf deliberately deprives us of much of his thought. Instead of Joyce's internal focus on the young protagonist, Woolf gives us very little of Jacob's interior life; we see him almost exclusively through the eyes of the narrator and other characters. If Stephen is a complicated and full, experiencing center of consciousness surrounded by "hollowsounding" (II.844) voices, Jacob is himself a blank surrounded by characters and a narrator whose main task is to try to interpret him. To paraphrase Stephen, Jacob himself may very well be the uncreated conscience of his race. Woolf has been criticized for her failure to create real characters in the novel, but the absence of this definitive male ego seems to me intentional. Throughout her works, Woolf subverts the stability of character, that "old stable ego" of which Lawrence, too, complained. As Maria DiBattista says in *Virginia Woolf's Major Novels: The Fables of Anon,* Woolf's work reflects a "critique of [the] presumptuous powers" found in earlier forms of narrative.[8] We can see this critique not only as modernist, but as feminist as well, for the world of the self is for Woolf patriarchal, the

---

7. In *The Narrative Act: Point of View in Prose Fiction* (Princeton: Princeton UP, 1981), Susan Sniader Lanser presents a "descriptive poetics of point of view," which, although somewhat overelaborate, does demonstrate that the components of narrative status and stance involve complex questions of power that are unaccounted for in traditional debates about the narrator's attitude. See chapter 4, in particular.

8. (New Haven: Yale UP, 1980), 21.

realm of the male. In part at least, Woolf's decision not to provide a traditional protagonist is a feminist gesture; to quote Jane Marcus, it is evidence of her "feminist attack on the ego as male false consciousness."[9]

Thus, in contrast to Stephen Dedalus, Jacob experiences no epiphanies, no rebellions, no real development in the course of the novel.[1] Unlike Stephen, he doesn't ask himself many questions about the purpose of life: "'What for? What for?' Jacob never asked himself any such questions, to judge by the way he laced his boots . . ."[2] The narrator's explanation for this lack of curiosity is striking: "He was young—a man" (161). The attributes that for Joyce help to certify Stephen as an interesting center of consciousness seem to disqualify Woolf's protagonist. Jacob is, the narrator tells us, "amiable, authoritative, beautifully healthy" (92), and somehow all this prevents him from being a sensitive interpreter of his surroundings.

Significantly, the main interpreter in this novel of education is a woman, ten years older than Jacob and, by virtue of her sex, excluded, as was Woolf, from the very kind of education he is free to obtain. After describing Jacob's face as he sees his girlfriend walk down the street with another man, the narrator says, "This was in his face. Whether we know what was in his mind is another question. Granted ten years' seniority and a difference of sex, fear of him comes first; this is swallowed up by a desire to help . . ." (94–95). The narrator is not a character in the drama of the plot, but the mixture of sarcasm and awe, resentment and solicitude in her tone, and the presence of rhetorical questions and sudden outbursts of self-reference indeed give her a distinct personality.

Unlike Joyce's cool and unobtrusive narrator, who shares Stephen's experiences, Woolf's narrator serves as a kind of voyeur of the male personality. Here is her description of Jacob at Cambridge: "The young men were now back in their rooms. Heaven knows what they were doing. What was it that could *drop* like

---

9. *New Feminist Essays on Virginia Woolf*, ed. Jane Marcus (Lincoln: U of Nebraska P, 1981), 9.

1. For a discussion of Woolf's "playful yet serious rebellion" against the traditional *Bildungsroman*, see Judy Little's very interesting essay "*Jacob's Room* as Comedy: Woolf's Parodic *Bildungsroman*" in *New Feminist Essays on Virginia Woolf*, ed. Jane Marcus (Lincoln: U of Nebraska P, 1981), 105. Little is very good on Woolf's ironic treatment of the conventions of the *Bildungsroman*, but I quarrel with her essay on three major points: she fails to distinguish Joyce's *A Portrait* from more traditional *Bildungsromane* and therefore slights Joyce's own brand of "rebellion" against the traditional form; she sees a good deal of identification between narrator and protagonist, whereas to me the gap between them is one of the most significant aspects of the novel; and, finally, I find that the word "comic" does not quite capture the tone of Woolf's attack, which sometimes seems more bitter than the "mild, even cheerful feminism" that Little describes.

2. Virginia Woolf, *Jacob's Room* (1922, rpt. Harcourt Brace Jovanovich, 1978), 161.

that?" (42); and, "Was it to receive this gift from the past that the young man came to the window and stood there, looking out across the court? It was Jacob" (45). Nose pressed to the window of that bastion of male privilege, the narrator speculates, chats, comments, all from an excluded position. Jacob's room is precisely the "room of one's own" disallowed to women; "If one is a woman," Woolf writes in *A Room of One's Own,* "one is often surprised by a sudden splitting off of consciousness, say in walking down Whitehall, when from being the natural inheritor of that civilisation, she becomes, on the contrary, outside of it, alien and critical" (101).

The relation between the female narrator and her young male protagonist embodies this splitting off of consciousness, this estrangement and alienation from tradition. Because we are given almost a physical image of the exclusion of the narrator from tradition, "locked out" of the room and, occasionally, the mind of her young male protagonist, technical terms like "narrative distance" and "point of view" take on added meaning. The female narrator's cultural exclusion and aesthetic distance converge, as sexuality creates a gap between character and narrator. "Then consider the effect of sex," the narrator advises us at one point, "how between man and woman it hangs wavy, tremulous, so that here's a valley, there's a peak, when in truth, perhaps, all's as flat as my hand. Even the exact words get the wrong accent on them" (73). Through irony, Joyce's narrator keeps some distance from Stephen, who, in turn, exiles himself from his society, but Woolf's female narrator is already estranged from the tradition she describes *and* the young man who should inherit the privileges of that tradition. Indeed, images of exclusion recur in Woolf's writing, whether in the form of Miss Latrobe, the artist in *Between the Acts,* who hides behind the bushes while her play is presented, or the speaker in *A Room of One's Own,* who is told to keep off the grass, an admonition that reflects larger issues of cultural interdiction, or Lily Briscoe [in *To the Lighthouse*], feeling, as she paints her picture, that she is positioned "on the fringe of the lawn" which is "the world."

Thus, in *Jacob's Room,* Woolf translates female cultural exclusion into a narrative principle. Unlike the restrained but powerful narrator in *A Portrait,* Woolf's narrator overtly abdicates her power. She offers disclaimers, reservations, even retractions. After describing Jacob's appearance, she says "but surely, of all futile occupations this of cataloging features is the worst. One word is sufficient. But if one cannot find it?" (71). And after interpreting Jacob's expression at one point, she retracts her analysis: "But whether this is the right interpretation of Jacob's gloom . . . it is impossible to say; for he never spoke a word" (49). Through her female narrator, Woolf deliberately limits narrative hegemony and the godlike powers of the Joycean narrator.

This reduction of narrative authority is, I think, a strategy to circumvent and expose the pitfalls of the egotism of traditional narration. Instead of the filiality of narrator and protagonist, we find the gap of sexuality, and admittedly fallible observation replaces the knowledge of the protagonist's every thought. In part this may be a bid for a greater realism, a way of writing that acknowledges human fallibility and the enigma of personality. Certainly, Woolf's other novels return to this theme of the mysteriousness of human personality—we can't write about other people definitively because in life we can't really know anyone else. But the self-conscious abdication of authority suggests a further purpose here: an experiment with a feminine alternative to egotistical narration, a transformation of cultural exclusion into an aesthetic boon. The language of gesture Woolf develops in the novel creates a dramatic perspective; exclusion from Jacob's mind forces us to develop our skills of observation and to learn to read a face or gesture, without the privileged access sanctioned by tradition and gender. For Woolf, the other side of female exclusion is the freedom of imagination that comes with being "locked out."

Woolf's deliberate renunciation of power, however, is not, to my mind, her most successful alternative to "egotistical narration." I prefer the wonderfully fluid narration in *Mrs. Dalloway* and *To the Lighthouse,* which does allow privileged entry into the minds of the main characters *and* avoidance of the egotistical narrative self. In her essay "The Narrow Bridge of Art," Woolf alludes to this possibility of access without the arrogance that sometimes accompanies such privilege. She describes the possibilities for prose in the novel of the future, a novel which "will clasp to its breast the precious prerogatives of the democratic art of prose; its freedom, its fearlessness, its flexibility. For prose is so humble that it can go anywhere; no place is too low, too sordid, or too mean for it to enter. It is infinitely patient, too, humbly acquisitive. It can . . . listen silently at doors behind which only a murmur, only a whisper, is to be heard. With all the suppleness of a tool which is in constant use it can follow the windings and record the changes which are typical of the modern mind."[3] In novels like *Mrs. Dalloway* and *To the Lighthouse,* an incarnation occurs in the narrative; consciousness slips in and out of the minds of multiple characters and, thus, inclusion rather than exclusion predominates—our sense of the mystery of personality results from our exposure to the complexity of character rather than our exclusion from interior views. It is the richness, ambiguity,

3. Virginia Woolf, *Granite and Rainbow* (London: Hogarth P, 1958), 20.

and depth of a Mrs. Ramsay that make her remain a mystery, despite our access to her thoughts.[4]

Nevertheless, the narrative distance between male character and female narrator in *Jacob's Room* provides a fascinating version of the female writer's estrangement from patriarchal tradition. Perhaps the best emblem within the novel for the marginality of female writing, and a good contrast to Stephen's view of the male "God of creation" "within or behind . . . his handiwork," is the letter Jacob's mother writes to her son. It sits unopened on his desk outside the bedroom where he and his girlfriend make love. Although the narrator cites some male writers who have "addressed themselves to the task of reaching, touching, penetrating the individual heart" in letters (93), she identifies these more private, unofficial messages primarily with women. "Poor Betty Flanders' letter" (87), the narrator says, and goes on to describe letters as "the unpublished works of women, written in pale profusion." Within this published novel written by a woman, given over to a female narrator, Woolf reminds us that female writing is often excluded from centers of male power.

Of course, it might be argued that women are not the only ones excluded from power; it is true that Joyce regarded the Irishman as the "servant" of two masters, England and Rome. As he listens to the English dean of studies, Stephen Dedalus thinks, "the language in which we are speaking is his before it is mine" (V.553–54). Woolf and Joyce shared a sense of exclusion from the dominant English culture—an Irishman and an Englishwoman are both second-class citizens vis-à-vis British patriarchy. However, in *A Portrait*, Joyce had not yet begun to question certain central patriarchal ideas. It is not until *Ulysses* and *Finnegans Wake* that he mounts a more radical attack on the notions of privilege, authority, and identity, and the whole notion of fathering forth or authoring a text.[5] Also, the types

4. It is not simply that Woolf gives up representing the inner lives of men. Interestingly, she does portray male consciousness in subsequent novels where the male mind is somehow linked closely to an equally dominant female consciousness. The protagonist in *Orlando*, whose consciousness is recorded by the narrator, metamorphoses from male to female; Septimus Smith in *Mrs. Dalloway* is, as Woolf herself remarked, a "double" for Clarissa; and Bernard, Louis, and Neville in *The Waves* provide the male counterparts to the female chorus of Susan, Jinny, and Rhoda. No longer opaque to narrative scrutiny, the male mind in these novels is presented from the inside as a part of the androgynous consciousness.
5. In a fine essay entitled "Polytropic Man: Paternity, Identity and Naming in *The Odyssey* and *A Portrait of the Artist as a Young Man*," Maud Ellmann suggests that the ultimate authority of paternity is, in fact, disputed in *A Portrait* and claims that the novel is "omphalocentric." While her individual discussions of certain images are fascinating (for example, her treatment of the word "Foetus" carved in a school desk), nevertheless, the dominant metaphors for artistic creation and for the development of the protagonist seem to me overwhelmingly male-centered (i.e., the "priest of the eternal imagination") and, for the most part, patriarchal. See *James Joyce: New Perspectives*, ed. Colin MacCabe (Bloomington: Indiana UP, 1982), 73–104. For a discussion of Joyce's subversion of the patriarchal in *Ulysses*, see Karen Lawrence, "Paternity: The Legal Fiction," in Weldon Thornton and Robert Newman, eds., *Joyce's "Ulysses": The Larger Perspective* (U of Delaware P, 1987).

of rebellion against society waged by Joyce and Woolf in *A Portrait* and *Jacob's Room* are very different: Woolf felt oppressed by institutions that tried to lock her out; Joyce (as well as Stephen) felt oppressed by institutions that sought to include him. In fact, Stephen's sense that his artistic consciousness is preempted by the patriarchal institutions seeking to include him sheds some light on Woolf's ability to make the position of marginality a creative source. The different narrative strategies and treatments of patriarchal tradition in *Jacob's Room* and *A Portrait* reflect, in part at least, differences in the writers' perceptions of sexual privileges and burdens.

MAUD ELLMANN

Disremembering Dedalus:
A Portrait of the Artist as a Young Man†

A stranger once came up to Joyce in a café and cried, "Let me kiss the hand that wrote *Ulysses!*" Joyce promptly replied, "It's done a lot of other things too." In *A Portrait of the Artist as a Young Man*, a thought occurs to Stephen which seems, curiously, to anticipate this joke without—for the thinker—being jokey:

> If ever his soul, re-entering her dwelling shyly after the frenzy of his body's lust had spent itself, was turned towards her whose emblem is the morning star, *bright and musical, telling of heaven and infusing peace,* it was when her names were murmured softly by lips whereon there still lingered foul and shameful words, the savour itself of a lewd kiss. (III.116–21)

What appalls Stephen—as it amuses Joyce—is the way lust and language may converge in a single bodily member. The hand, in the one case, and the lips, in the other, are stained by their intimacy. These organs are puns in bad taste. They betray, between the text and sexuality, an intercourse more cunning than a rhyme.

How, then, can these members remember? Among the things the hand that wrote *Ulysses* did was to write *A Portrait of the Artist*. In fact, it wrote three portraits of him: a first draft, whose rejection

---

† From *Untying the Text: A Post-Structuralist Reader*, ed. Robert Young. Boston and London: Routledge & Kegan Paul, 1981, 189–206. Used by permission of the editor. The author's "Further Reading" list has been omitted. Some of the author's notes have been omitted. Page references have been replaced with part and line numbers of this Norton Critical Edition. Some cited passages might differ slightly from the equivalent passages in this volume.

gave rise to *Stephen Hero* and to what we regard, teleologically,[1] as the final text. As for this last version, the indefinite article of its title suggests that it, too, may represent yet another Wordsworthian preparation to write.[2] It is *a* portrait, not *The Portrait*. At first, a repetition of the author's life, Joyce's autobiography seems henceforth destined to repeat itself. What can it be about self-portraiture, for Joyce as for Wordsworth, that makes them so reluctant to conclude?

To account, in the case of *The Prelude,* for the growth of a poet's mind, Wordsworth must read his own life backwards. Through memory, he must retrieve the seeds from which—organically speaking—the poem and the mind that wrote it grew. If memory is constructed in the present, the past, as such, can never be recovered. So we behold, in autobiography, a paradoxical procedure by which memory writes the past to discover how the past wrote and determined memory. In this sense, the autobiographer decomposes the present that the past composed: unwrites the hand that writes. Remembering becomes dismembering: or more precisely, "disremembering"—to borrow Davin's Irishism from *A Portrait* ["disremember," V.273]. It is to forget oneself—in the most indiscreet ways.

If *A Portrait* borrows from *The Prelude* any model of the poet's mind, it is not the metaphor of growth. Rather it is Wordsworth's notion of "spot of time" that fascinates the text. "Islands in the unnavigable depth of our departed time": the spot of time, which Wordsworth seems to use to mean a space, or place, or interlude, includes, among a plethora of definitions, the idea of a blemish, stain, or scar. And indeed, it is a scar which hollows out the "spot" in the Gibbet-Mast episode of Wordsworth's autobiography: the scar that remains of an identity.[3] This scar is the name of a murderer. Neither the name, nor the hand that carved it, is disclosed: all that the passage intimates is the act of cutting it and its indelibility. Naming is maiming. "To this hour," the text insists, the letters, "carved by some unknown hand," are "all still fresh and visible." *A Portrait*, too, as I shall try to show, conceives identity as a scar without an author, without an origin, and at last, without even a name. And this identity is a wound that constantly re-opens, so that its letters may remain "all fresh and visible."

It is important, however, to stress that *A Portrait* is not "about" a scar. To say that the text is "about" something reinstitutes the polarity of content and form which Joyce's writing constantly stretches and transgresses. Daedalus's labyrinth lurks in *A Portrait*'s imagery

1. From the perspective of the result, which seems, retrospectively, to have been intended [Editor].
2. In the mode of the English poet William Wordsworth (1770–1850), whose autobiographical, posthumously published poem *The Prelude* concerns his preparation to create poetry, including *The Prelude* [Editor].
3. *The Prelude* (1805), XI, 278–316.

as if to halt us in our hermeneutics.[4] For the secret of a labyrinth is only the way out, whereas I, for one, am looking for a way in. The scar is not a secret, but a principle of structure: a punctuation. Because it is a living scar, it constantly resurges and reiterates itself. And the signification of the text is lodged in the very blanks and repetitions that mark and mask its cicatrix. For the scar belongs not only to the subject but to the text itself, which both suffers and enacts the mutilation by which identity reconstitutes itself. Purloined letters, the lacunae of the narrative—its scars—are hidden only in that they are too blatant to be seen. Rather than the secret of *A Portrait*, the scar insinuates itself as a secretion: a word which describes at once the operations of hoarding, fission, and emission which undo the fixity of identity and hyphenate autobiography.

In this essay I shall pursue the notion of identity as process: in fact, as a series of processes, which *A Portrait* joins in a "brisure." "Brisure," which I borrow from Derrida,[5] encompasses the ambiguities of "cleaving" in the sense of splitting, and "cleaving" in the sense of joining or embracing. So in translation let's enflesh brisure by calling it a cleavage.

One process that proceeds from the cleavage of identity consists of scarrification. This has two sides, which could be described as nomination and punctuation. In the act of nomination, word is stained with flesh and flesh with word, for the name, like the name of Wordsworth's "murderer," emerges in this text as a cicatrix. Once named and maimed, the subject, rather than a plenitude, erupts henceforth as punctuation, as a gap or wound that rips the fabric of the text at irregular intervals.

Punctuation)   (repeats
)   SCAR   (
)   (
Nomination)   (secretes

Both aspects of scarrification make themselves felt in the fourth section of Chapter 2 (II.946–1275), the trip to Cork, which I shall take as a point of departure.

But we know the scar only by its secretion: by that which issues from and enters into it. What proceeds from scarrification is circulation: and *A Portrait* sets in motion a complex circulation of sexual and textual economies. The diagram will suggest, inevitably, a schematic rigidity: but if we keep in mind that each overlaps and

4. Theory and method of interpretation, though here referring to the act of interpretation [Editor].
5. Jacques Derrida (1930–2004), Algerian-born French philosopher and founder of deconstruction, which explores how meaning comes into being [Editor].

overleaps the others, to abstract them in this way may help us to discern their furious rhythm.

Circulation occurs in three forms, each of which involves the linguistic and corporeal equivalents that I have listed, respectively under WORD and FLESH. Each also corresponds to the strategies of disremembering that constitute the subject of autobiography.

SEXUAL/TEXTUAL ECONOMIES

	ECONOMY	FLESH	WORD
MARKET PLACE	1 Flows	dismembering emission	synecdoche
	2 Influence	remembering incorporation	metaphor or tautology
LITERATURE	3 "Detaining" Hoarding	retention chastity	lacunae and the "literal"

The first is an economy of flows, whereby the subject purges or evacuates himself, and issues forth in all kinds of secretions.

> His sins trickled from his lips, one by one, trickled in shameful drops from his soul, festering and oozing like a sore, a squalid stream of vice. The last sins oozed forth, sluggish, filthy. (III.1504–07)

Semen, blood, urine, breath, money, saliva, speech and excrement provide the currencies for this economy. Menstruation also figures among these flows, for the text at this level (though not at others) is as indifferent to gender as to the formal separation of excrement and sexuality. Not to mention vomit, which is a perpetual danger in this text—not only for Stephen but for his reader. Rhetorically, the economy of flows corresponds to the trope of synecdoche—the part for the whole—for through these flows, any notion of totality disintegrates, and the subject is dispersed into the fragments and the waste that stand for him.

What passes out of Stephen must, however, first pass into him. So, working in tandem with the rhythm of his flows is an economy of influence. Food, particularly the bread and wine of the Eucharist, figures in this economy, but on the whole it is Stephen's nose, rather than his mouth, that opens him to influence.

The odours that so besiege our hero's nose are more frequently noxious than sweet. In fact, they are the odours of mortality: of dead flesh, and, as I shall show, dead speech. The worst stench of all is that of writing—dead speech stored in literature—which passes into Stephen through his nose and passes through his mouth as speech again. So, "influence" retains its literary implications: Stephen inhales the literary tradition and re-members it in his secretions.

This transaction with the past resembles the Eucharist, which changes spirit into wine, until at last—as Mulligan [in *Ulysses*] mischievously adds—the wine becomes water again. It compares also to the other conversions which enthrall the text: of money into goods, lust into language, peristalsis into metre, or the gross earth into art. And vice versa. Trans-substantiation and digestion meet as the loci of metaphor. But Stephen's own transactions with influence tend to conclude, as we shall see, not in metaphor, but in repetition and tautology.

"Literature" is the name that Stephen gives to the third economy, the economy of hoarding. This baptism occurs in the context of a conversation with the English dean:

> —One difficulty, said Stephen, in aesthetic discussion is to know whether words are being used according to the literary tradition or according to the tradition of the marketplace. I remember a sentence of Newman's in which he says of the Blessed Virgin that she was detained in the full company of the saints. The use of the word in the marketplace is quite different. *I hope I am not detaining you.*
> —Not in the least, said the dean politely.
> —No, no, said Stephen, smiling, I mean . . .
> —Yes, yes: I see, said the dean quickly, I quite catch the point: detain. (V.494–504)

In this conversation, the word "detain" itself becomes "literature" when it elicits no response. "Detain," of course, is not unlike "retain" except, importantly, that its implications are less absolute. "Literature" consists of words and flesh detained, held back, withdrawn for a time from circulation. In opposition to the marketplace of flow and influence, literature detains language as the miser hoards his money and the petulant infant withholds what Lacan[6] calls his "gift of shit." Nor is it by accident that it is Mary, in this passage, who is detained: for her chastity also represents a form of hoarding. Speech in storage, "literature" functions as hiatus, blocking the exchange of word for flesh and flesh for words. Literature—to borrow a word from *Dubliners*—is the paralysis of language.

Stephen's proclaimed aesthetic of "silence, exile, and cunning" seems, like "scrupulous meanness,"[7] to bespeak the linguistic avarice of "literature." His *Portrait* too practises a politics of "detaining," hoarding words in the transcendentalised retentions of epiphany.

6. Jacques Lacan (1901–1981), French psychiatrist and psychoanalytic theorist, who reinterpreted and extended the work of Sigmund Freud (1856–1939), the founder of psychoanalysis [Editor].
7. Joyce's phrase describing the style of *Dubliners* (*Letters of James Joyce*, Vol. II, ed. Richard Ellmann. New York: Viking, 1966, 36) [Editor].

These occulted episodes erupt as blank spots in the narrative. In their very literality they refuse to flow, to undergo the exchange and transformation of synecdoche or metaphor.

But withdrawing words from circulation can bring about only a temporary pause, before the text embezzles them in new transactions. In the passage I shall presently discuss, the word "Foetus," paralysed as "literature," surreptitiously, and with explosive implications, reinfiltrates the text's economies. But before we embark on these semantics, let's survey the text's whole economic policy.

A capitalist economy operates by withdrawing funds from circulation in order, paradoxically, for money and commodities to circulate at all. All these economies depend upon the hoarding of the bank vault and the interest racket. Thus, in *A Portrait,* words and flesh take the place of money and commodities, and "literature" or hoarding mischievously completes the cycle of a capitalist economy in miniature.

I now turn to the further section of Chapter 2 (II.946–1275), which will provide a paradigm for the procedures of disremembering. Nomination, punctuation, and all the sexual and textual economies work their commerce here. What is more, the section represents an autobiography within an autobiography: for it describes Simon Dedalus's sentimental journey to his origins in Cork, and his struggle to remember his fugitive history. His nostalgia reaches its climax in the search for his own initials, carved as indelibly as the name of Wordsworth's "murderer" in the dark stained wood of a school desk.

But another scar precedes these initials, and in a sense pre-empts them: the word "Foetus," which I alluded to before, whose carved letters move Stephen to a horror as extreme as it is unexplained.

While the father's rehearsals of his past, and his excavation of his name, seem to represent a repossession of identity, the brute material motive of the journey belies his sentiment. For he returns to his origins only to sell them away. He is to auction his belongings, and to dispossess himself and his resentful son. Remembering reverts to disremembering.

Duplicity, indeed, begins with the opening sentence of the section.

> Stephen was once again seated beside his father in the corner
> of a railway carriage at Kingsbridge. (II.946–47)

"Once again" is a curious sleight of hand: Stephen has never shared a railway carriage with his father in the text before. This is a first time masquerading as a repetition. It recalls the first sentence of the whole autobiography: "Once upon a time and a very good time it was," where the first time turns out to be the beginning not of

Stephen's story, but of a story told to Stephen by his father. The trip to Cork is also an episode in which Stephen's story grafts itself upon his father's story, and they compete for autobiographies. We begin to suspect some relation between the father and false starts; and to suspect, perhaps, the very notion of beginning.

But some form of recollection is taking place here, which prevents the "once again" from startling us. In the second half of the paragraph, the reader undergoes a repetition:

> He saw the darkening lands slipping away past him, the silent telegraph poles passing his window swiftly every four seconds, the little glimmering stations, manned by a few silent sentries, flung by the mail behind her and twinkling for a moment in the darkness like fiery grains thrust backwards by a runner. (II.951–55)

This passage does not repeat a real event, but a dream that Stephen had at Clongowes:

> The train was full of fellows: a long long chocolate train with cream facings. The guards went to and fro opening, closing, locking, unlocking the doors. They were men in dark blue and silver; they had silvery whistles and their keys made a quick music: click, click: click, click.
>
> And the train raced on over the flat lands and past the Hill of Allen. The telegraph poles were passing, passing. The train went on and on. It knew. (I.465–72)

Just as the beginning of Stephen's story is another story, so here the real train evolves out of the dream. This order makes a fiction of experience.

What the reader undergoes, through the repetition of the dream-sequence, is the constitution of his own memory. The logic of repetition works backward in this text: the second episode reverts upon the first, and modifies its structure and its sense. In other words, it takes the second episode to activate the scar left by the first. This, perhaps, is why the text cannot begin. By the same strategy of repetition, text and reader are deprived of their originality. Like the autobiographer himself, we as readers are forced to read backwards: we, too, are disremembering.

We recall that the autobiographer must unwrite the present in order to write the past. These two passages capture the moment when remembering reverses into disremembering: when the present "passes" into memory and the past "presents" itself as desire. They enact the very process of "passing," a word invested in *A Portrait* with multiple reverberations, and which repeats itself insistently in these two homecomings:

> The telegraph poles were passing, passing. (I.471)

> He saw the darkening lands slipping away past him, the silent
> telegraph poles passing his window swiftly every four seconds.
> (II.951–52)

The two journeys themselves do not precisely represent events, but
passages between events: interstices between the present and the
past. They have no content: none, that is, but the passing and the
missing of a content: the landscape that slips past, and the stations
and the sentries flung behind. This train not only passes by content
but passes it out, evacuates and disremembers it. All that remains is
a wake: the trail of fiery flakes thrust backwards as by a runner.

*   *   *

What's left, then, of the subject after all this "passing," all this
evacuation? In the course of disremembering, a different kind of
subject emerges from the text: different, and radically opposed to
the tradition of the human subject and to the orthodox conception
of the subject matter of a text. The subject erupts as punctuation. As
the silence woven into music, the absence woven into vision: as the
pulsation of the unconscious. * * *

This punctuation establishes itself even prior to the dream at
Clongowes, in a series of what we might call ontological experiments:

> He leaned his elbows on the table and shut and opened the
> flaps of his ears. Then he heard the noise of the refectory every
> time he opened the flaps of his ears. It made a roar like a train
> at night. And when he closed the flaps the roar was shut off like
> a train going into a tunnel. * * * (I.223–28)

Is Stephen shutting the world out of himself, or himself out of the
world? This game reverts upon the player. While he seems to be mastering the world, controlling its presence and its absence, the child is
establishing his own intermittency, his own punctuation. This fiction uncreates the fabricator.

The punctuation of the earflap game gradually accrues to itself a
number of semantic oppositions which invest it with a form of rep-
resentability.

> First came the vacation and then the next term and then vaca-
> tion again and then again another term and then again the
> vacation. It was like a train going in and out of tunnels and that
> was like the noise of boys eating in the refectory when you
> opened and closed the flaps of the ears. Term, vacation; tunnel,
> out; noise, stop. How far away it was! (I.349–55)

Each time the scar recurs, it amalgamates another binarism. Now its punctuation leans upon the oppositions of in and out, home and school, vacation and term, and the train that enters and emerges from the tunnel, with its sudden roar. These alternatives articulate the scar, and constitute a bank of representatives to be embezzled by the dream.

Later in the book, the sermon seems to parody this process of accretion, when the priest gathers compound interest on the words "ever never":

> * * * and it seemed to this saint that the sound of the ticking was the ceaseless repetition of the words: ever, never; ever, never. Ever to be in hell, never to be in heaven; ever to be shut off from the presence of God, never to enjoy the beatific vision; ever to be eaten with flames, gnawed by vermin, goaded with burning spikes, never to be free from those pains; ever to have the conscience upbraid one, the memory enrage, the mind filled with darkness and despair, never to escape; ever to curse and revile the foul demons who gloat fiendishly over the misery of their dupes, never to behold the shining raiment of the blessed spirits. (III.1091–102)

Et cetera. This is the rhythm of exile from the sight of God; the music of mortality. Reading backwards—as the text demands—we can see that the former alternations also involve an ostracism: the punctuation and its representatives all bespeak Stephen's exile from home, and his desire to return to origins. Confounding the journey home with the ticking of eternity, this rhythm links the end to the beginning, staining with mortality the search for origins. And we too, reading backwards in pursuit of a first time—a return to origins—we, too, are caught in its furious music.

As punctuation, the subject is never fully present, but is always either coming into, or dying out of, being. "Coming" and "dying": both are orgasmic: and the rhythm of exile also resembles a "frottage."[8] The furious music of the train passes through Stephen to die in an "ejaculation." Most of Stephen's verses "come" in this way. He vacillates between two states described habitually as "unrest" and "weariness" (II.167, II.532–33, II.623, III.37), broken by ejaculations. This brings us to the first of the textual economies: the economy of flows.

Like the landscape that passes by Stephen on the train, passing out of him in foolish words, verses, throughout the book, associate themselves consistently with the circuitous itinerary of the verb "to pass":

8. Rubbing (French) [Editor].

> Such moments passed and the wasting fires of lust sprang up
> again. The verses passed from his lips and the inarticulate cries
> and the unspoken brutal words rushed forth from his brain to
> force a passage. (II.1392–95)

Lust, for the hand that wrote *Ulysses*, passes incessantly through language, staining flesh with words and words with flesh. The two can
scarcely be distinguished. No more can they detach themselves from
any other form of passing or evacuation. The streams and floods
which pass from Stephen's lips could be urethral, or menstrual, as
well as seminal: breath, blood, vomit and saliva also issue from this
orifice in the form of speech:

> * * * It broke from him like a wail of despair from a hell of suf-
> ferers and died in a wail of furious entreaty, a cry for an iniquitous
> abandonment, a cry which was but the echo of an obscene scrawl
> which he had read on the oozing wall of a urinal. (II.1409–13)

This cry is in the strictest sense a dirty word. It is a matter of indifference to the metaphor whether it "passes" or it "comes" from
Stephen's lips. A movement—orgasmic, bowel, or urethral—releases
it to die into a wail: to ooze into an echo of a scar on the wall of a
urinal. The subject's body is a mint which issues him in wakes,
trails, fragments and secretions. "Issue," a word the text relishes as
much as "passing," may be applied to publication, currency, or generation: and all the flows which "issue" from the subject constitute
the means by which he duplicates, or publishes, or coins himself.
These secretions—verbal or corporeal—invisibly depart, and enter
henceforth into circulation.

Everything that "passes" through Stephen's consciousness "issues"
forth emptied or dismembered. In one of his attempts at poetry:

> * * * The verses told only of the night and the balmy breeze
> and of the maiden lustre of the moon. Some undefined sorrow
> was hidden in the hearts of the protagonists as they stood in
> silence beneath the leafless trees. . . . After this the letters
> L.D.S. were written at the foot of the page. (II.382–88)

Only the initials at the end of this verse receive direct quotation, as
Stephen, earlier, had halted, blocked, at the initials of its dedication
(II.362). Apart from these detained letters ("literature") the passage
offers a paralyptical[9] account of the content of the verses: or rather, of
the voiding of their content. Also without content are the letters of a
different kind—epistles—which emerge as frequently from Stephen's
failures in verse:

9. Indirect [Editor].

> * * * But his brain had then refused to grapple with the theme
> and, desisting, he had covered the page with the names and
> addresses of certain of his classmates. (II.370–72)

These are letters that are never sent.

Both forms of reduction to the letter occur in the following
passage:

> He could scarcely interpret the letters of the signboards of the
> shops. By his monstrous way of life he seemed to have put him-
> self beyond the limits of reality. . . . He could scarcely recognise
> as his his own thoughts, and repeated slowly to himself:—I am
> Stephen Dedalus. I am walking beside my father whose name is
> Simon Dedalus. We are in Cork, in Ireland. Cork is a city. Our
> room is in the Victoria Hotel. (II.1142–54)

As well as the words he writes, the words Stephen reads are constantly disintegrating into a debris of letters. And he responds by
composing a letter to himself: his name and his address, without a
message. This is the art of disremembering.

An art of living. Just as the word is shattered into letters, so the
flesh decomposes into an inventory of its members and secretions.
Other people Stephen apprehends as voices, faces, eyes, hands,
clothes, glances, or footsteps. The woman he desires, for instance,
he perceives as breath, a glance, and the tapping of shoes:

> Her glance travelled to his corner, flattering, taunting, search-
> ing, exciting his heart . . . sprays of her fresh warm breath flew
> gaily above her cowled head and her shoes tapped blithely on
> the glassy road. (II.315–21)

The text, however, demolishes the flesh fastidiously. Here it reduces
the woman's body specifically to its exchange values. Not just any
parts are itemised, but the parts that issue forth in circulation. The
face, the gaze, the footstep and the voice represent the currency
through which the subject enters the economies of flow and influence.

But the text does not halt at mere dismemberment. The face, the
gaze, the footstep and the voice degenerate into images and echoes
of themselves. This is how, for instance, its rhetoric mutilates the
director:

> Stephen smiled again in answer to the smile he could not see
> on the priest's shadowed face, its image or spectre only passing
> rapidly across his mind as the low discreet accent fell upon his
> ear. (IV.285–88)

These are smiles of the order of the Cheshire cat. In this reverse
apotheosis, the priest dematerialises, leaving in his wake a trace in

Stephen's consciousness: an image or a spectre of an accent and a smile.

There seems to be no agency apart from consciousness that could assume responsibility for the priest's explosion. Yet Stephen's consciousness appears to be the victim of the fall-out too. His own gestures are not precisely self-determined actions, but mimetically return the images projected from the priest. Blinded by the shadows—which also are projections of the interlocutors—Stephen answers, rather than broaches, the first smile, whose image passes of its own accord across his mind, while the disembodied accent falls upon his passive ear. Both parties to this dialogue reflect, refract, and echo one another: each is the other's mirror, and the subject but the speculation of the object, in a triple sense. Dismembering reverts upon the disrememberer.

It is through an ambush of synecdoche that Emma Clery and the priest disintegrate into their exchange values. But it is also by means of this dismemberment that either gains admission to Stephen's consciousness as an "image." So that synecdoche represents a kind of rhetorical chewing which prepares experience for ingustation. This second process takes us into the domain of metaphor; or in fleshly terms, into the economy of influence. Flow and influence constantly converge, however, in that Stephen's overflows, spontaneous as they may be, are always derived from a previous source. Many of his verses are only paraphrased: but those few that the text vouchsafes directly tend to be quotations. Even the word "weariness," which terminates his feelings of "unrest," is recycled from Shelley and Ben Jonson (II.1269, III.37, V.86).[1] Or else "the soft speeches of Claude Melnotte" rise to his lips to "ease his unrest" (II.1386–87). Even Stephen's dirty word is the echo of the graffitto in the urinal, where the wake of language—writing—is stained by urine, the wake of the flesh. Every word that "passes" out of Stephen originates in "literature": from whence its stench conducts it to his nose, and issues henceforth from his lips. While the dirty word reeks of excrement, the legends in shop windows which confront him later stink of mortality:

> * * * every mean shop legend bound his mind like the words of a spell and his soul shrivelled up, sighing with age as he walked on in a lane among heaps of dead language. His own consciousness of language was ebbing from his brain and trickling into the very words themselves which set to band and disband themselves in wayward rhythms:

---

1. Percy Bysshe Shelley (1792–1822), English Romantic poet. Ben Jonson (1572–1637), English poet and dramatist [Editor].

> The ivy whines upon the wall,
> And whines and twines upon the wall,
> The yellow ivy on the wall,
> Ivy, ivy up the wall.

> Did anyone ever hear such drivel? Lord Almighty! Who ever heard of ivy whining on a wall? (V.169–81)

This is the smell of dead language. It is the smell of words which have been heaped up in mean shop legends: withdrawn from circulation and hoarded in writing. These words, like flesh, disintegrate in Stephen's consciousness into meaningless concatenations. He cannot help but absorb their deadly exhalations and pass them out again—in "drivel."

This passage, then, unfolds the interactions of all three economies: the "flow" of drivel; the "influence" of mortal odours; and the dead language, the "literature" which occasions these deferred effects. To complete the disremembering of Dedalus, we have only now to see how the letters of his name—his founding "literature"—also constitute, with their deferred effects, a cicatrix.

So, by this "commodious vicus of recirculation,"[2] we return to Cork. Stephen, now, is trying to track down the initials that stand for his father's name—and also, incidentally, his own:

> * * * On the desk he read the word "Foetus" cut several times in the dark stained wood. The sudden legend startled his blood: he seemed to feel the absent students of the college about him and to shrink from their company. A vision of their life, which his father's words had been powerless to evoke, sprang up before him out of the word cut in the desk. * * *
> Stephen's name was called. He hurried down the steps of the theatre so as to be as far away from the vision as he could be and, peering closely at his father's initials, hid his flushed face. (II.1049–55, 1060–62)

Concerned as this passage is with spotting, it also functions as a blank spot in the narrative. It remains, like the legend of the desk, unalterably literal: no trope can induce it into circulation. Neither Stephen, nor the reader, nor the text, can incorporate the word "Foetus," which erupts so inexplicably.

What the passage emphasises most about these letters is the act of cutting them. Like a scar, and like the dead letters in shop windows, this literature administers deferred effects. Clearly, it is not just a word that we are dealing with, but a wound: an old wound, indeed, that Stephen activates in reading it. He responds with an

---

2. James Joyce, *Finnegans Wake*. New York: Viking Press, 1939, 3.2. "Vicus" suggests, among other meanings, a road [Editor].

hallucination: he feels himself surrounded by the absent students who once scarred the desk with this uncanny legend. This word, unlike the father's memories, can resurrect the dead.

By two strategies, then, this word usurps the father's place: it emerges where the father's name should be; and it summons up a vision of the dead which his father's words—thinks Stephen—had been "powerless to evoke." But the initials that the word pre-empts are also the initials of Stephen Dedalus.

That the initials of the name of the father should present themselves as a scar is thinkable within a psychoanalytic frame of reference. In "Moses and Monotheism," Freud[3] connects the scar of circumcision to the patronym; and Lacan uses the term "Name of the Father" as a synonym for the Law of Castration. For the psychoanalytic critic, it is almost wearisome to find that SD has been made into a wound. But why, in this account of things, should another word achieve priority, and an earlier scar forestall the laceration of the name? And why is this word "Foetus"?

Why, if not because this first scar is a navel, to which the Foetus is, of course, attached? Attached, not to the father's name, but to the mother's namelessness? Why the horror, if not because the phallus has surrendered to the omphalos?[4]

In another autobiography, *The Interpretation of Dreams,* Freud's heuristics direct him to the navel as ineluctably as those of his Irish namesake:[5]

> There is often a passage in even the most thoroughly interpreted dream which has to be left obscure; this is because we become aware during the work of interpretation that at that point there is a tangle of dream-thoughts which cannot be unravelled and which moreover adds nothing to our knowledge of the content of the dream. This is the dream's navel, the spot where it reaches down into the unknown. The dream-thoughts to which we are led by interpretation cannot from the nature of things have any definite endings; they are bound to branch out in every direction into the intricate network of our world of thought. It is at some point where this meshwork is particularly close that the dream-wish grows up, like a mushroom out of its mycelium.[6]

---

3. See note 6, p. 393 [Editor].
4. Navel (Greek) [Editor].
5. Ellmann is linking Freud's surname, which means joy (German), with Joyce's. Although Freud's book is not literally autobiographical, Ellmann suggests that indirectly or in disguise it is a form of life writing. "Heuristics": speculative principles of investigation [Editor].
6. Sigmund Freud, *The Interpretation of Dreams,* Pelican Freud Library, Vol. 4, trans. James Strachey. Hammondsworth, Eng.: Pelican Books, 1976, 671–72 [Expansion of author's note. Editor].

According to this description, the navel represents at once the origin and essence of the dream—its wish—and yet contributes "nothing" to its content. At once a knot and a lacuna, where meaning, in its very density, dissolves, the navel is the seam of the dream. Strangely, this absence occurs where sense is most concentrated, in the closest tangle of the dream thoughts. If, as Freud suggests, the navel constitutes the dream's origin, it is, moreover, an incongruous metaphor for him to use. For even anatomically, the navel is the point at which the foetus was once fastened parasitically upon its mother: where, indeed, the body has no definite ending, nor beginning, but branches out in every direction into the intricate network of its amniotic world. The navel marks the spot at which identity dissolves.

* * *

A *Portrait* * * * incessantly short-circuits. In its repeated births, its repeated exiles, it compulsively returns to the moment of the fracture and the scar. After the phallus, then, and Derrida's corrective technics of the hymen, I proffer the navel as the prototype of Dedalus's scars.[7] A prototype, but not an origin: for already we have seen, in the knotting and entanglement of Freud's own metaphor, that the navel necessarily resists the very structures of priority, centrality, originality. Omphalocentrism is that movement which deflects, supplants, transverses and attenuates the notion of a first, or a last, instance. In *A Portrait,* the word "Foetus" does not "mean" navel, but rather carves the spot where word and flesh meet in a single scar. These scars, or letters, or "scarletters"—to contract Hawthorne's pertinent title[8]—are littered through the *Wake,* and weave also through *Ulysses* like an umbilical cord. "Gaze in your omphalos," Stephen counsels to himself in "Proteus":[9] and his *Portrait* is a contemplation of the navel, with all its narcissistic implications. As onanistic as the *Wake* is incestuous, the rhythms of *A Portrait* are not those of fluid interchange, but the rhythms of "ejaculation" in the loneliness of exile, those of a hundred wet and navelled dreams.

7. For "the technics of the hymen" see "La Double séance," in Jacques Derrida's *La Dissémination,* Paris, Seuil, 1972, pp. 199–317 [Author]. English translation: "The Double Session," in *Dissemination,* transl. Barbara Johnson. Chicago: U of Chicago P, 1981, 173–366 [Editor].
8. *The Scarlet Letter* (1850), a novel by the American writer Nathaniel Hawthorne (1804–1864) [Editor].
9. Third episode of eighteen in *Ulysses* [Editor].

BONNIE KIME SCOTT

[The Artist and Gendered Discourse]†

[*Joyce and Muted Female Culture*]

* * * Joyce's present availability owes much to the industry and support of women in publishing. Joyce's nurturing by females was not just a fortunate fall into female altruism. He was selected from other modernists because the women involved found revolutionary affinities in Joyce. Joyce began under male patronage—his father's. John Joyce had his son's poem on Charles Stuart Parnell published privately. Presumably, it echoed the father's sense of history. Next, the prestigious British periodical *The Fortnightly Review* published his review on Ibsen (1900). With the exception of the relatively conventional poems in *Chamber Music* (1907), Joyce's increasingly experimental and iconoclastic works met with rejections. *St Stephen's*, his college newspaper, censored his attack on the Irish literary revival, "The Day of the Rabblement," and Joyce published it privately with an equally marginal essay on women's education by Irish feminist and friend Francis Skeffington. The bourgeois readers of *The Irish Homestead* objected to the stories that became *Dubliners*, so publication ceased after three. With *Dubliners* still unpublished, Joyce's prospects for *A Portrait* seemed gloomy until Ezra Pound put him in touch with the daring women editors of *The Egoist*. Dora Marsden and Harriet Shaw Weaver were willing to deal with printers' fears of litigation, to defy the norms of established literature and the economics of the marketplace, as were other female editors of small, individualist magazines.

The gynocritical concept of a muted female culture applies well to the operations of women editors and publishers of Joyce. *The Egoist* was descended from suffragist periodicals (*The Freewoman*, later renamed *The New Freewoman*), and staffed by feminists, including Rebecca West, H.D., and Bryher (Winnifred Ellermann). As writers, these women were neglected during the years when Joyce studies grew into an industry, but their muted modernist tradition has drawn the attention of feminist critics and publishers * * * . Joyce was living in Trieste when his work began appearing in *The Egoist*, and the only woman connected with the enterprise that he came to

† From *James Joyce*. Atlantic Highlands, N.J.: Humanities Press International, 1987, 16–17, 20–22, 31–33, 47–53, 86–88, 112–16, 120, 128–29. Used by permission of the author. Some of the author's footnotes have been omitted. Information from her bibliography has been incorporated into her footnotes. Page references for *A Portrait* have been replaced with part and line numbers of this Norton Critical Edition. Some cited passages might differ slightly from the equivalent passages in this volume.

know personally was Weaver. If so disposed, he could have read the work of Weaver, West and H.D. in *The Egoist*.

Weaver re-made the quaint role of literary patronage in a style of her own, learned partially from her participation in Victorian women's roles. She avoided poses of authority and airs of social superiority, offering instead common sense, practical nurture, and the psychological support that came from utter dependability and loyalty. Weaver's support of Joyce began with handling the details of periodical publication of *A Portrait*, including the same sort of haggling with printers that so delayed *Dubliners*. She eventually changed from periodical publishing to book publishing. The Egoist Press was established "on non-commercial lines" with the aim of making "operative an influence capable of transforming our entire world of form-thought and action."[1] Its Joyce list included several editions of *A Portrait*, as well as English editions of *Ulysses, Exiles, Dubliners,* and *Chamber Music*. Weaver also published T.S. Eliot, Wyndham Lewis, Ezra Pound, Marianne Moore, H.D. and Dora Marsden, a list with a generous presence of women writers.

* * *

[*Stephen, History, and Literature*]

In *A Portrait of the Artist as a Young Man,* Stephen Dedalus begins early to absorb the lessons on the Romans, the Greeks and Napoleon. He thinks that there are right answers about history, and examples of greatness to be followed, even in family life. There should be simple monological solutions to problems involving gender, like the question posed by the bully, Wells, "Do you kiss your mother before you go to bed?" (I.246–47). Personal application of male historical paradigms is evident in the aftermath of the pandy-bat incident. A priest has beaten Stephen's hand as punishment for Stephen's having broken his glasses. The dynamics of phallic power over excised or castrated vision invite gender-based interpretations, but the boys cannot articulate them. Stephen's peers state his grievance in classical historical terms: "The senate and the Roman people declared that Dedalus had been wrongly punished" (I.1625–26). Stephen responds:

> He would go up and tell the rector that he had been wrongly punished. A thing like that had been done before by somebody in history, by some great person whose head was in the books of history. . . . Those were the great men whose names were in Richmal Magnall's Questions. History was all about those men

1. *The Egoist*, December 1919, 71.

and what they did and that was what Peter Parley's Tales about
Greece and Rome were all about. (I.1635–45)

On his way to secure justice from the highest school authority,
Stephen displays internalized male-biased values that allow him to
feel superior to his punisher. His name, Dedalus, connects him to
the great men of the classics he has studied: "The great men in the
history had names like that and nobody made fun of them. . . . Dolan:
it was like the name of a woman that washed clothes" (I.1701–04).
Stephen has learned that women in domestic service deserve low
regard; great men in history are respectable. * * *
    Stephen develops a reputation as a prize-winning student over the
years. His memory is excellent; his knowledge of the catechism can
be used later to divert a priestly instructor from unprepared lessons
(III.131–33). The Jesuits of Belvedere are convinced that they have
a potential recruit (IV.362–66). But long before he must use a "habit
of quiet obedience" (IV.326) to disguise other interests from the
priests, the young Stephen searches out different angles, de-centering
Jesuit-style learning. Stephen tries, but only half-heartedly, to compete on one of two teams named (with significant indifference to
Irish nationalism) for the historical English factions of York and
Lancaster in the Wars of the Roses. Due to illness, Stephen's mind
works feverishly, eluding a more customary discipline. On a more
normal day, Stephen had listed his name at the head of a hierarchy,
ranging from self to universe (I.300–08). But on this day, Stephen's
mind wanders from manly competition to colour, rearranging and
inventing. Stephen displays little respect for the hierarchy of colours
accorded to high and low places. He thinks of the flower (usually a
female emblem) originally attached to the colour symbolism. He
introduces off-shades and plays with a chiasmic structure (paral-
lelism in reverse order that achieves symmetry rather than hierarchy): "White roses and red roses: those were beautiful colours to
think of. And the cards for first place and second place and third
place were beautiful colours too: pink and cream and lavender.
Lavender and cream and pink roses were beautiful to think of"
(I.191–95). At his second school, Belvedere, Stephen cannot attend
to a typical history lesson; he is troubled by the concentration on
names which veil and mute what interests him: "royal persons,
favourites, intriguers, bishops passed like mute phantoms behind
their veil of names" (III.845–46). His mind is diverted at this time
by his own mysteries—a sense of sin with a prostitute, and concern for his soul * * * (III.479–501). Stephen grows more openly
critical of the educational process at University College. He cuts
his English lecture, but imagines his peers at their Jesuit rituals,
their heads "meekly bent as they wrote in their notebooks the

points they were bidden to note, nominal definitions, essential definitions and examples or dates of birth or death, chief works" and so
on (V.134–37). Stephen turns the available instruction toward a different form of history. He seeks social rather than political, militant
history, often finding his cues in language, however ill-chosen by his
instructors:

> The crises and victories and secessions in Roman history were
> handed on to him in the trite words *in tanto discrimine* and he
> had tried to peer into the social life of the city of cities
> through the words *implere ollam denariorum* which the rector
> had rendered sonorously as the filling of a pot with denaries.
> (V.194–98)

His new history of pots rather than battles has affinity with feminist
history, as defined by feminist historians like Gerda Lerner. *Ulysses*
offers many discussions of military engagements, but Stephen figures in them peripherally, if at all. He is less involved in the historical debates of the "Eumaeus" episode than is Leopold Bloom, though
they agree momentarily on the values of pacifism. As if to emphasize
his distaste for the subject, he requests, rather affectedly, "O, oblige
me by taking away that knife. I can't look at the point of it. It reminds
me of Roman history" (*U* 16.814–6).[2]

*   *   *

Though Stephen is indebted to classicism and scholasticism, and
though he makes the canonized British master Shakespeare the subject of his central literary discourse in *Ulysses,* these authorities receive
significant challenges from Stephen, his audience, and Joyce, as the
arranger of *Ulysses*. Stephen is not even prepared to say he believes
in the theories he expresses on Shakespeare. In *A Portrait,* Stephen
acknowledges weariness after searching the "spectral words of Aristotle and Aquinas," and is relieved by "the dainty songs of the Elizabethans," and gladdened by his passage through "the squalor and
noise and sloth of the city" (V.88, V.89, V.110). Stephen is "disheartened" by "the firm dry tone" of the dean of studies, outlining a
Jesuitical method of exploring beauty through a set of distinctions
(V.565–93). He is not eager to become an "unlit lamp" or a "faithful
servingman of the knightly Loyola" (V.488, V.586).

Clearly without Jesuit endorsement, Stephen had sought out romantic texts like Dumas' *The Count of Monte Cristo*. One appeal of these
texts was their romantic visions of women like Mercedes. Stephen
has prized other romantic writers who offer comparable distanced
female inspirational figures for questing. Foremost is Byron, who

2. *Ulysses,* ed. Hans Walter Gabler. New York: Vintage, 1986 [Editor].

provides the form for Stephen's poem to E.C. (II.361–64), and for whom Stephen sustains a beating by virile schoolfellows. Byron had been denounced by Stephen's schoolmate Heron as immoral and heretical.

In Blake, Stephen encountered a profoundly radical critique of cultural hegemony, one which contributed to his re-vision of history * * * . "The most enlightened of Western poets" referred to in an essay Joyce wrote in 1902 was Blake, according to Joyce's brother, Stanislaus (CW 74–5).[3] Interestingly, Blake was ensconced alongside Joyce in Sylvia Beach's bookshop. The romantic temper, with its heritage of the French Revolution, its denial of hierarchies, and its greater interest in subjective and unconscious human experience, added new dimensions to Joyce and to his persona, which brought him closer to the sensibilities of revolutionary women writers like Mary Wollstonecraft, Mary Shelley and Charlotte Brontë.

Even in his pursuit of classical male writers, Stephen adopted his own course. The final chapter of A Portrait shows Stephen decentring classical teaching to suit his interests. He reads Ovid and Horace with the Jesuits, but is distracted by the whimsical words used to translate Ovid and by the human imprint of the "timeworn pages" of his copy of Horace (V.199–203). In John Henry Newman, Stephen admires a writer approved for the modern Jesuit canon, but values, not the theology, but the "silver-veined prose." Stephen also seeks out the heretics of ecclesiastical history. He defends Bruno of Nola to the dean of students, just as he had defended Byron with his contemporaries. Stephen is not physically punished for this allegiance, but he reminds the dean that Bruno was brutally burned. In a book review on Bruno (1903), Joyce agrees with the author's view of Bruno as a revisionist of scholasticism. Joyce appreciates Bruno's pluralist attitude * * * . Bruno's system has various poles, "by turns rationalist and mystic, theistic and pantheistic." Joyce reiterates Coleridge's identification of Bruno as a "dualist" (CW 133–4). Thus Bruno offers a greater sensitivity to alternative paradigms than the more monological scholastic thinking, but we should recall that dualistic thinking is also suspect as a male-generated paradigm by Marxist and post-structuralist feminists. Where Brunonian binaries operate in Joyce, their function must be deconstructed; where they are synthetic or question the usual hierarchy, they may offer a positive paradigm. Bruno's supposed abhorrence of the multitude is endorsed by Joyce in "The Day of the Rabblement." This supports the pose of aloof, romantic artist, and is more difficult to accommodate to a feminist position. The multitude scorned by Bruno and

3. *The Critical Writings of James Joyce*, ed. Ellsworth Mason and Richard Ellmann. New York: Viking, 1959 [Editor].

Joyce, however, may be most objectionable for its mindless support of hegemonic culture.

Stephen's thoughts are also crossed by the modern continental playwrights Gerhart Hauptmann and Henrik Ibsen, who are serious alternatives to the classical curriculum of the Jesuit university. Interestingly, Joyce specialized, not in the classics but in modern literature, the subject usually chosen by female students. Ibsen has surprisingly little place in A Portrait, considering Joyce's substantial effort to claim his place in the dramatic canon in such essays as "Drama and Life," "Ibsen's New Drama," "Catalina," and "The Day of the Rabblement." Joyce's major performance at the university was not on the well-canonized Shakespeare, Stephen's choice for the library discourse [in Ulysses], but on Ibsen. In "Drama and Life," Joyce notes that the "Shakespearean clique" had toppled an already failing classical dramatic tradition. Yet he sets about dismissing Shakespeare in turn, finding him a writer of "literature in dialogue." Ibsen is preferable as a writer of a higher and more collective "dramatic" art (CW 39, 45ff.). Stephen's few thoughts on Hauptmann and Ibsen suggest that they provide him with images and attitudes not available in the canon. Thoughts of Hauptmann come to Stephen from the sensuous "rainladen trees," evocative of the girls and women in his plays. Ibsen is a revolutionary "spirit" that "would blow through him like a keen wind, a spirit of wayward boyish beauty" (V.71–73, V.81–83). * * *

[The Discourse of the Father]

* * * While examining issues of canonical history and literature, we charted Stephen Dedalus' acquisition of academic male discourse from the classical and theological education provided by the Jesuits. [Stephen absorbs] a second male discourse [from] his father, Simon. * * *

Simon Dedalus offers his son's first rhetorical model in the storytelling at the opening of A Portrait of the Artist as a Young Man. Lacanian theory[4] associates the paternal phallus with the logos or word, as well as the laws by which society operates, hence the importance of this narration in supplying Stephen with the rules of discourse. By making "Baby Tuckoo" or Stephen the subject or centre of his narrative, Simon encourages the self-centred, egotistical, solipsistic narrative so obvious throughout Stephen's artistic development. The early story-telling is one in a series of vignettes where Stephen witnesses a performance, a personal or political discourse by his father, and is moved to sort out his own personal history and

4. In the work of the French psychiatrist Jacques Lacan (1901–1981) [Editor].

eventually his artistic course. Mrs Dedalus, on the other hand, has had most of her performances edited out of A *Portrait*. Dialogues are recalled, not recorded at length. She complies generally with the stereotypically feminine roles of accompanist and observer, displaying a muted and inhibited discourse, or providing a mouthpiece for the words of the father or the patriarchal church.[5] We see her teamed with Stephen's Aunt "Dante," but never in exclusively female company.

Simon's major performances include the Christmas dinner scene, where he is patriarchal host—wielder of the knife, dispenser of the sauce, and instigator of the political discussion that divides the family along gender lines and sunders Stephen's sense of a moral world order. Simon is again on stage in Cork (II.946–1275), where he sentimentally recalls his personal past, including his prowess with women and his attachment to his father. In another scene, Simon makes a political speech outside the former Irish House of Commons, regretting the diminishment of public men (II.1276–1301). Scattered through A *Portrait* are his pearls of paternal wisdom. To facilitate Stephen's male-bonding at school, Simon advises "never to peach on a fellow" (I.86). Simon's discourses have their antecedents in *Dubliners* in the speech of Joe Hynes in "Ivy Day in the Committee Room" and the banquet address of Gabriel Conroy in "The Dead." Simon says less in *Ulysses*, but he moves about the male preserves of the city, and everywhere he is or has been, we find recollections and repetitions of his discourse. Significantly, so does Stephen. The rhetorical tropes of the headlines printed in "Aeolus" are related to his discourse. Simon's sort of talk culminates in the "Cyclops" chapter of *Ulysses*[6] but echoes still in the *Finnegans Wake* speeches of the four chroniclers and Shaun as "Jaun the Boast" (*FW* 469.29)[7] with his "barrel of leaking rhetoric" (*FW* 429.8), "stone of law" (430.6), and ["preaching to himself" (467.9)]. Hugh Kenner describes the spectacle of a man speaking in public as "a paradigmatic communal act, offering to make sense of what he and his listeners confront together." He suggests that Dublin men simply lack the sense of history needed to carry off more than "pieces of inappropriate virtuosity" or "Pyrrhonism in the pub."[8] I suggest that their failures lead us on to deconstruct the male speech act itself, and to recover alternate acts and conceptions of community more inclusive of women, and less characterized by forced unities.

Even though his economic prowess steadily declines in A *Portrait*,

5. Colin MacCabe suggests that the father's authority as narrator is juxtaposed by the sound of the mother in this opening scene. See *James Joyce and the Revolution of the Word* (London: Macmillan, 1979), 55–6.
6. The twelfth episode of that novel; "Aeolus" is the seventh [Editor].
7. New York: Viking Press, 1939 [Editor].
8. *Joyce's Voices* (Berkeley: U of Calif. P, 1978)

Simon clings to a rhetoric of masterful command. When he can no longer afford to send Stephen to prestigious Clongowes Wood College, Simon takes pride in having arranged with Father Conmee for Stephen's place in the local Jesuit school, Belvedere. His self-satisfaction comes from a sense of knowing and manipulating a system and implies complicity in social and intellectual hierarchies and male networks. He performs for the family, with Mrs Dedalus as his assistant. The narrator implies criticism, with references to his busy tongue and calculations of Simon's repetitions:

> One evening his father came home full of news which kept his tongue busy all through dinner. . . .
> —I walked bang into him, said Mr Dedalus for the fourth time, just at the corner of the square.
> —Then I suppose, said Mrs Dedalus, he will be able to arrange it. I mean about Belvedere.
> —Of course he will, said Mr Dedalus. Don't I tell you he's provincial of the order now?
> —I never liked the idea of sending him to the christian brothers myself, said Mrs Dedalus.
> —Christian brothers be damned! said Mr Dedalus. Is it with Paddy Stink and Mickey Mud? No, let him stick to the jesuits in God's name since he began with them. They'll be of service to him in after years. Those are the fellows that can get you a position. (II.392–410)

The most extensive, varied, virtuoso performance by Simon is the earlier Christmas dinner scene, which also marks an epoch in Stephen's cultural passage into manhood. Stephen has survived the anxieties of the young male world at Clongowes and is fulfilling a dreamed-of return home. Triumphal return to the family from the larger, public world of Clongowes was a male pattern and freedom in that era. * * * Stephen also takes on the privileges of an adult occasion and an Eton suit, a uniform of social prestige, notably of British public school design. Simon's tears at seeing the suit betray a male identification, Simon thinking back to his father (I.812–16). Stephen recalls the suit years later, and Leopold Bloom has a vision of his long-dead son in similar garb in *Ulysses*.

The argument which develops at Christmas dinner is strongly marked by gender. Simon has been out walking with his radical nationalist friend Mr Casey. The Sunday or holiday walk is another male institution. Politics is a usual topic, and a suburban pub is a probable destination, since drinking laws limited serving to bona-fide travellers. Stephen joins his father and Uncle Charles on their constitutionals. He listens and thinks that he is finding a future for himself.

> Trudging along the road or standing in some grimy wayside publichouse his elders spoke constantly of the subjects nearer their hearts, of Irish politics, of Munster and of the legends of their own family, to all of which Stephen lent an avid ear. . . . The hour when he too would take part in the life of that world seemed drawing near and in secret he began to make ready for the great part which he felt awaited him. . . . (II.79–88)

Simon Dedalus comes to Christmas dinner prepared by discussion with a like-minded Parnellite to vindicate his fallen political hero. In this territory of mixed gender, Simon meets opposition in Mrs Riordan (Dante), whom Stephen takes as a figure of some intellectual and moral authority, but already sees as subordinate to males and a disappointment in life. He assumes she knows less than priests and recalls his father's assessment of her as a "spoiled nun" (I.996). Stephen is clearly more interested in Mr Casey, an exotic from a sphere of male action and violence, while Dante is a regular domestic feature. Stephen imagines Casey's bold adventures and dangerous connections through the half-told recollections cherished by his father. He likes to sit by Casey and looks "with affection" at his face, which has the same "fierce" appeal that attracted the boy of "An Encounter"[9] to the exotic female figures of detective fiction (I.990–92). Thus Stephen enters the dinner scene with a male bias. At the end, when Dante storms out consoled and accompanied by Mrs Dedalus, Stephen is fixed with the men.

Simon Dedalus has an array of rhetorical devices. Cryptic allusions to tales shared with Mr Casey give them mysterious attractiveness and exclude Dante. Simon's first remark to her accentuates their different worlds:

> —You didn't stir out at all, Mrs Riordan?
> Dante frowned and said shortly:
> —No. (I.748–50)

Dante's curtness suggests pre-existing difficulties; perhaps she anticipates the baiting techniques that regularly appear in Simon's apparently jovial discourse. Simon does arouse her finally with an anticlerical recollection to the appreciative Mr Casey. Simon admires a "good answer" made to a canon who had spoken of politics from the pulpit. Dante is alone in her defence of the role of the church, though Mrs Dedalus seems a sympathizer, silenced by her husband's domination. Dante comes across as a defender of strict moral priorities. Her thinking and even her rhetoric derive from church fathers, not from any female culture. The defence, once summoned, is relentless

---

9. Second story in *Dubliners*.

and ends in the apocalyptic, vengeful discourse of a hell-fire sermon: "Devil out of hell! We won! We crushed him to death!" It is impossible to idealize this discourse or identify it as a feminist alternative to Simon's. Its product is sex war.

Simon's speech is far more amusing than Dante's and his tearful breakdown at the end of the scene tends to evoke the reader's sympathy. His discourse is just as sinister as Dante's, however. We have seen two examples of baiting. There are others, calling the turkey's tail "the pope's nose," and a reference to "strangers" in the neighbourhood (foreign intruders, to an Irish audience) (I.903, I.912–13). Simon moves on to *ad hominem* invective against priests: "Respect! he said. Is it for Billy with the lip or for the tub of guts up in Armagh? Respect!" Simon adds the dimension of physical mimicry, "a grimace of heavy bestiality and . . . a lapping noise with his lips" (I.923–24, I.932–33). In the late parts of his performance, Simon receives his friend's support, Mr Casey providing useful nods and reinforcing echoes of Simon's opinions. To Dante's charge of "renegade" Catholicism, Casey embraces a significantly male-identified Catholicism: "I am a catholic as my father was and his father before him . . ." (I.970–71). Indeed, Catholicism does have different male and female versions in Ireland, Joyce suggests repeatedly.

Casey's own narrative performance is the story of "the famous spit." Casey creates himself as the hero at the centre of his narrative. As in the larger Christmas dinner scene, there is female opposition, an old woman, who like Dante lacks the wit so apparent in the men. Casey prepares his response, holding off through several of her verbal assaults, the delay in the narrative arousing the curiosity of his audience and Simon's appreciative prompting. The woman plays right into his hands, presenting her face for his *"Phth!,"* which Casey delivers twice, for effect, in his narrative. Like Simon, he also has skills of mimicry, which he turns toward the representation of her screams and exclamations (I.1047–52). Casey's spit offers paradigms of male physical and sexual assault upon a woman grown despicable by age as well as speech. Male production denies female speech. The old woman's message, a condemnation of Parnell's extramarital love, Kitty O'Shea, shows complicity in the moral norms of male hegemony, a familiar aspect of woman's consciousness in the shared culture, to which Joyce was sensitive.

Simon's final subject at Christmas dinner, the fall of the great man of Irish history, Charles Stuart Parnell, [reveals his] version of Irish history[.It] is peopled by great and infamous men, and treats of a series of wars and political struggles, much like the Roman history studied by young Stephen * * *. In Ireland, as Kenner notes, defeat and betrayal are recurrent outcomes, and the discourse takes on tones of regret and nostalgia for bygone greatness.

Simon's lists of former heroes and gross betrayers are long and embellished, the heroes including his male ancestors. He began his Christmas remarks with a gesture toward the portrait of his grandfather, "condemned to death as a whiteboy" (I.1086). In Cork, Simon reminisces tearfully about his father. In the street by the old House of Commons, he recalls Flood, Grattan and other parliamentarians predating the Act of Union (a parliamentary unification of Ireland with England which occurred in 1800). Simon follows his citation of the heroic grandfather with a well-prepared list of traitor priests:

> —Didn't the bishops of Ireland betray us in the time of the union when bishop Lanigan presented an address of loyalty to the Marquess Cornwallis? Didn't the bishops and priests sell the aspirations of their country in 1829 in return for catholic emancipation? Didn't they denounce the fenian movement from the pulpit and the confessionbox? And didn't they dishonour the ashes of Terence Bellew MacManus? (I.1101–07)

Simon's final tearful utterances on Parnell are familiar to readers of "Ivy Day in the Committee Room," where Joe Hynes shares both the subject and the discourse, as he will again on the all-male occasion of the funeral in the "Hades" chapter of *Ulysses*. Stephen's memories of Paris in the "Proteus" episode of *Ulysses* are haunted by a fallen Fenian father, Kevin Egan.

*   *   *

[*Stephen and Women*]

Joyce's mythical explorations of the construction of the psychological subject greatly favour the male subject, beginning with ones resembling himself—the male persona of *Chamber Music*, the boys in *Dubliners*, and of course Stephen Dedalus. Hélène Cixous suggests that the becoming of the subject is a perpetual theme in Joyce, starting her analysis with "The Sisters,"[1] but extending it to include Stephen.[2] This is a concept which helps us around Stephen Dedalus' classic Aristotelian value of "stasis," and his apparent identification with the father, and one that moves him toward the mythic principle of "transitionality" that Lauter has found in women poets.[3] We have considered the male cultural influences on Stephen's development * * *, and can leave his development in terms of

1. First story in *Dubliners* [Editor].
2. Hélène Cixous, 'Joyce: the (r)use of writing', in *Post-structuralist Joyce,* ed Derek Attridge and Daniel Ferrer (Cambridge, Eng.: Cambridge UP, 1984), 15–30.
3. Estella Lauter, *Women as Mythmakers*. Bloomington: Indiana UP, 1984 [Editor].

identification with the father to Joyce's Freudian critics.[4] What seems more controversial in feminist terms is his mode of rejecting his mother and other women. Feminists, led by Florence Howe, have been particularly troubled by Stephen's viewing of female subjects like the bird-girl as "other," as defined by Simone de Beauvoir in *The Second Sex*.[5]

Stephen makes some rather artificial, literary constructions of woman as "other" or distant muse that are less constructive than deeper, psychological contacts that spring from his mother. The artificial literary constructions show the immature artist's handling of male-devised literary and liturgical conventions, and are what was found deficient in early feminist critiques. In *Stephen Hero*, when Stephen has his first significant contact with a lively, desirable young woman, Emma Clery, he finds her "image" incongruous to his aesthetics and the verses he has composed: "He knew that it was not for such an image that he constructed a theory of art and life and a garland of verses and yet if he could have been sure of her he would have held his art and verses lightly enough" (*SH* 158).[6] Joyce had a comparable feeling of incongruity between Nora Barnacle[7] and the image he had cultivated for *Chamber Music*.

Joyce's early verses idealize the parts of woman he has seen emphasized by the decadents (her golden hair [*CP* 13],[8] her bosom, which is good for male reclining [14]), or in icons of the Virgin Mary (the sombre eyes, the snood, the colour blue [19]), or in Elizabethan songs (the "merry green wood" and her "pretty air" [16–18]). Joyce's maiden has a "little garden" (21) but, unlike the stronger Eve, she doesn't cultivate it. She must be summoned or sung to as she sits at a window. "Love" is a solitary male persona, who at one point in the cycle upbraids the beloved for destroying male friendship or perhaps access to a male god: "He is a stranger to me now/Who was my friend" (25). Throughout, the adored but distrusted maiden is more absent than present, a distant object of conventional, not physical, desire.

Stephen's musing on the unencountered, literary Mercedes is comparable. He finds passive brooding is preferable to interactions with real, noisy children:

---

4. I recommend Edmund Epstein, *The Ordeal of Stephen Dedalus* (Carbondale: Southern Illinois UP, 1971) and Sheldon Brivic, *Joyce between Freud and Jung* (Port Washington, N.Y.: Kennikat, 1980).

5. Florence Howe, "Feminism and Literature," in *Images of Women in Fiction: Feminist Perspectives*, ed Susan Koppelman Cornillon (Bowling Green, Ohio: Bowling Green U Popular P, 1972), 260.

6. Ed. John J. Slocum and Herbert Cahoon. New York: New Directions, 1963 [Editor].

7. James Joyce's companion (1884–1951), muse, and then wife, who was from the west of Ireland [Editor].

8. *Collected Poems*. New York: Viking Press, 1957 [Editor].

He did not want to play. He wanted to meet in the real world
the unsubstantial image which his soul so constantly beheld.
* * * They would be alone, surrounded by darkness and silence:
and in that moment of supreme tenderness he would be transfigured . . . Weakness and timidity and inexperience would fall
from him in that magic moment. (II.173–85)

The bird-girl Stephen views at the close of chapter 4 of *A Portrait*
is gazed at (to use Irigaray's[9] concept of basic Greek aesthetics) and
rendered poetic, but she is not psychologically encountered. Compared to the *Chamber Music* girl, there is a slightly fuller catalogue
of her body, slender legs and full thighs. But the dove she is transformed to was in *Chamber Music* and is a suspiciously religious
icon; her likeness to the Virgin Mary is even more strikingly rendered. Though Stephen claims that "her image had passed into his
soul forever" and he experiences an ecstasy that is at least partly sexual ("His cheeks were aflame; his body was aglow; his limbs were
trembling"), Stephen still represents a woman in conventional terms
of the religious call to a vocation. His much-analysed "Villanelle of
the Temptress," with its reliance on eucharistic trappings, is a comparable failure. The eucharistic metaphor is troubling, not just
because of its religious conventionality, but because of its mixture of
spiritual selfishness with the implicit intention to consume the host.
A more significant journey into the unconscious comes after
Stephen's bird-girl construction has vanished. He reclines on a nurturing mother earth, then falls into a sleep that is also a fall into a
flushed womb through rose-like labia:

> * * * the earth beneath him, the earth that had borne him, had
> taken him to her breast.
> He closed his eyes in the languor of sleep. * * * A world, a
> glimmer, or a flower? Glimmering and trembling, trembling and
> unfolding, a breaking light, an opening flower, it spread in end-
> less succession to itself, breaking in full crimson and unfolding
> and fading to palest rose, leaf by leaf and wave of light by wave
> of light, flooding all the heavens with its soft flushes every flush
> deeper than the other. (IV.901–13)

*   *   *

From the very first scene of *A Portrait,* Stephen takes note of his
father's stories. But using a variety of his senses, he also carefully
notices his mother's emissions. She has a nice smell; she plays music
and encourages his dance, an art form usually associated with
women in Joyce. At Clongowes Wood College, he remembers "her

9. Luce Irigaray (b. 1930), Belgian psychoanalyst and feminist cultural theorist.

feet on the fender and her jewelly slippers were so hot and they had such a lovely warm smell" (I.15–16, I.129–31). She has an erotic relation to language. Her image serves his definition of the word kiss: "His mother put her lips on his cheek; her lips were soft and they wetted his cheek; and they made a tiny little noise: kiss" (I.278–80). This begins Stephen's focus upon maternal lips.[1] Described as soft and wet, the lips suggest not just her mouth, but her vulva, and both are "they" or two. Irigaray focuses upon the diffuseness of sexuality women experience in their bodies. The two lips of the vulva are only one aspect of the multiple sites and surges of female libidinal energy, as opposed to the singular identity and orgasm of the male's penis and corresponding phallocentric language.[2] The lips produce minimal sound, and no word. This is fitting as an aspect of female silence. Yet the sound which is not a word is onomatopoetic and becomes the partial source of the word for Stephen.

Mrs Dedalus elicits written words in the form of a letter from young Stephen at Clongowes; he is ill and wants to return to his primary source of nurture. Stephen asks, "Please come and take me home" (I.586–87). This is classically Oedipal, but also offers an intriguing relationship between language and the maternal body. Stephen closes A Portrait with another female writing form, the diary, which contains a number of entries on his mother as well as Emma, but, at this stage, expresses a determined leave-taking.

Nancy Chodorow's revisions of the theory of the Oedipus complex suggest that young men are helped in resolving their desire for the mother by replacing her with the women they encounter as prospective and actual mates.[3] Stephen continues to read the semiotics of the maternal body in the girls and women he meets, and to note occurrences of silence and suggestions of alternative languages. His own imagery re-creates female pulsions and genital forms. Stephen notices water "falling softly in a brimming bowl" at the culmination of chapter 1 of A Portrait (I.1848). He reads, almost as language, the look in the eyes of a girl and the pressure of her hand; her nonverbal expressions have a fluid, soothing effect that reaches to his brain and body even in memory, setting a pattern for future reception of female semiotics.

> He could remember only that she had worn a shawl about her head like a cowl and that her dark eyes had invited and unnerved him. . . . Then in the dark and unseen by the other two he

1. Maud Ellmann works with language and lips, Stephen's as well as his mother's, in "Disremembering Dedalus: A Portrait of the Artist as a Young Man" [p. 389 in this volume].
2. Luce Irigaray, from "This sex which is not one," in New French Feminisms, ed Elaine Marks and Isabelle de Courtivron (U of Massachusetts P, Amherst, 1980), 100–1, 103.
3. Nancy Chodorow, The Reproduction of Mothering (Berkeley: U of Calif. P, 1978), 167.

rested the tips of the fingers of one hand upon the palm of the
other hand, scarcely touching it and yet pressing upon it lightly.
But the pressure of her fingers had been lighter and steadier:
and suddenly the memory of their touch traversed his brain and
body like an invisible warm wave. (II.807–16)

Stephen's first encounter with a prostitute involves more communication by gesture and pressure than actual language on her part, or
significantly, on his:

* * *

* * * Her round arms held him firmly to her and he, seeing
her face lifted to him in serious calm and feeling the warm
calm rise and fall of her breast, all but burst into hysterical
weeping. Tears of joy and relief shone in his delighted eyes and
his lips parted though they would not speak.

* * *

With a sudden movement she bowed his head and joined
her lips to his and he read the meaning of her movements in
her frank uplifted eyes. It was too much for him. He closed
his eyes, surrendering himself to her, body and mind, conscious of nothing in the world but the dark pressure of her
softly parting lips. They pressed upon his brain as upon his
lips as though they were the vehicle of a vague speech; and between them he felt an unknown and timid pressure, darker
than the swoon of sin, softer than sound or odour. (II.1437–42,
1450–58)

Stephen begins with an effort to control the situation by speech
but the prostitute's own "vehicle of a vague speech" moves him to
uncharacteristic silence, submission and almost to hysterical
weeping. "Hysterical," derived from "hyster," the Greek word for
womb, is a negative symptom attributed particularly to women by
Freud; it has been rehabilitated in some feminist theory as an
expressive and useful form for organizing language.[4] Stephen
ceases his gaze and opens his brain and body to an alternative experience, which is articulated in terms of the female body's
warmth, the rise and fall of her breast, the pressure of her soft
parted lips, experiences darker and softer than the intellectual,
moral or sensuous experiences he has known in the world, but
reminiscent of his mother's early kiss.

Even during his reactionary period of self-imposed asceticism,
Stephen is receptive of muted voices merged with female form, the

4. Robin Tolmach Lakoff, "Women's language," in *Women's Language and Style*, ed. [Dou-
glas] Butturff and [Edmund L.] Epstein (Akron: L&S Books, 1978), 152.

ubera or breasts. He takes as his text the other-worldly "Song of Songs":[5]

> A faded world of fervent love and virginal responses seemed to be evoked for his soul by the reading of its pages . . . An inaudible voice seemed to caress the soul, telling her names and glories, bidding her arise as for espousal and come away, bidding her look forth, a spouse, from Amana and from the mountains of the leopards; and the soul seemed to answer with the same inaudible voice, surrendering herself: *Inter ubera mea commorabitur*. (IV.180–88)

Stephen's soul is feminine in pronoun and behaviour. The final surrender unites feminine soul with maternal bosom, an expression of primal feminine affinity, even lesbianism. Stephen's production of language or art is frequently inspired by the maternal, female body, the muse as semiotician. In his discourse with Lynch, Stephen admits that scholasticism is not enough to go beyond asthetics to actual creation:

> So far as this side of esthetic [*sic*] philosophy extends Aquinas will carry me all along the line. When we come to the phenomena of artistic conception, artistic gestation and artistic reproduction I require a new terminology and a new personal experience. (V.1268–72)

Lynch enjoys the sexual metaphors, but postpones the discussion—forever, as far as *A Portrait* goes. In the scene where Stephen composes his villanelle, the word emerges from the womb: "O! In the virgin womb of the imagination the word was made flesh. Gabriel the seraph had come to the virgin's chamber" (V.1543–45).

Stephen's openness to female semiotics as a marginal form of communication is in keeping with his feelings of marginality as an Irish speaker of English:

> * * * His language, so familiar and so foreign, will always be for me an acquired speech. I have not made or accepted its words. My voice holds them at bay. My soul frets in the shadow of his language. (V.556–59)

Notably, it is the soul, the female aspect of himself, that frets. Stephen also recognizes that he has special and different things to do with words. He meditates upon a phrase he has made, "A day of dappled seaborne clouds":

> * * * was it that, being as weak of sight as he was shy of mind, he drew less pleasure from the reflection of the glowing sensi-

5. See note 7, p. 132.

ble world through the prism of a language manycoloured and richly storied than from the contemplation of an inner world of individual emotions mirrored perfectly in a lucid supple periodic prose? (IV.698–703)

Stephen's interests here, though not comprehensive of Joyce, bear elements of what has been identified as male as well as female literary form. His direction toward an "inner world" diverts him from the masculine realm. His multiple interests, his fascination with rhythm, his willingness to watch colours in the process of changing, and his "supple periodic prose" suggest multiplicity, fluidity and recycling, aspects attached to the female body and female writing. But the "periodic" also suggests what Virginia Woolf called the masculine sentence;[6] at this point Stephen aspires to the exact and culminating phrase, a control of language and desire for representation (though different in its inward direction) that has been identified with male language. Stephen's habit of imposing Latin on an encounter with a young girl, *mulier cantat* (V.2479), and mother love, *amor matris* (U 2.165), is also questionable as a form of linguistic distancing, learned through the church.

* * *

[Joyce and Women's Language]

The language of flowers is one way that the female body is "written" (as Cixous and practitioners of *écriture féminine*[7] put it) in Joyce, though it is not exclusively identified with female writers. In [one] passage in *A Portrait* * * * a rosy glow seems to open into a metaphorical journey into labia for Stephen. Molly Bloom takes up her husband's identification of her body with flowers, "Yes he said I was a Flower of the mountain yes so we are flowers all a womans body yes that was one true thing he said in his life" (U 18.1576–7). Bloom's gift of eight poppies was effective in wooing Molly. As "Henry Flower," Bloom gives Martha Clifford a subject to write about, and he thinks again of the affinity of women to flowers in terms of silence: "language of flowers. They like it because no-one can hear" (5.261). ALP, in encouraging HCE near the end of the *Wake*, describes her hands "in the linguo of flows" (621.22). Issy's accompanying girls are written as flowers and flowers typically triumph over ruins in the *Wake* landscape.

In *Finnegans Wake*, female identities write themselves in several ways. This is somewhat surprising in the case of the mother, whom

6. Virginia Woolf, *A Room of One's Own* (1928; New York: Harcourt Brace and World, 1963, 79).
7. Female writing (French) [Editor].

we have seen written but not writing in early Joyce. According to
Susan Rubin Suleiman, female as well as male writers offer a written, but not a writing mother.[8] The "Mamafesta"[9] or hen's letter is
probably the most obvious woman's writing, though there is constantly the issue of forgery by Shem or Issy,[1] or even T.S. Eliot,
where the language of "The Waste Land" seems evident. The text is
written, written over and analysed, becoming a collective expression
of both genders, a palimpsest, an anastomotic text.[2]

* * *

Woman's language has some variants in Joyce. It may be as ancient
as the cuneiform wedge or as common as Molly's *lingua franca*. It
makes do with available surfaces, an egg or a rock. It is an essential
variant for the male writer, and allows him a measure of self-
criticism. Female modernism, as constructed by Joyce, does not
show off with densities and portmanteau words: "But how many of
her readers realise that she is not out to dizzledazzle with a graith
uncouthrement of postmantuam glasseries from the lapins and the
grigs" (*FW* 112.36–113.2). Though he may raise a "meandering
male fist" of control, the action is sure to be mocked by his own
female writer. Female language may flow in and from the body, or be
woven or played as music. The aesthetic of women's language is sufficiently broad to embrace both the goddess and Stephen Dedalus in
the artistic life-sustaining process: "As we, or mother Dana, weave
and unweave our bodies, Stephen said, from day to day, their mole-
cules shuttled to and fro, so does the artist weave and unweave his
image" (*U* 9.376–8). We find ALP a musician-weaver. "Windaug,"
she weaves like Penelope, making music as did Mrs Dedalus in
Stephen's first perceptions of her. She also unweaves, flowing away
into impersonality and recombination of gender, as she rejoins her
sky mother and sea father. ALP is allowed lush sound, but no personal ambition. There is no culminating, final sentence. Her language is as interrupted, interruptable as the final half-sentence of
Finnegans Wake. Yet her feminine language is what provides the
umbilicus, the "vicus" of recirculation,[3] and offers a new politics of
relationship and authorship. As she flows to the sea, Anna thinks of

8. "Writing and Motherhood," in *The (M)other Tongue: Essays in Feminist Psychoanalytic
Interpretation*, ed Shirley Nelson Gardner, Claire Kahane, and Madelon Sprengnether
(Ithaca, N.Y.: Cornell UP, 1985), 356–60.
9. Word from *Finnegans Wake* that suggests both the mother and a manifesto [Editor].
1. In the Earwicker family of *Finnegans Wake*, Shem is one of the male children, and Issy, or
Iseult, is the only female child [Editor].
2. Characterized by anastomosis, the connection among individual parts of a branching system into a network, as in the capillary connections in the vessel network of the human
circulatory system [Editor].
3. "Vicus of recirculation" (*FW* 3.2). "Vicus" suggests, among other meanings, a road
[Editor].

the writer of "work in progress" (the working title Joyce used for *Finnegans Wake*) and says with confidence, "But it's by this route he'll come some morrow" (625.13–14).

Anna's route cannot fully satisfy the woman writer or gynocritic who has a shaping vision, a self-defining ambition and tradition, along with her physical female form, to equate with language. Still, the French feminist paradigms of writing the feminine enrich our reading of Joyce, taking us beyond Freud and beyond structuralism. A troubling possibility is that Joyce's writing of woman still serves a male author's ego, proving he can move into "other" forms. On the other hand, if the move is made, not in the spirit of epic conquest, but as wanderer-gatherer and re-viewer of writing, we should wish for more male writers who will follow in Anna's wake.

JOSEPH VALENTE

Thrilled by His Touch: Homosexual Panic and the Will to Artistry in *A Portrait of the Artist as a Young Man*†

* * *

The modern educational system in general and the elite boarding school in particular, where boys learned the ways of male entitlement under the pressure of powerful and labile erotic pulsions, have afforded a prototypical arena for the experience of homosexual panic.[1]

Joyce not only betrays just this sort of sexual unease in his private correspondence, but, I will be arguing, he communicates these attitudes to his fictive alter ego, Stephen Dedalus, in a more explicitly "panicky" mode, which affects the most crucial decisions Stephen enacts: his appeal to Conmee, his refusal of the priesthood, his

---

† From *James Joyce Quarterly* 31:3 (Spring 1994): 167–88. Reprinted with permission of the publisher. Some of the author's notes have been omitted. Page references for *A Portrait* have been replaced with part and line numbers of this Norton Critical Edition. Some cited passages might differ slightly from the equivalent passages in this volume.

1. [On homosexual panic, see] Eve Kosofsky Sedgwick, *The Epistemology of the Closet* (Berkeley: Univ. of California Press, 1990), pp. 182–212, and *Between Men* (New York: Columbia Univ. Press, 1985), pp. 83–96. On page 195 of *Epistemology*, Sedgwick doubts whether the "arguably homosexual" objects of her own analysis properly bear out or embody the experience of homosexual panic, which "is proportioned to the non-homosexual identified elements of . . . men's character." Accordingly, she continues, "if Barrie and James are obvious authors with whom to begin an analysis of male homosexual panic, the analysis I am offering here must be inadequate to the degree that it does not eventually work just as well—even better—for Joyce, Faulkner, Lawrence, Yeats etc." In this respect, my essay can be seen as a continuation of Sedgwick's project, an attempt not only to explore Joyce's writing by way of her conception but also to demonstrate the adequacy of her conception by way of Joyce's writing. Further references to these works will be cited parenthetically in the text as *Closet* and *Men*.

assumption of an aesthetic vocation, his self-exile. A number of critics have, over the years, pointed to the emergence of homoerotic
energies in A Portrait, for example, in the smuggling episode or in
Stephen's final interview with Cranly, and several have even asserted
the importance of these same energies as a component of Stephen's
psychology.[2] What I would like to demonstrate is that Joyce's phobic
denial or denegation[3] of his own homoerotic energies makes its way
into the novel as a *fundamental determinant* of its basic narrative
structure and hence of Stephen's destiny. By taking this approach, I
do not mean to imply any simple autobiographical identification
of the figure of Dedalus with that of Joyce. I do mean to propose,
however, that the combination of projection, disavowal, and self-
awareness connecting author and alter ego comprises a certain homoerotic ambivalence whose operation in the text helps to demystify
Stephen's strongest claim to being Joyce's surrogate, his will to
artistry.

The very title of the novel invokes the homoerotic scenario and
does so in a characteristically Joycean fashion, by establishing, at
the outset, the text as intertext. As Vicki Mahaffey suggested to me,
the phrase "a portrait of the artist" is a quite peculiar locution,
which makes its derivation from one work in particular, Oscar
Wilde's *The Picture of Dorian Gray*, that much more assured, especially since Dorian's portrait *keeps* him at the age of a young man.
During the opening scene of Wilde's famous novel, Basil tells
Henry:

> [E]very portrait that is painted with feeling is a portrait of the
> artist, not of the sitter. The sitter is merely the accident, the
> occasion. It is not he who is revealed by the painter; it is rather
> the painter who . . . reveals himself.[4]

In this light, Stephen can be taken either as a self-portrait in the
ordinary sense or as a self-portrait strictly by virtue of being "a portrait painted with feeling," a condition likely to disfigure the ordinary self-portrait with a certain self-indulgence. Stephen must,
therefore, not only be seen as both Joyce and not Joyce, but he must
also be seen as revealing Joyce precisely to the extent that he is *not* a
self-depiction (being instead merely a portrait painted with feeling)

2. These critics include James F. Carens, "A Portrait of the Artist as a Young Man" in *A Com-
panion to Joyce Studies*, ed. Zack Bowen and James F. Carens (Westport: Greenwood
Press, 1984), pp. 255–359; Jean Kimball, "Freud, Leonardo and Joyce" in *The Seventh of
Joyce*, ed. Bernard Benstock (Bloomington: Indiana Univ. Press, 1982), pp. 57–73;
Chester Anderson, "Baby Tuckoo: Joyce's Features of Infancy," in *Approaches to Joyce's
"Portrait": Ten Essays*, ed. Thomas F. Staley (Pittsburgh: Univ. of Pittsburgh Press, 1970),
pp. 136–42. Further references to these works will be cited parenthetically in the text.
3. Freud's term for admitting to consciousness by denying [Editor].
4. Oscar Wilde, *The Picture of Dorian Gray* [See p. 303 in this volume. Editor].

and disfiguring Joyce to the extent that he *is* a self-depiction, altered by that feeling.

But Joyce's interest in the intercourse between revelation and representation in Wilde exceeded questions of the pragmatics of self-portraiture. It had a nakedly ethico-political edge as well. Joyce's primary response to *The Picture of Dorian Gray* was disappointment that Wilde had dissembled in presenting the homosexual charge binding Dorian, Basil, and Henry, that Wilde's own complex self-representation had not been more of a (sexual) revelation.

> I can imagine the capital which Wilde's prosecuting counsel made out of certain parts of it. It is not very difficult to read between the lines. Wilde seems to have had some good intentions in writing it—some wish to put himself before the world— but the book is rather crowded with lies and epigrams. If he had had the courage to develop the allusions in the book it might have been better. I suspect he has done this in some privately-printed books.[5]

Like this letter, however, which conspicuously declines to develop "the allusions in the book" any more than Wilde does, leaving the homosexuality therein an "open secret," Joyce's title repeats the gesture of circumspection, leaving the *homotextual* relations between his novel and Wilde's at the level of "epigram." Or perhaps it would be truer to say, Joyce's title answers Wilde's conscious circumspection with an unconscious disavowal; it simultaneously reveals and conceals the intense homotextual relation between his *Bildungsroman* and his precursor, revealing the "textual" affinity, in its most Derridean sense,[6] while concealing or eliding the "homo." Whereas the "feeling" that makes Dorian's portrait a "portrait of the artist" involves Basil's homoerotic attraction to his "sitter," as Joyce recognizes, Joyce's "feeling" for his "sitter" could only be construed as narcissistic, a modality of desire properly understood as the precondition for any object relation, homo- or hetero-. That is to say, by remaining at the level of epigram, *A Portrait of the Artist* translates the "open secret" of *Dorian Gray*'s sexual economy into an open option or open possibility.

A similarly displaced homotextual relation reveals itself in the symbol of Stephen's Irish art * * * , the impossible green rose. Stephen's aesthetic career begins on a significant pun, significantly repeated.

> *O, the wild rose blossoms*
> *On the little green place.*

5. *Selected Letters of James Joyce*, ed. Richard Ellmann. New York: Viking, 1975, 96 [Editor].
6. Jacques Derrida (1830–2004), Algerian-born French philosopher and founder of deconstruction, which explores how meaning comes into being [Editor].

He sang that song. That was his song. (I.9–11)

And again,

> Perhaps a *wild* rose might be like those colors. And he remembered the song about the *wild* rose blossoms on the little green place. (I.195–97, my emphasis)

Joyce underlines and clarifies the pun in *Finnegans Wake,* where it serves to stake the process of history on the wages of illicit sexuality:

> has not levy of black mail from the times the fairies were in it, and fain for *wilde* erthe blothoms followed an impressive private reputation for whispered sins? (*FW* 69.02–04, my emphasis)[7]

With this in mind, Stephen's subsequent musing—"But you could not have a green rose. But perhaps somewhere in the world you could" (I.197–98)—unmistakably recalls Wilde's famous "green carnation," which was the symbol both of the artifice of the imagination, the conventional reading of Stephen's rose, and a badge of the homosexual subculture of *fin de siècle* England,[8] a sense that Stephen's flower intimates *sotto voce.* At a certain level, Joyce is grounding Stephen's aesthetic vocation in an inarticulate homoeroticism or rather, as we shall see, in an inability or unwillingness to articulate his homoerotic cathexes directly, a simultaneous experience, denial, and diversion of them, rooted in his Clongowes education.

Stephen's thoughts on the green rose immediately follow his ruminations on Simon Moonan, the homoerotic implications of which are, of course, patent * * *:[9]

> —We all know why you speak. You are McGlade's suck.
> Suck was a queer word. The fellow called Simon Moonan that name because Simon Moonan used to tie the prefect's false sleeves behind his back and the prefect used to let on to be angry. But the sound was ugly. Once he had washed his hands in the lavatory of the Wicklow Hotel and his father pulled the stopper up by the chain after and the dirty water went down through the hole in the basin. And when it had all gone down slowly . . . [it] made a sound like that: suck. Only louder. . . . There were two cocks that you turned and water

7. New York: Viking, 1939 [Editor].
8. In his own words, Wilde "invented that magnificent flower," the green carnation, as a "work of art"—Richard Ellmann, *Oscar Wilde* (New York: Vintage, 1987), pp. 424–25. The green carnation became a symbol of aestheticism, memorialized in Robert Hichens, *The Green Carnation* (New York: Dover Publications, 1970).
9. See [Kimball (66) and] Leonard Albert, "Gnomonology: Joyce's 'The Sisters,'" *JJQ,* 27 (Winter 1990), 360–61.

came out: cold and hot. . . . and he could see the names printed
on the cocks. That was a very queer thing. (I.149–63)

I have quoted this passage at length because:

1. through the repeated use of terms like suck, queer, cocks,
   and so forth,[1] it establishes a psychosymbolic association
   among Stephen's developing fever, his long-standing fascination with and aversion to standing water and waste, and
   an embryonic homosexual possibility and panic;

2. it sets an erotic context for understanding the sort of homosocial roughhousing that lands Stephen in the square ditch and
   causes his fever. Stephen, remember, a designated mama's
   boy, will not trade his dandyish "little snuffbox" for Wells's
   macho "hacking chestnut, the conqueror of forty" (I.124–25);
   the box and the nut function as genital symbols for the
   respectively feminized and masculinized positions of Stephen
   and Wells. Since the incident exemplifies the sexualized
   aggression that Joyce attributed to English boarding school
   activities, and since Joyce was likewise shouldered into the
   ditch, with similarly febrile consequences (*JJII* 28),[2] it is
   worth noting that the square ditch runs along the perimeter
   of Clongowes and forms its boundary with the old English
   pale.[3] It is, in other words, a border zone where the masculinized Anglo-Saxon "conqueror" and the feminized Irish conquered meet and, partly as an effect of the conquest itself,
   where their ethno-racial differences are both marked, even
   exaggerated, and overridden, even erased. With respect to
   Joyce's cherished distinction between the rampant homoeroticism of English public school life and the comparative innocence of its Irish counterpart, the square ditch constitutes an
   objectified instance of "the proximate"[4] itself, in effect, a thin
   margin of dissociation into which the subject might always
   land or be pushed and his kinship with the other be uncom-
   fortably reaffirmed;[5]

1. Elaine Showalter correctly contends that the term "queer" had homosexual connotations
   before the yellow nineties, let alone the twentieth century, began. All subsequent references to and uses of the term will assume a distinct homosexual valence—*Sexual Anarchy*
   (New York: Viking, 1990), p. 112.
2. Richard Ellmann, *James Joyce* (N.Y.: Oxford UP, 1982) [Editor].
3. For this information, I am grateful to Vicki Mahaffey, who gathered it on a visit to Clongowes in 1992.
4. On "the proximate," see Jonathan Dollimore, *Sexual Dissidence* (New York: Oxford Univ.
   Press, 1991), pp. 14–17 [Expansion and relocation of author's note. Editor].
5. This dynamic of proximate-ness played itself out quite humorously in Joyce's indirect dialogue with H. G. Wells. Wells objected to the "'cloacal obsession'" of *A Portrait*. Joyce's
   reply to Frank Budgen reveals the kind of ethno-racial dichotomy that we have been adduc-
   ing: "'Why, it's Wells's countrymen who build water-closets wherever they go.'" But in a private comment to another friend, Joyce acknowledged, "'How right Wells was!'" (*JJII* 414).

3. it establishes a basis on which to overcome an inveterate critical assumption—an Enlightenment prejudice really—that because Stephen does not fully grasp the implications of the "smugging" scandal until later on, he is not really party to the homosexual energies circulating among the Clongowes students as they remember or recount the "crime" and anticipate the similarly titillating punishment.

As it turns out, these three narrative functions are strictly correlative. For it is not the appropriately named Athy's prosaic specification of Moonan and Boyle's offense ("smugging") nor even his poetic acting out of their chastisement ("It can't be helped;/It must be done./So down with your breeches/And out with your bum"—I.1325–28) that most powerfully eroticizes the scene. It is instead the way that Stephen elaborates upon these accounts and the way that his elaborations interact with other environmental cues like the sound of the cricket bats.

Regarding the crime, it is Stephen who seeks to exculpate Simon Moonan and, in the process, reveals the direct libidinal impact that young man has had upon him:

> What did that mean about the smugging in the square? . . . It was a joke, he thought. Simon Moonan had nice clothes and one night he had *shown him a ball of creamy* sweets that the fellows of the football fifteen had rolled down to him along the carpet. . . . It was the night of the *match against the Bective Rangers* and the ball was made just like a red and green apple only it opened and it was *full of the creamy sweets*. (I.1244–52, my emphases)

Stephen's earlier fantasy about leaving on vacation already incorporated his experience with Moonan in a plainly, if unconsciously, homoerotic fashion: "The train was full of fellows: a *long, long chocolate train* with *cream facings*" (I.465–66, my emphases). This is a classic instance in which commonplace homosocial reinforcement, highlighted by the affiliation with team sports, merges almost seamlessly with the "most reprobated" sexual imagery and investments. Once again, Stephen undergoes the panic that this double bind arouses as * * * a dread associated with waste and sitting urine:

> But why in the square? You went there when you wanted to do something. It was all thick slabs of slate and water trickled all day out of tiny pinholes and there was a queer smell of stale water there. (I.1270–73)

Being the site of a certain mutual genital exposure, the male lavatory space always carries some homoerotic potential; as a result, the introduction of an *explicitly* sexual element, tapping as it does Stephen's existent fear and confusion, renders the excremental function itself "queer" and therefore unspeakable for him. You went to the lavatory to "do something" that apparently dares not be named.

Regarding the punishment, Stephen's dread and Stephen's desire are simultaneously on display.[6] He imagines the prospect of being caned less in terms of pain than in terms of "chill": "It made him shivery to think of it and cold. . . . It made him shivery" (I.1337–39). That this chill bespeaks a sexualized *frisson* becomes immediately evident in Stephen's focus on the ceremonial unveiling of the "vital spot" (I.1321): "He wondered who had to let them [the trousers] down, the master or the boy himself" (I.1342–43). Stephen's speculation on the protocol involved suggests a mutuality of participation in the act of undressing that bares the sexual energy animating the exemplary discipline. His subsequent vision of the caning itself implies a literalized dialectic or reciprocity between beater and beaten that issues in a sense of positive and implicitly homoerotic pleasure:

> [Athy] had rolled up his sleeves to show how Mr Gleeson would roll up his sleeves. But Mr Gleeson had round shiny cuffs and clean white wrists and fattish white hands and the nails of them were long and pointed. Perhaps he pared them too like Lady Boyle. . . . And though he trembled with . . . fright to think of the cruel long nails . . . and of the chill you felt at the end of your shirt when you undressed yourself yet he felt a feeling of queer quiet pleasure inside him to think of the white fattish hands, clean and strong and gentle. (I.1346–57)

As the passage mushrooms into a full-blown, if displaced, sexual fantasy, Stephen takes center stage as the subject of warring sensations, an outer chill and an inner glow, an anticipated pain and an experienced pleasure, an involuntary engagement but a voluntary imagining, a sexual affect at once savored and denied. Indeed, Joyce exploits the equivocality of the word "queer" in this passage in order not only to mark the homoerotic nature of Stephen's ambivalence but also to mark the ambivalent, uncanny impact of the homoerotic upon Stephen, his mixture of fear and fascination, attraction and repulsion, which is the recipe for a "panic" borne of "proximate-ness."

This proximate-ness, in turn, with its ambivalent affect, gives a sharply ironic twist to Stephen's subsequent pandying. It is not just that Stephen receives punishment for something he never did, scheme to break his glasses, nor even that he is made the scapegoat for a sexual scandal he imperfectly comprehends, which is how he comes to

---

6. Carens speaks of the Clongowes episode as denoting an element of sexual ambivalence in Stephen (p. 319).

interpret the matter (I.1659–68); no, what is ironic is that, in the unconscious, where the thought or the wish can stand for the deed and carry the same transgressive force,[7] there is indeed a certain symmetry, if not equity, to Stephen's chastisement. If, as Stephen and the other boys suspect, the pandyings actually respond to the homoerotic indulgences of the smugging "ring," then Stephen can be seen as an accomplice after the fact, participating vicariously in these indulgences through his fantasy-construction of Mr. Gleeson's discipline. In fact, the imagined caning and the real pandying communicate with one another precisely through Stephen's erotic preoccupation with his masters' hands. Having taken a "queer quiet pleasure" from the contemplation of Mr. Gleeson's "white fattish hands, clean strong and gentle," Stephen seems to expect something of the same gratification from the prefect's fingers, in which he initially discerns a like quality, and Stephen finds Father Dolan's betrayal of this sensual promise to be, in some respects, the most galling aspect of the whole episode. His mind returns to it obsessively in the aftermath.

> [H]e thought of the hands which he had held out in the air with the palms up and of the firm touch of the prefect of studies when he had steadied the shaking fingers. (I.1559–62)

> He felt the touch of the prefect's fingers as they had steadied his hand and at first he had thought he was going to shake hands with him because the fingers were soft and firm: but then in an instant he had heard the swish of the soutane sleeve and the crash. (I.1586–90)

> And his whitegrey face and the nocoloured eyes behind the steelrimmed spectacles were cruel looking *because* he had steadied the hand first with his firm soft fingers and that was to hit it better and louder. (I.1597–1600, my emphasis)

Since we are dealing with Stephen's *perception* of the scene, the insistent, fetishistic repetition of "soft," "firm," "fingers," "touch," and "steadied," along with the bizarre causal priority accorded Dolan's duplicitous touch, must be seen as registering some sort of baffled desire as well as trauma or rather an overlapping of the two psychic movements. Stephen's trauma at the pandying fixates upon the master's touch because that is where Stephen's unconscious wishes insert themselves into both the smugging scandal and the larger homosocial-sexual economy of Clongowes. It is the point at

---

7. This is what Freud means by the omnipotence of the unconscious wish, a crucial motif everywhere in his work. See, in particular, chapter 3 of *Totem and Taboo*, [*The Standard Edition of the Psychological Works of Sigmund Freud,* ed. James Strachey (London: Hogarth P, 1961)], vol. 13, pp. 94–124.

which he has eroticized, and so from a certain point of view merited, the priests' brutal sanctions on such eroticism.

Stephen's subsequent protest at the injustice of his thrashing likewise belies his fascination with the male body, which is, of course, the vice being penalized.

> [A]nd the fifth was big Corrigan who was going to be flogged by Mr Gleeson. That was why the prefect of studies had called him a schemer and pandied him for nothing. . . . But he [Corrigan] had done something and besides Mr Gleeson would not flog him hard: and he [Stephen] remembered how big Corrigan looked in the bath. He had skin the same colour as the turf-coloured bogwater in the shallow end of the bath and when he walked along the side his feet slapped loudly on the wet tiles and at every step his thighs shook a little because he was fat. (I.1662–73)

Stephen wants to assert a distinction between guilty, robust Corrigan and poor little innocent Dedalus. But in doing so, he discloses a familiarity with Corrigan's physique apparently gleaned from watching his "every step" "in the bath," and the desire such familiarity would suggest seems further corroborated by the way Corrigan's bodily image simply takes over Stephen's juridical meditation. At the same time, his comparison of Corrigan's pigmentation to the dirty water in the bath recalls his own immersion in the square ditch and so indicates how profoundly this desire interfuses with dread.

Far from resolving this double bind, Conmee's vindication of Stephen and his schoolmates' ensuing homage only cements it. After his interview with the rector, Stephen is "hoisted" and "carried . . . along" (I.1824–25) in a homosocial bonding ritual that obviously makes him quite uncomfortable, for he immediately struggles to extricate his body from their grasp. And it is only once "[h]e was alone" that "[h]e was happy and free" (I.1833–34). He then proceeds to dissociate himself in a categorical fashion from any sense of triumph over the prefect and so, by extension, from the celebratory fellowship of his peers. The reason is not far to seek. The very image in which his sense of gratification crystallizes, a sound "like drops of water in a fountain falling softly in a brimming bowl" (I.1847–48), is but the inverse of his image of the dreaded "smugging" square, "all thick slabs of slate and water trickled all day out of tiny pinholes." The aestheticized emblem of personal fulfillment thus encodes and carries forward the cloacal image of taboo sexual longing. Just as the prospect of painful social humiliation—being singled out for a caning—triggers in Stephen a "queer quiet pleasure" amid anxiety, owing to its homoerotic undercurrents, so the fruits of Stephen's social victory trigger an unconscious anxiety amid validation, an anxiety registered along the associative chains of Stephen's mental imagery.

In this regard, the fact that this ambivalent water rhapsody actually emanates from a game of cricket, a sport exported from the elite playing fields of England to those of Ireland, implicates the author's unconscious as well in the structure of homoerotic disavowal. As Trevor L. Williams has argued, Joyce frames Stephen's success with a motif of colonial-cultural hegemony as a way of qualifying or undercutting its ultimate meaningfulness, in keeping with the alternating elevation/deflation mechanism of the narrative as a whole.[8] But in the process, Joyce necessarily undermines his own cherished distinction between the athletic customs of English and Irish boarding schools at precisely the moment when the sexual anxiety that distinction was intended to forestall infiltrates the crowning symbol of Stephen's young life—the brimming bowl.

Stephen's failure to resolve his "homosexual panic," in spite of his social victory, presages Joyce's treatment of the issue through the remainder of the novel, beginning with Stephen's entry into nominally heterosexual activity, from courtship rituals to whoring practices. Joyce consistently surrounds Stephen's participation in these things with forms of gender inversion, which, by the end of the century, was the dominant model of homosexuality in both the popular imagination and in the work of prominent sexologists like Havelock Ellis, Richard Krafft-Ebing, Edward Carpenter, and Freud (all of whom Joyce read).[9] As an effect of this pattern, the homoerotic surfaces in the text neither as a simple alternative to nor an anomalous deviation from some naturalized heteroerotic incitement, but as an element uncannily symbiotic with that incitement and menacing to its normalization.

First, just *before* the Harold's Cross children's party—Stephen's "coming out" as a heterosexual male—an old woman, possibly a relative of Stephen's, with a "whining voice" mistakes him for a female, repeating the phrase "I thought you were Josephine" several times (II.290, II.300). Often treated as an isolated epiphany, this interlude has little if any pertinence to the rest of the narrative, other than being the first of several instances in which gender inversion attaches specifically to Stephen. As such, it can be read as one of those incompletely processed "lumps" in which the subterranean

---

8. Trevor L. Williams, "Dominant Ideologies: The Production of Stephen Dedalus," in *The Augmented Ninth*, ed. Bernard Benstock (Syracuse: Syracuse Univ. Press, 1988), p. 316.
9. Havelock Ellis and J. A. Symonds, *Studies in the Psychology of Sex*, vol. 1, *Sexual Inversion* (London: Wilson & MacMillan, 1897); Edward Carpenter, *The Intermediate Sex* (Manchester: Labour Press, 1896); Baron Richard Von Krafft-Ebing, *Psychopathia Sexualis* (London: F. G. Rebman, 1892); Freud, *Three Essays on Sexuality, Standard Edition*, vol. 7, pp. 136–48; see Richard Brown, *James Joyce and Sexuality* (Cambridge: Cambridge Univ. Press, 1985), pp. 78–107.

concerns of a text concentrate themselves in a nearly illegible form. In support of this thesis, I would note that just *after* the party, Stephen actually bears out this gender (mis)identification in terms of the standard Victorian sexual typology.[1] On the tram ride home with E__ C__, he assumes what was though to be the essentially, even *definitively* feminine role of sexual passivity and withdrawal, receiving without responding to her sexual advances.

Once again, just before E__ C__'s attendance at Stephen's Whitsuntide performance, their first encounter since the party, a significant instance of gender misidentification supervenes. There appears backstage "a pinkdressed figure, wearing a curly golden wig and an oldfashioned straw sunbonnet, with black pencilled eyebrows and cheeks delicately rouged and powdered" (II.501–03). The presiding prefect asks facetiously, "Is this a beautiful young lady or a doll that you have here, Mrs Tallon?" (II.508–09). It turns out, of course, to be the "girlish figure" of a boy, "little Bertie Tallon," a circumstance that provokes "a murmur of curiosity" and then "a murmur of admiration" from the other boys (II.505, II.512, II.504, II.514–15). In Stephen, however, this transvestite spectacle precipitates a telling "movement of impatience. . . . He let the edge of the blind fall and . . . walked out of the chapel" (II.517–19). Why would Stephen react or overreact in this fashion? Perhaps because the superimposition of the signifiers of feminine desirability upon a schoolboy's already "girlish figure," the accompanying expression of the other schoolboys' admiration, and the disingenuous participation of the prefect combine to tap the ambivalence at the heart of Stephen's sexual desire (Carens 304–05), by recalling the roots of that ambivalence in his own school experience as the "little" boy, the mama's boy, the feminized boy. A subsequent passage, however, indicates that still more is at stake.

> All day he had thought of nothing but their leavetaking on the steps of the tram at Harold's Cross. . . . All day he had imagined a new meeting with her for he knew that she was to come to the play. The old restless moodiness had again filled his breast as it had done on the night of the party but had not found an outlet in verse. The growth and knowledge of two years of boyhood stood between then and now, forbidding such an outlet: and all day the stream of gloomy tenderness within him had started forth and returned upon itself in dark courses and eddies, wearying him in the end until the pleasantry of the prefect and the painted little boy had drawn from him a movement of impatience. (II.612–25)

1. Freud actually declares, "He understood now that active was the same as masculine, while passive was the same as feminine"—*An Infantile Neurosis, Standard Edition,* vol. 17, p. 47.

THRILLED BY HIS TOUCH 433

And why does the moodiness attached to Stephen's sexual "growth and knowledge," not to mention the restlessness accumulated over his day of brooding on Harold's Cross, vent itself *specifically* in response to a schoolboy's drag performance? Perhaps because Stephen's sexual ambivalence, tapped by this transvestic scenario, persists in such a way as to disturb the ease of his enlistment in the rolls of compulsory heterosexuality, his dalliance with E__ C__ being a critical step in this process. Notice, in this respect, that Stephen figures his feelings for E__ C__ as a "stream of gloomy tenderness" moving "in dark courses and eddies," a metaphor that unmistakably keys into and recirculates the homoerotic valences and associations of Stephen's past experience with dark or eddying courses of water: the square ditch, the sink at the Wicklow Hotel, the shallow end of the bath at Clongowes. Given this commingling of the "streams" of heterosexual affect with the "courses" of (water)closeted homosexual desire, Stephen's prescription for calming his heart after he misses E__ C__, the "odour" of "horse piss and rotted straw" (II.943–44), seems a recognizable enough displacement.

Finally, Stephen's venture into the brothel area is characterized by a literal and symbolic inversion of the phallic mode of heterosexual activity. He serves as the object or locus rather than the agent of penetration. First, "subtle streams" of sound "penetrated his being." Then, "[h]is hands clenched convulsively and his teeth set together as he suffered the agony of . . . penetration" (II.1404–06). Upon entering the prostitute's room, it is Stephen who becomes "hysterical," Stephen who is "surrendering himself," and Stephen who is penetrated by "the dark pressure of her softly parting lips" (II.1453–55). Moreover, Joyce frames Stephen's long anticipated (hetero)sexual transfiguration with lavatory motifs familiar from Clongowes. He depicts Stephen prowling "dark slimy streets" (II.1396), being penetrated by the "subtle streams" of sound, and issuing "a cry which was but the echo of an obscene scrawl which he had read on the oozing wall of a urinal" (II.1411–13). In this way, Joyce unsettles the popular *Bildungsmythos* of a young man's self-conscious graduation from homosexual play to heterosexual maturity and (re)productivity, and he replaces it with an ambivalent complication, a progressive overlapping and interfolding of sexual preferences that is registered at one level of self-narration only to be denied or externalized at another. Such interfolding even extends to Stephen's repentance for these sexual excesses at the religious retreat. For his nominally *heterosexual* sins, he imagines an eternal punishment expressive of his profound dread at his unacknowledged *homosexual* desires: a weedy field of "solid excrement" populated by bestial creatures with long phallic tails and faces whose similarity to and contact with the field give them an anal cast (III.1263, III.1267–82).

Keeping this sexual ambivalence at bay (what we might call the normative working through of homosexual panic) exerts a subtle yet potent pressure on the subsequent course of Stephen's development. On the one hand, his unconscious anxiety about the homoerotic component of his sexual drives can be seen as fueling his repentance and the renunciation of their illicit enactment. On the other hand, and more importantly, a gradual accretion of images and associations of sexual inversion and memories of the homosocial interplay at Clongowes work to hold Stephen back from the logical terminus of his recovered piety, turning his consideration of the religious life toward a relieved demurral.

The latter point becomes evident over the course of his vocational interview with the director of Belvedere. The director opens the interview with a comment on "the friendship between saint Thomas and saint Bonaventure" and goes on to criticize the feminine design of "[t]he capuchin dress" (IV.264) known as *"[l]es jupes"* (IV.279–80). Stephen's silent embarrassed response is a meditation upon the "soft and delicate stuffs" (IV.292) of women's clothing followed by a meditation on the Jesuit body, in both senses of the term:

> His masters, even when they had not attracted him, had seemed to him always intelligent and serious priests, athletic and high-spirited prefects. He thought of them as men who washed their bodies briskly with cold water and wore clean cold linen. (IV.308–12)

In a context thus informed by questions of homosocial affection and institutionalized cross-dressing, the director's ensuing gesture of releasing the blindcord suddenly cannot but trigger, in both Stephen and the reader, the unconscious memory of Bertie Tallon in drag and Stephen's own impatient responses: letting the edge of the blind fall.

As Stephen leaves the director, he begins to envisage his daily life as a priest in more concrete detail, and the (homo)eroticized traces of the past gather more thickly and affect him more intensely:

> The troubling odour of the long corridors of Clongowes came back to him. . . . At once from every part of his being unrest began to irradiate. A feverish quickening of his pulses followed. (IV.483–87)

An olfactory cue, always the strongest for Stephen, puts him in the grip of an excitement that cannot be explained on a purely nonsexual basis or in terms of simple attraction or repulsion, but only by way of the annihilating proximate-ness of a taboo desire, its alien and alienating intimacy. The memory of the bathhouse atmosphere at Clongowes returns to Stephen with precisely this quality, being *in* and yet not *of* him:

> His lungs dilated and sank as if he were inhaling a warm moist
> unsustaining air . . . which hung in the bath in Clongowes
> above the sluggish turfcoloured water. (IV.489–92)

The last phrase, it should be noted, substantially repeats Stephen's
mesmerized description of big Corrigan's naked body. So when
Stephen goes on to ground his refusal of the clerical life on "the pride
of his spirit which had always made him conceive himself as a being
apart in every order" (IV.503–05), he represses one of his libidinal
aims in the service of the larger economy of desire that feeds his
"panic." Stephen does not, as he later thinks, refuse the priesthood
by obedience to a "wayward instinct" (IV.654) but rather by the fear
of yet another "wayward instinct" implicated in his possible acceptance. This misprision resonates specifically in the odd, ambiguous
phrase "apart in [not from] every order" (IV.504–05). To be "apart
in" an order, after all, is also to be "a part in" that order; it is to find
oneself in a situation of belonging and estrangement simultaneously,
the condition of the proximate.

That Stephen's professedly homosocial discomfort cannot be dis-
sociated from homosexual anxiety grows even clearer during the climactic scene on the strand, where he receives his "true" calling. His
fetishistic (which is to say implicitly misogynistic) overvaluation of
the bird girl's physical presence follows a correspondingly aversive
overreaction to the physical presence of his unclothed schoolmates.

> It was a pain to see them and a swordlike pain to see the signs
> of adolescence that made repellent their pitiable nakedness.
> Perhaps they had taken refuge in number and noise from the
> secret dread in their souls. But he, apart from them and in
> silence, remembered in what dread he stood of the mystery of
> his own body. (IV.758–63)

The phallic ("swordlike") nature of Stephen's pain, his confounding of
his dread of others with a dread of self, and finally the now familiar
solace that he takes in a fantasy of dignified solitude, all indicate a recurrence of Stephen's homosexual panic. The representation of his
state of being upon removing himself from the spectacle of his naked
classmates even recalls the description of his state of being upon extri-
cating himself from his classmates' celebratory embrace at Clongowes.

> He was alone. He was unheeded, happy and near to the wild
> heart of life. (IV.848–49)

> He was alone. He was happy and free. (I.1833–34)

The crucial development on this occasion is that Stephen is able to
legitimate his resource of splendid isolation through the romantic
myth of the artist.

* * *

Here we have then the erotic hinge on which the *Künstlerroman* aspect of the narrative can be said to turn. Whereas the religious life figures for Stephen the perilous slide of homosocial relations toward homosexual exposure, prompting his flight, the aesthetic vocation figures the sublimation of homosocial ties through the elaboration of a heteroerotic ideal. It thus serves as a kind of supplement to the heterosexual imperative, a subsidiary distancing or mediating agency of homosocial bonds. That the heterosexual imperative should need the supplement of aesthetic transformation, however, is a sign of its ultimate vulnerability.

Such vulnerability is borne out in Stephen's friendship with Cranly, which features the closest thing *A Portrait* has to a French triangle: Stephen projects upon Cranly a mutual competitive interest in E__ C__. This triangle is modeled in turn onto an oedipal triangle, in which the paternalistic Cranly remonstrates with Stephen over the proper devotion to be paid his mother. We seem, in other words, to be moving toward what Sedgwick would see as a normative heterosexual/homophobic resolution. But it does not work. For if Stephen requires a heteroerotic ideal to sublimate his stubborn homoerotic ambivalence, his rarefaction of E__ C__ paradoxically renders her too shadowy and insubstantial a figure to mediate his powerful homosocial relationship with Cranly. Stephen's fleeting sense of romantic rivalry notwithstanding, Cranly increasingly comes to *take over* the place of E__ C__ as Stephen's object of affection. True to the terms of the novel outlined thus far, this transfer of erotic intensity and intimacy to a male figure passes through the register of religious intercourse.

Shortly before Stephen's initial thoughts of Cranly, there occurs a moment of gender misidentification of the sort that occurs prior to Stephen's first date with E__ C__. Stephen's father adverts to him as a "lazy bitch" (V.41). Joyce hereby intimates a structural parallel between Stephen's relations with E__ C__ and Cranly, a sort of dueling courtship. Stephen's thoughts themselves are fairly bursting with a barely repressed homoeroticism. He begins by wondering:

> Why was it that when he thought of Cranly he could never raise before his mind the entire image of his body but only the image of his head and face? (V.146–48)

The habit of mind Stephen observes would seem to locate Cranly, like the aestheticized image of Venus, exclusively "in a mental world" (V.1136), in this case by substantially blotting out his bodily existence. But the "mental world" in which Stephen would cloister his friend is sacerdotal rather than aesthetic; as the following passage indicates, Stephen's identification of the clerical orders with marked homosocial-sexual bonding has survived his rejection of them:

> The forms of the community emerged from the gustblown vestments. . . . They came ambling and stumbling, tumbling and capering, kilting their gowns for leap frog, holding one another back . . . smacking one another behind . . . calling to one another by familiar nicknames . . . whispering two and two behind their hands. (V.646–61)

The largely confessional nature of Stephen's mental intercourse with Cranly, in which he recounts "all the tumults and unrest and longings in his soul" (V.156–57), plugs directly into this homoerotic fantasy of church life, too directly, in fact, to escape Stephen's notice altogether. Even as he contemplates Cranly's "priestlike face," Stephen is brought up short remembering "the gaze of its dark womanish eyes," and "[t]hrough this image" of gender inversion, "he had a glimpse of a strange dark cavern of speculation" (V.152–63)—the very cavern, I would submit, that the present essay has traversed.

Stephen does not really explore this "cavern" until his last interview with Cranly, when he announces his imminent departure from Ireland. Most readers of this scene have followed Richard Ellmann in taking the "homosexual implications" to emanate largely, if not entirely, from Cranly—"Stephen's friend is as interested in Stephen as in Stephen's girl" * * *.[2] But Stephen is the one taken with Cranly's "large dark eyes" (V.2509), which he earlier finds "womanish"; Stephen is the one who inquires, with significant double entendre, "[A]re you trying to make a convert of me or a pervert of yourself?" (V.2429–30); and Stephen is the one whose sexual interests are left most ambiguous:

> Yes. His face was handsome: and his body was strong and hard. . . . He felt then the sufferings of women, the weaknesses of their bodies and souls: and would shield them with a strong and resolute arm and bow his mind to them.
>
> Away then: it is time to go. A voice spoke softly . . . bidding him go and telling him that his friendship was coming to an end. (V.2509–16)

Stephen here follows the cultural script of placing the figure of woman between himself and his homosocial counterpart, just as he did with the swimmers and with Lynch, but beside Cranly she disappears into a vapid generality. By the end of the passage, in fact, it is hard not to see Cranly as Stephen's *real* object of sexual rivalry rather than a rival for the favor of another. As if to emphasize this gender inversion, when an actual woman appears further on, mediating the "strife of their minds," Stephen perceives her in masculine

2. [Ellmann, *James Joyce*, 117.] An exception is Carens, who takes specific issue with Ellmann, arguing that Stephen is "drawn" to Cranly and partakes of "the current of latent homosexuality in the scene" (pp. 304, 323).

terms; he sees her "small and slender as a boy" and hears her voice "frail and high as a boy's" (V.2483–87). That the transferential woman now figures in Stephen's mind as male reflects the preeminence of Cranly in his affections.

Finally, if Cranly initiates the physical contact in this encounter, Stephen is the one who responds positively to it. Moreover, having eroticized the priestly office since his time at Clongowes, Stephen insistently positions Cranly as a cleric manqué, a priest without portfolio or the "power to absolve" (V.160). In this way, Stephen can himself experience sexual *frisson* without institutional subordination. This may, in fact, be the key to Stephen's relationship with Cranly. In order that Stephen may resolve the trauma of the doubtful or duplicitous "touch" of his masters, such as Father Dolan, he enlists Cranly to extend to him the "touch" of a doubtful mastery, a touch that elicits a less immediate sense of dread. But precisely because Stephen can be so "thrilled by his touch" (V.2585–86), Cranly embodies the most profound danger yet to Stephen's heterosexual self-conception. He not only represents the persistence of Stephen's religious sensibility in and despite his apostasy ("your mind," he says, "is supersaturated with the religion in which you say you disbelieve"—V.2335–36), but he also represents the persistence of its homoerotic attractions in and despite Stephen's aggressively heterosexual aesthetics.

As the vessel of this persistence, I would suggest, Cranly plays *the* decisive role in motivating Stephen's self-exile. For at this point Stephen can only reconstruct the aesthetic mission as a safely heterosexual adventure by making its completion somehow contingent upon separating himself from the "one person . . . who would be more than a friend" (V.2599–600), however much Stephen would like to project that sentiment onto Cranly alone. Surely it is no coincidence that this pivotal conversation with Cranly breaks off, assuring Stephen's departure, just when the issue of homosexual attraction and involvement, which has been diverted, displaced, and misrecognized throughout the novel, is finally if inconclusively broached. Stephen's last unanswered question, "Of whom are you speaking?" (V.2607), virtually epitomizes homosexual panic as a neurotic obsession with the identity, status, and location of homo-hetero difference and virtually defines Stephen as its captive.

Can we extend the diagnosis to Joyce and to his leavetaking? This question can only return us to the pragmatic riddles concerning self-revelation and fictional representation introduced at the outset of this essay. The unstable differential equation between Stephen and Joyce, wherein the protagonist conceals the author by standing for him, means that self-portraiture is its own refuge, requiring no deliberate forms of secrecy. All of the disclosures that Joyce might have packed or wanted to pack into his depiction of Stephen, includ-

ing the display of homoerotic desires and discomforts, ultimately
prove indistinguishable from the exercise of poetic license as a mode
of denial. That is to say, regarding such things as erotic preferences,
the ontology of self-portraiture makes the candor Joyce demanded
of authors easy because it makes the credulity of the reader impossible. A portrait of the artist is an open closet.

MARIAN EIDE

The Woman of the Ballyhoura Hills:
James Joyce and the Politics of Creativity[†]

The Irish Revival[1] was in its ascendancy when James Joyce embarked
on his career as a writer. And while there is increasing evidence that
he had sympathy with the movement's expression of revolutionary
Irish politics and its attempt to recreate an Irish national culture,[2]
his differences with specific positions and attitudes represented by
proponents of Irish nationalism are dramatized throughout his writings. In A Portrait of the Artist as a Young Man, Joyce addresses the
nationalist personification of Ireland as either an idealized woman
(Mother Ireland or the beautiful queen) or a degraded seductress
(the woman who invites a stranger into her bed) by creating his
own, resistant personification of Ireland in the woman of the Ballyhoura hills. This Irish peasant woman presents a brief though
complexly realized figure of the nation. In rendering her portrait,
Joyce indicates his strong commitment to an esthetic practice
grounded both in an Irish national identity and in a progressive sexual
politics. Joyce's version of national identity demands full consciousness as the basis for a morality comprised of equal parts responsibility and desire, without the bonds of repression or hypocrisy. Joyce,
then, counters a stereotypical morality that would equate responsibility and repression. In Portrait, his Irish national artist models full
consciousness in the act of creativity.

Readers might recognize Joyce's investment in the connection
between an artist's sexual experience and the esthetics that would
express a nation's identity emerging in a notebook Joyce kept in Trieste

---

† From Twentieth Century Literature 44:4 (Winter 1998): 377–93. Reprinted with the permission of the publisher. Some passages and notes have been modified or omitted. Information from the author's Works Cited list has been incorporated into her footnotes and
  new ones; some Works Cited entries have been omitted. Page references for A Portrait
  have been replaced with part and line numbers of this Norton Critical Edition. Some
  cited passages might differ slightly from the equivalent passages in this volume.
1. See, for example, the 1884 and 1893 entries in "Key Dates, Events, and Figures" (p. 229).
2. Vincent Cheng makes this argument compellingly in Joyce, Race, and Empire (New York:
   Cambridge UP, 1995).

while revising *Portrait*. In one entry he expresses concern over the
prevalence of sexual repression in Irish culture: "One effect of the
resurgence of the Irish nation would be the entry into the field of
Europe of the Irish artist and thinker, a being without sexual education."[3] * * * This entry records Joyce's belief that Irish writing will
have a separate and particularly national identity and that it will
have to compete in the field of European thought. The idea of a sexually inexperienced Irish artist concerns Joyce, and he counters this
type through the variety of sexual encounters Stephen Dedalus experiences. Through Stephen's sexual preoccupations Joyce associates
sexual and intellectual expression. Esthetics, national politics, and
sexuality are for Joyce mutually informing forces that Irish national
literature must address.

Mary Reynolds has pointed out that the inception of Joyce's career
was marked by his competition with the more idealist writers of the
Irish Revival, and with Yeats and Synge specifically. The substance
of that competition was to be his rival representation of the Irish
nation. In "The Day of the Rabblement," Joyce writes that the Irish
Literary Theatre has succumbed to the popular, unthinking nationalism of the crowd and to "the contagion of its fetishism and deliberate self-deception."[4] * * * In "The Holy Office," he rehearses his
role in Irish art as a counter to the idealism of his predecessors, a role
that makes him "the sewer of their clique. / That they may dream
their dreamy dreams / I carry off their filthy streams" (*CW* 151). In
Finnegans Wake, Joyce takes direct aim at the movement by calling it
the "cultic twalette" * * * , a phrase that both parodies Yeats's book
The Celtic Twilight and names Joyce's role as the sewer of an idealist movement.[5] In *Portrait*, his critique is more indirect. Resisting
the idealism of the Revival, *Portrait* responds with a myriad of representations that express an ambivalent view of the emerging nation.
Several emblems of creativity preoccupy Stephen and, as I will argue,
inform the political dimension of his developing esthetic theory in
the fifth part of *Portrait*. The first emblem is the ambiguous image
of a pregnant woman who stands in the doorway of her lighted

3. "The Trieste Notebook," *The Workshop of Daedalus: James Joyce and the Raw Materials for "A Portrait of the Artist as a Young Man,"* ed. Robert Scholes and Richard M. Kain. Evanston, Il.: Northwestern UP, 1965, 100 [Editor].
4. *The Critical Writings of James Joyce,* ed. Ellsworth Mason and Richard Ellmann. New York: Viking, 1959, 79. Hereafter abbreviated as *CW* [Editor].
5. *Finnegans Wake*. New York: Viking, 1939, 344.12. Hereafter abbreviated as *FW*. References provide page and line numbers [Editor]. Joyce's pun on *The Celtic Twilight* as "cultic toilette" signals the cult influence of Irish nationalism, a label that would indicate both the unexamined adherence of its members and the movement's transience. The French *toilette* gestures toward the hypocritical purism of the movement. *Les toilettes* are water closets and indicate Joyce's role as the sewer into which the movement deposits the more undesirable and unacknowledged aspects of experience. *La toilette* refers to a woman's clothing or outfit and indicates the extent to which this cult dresses up, clothes, and disguises the actual corpus of Irish experience [Author].

cottage inviting a stranger into her bed. The second recalls Shelley's idea of a fading coal brought partially to light by an inconstant wind. These images, in turn, ground Joyce's esthetics in both national and sexual politics.

While Joyce's objections to the politics of the Irish Revival led some contemporary readers to label him an estheticist (placing art above the quotidian concerns of politics or morality), Joyce actually dramatizes both the nationalist and the estheticist points of view * * * in such a way as to declare his subtle differences from both and to mark out a national politics that informs his esthetic approach.

* * *

Joyce is not * * * completely dismissing the claims of the Gaelic League by representing Stephen's difficult relations with their program. He is sympathetic, though not ultimately in agreement, with their rebellion against the imposition of the English language in Ireland. Stephen's esthetic objectives encompass a complex desire for liberation (both erotic and political) that must be based on a coherent and independent identity for the Irish nation. In Stephen's view it is the responsibility of the Irish artist to "forge" a "conscience" for the Irish nation. In other words, the Irish artist creates a way for the Irish to understand themselves as separate from the double colonizing forces of Roman Catholicism and British imperial rule.[6] The artist must also imagine an independent morality that is not constrained by the dominant paradigms created by these two institutions. In forging such a conscience, Stephen uses the English language as his medium. Yet he is aware that this language is itself a symptom of external controls. In creating an esthetic theory compatible with his national conscience, Stephen must consider the problem of language: how does an artist write in the language of the master without acceding to the colonial influence of the master's own esthetic?

In a conversation that introduces and informs Stephen's discussion of esthetics, Joyce dramatizes the loss of the Irish language as a loss to the nation and the national artist. Talking with the dean in the physics theater before class, Stephen discovers that they use different words to refer to an instrument for filling lamps. The dean calls it a funnel while Stephen calls it a tundish, a word that the dean, who is English, assumes to be Irish. Stephen notes their different relations to the English language and is troubled by the implications:

6. In *Ulysses* (Ed. Hans Walter Gabler. New York: Vintage, 1986, lines 638–44), Stephen, quoting Jesus, describes himself as a servant to two masters and refers explicitly to the Roman Catholic church and the imperial British state.

> —The language in which we are speaking is his before it is
> mine. How different are the words *home, Christ, ale, master,* on
> his lips and on mine! I cannot speak or write these words with-
> out unrest of spirit. His language, so familiar and so foreign,
> will always be for me an acquired speech. I have not made or
> accepted its words. My voice holds them at bay. My soul frets in
> the shadow of his language. (V.553–59)

Recognizing English as a colonial language and one in which his
particularly Irish thoughts might not easily be spoken, Stephen
nonetheless realizes that this language is his "native" tongue, the
first he learned to speak. Like many Irish, he does not speak * * *
his "own language." The result is that the medium of Stephen's
esthetic expression will always be foreign for him; he speaks in an
acquired speech and writes in an acquired script.

Even the possibility of an Irish influence within the English language is minimized by Stephen's later realization:

> That tundish has been on my mind for a long time. I looked it
> up and find it English and good old blunt English too. Damn
> the dean of studies and his funnel! What did he come here for
> to teach us his own language or to learn it from us? (V.2740–44)

Stephen's realization of the loss of his national language and his initial thoughts about the effect of this loss on his writing, however, do
not spark an attendant nationalist politics. He presents the issue of
lost language in conversation with his friend Davin in the context of
his refusal to serve a nationalist cause: "My ancestors threw off their
language and took another . . . They allowed a handful of foreigners
to subject them. Do you fancy I am going to pay in my own life and
person debts they made?" (V.1031–34). Yet Stephen's attempt to
create an Irish art that will forge a national conscience is a version
of the sacrifice he refuses at this moment.

                              *   *   *

In *Portrait,* Joyce presents Stephen's esthetic theory in a private
conversation with one sympathetic though distracted listener.
Lynch admits to eating dung as a child, swears in "yellow," and rubs
his groin when amused. Readers might initially wonder why Joyce
chooses this crass character (rather than the more cerebral Cranly, for
example) as a respondent to Stephen's ideas on the apprehension of
the beautiful. Yet Lynch asks the pivotal question that reveals Joyce's
difference from estheticism and suggests Stephen's national and
political investments.

> —What do you mean, Lynch asked surlily, by prating about
> beauty and the imagination in this miserable Godforsaken island?

No wonder the artist retired within or behind his handiwork
after having perpetrated this country. (V.1474–77)

Lynch's witty heresy temporarily masks his significant contribution
to the discussion by suggesting that art must take into account its
context: "this miserable Godforsaken island." While God may have
absented himself after the creation of the universe, the more earthly
artist must create within and in response to those conditions.

Stephen realizes this necessity most concretely in concerns about
his audience. It is clear that he wants to write for Irish readers and
to have a measurable effect on their thought, and through his recollection of Davin's story he links this responsibility with sexual experience.

> How could he hit their conscience or how cast his shadow over
> the imaginations of their daughters, before their squires begat
> upon them, that they might breed a race less ignoble than
> their own? * * * A woman had waited in the doorway as Davin
> had passed by at night and, offering him a cup of milk, had all
> but wooed him to her bed; for Davin had the mild eyes of one
> who could be secret. But him no woman's eyes had wooed.
> (V.2265–75)

Given his spotty record in romance, Stephen despairs of the influence he might have through creativity in parenting. But he demands
of his art a greater influence, that it might parent an altered Irish
race. Stephen thinks about his art and its audience in immediate
association with Davin's encounter with a woman in the Ballyhoura
hills. For Stephen, she represents a troubling yet auspicious alternative view of the nation he is writing for and about. This woman
acts from a conscience that is freed from the repressive demands of
traditional morality and that also metaphorically addresses the status of Ireland as a colony that demands its independence. In her
figure and her choices, Stephen finds a model for his national esthetics as a coming into consciousness by way of an altered understanding of morality. The woman of the Ballyhoura hills is neither
the Irish temptress who betrays her nation by bedding the English
stranger, nor the devouring Irish mother who demands a blood sacrifice of her children and then betrays them to the conqueror, the
"old sow that eats her farrow" (V.1055). Stephen's "Mother Ireland" is a figure of the plenitude and excess of creativity; hers is an
erotic abundance that a nationalist might reject but Joyce clearly
embraces.

While walking through Dublin streets to the university one morning, Stephen remembers the story about the Ballyhoura woman that
Davin confided only to him. One night, stranded after a late-ending
hurling match, Davin chose to walk the entire way home. On his

way he grew thirsty and stopped at a lighted cottage to ask for a
drink. Stephen recollects Davin's account of what followed:

> I spied a little cottage with a light in the window. I went up
> and knocked at the door. A voice asked who was there and I
> answered. . . . After a while a young woman opened the door. . . .
> She was half undressed as if she was going to bed when I
> knocked and she had her hair hanging; and I thought by her fig-
> ure and by something in the look of her eyes that she must be
> carrying a child. She kept me in talk a long while at the door and
> I thought it strange because her breast and her shoulders were
> bare. She asked me was I tired and would I like to stop the night
> there. * * * I didn't go in, Stevie. I thanked her and went on my
> way again all in a fever. At the first bend of the road I looked back
> and she was standing at the door. (V.305–26)

Davin's recollection is marked by a wistful ambivalence. His gaze
returns to the woman even as he walks away into the night. He
describes the woman as pregnant, though his evidence is slight. He
shores up the equivocal testimony of her figure with the more ambiguous observation of the "look in her eyes." It is as though he must guard
against his own sexual longings by transforming this woman into the
erotically inaccessible ideal of Irish motherhood. The simultaneous
belief in her pregnancy and in the sexual intentions underlying her
invitation drive Davin's account. Stephen's recollection of the incident highlights these two elements and by doing so reminds us of his
own varying and conflicted reactions to women. The peasant woman
emerges in *Portrait* as a fantasized projection that reveals more
about Davin and Stephen than about the woman herself. It is precisely the conflict and ambivalence through which Joyce recounts
the incident that become the vehicle for a reworking of traditional
myths about Irish colonization. The woman of the Ballyhoura hills
presents an altered version of the conventional representation of Ireland as a woman who invites the colonizing stranger into her bed.

In 1152, Devorgilla, the wife of nobleman O'Rourke, deserted her
husband to join her lover, the rival lord MacMurrough. O'Rourke,
furious at her adulterous defection and unwilling to allow her release
from their marriage, decided to attack his rival. After being driven
into exile by O'Rourke, MacMurrough called on the famous English
soldier Strongbow. Unfortunately for Ireland, Strongbow took as his
spoils a portion of Irish territory, and that, as some of Joyce's characters theorize, was the opportunity that facilitated English colonization of the island.[7] From this historical event grew the legend

---

7. Accounts of this conflict vary widely. Some historians claim that Devorgilla was kid-
   napped. See R. F. Foster, *The Oxford History of Ireland*. Oxford: Oxford UP, 1989, 47–48
   [Editor].

that attributed to Devorgilla's desertion the invasion of foreign forces. That early legend initiated the clichéd image of Ireland as a betraying woman, an image that has endured as a mythical explanation for Ireland's colonial history under English rule.

*   *   *

Through Davin's experience, Joyce's narration debunks this misogynist explanation of Ireland's colonization. In *Portrait,* the stranger to whom the Irish woman opens her door is, of course, not a stranger. Rather, Davin is depicted as a particularly Irish figure; his proficiency in Gaelic, his dedication to Irish nationalist politics, and his rural past mark him significantly as a native:

> the young peasant worshipped the sorrowful legend of Ireland. The gossip of his fellowstudents which strove to render the flat life of the college significant at any cost loved to think of him as a young fenian. His nurse had taught him Irish and shaped his rude imagination by the broken lights of Irish myth. (V.244–49)

Davin is distrustful of foreign ideas and influences, and especially of the English. In fact, Stephen has discovered a cache of violent nationalist literature in Davin's room and taunts him with excerpts: "Long pace, fianna! Right incline, fianna! Fianna, by numbers, salute, one, two!" In his defense, Davin describes himself as an Irish nationalist "first and foremost" (V.989–92). Davin, assuming the role of the foreign invader in the paradigmatic encounter with the native woman, inverts the structure because he is so clearly a compatriot.

Davin's national politics are paired with sexual purism and so his friendship with the more sexually adventurous and politically ambiguous Stephen is a challenge for the patriot. When Davin questions Stephen's allegiances, his argument is based in part on his politics but almost equally on his unorthodox sexual history. Davin admits that the thought of Stephen's sexual experiences temporarily prevented him from eating and sleeping. Stephen's response is unexpected; he defends himself by claiming that "This race and this country and this life produced me" (V.1027). In other words, it is not only personal experience that structures political vision; the national political situation shapes even the most personal experiences. Understanding this claustrophobic arrangement, in which the moral hypocrisy of the Irish nation produces a sexual underclass and prevents the honest expression to which his art aspires, Stephen protests:

> When the soul of a man is born in this country there are nets flung at it to hold it back from flight. You talk to me of nationality, language, and religion. I shall try to fly by those nets. (V.1047–50)

The nationalist vision of Ireland, as represented in *Portrait* by Davin and in Joyce's life by the writers of the Irish Revival, was a vision that both Stephen and Joyce saw as typical of Irish repression, a restraint from flight. It is possible to interpret Stephen's comment, "I shall try to fly by those nets," as an indication of his objective "to fly by" or beyond the constraints that the Irish nation places on his creativity. But it is also possible to understand Stephen's metaphor to mean that he will use the very restraints presented by Irish culture as the means for his flight; he will fly by means of those nets. Such a choice is figured by the exile that Joyce chose, an exile that always returned his gaze to Ireland. Just as his reading of the repressive accusation against Ireland's prostitution became the opportunity for him to read subversive potential into the actions of the woman of the Ballyhoura hills, the nets that his nation places on him become the means for a subversion of both imperialist and nationalist politics.

* * * This pregnant Helen of the Ballyhoura hills does not cross national boundaries or incite war.[8] Insofar as sexual activity is limited within the confines of her Catholic culture to the goal of reproduction, her putative pregnancy renders the erotic invitation she extends to Davin a sort of redundancy, an excess. Because another (marital) sexual encounter has apparently already taken place, she simultaneously plays the roles of Ireland as mother and as whore, undermining the validity of each of these familiar types with her doubled gesture. While I am tempted to read the woman's invitation as a gesture of abundance and eroticism, Stephen's memory is not explicit in this way. Her erotic gesture could just as easily be motivated by loneliness or revenge. Whatever the unnamed catalyst, her actions introduce an excess into the expected economy of a monogamous Catholic marriage; her desire is inherently subversive of the institution by which she is bound.

The woman's erotic impulse also serves to remind us that occupation (marital or colonial) does not promise either control or permanence. The marriage laws that have promised her absent husband ownership of his bride are easily broken. Even while the mark of that ownership lies on her body, even as her pregnancy provides a visible sign of occupation by his seed and their progeny, her actions exceed the control of ownership or occupation. She can repeat the sexual act that promised her husband dominion over her body. By initiating that act with another she insures that neither man will have permanent control. Her promiscuity gives new meaning to the traditional notion of Ireland as a prostitute who invites the stranger

8. In Greek mythology, Helen was noted for her beauty; her abduction by Paris, son of the king of Troy, resulted in the Trojan War [Editor].

into her bed. The very prostitution that seduces the stranger also promises the impermanence of his reign and ultimately guarantees her own sovereignty. The pregnant woman's sexual invitation recalls the multiple colonial occupations whose progeny became the hybrid nation of modern Ireland. In *Finnegans Wake*, for example, Joyce describes Ireland as a nation of "Miscegenations on miscegenations" (*FW* 18.20).

If Davin had chosen to occupy this woman's bed, he would have filled that role only temporarily. The seduction and its outcome are limited by evidence that this occupation is only the most recent in a series. Nor does the woman's pregnancy give primacy to her husband's previous occupation of her bed. On the contrary, impregnation facilitates her adulterous longing as it makes her new erotic encounter safe from the worry of procreative repercussions.

When Davin declines the woman's invitation, the myth is displaced once more and emphasis is shifted from the blame placed on a promiscuous woman to the burden of choice that devolves on her suitor. It is not that her pregnancy makes the woman seem more virtuous. Perhaps the opposite is true. Rather, as we understand the experience mediated through Davin's perspective, we are made aware of his responsibility in the thwarted coupling. * * * Davin's refusal indicates his shared responsibility. Davin is specifically presented as an Irish nationalist, highlighting a rarely noted aspect of Devorgilla's mythic betrayal. Her erotic pursuits did not lead her to the bed of an Englishman but to a rival Irish leader.

Colbert Kearney indicates another context through which Davin's encounter with the woman of the Ballyhoura hills may be read. Kearney associates this encounter with the aisling tradition, which he defines as:

> a species of visionary poem with a clear political allegory. . . . In a typical *aisling*, the poet is lost in the mist or twilight when he is confronted by a woman of superhuman beauty. He asks if she is one of the fairy spirits or one of the classical goddesses or one of the legendary beauties. She replies . . . that she is Ireland and that she is imprisoned by a brutal tyrant and will remain so until her true love comes from overseas and liberates her. The poet pledges himself to her and promises to do all in his power to expedite her liberation.[9]

According to Kearney, Davin fails to recognize the Ballyhoura peasant woman as Ireland herself because he has been too rigidly trained in a rude nationalism that romanticizes Ireland. His particular politics place a strong restriction on the sexual adventure this woman

9. Colbert Kearney, "The Image of Ireland in Joyce's *Portrait*," *The Artist and the Labyrinth*, ed. Augustine Martin. London: Ryan, 1990, 108 [Editor].

offers. In other words, it is precisely Davin's nationalist training that prevents him from taking the romantic role of the poet in the aisling who recognizes and liberates the Irish nation.[1] In rendering the incident, Joyce highlights the connection between sexual liberation and national independence.

The figure of this woman as a representation of Ireland subverts common assumptions about the role of gender in the politics of colonization. She is not recognizable as the beautiful woman to whose side the nationalist poet rushes, nor does she fit the type of the temptress in historical legends. She is a distorted combination of these two, equal parts dark and light. (Joyce presents this mingling of oppositional categories metaphorically by the woman's placement in the vestibule between the lighted cottage and the darkened landscape.) And Stephen, in remembering Davin's confidence, processes the memory in a peculiar way that continues to subvert the hackneyed view of Mother Ireland as the woman who welcomes the colonist into her homeland only to find she needs the poet to rescue her from her plight. Davin's encounter recalls these myths at the same time that it undermines the assumptions arising from them.

> The last words of Davin's story sang in his memory and the figure of the woman in the story stood forth, reflected in other figures of the peasant women whom he had seen standing in doorways at Clane as the college cars drove by, as a type of her race and his own, a batlike soul waking to the consciousness of itself in darkness and secrecy and loneliness and, through the eyes and voice and gesture of a woman without guile, calling the stranger to her bed. (V.327–34)

The description of the peasant woman as a "batlike soul waking to the consciousness of itself in darkness and secrecy and loneliness" anticipates precisely the words Stephen later uses in thinking about E.C.: "she was a figure of the womanhood of her country, a batlike soul waking to the consciousness of itself in darkness and secrecy and loneliness" (V.1666–69).[2] Given Stephen's puerile comparison

---

1. Mary Reynolds offers a different explanation for Davin's refusal in "Davin's Boots: Joyce, Yeats, and Irish History," *Joycean Occasions: Essays from the Milwaukee James Joyce Conference*, ed. Janet E. Dunleavy, et al. Newark: U of Delaware P, 1991, 218–34. She points out that his reaction is partly defined by years of English terrorism among Irish peasants. For although the Irish countryside at *Portrait*'s narrative time, 1902, was prosperous (as indicated by Davin's well-made boots), the people who resided there still reacted to centuries of English oppression. "Stephen realizes that what repels him in his peasant friend . . . is Davin's slow reluctance of speech and deed—these qualities are actually a survival of the peasant response to English terror, a dehumanizing effect . . ." (231).
2. Vincent Cheng * * * explores this bat metaphor by drawing on its implication of prostitution. Certainly the element of prostitution in national and sexual politics is a strong part of the material with which Stephen struggles in assessing Davin's story. Stephen's metaphor questions whether Ireland prostitutes herself or expresses desire. See his " 'The Bawk of Bats' in Joyce's Belfry: The Flitter in the Feminine," *Joycean Occasions*, 125–37.

of women with marsupials in the draft form of this novel, this observation can be read as purely misogynist.[3] But I think his comment is
complicated by his realization at this moment that he has wronged
E.C., who has the right both to her innocence and to her desires.
The comment is also complicated by the identification with the
batlike woman as a "type of her race and his own." Stephen is not
necessarily thinking that sexually experienced women are either
mothers (marsupials) or whores (bats), nor is his metaphor solely an
attempt to imply an animal lack of consciousness. Rather, her mind,
like his, and like that of their common "race," is waking into consciousness of itself.

It is precisely this trajectory from the unconscious into consciousness that Stephen associates with the act of artistic creativity later
in the fifth chapter, when he culls from Percy Shelley's "Defense
of Poetry" the idea of the fading coal that is for both Shelley and
Stephen the image of the mind in the act of creation. In the
"Defense," Shelley writes:

> Poetry is not like reasoning, a power to be exerted according to
> the determination of the will. A man cannot say, "I will com-
> pose poetry." The poet cannot even say it; for the mind in cre-
> ation is as a fading coal, which some invisible influence, like an
> inconstant wind, awakens to transitory brightness; . . . and the
> conscious portions of our natures are unprophetic either of its
> approach or its departure.[4]

Shelley proposes that the impulse for poetic expression has its origins in the unconscious. When an inconstant and unpredictable
wind lights on the coal, it glows. He draws this image, in his bril-
liantly literal-minded way, from the word *inspire,* which means "to
blow into." Creativity, then, is a record of the invisible movement of
unconscious thought into conscious expression (just as pregnancy
is the sign, partly visible and partly invisible, of the movement
of potential creativity into actual creation in the biological context). As Stephen explains it in his conversation with Lynch, "This
supreme quality" (by which Stephen means "radiance," the last in
his four phases of apprehension) "is felt by the artist when the
esthetic image is first conceived in his imagination. The mind in
that mysterious instant Shelley likened beautifully to a fading coal"
(V.1395–98).

3. *Stephen Hero,* ed. John J. Slocum and Herbert Cahoon. New York: New Directions, 1944,
1963, 176. Suzette Henke eloquently presents this point of view. See her "Stephen
Dedalus and Women: A Portrait of the Artist as a Young Misogynist," *Women in Joyce,* ed.
Suzette Henke, et al. Urbana: U of Illinois P, 1982, 82–107.
4. Percy Bysshe Shelley, "A Defense of Poetry," *Shelley's Poetry and Prose,* ed. Donald H.
Reiman and Sharon B. Powers. New York: Norton, 1977, 503–04.

Stephen might not consciously associate the radiant moment of apprehension with E.C. and the pregnant woman as types for the Irish race coming into awareness of itself. And some have made the argument that his point is precisely to delimit the creativity of women as a purely physical phenomenon. Judith A. Spector notes that:

> The message is clear; since women have physical wombs, they must be relegated to the realm of the physical. The female characters in *Dubliners, A Portrait,* and *Ulysses* are limited to their physicality and preoccupied with their sexuality; they are assuredly not intellectuals or artists.[5]

Spector argues that Joyce opposes women's physical creativity to men's intellectual creativity. But while Stephen may be guilty of such a simplified opposition, Joyce's objective is to reconcile physical and intellectual creation. Joyce draws an analogy between the woman's process of coming into consciousness and the artistic endeavor through the metaphor provided by pregnancy. And while pregnancy, labor, and delivery have long provided male writers with an image for their act of poetic creation, Joyce's version of this comparison is quite different. The pregnant woman, casting light into the shadows through her open door and moving between consciousness and its lack, replicates the movement of wind on Shelly's partially lit coal. The metaphor that balances light with dark in the woman's placement in the doorway and in the fading coal's brightened response to wind presents the woman's physical creativity as analogous to the poet's creativity, a waking into consciousness. The woman's role in creativity is not wholly subsumed by the author nor is she made a passive object in this representation. It is important to note also that Joyce does not imagine the pregnant woman as a muse. Nor is this woman a receptacle, merely, for the seed of masculine creativity. For it is not on her pregnancy that the representation of this memory lays its emphasis. Rather, our attention is drawn to her initiating erotic impulse as an act of creativity; the desiring impulse itself is coupled with the darkness and secrecy of her soul in the moment that it begins to waken to consciousness of itself.

It is curious that the text places the peasant woman in this liminal space between consciousness and its lack. Intuitively, I would be inclined to associate the political oppression of a colonized Irish woman with the structures of repression in the unconscious itself. We need look no further than May Dedalus to understand the oppression suffered by Catholic women in colonial Ireland. And

---

5. Judith A. Spector, "On Defining a Sexual Aesthetic: A Portrait of the Artist as Sexual Antagonist," *Midwest Quarterly* 26 (1984): 83.

Joyce's texts abound with examples of such women: visibly suffering the ill effects of a repressive culture that confines them to a few, preferably invisible and certainly restraining, roles. But in following that intuitive judgment, I would be guilty of precisely the error that Stephen makes more flamboyantly in calling women marsupials. I would assume that social oppression relegated Irish women clearly and irretrievably to the territory of darkness and mute physicality. Joyce draws our attention to the peasant woman to indicate that there is always excess that erupts beyond the borders of any oppression. While the conditions in which the woman lives demand monogamy and fertility, her sexuality moves against and distorts these cultural boundaries. She uses her pregnancy to mark her husband's absence with an expression of desire that transgresses community sanctions.

Joyce marks the porous borders of repression with the sign of creativity in the same gesture that marks the woman's body with the sign of biological creation. The transition between the pregnant woman's reproductive function and her erotic impulse, as differing signs of creativity, marks a portal of escape from repression, an opportunity to "fly by those nets." From that portal of escape, Joyce traces the barely perceptible movement of creativity along subversive pathways away from the reservoirs of cultural oppression, whether it is imperialist or nationalist. Stephen's remembrance of the woman subverts the clichéd stories that frame her choices. Joyce's image equates the coming into consciousness of a nation with the coming into consciousness of desire. Davin's withdrawal from desire reminds readers that for Joyce, Irish nationalism, like the literary movements that support it, is hampered by an investment in sexual repression, and that esthetic creativity requires creative receptivity.

PERICLES LEWIS

The Conscience of the Race: The Nation as Church of the Modern Age†

Joyce's Stephen Dedalus and by extension Joyce himself have gained a reputation among some literary critics as apolitical "individualists" because Stephen rejects overtly nationalistic art.[1] Yet, even as he

† From *Joyce through the Ages: A Nonlinear View*, ed. Michael Patrick Gillespie. Gainesville: UP of Florida, 1999, 85–106. Reprinted with permission of the University Press of Florida. Some cited passages, some parenthetical citations, and some notes have been abridged or omitted, and the author has provided some additional notes. Page references for *A Portrait* have been replaced with part and line numbers of this Norton Critical Edition.
1. Vincent Cheng, *Joyce, Race, and Empire* (Cambridge: Cambridge UP, 1995), 74.

refuses to learn Irish or to endorse the program of the Gaelic League, Stephen affirms the importance of his nationality to his art: "This race and this country and this life produced me. . . . I shall express myself as I am" (V.1027–28). This budding artist proposes to use the fact that he himself is a product of a particular race and country as a means of achieving a new sort of freedom. This freedom will consist in using his experience and his self-expression to embody the fate of the race that has created him. * * * Although Stephen does not endorse the nationalist political program, he does set himself the typically nationalistic goal of reviving his nation-race. He hopes to do so, however, not through traditionally political activity but by searching within his own soul and, through his writing, affording his race an opportunity for rebirth. Joyce's narrative technique emphasizes the close relationship between Stephen and the Irish race. In revising the traditional plot structure of the novel of disillusionment, Joyce attempts to overcome the radical distinction between the God's-eye-view of the omniscient narrator and the limited perspective of the individual character. It is through the fusion of these two perspectives at the end of the novel, with Stephen's ascension to the role of narrator, that Joyce inaugurates a radical revision of the novelistic tradition. At the same moment, Stephen attempts to overcome his own subjectivity by merging it in the larger fate of his nation. Thus, I will argue, the aim of rebuilding the nation plays an important role in the formal structure of the novel and is not merely a secondary thematic concern.

A *Portrait of the Artist as a Young Man* tells the story of Stephen's emergence into consciousness as an entrance into Irish history. Political events that play a crucial role in Stephen's conception of his place in history, such as the fall of Parnell, precede Stephen's conscious understanding of Irish politics, and Stephen's attempts to understand such events are part of the novel's drama. From the first page of the novel, references to the Irish historical and political situation fill Stephen's growing mind. Dante's two brushes—a maroon one for the radical Michael Davitt and a green one for the moderate Parnell—color his childhood perceptions before he even knows what the colors may signify. As a child, Stephen cannot solve the problems that theology and politics raise for him: "It pained him that he did not know well what politics meant and that he did not know where the universe ended. He felt small and weak" (I.345–47). Stephen is conscious of growing up in a world in which politics and history weigh upon the brains of the living. He is surrounded by discussions of Irish politics and particularly of Parnell's campaign for Home Rule. Already Stephen's awakening consists in his becoming conscious of his entrapment in the nightmare of Irish history. Without being able to articulate the reasons for his fate, the young hero feels himself to be growing up as part of what his father calls a "priest-ridden Godforsaken race" (I.1081). When he goes to the rector to complain of having been beaten by Father Dolan, he sees himself as a historical personage: "A thing like that had been done before by somebody in history, by some great person whose head was in the books of history. . . . History was all about those men and what they did" (I.1637–44). To find his own place in history, Stephen places Irish history in the context of a mythical religious pattern that culminates in his own person.

Stephen's entrapment in the nightmare of Irish history and his living out of its logic make him the potential author of an Irish national epic. Stephen proposes to do rather more, however, than simply justify the ways of God to Irishmen. In this potential epic, the artist himself will play the role of the redeeming hero who, by his mystical union with the conscience of the race, helps to transform the Irish people. Stephen ends his diary entry for 26 April with the famous declaration that could stand as a motto for many of the novelists of his day: "Welcome, O life! I go to encounter for the millionth time the reality of experience and to forge in the smithy of my soul the uncreated conscience of my race" (V.2788–90). The conjunction "and" in this little manifesto suggests the close but oblique relationship between the two goals the aspiring novelist has set for himself. The encounter with experience seems deeply personal, while the forging of the conscience of the race has important political implications. Yet Stephen links the personal and political goals by claiming that the forging will take place in the smithy of his soul. The problem that has faced many literary critics in interpreting Stephen's project has been that the quest for an authentic form of a pure, inner experience seems at variance with the desire to transform the "race." If Stephen really wants to serve his race, then why does he leave Ireland and bury himself in books? Why does he not join the nationalist movement and fight for political independence? Or why not, at least, write a work that will rouse other Irishmen to political action?

Answers to these questions depend on a rather odd form of theology in which the idea of the racial conscience takes the place preserved in the Catholic tradition for the idea of God, the only "uncreated" being in Christian theology, while the actual living members of the Irish nation become the Church of this new religion. Stephen himself plays the role of Christ in this nationalist theology, redeeming by reshaping the conscience of his race. This theology, I shall argue, places an emphasis on the role of the race in shaping the individual's experience that has often been ignored in Joyce criticism.

Stephen's use of the expression "uncreated" has often been taken to imply that Stephen plans to create a brand new racial conscience from nothing (to "forge" in the sense of "inventing"). Most critics assume that Stephen wishes to break free from Irish tradition and to invent something entirely new, in a Godlike *creatio ex nihilo*.[2] * * * It is true that in 1912, Joyce spoke of himself as "one of the writers of this generation who are perhaps creating at last a conscience in the soul of this wretched race."[3] By the time he finished *A Portrait of the Artist as a Young Man* in 1914 or 1915, however, Joyce came to a more significant theologic formulation of the relationship between the artist and the people that seems to imply a rather different conception of the role of the artist. For Joyce, I shall argue, the artist's work involved not a *creatio ex nihilo* but a reconfiguration of the eternal forces that had formed the racial conscience. The artist's role was not to invent a new consciousness for the race but to epitomize the age-old racial conscience that created both the artist and his people.

There are a number of reasons to suspect that Stephen's project involves not so much the creation of something new as the reshaping of what is old. The *Oxford English Dictionary* notes that, in Christian dogma, *uncreated* is originally and most commonly used to refer to the Creator, who is "of a self-existent or eternal nature," who precedes creation, and who is the source of the entire created world. By calling the racial conscience "uncreated," Stephen suggests not that this collective soul remains to be invented, but rather that it is itself the source of all experience, something permanent like God and unlike all mortal creatures. Ibsen's Brand, to whom Stephen alludes in this diary entry, says, for example: "I do not aim at anything that's new, / I stand to champion the eternal law . . . / There is an end to all created things . . . / But there is one thing indestructible. / *That* is the uncreated soul of man . . ."[4] Both Brand and Stephen are proposing heretical views, since the soul of man and the conscience of the race are properly, in Catholic theology, created things, while God alone is uncreated.

Stephen himself is highly conscious of the theological implications of his language and particularly of the theology of creation. Earlier in the novel, he has listened to a sermon that dwelt on the problem of creation. The preacher tells him that God is "the supremely good and loving Creator Who has called [the] soul into existence from nothingness" and refers to the torment into which "the created soul" falls upon separation from God (III.932–39). When Stephen later proposes to forge in the smithy of his soul the

---

2. "Creation of the universe out of nothing" (Latin) [Editor].
3. Richard Ellmann, *James Joyce,* Rev. ed. (New York: Oxford UP, 1982), 344.
4. Henrik Ibsen, *Brand,* trans. G. M. Gathorne-Hardy (Seattle: U of Washington P, 1966), Act 1 scene 1, p. 49.

uncreated conscience of his race, he is placing the conscience of the race on a level with God, the uncreated, in opposition to his own soul, which is merely created. In "forging" the "uncreated" conscience of his race, then, Stephen will not be inventing something entirely new, but reenacting and thus reshaping an eternal substance that precedes and conditions all his personal experiences. Stephen's experience, like the flames of the smithy, will give a new form to this substance, which he has inherited and which inhabits his soul.

Stephen's obsessive concern with the debate between free will and determinism shows the importance of interpreting Stephen's final gesture as I have suggested. Stephen's ruminations on the idea of a first cause for the entire created world militate against the idea that he can create something new. Throughout the novel, Stephen is moved by the idea that his actions are at once free and determined, both the actions of his own will and the products of an endless chain of circumstances. The theological resonances of Stephen's plan to "forge in the smithy of my soul the uncreated conscience of my race" fit in well with Stephen's search for a solution to the problem of free will. In coming to a vision of himself as a Christlike redeemer figure at the end of the novel, Stephen believes he has resolved this problem. Rather than claiming that his creative activity can invent something new, Stephen sees his action in terms of metaphors of shaping and remodeling the inert matter that has been granted to him by his Creator. He conceives of himself as "a priest of eternal imagination, transmuting the daily bread of experience into the radiant body of everliving life" (V.1677–79). What makes this transubstantiation possible is the mystical unity of the priestlike artist with the "conscience of [his] race." Yet Stephen's ambition passes beyond that of the imaginative priesthood. In the novel's final chapter, he hopes to become a more powerful mediating figure between the eternal world of ever-living life and the daily bread of experience. In Christianity, the only "uncreated" being is God. In Stephen's theology, it is "the conscience of [his] race" that is uncreated, and Stephen himself is its prophet, or perhaps its redeemer.

The religious crises that play such a central role in the novel lead Stephen toward his conception of himself as a priest or redeemer of the secular world and the race. At the end of *A Portrait of the Artist as a Young Man*, Stephen rejects his mother, noting that Jesus did the same: "Jesus, too, seems to have treated his mother with scant courtesy in public" (V.2417–18). In a debate with his mother, he holds up "relations between Jesus and Papa against those between Mary and her son" (V.2640–41). He thinks of his relationship to his own family as comparable to the "mystical kinship of fosterage," akin presumably to Jesus' relationship to Joseph and Mary (II.1359). Read in this light, even the final sentence of the novel seems to recall the relations between Christ and God the Father as much as those between Icarus and Daedalus: "Old father, old artificer, stand me now and ever in good stead" (V.2791–92). Even as Jesus stands in the place of humanity on the cross, He fears that His Father has forsaken Him. Just as Christ stands for all humanity in His death on the cross, Stephen plans to become a Christ-figure, redeeming his "Godforsaken" race by symbolically standing for the Irish nation. Like Christ, he is at once a creature (one who has been created) and one with the power to reshape the raw material with which the racial conscience has provided him. The racial conscience conditions Stephen's experience, but, as a great soul, he in turn transforms the racial conscience. The encounter with reality that Stephen plans for Paris has not only a personal but a racial and national significance.

If Stephen sees himself as a Christ-figure, then the "uncreated conscience of [his] race" appears to be God, and the "race" approximates the church, the body of faithful in need of redemption. Conceptions of the Christ-figure as embodying the genius of the race may owe something to Joyce's reading (in 1905) of Ernest Renan's *Life of Jesus* and possibly also David Friedrich Strauss's work of the same name.[5] Strauss elaborated a Hegelian interpretation of the Incarnation, emphasizing the dialectical nature of the Christ-figure who shares the infinite capacities of God and the finitude of humans.[6] Renan conceived of Jesus as embodying the characteristics of his race at the moment when it was being decisively transformed by its contact with Greco-Roman civilization. Stephen's conception of the "race" mixes notions of historical fate, biological inheritance or blood, and spiritual unity.

In his new theology, Stephen finds a place for a number of doctrines of the Roman Catholic Church. The *creatio ex nihilo,* God's creation of the universe out of nothing, concerns him first in the class of elements at Clongowes Wood when he ponders his own place in the universe, having written in his geography book, on successive lines, his location (I.300–08). Stephen wonders what belongs before the universe: "It was very big to think about everything and everywhere. Only God could do that" (I.321–23). Here, Stephen

---

5. Ellmann, *James Joyce,* 200; Michael Patrick Gillespie, *Inverted Volumes Improperly Arranged: James Joyce and His Trieste Library* (Ann Arbor: UMI Research P, 1983), 20.
6. "Hegelian interpretation": an understanding like that advocated by Georg Wilhelm Friedrich Hegel (1770–1831), the German philosopher who claimed that absolute knowledge involves deriving a higher unity from apparent contradictions. "Dialectical": term used by Hegel and philosophers influenced by Hegel for the interaction of opposing elements that produces a third, blended phenomenon [Editor].

understands God as a first cause of the universe, in a version of the ontological proof of Saint Anselm.[7]

What troubles Stephen next is that God has different names in different languages, a problem he eventually abandons after thinking, "though there were different names for God in all the different languages in the world and God understood what all the people who prayed said in their different languages still God remained always the same and God's real name was God" (I.328–32). Stephen accepts that there must be some ultimate cause at the root of the way in which the world is ordered. The problem for Stephen seems to be that each person can imagine God only in language, and that each language gives God a different name.

Stephen's very specific location has of course shaped his conception of God. A number of other aspects of the passage call attention to the shaping of Stephen's conception of the world by his nationality and particularly by Irish politics. Across from his "address" in the geography book, Stephen's classmate Fleming has written:

> Stephen Dedalus is my name,
> Ireland is my nation.
> Clongowes is my dwellingplace
> And heaven my expectation. (I.311–14)

Fleming has also colored in the picture of the earth in the geography book in maroon and green, which reminds Stephen of Dante's maroon brush for Davitt and green brush for Parnell. Stephen contemplates the coincidence: "But he had not told Fleming to colour them those colours. Fleming had done it himself " (I.291–92). The lesson is that Fleming and Stephen get their values, including aesthetic ones, from their nation. When he comes to embrace the "conscience of [his] race" as that which is "uncreated," he will see in the values he has learned from his nation, rather than in a universal God, the first cause that has called his soul into existence from nothingness.

In college, Stephen's teacher Mr. Tate accuses him of heresy for his statement in a paper "about the Creator and the soul" that the soul should strive to imitate the perfection of the creator "without a possibility of ever approaching nearer" (II.690). Stephen quickly corrects himself: "I meant without a possibility of ever reaching" (II.693). In the final chapter of the novel, Stephen finally devotes himself to an imitation of Christ that implies the opposite heretical position: that he can actually reach divine perfection, and become God the Son.

Stephen, then, proposes not an absolutely original creation but a transformation of the ideal racial conscience he embodies through

7. St. Anselm, *Proslogium,* chapter 5, in *Philosophical Problems: Selected Readings,* ed. Samuel Enoch Stumpf (New York: McGraw-Hill, 1971), 93–104.

yet another encounter with the reality of experience. On the one hand, he wants to believe himself free to make his own moral choices. On the other hand, he sees that his very being, his moral agency, is the product of a personal and national history that he did not choose. Viewed subjectively from an ethical, "first-person" standpoint, Stephen is a free agent. Viewed objectively, from a sociological, "third-person" perspective, Stephen is the product of the laws of history, psychology, and biology. It is the intense conflict between his deterministic conception of the laws of the mind and his desire for autonomy that leads Stephen to seek in a dialectical conception of "experience" an escape from this central dilemma of human freedom.

Stephen's relation to his society shows an extreme form of a tension between determinism and free will, and his mystical unity with the race will allow him to resolve this tension. Stephen continually asserts that he can overcome his shaping by society: "You talk to me of nationality, language, religion. I shall try to fly by those nets" (V.1049–50). He tells his friend Cranly that he aims "[t]o discover the mode of life or of art whereby [his] spirit could express itself in unfettered freedom" (V.2542–44). He sets himself the goal of complete autonomy, serving no end but his own. These statements have contributed to the conception of Stephen as an "individualist," or an adherent of "art for art's sake." Yet Stephen just as often expresses a conviction that his actions are part of a teleological plan that he himself can only vaguely sense. As a child, he is conscious of having been born to serve an unknown end: "in secret he began to make ready for the great part which he felt awaited him, the nature of which he only dimly apprehended" (II.87–89). He frequently senses throughout the novel that his life is headed toward a predestined goal, "the end he had been born to serve yet did not see" (IV.634–35). * * *

He couples this sense of destiny with a skepticism of the capacity of the human mind to act in ways that are new. Toward the end of the novel, Stephen tells the dean of his college that he is "sure there is no such thing as free thinking inasmuch as all thinking must be bound by its own laws" (V.462–64). If the mind does obey "its own laws," it meets the formal definition of "autonomy" (self-rule), but this autonomy does not constitute a Kantian freedom,[8] since it involves no active will on the part of the thinker; thought is an automatic process, like breathing or the circulation of the blood. Stephen seems trapped in a determinism that suggests that his own thoughts can develop only in accordance with his instincts, his previous experience, and the nets in which that experience has captured him:

8. As formulated by the German philosopher Immanuel Kant (1724–1804) [Editor].

"this race and this country and this life produced me. . . . I shall express myself as I am" (V.1027–28).

Joyce expressed himself in words similar to Stephen's when discussing Irish independence with Frank Budgen: "Ireland is what she is and therefore I am what I am because of the relations that have existed between England and Ireland. Tell me why you think I ought to wish to change the conditions that gave Ireland and me a shape and a destiny."[9] Today, we might refer to this shaping of the individual by the nation as an effect of "culture," but people in the first decades of the twentieth century tended to talk of nationality in terms of "race." Like Stephen, they tended to use the word "race" to refer to the complex amalgam of biological and cultural factors that made up their conception of the nation.

To overcome this persistent tension between determinism and free will, Stephen comes to understand the development of his personality as a dialectic; as his consciousness encounters reality, it actively transforms the world it perceives according to the categories it has derived from experience. While this reality conditions how Stephen's consciousness will perceive the outside world, each new encounter adds to Stephen's store of experience and thus transforms his consciousness. All experience is new in as much as it does transform Stephen's mind, but it is also old in that Stephen can interpret it only in accordance with the hundreds of thousands of encounters that have already created him. For this dialectical notion to allow Stephen a sense of meaningful freedom, Stephen must believe that the encounter between his consciousness and experience can create something essentially new, a synthesis of his mind with external reality that can allow him to do something more than enact the inevitable logic of history.

Stephen's capacity to live and create art in "unfettered freedom" depends on the transformation of "experience" into "everliving life." In order to accomplish this synthesis, he must find freedom in the knowledge that he has been shaped by forces beyond his control. The narrator-protagonist becomes, in Stephen's vision, the focus for a reawakening of national consciousness centered on the awareness that individuals are both subjects and objects of historical processes. He must find in the fact that his soul derives from an "uncreated" racial conscience the condition for a new type of freedom. He must think of himself as a type of world-soul, who in his individual actions also lives out the fate of the entire nation-race. He must awake from the nightmare of Irish history, not by escaping from that history but by allowing it to speak through him. Like the Christ described by

9. Frank Budgen, *James Joyce and the Making of Ulysses* (Bloomington: Indiana UP, 1960), 155.

Renan,[1] Stephen must embody the genius of his entire race in order to be able to redeem it.

The idea of the novelist as national redeemer contributed to Joyce's reworking of a literary archetype of nineteenth-century realism, the novel of disillusionment. The disillusionment plot, of which Balzac's *Lost Illusions* is the prime example, brings the protagonist into conflict with a world of contingent reality * * * . The protagonist goes out into the world expecting to conquer it, but instead finds that it conquers him. In *Lost Illusions,* the hero is Lucien de Rubempré, from whom Stephen borrows his motto "silence, exile, cunning."[2] * * *

Joyce's reworking of the disillusionment plot typified the modernists' rethinking of the logic of realist narrative forms. Novelists like Balzac developed a set of techniques for describing the complex interplay of personal identity and social role within a newly liberalized, industrial society. These techniques included the radical separation between the third- and first-person perspectives on the actions of individuals. This bifurcation corresponded to a liberal model of the nation-state. Individuals pursued their own private interests in the context of a shared public reality; these were the characters of the traditional realist novel, with their limited, first-person perspectives. On the other hand, the omniscient narrator acted as a neutral arbiter of the shared reality within which the characters interacted. The third-person narrator played a role similar to that of the state in liberal political thought, standing above and outside the various individuals who make up society. Modernists radically reconsidered the role of the omniscient narrator, guarantor of public reality. They scrutinized the distinction between an objective narrator and subjective characters with limited perspectives, giving life to a whole generation of narrator-heroes who, like Stephen, forged social realities in their own images. Their various attempts to unify the first- and third-person perspectives demonstrated the power of national myths to shape even apparently "objective" perceptions of reality.

Hugh Kenner, Wayne Booth, and others have noted the mingling of the character's and the narrator's voices in *A Portrait of the Artist as a Young Man,* what Kenner has called Joyce's "doubleness of vision."[3] This formal technique, the mingling of third- and first-person perspectives on Stephen's actions, serves to undermine the social and political assumptions of the realist novel. In *A Portrait of*

1. Ernest Renan (1823–1892), French philosopher, who wrote *Vie de Jésus* (*Life of Jesus*; 1863) [Editor].
2. Ellmann, *James Joyce,* 385.
3. Hugh Kenner, *Joyce's Voices* (Berkeley: U of Calif. P, 1978), 82. Wayne Booth, *The Rhetoric of Fiction,* 2nd ed. (Chicago: U of Chicago P, 1983), 323–36.

the Artist as a Young Man the intertwining of narrator's and characters perspectives makes the existence of the mature, socially sanctioned perspective problematic. The distinction between the outer world and the mind of the protagonist is vague, and it is not always possible to separate perception from reality.

The most remarkable formal innovation of *A Portrait of the Artist as a Young Man* is the disappearance of the narrator's "objective" social knowledge. * * * For Joyce, the shaping effects of consciousness are so important that the hero, by virtue of his perceptions, effectively transforms the outside world. This becomes clear in Joyce's use of a heightened form of novelistic irony, in which it is very difficult to separate the perceptions of the narrator from those of the protagonist. *A Portrait of the Artist as a Young Man* mingles objective, third-person accounts with the subjective impressions of the growing artist. Not only does Joyce do away with quotation marks when relating the character's impressions, but he also severely limits his use of verbal markers, such as "Stephen thought." This narrative voice, then, represents an "objectivity" itself shaped by the same forces that shape the hero.

This collapsing of the distinction between objectivity and subjectivity allows Joyce to convert the disillusionment plot from a single, momentous event in the life of the protagonist into an indefinite process, coextensive with life itself. Stephen proclaims his desire to go to Paris and "encounter for the millionth time the reality of experience" at the end, not the beginning, of the novel, after he can already claim to have encountered experience 999,999 times. Whereas Balzac presents the reader with fully formed young adult characters who are ready to leave home for Paris, Joyce starts with an infant. Joyce thus presents the formation of character itself as a product of social forces, rather than (as in Balzac) the unique function of the intimate household.

The role of language itself in *A Portrait of the Artist as a Young Man* emphasizes the lack of a dividing line between the household and society at large. The novel begins with the protagonist's first attempts to make sense, in language, of the reality of experience, and it is through his many encounters with reality, always mediated by language, that his consciousness develops. As Stephen learns language, he also learns his place in history and in geography. Thus even his nursery song about a "wild rose" blossoming on a "little green place" leads him a little later in life to muse half-consciously on the possibility of Irish nationhood: "you could not have a green rose. But perhaps somewhere in the world you could" (I.197–98). As Stephen remarks to his friend Davin, "When the soul of a man is born in this country there are nets flung at it to hold it back from flight" (V.1047–48). One of these nets is language, which captures the soul in a particular way of encountering reality. Yet Stephen transforms this consciousness of the individual's shaping by society into the material for a transfiguration of society through the individual. Through his manipulation of language in writing, Stephen hopes to overcome the dynamic of disillusionment and to convert the hostile, contingent "reality of experience" into the material of his own meaning-making process.

Around the time that he was completing *A Portrait of the Artist as a Young Man*, Joyce read Vico, who argued that "the world of civilization has certainly been made by men . . . and its principles are to be found in the modifications of our own human mind."[4] Stephen attempts something similar in finding in his own mind the ultimate product of the laws immanent in the world of civilization. Joyce also read Marx, who argues that while humans make their own history, they do not do so under circumstances of their own choosing. By recognizing that the ethical self he is now is a product of the historical forces at work in human society, that his mind is a product of human history, and human history is a product of the human mind, Stephen hopes to overcome the dynamic of disillusionment. His coming to consciousness is a gradual process that culminates in the epiphanic moments of the novel's final chapter, a fulfillment of historical laws that will also lead to their transfiguration. It will allow him to achieve the unity with the Irish race that raises his experience above the level of mere necessity and contingency.

Parnell's adultery, fall from power, and death will play something like the role of original sin in Stephen's Irish eschatology. Stephen hears of Parnell on the first page of the novel. He learns of Parnell's death as he lies in the school infirmary where he has been imagining his own death (I.591–604, I.709–12). Later, he recalls that moment: "But he had not died then. Parnell had died. There had been no mass for the dead in the chapel and no procession" (II.1167–69). At the Christmas dinner, Stephen struggles to understand the argument between Dante, a family friend who condemns Parnell, and John Casey, who glorifies Parnell as "my dead king," while Simon Dedalus bemoans the fate of his "priestridden Godforsaken race" (I.1148, I.1081). The next morning, Stephen attempts to write his first poem, a commemoration of Parnell (II.359–70). Parnell, for Stephen, is both an Adam whose fall has terrible consequences for his entire (Irish) race and a failed Christ, who might have redeemed Ireland. Stephen imagines Parnell, like Christ, dying in his place. Parnell

---

4. Giambattista Vico, *The New Science*, trans. Thomas Bergin and Max Fisch (Ithaca: Cornell UP, 1984), paragraph 232. On the relationship between Vico and *A Portrait*, see John Bishop, *Joyce's Book of the Dark* (Madison: U of Wisconsin P, 1986), 180–81.

inspires Stephen, and Stephen imagines himself as capable, through his writing, of redeeming Parnell's fall and repaying Parnell for having died in his place. Through his writing, then, Stephen will offer the sacrifice of his own soul to Ireland. Just as this act of martyrdom will save the Irish, however, it will also allow Stephen to achieve unfettered freedom because, in embracing his moral unity with the Irish race, he will reconcile his ethical self with his socially constructed identity. He will become both the first-person character who pursues his own ends and the third-person narrator who sees that all apparently free acts are in fact products of historical circumstance.

Stephen's choice of the word *race* to describe the source of the identity of his ethically free and sociologically determined selves points to his concern with achieving a moral unity of the nation as the basis for the new form of freedom he hopes to achieve through his writing. Stephen has promised to fly by the "nets" of "nationality, language, religion" before dedicating himself to the "conscience of [his] race" (V.1049–50, V.2790), leading to much critical confusion. (One good reason for the confusion is the virtual impossibility of clearly distinguishing Joyce's own voice from that of Stephen on any internal textual evidence.[5] I have written throughout of Stephen's project, except where referring to specific technical devices employed by Joyce.) His choice of vocabulary seems rather shocking since to affirm "racial" ties seems to involve accepting the idea of a biological essence of the nation, as opposed to the purely legal or political notions of membership in the community implied, for example, by the term "citizenship."

The biological content of Stephen's ideal does not sit well either with the older critical conception of Joyce as an apolitical individualist or with more recent attempts to find in Joyce a progressive, antiracist critic of capitalism, patriarchy, and imperialism. In his groundbreaking *Joyce's Politics,* Dominic Manganiello summarizes and attacks the traditional view of Joyce as an apolitical artist. From Manganiello's discussion of Joyce's interest in anarchism emerges the conception of Joyce as a sort of ultraindividualist, a point of view very much in line with the earlier idea of Joyce as an apolitical defender of "art for art's sake": "For Joyce, the freeing of the individual was the main issue, indeed the only one."[6] ***

Two more recent attempts to find a different sort of politics in Joyce are Vincent Cheng's *Joyce, Race, and Empire* and Emer Nolan's

---

5. Booth, *The Rhetoric of Fiction,* 323–36.
6. Dominic Manganiello, *Joyce's Politics* (London and Boston: Routledge & Kegan Paul, 1980), 232.

James Joyce and Nationalism. These two works share a salutary emphasis on Joyce's criticisms of liberal individualism, but whereas Cheng focuses on Joyce's opposition to imperialism throughout the world, Nolan is concerned primarily with Joyce's links to Irish nationalist cultural movements. Neither offers a satisfactory account of Stephen Dedalus's devotion to the "conscience of [the] race." Nolan notices the kinship with the Irish nationalist project but still sees Stephen as involved in a "resolutely individualistic self-fashioning" and, in line with most previous criticism, considers Stephen simply an aesthete.[7] Cheng tends to consider race primarily in terms of biological racial theory rather than in its full range of application, which could include cultural as well as biological phenomena. He therefore expects Joyce to oppose any notion of race, and in particular sees in Stephen's conception of race an overturning of an "English/Irish dialectic."[8] Cheng concludes that Stephen "certainly runs the risk of an apolitical aestheticism (such as Joyce has been accused of) in his concerns with an Aristotelian/Thomistic aesthetic theory."[9]

Manganiello, Nolan, and Cheng all seem bent on reclaiming Joyce for progressive politics * * * . The Stephen of *A Portrait of the Artist as a Young Man* seems at any rate to have much in common with the younger Joyce, who wrote of the artist's role as a sort of midwife for the "nation that is to come." In "A Portrait of the Artist," the first sketch of what later would be the novel, Joyce uses the word *nation* in a sense akin to Stephen's use of the word *race:* "Man and woman, out of you comes the nation that is to come * * * the confederate will issues in action."[1] Several of Joyce's youthful critical statements seem similarly to participate in Stephen's "racial" conception of the Irish, notably his reference to the Irish, in "The Day of the Rabblement," as "the most belated race in Europe."[2] What, then, does Stephen mean by "race" and how can serving the race be linked to the project of individual freedom?

Stephen looks at the race as a body with which he can identify more fundamentally than with any other social group. His references to "race" contain echoes not simply of modern racist tracts like Arthur de Gobineau's *The Inequality of Human Races,* but also of older, "pre-scientific" conceptions of "race" as a group sharing a common lineage and fate. It is in this latter sense that Milton's fallen angels frequently refer to the competition between their race

7. Emer Nolan, *James Joyce and Nationalism* (London: Routledge, 1995), 38, 44.
8. Cheng, *Joyce, Race, and Empire,* 64.
9. Cheng, *Joyce, Race, and Empire,* 74.
1. James Joyce, "A Portrait of the Artist," *The Workshop of Daedalus,* ed. Robert Scholes and Richard M. Kain (Evanston, Il.: Northwestern UP, 1965), 68.
2. "The Day of the Rabblement," *Critical Writings,* ed. Ellsworth Mason and Richard Ellmann (New York: Viking, 1959), 70.

and the race of mankind: "Shall we then live thus vile, the race of Heaven / Thus trampled, thus expelled to suffer here these / Chains and these torments?"[3] Part of the difficulty for Joyce's critics lies too in a confusion about the contemporary meaning of the word *race* * * * as an amalgam of cultural and biological factors. The resulting amalgam did carry elements of the rigid biological determinism that, according to Vincent Cheng, Joyce "rejects and reverses" in his later fiction.[4] Yet the concept of "race" still had the flexibility, in the early twentieth century, to refer not just to a rigid biologism but also to the "moral" factors, such as customs and institutions, that later anthropologists would distinguish as "culture."[5] In common parlance, the concept "race" blurred the boundaries between the terms that the later liberal tradition would confidently differentiate as "race" and "culture."

* * * Today, the "natural" or appropriate response to the history of racial stereotypes of the Irish might seem to be to reject racial stereotyping outright. For Stephen Dedalus, however, and apparently also for Joyce, there was another possible response: to affirm Irish "racial" difference and find in it a source of strength. In doing so, Stephen shares many of the crucial assumptions of Irish nationalists whose overt political and cultural agenda he opposes. In particular, he rejects political activism in favor of cultural renewal and associates this cultural renewal with expressing the essence of the Irish race.

Apart from the fact that he has inherited the notion from his father, one of Stephen's reasons for conceiving of the Irish nation as a "race" apparently stems from his conception of the race as a community to which a person belongs even before learning a language. Part of the fallen condition of the Irish race is that it has abandoned its own language in favor of the language of the conquerors. * * *

"Language" is one of the nets in which the Irish soul is captured upon birth. Stephen hopes to return to something even more primary, although he recognizes that he can do so only through language. Thus, he accepts the Gaelic League's conception of the Irish as alienated from themselves by their use of English, but rejects the solution of a return to Irish. Working out the implications of this alienation rather than seeking a nostalgic return to a lost origin will bring Stephen's soul out of the shadows.

---

3. Belial's speech at the conclave of the fallen angels, *Paradise Lost,* book 2, lines 194–96. "Race" has a wide range of cultural resonances, illustrated by the various definitions offered of it in the *Oxford English Dictionary.*
4. Cheng, *Joyce, Race, and Empire,* 27.
5. See in particular the discussion of Leslie Stephen in George Stocking, *Victorian Anthropology* (New York: Macmillan, 1987), 137–43.

Similarly, Stephen rejects the term *nationality* and much of the rhetoric of national renewal. Here again, he seems to be searching for a conception of Irish identity prior to its identification with the formal politics of citizenship in a modern liberal state. In this respect, again, he models his concept of membership in the race on notions of community he has inherited from the church. As Cranly tells Stephen just before he rejects Christianity, "[t]he Church is not the stone building nor even the clergy and their dogmas. It is the whole mass of those born into it" (V.2527–29). In the race, Stephen finds an even more primary source of communal identity. He embraces the concept of the "race" because one belongs to the race by right of birth, before learning a language or being baptized. Whether it depends primarily on one's blood or on one's being born in a particular location is a problem that Stephen considers without resolving. It seems likely, from the evidence of *Ulysses* and *Finnegans Wake*, that Joyce himself gradually broadened his definition of the race to which he belonged.

Most of the eleven uses of the word *race* in *A Portrait of the Artist as a Young Man*, which have been enumerated by Vincent Cheng, confirm this association of the racial conscience with an identification prior to all other forms of membership in social groups.[6] * * * Because he has rejected the intimate sphere, Stephen's own contribution to the race will be strictly spiritual, but he nevertheless links it closely with reproduction. It is in women, and especially peasant women, that he expects to find the racial conscience embodied. He listens with fascination to Davin's story of a peasant woman who had asked him to spend the night with her. Stephen pictures this peasant woman as "a type of her race and of his own, a batlike soul waking to the consciousness of itself in darkness and secrecy and loneliness" (V.330–32).

* * *

Stephen's hostility to politics, whether democratic and progressive or organic-nationalist, confirms this association of race with the inheritance of a group membership prior to all cultural associations. The racial conscience is "natural," not in the sense that it belongs outside history or culture, but in the sense that it precedes the individual's formal incorporation into the cultural groups associated with the nets of "nationality, language, religion." Stephen recognizes the significance of formal politics, and particularly of Parnell, in having shaped the Irish race, but he seems to view politics as a lost opportunity and thus treats with skepticism any attempts at political renewal. * * * Stephen even seems to sense this irrelevance of his

6. Cheng, *Joyce, Race, and Empire*, 17.

forging of the racial conscience to formal politics somewhat guiltily in his various exchanges with the democrat MacCann.

While Stephen's own theory of the race does not serve any explicitly political agenda, it nonetheless participates in a number of contemporary political trends.[7] In particular, his conception of himself as a redeemer eerily prefigures the sacrificial language surrounding the uprising of Easter, 1916, the year of publication of *A Portrait of the Artist as a Young Man*. In seeking to forge in the smithy of his soul the uncreated conscience of his race, Stephen draws upon the organic nationalist conception of the intimate relationship between the individual and his ethnic group, which precedes all cultural ties and fundamentally conditions the individual's experience. It is more primary than culture, but it necessarily implies a combination of historical, cultural, biological, and spiritual conditions.

In this ultimate existential unity between the individual and the race, Stephen, much like the Gaelic nationalists whose merely superficial nationalism he opposes, seeks to overcome the conflict between the individual's moral autonomy and his status as a product of a given set of historical and social forces. Stephen rejects religion because it proposes a false standard of human conduct, language because it is a purely conventional social structure that for the Irish in particular always involves oppression, and nationality because it reflects the merely formal, institutional conception of community implicit in modern liberal politics. He seeks instead a moral unity not with all of humanity nor with the principle of individuality, not with the nation nor the fatherland, but with the conscience of his "Godforsaken priestridden race."

Joyce's narrative technique seems to offer some hope that Stephen will succeed in achieving this mystical union. At the end of the novel, the transcription of Stephen's diary, written in the first person, offers an apparent resolution of the tension between first- and third-person modes of narration; the young man with his subjective impressions becomes the narrator and a purely subjective first-person account replaces the tainted objectivity that has constituted the narrative up to that point. The intensified conflict between the third- and first-person perspectives in *A Portrait of the Artist as a Young Man* leads to a collapsing of the two voices, and this collapsing corresponds to Stephen's attempt to overcome the bifurcated perspective on life in this world implied by the realist literary tradition and by liberal politics. * * * Stephen comes to realize the retrospective unity of his whole life. The fact that his entire experience has contributed to the formation of his present identity seems to

---

7. On the sacrificial language surrounding the Easter, 1916, uprising, see Roy Foster, *Modern Ireland* (New York: Penguin, 1989), 477–84.

lend his current subjective impressions an air of objective necessity. The diary represents the final step in Stephen's coming to consciousness of his own destiny and his overcoming of the bifurcation between his social and ethical selves.

Stephen's statement of his own aesthetic theory suggests that Joyce saw his experiments with narrative technique as aspects of an attempt to overcome the bifurcation I have described between sociology and ethics, between the third- and first-person perspectives on human action. Stephen suggests that the "epical form" emerges "out of lyrical literature when the artist prolongs and broods upon himself as the centre of an epical event and this form progresses till the centre of emotional gravity is equidistant from the artist himself and from others. The narrative is no longer purely personal" (V.1448–53). He gives as an example the "old English ballad Turpin Hero which begins in the first person and ends in the third" (V.1456–58). Stephen compares this transformation to the creation. *A Portrait of the Artist as a Young Man* proceeds in the opposite direction, from the third person to the first person. At the end of the novel, Stephen begins his diary and thus becomes the narrator. Joyce is not retreating from the "epical" to the "lyrical," so much as reuniting the lyrical "I" with the epical third person (or, in the terms I have been using, the ethical, subjective "I" with the sociological, objective third person).

In *A Portrait of the Artist as a Young Man* the artist reenters his creation to overcome the distinction between lyric and epic. If the accomplishment of the epic resembles in Stephen's theory the mystery of creation, the achievement of Joyce's modernism resembles the mystery of God's incarnation, which permits redemption. After Stephen has explained his aesthetic theory, he and Lynch take shelter under the arcade of the national library. Lynch complains: "What do you mean by prating about beauty and the imagination in this miserable Godforsaken island? No wonder the artist retired within or behind his handiwork after having perpetrated this country" (V.1474–77). The echo of Stephen's father's complaint about the "Godforsaken priestridden race" is unmistakable. Stephen will resolve on a new type of art in which the artist enters into his creation and in doing so he will redeem the Godforsaken island. The debate with Lynch outside the National Library seems an essential step in Stephen's development of his theory of a new type of art that will allow him to forge the racial conscience, and such an art must, like *A Portrait of the Artist as a Young Man*, achieve a synthesis between purely lyrical subjectivity and epical objectivity, must reinsert the creator in his creation, must reunite the artist with his country.

Stephen's other main statement of his aesthetic theory * * * confirms the centrality of the problem of race to his literary experiments. In expounding aesthetics to Davin, he points out that different races have different ideals of beauty (V.1227–28). One explanation of this variety is that aesthetics originates in a purely physiological impulse, which differs according to the different biological makeup of the various races (V.1230–33). Stephen rejects this explanation as leading to "eugenics rather than to esthetic." He denies the reasoning he associates with Darwin, which ultimately reduces the differences among races to purely physical terms.

Stephen does not, however, propose as an alternative that beauty itself inheres in aesthetic objects or in women or that beauty can be judged universally. Rather, he suggests that each beautiful object appeals to a certain common set of relations presumably present in human minds: "though the same object may not seem beautiful to all people, all people who admire a beautiful object find in it certain relations which satisfy and coincide with the stages themselves of all esthetic apprehension" (V.1255–58). This solution allows Stephen to reconcile the fact that each race interprets the world differently with a notion of a universal human nature. For if the beautiful differs for each race, then paradoxically the way to reach the universal in human nature may be to submerge oneself in the particularities of one's own race. Only by embodying a racially specific perspective as perfectly as possible can one arrive at an embodiment of the shared human condition of belonging to a particular race. This suggestion bears a resemblance to some modern multiculturalist theories and in particular to the notion of a "politics of identity," but it bears an equally striking resemblance to the racialist theories that Joyce's work is often seen as opposing.

Just as Balzac's disillusionment plot reproduces certain crucial assumptions of nineteenth-century liberalism, Stephen's proposal to overcome disillusionment embodies early-twentieth-century theories of the nation-state. In particular, like many contemporary "organic" nationalists, Stephen conceives of the individual not as autonomous but as largely (perhaps entirely) determined in all his actions by the circumstances of his birth and by membership in a given national community. For Joyce, this determining force works primarily through historical conditioning but also perhaps through biological inheritance * * *. The liberal conception of a necessary bifurcation between an intimate sphere dominated by ethics and true moral freedom and a social sphere operating according to purely material laws of necessity has disappeared for Stephen. The nation represents the cultural and genetic inheritance that cannot be overcome or ignored, and the nation speaks through the writer. The individual is a product of racial or historical forces that he does not control, but by embracing this condition, he can achieve the mystical union with his race that will allow him to convert his determination into a source of freedom.

In the novel generally, as Lukács[8] wrote, life is a going out onto an earth in which we are exiled from God, a world ruled by merely conventional morality, with no divine sanction for authority or divine guarantee of justice. A redemption on the earth is impossible in the realist novel; the world is only the world and cannot become paradise. In the modernist novel, the possibility of regaining paradise on earth becomes central again, and the nation becomes the means for this redemption. The national bond represents the possibility of transcending the apparent meaninglessness of life on earth, of "transmuting the daily bread of experience into the radiant body of everliving life" (V.1677–79). Through the novelist-hero's mystical union with the racial conscience, the experience of life in a world abandoned by God is redeemed and the word again made flesh.

JONATHAN MULROONEY

Stephen Dedalus and the Politics of Confession[†]

I

In the spring of 1907 James Joyce, tutor, writer, and (sometime) bank clerk delivered a series of three public lectures at the Universita Popolare in Trieste. In those lectures, the first two of which survive, the young Joyce expressed strong reservations about the misplaced zeal of twentieth-century Irish nationalism. Anglo-Irish attempts to promote a national recovery of Celtic culture had served, in Joyce's estimation, only to limit the advancement of Irish art and thought. "The economic and intellectual conditions that prevail in [the Irishman's] own country do not permit the development of individuality," he lamented in *Ireland, Island of Saints and Sages*. "No one who has any self-respect stays in Ireland, but flees afar as though from a country that has undergone the visitation of an angered Jove" (*CW*, p. 171).[1] With a catalogue of Ireland's past contributions to world culture, Joyce warned that the Irish had betrayed their legacy as vital players in the European cultural theater by embracing artificial national identities.

---

8. György Lukács (1885–1971), also known as Georg Lukács, Hungarian Marxist philosopher [Editor].

† From *Studies in the Novel* 33:2 (Summer 2001): 160–79. Reprinted by permission of the publisher. Some notes have been abridged or omitted. Page references for *A Portrait* have been replaced with part and line numbers of this Norton Critical Edition. Some cited passages might differ slightly from the equivalent passages in this volume.

1. *The Critical Writings of James Joyce*, ed. Ellsworth Mason and Richard Ellmann (New York: Viking, 1959), 171. Identified hereafter as *CW*.

Joyce's description of the Irish situation in these early lectures reflects the differences that separated him from most of his older contemporaries. Yeats's revival sought in the Celtic legacy of Ireland an artistic and political alternative to the shackling dominance of Catholicism. Resistant to the conception that, in F. S. L. Lyons's words, any Irish work "that claimed to be 'national' would be judged according to whether or not it conformed to the stereotype which ascribed to Catholic Ireland the virtues of purity, innocence, and sanctity," the Yeatsian artist allied himself with a history that neither England nor Rome could claim as its own.[2] For Joyce, though, the wholesale rejection of Catholicism merely exchanged one problem for another. In an effort to challenge Catholicism's influence over the lives of the Irish population, the Celtic renaissance had constructed a national fiction equally ill-equipped to represent Ireland's complex modern culture. Revival of the Irish language, retrieval of Celtic mythology, and the infusion of old mysticisms into contemporary literature were measures that Joyce believed to be as limiting to the development of a free Irish consciousness as any Catholic nationalism. To turn from the "coherent absurdity" of Catholicism to a cultural identity that was "dead just as ancient Egypt is dead" (*CW*, pp. 168, 173) could result only in another impotent aesthetic and political agenda. Lashing themselves to the mast of uncritical nationalism in a desire for collective strength, Irish artists were in Joyce's mind submitting to a ruining power that would limit the nation's options for self-determination and wreck Ireland's journey to renewed cultural prominence.

Scholars have long recognized Joyce's ambivalence regarding the attempts of the Irish literati to Celticize Ireland's culture. Much recent work, though, has taken up the question of how Joyce's texts treat nativist and specifically Catholic nationalisms. Yet this discussion has focused almost entirely on the later writings. Postcolonialists concerned with evaluating the politics of Joyce's modernism have chosen *Ulysses* and to a lesser extent *Finnegans Wake* as their preferred texts. *A Portrait of the Artist as a Young Man*, at least from this perspective, has been largely ignored. In the novel that Joyce was composing at the time of the Trieste lectures, he produces a crucial text for assessing his development of a uniquely Irish modernism. *A Portrait* publicly rejects Catholic nationalism's claims to speak for all Ireland, even as it resists the solution of transnationalism by manifesting a sustained engagement with the Irish-Catholic discourses of Joyce's youth. That the illusion of literary independence offered by the Anglo-Irish Celtic revival held little charm for

---

2. F. S. L. Lyons, *Culture and Anarchy in Ireland: 1890–1939* (Oxford: Clarendon, 1979), p. 51.

the young Joyce is well established; that the security of nativist Catholicism was to his mind equally inadequate appears to need further assertion at this point in Joyce studies. Stephen Dedalus's growth toward a lyric self-narration, which culminates in the final defiant artistic stance of *A Portrait,* relies on Catholic modes of expression to the exclusion of all others and marks the surrounding text's multiple narrative techniques as a more authentic Irish literary form. The limitations of Stephen's confessional lyricism thus represent to Joyce's readers the inadequacy of essentialist notions of Irish identity, and the need for critical engagement with the nation's complex cultural legacies.

The debate over Joyce's nationalism has developed out of a consideration, expressed most consistently in the work of David Lloyd, of the ways that postcolonial texts simultaneously represent and critique the marginalized conditions of their production.[3] Focusing on the subversiveness of an Irish "minor" literature, Lloyd, like other postcolonial scholars, politicizes the development of Irish literary form. He describes an increasingly successful mediation of the modes of production inherited from colonial tradition and those offered by nativist nationalisms. Not surprisingly, the idea of a transnational modernist Joyce, or a Joyce who at the very least eschews Irish Catholicism's totalizing cultural narrative, stands at the forefront of such a concern. In a 1993 essay, "Adulteration and the Nation," Lloyd renders an exemplary reading of *Ulysses* along these lines: because Joyce's work "dismantles voice and verisimilitude in the same moment," it "insists . . . on a deliberate stylization of dependence and inauthenticity, a stylization of the hybrid status of the colonized subject as of the colonized culture."[4] What Enda Duffy has similarly called the "relentless interrogativity" of Joyce's texts has come to be understood as the triumph of modern Irish writing: the production of literary form that successfully negotiates, through its conspicuous hybridity, the colonial and native essentialisms that would otherwise threaten its efficacy as a representative text of fractured post-colonial culture.[5]

These critical formulations have met recently with significant resistance. In her provocative 1995 study *James Joyce and Nationalism,* Emer Nolan argues that, because of its zeal for a pluralism that

3. For example, in his study of James Clarence Mangan, *Nationalism and Minor Literature: James Clarence Mangan and the Emergence of Irish Cultural Nationalism* (Berkeley: Univ. of California Press, 1987), Lloyd states that postcolonial nationalist literature is "produced dialectically out of the very damage suffered by a colonized people" (p. x).
4. David Lloyd, "Adulteration and the Nation," *Anomalous States: Irish Writing and the Post-Colonial Moment* (Durham: Duke Univ. Press, 1993), pp. 109, 110.
5. Enda Duffy, *The Subaltern "Ulysses"* (Minneapolis: Univ. of Minnesota Press, 1994), p. 3. Like David Lloyd's critique, Duffy's attempt to "reclaim *Ulysses* . . . for Irish readers as *the* text of Ireland's independence" politicizes the formal operation of Joyce's modernism (p. 1).

can be deployed as a solution to the ongoing Irish question, post-colonial Irish criticism has obscured Joyce's real nationalist commitments. By positing that "explorations of language, personal identity and history are simply incompatible with the reverence displayed for tradition and community in nationalist ideology," Joyce scholars "do not acknowledge that nationalisms vary, and are internally divided and disputatious." For Nolan, Joyce's "rejection of Revivalism is a characteristic gesture of the world of native Catholic nationalism—the world within which he was brought up."[6] Hence, explanations of his antagonism toward the Celtic revival as both a desire for the greater psychic space of European "transnational modernity" and as a rejection of nationalism in all its forms must be judged as oversimplified and inadequate. Joyce's texts, while undeniably modern, "record or lament the progressive abolition of local difference in the modern world." In this way, Nolan argues, "Joycean modernism and Irish nationalism can be understood as significantly analogous discourses, and the common perception of them as unrelated and antagonistic begins to break down."[7]

But the Ireland Joyce envisioned in the 1907 lectures was a nation of agents free from the over-determined identity of subjection to the English monarchy, to the Celtic revival, *and* to the Catholic Church. No longer "island of saints and sages," the new Ireland would include the very peoples the old nation had alienated, for "to exclude from the present nation all who are descended from foreign families would be impossible, and to deny the name of patriot to all those who are not of Irish stock would be to deny it to almost all the heroes of the modern movement" (*CW*, pp. 161–62). In the final lines of his first lecture, Joyce employed the image of language itself to describe both Ireland's cultural servitude and the process by which it could be thrown off. "It is well past time for Ireland to have done once and for all with failure," he urged, for "though the Irish are eloquent, a revolution is not made of human breath and compromises. Ireland has already had enough equivocations and misunderstandings" (*CW*, p. 174). What was needed instead was for the Irish to reconceive their own nation, creating an environment in which the multitude of cultural discourses present in Ireland could freely inform the practices of the nation's political and aesthetic life. Only when the "convenient fiction" of Celtic and Catholic nationalisms had been recast into a "nationality [that] must find its reason for being rooted in something that surpasses and transcends and informs changing things like blood and the human word" (*CW*, p. 166) would Ireland "put on the play we have waited for so long" (*CW*, p. 174). What

6. Emer Nolan, *James Joyce and Nationalism* (London: Routledge, 1995), pp. ix, xiii, 48.
7. Nolan, p. xii.

Joyce wanted in 1907 was, in a very practical sense, a common recognition of Ireland's complex and diverse cultural situation, and the realization of a truer (if less convenient) national fiction to represent that situation. "[T]his time," he wrote, "let it be whole, and complete, and definitive."

In the second Trieste lecture, Joyce described the revolutionary role literature would need to take if Ireland were to enact her whole and complete play on the world stage. Qualifying a more enthusiastic position he had expressed five years before on his chosen subject, Joyce offered James Clarence Mangan as an example of the typically limited Irish artist, one whose identity was beholden to an uncritical and "hysterical nationalism" (CW, p. 186). The positive aspects that David Lloyd can now find in Mangan's fractured communication of native Irish culture, Joyce saw in 1907 only as weakness. Although he was "the most significant poet of the modern Celtic world" (CW, p. 179), Mangan had no critical perspective on his own culture because "the history of his country encloses him so straitly that even in his hours of extreme individual passion he can barely reduce its walls to ruins" (CW, p. 185). When his perspective on Ireland did break through, it was only as a fiery representative of a solely Celtic racial consciousness. Embodying an Irish aesthetic that Joyce found inadequate, Mangan was in the end a slave to his limited idea of Irishness, and the singular perspective of his lyric poetry revealed the shortcoming.

Taken together, the two surviving Trieste lectures powerfully represent the young Joyce's ambivalence toward contemporary Irish identity politics in both its Celtic and Catholic versions, and his desire to construct a culturally critical aesthetic that was yet uniquely Irish as part of an alternative to those politics. For Joyce, the revolutionary "play" of national identity would arise out of a literary and indeed novelistic portrayal of the true composition of Irish culture, a portrayal incorporating all aspects of the culture as they existed in Irish daily life. Joseph Valente has remarked that the collision of so many varying cultural discourses (English, Catholic, Celtic) made Joyce's Ireland "acutely sensitive to the relativity of language."[8] In my reading of the lectures, the problem as Joyce saw it in 1907 was precisely that most Irish *chose not* to admit any relativity in their cultural situation, and instead embraced the security of simplistic notions of what it meant to be Irish. What Anglicized Celticism was for the Irish intelligentsia, Catholicism was for the mass of unschooled Irishmen: an essentialized collective identity, complete with its own way of perceiving, and speaking about, and living in the world.

---

8. Joseph Valente, "The Politics of Joyce's Polyphony," in *New Alliances in Joyce Studies*, ed. Bonnie Kime Scott (Newark: Univ. of Delaware Press, 1988), p. 59.

For Joyce, as for Mikhail Bakhtin, the novel is the genre that explodes the illusion of linguistic homogeneity in any community. When individuals encounter different formal manifestations of language in their everyday interactions, they gain the ability "to regard one language (and the verbal world corresponding to it) through the eyes of another language (that is, the language of everyday life and the everyday world with the language of prayer or song, or vice versa)." The consequence of such a "critical interanimation of languages" is a developed notion of personal identity as a process, in which "the inviolability and predetermined quality of these languages [comes] to an end, and the necessity of actively choosing one's orientation among them beg[ins]."[9] The novel can formalize this cognitive process by portraying the influence of various languages on an individual consciousness; and the novel's textual portrait in turn becomes a locus of subjective transformation for readers. With its depiction of Ireland's grand linguistic interplay, Joyce's true Irish literature would in just this way imagine for its readers a nationality rooted not in any single inherited blood or language, but in the multiplicity of bloods and languages that were present in Ireland working upon the consciousness of the Irish people.

Joyce advocated in the Trieste lectures a political consciousness-raising accomplished through literature, in which reading audiences would be invited to consider the arbitrary relation commonly imagined between their social practices and any abstract or essentialist concept of Irishness. As Cheryl Herr has written, "much of Joyce's effort is . . . to erode the concept of nature and to indicate the fabricated quality of all social experience."[1] The Joycean poet, in revolt against the collective torpor that accepted Ireland's role as the "island of saints and sages," could not be merely a passionate Manganian spokesperson for "the succession of the ages, the spirit of the age, the mission of the race," regardless of whether the race was conceived as exclusively Celtic, or Catholic, or anything else (CW, p. 185). Rather "the poet's central effort is to free himself from the unfortunate influence of these idols that corrupt him from without and within": to become not the servant, but the critic of the cultural perspective his language expresses. Joyce's portrayal of Stephen Dedalus dramatizes for readers how the young artist's insufficiently sophisticated reliance on an inherited mode of subjectivity prevents his achieving precisely this kind of critical aesthetic consciousness.

9. M. M. Bakhtin, *The Dialogic Imagination: Four Essays,* ed. Michael Holquist, trans. Caryl Emerson and Michael Holquist (Austin: Univ. of Texas Press, 1981), p. 296.
1. Cheryl Herr, *Joyce's Anatomy of Culture* (Chicago: Univ. of Illinois Press, 1986), p. 5. Dominic Manganiello has similarly noted in *Joyce's Politics* (London: Routledge, 1980) the critical capacities Joyce saw in fiction "for altering men's minds" (pp. 38–39).

Only when the Irish writer's words revealed themselves as a nexus of cultural interplay would Ireland begin to emerge from its self-imposed cultural tutelage. By fashioning his text to reveal the irreducible complexity of Irish social and cultural life, Joyce exposes the fallacy that any singular discourse can wholly and completely embody Irish culture. The stylistic and narrative shifts that characterize A Portrait synecdochically represent to the novel's audience a fuller understanding of Ireland's uniqueness than had previously been attempted in Irish literature, and seek nothing less than a revolution of the national mind.

II

In A Portrait of the Artist as a Young Man, Joyce's novelization of a new Irish aesthetic centers around Stephen Dedalus. Stephen's portrait is at the same time the portrait, as Joyce conceived it, of the Irish artist's attempt to navigate out of cultural subjection into a position of economic and intellectual freedom. Language, not surprisingly, plays a vital role in that attempt. The linguistic practices to which Stephen is exposed as a young man represent to him (and to readers of the text) various methods to perceive and communicate, that is, to figure, reality. Throughout the novel, Stephen struggles to find his own voice amidst the others he encounters. The degree to which Stephen constructs a voice that does not merely reproduce the linguistic norms with which he was raised is the degree to which he resembles the kind of critical artist Joyce seeks. The language of the Portrait journal entries seemingly shows Stephen as finally the author of his own reality. Going forth to "forge in the smithy of my soul the uncreated conscience of my race" (V.2789–90), Stephen is presumably free from the political and religious strictures of "nationality, language, religion" that have tormented his younger years (V.1049). He has throughout the book's final sections moved steadily away from any practical enactment of Catholic morality: "Cannot repent. Told her so . . ." he remembers of his mother (V.2646). And in dismissing Yeats's symbolic Michael Robartes and the "forgotten beauty . . . which has long faded from the world" in favor of "the loveliness which has not yet come into the world," Stephen summarily rejects the cultural archeology of the Irish national literary revival (V.2723–27). In Dominic Manganiello's words, "Stephen recognizes no anterior logos, no authoritative word other than his own."[2] On the threshold of fully engaging a unique artistic identity, Stephen seems free at last from the "nets" of his Irish boyhood. In

---

2. Dominic Manganiello, "Reading the Book of Himself: the Confessional Imagination of St. Augustine and Joyce," in Biography and Autobiography: Essays on Irish and Canadian History and Literature, ed. James Noonan (Ottawa: Carleton Univ. Press, 1993), p. 159.

his vision only Paris and the guiding aesthetic genius of his namesake stand before him.

But Stephen's strident declaration at the novel's end demonstrates that his struggle for independent artistic identity remains as
yet unfulfilled. His expressive stance is a lyric one that has so deep an
investment in the linguistic formulations of a Catholic confessional
identity as to be inseparable from them. While Stephen's effort to
gain a personal voice strategically resists the dominant cultural
influences of his boyhood, the lyric language of that resistance,
when contrasted to the surrounding narrative's formal representation of multiple Irish discourses, cannot finally be accepted as a
complete and definitive Irish perspective. It is, quite simply, too
much an exercise in personal identity formation. John Paul
Riquelme has argued that Stephen's increasing command as a teller
of his own experience, when juxtaposed to the shifting narrative perspective of the text as a whole, creates an ambiguity that makes
authorship the central problematic of A Portrait. For Riquelme, the
ambiguity is resolved (though not erased) as we see the growth of
Stephen's poetic powers. Constructing the villanelle, creating the
journal, Stephen begins to claim A Portrait as his own book. As
Stephen's language breaks through to form an independent voice,
"we discover that the fulfillment of the process of becoming an
author occurs in the act of writing."[3] In its denial of any social and
political reality beyond the personal, though, the same lyric voice
that frees Stephen from cultural bondage finally leads him into a
static, and literally pronounced, artistic solipsism. Concerned with
individual identity more than anything else, Stephen denies himself
the interactions with others that would enable him to create an
authentic aesthetic representation of Ireland's culture. Isolated by
his self-authorship, Stephen renders himself incapable of speaking
for all Ireland.

* * *

Considering the less than successful outcome [presented in
Ulysses] of Stephen's journey abroad, the development of narrative
control in A Portrait, which has at times in its critical history been
seen as an all-encompassing political and artistic emancipation, appears rather to be the shaping of a particular subjective position that
limits Stephen even as it empowers him. Throughout A Portrait, and
particularly at novel's end, the text details Stephen as the inhabitant
of what Michel Foucault has famously called "disciplinary space."[4]

3. John Paul Riquelme in Teller and Tale in Joyce's Fiction: Oscillating Perspectives (Baltimore: Johns Hopkins Univ. Press, 1983), p. 51.
4. Michel Foucault, Discipline and Punish: The Birth of the Prison, trans. Alan Sheridan (New
   York: Vintage, 1977), p. 143. Foucault details how discipline operates materially (p. 167).

This is to say that Stephen develops a conception of reality, a consciousness, that is informed and indeed created by the continual regimented experience of his Irish Catholic family, school, and church environment. Seizing control of *A Portrait*'s narrative, Stephen merely repositions himself in a system of social relations which, in Foucault's words, "produces reality" by "produc[ing] . . . rituals of truth."[5]

The presiding ritual that locks Stephen into his limited Irish subjectivity is that of confession. Both the explicit Catholic (and specifically Ignatian)[6] practice of imaginative self-examination, as Joyce conceives it, and the development of Stephen's limiting lyric stance continually enact a subjectivity in which the speaker reveals his examined inner self to an imagined audience. Stephen's poetic lyricism is a performative self-positioning, a ritual that takes its cue from the method of Catholic sacramental confession where the penitent must engage in "the nearly infinite task of telling—telling oneself and another, as often as possible, everything that might concern the interplay of innumerable pleasures, sensations, and thoughts."[7] The rituals of truth prescribed by Irish Catholicism make it impossible for Stephen to produce literary texts embodying a critical Irish aesthetic. Although Stephen theorizes a mature aesthetic perspective in the latter stages of *A Portrait* that is essentially identical to Joyce's discussion in the Trieste lectures, his confessional self-conception prevents him from ever speaking about experience, or speaking with a voice, other than his own. Just as the aesthetic theory to which Stephen turns as a method of emancipation from Catholicism "depends to a very large extent on the religious vocabulary in terms of which it is formulated,"[8] so the artistic identity informing his lyric stance is rooted in the methodology of Catholic self-examination. The repeated ritual practice of the confessional refines the strategies of self-narration Stephen learns in his earliest days, shaping his notions of identity to the degree that, when Stephen leaves the actual practice of sacramental confession behind, his identity as a confessor remains. His writing becomes so charged with the force of confessional method that he cannot create, as he desires, an art critical of the Irish Catholic culture he proposes to redeem. Stephen cannot go beyond the practice of lyric confession, because he will in the same act dismantle the only self he has ever known.

5. Foucault, *Discipline and Punish*, p. 194.
6. See the daggered footnote for St. Ignatius of Loyola, *The Spiritual Exercises* (p. 277) [Editor].
7. Michel Foucault, *The History of Sexuality, Volume I*, trans. Robert Hurley (New York: Vintage, 1978), p. 20.
8. Joseph A. Buttigieg, *A Portrait of the Artist in a Different Perspective* (Athens, Ohio: Ohio Univ. Press, 1987), p. 107.

III

Stephen's *will to lyricism,* that is, his compulsion to continue narrating his own subjective position to the exclusion of others, originates in the way he situates himself psychically in response to his
earliest sensations by constructing a personal narrative. Consider
the short, story-like sequence that opens *A Portrait:* "Once upon a
time and a very good time it was there was a moocow coming down
along the road and this moocow that was coming down along the
road met a nicens little boy named baby tuckoo" (I.1–4). Young
Stephen appropriates the narrative context imparted by these words
as a structure after which he models his own narrative. The boy
fashions a story in the image of his father's, reordering the elements
in relation to the central social position he imagines for himself. In
his own story, Stephen, the narrator, is the most important character. Even the teller of the original tale is refigured as an element
revolving around Stephen: "*His* father told *him* that story: *his* father
looked at *him* through a glass . . . *He* was baby tuckoo" (I.5–7, emphasis added). Later in *A Portrait,* when Stephen encounters competing
symbolic systems, the egotism of his first little tale gives way to a
recognition that he is not the center of those systems or their narratives: his self-narrative is one of many on a vast cultural landscape.
The almost binary cognitive operation of countering his father's
story with his own develops accordingly into a complex practice of
self-orientation attentive to the social and political implications of
encountered narrative methods. Like Bakhtin's developing individuals, Stephen is continually "choosing [his] orientation among"
those methods by appropriating various aspects of their figurations
of reality as his own.[9] The task of self-narration remains quite the
same throughout his growth, but the nature of his personal narrative, insofar as it reproduces or does not reproduce elements of the
discourses Stephen encounters, tells who Stephen is and how he
changes.

   Throughout *A Portrait* Stephen is surrounded by the discourses of
family, school, and church. The Dedalus family's dinner conversation, the ribald debates of his classmates, and the severe homily of
the Jesuit spiritual director represent to Stephen the changing social
function of language. Amidst the din of these discourses he tries to
create an independent self. In the beginning his voice is, as he himself recognizes, small and weak; he cannot master and appropriate
the narrative strategies he encounters. The dominant narrative structure early in the text is consequently the interaction of his family's
voices. Stephen is only a listener:

9. Bakhtin, p. 296.

—That was a good answer our friend made to the canon.
What? said Mr. Dedalus.

—I didn't think he had that much in him, said Mr. Casey.

—*I'll pay your dues, father, when you cease turning the house of
God into a pollingbooth.*

—A nice answer, said Dante, for any man calling himself a
catholic to give to his priest. (I.837–43)

The dialogue is, of course, charged with the political and religious
vocabulary of Irish Catholicism. Stephen's growing narrative power,
as Joyce portrays it, is not simply a struggle for existential determination, an attempt to gain a voice that, once possessed, will empower
him to be a self-sustaining *logos*. Rather, Stephen's self-telling is an
ongoing process of social positioning within the world of cultural
narratives the text comprises.

Even Stephen's earliest private musings (that is, his earliest
attempts to move beyond the position of listener) are shaped by a
concern for enacting the "right" social role through a proper public
expression of the self. Tormented by his classmates' questions of
whether or not he kisses his mother at night, Stephen wonders
"What was the right answer to the question? He had given two and
still Wells laughed. But Wells must know the right answer for he was
in the third of grammar" (I.260–63). As Augustine Martin has
noted, Stephen's "crisis of conscience is Irish and Catholic in its terror, its ardour and its intensity," even in its minutest aspects.[1] The
self Stephen conceives and tells is primarily concerned with its own
social function within those communities, and it is told through
their language. That the apparently simple self-examination just
described gives way to a complex religious and political meditation
in which Stephen tries to determine his relation to the larger cultural norms of Irish Catholicism is thus not surprising. He seeks to
understand his imagined self as a relation to God ("God was God's
name just as his name was Stephen") and to Irish politics ("He wondered which was right, to be for the green or for the maroon")
(I.324–25, I.336–37). In this attempt, Stephen fails: "He felt small
and weak. When would he be like the fellows in poetry and rhetoric?
They had big voices and big boots and they studied trigonometry"
(I.346–49).

As Stephen grows, he more consciously appropriates and discards
aspects of the voices he perceives. To the degree that he appropriates the language of any encountered discourse, represented to him
(and to the novel's readers) by the voices of other characters, he

---

1. Augustine Martin, "Sin and Secrecy in Joyce's Fiction," *James Joyce: An International Perspective,* ed. Suheil Badi Bushrui and Bernard Benstock (Totawa, NJ: Barnes and Noble,
   1982), p. 147.

gains for himself a vocabulary and a grammar with which he can express his identity. When his self-conception is in harmony with the narrative methods he encounters, the dominant voice of *A Portrait* becomes Stephen's. The most striking example of this is his specific appropriation of Catholic confessional language. Because the Jesuit rector's direct and powerful rhetorical method models for Stephen a use of language radically different from the dialogues he has encountered at home and school, it offers a radically different conception of how language creates identity. The interplay of voices at the family dinner table, a linguistic setting that allows for the mutual enactment of social identity by its participants, disappears, replaced by an arena where the self is methodically scripted by the formulaic, unyielding, singular voice of ecclesiastical Irish Catholicism: "The soul tends towards God as towards the centre of her existence. Remember, my dear little boys, our souls long to be with God. We come from God, we live by God, we belong to God: we are His, inalienably His" (III.923–25). There is little opportunity here amidst sermons and rote responses for an individual to join in a dialogue, little room for identity-as-process.

The Ignatian spirituality the rector exemplifies is defined by interdependent rituals of self-examination and imaginative meditation that enable the sinner to renew himself and his relation to God. The *Spiritual Exercises* of Ignatius require both a "daily particular examination of conscience" in which the exercitant "should demand an account of himself with regard to the particular point he has resolved to watch in order to correct himself and improve," and a "general examination of conscience" in which the exercitant is to "demand an account of [his] soul from the time of rising up to the present examination" by fully considering sins of "thoughts," "words," and "deeds."[2] Yet in the Ignatian context confession is not simply the creation and expression of a moral inventory. Rather, it is one component of an ongoing ritual in which the "mental representation" of scenes from the life of Christ enable the exercitant to "see in imagination" the fullness of his human condition and his relation to the eternal other of God.[3] The applied intellect becomes a means of transforming the sinner's entire ontological orientation. And confession becomes the central practice through which the newly imagined—and newly imaginative—being must manifest itself in language.

The rector's sermon, with its highly detailed imagery of hell and its exhortations to self-examination and repentance, is the product of this Ignatian spiritual model. Whether or not Stephen finally

2. Ignatius of Loyola, *The Spiritual Exercises of St. Ignatius,* trans. Louis J. Puhl, S.J. (Westminster, Maryland: Newman Press, 1951), pp. 15, 23.
3. Ignatius, p. 25.

accepts the doctrines communicated by the rector's voice, he learns from that voice a self-conception that comes to define his every imaginative act. The impulse toward imaginary self-examination by which Stephen situates himself with regard to the discourses of family and school gains new rigor when, appropriating the formal language of Irish Catholicism, he learns to confess (and therefore enact) new and greater social transgressions and to conceive of himself as a particular kind of self-examining social, and, in the face of God, essential being:

> No escape. He had to confess, to speak out in words what he had done and thought, sin after sin . . . The thought slid like a cold shining rapier into his tender flesh: confession. But not there in the chapel of the college. He would confess all, every sin of deed and thought, sincerely: but not there among his school companions. Far away from there in some dark place he would murmur out his own shame. (III.868–75)

The sacramental recital of the Act of Contrition, repeated verbatim after the priest, occasions a crisis of identity that can be resolved only by an extrasacramental telling of the imagined Catholic self. Stephen longs "[t]o be alone with his soul, to examine his conscience, to meet his sins face to face, to recall their times and manners and circumstances, to weep over them" (III.1231–33). The diction here is strikingly evocative of the rector's ritualistic language, and its vocabulary is tellingly Ignatian. Throughout the book's central sections, Stephen is constantly in this state of self-examination and narration; he catalogues his every action as good or evil and defines his identity solely within the parameters of Catholicism's master discourse. Confession reestablishes his social role within the Catholic milieu by distancing his imagined self from actions that represent any experience outside dogmatic Catholicism's figured reality: "He had confessed and God had pardoned him. His soul was made fair and holy once more, holy and happy" (III.1548–50).

In section four of *A Portrait,* the experiences Stephen once marked as deviant aspects of his confessional Catholic identity become the basis for recasting that identity in terms of a supposedly asocial alliance with transcendent beauty. Called into the rector's office after having "amended [his] life" (IV.235), Stephen is faced with the impending consequence of his continued acceptance of Catholic self-scripting: "the Reverend Stephen Dedalus, S.J." (IV.506). He leaves the office and enters into yet another ruminative self-examination. This one, though, leads him to reject his life in Catholic Ireland, and gives rise to a visionary state in which he refigures his identity with language free from the limiting formulas of Catholic doctrine:

> His soul had arisen from the grave of boyhood, spurning her
> graveclothes. Yes! Yes! Yes! He would create proudly out of the
> freedom and power of his soul, as the great artificer whose
> name he bore, a living thing new and soaring and beautiful,
> impalpable, imperishable. (IV.809–13)

The identity reformation this language represents is an attempt to
throw off all the social orientations Stephen had previously chosen.
Brooding over himself in an unending examination, he rejects utterly
his social position as an Irish Catholic by becoming the confessor-
prophet of an alternative discourse, that of beauty. Yet Stephen's
visionary language, while not doctrinally beholden to his former
Catholic identity, unselfconsciously demonstrates Catholic confessional method as it seizes control of *A Portrait*'s narrative: "Where
was his boyhood now? Where was the soul that had hung back
from her destiny . . . Or where was he? . . . He was alone. He was
unheeded, happy and near to the wild heart of life. He was alone
and young and wilful and wildhearted" (IV.843–50). All of Stephen's
experiences continue to be transformed into language that has as its
ultimate referent only Stephen Dedalus. Even the sublime encounter
with the bird-girl, which would seem to stand outside of language, is
figurally contained by Stephen's lyrical-confessional egotism:

> Her image had passed into his soul for ever and no word had
> broken the holy silence of his ecstasy. Her eyes had called him
> and his soul had leaped at the call. To live, to err, to fall, to tri-
> umph, to recreate life out of life! A wild angel had appeared to
> him, the angel of mortal youth and beauty, an envoy from the
> fair courts of life, to throw open before him in an instant of
> ecstasy the gates of all the ways of error and glory. On and on
> and on and on! (IV.883–90)

The bird-girl, in Stephen's mind, exists only for him, becoming, as
do all his experiences, an impetus for his continuing self-absorption.
  An artist sworn in fealty to beauty, Stephen now seeks to awaken
in others a similar knowledge of transcendence. "Beauty expressed
by the artist," he asserts, "awakens, or ought to awaken, or induces,
or ought to induce, an esthetic stasis, an ideal pity or an ideal terror,
a stasis called forth, prolonged and at last dissolved in what I call the
rhythm of beauty" (V.1147–52). That rhythm is a sort of aesthetic
apotheosis, a movement out of the realm of the social to a state
where "the mind" perceives in an object only the Thomistic virtues
"*integritas, consonantia, claritas*," and enters into "the luminous
silent stasis of esthetic pleasure" (V.1346–47, V.1401–02). In the final
stages of *A Portrait*, Stephen theorizes just how the artist accom-
plishes his task. He proposes an aesthetic hierarchy, the measure of
which is the artist's ability to transcend his personal social identity

and remain "within or behind or beyond or above his handiwork, invisible, refined out of existence, indifferent" (V.1467–69). The lowest rung on this hierarchy is the "lyrical form," which "is in fact the simplest verbal vesture of an instant of emotion" (V.1444–45). Because the lyrical artist is unaware of the symbolic or social significance of his experience, he "is more conscious of the instant of emotion than of himself as feeling emotion" (V.1447–48). As the artist realizes that the central role he fashions for himself in the lyrical mode is in fact a solipsistic fallacy, the artistic text becomes less a straightforward expression of personal identity and more a critical portrayal of the conditions that produce that identity. In the "epical form," which "is seen emerging out of lyrical literature when the artist prolongs and broods upon himself as the center of an epical event . . . the narrative is no longer purely personal. The personality of the artist passes into the narration itself" (V.1448–54). Finally, as the artist entirely removes his own experience as the centerpiece of the aesthetic form, his personality "refines itself out of existence" in favor of a depiction of the vital interplay of others' experiences: "The dramatic form is reached when the vitality which has flowed and eddied round each person fills every person with such vital force that he or she assumes a proper and intangible esthetic life" (V.1458–61). What Stephen describes here is the growth of an artistic consciousness able to formalize experiences other than those of its own imagined social centrality, to enact the very poetic method Joyce finds lacking in an artist like James Clarence Mangan or, ironically enough, in Stephen Dedalus himself.

Stephen is, finally, so acculturated to conceive of himself as a confessional being that he cannot forsake lyric expressions of his experience for an aesthetic form manifesting an interplay of conflicting social realities. He remains at book's end unable to move into the dramatic stage of artistry he has theorized. The narrative relating his production of the villanelle is scrupulously infused with Catholic vocabulary, including "O! In the virgin womb of the imagination the word was made flesh" (V.1543–44), and later "The earth was like a swinging smoking swaying censer, a ball of incense, an ellipsoidal ball" (V.1571–72), and still later "The radiant image of the eucharist united again in an instant his bitter and despairing thoughts, their cries arising unbroken in a hymn of thanksgiving" (V.1680–82). But the images work their way into the poem only as figurations of Stephen's personal desire. "[T]he fallen seraphim . . . the smoke of praise . . . one eucharistic hymn . . . [t]he chalice flowing to the brim": these are in the villanelle simply devices rendering a confession of sensual love (V.1750, V.1755, V.1759, V.1762). Stephen's singular perspective, his alliance to a perfect formal beauty, limits his ability to render as independently valid the discourses he has now disdained. In the villanelle, as in the visionary narratives that are its substance, we hear only Stephen's voice.

The final journal most clearly crystallizes into textual form the confessional artistic self Stephen has adopted. There, he figures all discourses of Irish social reality that are incompatible with his perspective as "dead" (V.2630–31). What results is an identity that denies the ongoing process of social orientation so vital to the formation of the Joycean artistic perspective. The lyric posture that once uncritically shaped Stephen's understanding of the discourses of "nationality, language, religion" now just as uncritically shapes his antagonism ("*non serviam*") towards them. Because Stephen's narrative method subordinates all other voices to his own, those who represent alternative voices of Ireland become figures that he uses only to punctuate his development. On *20 March* Cranly is the "child of exhausted loins," and on *21 March* "he is the precursor," to be overcome (V.2620, V.2623). On *24 March* Stephen's religious discussion with his mother, "Subject: B.V.M.," leads to his refusal of repentance. On *6 April* comes the dismissal of Michael Robartes, and on *13 April* the disdain for all things English: "Damn the dean of studies and his funnel! What did he come here for to teach us his own language or to learn it from us? Damn him one way or the other!" (V.2742–44). Most tellingly, on *14 April* Stephen expresses anxiety about Mulrennan's old man of the West, who speaks from a rural Irish perspective about which Stephen knows nothing:

> John Alphonsus Mulrennan has just returned from the west of Ireland . . . He told us he met an old man there in a mountain cabin. Old man had red eyes and short pipe. Old man spoke Irish. Mulrennan spoke Irish. Then old man and Mulrennan spoke English. Mulrennan spoke to him about universe and stars. Old man sat, listened, smoked, spat. Then said: Ah, there must be terrible queer creatures at the latter end of the world. (V.2745–53)

Here is language that could most certainly disrupt the power of the artist's lyrical impulse, and Stephen knows it: "I fear him. I fear his redrimmed horny eyes. It is with him that I must struggle all through this night till day come, till he or I lie dead, gripping him by the sinewy throat till . . . Till what? Till he yield to me? No. I mean him no harm" (V.2754–57, Joyce's ellipses). What cannot be conquered must be dismissed, in the hope that it will ignore the lyric artist, as he ignores it. What Stephen is left with, then, when all else is stripped away, is himself alone. The "uncreated conscience" he will examine and confess is his, and only his. He is a race of one.

In shirking the Irish artist's duty to wrestle continually with Ireland's multiple cultural legacies, Stephen chooses instead to ally himself with an asocial Daedalian aesthetic, to rejoice in "the loveliness which has not yet come into the world" (V.2726–27). But the journal confirms Stephen's subjection to the lyricism he earlier rejected as aesthetically incomplete. Stephen Dedalus, disciple in the sodality of beauty, committed intellectually to an art that valorizes the dissolution of the egotistical artist, is in the end as entrapped as ever he was in a psychic cloister fashioned by Catholic self-representation. Contrasted to the form of A Portrait, in which narrative alters in structure and style to represent Ireland's multifaceted culture (a form that will come to fruition with Ulysses), the lyrical stance of Stephen's journal destines him for artistic failure. While Joyce himself remains critically engaged with the Catholicism of his youth, Stephen embraces a position as limited as the one Joyce criticized in Mangan: he is a lone Irish troubadour rebelling against cultural oppression with an uncritical alliance to a falsely essentialized identity. Like the Irish artists that preceded him, Stephen's language owes its grammar to the governing rituals with which he was raised. * * *

* * * Stephen's self-expression stands as a conspicuous measure against which, if we rely on the young Joyce's aesthetic standards, the encompassing narrative style of A Portrait should be favorably compared. The political implications of this are clear. Rather than rejecting Irish nationality, language, and religion by creating a voice of solipsistic lyricism as Stephen does, Joyce accepted those discourses and refigured them in A Portrait into a novelistic text that brings out the potential for dynamic cultural interplay in modern Ireland. As witnesses of that interplay, and as witnesses of Stephen's failure to recognize its vitality, A Portrait's audience inherits the urgent task of reconceiving themselves, and their nation, as free.

Selected Bibliography

Joyce's Writings

Long Narratives

Stephen Hero (incomplete; published posthumously, 1944)
A Portrait of the Artist as a Young Man (1916)
Ulysses (1922)
Finnegans Wake (1939)

Short Stories

Dubliners (1914)

Essays and Other Prose (posthumous collections)

The Critical Writings of James Joyce. Ed. Ellsworth Mason and Richard Ellmann. New York: Viking, 1959.
Occasional, Critical, and Political Writing. Ed. Kevin Barry. Oxford, Eng.: Oxford UP, 2000.
Poems and Shorter Writings: Including Epiphanies, Giacomo Joyce, *and "A Portrait of the Artist."* Ed. Richard Ellmann, A. Walton Litz, and John Whittier-Ferguson. London: Faber and Faber, 1991.
The Workshop of Dedalus: James Joyce and the Raw Materials for A Portrait of the Artist as a Young Man. Ed. Robert Scholes and Richard M. Kain. Evanston, Il.: Northwestern UP, 1965.

Poetry and Drama

Collected Poems (1936; consists of *Chamber Music, Pomes Penyeach,* and *Ecce Puer*).
Exiles, A Play in Three Acts (1918).

Other Materials

The James Joyce Archive. 63 Volumes. Ed. Michael Groden et al. New York and London: Garland Publishing, 1977–79. [Reproduces prepublication material in photographic facsimile.]
Letters of James Joyce. Vol. I. Ed. Stuart Gilbert. New York: Viking, 1957, rev. 1966. Vols. II–III. Ed. Richard Ellmann. New York: Viking, 1966.
Selected Letters of James Joyce. Ed. Richard Ellmann. New York: Viking, 1975. [Contains letters not previously collected.]

Bibliographies

Slocum, John J. and Herbert Cahoon. *A Bibliography of James Joyce, 1882–1941*. New Haven: Yale UP, 1953.

Biographies

Ellmann, Richard. *James Joyce*. New and rev. ed. New York: Oxford UP, 1982.
Jackson, John Wyse and Peter Costello. *John Stanislaus Joyce: The Voluminous Life and Genius of James Joyce's Father*. New York: St. Martin's P, 1998.
Joyce, Stanislaus. *My Brother's Keeper: James Joyce's Early Years*. Ed. Richard Ellmann. New York: Viking, 1958.
Maddox, Brenda. *Nora*. Boston: Houghton Mifflin, 1988. [Biography of Joyce's wife.]
McCourt, John. *The Years of Bloom: James Joyce in Trieste, 1904–1920*. Dublin: Lilliput P, 2000.

Criticism

• indicates works included or excerpted in this Norton Critical Edition.

Attridge, Derek. "'Suck was a queer word': Language, Sex, and the Remainder in *A Portrait of the Artist as a Young Man*." *Joyce Effects: On Language, Theory, and History*. Cambridge, Eng.: Cambridge UP, 2000. 59–77.
Benstock, Shari. "The Dynamics of Narrative Performance: Stephen Dedalus as Storyteller." *English Literary History* 49:3 (1982): 707–38.
Bloom, Harold, ed. *James Joyce's* A Portrait of the Artist as a Young Man. Modern Critical Interpretations. New York: Chelsea House, 1988.
Booth, Wayne C. "The Problem of Distance in *A Portrait of the Artist*." *The Rhetoric of Fiction*. 2nd ed. Chicago: U of Chicago P, 1983. 323–36.
Brady, Philip and James F. Carens, eds. *Critical Essays on James Joyce's* A Portrait of the Artist as a Young Man. New York: G. K. Hall, 1998.
Brivic, Sheldon. "Gender Dissonance, Hysteria, and History in James Joyce's *A Portrait of the Artist as a Young Man*." *James Joyce Quarterly* 39 (2002): 457–76.
Brockman, William S. "*A Portrait of the Artist as a Young Man* in the Public Domain." *The Papers of the Bibliographical Society of America* 98:2 (2004): 191–207.
Brown, Richard. *James Joyce*. New York: St. Martin's P, 1992.
• Burke, Kenneth. "Fact, Inference, and Proof in the Analysis of Literary Symbolism." *Terms for Order*. Ed. Stanley Edgar Hyman. Bloomington: Indiana UP, 1964. 145–72.
Buttigieg, Joseph A. *A Portrait of the Artist in a Different Perspective*. Athens: Ohio UP, 1987.
Carens, James F. "*A Portrait of the Artist as a Young Man*." *A Companion to Joyce Studies*. Ed. Zack Bowen and James F. Carens. Westport, Conn.: Greenwood, 1984. 255–359.
Castle, Gregory. "*Bildung* and the Bonds of Dominion: Wilde and Joyce." *Reading the Modernist Bildungsroman*. UP of Florida, 2006. 126–91.
———. "Confessing Oneself: *Homoeros* and Colonial Bildung in *A Portrait of the Artist as a Young Man*." *Quare Joyce*. Ed. Joseph Valente. Ann Arbor: U of Michigan P, 1998. 157–82.
Cheng, Vincent J. "Coda [to 'Catching the Conscience of a Race']: The Case of Stephen D(a)edalus." *Joyce, Race, and Empire*. Cambridge, Eng.: Cambridge UP, 1995. 57–74.
Church, Margaret. "The Adolescent Point of View toward Women in Joyce's *A Portrait of the Artist as a Young Man*." *Irish Renaissance Annual* 1. Ed. Zack Bowen. Newark: U of Delaware P, 1981. 158–65.
• Cixous, Hélène. "Reaching the Point of Wheat, or A Portrait of the Artist as a Maturing Woman." *New Literary History* 19:1 (Autumn 1987): 1–21.
Connolly, Thomas E., ed. *Joyce's Portrait, Criticisms and Critiques*. New York: Appleton-Century-Crofts, 1962.
Deane, Seamus. "Joyce and Stephen: The Provincial Intellectual." *Celtic Revivals: Essays in Modern Irish Literature, 1880–1980*. London: Faber and Faber, 1985. 75–91.
Deming, Robert H., ed. *James Joyce: The Critical Heritage, Volume One, 1902–1927* and *Volume Two, 1928–1941*. New York: Barnes and Noble, 1970.

• Eco, Umberto. *The Aesthetics of Chaosmos: The Middle Ages of James Joyce*. Transl. Ellen Esrock. Cambridge, Mass.: Harvard UP, 1989.
• Eide, Marian. "The Woman of the Ballyhoura Hills: James Joyce and the Politics of Creativity." *Twentieth Century Literature* 44:4 (Winter 1998): 377–93.
• Ellmann, Maud. "Disremembering Dedalus: *A Portrait of the Artist as a Young Man*." *Untying the Text: A Post-Structuralist Reader*. Ed. Robert Young. Boston and London: Routledge & Kegan Paul, 1981. 189–206.
Epstein, Edmund. *The Ordeal of Stephen Dedalus: The Conflict of Generations in James Joyce's* A Portrait of the Artist as a Young Man. Carbondale, Il.: Southern Illinois UP, 1971.
Feshbach, Sidney. "A Slow Dark Birth: A Study of the Organization of *A Portrait of the Artist as a Young Man*." *James Joyce Quarterly* 4:4 (1967): 289–300.
Froula, Christine. *Modernism's Body: Sex, Culture, and Joyce*. New York: Columbia UP, 1996.
Gabler, Hans Walter. "The Genesis of *A Portrait of the Artist as a Young Man*." *Critical Essays on James Joyce's* A Portrait of the Artist as a Young Man. Ed. Philip Brady and James F. Carens. New York: G. K. Hall, 1998. 83–112.
Gifford, Don. *Joyce Annotated: Notes for* Dubliners *and* A Portrait of the Artist as a Young Man. Second Ed. Berkeley. U of Calif. P, 1982.
Gose, Elliott B., Jr. "Destruction and Creation in *A Portrait of the Artist as a Young Man*." *James Joyce Quarterly* 22 (1985): 259–70.
Harkness, Marguerite. A Portrait of the Artist as a Young Man: *Voices of the Text*. Boston: Twayne, 1990.
Henke, Suzette. "Stephen Dedalus and Women: A Portrait of the Artist as a Young Narcissist." *James Joyce and the Politics of Desire*. New York and London: Routledge, 1990. 50–84.
Howes, Marjorie. "'Goodbye Ireland I'm going to Gort': geography, scale, and narrating the nation." *Semicolonial Joyce*. Cambridge, Eng.: Cambridge UP, 2000. 58–77.
Jacobs, Joshua. "Joyce's Epiphanic Mode: Material Language and the Representation of Sexuality in *Stephen Hero* and *Portrait*." *Twentieth-Century Literature* 46:1 (2000): 20–33.
Kenner, Hugh. "The Cubist *Portrait*." *Approaches to Joyce's "Portrait": Ten Essays*. Ed. Thomas F. Staley and Bernard Benstock. Pittsburgh: U of Pittsburgh P, 1976. 171–84.
• ———. "Joyce's *Portrait*—A Reconsideration." *The University of Windsor Review* 1:1 (Spring 1965): 1–15.
——. "The *Portrait* in Perspective." *Dublin's Joyce*. Bloomington: Indiana UP, 1956. 109–33.
Kershner, R. B. "The Artist as Text: Dialogism and Incremental Repetition in *Portrait*." *English Literary History* 53:4 (1986): 881–94.
Klein, Scott. "National Histories, National Fictions: Joyce's *A Portrait of the Artist as a Young Man* and Scott's *The Bride of Lammermoor*." *English Literary History* 65:4 (1998): 1017–38.
• Lawrence, Karen. "Gender and Narrative Voice in *Jacob's Room* and *A Portrait of the Artist as a Young Man*." *James Joyce: The Centennial Symposium*. Ed. Morris Beja, et al. Urbana: U of Illinois P, 1986. 31–38.
Leonard, Garry. "When a Fly Gets in Your I: The City, Modernism, and Aesthetic Theory in *A Portrait of the Artist as a Young Man*." *Advertising and Commodity Culture in Joyce*. Gainesville: UP of Florida, 1998. 175–207.
Levenson, Michael. "Stephen's Diary in Joyce's *Portrait*—The Shape of Life." *English Literary History* 52:4 (1985): 1017–35.
• Lewis, Pericles. "The Conscience of the Race: The Nation as Church of the Modern Age." *Joyce through the Ages: A Nonlinear View*. Ed. Michael Patrick Gillespie. Gainesville: UP of Florida, 1999. 85–106.
Lowe-Evans, Mary. "Sex and Confession in the Joyce Canon: Some Historical Parallels." *Journal of Modern Literature* 16:4 (1990): 563–76.
Mahaffey, Vicki. "Père-version and Im-mère-sion: Idealized Corruption in *A Portrait of the Artist as a Young Man* and *The Picture of Dorian Gray*." *Quare Joyce*. Ed. Joseph Valente. Ann Arbor: U of Michigan P, 1998. 121–38.
——. *Reauthorizing Joyce*. Cambridge, Mass.: Cambridge UP, 1988.
Manganiello, Dominic. *Joyce's Politics*. Boston and London: Routledge & Kegan Paul, 1980.
——. "Reading the Book of Himself: the Confessional Imagination of St. Augustine and Joyce." *Biography & Autobiography: Essays on Irish and Canadian History and Literature*. Ed. James Noonan. Ottawa: Carleton UP, 1993. 149–62.
Muller, Jim. "John Henry Newman and the Education of Stephen Dedalus." *James Joyce Quarterly* 33:4 (1996): 593–603.

Mullin, Katherine. "'True Manliness': Policing Masculinity in *A Portrait of the Artist as a Young Man*." *James Joyce, Sexuality and Social Purity*. Cambridge, Mass.: Cambridge UP, 2003. 83–115.

• Mulrooney, Jonathan. "Stephen Dedalus and the Politics of Confession." *Studies in the Novel* 33:2 (Summer 2001): 160–79.

Nolan, Emer. *James Joyce and Nationalism*. London and New York: Routledge, 1995.

Noon, William T. *Joyce and Aquinas*. New Haven: Yale UP, 1957.

Norris, Margot. "Stephen Dedalus, Oscar Wilde, and the Art of Lying." *Joyce's Web: The Social Unraveling of Modernism*. Austin: U of Texas P, 1992. 52–67.

Parrinder, Patrick. *James Joyce*. Cambridge, Eng.: Cambridge UP, 1984.

Peake, C. H. *James Joyce: The Citizen and the Artist*. Stanford, Calif.: Stanford UP, 1977.

Rabaté, Jean-Michel. *James Joyce: Authorized Reader*. Baltimore: Johns Hopkins UP, 1991.

Radford, F. L. "Dedalus and the Bird Girl: Classical Text and Celtic Subtext in *A Portrait*." *James Joyce Quarterly* 24:3 (1987): 253–74.

Riquelme, John Paul. "Desire, Freedom, and Confessional Culture in *A Portrait of the Artist as a Young Man*." *A Companion to James Joyce*. Ed. Richard Brown. Oxford: Blackwell, 2007.

———. "*Stephen Hero* and *A Portrait of the Artist as a Young Man*: Transforming the Nightmare of History." *Cambridge Companion to James Joyce*. Second Ed. Ed. Derek Attridge. Cambridge, Eng.: Cambridge UP, 2004. 103–21.

• ———. *Teller and Tale in Joyce's Fiction: Oscillating Perspectives*. Baltimore and London: Johns Hopkins UP, 1983.

Roche, Anthony. "'The strange light of some new world': Stephen's Vision in *A Portrait*." *James Joyce Quarterly* 25:3 (1988): 323–32.

Rossman, Charles. "Stephen Dedalus and the Spiritual-Heroic Refrigerating Apparatus: Art and Life in Joyce's *Portrait*." *Forms of Modern British Fiction*. Ed. Alan Warren Friedman. Austin: U of Texas P, 1975. 101–31.

Scholes, Robert. "Stephen Dedalus, Poet or Esthete?" *PMLA* 89 (1964): 484–89.

Schwarze, Tracey-Teets. "Silencing Stephen: Colonial Pathologies in Victorian Dublin." *Twentieth-Century Literature* 43:3 (1997): 243–63.

Schutte, William, ed. *Twentieth-Century Interpretations of 'A Portrait of the Artist as a Young Man.'* Englewood Cliffs, N.J.: Prentice-Hall, 1968.

• Scott, Bonnie Kime. *James Joyce*. Atlantic Highlands, N.J.: Humanities P International, 1987.

Seed, David. *James Joyce's A Portrait of the Artist as a Young Man*. New York: St. Martin's P, 1992.

Seidel, Michael. *Exile and the Narrative Imagination*. New Haven: Yale UP, 1986.

Senn, Fritz. "The Challenge: *ignotas animum* (An Old-fashioned Close Guessing at a Borrowed Structure)." *James Joyce Quarterly* 16:1–2 (1978–79): 123–34. Repr. in *Joyce's Dislocutions: Essays on Reading as Translation*. Ed. John Paul Riquelme. Baltimore and London: Johns Hopkins UP, 1983. 73–84.

Sosnoski, James J. "Reading Acts, Reading Warrants, and Reading Responses." *James Joyce Quarterly* 16:1–2 (1978–79): 43–63.

Spoo, Robert. *James Joyce and the Language of History*. New York: Oxford UP, 1994.

Spurr, David. "Colonial Spaces in Joyce's Dublin." *James Joyce Quarterly* 37:1–2 (1999–2000): 23–42.

Staley, Thomas F. and Bernard Benstock, eds. *Approaches to Joyce's "Portrait": Ten Essays*. Pittsburgh: U of Pittsburgh P, 1976.

Thomas, Calvin. "Stephen in Process/Stephen on Trial: The Anxiety of Production in Joyce's *Portrait*." *Novel* 23:3 (1990): 282–302.

Valente, Joseph. "The Politics of Joyce's Polyphony." *New Alliances in Joyce Studies*. Ed. Bonnie Kime Scott. Newark: U of Delaware P, 1988. 56–69.

• ———. "Thrilled by His Touch: Homosexual Panic and the Will to Artistry in *A Portrait of the Artist as a Young Man*." *James Joyce Quarterly* 31:3 (Spring 1994): 167–88. Rev., exp. in *Quare Joyce*. Ed. Joseph Valente. Ann Arbor: U of Michigan P, 1998. 47–75.

Williams, Trevor L. "Dominant Ideologies: The Production of Stephen Dedalus." *James Joyce: The Augmented Ninth*. Ed. Bernard Benstock. Syracuse: Syracuse UP, 1988. 312–22.

Wollaeger, Mark A. *James Joyce's A Portrait of the Artist as a Young Man: A Casebook*. Oxford, Eng.: Oxford UP, 2003.